Cognitive Psychology

Third Edition

Cognitive Psychology

Third Edition

Douglas L. Medin
Northwestern University

Brian H. Ross
University of Illinois

Arthur B. Markman
University of Texas

Harcourt College Publishers

Fort Worth   Philadelphia   San Diego   New York   Orlando   Austin   San Antonio
Toronto   Montreal   London   Sydney   Tokyo

To Linda and Liberty, in that order. —Douglas Medin
In memory of my father, Martin. —Brian Ross
To my parents, Ed and Sondra Markman, for teaching me the power of thinking. —Arthur Markman

Publisher	Earl McPeek
Acquisitions Editor	Bradley J. Potthoff
Market Strategist	Katie Matthews
Developmental Editor	Peggy Howell
Project Editor	Elaine Richards
Art Director	David A. Day
Production Manager	Linda McMillan

Cover credit: © Digital Vision Ltd.

ISBN: 0-15-508057-1
Library of Congress Catalog Card Number: 00-102762

Address for Domestic Orders
Harcourt College Publishers, 6277 Sea Harbor Drive, Orlando, FL 32887-6777
800-782-4479

Address for International Orders
International Customer Service
Harcourt, Inc., 6277 Sea Harbor Drive, Orlando, FL 32887-6777
407-345-3800
(fax) 407-345-4060
(e-mail) hbintl@harcourt.com

Address for Editorial Correspondence
Harcourt College Publishers, 301 Commerce Street, Suite 3700, Fort Worth, TX 76102

Web Site Address
http://www.harcourtcollege.com

Harcourt College Publishers will provide complimentary supplements or supplement packages to those adopters qualified under our adoption policy. Please contact your sales representative to learn how you qualify. If as an adopter or potential user you receive supplements you do not need, please return them to your sales representative or send them to: Attn: Returns Department, Troy Warehouse, 465 South Lincoln Drive, Troy, MO 63379

Printed in the United States of America

1 2 3 4 5 6 7 8 9   0 3 9   9 8 7 6 5 4 3 2
Harcourt College Publishers

PREFACE

What are the most interesting questions that the human mind can ever pose and hope to answer? How the mind works is certainly one of them. How is it that the billions of neurons in our brains are organized such that we can move around the world, pursue goals, and interact with others? What gives rise to conscious experience? How is knowledge stored in the brain? Cognitive psychology is the study of the human mind; its domain includes questions concerning how people perceive the world, remember information, access and use knowledge, understand language, reason, learn, solve problems, and make decisions.

For most of us, our everyday experience seems quite unremarkable. We have the subjective experience of seeing the world as it is. We normally have no difficulty making sense of our world, and we don't have to worry about how to think, form sentences, and act; we just do them. When we look beneath the surface of everyday experience, however, we see that what our cognitive system accomplishes is nothing short of amazing. In this book we will examine the what, why, and how of these accomplishments.

What exactly is so amazing? As we shall see, the world continually confronts us with situations that offer too little information about what is going on and too many possibilities about what to do. For example, as we shall see in the chapter on perception, any visual input is consistent with an unlimited number of interpretations. The challenging question is how the perceptual system functions such that we normally are unaware of any ambiguity. Our experience is simply that of seeing things the way they are. The reason for this is that, instead of considering all the logical possibilities, our conceptual system comes prepared with expectations that greatly influence what we consider and how we act. We do not experience uncertainly and ambiguity because we typically do not consider alternative possibilities. These sorts of expectations or "constraints" occur in all facets of cognition. Constraints represent an adaptation to our world and therefore should be thought of as guiding principles rather than limitations.

It is as if the conceptual systems make bold guesses about the way things are, guesses that are accurate enough often enough that we can act intelligently. Perhaps the most important characteristic of the mind is that it is exquisitely adapted, "tuned" to life on earth.

Goals

Ambiguity and adaptive responses to it provide some broad themes that serve to organize this book. We hope to provide the framework *to allow students to better appreciate not just a series of interesting phenomena in different areas of research but some basic commonalities that cut across these areas.*

A second, closely related goal is *to encourage the student to gain an appreciation for methods by which researchers study the mind.* Although we can gain some insight by thinking about how we think, this understanding is very limited. Much of cognition occurs so quickly that we are not able to reflect on it; for example, how do people read words, understand speech, or decide something is a bird? Even for slower processes, such as solving a math problem or deciding where to go to college, an examination of what people are thinking often leads to many possible interpretations. *Cognitive Psychology* examines a wide variety of activities and tries to provide an understanding that captures many of them.

A third goal of the book is *to convey challenges and open questions associated with the field of cognition.* Research on cognition has led to some striking and counterintuitive findings that have important practical implications. Nonetheless, we will be disappointed if students focus only on answers and conclusions and ignore the many deep puzzles that remain.

Features/Organization

In each chapter we have included three boxes: "An Enigma," "A Debate," and "An Application." An Enigma highlights a strange or unexplained result in an area; A Debate focuses on an ongoing research debate; and An Application points to the ways in which research in an area has been applied either outside the lab or in another area of science.

To further help in giving some structure to the research area, the book, following a general introduction to the themes and methods of cognitive psychology, is organized into five parts. Part I is an overview; Part II (chapters 2, 3, and 4) examines how information is acquired, including basic learning processes, perception, and attention. Part III (chapters 5, 6, 7, and 8) addresses fundamental issues of memory and representation of knowledge, including how it is used in real-world cases and for imagery. Parts IV and V (chapters 9 through 14) begin with an examination of language and then address thinking, with a discussion of concepts, reasoning, problem solving, expertise, creativity, and decision-making.

This book is intended for a one-semester course in cognitive psychology. We have attempted to place the chapters in a logical sequence, but other orderings are possible. Your instructor may choose not to cover a chapter or two for reasons of interest, overlap with other courses, or shortage of time. Nonetheless you will get a lot of exposure to the important themes that provide the framework for this book.

It is probably important that the opening chapter outlining the themes be read first. Other than that it would probably be best to read chapter 5 before the other memory chapters and chapter 12 before 13. Although we tie together material across chapters, the overall themes permit an instructor to skip certain early chapters (e.g., Learning, Perception) without too much loss of continuity.

New to This Edition

This third edition of *Cognitive Psychology* represents a substantial revision. The single most important change is that Arthur Markman has joined the team of authors. It was important to this edition of the text to add new energy without sacrificing the conceptual framework that makes this book unique. Markman has known Medin and Ross and has collaborated with them for many years; he shares their vision of cognitive psychology as a field. His contributions are compatible, and his enthusiasm for cognitive psychology is reflected in every chapter in the new edition.

How has the current edition been changed? Each of the three authors has worked on each of the chapters and we think there is a visible improvement in clarity, even though we have not shied away from presenting technical details in many sections. Every chapter has been systematically updated and new material has been added, especially concerning new developments in cognitive neuroscience. In addition, based on extensive reviews, we have made a number of major changes from the second edition. Most notably, we have greatly reorganized the four memory chapters to make the presentation more coherent, and we have deleted the chapter on language acquisition to enable us to expand coverage in other areas.

We have also carefully developed a new test bank for instructors to use. Authored by Wendy Domjan, the new test bank provides 50% more questions and identifies them by type: factual, application and conceptual. *Computerized test banks are available for Windows and Macintosh.*

Acknowledgments

We have received much help in writing this book. For this third edition we wish particularly to acknowledge the help of our developmental editor at Harcourt, Peggy Howell. She helped us overcome a variety of obstacles and brought us to the finish line in excellent time. We also thank art director David A. Day, project editor Elaine Richards, production manager Linda McMillan, copyeditor Beth Alvarez and proofreader Steven Baker, all of whom helped move this edition smoothly through production.

We also wish to thank the thoughtful and constructive comments of those who reviewed this edition of the book: James I. Chumbley, University of Massachusetts; Kenneth D. Kallio, SUNY–Geneseo; Steven M. Smith, Texas A & M University; Jerry Hauselt, Southern Connecticut State University; W. Daniel Phillips, The College of New Jersey; Tom Alley, Clemson University; Pamela Tsang, Wright State University; Kevin B. F. Thomas, University of Arizona–Sierra Vista; Patricia E. O'Neill, University of Mississippi; M. John Lutz, East Carolina University; and Thomas Sanocki, University of South Florida. Thanks also to earlier reviewers Woo-Kyoung Ahn, Neal Cohen, Gary Dell, Stephanie Doane, Evan Heit, Phillip Johnson-Laird, Gordon Logan, Harold Pashler, Javier Sainz, and David Swinney. A special thanks goes to Caryn Carlson, Bill Geisler, and Todd Maddox for helpful suggestions in their areas of expertise. We would also like to thank people who may not have helped directly with this book but who have had large influences on our thinking about cognition: James Anderson, John Anderson, Scott Atran, Larry Barsalou, Gordon Bower, William K. Estes, Dedre Gentner, Thomas Landauer, Gregory Murphy, Elissa Newport, Edward Smith, Edward Wisniewski, (and each other). Special thanks are due to Greg Hand, who helped in all phases of manuscript preparation. Greg, you are amazing.

Finally, we acknowledge a great deal of tangible and intangible support on the home front. For their love, support and patience Doug, Brian, and Art would like to thank Linda, Cheri, and Betsy, respectively.

—Douglas Medin, Brian Ross, and Arthur Markman

TABLE OF CONTENTS

Preface   v

Part I Overview   1

**Chapter 1 Possibilities, Information, and
    Approaches to the Study
    of the Mind**   3
Introduction   4
    Domain of Cognitive Psychology   4
    Puzzles   5
    Possibilities   7
    A Framework   8
    A Closer Look   9
    Themes and Implications   11
Knowledge and Experience   11
    Ways of Knowing   11
    Experimentation   15
    Cognitive Psychology and
      Experimentation   16
Roots of Cognitive Psychology   17
    Introspectionism   18
    Behaviorism   18
    Critique of Behaviorism   19
Cognitive Psychology   22
    The Emergence of Cognitive Science   24
    Cognitive Neuroscience Techniques   26
    Event-Related Potentials   27
    Positron Emission Tomography   27
    Functional Magnetic Resonance
      Imaging   28
Levels of Analysis   31
    Marr's Three Levels   31
    Recursive Decomposition   33
Diversity of Approaches   34
    Degree of Formalism   34
    Explicit Versus Implicit Structure   35
    Connectionist Models   36
Ecological Validity   40
Summary   42
Key Terms   43
Recommended Readings   43

Part II Acquiring Information   45

Chapter 2 Learning   47
Introduction   48
    The Challenge of Learning   48
The Biological Backdrop of Learning   49
    Fixed-Action Patterns and Releasers   50
    Critical Periods and Imprinting   52
    Constraints on Learning   57
Basic Learning   59
    Habituation   59
    Classical Conditioning   60
    Trial-and-Error Learning or
      Instrumental Learning   66
    Paired-Associate Learning   68
Implications   71
    The Learning-Performance Distinction   71
    Contingency Learning and Illusory
      Correlation   72
    Content and Meaningful Learning   75
Summary   78
Key Terms   79
Recommended Readings   79

Chapter 3 Perception   80
The Problem of Perception   81
Visual Perception   82
    Low-Level Vision   83
    Localization   87
High-Level Vision   96
    Feature Detection Theories   96
    Structural Theories   99
    Template Matching and Alignment   104
    Face Recognition and Visual
      Subsystems   105
**Levels and the Integration of Information
    in Perceptual Context Effects**   108
    The Word Superiority Effect   109
Summary   113
Key Terms   114
Recommended Readings   114

Chapter 4 Attention 115
Introduction 116
Initial Observations in Perceptual
   Attention 117
     Sensory Stores 117
     Evidence for Capacity Limitations 118
     Focused Attention 121
Capacity and Attention 123
     Bottleneck Theories 124
     Late Selection 126
     Capacity Theories 126
Feature Integration Theory 130
Attention in Complex Tasks 133
     Capacity and Automaticity 136
Central Executive Functions 141
     Dual-Task Interference 141
Attention and the Brain 144
Summary 147
Key Terms 147
Recommended Readings 148

Part III Memory 149

Chapter 5 Memory: Remembering
   New Information 151
Introduction 152
     Centrality of Memory 152
     Uses of Memory 152
Short-Term Memory 154
     Introduction 154
     Characteristics of Short-Term
       Memory 155
     Working Memory 158
     Summary 164
Long-Term Memory 164
     Introduction 164
     Encoding 166
     Retrieval 170
     Encoding-Retrieval Interactions 171
     Forgetting 181
     Summary 185
Models of Memory for New Information 186
     General Approach 186
     Simple Association Models 187
     The SAM Model 189

Summary 194
Key Terms 195
Recommended Readings 195

Chapter 6 Memory Systems and
   Knowledge 196
Introduction 197
Semantic Knowledge 197
     Characteristics of Semantic Memory 197
     The Hierarchical Model 198
     Evaluation of the Hierarchical Model 200
Episodic Memory 202
     Are Episodic and Semantic Memory
     Distinct Memory Systems 202
Procedural Memory 208
Implicit and Explicit Memory 210
     Spared Learning in Amnesia 211
     Implicit and Explicit Memory with
       Normal-Memory Adults 215
     Evaluation of the Implicit-Explicit
       Distinction 218
     Two Models of Memory 220
     Introduction 220
     The ACT Theory 220
     A Parallel Distributed Processing
       Model of Memory 229
Summary 240
Key Terms 241
Recommended Readings 241
Appendix: Learning in a Parallel
   Distributed Processing
   Model 243

Chapter 7 Remembering New Information:
   Beyond Basic Effects 248
Introduction 249
Schemas: Understanding and
   Remembering Complex Situations 250
     Introduction and Motivation 250
     Understanding 253
     Schemas 254
     Scripts 257
     Schema Activation 261
     Problems with Schemas 262
     Summary 262

Reconstructive Memory 263
  Encoding-Retrieval Interactions
    Revisited 263
  Schemas and Stereotypes 265
  Summary 267
Memory in the World 267
  Introduction 267
  Eyewitness Testimony 268
  Flashbulb Memories 273
  Recovered Memories 278
  Summary 282
Knowing Your Memory 284
  Introduction 284
  Strategies and Knowledge 284
  Metamemory 287
  Summary 290
Summary 290
Key Terms 291
Recommended Readings 291

**Chapter 8 Spatial Knowledge, Imagery,
    and Visual Memory** 293
Introduction 294
Representations 295
  Relations Between Representations
    and Referents 295
  Analog Representations 296
Summary 298
Spatial Knowledge 299
  Maps and Navigation 299
  Spatial Representations From
    Descriptions 300
  Hierarchical Representations of Space 302
  The Brain and Spatial Cognition 305
  Spatial Representations and
    Development 305
  Summary 305
Imagery 306
  Evidence for Use of Visual Imagery 307
  Representation of Images 310
  Summary 314
Visual Memory 315
  Remembering Details 315
  Memory for Pictures 316
  The Picture-Superiority Effect 319

  Memory for Faces 322
  Summary 322
Summary 322
Key Terms 324
Recommended Readings 324

Part IV Language and
    Understanding 325

Chapter 9 Language 327
Introduction 328
Language and Communication 328
  Principles of Communication 329
  The Given-New Strategy 330
  Presupposition and Assertion 330
  Conversational Maxims 331
  Summary 332
The Productivity of Human Languages 333
  Productivity and Novelty 333
  Ambiguity 334
Phonology 335
  Phonological Rules 335
  Speech Perception 339
  Summary 343
Syntax 343
  The Need for Structure 343
  Structure 344
  Phrase Structure 345
  Transformations 347
  The Psychological Reality of Syntax 349
  Summary 350
Understanding Language 350
  Heuristics and Strategies 351
  Minimal Attachment 353
Text Comprehension 356
The Brain and Language 360
Summary 362
Key Terms 363
Recommended Readings 364

**Chapter 10 Concepts and Categories:
    Representation and Use** 365
Introduction 366
  Why Categorize 366
  Computational Complexity 366

Functions of Concepts   367
Concepts and Misconceptions   369
Summary   371
Structure of Natural Object Categories 371
The Classical View   372
The Probabilistic View   373
Between-Category Structure   382
Does Similarity Explain
   Categorization   386
Concepts as Organized by Theories   390
Putting Similarity in Its Place   391
Are There Kinds of Categories   393
Summary   395
Use of Categories in Reasoning   396
Goals and Ad Hoc Categories   396
Conceptual Combination   396
Categories and Induction   397
Summary   399
Key Terms   400
Recommended Readings   400

Part V Thinking   403

Chapter 11 Reasoning   405
Introduction   406
Logic and Reasoning   406
Validity and Truth   408
Deductive Versus Inductive
   Reasoning   409
Summary   410
The Psychology of Deduction   410
Conditional Reasoning   411
Conditional Reasoning in Hypothesis
   Testing: The Selection Task   414
Summary   418
The Psychology of Inductive Reasoning 419
Probabilistic Reasoning   420
Test Quality: A Case Study of
   Base Rates   421
Base Rate Neglect   423
Confusing Conditional Probabilities   424
Argument Structure and Relevance   425
Summary   427
The Importance of Content   427
Analogy and Similarity   427

An Example of Mapping   431
A Return to Similarity   431
Summary   433
Mental Models and Intuitive Theories   434
Intuitive Theories   438
**Hypothesis Testing and Scientific
   Reasoning**   441
Summary   444
Key Terms   445
Recommended Readings   445

Chapter 12 Problem Solving   446
Introduction   447
Problems, Problems, Problems   447
What Is a Problem   447
Types of Problems   448
Methods for Studying Problem
   Solving   448
Summary   452
**Problem Solving as Representation
   and Search**   452
Introduction   452
The Problem Space Analysis   453
Problem Solving as Search   456
Problem Solving as Representation   461
Summary of Problem Solving as
   Representation and Search   469
Reliance on Specific Relevant Knowledge 470
Introduction   470
The Influence of Related Problems   470
Summary   478
Summary   479
Key Terms   479
Recommended Readings   480

Chapter 13 Expertise and Creativity 481
Introduction   482
Expertise   482
Introduction   482
Comparing Experts and Novices   482
Developing Expertise   492
Expert Systems   500
Adaptive Expertise   503
Summary   504

Creativity 505
  Introduction 505
  The Traditional View 507
  Some Recent Views of Creativity 509
  Summary 514
Summary 516
Key Terms 516
Recommended Readings 517

**Chapter 14 Judgment and Decision
    Making** 518
Introduction 519
Rational and Normative Models 520
  Expected Value Theory 521
  Expected Utility Theory 522
**Limitations of Expected Utility and
  Alternatives to It** 523
  Violations of Expected Utility 523
  Prospect Theory 529
  Regret Theory 531
  Decision Making Over Time 532
  Summary 534
Dealing With Complexity 534
  Strategies for Dealing With
    Complexity 535

  Adaptive Decision Making 535
Further Heuristics and Biases 536
  Availability Heuristic 537
  Representativeness Heuristic 540
  Anchoring and Adjustment 541
  Causal Schemas 541
  Hindsight Bias 542
  Overconfidence 542
  Relativity of Judgment and
    Use of Norms 543
  Summary 544
Are There Kinds of Decisions 545
  Mental Accounting 545
Summary 548
Key Terms 548
Recommended Readings 549

Glossary 551
References 563
Credits 613
Author Index 617
Subject Index 627

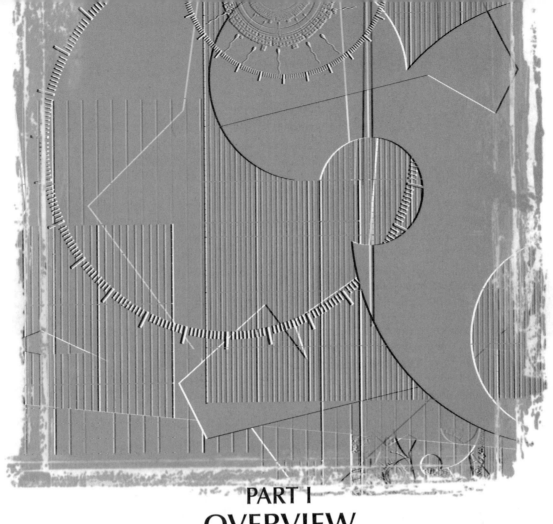

PART I
OVERVIEW

Chapter 1
**Possibilities, Information, and Approaches
to the Study of the Mind**

Chapter 1

Possibilities, Information, and Approaches to the Study of the Mind

Introduction
Domain of Cognitive Psychology
Puzzles
Possibilities
A Framework
A Closer Look
Themes and Implications

Knowledge and Experience
Ways of Knowing
Experimentation
Cognitive Psychology and Experimentation

Roots of Cognitive Psychology
Introspectionism
Behaviorism
Critique of Behaviorism

Cognitive Psychology

The Emergence of Cognitive Science

Cognitive Neuroscience Techniques
Event-Related Potentials
Positron Emission Tomography
Functional Magnetic Resonance Imaging

Levels of Analysis
Marr's Three Levels
Recursive Decomposition

Diversity of Approaches
Degree of Formalism
Explicit Versus Implicit Structure
Connectionist Models

Ecological Validity

Summary

Key Terms

Recommended Readings

All nature is but Art, unknown to thee;
all chance, direction, which thou canst not see.
—Alexander Pope

INTRODUCTION

Domain of Cognitive Psychology

As you read this, you are engaged in information processing. In fact you've spent much of your life processing information as you attend, perceive, learn, solve problems, and reason about your world. In short you have been doing exactly what cognitive psychologists attempt to understand—how people acquire, store, retrieve, and use knowledge. If we are going to spend a whole book talking about **cognitive psychology,** then we ought to take a moment to think about what cognitive psychology is. Simply put, cognitive psychology is the study of thought. Thought goes all the way from the ability to perceive the world around us by sight, hearing, touch, and smell, through our ability to reason, to solve problems, to use language, to learn and remember, and to move and act in the world.

One might think that the fact we've spent our lives processing information would give us some special insight into how people think. Given that we all spend a great deal of time explaining other people's behavior as well as our own, we should all be experts on cognition. But it's not so simple. We also have spent all of our lives eating food—does that mean we are all experts on digestive processes, liver functioning, and the like? Probably not. Still it is hard to resist the idea that everyone knows quite a bit about thought because we've done so much of it.

Intuitions about how the mind works may be helpful sometimes but at other times they are useless or even very misleading. One of our strongest intuitions is that perception involves nothing more and nothing less than seeing the world as it is, a view known as **naïve realism.** There are two serious problems with this view. One is that it is wrong. A clear demonstration of this fact comes from a study conducted by two social psychologists who asked undergraduates to view a film of a football game and rate the behaviors of the competing teams (Hastorf & Cantril, 1954). The game in question pitted two long-term rivals, Princeton University and Dartmouth College, and the game was very rough. Numerous fights and penalties punctuated the hard-fought game. Princeton and Dartmouth undergraduates who were shown the film of the game a month later gave strikingly different responses. Princeton students saw a succession of Dartmouth violence and poor sportsmanship, with Princeton players sometimes retaliating out of self-defense. Dartmouth students saw the teams as equally aggressive and interpreted their team's infractions as reasonable responses to the brutality of the Princeton players. The Princeton and Dartmouth students literally saw two different games. Still it is hard to resist the impression that we are just seeing things the way they truly are.

The other problem with naïve realism is that it doesn't provide any explanation of how perception is actually accomplished. It is only when researchers have tried to provide an information processing account of perception that we have come to realize just how complex it is. In fact, there is a real sense in which perception is impossible! Therefore, it is a deep puzzle how we are able to do it. More generally, much of cognition involves these sorts of challenges. In the rest of this chapter we will provide an overview of these puzzles and then offer a framework for understanding them.

Puzzles

This book is about the obvious and the nonobvious. Hidden under the cognitive tasks that people find natural and easy are some of the most challenging and mysterious puzzles concerning human intelligence. Most people do not spend a lot of time thinking about how we perceive objects and events in our environment. Our experience is of seeing the world more or less directly. But there is a great deal more to perception than meets the eye. So much information is lost during the imaging process that projects light from the three-dimensional world into two-dimensional images on the retina of the eye that any perceptual experience has an unlimited set of possible interpretations. So how do we see the world accurately enough to make our way through it? To deal with ambiguity, the perceptual system appears to make assumptions about the nature of the world (see, for example, Poggio, Torre, & Koch, 1985).

Look at the shaded objects in Figure 1.1 (taken from Kleffner & Ramachandran, 1992). They appear to fall into two natural groups, one type being concave (curving inward) and one type being convex. Now turn your book upside down. The objects that before appeared to be concave now appear convex and vice versa. Why does this happen? According to Kleffner and Ramachandran, the visual system assumes that the light source is from "above." Consider the object in the lower right-hand corner. If light came from above, the pattern of shading would make sense if the object were concave. The shading pattern for the object in the lower left-hand

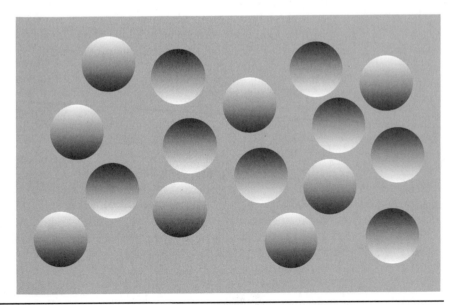

Figure 1.1   **A Mixture of Shaded Objects With One of Two Patterns of Illumination** The objects that are lighter on top appear to be convex and those lighter on the bottom appear to be concave.

Source: Kleffner & Ramachandran, 1992.

corner is consistent with a convex figure (as long as the light source is from above). If you turn your book sideways, the objects appear more ambiguous and it is less easy to see them as two distinct groups. In this case the pattern of shading is inconsistent with a single light source. Note that the default assumption that the source of illumination is from above is usually (but not always) correct.

The assumptions that the perceptual system makes are accurate enough that we can successfully get along in our environment, but they are not infallible. When these assumptions fail, they may give rise to perceptual illusions that demonstrate that we do not just simply see things the way they are. For example, our visual system is structured so that the apparent shape of objects does not change across a variety of viewing conditions that produce different images on the retina. If you hold a pen or pencil in your hand and rotate it, it does not appear to stretch or shrink in size as you shift from a broadside view to more of an end view. This phenomenon, known as *shape constancy,* generally serves us well. But now consider the shaded parallelograms in Figure 1.2.

Although parts A and B are two-dimensional, the connected lines provide cues to depth, and we see the top ends of each figure to be farther from us than the bottom ends. That is, we see the objects as three-dimensional. The processes that allow us to achieve shape constancy operate on the retinal image such that we see the vertical component of the shaded parallelograms in parts A and B as being longer than they really are. Therefore, we are surprised to find that the horizontal part of A's parallelogram is equal to B's vertical component and that B's horizontal component is exactly as long as A's vertical component. This is a powerful visual illusion that does not disappear when we realize that it is an illusion. In fact, you may not believe that the two shaded parallelograms are congruent (would fit on top of each other) until you measure it for yourself.

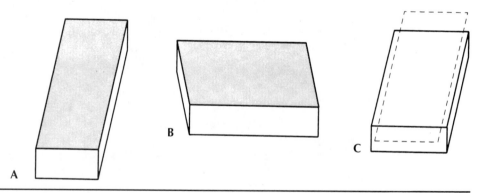

Figure 1.2   **A Shape Constancy Illusion**   The shaded parallelogram in part B is congruent with the one in A and with the dashed outline in C (that is, if you cut out the shaded area in A it would fit exactly on the shaded area in B). If you are skeptical, try tracing the outlines of these parallelograms on thin paper and placing them on top of one another.

Source: Shepard, 1981.

Normally we are not aware of the assumptions made by our perceptual system; we seem to just see things the way they are directly. The point of these examples is not that the eye sometimes can be tricked; instead they illustrate the fact that the perceptual system is normally faced with ambiguous information which it interprets by making assumptions that resolve the ambiguity. The remarkable thing is that these assumptions are usually (but not always) close enough to the truth that our experience is of seeing the world as it is.

As a general rule, tasks that seem natural and easy to us have proven to be among the most difficult to understand and implement in a machine. Although we may be impressed by computers that perform complex calculations at great speed, it is far more challenging to program common sense into a computer. The sort of plausible inferences that we take so much for granted are notoriously difficult to build into computer programs associated with **artificial intelligence** (the science of writing programs that do intelligent things). Consider the question, "Why did John roller-skate to McDonald's last night?" People have no difficulty realizing that the topic of the question is probably the roller-skating and that "because he was hungry" and "because he was busy during the day" are not relevant answers. But if the question is changed to "Why did John drive to McDonald's last night?" people understand that the topic is not driving. Furthermore, an intelligent system would have to realize that John drove some vehicle and that the vehicle was probably a car, possibly a truck, and certainly not a tank or a sled pulled by a team of huskies. We make such assumptions and inferences so naturally that we are scarcely aware of them.

Possibilities

Life is full of possibilities. In fact, the richness of life's possibilities places limitations on the ability of an organism to reason and act intelligently. Intelligent actions require information, and organisms are faced with a chronic shortage of relevant information concerning the past, present, and future.

We should clarify what we mean by *information*. Sometimes when discussing our complex society, people talk about the problem of "information overload." What they normally mean is that it's hard to filter through all this information to focus on the part that is useful or personally relevant. Informally speaking, we could say that more possibilities mean more information as long as we are talking about *potentially* useful information. But if we focus on information that is actually relevant, it's easy to see that we are challenged by the large set of *potentially* useful information; the problem is that there are many possibilities to be ruled out before we can be sure that we have determined which information is relevant. In short, the more possibilities or potential information, the harder it is to single out what is relevant.

Suppose you are considering buying a car. Some of the information needed to make an intelligent decision is straightforward: how much the car will cost, how much money you have to purchase the car, how the car performs, what kind of mileage it gets, the likelihood that expensive repairs will be needed, and so on. Other potentially relevant information is not so obvious. For example, the future health of your grandmother might be important, because you might need to drive a long distance to visit her and the best car to buy might depend on the relative amount of city versus country driving that you anticipate. A sudden interest in anthropology could lead you to long for a jeep to take on field trips. A chance to work in New York City could obviate the need for a car altogether. If you postponed the decision until you examined and evaluated all potential relevant information, you would never make the decision. The point is that you cannot anticipate *all* possibilities so as to guarantee that you will purchase the "best" car.

Even when the possibilities can be systematically enumerated, there may simply be too many to allow an exhaustive search. Consider the game of chess. The number of ways in which the first 10 moves can be played is on the order of billions, and there are more possible sequences for the game than there are atoms in the universe! Obviously neither humans nor machines can determine the best moves by considering all the possibilities. In fact, grand master chess players typically report that they consider only a handful of the possible moves and "look ahead" for only a few moves. In contrast, chess computers are capable of examining more than 100,000 positions per second and can search quite a few moves ahead. The amazing thing is that the best grand masters (as of this writing) still can defeat the best computers (though in 1997 world champion Gary Kasparov lost a two-game exhibition match to Deep Blue, a computer dedicated to chess, so the margin is narrowing). The next generation of chess-playing computers will be an order of magnitude faster, will be able to search further, and may well surpass the best chess player, but just how grand masters select the best lines of play after very limited search remains a mystery.

A Framework

This book is organized around the idea that much of intelligent behavior can be understood in terms of strategies for coping with too many possibilities for what might be relevant. As we shall see, problems of **computational complexity** arise in all the major domains of cognitive psychology: learning, perception, memory, concept formation, decision making, and problem solving. In each case, there are too many possibilities to be considered (that's computational complexity) and no general-purpose way of resolving ambiguity. A fundamental goal in each of these areas is to identify guiding principles or **constraints** that allow organisms to explore the better (or at least satisfactory) possibilities. In short, human cognition is a specialized form of intelligence, one adapted to interactions in the world.

Cognitive psychology relies heavily on two metaphors. One is to view people as being like computers in the sense that we store, retrieve, and use information. This metaphor has been enormously useful for cognitive psychology, because computers are really the first devices created by people that are designed to process information in complex ways. Thus, the computer has given us a way of thinking about how humans might operate as an information processing device. This metaphor is limited, however, because it does not acknowledge that human beings are biological organisms that have evolved for life on Earth. That is, much of human cognition is in the service of adaptive or functional behaviors. We are not general purpose computational devices but rather special purpose devices exquisitely attuned to the demands of our environment. If nothing else, we hope that this book will give you a greater appreciation of this fact. We are able to cope with computational complexity precisely because we do not examine all the possibilities—instead we have evolved to pursue only a few paths, the ones that are most promising. Let's turn to some examples.

A Closer Look

Learning

Consider the problem of learning names for things. It may seem obvious that when a parent points to a rabbit and says, "Rabbit," a young child ought to be able to associate the sound with the object. But the situation is far more ambiguous. First of all the infant must attend to the relevant object. Have you ever tried to get your dog to attend to where you are pointing only to find that your dog is staring at your finger? The problem of joint attention is far from trivial (see Baldwin, 1993, for evidence on infants' ability to do so). Even if baby and parent are attending to the same object, how should the infant know the word *rabbit* is referring to the object? The word could refer to small or white or furry or pink-eyed or hopping. Or the word could be a proper name, refer to a role (as in *pet*) or a superordinate (as in *animal*), or even be some combination of the rabbit and other properties in the scene. It would take many, many examples to disentangle these possibilities

To cope with the possibilities or ambiguities, organisms seem to come prepared with certain biases or expectations. Consider a rat that eats some contaminated food in the morning, wanders around its environment, sees a cat, hears thousands of sounds, scratches its fleas, and then gets sick late in the day. To what should the rat attribute its illness? Seeing the cat? Hearing rattling garbage can lids? Drinking water in the early afternoon? There are limitless possibilities, but laboratory research suggests that the rat would associate illness with the smell and taste of the food eaten in the morning and acquire an aversion to it. And, of course, in this case the bias toward associating tastes and smells with illness serves the rat quite well. Pigeons, in contrast, readily link visual cues with food (Shapiro, Jacobs, & LoLordo, 1980). The cost of this bias or preference is that when the true association conflicts with a bias, learning may be difficult. This potential cost holds for all organisms, including humans, who have preferences that make some things easier and other things harder to learn. Ideally, we are biased to learn the things that we should learn. For example, young children who are learning words appear to have a bias for assuming that novel labels refer to names for whole objects rather than individual parts or complex scenes (Markman, 1989), and generally this inference is correct. In order to understand learning, we need to identify the natural biases or guiding principles that predispose organisms for making some associations rather than others.

Experience and Reasoning

Ordinary experience is extraordinarily challenging with respect to learning. Consider a simple social interaction. John greets Mary warmly, and she replies in kind. Why is Mary friendly? One possibility is that she is friendly to everyone by virtue of her occupation or social role or because her natural disposition is to be friendly. Another possibility is that whether Mary is friendly depends on her mood, and she happens to be in a good mood. Yet another explanation is that Mary's reaction is a response to John's warmth. Or Mary could be feigning friendliness to conceal underlying anger or resentment. The possibilities go on.

Which of these explanations of Mary's behavior is the correct one? We don't know, and the point is that John does not know either. John cannot re-create exactly the same situation and systematically vary his behavior to evaluate his role in Mary's response. (You may have seen the movie *Groundhog Day,* where the star, Bill Murray, keeps reliving February 2nd until he successfully handles relationships with other people. Part of what makes the movie so funny is that in our lives there is no resetting or chance to systematically explore alternatives.) Of course, psychologists can study the types of assumptions or guesses people make in explaining behavior (e.g., what characteristics are attributed to a person who helps someone cheat on an exam? Helpful? Dishonest? Both?).

People do not, in general, have sufficient information to choose between competing explanations. Therefore, people must adopt certain strategies in order to make attributions about other people's beliefs and behaviors. One idea is that people attempt to identify what is unusual in a situation and bias their causal attributions toward these abnormal conditions (see, e.g., Hilton & Slugoski, 1986). For example, if John has a car accident while driving home on a rainy evening, we might believe that the unusual rainy conditions were at least partly responsible for the accident. If John lives in a climate where it rains every evening, however, we would be much less likely to assume that rain was the cause. In the absence of definitive information, we cannot ask whether these attributions are logically justified (they are not, in almost all cases) but rather whether they are accurate often enough to prove useful. By analyzing ordinary experience in terms of principles of experimental design, one may readily see that experience might fail to provide relevant information or that experience might even provide misinformation.

Memory

People do scarcely anything without relying on their past experience, which, by definition, involves memory, and not simply memory, but accessing relevant memories. How do people access and use knowledge efficiently, and how do they determine relevance? If you are doing some rock climbing and come upon a snake, you need to access the knowledge that it is potentially dangerous; it would not be helpful to retrieve the facts that a snake's motion and traffic flow are sometimes analogous, that snakes molt, or that *snake* rhymes with *snowflake*. But determining relevance is not easy, and the set of observations that are potentially useful in a given situation is so large that there is the danger of getting lost in thought. A central problem in memory research is to discover just how memory is organized so as to provide relevant knowledge when it is needed.

Themes and Implications

Obviously, people cannot consider all the possibilities in a given situation. Much of human cognition can be seen as a response to information processing demands. Therefore, it should not be surprising that perception, learning, memory, and reasoning are riddled with, if not organized around, strategies and heuristics (general guidelines or shortcuts) for simplifying situations. Rather than striving for the "best" or optimal decisions, people are more pragmatic and settle for the "pretty good" or simply satisfactory. In Herbert Simon's terms, they **satisfice** (Simon, 1957). Measured against the standard of optimality, human cognition falls short, oversimplifies, and leads to systematic misperception. Measured against the problems of determining relevance, and inadequate information, however, human cognition can achieve marvels.

KNOWLEDGE AND EXPERIENCE _____

The goal of cognitive psychology is to understand how the mind works. To set the stage for describing how researchers address this challenging question, we first outline the variety of ways that people might acquire knowledge, describe the general framework for scientific experimentation, and then review the history of approaches to the study of the mind. We turn attention to some general observations on research in cognition.

Ways of Knowing

Nonempirical

Not all knowledge is gained through observation and experience. Much of what we believe to be true we derive from logic, judgments of reasonableness, other authorities, or faith.

DEDUCTIVE LOGIC   We use logic when we use a set of facts to derive other facts that are logical consequences. For example, given the premise "if it rains there will be no baseball game" and the premise that "it is raining," we can conclude that (it follows that) there will be no baseball game. Of course, logic can be misused. For example, it is tempting to take the observation that there was no baseball game as proving that it rained when, in fact, no baseball game was scheduled. Furthermore, observations that are logically correct may not be sensible in normal discourse. The statement "if two plus two equals five, then the president of the United States is a Martian" is logically correct but has no useful content.

REASONABLENESS   A major way in which we know or accept something to be true is by evaluating the plausibility of what is true. If it sounds reasonable, it is probably true. For example, someone might accept the statement that "the threat of punishment deters crime" as being true because it seems reasonable that people would want to avoid being punished. Although whether punishment really does reduce crime would seem to be an empirical issue, people may find the statement to be so transparently correct that it is treated as an a priori or self-evident truth.

Very often, results from psychological experiments make intuitive sense, so much so that one is tempted to dismiss psychology as nothing more than common sense. But intuition is far from an infallible guide. For example, in our culture there is a widespread belief that hypnotism can be used to improve eyewitness accuracy. The evidence from laboratory research, however, is that eyewitness accuracy may be *worse* when hypnotism is employed (Sanders & Simmons, 1983; see also Chapter 7).

Probably the safest conclusion about reasonableness judgments is that they are close enough to the truth to be correct much of the time but that occasionally reasonableness is very misleading. For example, in earlier centuries when people drew an even sharper distinction between body and mind, explanations of mental disorders were stated in terms of possession by demons. The idea that unusual behavior might be caused by a brain tumor or a biochemical imbalance would have been dismissed as wildly implausible.

AUTHORITY   Establishing knowledge by appeal to authority amounts to taking someone else's word for the truth. The dictionary is commonly used as the authority for how words are spelled. Children (for a short time, at least) usually assume that whatever their parents tell them is true, and, as adults, we usually accept the word of experts as correct. We could not get along without authorities, even if experts are not infallible.

FAITH   By definition, faith is a firm belief in something for which there is no proof. Religious beliefs are the most common example of faith. Faith in something is not an empirical issue, even if it is based on experience. For example, someone who believes that prayer heals the sick probably would not want to fund research that would compare the recovery rates for people who were or were not prayed for (though recently this issue has been a topic on television talk shows). One suggestion is that public figures ought to have a better prognosis than less-known people because public figures have more people praying for them. (A cynic might note that they also have more people praying against them!) Whatever sense this might make, it is not a good experimental design because the two groups would differ in quite a few ways other than the number of prayers said for them.

Empirical

In the present age of modern science, we take observation and experimentation as a natural road to truth. This attitude toward **empiricism** (the view that knowledge is derived directly from experience) has not always been held. Francis Bacon, one of the founders of British empiricism in the 16th century, was severely chastised by fellow debaters for suggesting that the answer to the question of how many teeth a horse has might best be obtained by looking into the mouth of a horse. (This story may be apocryphal.)

EXPERIENCE   Much of our knowledge comes from generalizations we have drawn from our experiences. For example, based on our interactions with people, we might come to the conclusion that people who are polite and friendly are also honest. Some of these generalizations are based on limited experience. If the first three people from Bolivia that we meet are musically talented, we may be ready to conclude that most or all Bolivians are musically talented.

If our initial impressions are not representative or accurate, they should be corrected. A serious problem with taking experience as a guide is the tenacity of our beliefs, which may lead us to search for information in a biased manner. A person who thinks Bolivians are musical may find it natural to elicit information that will reinforce that belief. This tenacity is particularly evident when people have conflicting beliefs or attitudes. Consider the following study conducted by psychologist Lee Ross and his colleagues (Ross, 1977; Ross, Lepper, & Hubbard, 1975). They identified people who had different beliefs about some controversial issue. In one study people were selected who either believed that marijuana had no harmful effects or thought it was very unhealthy. Both groups were then presented with the same set of information that consisted of descriptions of research studies showing a somewhat mixed picture. Their beliefs were measured again after they had read the material. One might expect the attitudes of the two groups to tend to converge toward a moderate position, but surprisingly the beliefs became still more extreme! Apparently, people tended to see flaws in the studies whose results did not fit their views and did not see any problems with the studies that supported their views. A biased search for information can lead to a distorted view of the evidence.

A second factor that serves to increase tenacity is the phenomenon of **self-fulfilling prophecy.** That is, people may act on their beliefs in such a way that they bring about the expected state of affairs. For example, a person who thinks that someone is going to be hostile may act in a guarded manner toward that person, which may indeed be met with coolness. A striking demonstration of this phenomenon comes from an experiment by social psychologist Mark Snyder and his colleagues (Snyder, Tanke, & Berscheid, 1977). The experiment involved men and women talking on the phone, ostensibly to evaluate whether they might wish to date each other. The men were shown a picture of the woman they were conversing with. Two different men talked with each woman (at different times). Although the pair of men conversed with the same woman, they were shown different photographs: One photograph showed a woman of average appearance, and the other showed a woman who was quite attractive. The photographs might well influence how much the men wanted to date the woman, but in this study the focus was on how the men's expectations influenced the conversations. An independent set of raters did not see any photographs but simply judged the woman's attractiveness based on hearing her half of the telephone conversation. The results indicated that the woman was rated to be more attractive when engaged in a conversation with a man who had been shown an attractive photograph than with a man who had been shown the less attractive photograph. Apparently, the photographs changed the manner in which the men interacted over the phone and, as a consequence, also affected the way in which the woman interacted over the phone. Expectations are not just predictions; they also influence our behavior in such a way as to confirm them.

Personal experience is often accurate, provides lots of ideas or hypotheses to be more systematically explored, and provides a proof that often refutes generalizations or stereotypes. For example, if one has read or been told that New Yorkers are unfriendly, then a personal encounter with a helpful, friendly New Yorker may be valuable in correcting one's beliefs about people who live in New York. Then again, people often are willing to let specific experiences override massive amounts of statistical information. One may read about a survey of 10,000 automobile owners indicating that some make of car has low repair costs, only to disregard this information when a friend says, "I bought one of them and I've had nothing but problems."

Systematic Observations in Natural Settings   All good science begins with observation. In many cases these observations take the form of **correlations.** A correlation is a relationship between two things we measure. If the value of one measurement tends to be high when the other is high and low when the other is low, then the values are *positively correlated*. If the value of one measure is high when the other is low and low when the other is high, then the values are *negatively correlated*. If you cannot predict one value from the other, then the values are *uncorrelated*. As an example, we might note a negative correlation between how much people smoke and how long they live. It is important to realize that correlation cannot be equated with causation. There is a positive correlation between ill people going to a hospital and their dying, but going to the hospital does not cause them to die. At the same time, one cannot simply rely on plausibility as a guide for interpreting correlations. For example, prior to the germ theory of disease, it did not occur to people that there would be a correlation between operating room cleanliness and surviving surgery.

Scientific Observation   Just because we call an observation scientific does not mean we are immune from bias, but it does involve a commitment to a set of principles for evaluating observations. First, scientific observation is public, by which we mean that in principle different people could make the same observation under the same conditions. That is, observations should be repeatable. Observations that are not public have far less credibility, according to scientific standards. Consider, for example, certain paranormal phenomena such as levitation or telekinesis (e.g., lifting a book by thinking about it). Sometimes it is claimed that these phenomena are real but that they will not occur if any "nonbelievers" are present. If nonbelievers cannot observe telekinesis, then it is no longer a public, reliable event. It is conceivable that there are such paranormal phenomena and that they truly do not appear when nonbelievers are present, but an alternative view is that believers simply are not evaluating their observations carefully. The latter view is reinforced by the fact that professional magicians can produce many, if not all, of these phenomena by methods that are anything but paranormal. (Suspiciously, one noted psychic, Yuri Geller, was a professional magician earlier in his career.)

A second major feature of scientific observation is that it is, in principle, *self-correcting*. That is, we require that observations and theories be testable. The initial observation that the earth is apparently flat has been replaced by the idea that the earth is a sphere. The flat-earth theory was falsifiable. One criticism of Freud's description of personality in terms of id, ego, and superego is that it can explain any observation after the fact (e.g., "he cheated because his superego was weak" versus "he did not cheat because his superego was strong") but that, since it can explain anything, it explains nothing. Commonsense aphorisms tend to cover all bases and not be testable. For example, we are told that "haste makes waste" and "a stitch in time saves nine" as well as "absence makes the heart grow fonder" and "out of sight, out of mind." All of these aphorisms are true some of the time, but just exactly when? A person committed to scientific observation must be prepared for the possibility that what seems intuitively obvious may not be true. To go back to an earlier example, the threat of punishment may not deter crime at all.

Experimentation

Experimentation can be distinguished from observation by the fact that some factor or factors are explicitly varied while some other factor or factors are measured. The factors that are varied by the experiments are known as **independent variables,** and the factors measured are the **dependent variables.** For example, in a study examining how caffeine affects memory, caffeine would be the independent variable and the amount of caffeine given would be varied; memory would be the dependent variable and would be measured.

Experiments are an excellent tool for interpreting naturalistic observations. Suppose one observes the amount of time students spend studying and correlates study time with test performance. If the better students study more efficiently and need less time to prepare, one might find either zero correlation or even a negative correlation between time spent studying and test performance. Does this mean that students should study less? Obviously not, but one way to demonstrate this unequivocally would be to run an experiment in which different groups of students would be allowed to study for different amounts of time. Under these conditions one would almost surely find a positive correlation between study time and test performance. The problem with the naturalistic observation is that study time might have been confounded with ability if the better students studied less. Thus student ability would be a **confounding factor** that would provide a misleading picture of the effects of studying. Indeed, one of the main justifications for psychological research is that it allows us to disentangle potential confounding factors.

Cognitive Psychology and Experimentation

Cognitive psychology is a branch of experimental psychology. This means that researchers in this area are committed to relying on systematic experimentation and empirical tests of ideas. Many of people's intuitions about human cognition may be correct but cognitive psychologists believe that carefully controlled experiments are needed to determine the validity of intuitions.

Frequently, cognitive processes are either nonconscious or take place so rapidly that intuitions provide no guide at all. For example, as you read this sentence, you are automatically accessing the meanings of words, rules of grammar, and routines for recognizing patterns of dark and light as individual letters and words. How do you do it? Introspection just doesn't help.

How do cognitive psychologists study and hope to understand complex information processing acts such as sentence comprehension? There's no simple way to peek into the brain and gets answers. And just watching people read doesn't seem like the solution either. In many cases researchers have had to develop and rely on measures that are quite subtle and indirect to develop theories of cognition. For example, one very common measure is *reaction time;* that is, the length of time it takes people to do something of interest. For example, suppose we show people a picture of a robin and we find that people can verify that it is a robin faster than they can verify that it is a bird. Such an observation might suggest that perceptual categorization leads us to first recognize the animal as a robin and we then verify it as a bird because we retrieve the knowledge that robins are birds. Of course, this sort of theory would need to be tested and only if it accounted for a wide range of observations on how quickly people do perceptual categorization would we believe that it was a promising theory. Later on we'll consider reaction time and other measures of cognitive processes in more detail.

One reason why research on cognition is hard to do is that we must use indirect measures of cognitive processing. As you will see, cognitive psychology can be quite abstract and it is not always easy to understand (as we keep saying, your own intuitions may be of no help or even misleading). We believe, however, that you are equal to the challenge and that you will come to see something of the cleverness of researchers in being able to use subtle measures to advantage. And more to the point, this book may also be something of a road map to the subtle operation of the human mind.

Summary

We began this section by noting that there may be different ways of fixing belief or acquiring knowledge. One particularly important way of learning is on the basis of experience. We noted, however, that learning from experience may be far from easy because of our inability to control for potentially confounding factors. Cognitive psychology attempts to address these problems by conducting systematically controlled experiments. Of course that still leaves the question of what we should measure and how we might measure it.

ROOTS OF COGNITIVE PSYCHOLOGY _____

 We now turn to an overview of different approaches to the study of the mind. In this section our focus will be on the following question: How exactly can one use experiments to learn about human cognition? In addition to the main text, this and the remaining chapters will introduce a debate, an application, and what we call an enigma. The debate will reinforce the view that researchers don't always agree, the application will serve to point to the real-world relevance of research, and the enigma will convey something of the fascination that researchers have concerning these challenging issues.

It is one thing to be interested in studying how the mind works but quite another to figure out how to go about it. Some people balk at the very idea of trying to understand human beings because the complexity and uniqueness of individuals seem to defy analysis. Indeed, not until the latter half of the 19th century did people begin to apply the scientific method to human thought and behavior. Wilhelm Wundt is credited with founding the first laboratory for psychological research at Leipzig, Germany, in 1879.

Suppose that, like Wundt, you decided that the study of the human mind should be attempted. You might begin by wondering why people behave the way they do. Suppose you wanted to know why some people are better at remembering where they parked their car than others. The most straightforward procedure might be to ask people how they try to remember where they parked. You might learn about some interesting strategies but it's also possible that people who remember easily might say "I don't know how, I just do it." We think it is unlikely that this sort of survey would provide deep insights into spatial memory. The problem is that we often don't have conscious awareness of cognitive processes. Therefore, the scientific study of the mind often involves finding indirect ways to ask questions about thinking.

Alternatively, you might study why some people have difficulty making decisions. The questions about memory and about decision making are concerned with individual differences. Although cognitive psychologists are interested in individual differences, they usually believe that it is at least as important to study characteristics that people tend to share, since we cannot understand differences without first understanding similarities. That is, psychologists try to learn the principles underlying human thought and behavior that might give rise to these individual differences. As we shall see, in many cases individual differences can help researchers formulate more accurate general theories. Just as genetic abnormalities such as Down's syndrome are best understood against the background of the science of genetics, we believe that individual differences in thought and behavior are best understood from the perspective of cognitive psychology.

In the following sections we will review several approaches to the study of the mind. Some of the methods seem straightforward; others are quite subtle. Some appreciation of the history of psychology is necessary to understand contemporary cognitive psychology (and to avoid repeating mistakes). Lack of uniformity is probably a good thing because of the different levels at which one may understand cognition. But we are getting ahead of ourselves. Let us first turn to a little history.

Introspectionism

It would seem that we are all potential experts on how the mind works because we have a lot of firsthand experience with our own thoughts and other people's behavior. We often make inferences about other people's beliefs, desires, and intentions, and we seem to have privileged, direct access to our own thoughts. Therefore, what better source of information about the mind than introspection?

Introspectionism was one of the first methods used to study the mind. It was adopted about a century ago when experimental psychology was getting its start in Germany. Wilhelm Wundt believed that just as physical things can be analyzed into their parts and elements, so too could thought be analyzed into its substructures or elements. Early research and debate included such issues as whether thoughts necessarily were or were not accompanied by images (see Boring's [1950] discussion of the Wurzburg school). In the United States, Edward Titchener attempted to establish rigorous procedures for introspection that focused on separating direct sensations from inferences drawn from them (that is, he wanted to eliminate information that goes beyond what was given directly). The goal was to understand the basic structure of perception and thought.

Introspectionism was quickly buffeted with severe challenges. Hermann Helmholtz argued that perceptual processes involve unconscious inferences, and Sigmund Freud emphasized the pervasiveness of unconscious influences on behavior. If psychology were limited to the study of what is available to consciousness, then it would miss out on critical determinants of behavior. Even within the school of introspectionism there were problems. Observations by Marbe at Wurzburg suggested that there were severe limitations on the data that could be obtained from introspection (again see Boring, 1950). Marbe asked people to lift two weights and judge which was the heavier. The participants noted numerous sensations and images but were not able to report any of the processes that actually generated or justified their judgments. In other words, the judgments came to mind, but the participants could not say how they got there. Introspection did not seem to reveal the structure of thought in the way that Wundt and others had hoped. An equally serious problem was that results from different laboratories often disagreed. These difficulties paved the way for a reaction against using introspection—behaviorism.

Behaviorism

Behaviorism, true to its name, takes psychology to be the study of behavior. John B. Watson, its founder, argued that behavior is objective and observable and that the agenda for psychology consists of formulating laws relating stimulus conditions to behavior. Consciousness, introspection, and the mind were to play no role in this science of behavior. His views were reinforced by the logical positivist movement in philosophy. Logical positivism emphasized *operational definitions;* that is, the idea that theoretical notions or constructs should always be tied to specific operations or observations. For example, thirst might be defined as going for 24 hours without taking in any fluids.

B. F. Skinner, another prominent behaviorist, helped promote behaviorism both by argument (his debates with Carl Rogers in the 1960s concerning free will received wide attention) and by the development of procedures for studying behavior. Skinner maintained that behavior is determined by reinforcements or rewards, not by free will. One of his notable findings was that, under tightly controlled learning conditions (taking place in what is known as the Skinner box, which we will describe in Chapter 2), rats, pigeons, and monkeys displayed very similar learning curves. Skinner's brand of behaviorism had no place for theories (Skinner, 1950). He argued that the science of behavior consists of describing relationships between patterns of reinforcement and behavior. Skinner collaborated with Charles Ferster on a book that consists of nothing but hundreds of graphs of behavior under different schedules of reinforcement (Ferster & Skinner, 1957). No reference to internal processes of organisms was permitted.

Although behaviorism did help to promote psychology as a science, its strictures on what could and could not be studied were too severe. There were always pockets of resistance to behaviorism, and, as attention shifted from studying simple learning in tightly controlled (and impoverished) situations to more complex learning, the inadequacies of behaviorism became increasingly apparent.

Critique of Behaviorism

Although people talk about the replacement of behaviorism by the "cognitive revolution," it is probably more accurate to say that behaviorism gradually declined because of a series of related inadequacies. Skinner's demonstration that rats, pigeons, and monkeys showed similar behavior in the Skinner box may tell us more about the limitations of Skinner boxes than about the generality of animal learning. One serious problem with behaviorism is its tendency to equate learning with performance. Memory was assumed to be simply the performance of a learned act. This view is inadequate. An early demonstration of the need to distinguish between memory and performance comes from studies by Tinklepaugh (1928, 1932) using chimpanzees and monkeys as subjects. Tinklepaugh studied what is known as a "delayed response." An animal would be shown where either lettuce or a banana was hidden and then, after a delay, be allowed to choose among several response sites (including the correct one). If the chimpanzee found the reward, it was allowed to eat it. Everything proceeded normally in trials in which lettuce was hidden and was the reward and when a banana was hidden and was the reward. But Tinklepaugh also ran trials in which a banana was hidden and then lettuce was surreptitiously substituted as the reward. In these trials the chimpanzees would select the correct location, but then—with an expression that can be described only as puzzlement—they would ignore the lettuce and search for the banana that should have been there! The chimpanzees were learning and remembering not just what to do but also what the reward was. It is not clear how a behaviorist could account for these observations. (Other problems with equating learning with performance are described in Chapter 2.)

A DEBATE
Rewards, Intrinsic Motivation, and Creativity

According to Skinner and other reinforcement theorists the best way to increase the probability of some behavior is to reward it. One criticism of this view draws on a distinction between intrinsic and extrinsic motivation. Intrinsic motivation is activity engaged in for its own sake (e.g., playing basketball, watching a movie) whereas extrinsic motivation involves incentives that are not inherently part of the activity (e.g., a parent giving ice cream to a child as a reward for studying hard for a test). Critics have suggested that external rewards may backfire because they reduce intrinsic motivation (e.g., Deci, 1971; Lepper, Greene, & Nisbett, 1973).

What is the evidence that rewards decrease intrinsic motivation? A common research paradigm involves participants being given an interesting task such as solving puzzles. Participants are randomly placed into an Experimental group or a Control group. The Experimental group receives rewards such as praise or money for doing the task, and the Control group receives no reward. After this initial period, both groups are observed during a nonrewarded period in which participants have a choice between continuing to engage in the task or switching to some alternative activity. This provides a measure of intrinsic interest. A typical result is that participants in the Experimental group spend less time on the activity than does

(Continued)

Behaviorism also never got very far in accounting for complex learning. Skinner did attempt to describe language learning in terms of reinforcement principles. For example, some speech utterances make requests or demands that are rewarded when the hearer complies. Thus, a child who says, "I wanna cookie!" is reinforced when the parent hands over a cookie. Another use of speech involves naming different objects. A child who hears what different things are called (often in response to the question "What's that?") can learn the meaning of words by abstracting the relevant properties. Thus a child knows that *dog* cannot refer to *color* because animals with very different colors are called dogs.

Skinner also described the acquisition of syntax or grammar. He proposed that learners abstract certain word-position frames to generalize to new utterances. For example, after hearing "the woman's dog," "the man's desk," and "the child's desk," the learner would begin to form the possessive frame and then generalize to a novel combination such as "the man's dog" or "the woman's desk."

A DEBATE

Rewards, Intrinsic Motivation, and Creativity *(Continued)*

the Control group, and this finding is taken as indicating that reward undermines intrinsic motivation.

These results have been widely accepted in both the research literature and the popular media. Teaching manuals warn against "killing creativity" by introducing external rewards. It seems to be common knowledge. We have heard cognitive psychologists complain about a small increase in salary by saying (sarcastically), "It's a good thing the administration didn't give me such a big raise that I would lose all interest in psychology." Recently, however, Robert Eisenberger and Judy Cameron (1996) have challenged this view.

Eisenberger and Cameron argue that the generality of the phenomenon has been much exaggerated. They claim that detrimental effects of rewards occur only under highly restricted, easily avoided conditions. For example, rewards that are based on the quality of performance may increase rather than decrease motivation. Eisenberger and Cameron are not strict behaviorists; instead they believe that understanding the effects of rewards will require a synthesis of reinforcement theory, personality and social psychology, and cognitive psychology. We suspect, however, that the issue of the role of rewards on motivation will remain controversial and that we haven't heard the last word on this issue. The Eisenberger and Cameron article is well worth reading whether you agree with their arguments or not.

Although Skinner's analysis seems to provide a reasonable beginning, it never proved influential. Quite early Skinner's book *Verbal Behavior* (1957) was subjected to an extremely effective critique by the linguist Noam Chomsky (1959). Chomsky's most telling arguments concern the problems with giving a description of the stimuli and responses solely in terms of observable behaviors. As one example, Skinner said that the past-tense suffix *-ed* is controlled "by that subtle property of stimuli that we speak of as action-in-the-past" (Skinner, 1957, p. 121). But "action-in-the-past" is not some objective stimulus such as a red light turning on in a Skinner box. By directly postulating some "action-in-the-past" stimulus, Skinner was abandoning the behaviorist principle of describing learning in terms of objective, external stimuli. In short, the stimulus-response account was empty and circular.

This neglect of internal processes mediating between stimulus and response eventually led experimental psychologists to move away from behaviorism. It soon became clear that one could analyze internal processes without running into the difficulties that plagued the early introspectionists.

Summary

Although the extreme forms of behaviorism and introspectionism have been abandoned, each has left a valuable legacy. In an important sense, psychology is the science of behavior, and this focus on behavior has led to many important insights. But psychology is also the science of mind, and we have learned that internal processes such as thoughts can be studied scientifically. Although introspection is not an infallible window to the mind, psychological research is leading to principles that suggest when verbal reports are likely to accurately reflect thinking (e.g., Ericsson & Simon, 1993) and when they are misleading or interfere with it (Wilson & Brekke, 1994). Finally, we are continuing to learn how mental processes can be studied using very subtle measures such as reaction time.

COGNITIVE PSYCHOLOGY

The decline of behaviorism began around the time of World War II. Psychologists such as Donald Broadbent in England were called on to improve human skills and performance in complex tasks such as piloting an airplane. Early observations made it clear that pilots were incapable of picking up all the information on the various dials and gauges of an airplane's instrument panel. One task for the psychologists was to suggest how instrument panels might be redesigned to improve performance; another was to better understand the human side of human performance. A key factor in this understanding was the notion of information and information transmission.

The term *information* was also being formalized by C. E. Shannon and others who were developing mathematical theories of communication at about this time. Communication was viewed in terms of sending information over potentially "noisy" channels. These channels might be physical devices such as radio transmitters or radar screens, but human beings could also be viewed in terms of channels for receiving and transmitting information. Broadbent and others began to develop and test theories of attention in terms of channels and information. It proved to be very useful to think of human performance as **information processing** in a manner analogous to these communication devices.

The information processing metaphor served as a rallying point in the development of cognitive psychology. The initial inspiration from communication theory was strongly reinforced by the development of computers and the corresponding theory of computation. Computers also provided a rich set of analogies for theorizing about human cognition. One could talk about buffers (locations where temporary results were kept and integrated), information storage, and information retrieval in describing the function of both machines and human beings. In short, one could theorize about internal processes without retreating into subjectivism. Terms like *storage* and *retrieval* became essential ingredients in theories of memory, and psychologists began to ask questions about information processing capacity. In a classic paper, George Miller (1956) noted that human short-term memory capacity seemed to conform to "the magical number seven, plus or minus two" **chunks** of information. He was referring to the finding that people can remember a series of seven words as well as a series of seven letters, even though those words are comprised of many more than seven letters. Miller's paper showed that generalizations about capacity must take into account how the learner organizes that information into chunks or units (see Chapter 5). His paper also underlined the role of the information processor in organizing its experience.

Cognitive psychology became predominant in the late 1960s. One touchstone was Ulric Neisser's (1967) book *Cognitive Psychology*, which summarized a body of work within what is known as an information processing framework. A central factor was the development of techniques that allowed researchers to use indirect measures such as response times to reveal the workings of the mind. For example, Neisser's early research involved asking people to search through lists of letters to detect particular letters. He reasoned that if people can search for any one of five letters (for example) as rapidly as they can for a single letter, then people must be able to make comparisons at once (i.e., in parallel) rather than one at a time (i.e., serially).

The rationale for using reaction time to study how the mind works comes naturally from an information processing framework. Information processing models conceive of cognitive activities as involving a series of steps, procedures, or processes that take time. It is important to note that the times involved are often quite short (e.g., on the order of a tenth of a second), too short for people to reliably introspect about what they are doing. Therefore, researchers turn to information processing analyses to make suggestions about what processes people are using to carry out a cognitive task. Each information processing step is assumed to take some amount of time. Studies of the amount of time actually required to carry out a process can be used to test among competing theories. An excellent overview of research that uses processing time to understand cognitive processes is provided by Meyer, Osman, Irwin, and Yantis (1988).

In some cases, experiments interrupt processing in order to see what information is available at different points in time. A nice example of this approach comes from a paper by Ratcliff and McKoon (1989). Participants learned lists of active and passive sentences such as "John hit Bill" and "Jeff was attracted by Helen" and then had to discriminate those sentences from new sentences like "Bill hit John." They were allowed varying amounts of time to decide if a sentence was old or new. Ratcliff and McKoon measured accuracy for discriminating different types of information as a function of time. They found that early in processing (responses between 0.3 and 0.7 seconds) people could discriminate previously studied sentences from sentences containing all new words. However, people were completely unable to discriminate between a new sentence like "Bill hit John" and an old sentence like "John hit Bill." Ability to discriminate on the basis of relational information (e.g., who hit whom) began after about 0.7 seconds and then increased systematically. In short, Ratcliff and McKoon found that different kinds of information became available at different times during the retrieval. The observation is important because it is inconsistent with numerous models or theories that do not distinguish between item information and relational information or assume that they become available in a unitary manner.

Another way to understand cognitive processes is to look at the pattern of errors that are made. For example, suppose a person is shown the letter string X, R, B, T and later on recalls X, R, V, C. The V and C do not seem visually similar to B and T, so this pattern of errors may seem puzzling. Note, however, that V and C are acoustically similar to B and T. This observation led psychologists to postulate an information processing step in which the initial visual code becomes converted into an acoustic code (see, e.g., Conrad, 1964).

Summary

The information processing framework offered a host of exciting questions to be asked and a sound experimental methodology for answering them. Early successes, coupled with the handy computer metaphor, prompted researchers to explore a greater variety of paradigms and to be willing to tackle more complex cognitive tasks. In doing so, cognitive psychologists laid the groundwork for their role in the emergence of cognitive science, a topic to which we now turn.

THE EMERGENCE OF COGNITIVE SCIENCE

We have already alluded to the development of computers and their influence on cognitive psychology. In addition to providing a technological tool and descriptive language for formulating information processing theories, the underlying theory of computation, notably the work of Alan Turing, had an enormous influence on how people think about the mind. Turing described a simple machine (called a Turing machine) that forms the basis for modern computer science.

A **Turing machine** consists of a tape of any length divided into cells in which a symbol (usually 1 or 0) can be written, and a device that can read the contents of a cell and then carry out some actions. The actions consist of replacing the current symbol with another symbol and then moving the tape one cell to the left or right. In addition, the machine has a finite list of states or conditions it can be in and a table that describes what action should take place for each of these states and what state should be entered after the action is completed. Turing (1936) showed that this simple device can do any computation that can be performed by a digital computer (as long as it has enough tape and enough time). More importantly, he showed that there were special machines (called universal Turing machines) that could carry out *any* computation. Computers are an example of a universal Turing machine.

From the standpoint of cognitive science, the most important property of universal Turing machines is that they are physical devices that carry out abstract computations. In short, these abstract computations are ways of processing information in a physical system. It is tempting to assert that the same principle holds for human beings. According to this functional analysis the nervous system can be viewed as a physical system that performs abstract computations, and that these computations are the cornerstone of intelligence. Part of the lesson of a Turing machine is that the way a machine is constructed physically is less important than what it can compute. Turing machines can be built using a variety of materials such as electrical relays (as in early computers) or silicon chips (as in modern computers). Thus, Turing's work suggested that it can be fruitful to study what the mind is doing without worrying about how the brain does what it does.

There is something subtle but important here. When people view the mind as being a computational device, that does not mean they think it is built like a computer. Modern computers have components such as a long-term storage device (like a hard drive), current memory (RAM), and a central processor (like the Pentium and Power PC chips at the heart of many computers). There is no reason to believe that the mind is set up at all like a computer. Nonetheless, it is possible that the brain is carrying out computations of the sort a Turing machine might perform. Thus, it is possible to say that the mind computes like a Turing machine does without believing that the mind is set up at all like a computer.

When computers began to be available in the 1950s, they were quickly put to use to do some fairly intelligent things. Herbert Simon and Allan Newell developed a program known as the Logic Theorist that could prove logical theorems and, furthermore, prove them in a way that resembled human performance. This work encouraged both the development of artificial intelligence (AI) and an interaction between cognitive psychology and artificial intelligence. And, of course, questions about whether computers can think are relevant to and informed by work on the philosophy of mind (see, e.g., Fodor, 1981; Putnam, 1960).

At roughly the same time, other developments led to increasing interaction between psychologists and linguists. Psychologists began to shift from an interest in memory for nonsense syllables and single words to memory for sentences, paragraphs, and stories. In addition, Chomsky's transformational grammar provided a rich source of ideas for researchers. Psychologists began to evaluate the psychological reality of some of the insights provided by linguists (see, e.g., Fodor, Bever, & Garrett, 1974; G. A. Miller, 1962).

The net effect of these developments was that some of the traditional distinctions among disciplines began to break down. A computer scientist, a philosopher, an anthropologist, a linguist, and a psychologist might all be interested in concept formation and bring insights from their disciplines to bear on the problem. Furthermore, the fact that brain damage appears to selectively affect categorization systems means that neuroscience also has a contribution to make. Philosophy, linguistics, AI, cognitive psychology, anthropology, and neuroscience have begun to formalize their similar interests under the banner of **cognitive science.**

Finally, Turing is also well known for his proposal for answering the question of whether machines can think. There used to be an English parlor game in which a person hid behind a screen and other players asked questions of the hidden person in order to determine whether they were a man or a woman. Turing suggested that if a computer were intelligent, it could play this game. One popular variant of this game, often referred to as the **Turing test** is to have a person communicate with a computer. If the person was unable to tell whether the computer was a computer or a person, then we ought to concede that the machine could think. The Turing test cuts through a lot of vagueness concerning what we mean by thought and encourages us to view intelligence in terms of functional rather than physical characteristics. That is, it encourages us to think about what the mind computes without worrying about how that computation is done.

Summary

Cognitive science is the interdisciplinary study of the mind. Important to its development is that computers not only provide a machine to use in research but also represent a model or abstract framework for thinking about the nature of intelligence. Much of intelligence can be seen as the representation and processing of information.

COGNITIVE NEUROSCIENCE TECHNIQUES

While computer science encourages us to think about what the mind is doing rather than how it is doing it, neuroscience provides pressure in the opposite direction. That is, neuroscience makes us think about how the brain is carrying out cognitive processes. Currently, one of the most exciting aspects of neuroscience (called *cognitive neuroscience*) uses techniques that allow us to study the way the brain operates without causing any harm to the organism. These techniques permit the study of the brain's operation in normal functioning humans. To give you a flavor of the kinds of techniques now available, we start with a description of a few aspects of the brain and then consider three techniques for studying (or imaging) the brain.

In order to understand something of the way cognitive neuroscience has affected psychology, it is necessary to say a few words about the brain. The brain is an amazingly complex organ consisting of many different kinds of cells. Probably the most important type of cell in the brain is the neuron. Neurons send electrical signals from the cell body to the other end of the cell. At the end of the cell are little baskets filled with chemicals (called neurotransmitters) that can affect the cells around them. When an electrical signal is sent from the cell body, the baskets of chemical are dumped out of the cell where the neurotransmitters make other neurons either more or less likely to send an electrical signal of their own (depending on the kind of chemical). It is believed that different areas of the brain are responsible for carrying out different functions. Thus, different cognitive processes may cause areas of the brain to have more or less electrical activity.

Cognitive neuroscience studies how the activity of the brain is related to different cognitive operations. What we would like are techniques that would allow us to study how human brains process information without actually having to open up people's skulls and insert electrodes. Modern technology has provided these sorts of techniques. However, there are (at least) two types of information about activity in the brain that we are interested in. First, we want to know where in the brain the activity is. Techniques with high *spatial resolution* give us good information about where activity is occurring. We also want to know when the activity occurs.

Techniques with good *temporal resolution* tell us when the activity is occurring. As we will see in the next sections, some current techniques have good spatial resolution, and some have good temporal resolution, but no techniques have both good spatial and good temporal resolution.

Event-Related Potentials

One way to gather information about electrical activity in the brain is to put a cap that has electrodes attached on the head of a subject. The electrodes are measuring devices that can detect very small voltages (another term for voltage is *electrical potential*). Electricity actually passes through the scalp and can be measured by these electrodes. This technique is called the electroencephalogram or EEG. Because the electricity passes through the scalp, it spreads out (or diffuses) and so the spatial resolution of EEG is poor. An electrical signal can only be localized within a few centimeters (huge by brain standards). However, EEG can detect rapid changes in electrical potential, and so the temporal resolution of EEG is quite good. Changes in activity over a few milliseconds can be detected.

An EEG technique that is used frequently in psychology is the *event related potential* (ERP). In this technique, the electrical activity at various electrodes on the scalp is measured starting with the time that a stimulus is presented on an experimental trial. Then, the activity from many different trials is averaged together, and the resulting pattern of voltages is examined. Because the pattern of voltages (or potentials) is related to the onset of the stimulus (the event), this technique is called the event related potential.

There are many different positive and negative voltage peaks (components) that have been observed in psychological studies. These components are distinguished by whether they correspond to a positive (P) or negative (N) voltage and by the time from the event that they occur (measured in milliseconds [ms]). Research suggests that ERP responses are sensitive to surprising or unexpected events. For example, Kutas and Hillyard (1984) found that an N400 wave (a large-amplitude negative component with a peak around 400ms after the stimulus) varied directly with the expectedness of words that ended a sentence. Osterhout and Holcomb (1992) reported that a different component, P600 (a positive peak 600ms after the stimulus), is responsive to syntactic (grammatical) anomaly or unusualness. These peaks provide information about how long it takes for the brain to compute that an event is surprising. In sum, ERP provides a very promising tool for analyzing the temporal aspects of cognitive processes on-line.

Positron Emission Tomography

Positron emission tomography (PET) uses the physics of radioactivity to trace chemicals in the brain. One prominent way to use PET to explore brain activity is to give a person small doses of a nontoxic radioactive substance that is then transported in the person's bloodstream. When a particular brain region is involved in cognitive processes, its neurons are more active, which causes the area to need more energy. Thus, more blood flows to that area. PET can be used to detect this increase in blood flow. PET has good spatial resolution (on the order of millimeters). However, because of the physics involved in detecting the radioactivity, the temporal resolution is poor, and so activity across a few seconds must be averaged together.

This technique represents an exciting tool for the localization of cognitive activities. Figure 1.3 shows different brain activity associated with hearing, reading, and generating words. As one might expect, seeing words is associated with activity in the visual cortex and hearing words with activity in the auditory cortex. More subtle differences can also be detected. For example, different regions of the brain appear to be activated when a person is shown a letter string that forms a word versus one that does not (S. E. Peterson, Fox, Snyder, & Raichle, 1990). Therefore, PET scans can provide evidence relevant to cognitive theories. For example, if some theory postulates that two systems are involved in a certain process, then the observation that two distinct neuronal regions are active during that process lends some support to that theory (Fiez & Peterson, 1993; Osherson, Perani, Cappa, Schnur, Grassi, & Fazio, 1998).

Functional Magnetic Resonance Imaging

Both ERP and PET methods represent exciting and promising developments. Even more powerful techniques are rapidly becoming available. One technique that has become more popular than PET in recent years is functional Magnetic Resonance Imaging (fMRI). In this technique, strong magnetic fields are created by large magnets. Detectors in the machine are able to track aspects of the behavior of hydrogen atoms in the magnetic field, which allows them to detect blood flow in the brain in much the same way that PET does. Like PET, fMRI has limited temporal resolution, but it has spatial resolution that is generally better than PET. Methods such as these are often expensive to obtain and use; the equipment alone runs into millions of dollars. For a review outlining the promise and progress associated with functional MRI see D'Esposito, Zarahn, and Aguirre (1999).

A potential difficulty with studying cognitive processing using PET and fMRI is in the way the techniques are interpreted. Despite what you may have heard as a child, you use all of your brain all of the time. Thus, a PET or fMRI scan reveals activity all over the brain. So how do you know which areas were *particularly* active when the person was doing the experimental task of interest? One popular way to do it is to have a *control task* that is like the experimental task you are interested in, but differs only in that the person is not actually doing the important part of the experimental task. For example, if you were interested in exploring the areas of the brain selectively involved in doing addition, you might show people a solved addition problem and have them press a button if the answer was correct. In a second task, the same people would read the addition problem and press a button when they were through reading. This control task would still require people

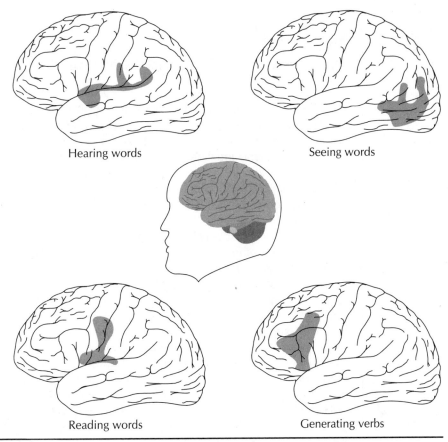

| **Figure 1.3** | PET scans showing increased blood flow associated with neural activity involved in hearing words, seeing words, reading words, and generating verbs. |

Source: Miller, 1995. Courtesy of Marcus Raichle, Department of Neurology, Washington University School of Medicine.

to read the numbers and to press a button, but not to do the addition problem. After performing these tasks, the activity in the brain in the control task is subtracted from the activity in the experimental task. That leaves us with a picture of the areas of the brain much more or much less active in the experimental task than in the control task.

The subtraction method is quite powerful and is the source of images like the one in Figure 1.3. However, it also demonstrates three important limitations of techniques like PET and fMRI. First, interpreting what the pictures mean requires knowing how good the experimental and control tasks are. If the control task differs from the experimental task in many ways, then it will be hard to know exactly why a particular brain region is active. Second, if a brain area is important to both the

AN ENIGMA
The Mind and the Brain and the Nature of Consciousness

We all know what consciousness is. Indeed, it seems to be at the very center of what it means to be a human being. We wouldn't be the same sort of entity without it. But what is it exactly? As far as we know, even the most powerful and intelligent computers lack consciousness. (Our intuitions about consciousness in animals are more variable but virtually everyone thinks that at least primates have consciousness.) How can consciousness be studied and what role should it play in theories of cognition? Intuitively, we know (or believe) that consciousness plays a causal role in information processing and behavior. If so, exactly how are we different from computers when it comes to information processing? Maybe it's just the case that conscious and unconscious intelligence are two paths to the same goal (getting along in the world).

Lately a number of cognitive scientists and neuroscientists have taken up questions about consciousness in hopes of systematically studying and understanding it. We know that molecules can give rise to emergent properties like liquid and solid states—maybe consciousness is an emergent property of brain activity (if so, maybe we shouldn't be so sure that computers can't have consciousness). Emergent properties can also have causal force—a brick that falls on your head can hurt you even though no individual molecule can do damage. And maybe we can make some progress by examining brain activity during consciousness (e.g., Crick & Koch, 1990). It is beginning to appear that we may be able to study consciousness empirically but as of yet it remains a mystery if not a miracle (for further discussion see Flannagan, 1998).

experimental and control tasks (though perhaps for different reasons), then it will not show up when the activation from the control task is subtracted from the activation in the experimental task. Finally, because the control task must be perfectly matched to an experimental task, only tasks of short duration are reasonable to test. It would be nearly impossible to generate a good control condition for exploring a long cognitive process like reading a paragraph. Thus, the techniques currently used are limited to studying processes that take place in a few seconds. Luckily, that still leaves us with a lot of cognition to explore.

Summary

It is a safe bet that cognitive neuroscience tools will increasingly provide insights into how the human brain performs cognitive operations. As we shall see, other researchers take the brain seriously because they believe that psychological theories should take their inspiration from neuroscience rather than from computer science. They believe that "brain-style" theorizing will ultimately prove more effective than theories that are not constrained by knowledge of the nervous system. In practical terms, this often means that neurally inspired theories aim to account for complex cognitive processes in terms of a large number of simple component processes. In this sense, complex behaviors are "reduced to" or explained by simple underlying processes. Before taking up a specific example of this approach, we describe two important perspectives for thinking about levels of analysis.

LEVELS OF ANALYSIS

A critical issue for cognitive science in general and cognitive psychology in particular is what level of analysis is likely to prove most fruitful. In cognitive psychology, the most common strategy has been to take a functional approach based on an information processing perspective. As we have seen, this approach is compatible with the development of computer science and artificial intelligence. But many researchers believe that it's a mistake to ignore how processes are actually implemented in living organisms. We've just noted some of the techniques that allow us to look at brain activity, and even the researcher dedicated to a functional analysis needs to be aware of developments in cognitive neuroscience. Furthermore, human beings are not simply computational devices but organisms whose intelligence is expressed in terms of adaptations to their environment. Thus, it may be useful to take an evolutionary stance and make predictions from the perspective of what is likely to be adaptive (e.g., see Buss, Haselton, Shackleford, Bleske, & Wakefield, 1998; Cosmides & Tooby, 1994; Tooby & Cosmides, 1990). A related strategy is to focus on the structure of information in the environment and assume that human cognition is sensitive to this structure (e.g., J. R. Anderson, 1990a; J. J. Gibson, 1979). In short, it is not so much that a functional analysis is wrong as it is that more than one level of analysis is needed. In reading about experiments and theories in this book it may be helpful to you to realize that theories may be directed at different levels of description and that these alternative levels yield different sorts of insights into how the mind works. In short, there's no single "correct" level. Let's take a moment to look at two specific ideas about multiple levels of analysis.

Marr's Three Levels

David Marr was a gifted vision scientist (who unfortunately died young). He pointed out that there are many ways to describe how something works. Consider asking why a cash register works the way it does. Depending on who is asking the question and why they wanted to know, we might respond by explaining the rules of addition. Alternatively, we might want to explain how cash registers represent numbers and how they increment those numbers. Finally, we might want to explain how electric current is passed through silicon chips to cause changes in electronic switches. Each of these levels of description might be the right one, depending on the nature of the question. Marr (1982) formalized the ideas that there may be many levels of description, and he outlined three levels that he thought were pertinent to the study of cognition.

The broadest level of analysis asks what the system or device does and why. That is, what is its purpose or function? What a cash register does is addition, so this level involves the theory of addition. This theory will tell us what is being computed in a way that is independent of both how numbers are written (e.g., roman versus arabic) and how the addition process will actually be executed. The why part of the question can be answered by noting that the constraints associated with making purchases correspond to the operation of addition. For example, if you buy nothing, you should pay nothing; there is a natural zero point; the total cost should depend neither on the order in which you purchase things nor on how things are grouped (the mathematical principles of commutativity and associativity); and if the purchaser returns an item, the net expenditure should be zero (i.e., there is a natural inverse). Questions about what is being computed and why characterize what Marr calls the **computational level,** and what it yields, in this example, is a computational theory of cash registers.

To actually perform the operation of addition, a system needs to have some form of representation (a formal system for being explicit about the information operated on) and an algorithm or procedure to accomplish the operation. This second level, the **algorithmic level,** specifies how the computations are done. For addition, a system might use arabic numerals for the representation, and the algorithm might follow the rules about starting with the least significant digits and "carrying" if the sum is greater than 9. Just which algorithm is appropriate depends on the representation selected. In general, a variety of different representations and algorithm pairs could accomplish the same computations (e.g., one could use either a decimal or binary system to do addition).

The third level of analysis is the **implementation level.** At this level the algorithm is physically realized. A child who adds arabic numerals in the manner we have described is using the same algorithm that is implemented by the wires and transistors in a cash register. Even different computers may realize the same algorithm in different ways; Marr points out that a program to play tic-tac-toe was implemented by W. K. Hissis and B. Silverman in a computer made from Tinkertoys!

These three levels are summarized in Table 1.1. Marr argues that to understand a complex system, scientists need to operate on all three levels. Knowing what is being computed often places important constraints on the algorithmic level (it must compute the right thing). Similarly, observations at the implementation level determine which algorithms can be realized. For example, studying brain function should provide important information on how cognitive processes are implemented in human beings.

Marr's three levels will come up again in later chapters. His framework allows us to see relationships among different research perspectives. As we shall see, Chomsky's theories of grammar apply at the computational level, research on language comprehension often corresponds to the algorithmic level, and a neurolinguist

Table 1.1   **The Three Levels at Which Any Intelligent System Carrying Out an Information-Processing Task Must Be Understood**

Computational Theory	Representation and Algorithm	Hardware Implementation
What is the goal of the computation and why is it appropriate?	How can this computational theory be realized? In particular, what is the representation for the input and output, and what is the algorithm that does the computation?	How can the representation and algorithm be physically implemented?

Source: From *Vision*, by D. Marr, ©1982, San Francisco: W. H. Freeman. Reprinted with permission.

focusing on the neural substrate of expressive aphasia (inability to speak associated with damage to Broca's area of the brain) can be seen as operating at the implementation level.

Recursive Decomposition

For many purposes, Marr's three-level distinction works fairly well. But a closer analysis suggests many possible levels of description, especially within Marr's algorithmic and implementation levels. Studies of how to present information to facilitate text comprehension are at a more abstract level than studies of how we access the meanings of individual words, which are, in turn, more abstract than studies of how people perceive individual letters. But all of these levels would fall under Marr's algorithmic level. Similarly, studies of brain damage and aphasia are several levels higher than single-cell recordings of brain activity and their underlying biophysics, though they all seem to be on the implementational side of things. Palmer and Kimchi (1986) suggest that information processing theories rely (among other things) on the principle of **recursive decomposition.** According to recursive decomposition, any complex (informational) event at one level of description can be specified more fully at a lower level of description by decomposing it into (1) a number of components and (2) processes that specify the relations among these components. Continuing an example, research on paragraph comprehension can be decomposed into sentence comprehension, word comprehension, letter perception, and so on. In some cases, theoretical models use multiple levels simultaneously and attempt to describe interactions within and across these levels.

Neither the Marr nor the Palmer and Kimchi descriptions of levels should be equated with the notion of **reductionism,** which assumes that the best or correct level of description is the most specific one (e.g., at the level of physics). Different levels of description are not just quantitatively simpler but may also be qualitatively different. This is most evident in Marr's analysis. In general, however, higher-level descriptions may manifest emergent properties that derive from how the system is organized. For example, we saw that many cognitive scientists think that consciousness is an emergent property of our nervous system and its functioning—consciousness derives from properties of groups or aggregates of nerve cells, not of individual nerve cells. In cognitive psychology, the ideal is to pick the level or levels that best illuminate the questions being asked. We say "levels," the plural, because there are likely to be limitations if only a single level of analysis is considered.

Summary

Research in cognitive psychology can be and is conducted at different levels of analysis. Some researchers choose to focus on the brain and cognition at what Marr would call the implementation level. Others argue that much is to be gained by attention to the function some cognitive process serves, Marr's computational level. Finally, a great deal of research is conducted at an intermediate (algorithmic) level as cognitive psychologists try to figure out how information is mentally represented and processed.

DIVERSITY OF APPROACHES

So far we have considered information processing from a fairly abstract level. When we look closer, we will see a range of styles of research and theorizing within this general framework. These styles generally fit within Marr's algorithmic level but may differ in the extent to which they are influenced by computational-level and implementational-level considerations.

Although most researchers subscribe to the information processing framework, that framework does not dictate exactly how research should be done. No single approach dominates cognitive psychology. Approaches tend to differ along two major dimensions: degree of formalism and explicit versus implicit structure.

Degree of Formalism

Cognitive psychologists perform experiments to answer questions, but the questions being asked vary enormously in terms of their formalism. At one end of the continuum are frameworks that attempt to describe general principles to organize research findings. No particular experiment really tests the framework, and the framework is not falsifiable in any formal sense. Rather, frameworks either are or are not useful in organizing research. An example of a useful framework is Tulving's encoding specificity principle (Tulving & Thomson, 1973; see Chapter 5).

The encoding specificity principle states that a retrieval cue will help memory only to the extent that it overlaps with the ways in which the material to be remembered was originally coded. Tulving, Thomson, and others produced a variety of observations that are consistent with this principle. For example, suppose that one studies the word *iron* in the context of steam and encodes *iron* as an "appliance" rather than as "a type of metal." Then recall of *iron* ought to be prompted by a context created by presenting *laundry* as a hint or cue but not prompted by hints such as *ore*. And that is what happens. Frameworks are not directly refutable, but they do provide general principles that can guide the development of testable theories.

At the other end of the continuum are computational or even mathematical models. Testability is one of the more salient characteristics of **mathematical models** of cognitive processes. Mathematical models, which attempt to represent processes in terms of mathematical equations and formulas, can vary considerably in their complexity, but they have in common the goal of predicting or "fitting" data. For example, according to some theories of decision making people always act in a way that is optimal. To see what this view predicts in a given situation, one simply calculates what would maximize gains (what is optimal). One advantage of this formal approach is that sometimes (e.g., Estes, 1986; Townsend, 1971) one learns that seemingly different models or theories are actually mathematical equivalents! More often the formal analysis points researchers toward situations in which the models in question make different predictions.

Probably the safest generalization is that the degree of formalism varies with the stage of development in an area. Initial observations make clear what the phenomena are; mathematical models might narrow attention prematurely to a subset of these phenomena. Frameworks serve to organize phenomena, but their lack of testability means that they may drift into circularity unless they inspire more specific theories. Formalism is also somewhat of a matter of taste—some people may not want to study some process if they can't put it into mathematical form. It is a testimony to the vitality of cognitive psychology that there seems to be plenty of room for varying degrees of formality.

Explicit Versus Implicit Structure

A common practice, if not goal, of many computer simulation programs is to make structure as explicit as possible. Information resides in discrete locations, and to understand how the program works, it is important to make transparent which structures are doing what. Of course, computer simulation may not represent plausible models of how the brain works, at least if one takes the analogy to be quite specific. For example, we know that information does not reside in single brain cells but rather is distributed across thousands of neurons. If information were completely localized, we might wake up unable to recognize Grandmother because the cell dedicated to recognizing her has "passed away." However, most computer programs that are generated as psychological models are assumed to be algorithmic level descriptions of a system (using Marr's terminology) rather than implementational level descriptions.

Recently there has been renewed interest in developing computational models that are more directly influenced by knowledge about how the brain functions. These models are variously referred to as neural networks, parallel distributed processing (**PDP**) models, or simply connectionist models. The majority of these models have a more implicit structure in that what corresponds to a piece of information is a pattern of activation across many nodes or over a network of interconnected cells. As we shall see, however, it is precisely the distributed nature of these representations that gives them many of their interesting characteristics.

Connectionist Models

Their implicit structure makes connectionist models (initially) difficult to understand. Here we begin by describing a very simple example. (Other examples will appear later on in this book in case your instructor may choose to skip this one.) The example does not illustrate many of the powerful features of connectionist models, but it may serve to indicate why so many researchers are intrigued by neural network models.

Look at Figure 1.4, and as rapidly as you can, read off the shade (gray or black) in which each word appears. (Normally, the task involves colors like red and green rather than shades, but you should get the effect for gray and black.) If you are like most people, you will be unable to completely ignore word form and will either make errors or slow down to avoid reading off the word rather than its color (Dunbar & MacLeod, 1984). (Interestingly, people can successfully ignore the colors if they are asked to just read the words.) This interference effect was first reported by Stroop (1935), and hundreds of studies using the Stroop task have been run to examine various aspects of attention. For example, Gotlib and McCann (1984) reported that depressed people were slower to name the color of words involving depressed content (e.g., worthless, inadequate) than the color of neutral words. Nondepressed people, even when exposed to a negative mood induction procedure (reading negative statements like "I want to go to sleep and never wake up") did not show this effect. It appears that being depressed heightens sensitivity to negative content.

Connectionist Account of the Stroop Effect

One approach to understanding the Stroop effect is seen in the parallel distributed processing model of J. D. Cohen, Dunbar, and McClelland (1990). The basic idea is that color and word shape information are simultaneously activated and compete for control of responding (reading aloud). Figure 1.5 illustrates the general idea of the network model.

Connectionist models consist of units (sometimes called nodes) and links. The units, which are shown as circles in Figure 1.5, are like neurons in the brain. The links, which are the lines that connect the units, are like the connections between neurons. Just as each neuron in the brain sends electrical signals that cause it to influence the neurons connected to it, units have levels of activation that affect

GRAY
BLACK
GRAY
BLACK
BLACK
GRAY
BLACK
GRAY
GRAY
GRAY
BLACK
BLACK
GRAY
BLACK
BLACK
GRAY

Figure 1.4   **An Example of the Stroop Task**   It is difficult to read out loud the shades in which the words appear, suggesting that people are unable to completely ignore word shape.

the activation of other units connected to it. If a link is excitatory, then activation of one unit tends to increase the activation of another. If a link is inhibitory, then activation of one unit tends to decrease the activation of another. The model in Figure 1.5 has input units at the bottom. These units are assumed to get their activation from the environment. The model also has response units at the top. These units get their value by having activation of the input units feed through connections to the middle units (called the hidden units because they are hidden between the input and response units) and then through a second set of connections to the response units.

In the model shown in Figure 1.5, the two leftmost input units are assumed to be activated by the color of the ink. If the ink color is gray, then the "gray" input node is activated. This activation leads to signals being passed onto the intermediate, hidden units. For example, when gray ink is presented, the input unit for the color gray sends an excitatory (+) signal to the intermediate unit directly above it and an inhibitory (−) signal to the adjacent intermediate unit. The leftmost intermediate unit, when activated, will, in turn, send an excitatory signal to the unit corresponding to "gray" at the response level and send an inhibitory signal to the response "black." So far, one can see that when gray ink is presented, the units that promote a response of saying "gray" become excited and that they, in turn, inhibit units associated with a response of saying "black."

The rightmost two input units are analogous to the ink color units except that they are responses to words rather than their color. When the word "gray" is presented (regardless of its ink color), it will excite one intermediate unit and inhibit the adjacent one, and the excited intermediate unit will send an excitatory signal to the response unit corresponding to "gray" and an inhibitory signal to the response units for "black." So far, so good?

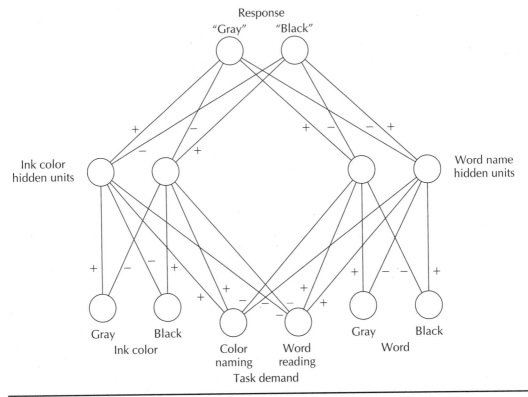

Figure 1.5   **The Network Architecture Applied by Cohen, et al. (1990) to the Stroop Task**   Units at the bottom are input nodes; units at the top are response or output nodes; and units at the middle level are hidden units that integrate multiple sources of information.

Source: J. D. Cohen, Dunbar, & McClelland, 1990.

Things become more complicated when we combine the ink color input units and the word shape and consider what happens when the word *gray* is presented in black ink. The ink color input unit will tend to activate the response "black" but the word input unit will tend to activate the directly opposing response, "gray." How is this conflict resolved? The network model adds two other input units corresponding to task demands to address this issue. For example, if the instruction is to name the ink color, it is assumed that the input unit corresponding to color naming is activated. As Figure 1.5 indicates, the color-naming input unit sends an excitatory signal to the left two hidden units (the ones that respond to ink color) and an inhibitory signal to the other two hidden units (the ones that respond to word shape).

Suppose, now, that the task is to read the color of words, and the stimulus is the word *black* presented in gray ink. The color-naming task demand unit will be activated, which will tend to facilitate the intermediate units that respond to color and inhibit the hidden units that respond to words. The gray color input unit and the black word input unit will also be activated. The gray color input unit and the task demand unit will both send excitatory signals to the hidden unit (leftmost intermediate unit), which in turn will tend to activate the correct response unit, "gray," and inhibit the incorrect response unit. Meanwhile, the rightmost hidden unit will receive a positive signal from the black word input unit but a negative signal from the task demand unit. Because this hidden unit is receiving both positive and negative signals, it will not send as strong a signal to the response units as it does when it receives only positive signals. In this instance, the "gray" response unit might well reach some threshold level of activation before the "black" response unit, and a correct response would have been made. All of the processes from input on take place in parallel. Activation from input units is passed on to hidden units, which in turn activate response units.

On some trials when the word *black* is presented in gray ink the black response unit may reach threshold first and then an error would be made. Even if no errors are made, it will take longer for "gray" to reach threshold first when it has to compete with the word unit activating "black." That is, the model predicts that people can name the ink color faster when the word presented is not a color term or corresponds to the ink color (as in the word *gray* presented in gray ink) than when the word corresponds to the incorrect ink color.

Why do words interfere with colors more than vice versa? The basic idea is that people spend a lot of time reading and that therefore the strength of connections between word input units and hidden units tends to be greater than that between color input units and hidden units. In addition, the strength of connections between hidden units and response units should also tend to be greater for hidden units that respond to words than for hidden units that respond to colors. People no doubt see colors all the time, but they don't typically name them. Words, in contrast, are frequently read (named). If this interpretation sounds informal, rest assured that J. D. Cohen et al. (1990) made specific assumptions about activation functions, trained the network, tested it, and showed that it could account for the basic Stroop effect and a variety of associated observations concerning things like practice effects (although our presentation seems complex, we've left out a lot of details).

We will not provide a separate chapter on connectionist models but we will incorporate their description into relevant content-oriented chapters. Many connectionist models, as well as the relationship between connectionism and neuroscience are described in the *Handbook of Brain Theory and Neural Networks,* edited by Michael Arbib (1995). One thing that has yet to be worked out is what level of description connectionist models apply to. At first glance, it would appear that connectionist models are implementational-level models, because they are talking about neuronlike units and connections. However, just as cognitive psychology sometimes uses a computational metaphor for thinking about cognition, it also may use a brain metaphor for understanding the brain. That is, connectionist models may be brainlike without actually being about the specific way the brain carries out cognitive processing. There are certainly plenty of differences between connectionist models and brains. For example, the units in connectionist models have levels of activation, but neurons change the number of electrical signals they send from the cell body to the end. Thus, many cognitive scientists now think of connectionist models as another kind of algorithmic-level description of cognitive processing.

AN APPLICATION
Schizophrenia

Interestingly, people with schizophrenia show larger than usual Stroop effects. Why might this be true? Is there a way to understand this intriguing finding in terms of an information processing model? Cohen and Servan-Schreiber (1992) interpreted these deficits within the framework of the neural network model we have just been discussing. They began by noting that one of the physiological correlates of schizophrenia is dopamine depletion (dopamine is a chemical involved in the transmission of nerve impulses). Cohen and Servan-Schreiber speculated that the effects of dopamine depletion would manifest themselves in the form of changing the activation pattern for network units. They then altered a network in this manner and were able to reproduce the pattern of deficits seen in people with schizophrenia.

Observations such as these both support the model and suggest that it may prove useful to understanding the effects of schizophrenia on cognitive processes. Although this research has yet to lead to a direct application, it has the promise of increasing our understanding of schizophrenia.

Summary

As we have just seen, there are strikingly different ways to study cognition. They range from general frameworks that guide and summarize large sets of studies to mathematical models that make very precise predictions, to neural network models that often produce emergent phenomena. All of these approaches fit within a general information processing framework and many researchers may use each of them at various points. Examples of these distinct styles of theorizing will be scattered throughout the remainder of this book. We conclude this chapter with one other fundamental issue with respect to the study of cognition: relations between (artificial) laboratory experiments and the natural world. This issue is important both for evaluating research and for linking our central themes to experimental research.

ECOLOGICAL VALIDITY

A common criticism of laboratory studies is that they are too artificial and lack ecological validity. We take **ecological validity** to refer to the idea of developing theories that describe cognitive processes operating in realistic, everyday situations. It is hard to fault this ideal.

One rather extreme position is that any laboratory experiment that fails to capture the full complexity of natural situations will necessarily produce invalid results. It certainly is possible to be so concerned with controlling variables that one creates a very artificial, even impoverished situation. Any important variable left out of an experimental situation may limit the generality of any result obtained. But to argue that results are necessarily invalid is to ignore much of the history of science. One often has to resort to highly artificial situations (such as forcing people to say whether a sentence is old or new after 400 milliseconds) to contrast the predictions of alternative theories. The other side of the issue is that ecologically valid situations are very likely (or even necessarily) experimentally invalid because one cannot tease apart the contributions of different correlated factors to performance. The critical issue is how to balance realism with the need to control variables.

One interesting perspective on ecological validity is provided by Shepard's (1984) analysis of the relation between evolutionary processes and methods for studying perception. Shepard begins by noting that higher organisms are active explorers and manipulators of their environment. Shepard argues that this exploration is not just random but is guided by internal models that allow one to anticipate as well as notice events. The ability to develop appropriate expectations may be vitally important when there is little information or little time available before an organism must act.

Shepard draws an analogy between the perceptual system and biological or circadian rhythms. The activity pattern of many animals is guided by day-night cycles and it seems natural to assume that these rhythms are directly under the control of the sun. Researchers found, however, that animals such as hamsters, when placed under conditions of constant illumination (in an artificial laboratory situation), continue to show cycles of 24 hours plus or minus only a few minutes. In short, the periodicity has become internalized so that it continues in the absence of the external stimulus, freeing an animal from directly depending on it. This would be advantageous for animals on cloudy days or in environments (e.g., in the safety of a burrow) where the cues from the sun are not directly available.

The same situation holds for the perceptual system, according to Shepard. The idea is that certain constraints associated with the environment (more properly, the interaction of organisms with their environment) may become internalized or embodied in the perceptual system. To see what these constraints are and to evaluate their significance, researchers need to put organisms into artificial situations where the information is ambiguous or undetermined. In these ambiguous situations, natural constraints may be observed, just as circadian rhythms are observed under the situation of constant illumination.

Shepard illustrates this framework by his research on apparent motion. In apparent motion, the rapid alternating presentation of different views of an object gives rise to the experience of one object smoothly transforming back and forth. In the case of a dot appearing in two locations, the experience is of a single dot that moves back and forth. In many situations there are a number of possible paths of motion (transformations), and the question is which ones are natural. Interestingly, just which path something appears to move along depends on whether it is a biological organism or a physical object (e.g., Chatterjee, Freyd, & Shiffrar, 1996). The point is that ambiguous situations, which take people out of their normally rich environment, allows natural biases or constraints to emerge and provides important clues to how the perceptual system functions.

We suggest that Shepard's framework may hold, not just for the perceptual system but for the cognitive system in general. Note that this is support for a procedure for understanding the relation of cognitive systems to their environment by using artificial situations, not a blanket endorsement of artificial situations as ends in themselves.

Summary

We believe that a concern with ecological validity is important not only to ensure that experiments generalize to real-world situations but also because ecological considerations may be crucial to understanding cognition. We have been arguing that cognition must be heavily constrained if it is to function effectively, and an analysis of natural situations provides a source of candidate constraints. Cognitive psychologists may profitably and explicitly violate ecological validity for certain purposes, but they cannot ignore ecological considerations.

Summary

This has been a pretty long introduction so a summary is clearly in order. We began by noting that there are major obstacles to learning from experience. Appropriate control or comparison conditions are almost always lacking. If our inferences are based only on outcomes or feedback, the information we receive may be systematically misleading (e.g., self-fulfilling prophecy). There are at least two morals to be drawn from these observations, one about human cognition and the other about studying it. One is that, in the face of inadequate information, the cognitive system must make some guesses about what inferences or attributions are likely to be correct. The other is that well-controlled experiments are critically important for understanding human thought and behavior. Intuitive judgments of reasonableness and informal observation are fallible guides.

Furthermore, random guesses about relevance or appropriate actions are too costly and too slow to allow organisms to learn which differences make a difference. To address this challenge, organisms have evolved in such a way that they favor some possibilities over others; that is, their learning is constrained. Although one might conclude that this paints a pessimistic picture of what people can hope to know or learn, we take a much more positive view. We have focused on fallibility to underline the inadequacy of experience but, in general, our guesses or biases appear to be nicely tied to the contingencies we face in the world. The quote from Alexander Pope at the beginning of this chapter sounds a theme that carries throughout this book.

We are a little uncomfortable with covering methods and approaches in such detail without talking very much about basic processes like learning, perception, memory, and problem solving. At the same time, however, we believe that you need a road map for the territory that we will be covering. The history of the development of cognitive psychology is important for understanding the logic of its methods and its ties with cognitive science and cognitive neuroscience. In reading the later chapters, you need to bear in mind questions about levels of description, kinds of theories, and relationships of experimental situations to real-world contexts. Our brief review of the history of cognitive psychology and the different approaches to studying cognition should make it clear that cognitive psychology is a dynamic, exciting field and not a lumbering, monolithic enterprise. We hope our road map will not only help you avoid getting lost but also provide a perspective for evaluating the material to follow.

Key Terms

algorithmic level	empiricism
artificial intelligence	implementation level
behaviorism	independent variable
chunks	information processing
cognitive neuroscience	introspectionism
cognitive psychology	mathematical models
cognitive science	naïve realism
computational complexity	PDP models
computational level	recursive decomposition
confounding factor	reductionism
connectionist models	satisfice
constraints	self-fulfilling prophecy
correlation	Turing machine
dependent variable	Turing test
ecological validity	

Recommended Readings

Cherniak's (1986) book, *Minimal Rationality,* does a nice job of analyzing the implications of computational complexity for what it means to be rational. For an overview of research on causal reasoning in the social domain, consult Kelly and Michela (1980) and Ross and Nisbett (1991). Finally, Rosenthal's (1967) review of experimenter expectancy effects provides a sobering reminder that the experimenter is not necessarily a neutral figure.

Robins, Gosling, and Craik (1999) present a recent review and analysis of approaches to psychology in general and the development of cognitive psychology in particular. The Eisenberger and Cameron (1996) paper gives a provocative analysis of different strategies for analyzing the relation of reward to motivation and creativity. A nice example of a technique for analyzing stages of processing appears in a recent paper by Love, Rouder, and Wisniewski (1999). David Marr's book

Vision (1982) provides a good overview of computational vision from an artificial intelligence perspective. He writes from a personal point of view that gives insight into how researchers think about problems. John Anderson's (1990) book illustrates the strategy of using computational-level considerations to constrain cognitive models. Useful discussions of the strong and weak points of the connectionist approach to modeling can be found in articles by McCloskey (1991) and Seidenberg (1993). Students with cognitive science interests will find Turing's (1936, 1958) articles to be fascinating reading. Shepard's (1984) paper is a very thoughtful analysis of an evolutionary approach to cognition. Finally, Chomsky's (1959) review of Skinner should be on the must-read list of any student of language.

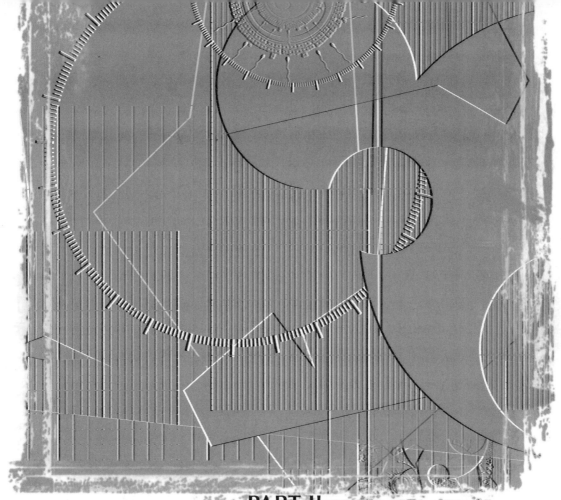

PART II
ACQUIRING INFORMATION

Chapter 2
Learning

Chapter 3
Perception

Chapter 4
Attention

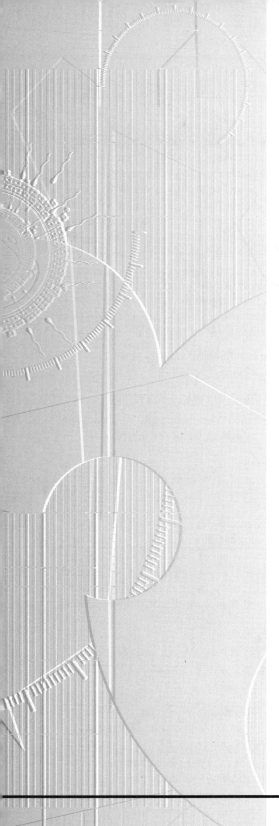

Chapter 2

Learning

Introduction
The Challenge of Learning
The Biological Backdrop of Learning
Fixed-Action Patterns and Releasers
Critical Periods and Imprinting
Constraints on Learning
Basic Learning
Habituation
Classical Conditioning
Trial-and-Error Learning or Instrumental Learning
Paired-Associate Learning
Implications
The Learning-Performance Distinction
Contingency Learning and Illusory Correlation
Content and Meaningful Learning
Summary
Key Terms
Recommended Readings

"Why do you walk in such a crooked way, my child?"
said an old crab to her son.
"You must learn to walk straight."
"Show me the way, mother," replied the young crab,
"and when I see you taking a straight course
I will try to follow."

—*Aesop's Fables*

INTRODUCTION

Typically, when we think about learning, our natural focus is on formal education. And it certainly is the case that the learning that takes place in school is vitally important and a central aspect of cognitive psychology. Material relevant to complex learning will be covered in chapters on memory, knowledge representation, concepts and categories, expertise and creativity, and problem solving. In this chapter we shall concentrate on basic learning processes and draw on examples from both human and animal learning. Whenever we study a complex behavior, it is important to know whether a simple learning procedure would be sufficient to understand it. As Braitenberg (1984) points out, sometimes very simple mechanisms can give rise to complex behavior.

This chapter is no substitute for a course on learning. Our coverage will necessarily be selective and often oversimplified. Furthermore, because learning is covered in several other chapters of this book, many instructors will choose to skip this chapter. The main reasons to include a separate chapter on learning are as follows:

1. Basic principles of learning such as conditioning are very powerful, not just in animals but also in human beings.

2. These learning principles also have important practical applications.

3. Questions concerning how even so-called "simple learning" is accomplished nicely illustrate the central organizing themes of this book.

The Challenge of Learning

A very common learning problem involves figuring out "what goes with what." How does the rat determine that it was the food it ate rather than the pigeons it saw that made it sick, and of the various foods it ate, how does it decide which one is the culprit? How does a bird learn the song of its own species rather than the song of many of the other kinds of birds it hears? In many cases organisms who must learn associations are faced with thousands and thousands of possibilities. Under these circumstances, it is surprising that learning ever takes place. Organisms cannot consider all logical possibilities; instead, they are born with certain biases so that learning some things is very easy. The cost of this bias is that learning other things is difficult, if not impossible. As we shall see, these constraints generally work in a way that is adaptive for the organism.

Although the types of learning we shall be considering are mainly simple associations, the conceptual issues involved in these forms of learning extend directly to complex learning. For example, in the branch of artificial intelligence concerned with machine learning (i.e., developing programs that can learn from examples rather than having knowledge directly programmed), one of the most important problems is **credit assignment.** When a program meets with success or failure, it has to figure out why it succeeded or why it failed in order to make adaptive modifications. Again, there are often many possibilities to be evaluated. Artificial intelligence (AI) researchers try to build into their programs biases that will lead their programs to pursue the most promising possibilities first. In the case of human and animal learning, nature has prepared us with certain heuristics (strategies) and biases that favor learning some things over others.

The word **learning** is familiar to everyone, yet means different things to different people. Asked what is meant by *learning,* a person might offer as a first definition "profiting by experience." *Learning* in this sense refers to improvement in performance or, more broadly, an increase in the organism's adaptation to its environment. This rough definition fits some cases well: a child learning to avoid a hot object, a puppy learning to find its water dish, a student acquiring facts and principles needed to pass an examination or the skills needed to compete in games. Of course, not all learning is adaptive. Consider a person who has come to be mortally afraid of elevators. Presumably this fear developed through some learning process, even though the person does not welcome the fear and may seek out the help of a therapist to overcome it.

Often we have reason to believe that a person or animal has learned something even though no specific change in performance can be identified. In this view, learning is conceived in terms of the storage of information in memory as a consequence of any experience the individual might have had. A separate set of principles will be needed to explain how information is retrieved from memory and translated into performance in new situations (see the chapters on memory in Part III).

Within this broadened framework, learning and memory are like two sides of a coin. We can never detect learning except by evidence that the organism remembers something. Conversely, there is no way to produce memory without learning. We separate these two aspects of a common basic process only for convenience. One of the main functions of living creatures—indeed, almost a defining property—is to process information continually from the environment and adjust behavior to take account of its significant aspects.

This chapter will focus on fundamental learning phenomena. Information-processing approaches to cognition often rely on analogies between humans and computers, but human beings are biological organisms with an evolutionary history. A major aspect of this history can be seen as responding to the need for constraints on learning in order to respond to complex problems in an adaptive manner. Nature helps with the problem of learning every step of the way.

THE BIOLOGICAL BACKDROP OF LEARNING _____

Early work on associative learning in the behaviorist tradition assumed that any response in an organism's repertoire could be conditioned (associated) with essentially any stimulus. We now know that some things are much easier to learn than others. One thing to keep in mind is that it is important not to learn the wrong things—the rat that learns to avoid pigeons because it got sick won't be very well adapted. As we shall see, nature has evolved mechanisms that help organisms learn what they need to know.

We can learn to drive an automobile without having the slightest idea as to what goes on under the hood. Nonetheless, some understanding of how the machine is built and how its components operate may help us appreciate its limitations and deal with malfunctions. Similarly, we can study learning purely by observing how the actions of animals or people change with experience, but there are advantages in taking into account other information about the nature of the "machine" we are observing. In particular, it is often useful to know what kinds of adaptive behaviors appear without specific learning, what kinds are easy, and what kinds are difficult or impossible to acquire through learning. Learning can provide flexible adaptation to environmental circumstances, but it also be risky. The danger is that learning will take too long—even one-trial learning can be too slow for prey avoiding a predator.

We should not be surprised, therefore, that many behavioral adjustments to the environment reflect evolutionary history in which preprogrammed action sequences become incorporated into genetic equipment and do not require new learning in each new generation. In some cases these behaviors are quite complex. For example, the long-tailed tailorbird sews two large leaves together and builds its nest inside (Figure 2.1). It is able to perform this complex task correctly on the first attempt. The ability is considered to be inborn because it appears suddenly (does not require practice) and with adaptive results. Older birds with more practice, however, may build better nests than those nesting for the first time (Wallace, 1973).

Fixed-Action Patterns and Releasers

Innate skills or behavior sequences that the animal does not have to learn are known as **fixed-action patterns.** Newborn humans are equipped with a number of these functional behavior patterns. One example is the grasping reflex of the hand. If you touch the palm of an infant's hand, its fingers close tightly around yours in an ordered sequence of movements. This grasping is strong when an infant is nursing and is especially reactive to the mother's hair. The reflex is later lost as the nervous system develops.

Most of these fixed-action reflexes are adaptive. Head-turning and sucking reflexes make it easy for newborn babies to be fed. Babies also have a respiratory occlusion reflex that is stimulated by a reduction of airflow: The first response is to pull back the head. If this is not effective, the baby will move its hands in a face-wiping motion. If this does not work, the baby will start to cry, and the resulting expulsion of air is often sufficient to remove whatever is obstructing the air passages. This exquisite pattern of reflexes is important for survival, but it may complicate breast feeding. If the mother presses the baby too close during feeding so that the baby's nostrils are covered by the breast, the respiratory occlusion reflex may be triggered. Therefore, successful nursing may require a bit of experience on the part of both baby and mother.

Fixed-action patterns are not limited to infants. For example, yawning may be triggered by the sight of another person yawning (Provine, 1986). Two characteristic features of fixed-action patterns are that they are initiated by quite specific stimuli or **releasers** and that then, once initiated, the behavior patterns often run their course almost automatically. If an egg is removed from the nest of the greylag goose,

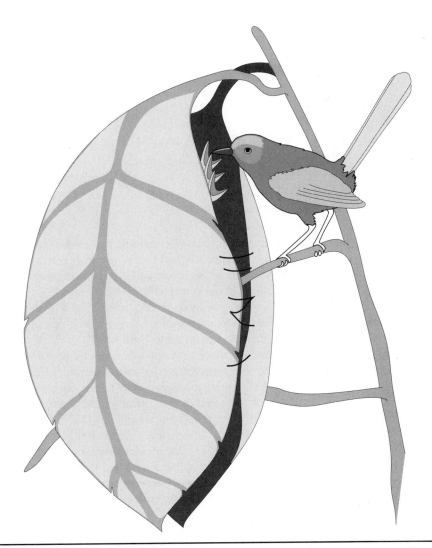

Figure 2.1   Tailor bird with its sewn nest. Its complex sewing behaviors are essentially innate.

Source: Wallace, 1973.

she will retrieve the egg by rolling it back under her bill. If the egg is removed by a human observer during this retrieval process, the goose will continue the egg-rolling motions until the egg would have been retrieved if it hadn't been removed. When slight alterations are made in environmental settings, the resulting behaviors often seem bizarre and inappropriate. For example, in many cases exaggerated or "supernormal" stimuli are preferred to normal stimuli. Oystercatcher birds prefer eggs that are larger than normal; if presented with artificial eggs, they will try to sit on ones that are much too large to incubate. The evolution of relatively inflexible patterns of behavior is based on the promise of stability in the environment. Where new circumstances do not intervene, these adaptations are quite effective. In some cases, members of one species exploit fixed-action patterns in other species. The female cowbird locates the nest of some other bird (typically a smaller one) and then quickly lays an egg when the other bird leaves its nest. When the owner returns, it often accepts the egg, incubates it, and hatches it. Furthermore, the baby cowbird is generally larger than its nest mates, and its size acts as a supernormal stimulus for (foster) parent feeding (Hamilton & Orians, 1965).

Critical Periods and Imprinting

Attachment

A compromise between built-in behavior patterns and totally flexible individual learning is the occurrence of especially rapid learning during certain favorable periods (usually early periods) in an organism's life. **Imprinting** refers to a type of learning that forms the basis of the young animal's attachment to its parents and, in many cases, later on controls its selection of a mate. A newly hatched duckling reared without its mother will follow a human being, a wooden decoy, or almost any moving object it sees shortly after its birth. Even brief periods of following may result in relatively permanent attachment to the "imprinting object," and the duckling will prefer the object even to a live mother duck. Imprinting has been found in dogs, sheep, and horses. Imprinting takes place only during certain sensitive or **critical periods.** It appears that the end of the critical period for imprinting coincides with the development of fear reactions to novel stimuli (Hoffman & Ratner, 1983).

Critical periods may occur in human learning as well. There is evidence that attachment or bonding between parents and their infants has a critical period and that early separation (such as might occur during extended hospitalization) may impair the development of emotional attachment (see, e.g., Bowlby, 1969). It has even been argued that the first minutes and hours after birth are important for bonding between mother and infant (Klaus & Kennell, 1976), a finding that often has been exaggerated and sensationalized in the popular media. More recent reviews (Kennell & Klaus, 1984; Myers, 1987) suggest that the critical period for bonding is on a broader time scale.

It is important to keep in mind that imprinting and other forms of constrained learning are not like switches that turn off and on. Critical periods don't necessarily have an abrupt onset and offset and learning may take place outside of a critical period (it's just that it's less likely or harder). It also is an oversimplification to categorize behaviors as innate versus acquired; it is more accurate to think in terms of interactions between innate tendencies and environmental factors jointly affecting learning and behavior.

Bird Song

Although mynah birds and parrots are known for their ability to mimic human speech, song learning in birds such as the white-crowned sparrow may actually show closer parallels to human language acquisition. The white-crowned sparrow will not develop a normal song if it does not hear the songs of other white-crowned sparrows as it matures. The sparrow must hear these songs when it is between 10 and 50 days old, even though it does not develop its own song until it is 150 to 200 days old (Marler, 1970). If a white-crowned sparrow is isolated from members of its species and exposed to tape recordings of normal white-crowned sparrow song, the song will be acquired. Tape recordings of the song of the closely related song sparrow, however, have no effect; the isolated bird neither imitates the song sparrow nor develops the song of its own species. If sparrows are given a choice of two recorded songs, one from their own species and the other from a bird species living in the same habitat, they learn their own song and ignore the other one (Marler & Peters, 1977). Different species of birds vary in how song learning is constrained, and these variations may be linked to local rearing conditions (Marler & Peters, 1988). For example, learning can be less constrained in environments that have few bird species with similar songs than in settings with many similar species and songs (see Ball & Hulse, 1998, for a general review of research on birdsong).

Can the study of song learning in birds tell us anything about human language learning? There are several intriguing possibilities. First, hearing particular songs at particular time periods is critical for the acquisition of bird song. Marler (1970) has suggested that birds have what he calls a "template" that acts as a crude guide for their species-specific song, much as other sign stimuli (chick distress calls) act as releasers for other behaviors (rescuing). By *template* he means some internal representation that can provide feedback to the bird concerning how well it is approximating the desired (species-typical) song. The auditory input must be in roughly the right form to influence the template, although there appear to be differences across species and perhaps even across individual birds (Marler & Peters, 1988; Marler & Sherman, 1983). Human infants select human speech sounds from the vast array of sounds to which they are exposed, and they may also have an auditory "template" that constrains their speech development. The fact that birds may learn their song from tape recordings in the absence of any other social stimuli or external sources of reinforcement suggests the possibility that song learning depends on an intrinsic feedback or reinforcement system (i.e., the template). That is, the bird may produce a variety of song components but the ones that correspond to the species-typical song may be more pleasing or rewarding for the bird such that it is more likely to repeat them. In a similar way, many aspects of human speech acquisition may not depend on external reward. Thus parents may teach their children language not by rewarding them with smiles and attention for speechlike behaviors but rather by providing the appropriate auditory environment in which the infant's own language acquisition system can operate (see J. L. Miller & Jusczyk, 1989, for a review).

Critical Period Effects and Language Learning

There is strong evidence that language learning has a critical period associated with it. Elissa Newport and Ted Suppalla have studied the signing abilities of deaf adults who had learned American Sign Language (ASL) at different ages. For all of the adults, ASL was their first full language; at best, they had only limited skills in

English. Although all groups were successful on basic word order tests, performance on tests for correct use of syntax decreased as the age at which language learning started increased (Newport, 1984, 1988, 1990). These differences in performance were very pronounced despite the fact that the adults had been using ASL for at least 10 years (Figure 2.2). Similar results are observed for ability to learn a second language as a function of when second language learning begins (J. S. Johnson & Newport, 1989). If one does not learn a language very early (during the critical period), one's language abilities may never be as good as those of someone who did. This is something of an enigma, because we think of adults as being better learners than children. Recently, research and theory have tried to address this puzzle.

Why should there be a critical period for learning a language? The most straightforward idea amounts to a redescription of the results—namely, that there is some language-learning capacity that is present only early in development. It is conceivable that neural development closes off some possibilities even as it opens up others.

Elissa Newport (1990) has offered an intriguing conjecture concerning language learning—the *less-is-more hypothesis*. The key idea is that the limited processing capacity of children may be precisely what allows them to learn a language. This possibility takes a little explaining. Following Newport (1990), consider a simple situation in which there are three sign components (call them a, b, and c) and three meaning components (call them m, n, and o). The learner has to figure out how sign components map into meaning components, and even in this very simple example there are 49 possibilities (the relevant sign components could be a, b, c, $a + b$, $a + c$, $b + c$, or $a + b + c$ and there are also seven ways to combine the meaning components to produce a total of 7×7 or 49 possibilities). For example, the sign components a and c together might correspond to meaning component m. For a slightly more complex sign with five components, there are nearly a thousand possible mappings.

So far we have only made things sound more challenging. The less-is-more hypothesis entails the idea that children will pick up fewer sign and meaning components than adults and examine many fewer possibilities. A child who encoded only sign component b and meaning components m and n could consider only a few possibilities (that b corresponds to m, that it corresponds to n, or to m+n). A child would be unlikely to encode enough sign and meaning components to consider the idea that abc as a whole corresponds to mno as a whole. In short, the child is able to search in only a tiny part of the space of possibilities. That's the "less" part. The "is more" part is that the tiny space of possibilities that a child can examine is more or less the right set of possibilities. In the case of ASL, the correct correspondences involve a one-to-one mapping of sign components to meaning components rather than any of the more complex combinations and possibilities that the child is unable to consider because of limited processing capabilities. Given that the more complicated possibilities are wrong, the child actually benefits from being unable to consider them. It is as if the infants limited learning ability forces them to "start simple," which for language is the right thing to do.

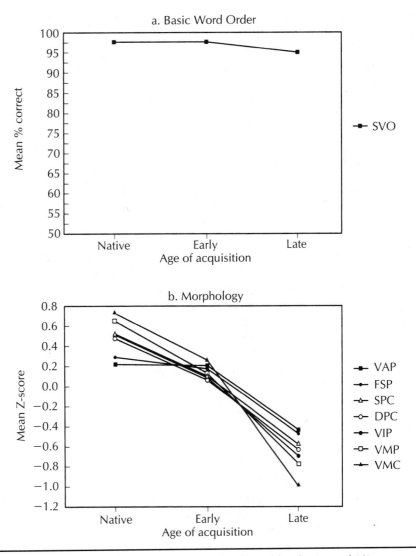

Figure 2.2   *(a)* Score on ASL basic word order for native, early, and late learners of ASL. Native signers were exposed to ASL from birth on. Early learners were first exposed to sign at ages 4 to 6, and late learners encountered sign after the age of 12. *(b)* Z scores on seven tests of ASL morphology (syntax) for native, early, and late learners of ASL. The Z-scores provide a measure of relative performance.

Source: Newport, 1990

At this point, the reader may wonder how children could know the right units or sign components. One answer is that ASL (and other languages) has developed linguistic components that correspond to natural perceptual segments. See Newport

AN APPLICATION
Chemotherapy and Taste-Aversion Learning

How can work on conditioning affect our lives? Actually there are some pretty important implications as is illustrated by some recent work on the use of chemotherapy in medicine. Chemotherapy often is an aversive experience, in part because of the nausea and vomiting associated with it. The unpleasant side effects of the drugs can also lead to taste aversions.

First of all, there is clear experimental evidence that chemotherapy treatments become selectively associated with tastes and odors. In one study, children in a clinic setting were allowed to eat a novel flavor of ice cream (a mixture of maple and black walnut) that was followed by a chemotherapy treatment. One control group did not receive the ice cream prior to treatment, and another control group received the ice cream but not the drug treatment. The children returned to the clinic a few weeks later and were given the choice of having ice cream or playing a game. Both control groups were more than three times as likely to choose the ice cream as the group that had the ice cream followed by the drug treatment (Bernstein, 1978). In short, the children who had the novel flavored ice cream and then received the treatment learned to dislike that flavor of ice cream.

Learned taste aversions can create serious practical problems because nutritious hospital foods may become targets for aversions and result

(Continued)

(1990) and Goldowsky and Newport (1993) for a detailed discussion of this point and some evidence bearing on it.

There is one very striking and counterintuitive prediction that seems to follow from this analysis: to help adults learn a language, one should make them more like children by interfering with or limiting their processing capacity. Although some researchers have speculated about this hypothesis, Cochran, McDonald, and Parault (1999) ran experiments that support it. They made up a novel sign language and trained adults in it under either normal learning conditions or while performing a concurrent task (that required processing resources). They found that adults learned faster under normal rather than concurrent-task conditions but, surprisingly, they made more errors in trying to generalize the language to new tasks. Other experiments suggest that the reason for this is that adults in normal conditions learned whole signs without analyzing them into their subcomponents. This is exactly the pattern of results that the less-is-more hypothesis predicts. If these laboratory results hold up, they would have important implications for adult language learning.

AN APPLICATION
Chemotherapy and Taste-Aversion Learning *(Continued)*

in loss of appetite. Viewing taste aversion from a learning perspecive has the virtue of suggesting remedies. In a follow-up study, Bernstein and her associates showed that a distinctive taste could serve as a "scapegoat." Children were given two different hospital meals, each of which was followed by a chemotherapy treatment. Along with one of the two meals, children were given a package of an unusual flavor of Lifesavers to eat (root beer or coconut). The idea was that the reaction to the chemotherapy might be associated with the distinctive flavor rather than with the meal. In fact, children were later twice as likely to eat foods from the meal that was followed by the candy than foods from the meal that was not (Bernstein, Webster, & Bernstein, 1982). As Bernstein puts it, one could say that the Lifesavers were prophetically named! For a review of relations between learned taste aversion and appetite loss, see Bernstein and Borson (1986). (See also Tyc, Mulhern, & Bieberich, 1997, for a recent overview of research on conditioning and coping with chemotherapy.)

Another characteristic of chemotherapy is that the nausea and vomiting do not appear solely after the drugs are given. After a few treatments, the nausea and vomiting may occur *before* the drugs are given. This suggests that conditioning has taken place. We will have more to say about chemotherapy and learning later in this chapter and we will consider some ways to prevent anticipatory nausea and vomiting.

Constraints on Learning

Critical periods and imprinting are one form of constrained learning. It is natural to ask whether other forms of learning are also constrained. Early laboratory research on learning assumed that constraints were not important. That is, this work was conducted from the perspective or belief that learning did not depend very much on the particular stimuli, responses, and rewards used. If a reinforcer worked for some particular stimulus or response, it apparently would work for virtually all stimuli and virtually all responses.

This generalization proved to be overdrawn. Rats can readily be trained to press a bar for food and to run away from a signal to avoid shock, but it is difficult to teach a rat to press a bar to avoid shock or to run away from a signal for food in order to receive food (Bolles, 1970). The animal's response system seems to be organized to approach desirable outcomes and avoid undesirable outcomes, and these tendencies greatly constrain learning.

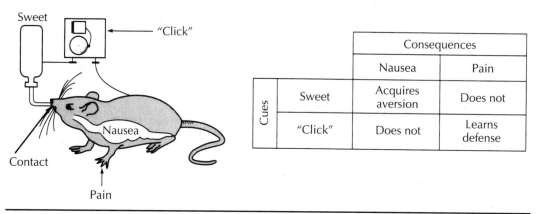

		Consequences	
		Nausea	Pain
Cues	Sweet	Acquires aversion	Does not
	"Click"	Does not	Learns defense

Figure 2.3 The effects of pairing a gustatory cue or an auditory cue with external pain or internal illness.

Source: Garcia, Hawkins, & Rusiniak, 1974.

A related experimental result is shown in Figure 2.3. The rat is electronically wired to a circuit that produces an audible click when the rat licks from the bottle containing sweetened water. The rat can be punished either by experimentally induced nausea or by electric shock administered to the paws. Thus there are two stimuli (the sweet taste and the click) and two outcomes (nausea and pain) that may be associated. This creates four possible associations (taste and pain, taste and nausea, click and pain, and click and nausea). Does the rat learn these associations with equal ease? The answer is "no"; the rat seems to learn only two of these four possible associations: the click with shock and the taste with nausea. The click comes to control whether the rat drinks if the rat is punished by shock; the sweet taste controls the rat's avoidance of drinking when illness induction is the punishment (Garcia, Hawkins, & Rusiniak, 1974). In short, what the rat learns is highly constrained by the particular cues and consequences. Sweetness can be associated with nausea but not pain, and the click can be associated with pain but not nausea.

Some constraints are species-specific and reflect what Seligman (1970) referred to as preparedness. For example, pigeons rely more on vision than taste to select food and pigeons readily associate visual cues with illness (Shapiro, Jacobs, & LoLordo, 1980). That is, organisms appear to be biased or prepared to learn associations that have biological relevance.

Summary

These various observations suggest that we should conceive of learning as involving a continuum of flexibility. Where the environment is stable and where there is no time for learning, behaviors may be innate or preprogrammed. Example of innate behaviors include fixed-action patterns that are triggered by releasers. Where the environment is less predictable and organisms need to be able to adjust to changing circumstances, learning may involve various degrees of flexibility. Critical periods, in which learning is confined to a stage of development (where the likelihood of learning the correct things may be maximized), represent an example of constrained learning. More generally, organisms appear to be predisposed to associate certain kinds of events with each other (e.g., tastes with nausea). In most cases these biases or constraints reflect useful adaptations to the environment. Overall, it appears that biologically relevant events often reflect some degree of constrained learning, even in human beings.

BASIC LEARNING

We continue our review of human beings as biological organisms by taking a brief look at basic learning. Certain forms of learning are so fundamental that we would expect them to be observed throughout the animal kingdom. Indeed, simple forms of learning occur even in single-celled organisms. In this case drastic differences in neurological organization make it unlikely that the neurophysiological basis could be the same. Scientists interested in the physiological basis of learning typically focus on simple organisms and simple learning, on the assumption that simple systems should be easier to understand than complex systems. Among the best examples of these simple forms of learning are habituation and conditioning.

Habituation

Habituation refers to the ability of an organism to reduce or discontinue its response to highly repetitive, predictable stimuli. Suppose a deer is feeding near a farm where the silence is frequently broken by the bleating sound of the farmer's sheep. Initially, one would expect the sounds to interrupt the deer's feeding and put it on the alert. If the sounds were very frequent, little feeding would take place if the deer responded each time. What would be an adaptive reaction on the part of the animal? Ideally, the deer would respond less and less strongly to successive occurrences of the same sound until it finally ignored the noises entirely and continued eating. (Of course, the deer would need to remain alert to other sources of sound.) You are familiar with similar examples from your own experience. The ticking of a loud clock can be very conspicuous when we first come into its vicinity, but we quickly "become used to the sound" and cease to hear it unless our attention is recalled to it for some reason.

The neurophysiological mechanisms responsible for habituation certainly cannot be the same in all species, for the process occurs in animals with and without nervous systems. It seems likely that in the very lowest organisms habituation is an independent process (in fact, almost the sole available learning process), but that in higher organisms it is simply a component of a more elaborate stock of related learning processes. (See Kandel, 1976; Kandel & Schwartz, 1982, for work on the biological basis of habituation.)

Although habituation is adaptive in its own right, it also may provide a useful bias for further learning. Suppose that some important event occurs, and the organism is trying to determine what might have predicted or caused it. For a moment let's go back to the example of a rat that becomes ill. We know that rats are biased to associate illness with tastes. But a rat may have tasted many things in the hours before it became ill. If rats habituate to familiar tastes, then they should tend to associate their illness with those tastes that are more novel or unusual. Indeed, they do (see, e.g., Rozin & Kalat, 1971). Given that tainted foods typically have a distinct taste, this bias for associating a novel event with a novel taste serves rats very well. This observation may also be relevant to human learning. For example, J. H. Holland, Holyoak, Nisbett, and Thagard (1986) argue that people generally follow an **unusualness heuristic** of linking surprising outcomes with unusual antecedent events.

Classical Conditioning

Predictiveness is an important part of learning in all organisms, including human beings. The basic nature of learning to anticipate events is seen most clearly in experiments on conditioning. **Classical conditioning** is associated for both laypeople and scientists with the Russian physiologist Pavlov, who observed that a dog salivates when it sees or hears some cue that means food is imminent. In classical conditioning a "neutral" stimulus (one that does not elicit a strong response) is paired with a biologically significant stimulus (e.g., food) that produces a response (e.g., salivation). Of interest is the change in response to the neutral stimulus. Figure 2.4 shows a typical classical conditioning experimental procedure. It starts with a stimulus, such as food, that produces a response prior to any learning. The stimulus is referred to as the **unconditioned stimulus** (US), and the response that is present prior to learning (salivation, in this case) is known as the **unconditioned response** (UR). This is shown in the top part of Figure 2.4.

Next, a second stimulus is selected that is originally neutral in that it does not lead to the unconditioned response. For example, dogs do not normally salivate when they hear a tone. Then the learning trials begin. On each of a series of conditioning trials the **conditioned stimulus** (CS) (a tone) is presented and followed by the US (food). We know that conditioning has occurred in one of two ways. The dog may start to salivate after the CS comes on and before the US is presented. Of course, there will be no time for this to happen if the US follows the CS too closely. In that event we may check for learning by presenting the CS without the US, and any salivation to the CS alone is considered to be a learned or **conditioned response** (CR).

Pavlov and others were able to use the classical conditioning procedure to learn a considerable amount about this form of learning. Is conditioning permanent? By no means. If the administration of food (US) is discontinued following a series of tone-food presentations, and the tone (CS) is repeatedly presented alone, then the tendency to respond to the tone declines much more precipitously. In this case, we speak of **extinction** of the conditioned response (CR).

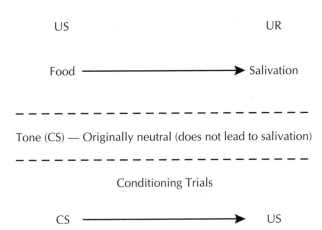

Classical Conditioning

Test for conditioning: CS alone

Figure 2.4 **Procedures Used in Classical Conditioning** US refers to unconditioned stimulus, UR to unconditioned response, CS to conditioned stimulus, and CR to conditioned response.

What Controls Conditioning?

Is conditioning automatic and unselective? Initially, researchers thought that conditioning does indeed occur automatically whenever some signaling stimulus precedes a biologically significant event such as the appearance of food, water, or pain. However, later studies have shown that the relationships between signals and signaled events must be such that the occurrence of the latter has some *information value* for the organism.

Consider an experiment reported by Leon Kamin (1969). In a baseline experiment, he used the well-established method for producing a "conditioned emotional response" by presenting rats with a certain stimulus A followed by shock. After only a few trials, he observed that presenting stimulus A when the animal was pressing a bar to obtain food produced a severe decrease in responding, signifying that the stimulus aroused fear of the impending shock. In a second condition, Kamin presented two stimuli—A and B (for example, a tone and a light)—together, followed by shock, and then tested the two stimuli separately and found that each gave evidence of eliciting fear. In a third and critical experimental condition, he first presented A followed by shock, then A and B together followed by shock, and finally tested A and B separately. The rather surprising observation was that in this last case stimulus B, when tested alone, showed no evidence of evoking fear. His interpretation was that the inclusion of stimulus B on the A-plus-B trials added no information as to when shock should be expected, and consequently conditioning to stimulus B was "blocked." **Blocking** is a robust phenomenon, even in humans (e.g., Wasserman, 1990a). We'd better add a hedge here. Blocking may not occur for stimuli that are biologically "prepared" to be associated in certain contexts (LoLordo, Jacobs, & Foree, 1982). Earlier we mentioned that pigeons have a propensity for associating visual cues with food (and food-related illness). Interestingly, pigeons do not appear to show blocking for visual cues even when other cues are more reliable predictors of food.

The idea that the information value of a CS regulates learning has had a major influence on our thinking about classical conditioning. Conditioning does not occur automatically whenever CS and US are paired; instead, the CS must predict the onset of the US. A dramatic illustration of this principle comes from an experiment by R. A. Rescorla (1967), which is outlined in Table 2.1. Four groups of rats were tested under different contingencies. For two groups, the probability that the US would follow the CS was high (80%), and for two it was low (40%). Also varied was the likelihood that the US would appear by itself in the absence of the CS. This manipulation allows a contrast of contingency and co-occurrence. The first two groups have higher co-occurrence than the second two but only in the second and fourth groups is there a contingency between the CS and US. The results showed that whether learning occurred depended not simply on the probability that the US would follow the CS (co-occurrence) but rather on this probability relative to the probability that the US would appear alone (contingency). Thus, the group for which the probability of the US was 80% in the presence of the CS and 80% in the absence of the CS showed no learning, whereas the group for which the US followed the CS only 40% of the time but did not appear in the absence of the CS did show conditioning. In short, conditioning of the CS was observed only when the CS had predictive value.

Although Rescorla's study shows that contingency is more important to conditioning than co-occurrence, others have argued that a different form of contingency plays a major role in conditioning. Specifically, the key factor may be the average

Table 2.1   **Outline of One of the Rescorla (1967) Conditioning Experiments**

Group	Probability That US Follows CS	Probability That US Occurs By Itself
1	.80	.80
2	.80	.40
3	.40	.40
4	.40	.00

Results: Groups 2 and 4 show conditioning.
            Groups 1 and 3 do not show conditioning.
Conclusion: The CS must predict the appearance of the US.

time delay between CS and US relative to the average delay between one US presentation and the next. If the former is shorter than the latter, then the CS helps to predict the occurrence of the US, and conditioning should occur (e.g., Gallistel, 1990; Gibbon & Balsam, 1981; Wasserman & Neunaber, 1986). In a typical conditioning experiment, the trial-by-trial contingency and the average relative temporal interval (from CS to US relative to US to US) are perfectly correlated, but it is possible to vary the intervals between trials to contrast simple contingency with time intervals. The important point, however, is that in all of these formulations the CS must have predictive value for conditioning to occur.

Conditioning as Adaptation

In general, classical conditioning seems to be a form of adaptation. For example, salivation may serve to aid the digestion of food. Other digestive processes also show conditioning. Insulin is released by the pancreas as an unconditioned response to the presence of sugar in the digestive tract. The taste of sugar can become conditioned to the release of insulin as an anticipatory conditioned response. Interestingly, after such conditioning, insulin may be released as an anticipatory response when subjects taste artificial sweeteners such as saccharin. This conditioned release of insulin causes a drop in blood sugar level and may account for the slight dizziness people may experience after drinking a diet soda on an empty stomach.

There is even evidence that the immune system is subject to principles of conditioning; that is, the presentation of a CS can influence the immune system, which suggests that the immune system is subject to neural control. Cyclophosphamide, a drug used to study conditioned taste aversions, also tends to suppress the immune system by interfering with the production of antibodies. Robert Ader and his colleagues have been able to demonstrate that this suppression of the immune system can also be produced as a CR to a taste stimulus (e.g., saccharin previously conditioned to cyclophosphamide as the US; Ader, 1982; Ader & Cohen, 1985 and commentary; see also MacQueen & Siegel, 1989). Even more recently, Siegel and his associates established conditioned enhancement of the immune system (MacQueen, Siegel, & Landry, 1990; see also Maier, Watkins, & Fleshner, 1994). This exciting work is leading to the emergence of a new interdisciplinary field known as psychoneuroimmunology. If the immune system can be conditioned, we may be able to use principles of classical conditioning to fight disease. At some point in the future, we may be able to undergo conditioning and then, when we become ill, present the CS from training in order to give our immune systems a boost. (See Kiecolt-Glaser, Page, Marucha, MacCallum, & Glaser, 1998, for a recent overview on the medical applications of psychoneuroimmunology.)

Conditioning as Stimulus Substitution

An early view of conditioning was that the CS comes to act as a "substitute" for the US and that the conditioned response (CR) takes exactly the same form as the unconditioned response (UR). For example, in Pavlov's experiments described earlier, both the UR and the CR were salivation. Today, we realize that this view is oversimplified. An alternative view is that the CR will take whatever form is most adaptive and may even be the opposite of the UR. There is some support for this compensatory response model. Consider the drug dinitrophenol. The UR to this drug is increased oxygen consumption and increased temperature. Because this drug would tend to disturb the body's homeostatic balance, the body might try to compensate for this disruption by attempting to restore oxygen consumption and body temperature to normal levels. Indeed, when dinitrophenol is used as a US in conditioning studies, the CR is decreased oxygen and decreased body temperature (Obal, 1966). In short, the CR takes the opposite form of the UR in the direction of what should be adaptive.

The compensatory response model has attracted a lot of attention because it may provide an explanation for the phenomenon of drug tolerance (Siegel, 1977a, 1977b; Solomon, 1977; Solomon & Corbit, 1974). Development of drug tolerance is often a serious problem because progressively higher dosages are required to produce a given effect. The key idea in the **compensatory response model** is that the CR to the cues associated with the administration of a drug (e.g., the needle, smells present in the context, and other CSs) tends to counteract the effect of the drug. Therefore, the response to the drug becomes attenuated. If this model is correct, then one ought to be able to alter the response to the drug if the CSs that elicit compensatory responses are absent. Siegel and his associates have found a considerable amount of support for this view. If an addict takes the same drug but in a different form so that the conditioned stimuli associated with drug tolerance are missing, then the same dosage that would have a very mild effect might produce an overdose (see Crowell, Hinson, & Siegel, 1981, for research based on this compensatory model, and Siegel, 1989, for a general review).

Attractive as the compensatory response model is, it does not provide a full account of the form that CRs will take in a conditioning situation (see, e.g., Flaherty & Becker, 1984). If one measures several response systems, one finds that some CRs are similar to the UR, and some are opposite to it. It appears that the exact form of a CR depends not only on adaptive value but also on the particular CS employed and innate behavior patterns in organisms (see Domjan & Burkhard, 1986; P. C. Holland, 1984; and Timberlake, 1994, for thoughtful discussions of this issue). What does seem clear is that classical conditioning is not an isolated phenomenon associated with primitive organisms but rather a form of adaptation relevant to human beings as well.

Research on conditioning is also important in that it may provide common ground for different approaches to learning and induction. For example, Sutton and Barto (1981) have pointed to close links between the contingency learning model of R. A. Rescorla and Wagner (1972) and the learning mechanisms of neural network models that have been widely applied in cognitive psychology. Contemporary approaches to conditioning span the range from biological models that directly incorporate constraints associated with the nervous system (e.g., see Hollis, 1997, for a review) to connectionist models, which are more loosely based on properties of neural networks (see Hawkins & Bower, 1989, for examples of these two approaches), up to theories of inductive learning in a rule-based system implemented in a traditional computer program (Holyoak, Koh, & Nisbett, 1989).

AN ENIGMA
Food and the Boundaries of Affective Conditioning

Although conditioning is a basic process that researchers have studied since the time of Pavlov, it still contains its share of mysteries. For example, it appears that taste-aversion learning may occur even in the absence of nausea and illness. Rozin (1986) reports that disgust may also act as an unconditioned stimulus (e.g., a person might acquire an aversion to chicken noodle soup from an incident where they were eating it and found a dead cockroach in it). Batsell and Brown (1998) provide suggestive evidence that forced consumption (e.g., a child being forced to sit at a table until he or she ate all of a serving of spinach) or even negative information (e.g., being told about the ingredients in a sausage) can produce disgust and corresponding food aversions.

These aversions seem to be more cognitive in character in that it's hard to identify a clear US. In addition, some researchers have suggested that a salient mental image can substitute for an external US in producing conditioning (e.g., Dadds, Bovbjerg, Redd, & Cutmore, 1997). Observations such as these suggest that conditioning may play an important role in eating disorders.

Although the potential applications of insights from affective conditioning to areas such as eating disorders are intriguing, at present we lack the core knowledge needed to establish more precise connections. First of all, it would be hard (though perhaps not impossible) to study conditioning in animals using mental images as the US and therefore, the relation between a large body of research on conditioning in animals and human affective conditioning is not so clear. In addition, recent reviews and experimental studies of affective conditioning in humans suggest that we do not know enough about it to accurately predict when it will or will not appear (e.g., Rozin, Wrzesiewski, & Brynes, 1998). In short, there may be important factors in affective conditioning that have not yet been identified and are not yet understood.

Summary

Classical conditioning continues to be fundamentally important to our understanding of learning. On the one hand conditioning shows many of the properties one would expect of an information processing system. Conditioning depends not on the number of times a CS and US are paired but on whether or not a CS is informative with respect to the US. Furthermore, conditioning often appears to be adaptive—the conditioned response does not necessarily mimic the unconditioned response and, if it is adaptive to do so, may even act in opposition to it (as a compensatory reaction). Finally, not all associations are equally easy to learn. Biological preparedness may be the rule rather than the exception. For example, it is easier to condition fear in people to a stimulus consisting of snake or a spider than to a gun (Mineka, 1992).

Trial-and-Error Learning or Instrumental Learning

We saw that in classical conditioning the unconditioned stimulus, or reinforcer, follows the presentation of the conditioned stimulus. In trial-and-error or **instrumental learning,** the experimenter arranges things so that the reinforcer is given only after some required action of the organism. For example, one may reward a dog for "shaking hands" by patting it on the head. The key idea is that a voluntary response is followed by some consequence designed to change the likelihood of the response (e.g., punishment may be used to try to decrease the probability that some response will be made).

Most psychologists think that much of everyday behavior is the result of instrumental learning and is under the control of **reinforcement.** Consider the following situation: A mother complains that her 3-year-old boy demands too much attention and that she never gets a minute's rest. When she tries to ignore his demands, the boy's behavior worsens until she finally loses her temper, screams at him, and ultimately complies with his request (perhaps feeling guilty about yelling).

How would you analyze the situation? The well-known psychologist B. F. Skinner viewed these episodes as comprising **operant behaviors** regulated by rewards. Operant behaviors are actions that "operate" on the environment to produce some effect. Skinner distinguished these acts from **respondent behaviors,** such as the knee-jerk reflex, which are under the control of specific stimuli and tend to occur regardless of their consequences. In the example, a distinct possibility is that the mother's attention, whether accompanied by positive or negative feelings, was rewarding to this little boy. If so, the mother should be able to change the boy's behavior by changing the payoffs. For example, she might pay special attention to her child when he engages in desired behaviors, such as independent play, and withhold rewards, either by ignoring demands or by removing the child from the situation (sending him to his room for 5 minutes), when her boy becomes overly demanding. In psychological jargon, she would be reinforcing desired behaviors and extinguishing undesired behaviors. As Krasner and Ullman (1965) have documented, these techniques are often effective and quite likely would work for the mother in our example.

Studying Operant Behavior

The mother-child interactions in this example are doubtless too complex to serve as a beginning point for deriving principles of learning and behavior. A typical laboratory setup for studying operant behavior employs a Skinner box, an apparatus in which a rat may be taught to press a bar for food or a pigeon may be taught to peck a key for food. The apparatus can be programmed to record automatically some operant behavior (e.g., bar presses or key pecks). Note that selecting a measure always involves ignoring lots of behavior—the recorder does not care whether the pigeon was standing on one foot or two when the key peck was made—it's just a key peck. If, by contrast, we tried to record all of the pigeon's behavior, we would probably conclude that behavior is infinitely variable and too complex to be studied in the laboratory. In practice, we try to strike a balance and observe classes of behavior that are both meaningful and open to practical analysis.

Mixtures of Classical and Instrumental Conditioning

Although experimental psychologists often act as if classical and instrumental conditioning can be easily separated, in almost all situations, both forms of learning ought to operate. We described operant behavior in the Skinner box as though it involved only instrumental learning. However, this analysis may not be complete. Not only is reward contingent on some prior response but also it is necessarily associated with the presence of certain stimuli, especially those occurring near where the response is made. These stimulus-reinforcer relations are just those conditions one uses in the study of classical conditioning.

This factor of stimulus-reward contingency can have a powerful influence on behavior. P. L. Brown and Jenkins (1968) studied a remarkably simple way of teaching a pigeon to peck a key, which has come to be referred to as **autoshaping.** The key was normally dark. At regular intervals, the key was illuminated, and free food was available in the food hopper. The light signaled when food was available, but the pigeon was not required to make any response to the key to get food. Yet the birds quickly came to peck the key when it was illuminated, even though that meant there was less time to eat the food. If the procedure is modified so that the illumination signals food only if the pigeon does *not* peck the key, pecking nonetheless develops and is maintained for hundreds of trials despite the fact that pecks cost the pigeons lots of rewards. As soon as the light starts to predict food, the pigeons begin pecking; when, as a result of pecking, the light predicts food less well, pecking decreases. But as pecking decreases, the light again becomes a better predictor of food, and the cycle repeats as the pigeons begin to peck once more (D. R. Williams & Williams, 1969).

The phenomenon of autoshaping illustrates the fact that stimulus-reinforcer relations are inevitably present whenever response-reinforcer relations are studied. Much as one might like to study classical conditioning and instrumental learning separately, almost inevitably they are closely interwoven. Observed performance may reflect the organism's knowledge of stimulus-reinforcer relations and not the simple, automatic running off of a stimulus-response association.

Recognizing that situations may contain elements of both classical and instrumental conditioning may help us to understand learning in some important applied settings. To illustrate this point we will return to the example of chemotherapy mentioned earlier in this chapter. Millions of people undergo chemotherapy as a treatment for cancer. As we mentioned before, chemotherapy is often a dreaded experience and particularly unpleasant is the anticipatory nausea and vomiting associated with it.

There is evidence that the chemotherapy situation contains important elements of classical conditioning. The odors and other cues (associated with the injection) may act as CSs, with the illness produced by the drugs acting as the US. Nausea and vomiting would be the initial UR and anticipatory nausea and/or vomiting are typical CRs. But the chemotherapy situation is quite different from the situation used by Pavlov in his studies. He arranged things so that the dogs would automatically be exposed to the tone CS. Dogs in the same situation with cotton in their ears might show no conditioning because they did not hear the CS. In the chemotherapy situation, people have at least some control over their exposure to potential CSs; therefore, at least part of this (learning) situation is under instrumental control. The theoretical implication of this fact is that classical and instrumental learning are not readily isolated, and the practical implication is that this observation can be used to suggest possible treatments for conditioned vomiting.

If anticipatory vomiting is a classically conditioned response, then if the CS is not perceived, the CR (vomiting) ought not to occur. This idea is the basis for some work by William Redd and his associates on patients undergoing chemotherapy. He employed a combination of relaxation and guided imagery techniques (e.g., imagine that you are on a beach on a nice, sunny day, etc.) that, on the present interpretation, distracted patients from attending to the cues associated with the administration of the toxic chemicals. These techniques proved to be remarkably successful (see Redd, Jacobson, Die-Trill, & Dermatis, 1987, for a more detailed report). Related techniques might also be tried. For example, presenting the CS many times prior to conditioning greatly slows down the rate of learning, a phenomenon known as *latent inhibition*. If the cues associated with drug administration are repeatedly presented without the drug, then when the drug is given later, the association between the drug cues and the drug ought to develop more slowly (see Dafters, Hetherington, & McCartney, 1983, for some evidence related to this point). Of course, it may occur to you that all that might happen is that conditioning will occur to other cues. For example, might not the imagined beach scene become associated with the drug? The principle of selective (constrained) learning mentioned earlier in this chapter seems to make it somewhat unlikely that this would happen. Tastes and odors are easily associated with illness and perhaps vivid, disgusting images may be as well (Dadds et al., 1997), but images of pleasant beach scenes should not readily come to be associated with illness.

We now turn to another case of learning, known as paired-associate learning. Originally, researchers conducted a large number of studies on paired-associate learning in humans with the idea in mind that it provided a close analog with instrumental learning in animals. But, as we will see, things didn't turn out to be so simple.

Paired-Associate Learning

Paired-associate learning is a simple procedure for studying how people form associations. Originally researchers thought that paired-associate learning provided a simple experimental analog to instrumental conditioning. The experimental technique involves pairing previously unrelated words in much the same way as in the traditional method of learning a vocabulary of foreign words. A student of a foreign language pairs English and foreign words, typically on the fronts and backs of flash cards, and practices anticipating the second member of each pair until eventually, when the foreign word is presented, its English meaning comes to mind.

A question of theoretical importance in the study of paired associates is exactly what is learned in the experimental situation. It is obvious that some sort of mental link between the stimulus and response terms is formed. Experiments have shown that this link can be bidirectional; that is, the presentation of the response word alone can evoke memory for the stimulus word (the opposite of the usual order of presentation).

Techniques that make this mental link more obvious can remarkably facilitate learning. Atkinson (1975) developed a keyword method to aid foreign language vocabulary learning. Starting with a foreign word, one finds an English word that sounds like some part of the foreign word. Using this English word as the keyword, the learner then forms a visual image associating the keyword with the English counterpart of the foreign word. For example, the Spanish word for duck is *pato* (pronounced something like "pot-o"). Using the English *pot* as the keyword, one could imagine a duck walking around with a cooking pot over its head. Although the method seems somewhat elaborate, people using the keyword method acquire a foreign vocabulary twice as fast as control subjects not using the technique.

An important question about the nature of associative learning concerns the effect of repetition on the learning process. In the paired-associate paradigm, the list of stimulus-response pairs is presented many times until all the pairs are learned. A common view is that each time a pair is repeated, the connection between the items is strengthened. However, the situation turns out not to be quite that simple. The graphs in Figure 2.5 help to illustrate the problem.

Paired-associate learning curves—for that matter, almost all learning curves—are an average of the results for a number of subjects. These average curves show a smooth and regular improvement. However, smooth curves may arise from individual curves being gradual and smooth, or they could as well arise from individual curves that exhibit an all-or-none transition from guessing to perfect learning. Indeed, paired-associate learning data collected by Bower (1961) conformed almost exactly to predictions arising from a model which assumed that learning was all-or-none (that is, on each trial either nothing was learned or the association was fully formed). A possible interpretation of this finding is that, even without special training in the keyword method, relatively sophisticated learners usually acquire a paired-associate item by searching their memories for a preexisting association linking the two members. For example, if an item were the word pair *car-ice,* one might recall a recent experience of skidding on an icy pavement. On this interpretation, an error merely signifies that the learner has not yet found a suitable mediating association. On the average, performance improves over trials in Bower's experiment, but the reason is apparently that additional trials provide additional opportunities for all-or-none learning. This all-or-none learning depends on selecting an appropriate unit of analysis. Obviously, we would not expect to learn the contents of a book on an all-or-none basis! One might, however, acquire isolated facts in an all-or-none manner. Although not everyone agrees on the relative importance of all-or-none versus gradual learning, looking at individual subject curves and even individual item curves can often yield important clues about the underlying learning process.

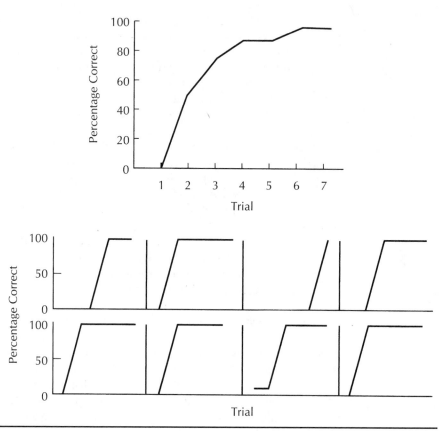

Figure 2.5   The bottom set of curves are data from a single subject learning eight different symbol-adjective pairs. The top curve is the average for that subject over all items. One can readily see that a gradual-appearing average curve does not imply that each item is learned gradually.

Source: Unpublished study by W. K. Estes.

Simple associative processes have turned out to be not so simple. Clearly, there is no process that automatically supplies a linkage between two words. Early work on paired-associate learning attempted to study learning in a pure form by using nonsense syllables as stimuli; instead of *car-ice,* pairs like *biv-goh* were used. The idea of using meaningless materials did not work, mainly because people are quite good at bringing their knowledge to bear to make nonsense materials meaningful. For example, one might note that *biv* provides the first letters of blue, indigo, and violet and that *goh* could be short for van Gogh, and then link *biv* and *goh* by the theme of painting. Learning depends on the strategies employed, and some words are much easier to associate than others. In short, there does not appear to be any learning process that forms associations independent of what is being associated. Selectivity in learning is the rule, not the exception. Psychologists no longer think of paired-associate learning as a procedure for studying "elementary learning processes" because the performance observed depends on the knowledge brought to bear on the situation, as we have just seen.

IMPLICATIONS

 Much of the progress in understanding learning has taken the form of overcoming limitations associated with certain forms of behaviorism. In particular, the ideas that learning consists of forming stimulus-response associations, that these associations are formed more or less automatically, and that any two things are equally easy to associate are incorrect. They are wrong because they ignore both the active role that organisms play in organizing their experience and bringing their knowledge to bear on it and the evolutionary adaptations that favor learning some things over others. Let's take one last look at these issues before moving on.

The Learning-Performance Distinction

Early learning theorists such as Thorndike assumed that rewards tend to strengthen stimulus-response associations directly and automatically. In other words, reinforcement is the glue that connects stimuli with responses. According to this viewpoint, any learning that takes place should be directly evident in changes in behavior; that is, performance directly reflects learning. But common experience tells us that not everything learned is immediately manifested in performance. When a dog refuses to perform tricks that his trainer has taught him by using dog biscuits as rewards, it may reflect the fact that the dog isn't hungry, not that the dog has forgotten how to do the tricks. Although learning is often inferred from performance, the absence of learning may not be inferred from the absence of performance.

Once we draw the **learning-performance distinction,** a natural question is whether reinforcement affects both learning and performance, mainly learning, or mainly performance. A variety of evidence suggests that reinforcement has its primary influence on performance rather than learning.

Expectancy

Our current view of reinforcement is that rather than enslaving behavior with its irresistible power, reinforcement seems to act as a source of information about relations between actions and consequences. One implication of this view is that the tendency for behavior to occur in a given situation is a function of the individual's expectation of reinforcement in that situation. In other words, anticipation of reward, or expectancy, influences which responses will be selected by the organism rather than which ones will be learned. An experiment reported by Estes (1969) illustrates this point. College students were given repeated opportunities to choose between pairs of cards that differed in their reward value.

However, the subjects' task was complicated; each card had two different reward values associated with it and in order to receive the reward, a subject had to choose the correct card and correctly guess the precise reward value associated with that card on that trial. For example, one card might be associated with either 7 or 9 points and another with either 4 or 6 points. Unknown to the participants the experiment was arranged such that on some cards they would never guess the reward amount correctly and on other cards they would always do so. This means that for some trials, they would receive more actual rewards from a card with low values (e.g., the 4, 6 card) than a card with high values (e.g., the 7, 9 card). After several runs through the cards, new pairings of the cards were given for transfer tests. Some of the transfer tests pitted a card of high value for which the reward had never been received (because the experimenter had arranged things so that the exact value had never been guessed) against a card of lower value for which rewards had been received. The results clearly indicated that choices were determined by the magnitude of the reward anticipated and not by the amount of reward previously received. This experiment is another source of evidence that reinforcement does not operate in a direct and automatic manner to strengthen response tendencies.

A related observation that illustrates a more cognitive approach to learning comes from the work of Levine (1971). He tested students on rule learning tasks where on each trial a stimulus was presented and the learner had to say whether it was or was not an instance of the concept. Of course, students are able to learn fairly difficult rules. In some of his experiments Levine gave students a hard problem followed by a trivially easy one (all red stimuli are instances of the rule, all green stimuli are not). He found typically students would go for many, many trials without learning the simple rule. According to Levine, the reason for this is that the students were looking for and evaluating very complex rules and not bothering with very simple rules. This suggests that the students only learned about the hypotheses they were evaluating. A simple reinforcement model of learning could not account for this failure to learn the simple rule.

We turn now to research on human contingency learning—the key problem of figuring out what goes with what. Although several of the ideas of the behaviorist framework appear to be incorrect, fundamental issues in associative learning continue to be interesting and important. As will be seen, associationism has had a significant influence on our understanding of contingency learning.

Contingency Learning and Illusory Correlation

Earlier we described Rescorla's studies showing that rats were sensitive to whether CS predicted something (contingency) rather than to the sheer number of times that a CS and US were paired (co-occurrence). Experiments have also examined people's judgments concerning contingency, and some surprising results have been observed. Smedslund (1963) asked nurses to look through 100 cards that provided information about whether a particular symptom was present and then whether a particular disease was present. The various possibilities and the different combinations are shown

Table 2.2   **Frequency (Out of 100) of Different Patterns of Presence or Absence of Symptom and Disease in Smedslund's (1963) Study**

		Disease		
		Present	Absent	Total
Symptom	Present	37	33	70
	Absent	17	13	30
	Total	54	46	100

in Table 2.2. The disease was indicated as being present on a little more than half (54) of the cards and the symptom was present on 70 of the 100 cards. The nurses were asked to judge whether there was a relationship between the presence of the symptom and the disease.

Table 2.2 shows essentially no relationship between the presence of the symptom and the disease. When the symptom was present, the disease was present a little more than half the time ($^{37}/_{70}$ or 53%). When the symptom was absent, the disease was also present a little more than half the time ($^{17}/_{30}$ or 57%). Even though there was no correlation between the symptom and the disease, 85% of the nurses judged that when the symptom was present is was more likely that the disease was also present. In short, they saw a contingency when none was present.

This difficulty in judging correlation may be quite general (see, e.g., Arkes & Harkness, 1983; Shaklee & Mims, 1982; Shanks, 1986, 1989; Ward & Jenkins, 1965; but also see Wasserman, 1990b, for a counterexample). A more abstract description of the covariation task is given in Table 2.3. One explanation of Smedslund's results is that the nurses may have based their judgments simply on the number of times that the symptom and disease were both present. The most frequent event (37 times) was the presence of both the symptom and the disease. This has come to be known as the "cell-a strategy" (again, refer to Table 2.3). Another possibility is that the nurses compared the frequency of the disease when the symptom was present versus when it was absent (cell a versus cell c, or 37 versus 17). This strategy has been documented (see, e.g., Arkes & Harkness, 1983; Shaklee & Tucker, 1980), but note that it misses the point that one also has to know how often the disease appears in the absence of the symptom. The fact that the outcome might occur 80% of the time when the predictor is present is not in itself informative, because the outcome might occur 80% of the time when the predictor is not present (or even 100%, which would produce a negative correlation!).

What is responsible for people's poor performance on contingency tasks? One possibility is that the cell-a (and cell a plus cell b) strategy works most of the time and that keeping track of four frequencies is much more difficult than keeping track of one or two. A related possibility is that the covariation task does not reflect the full complexity of most learning tasks. In general, there is an unlimited set of potential antecedents in more realistic contingency judgment tasks. We have already

Table 2.3   **Abstract Description of Information Relevant to Judging Correlation or Contingency**
The letters *a, b, c,* and *d* refer to frequencies.

		Property (e.g., Disease)	
		Present	**Absent**
	Present	a	b
Property (e.g., symptom)			
	Absent	c	d

seen that organisms have strong biases to select some antecedents over others (e.g., to associate illness with taste) in conditioning tasks. In more conceptually oriented domains, we might expect that people's theories or expectations would tend to narrow the set of potential antecedents. If the theory also included expectations concerning the strength of relationships between the predictor and the outcome, it might make sense to focus on cell a and cell b.

Actually, there is evidence that people's theories or expectations may dominate observations, leading observers to see correlations that are not objectively present. Consider a psychiatrist or clinical psychologist who gives a draw-a-person test (the patient is simply asked to draw a person) and is interested in whether characteristics of the drawing can be used to predict whether the patient is later diagnosed as paranoid or suspicious of others; that is, the basic question is whether there is a correlation between different properties of drawings and the diagnostic category. Tables 2.2 and 2.3 apply again. If some property, such as having significant body parts missing, is more likely to appear for patients later determined to be paranoid than for patients not found to be paranoid, then that property can be used to predict the presence of paranoia. In practice, however, as documented by Chapman and Chapman (1969), clinicians frequently fail to perceive correlations that are present and see correlations that are not objectively present. This latter phenomenon is known as **illusory correlation.** For example, in the case of the draw-a-person test, people "see" associations between how the eyes are drawn and paranoia that are not true correlations. That is, in the sample there is no association between how the eyes are drawn and the subsequent diagnosis. Illusory correlation is like a perceptual illusion in the sense that different clinicians tend to see the same illusory correlations as do undergraduate students presented with drawings and diagnoses.

Illusory correlations may represent an instance of how properties of the memory system affect memory for associated events. Words that are highly associated (e.g., table and chair) tend to cue each other. Similarly, the concept of suspiciousness tends to be associated in our culture with things like "shifty eyes." Consequently, it may be far easier to recall cases in which the eyes were drawn in an unusual way and the diagnosis of paranoia was given (cell a) than to recall cases in which paranoia was not the diagnosis (cell b). Contingency learning continues to be an active area of research, in part because it is directly relevant to how people combine their prior expectations with new information (see Shanks & Dickinson, 1988; Wasserman, 1990b, for reviews of contingency learning) and in part because contingency learning is thought to be a fundamental component of causal reasoning (Cheng & Novick, 1992; see the edited volume by Shanks, Holyoak & Medin, 1996).

Summary

Instrumental learning involves attempts to change voluntary behavior through reinforcement. Although originally researchers thought that rewards automatically increase response tendencies, modern theory suggests that rewards mainly function by providing information. Furthermore, it is important to distinguish between learning and performance because much of learning may not be immediately reflected in performance. We also noted that instrumental learning situations almost always contain contingencies corresponding to classical conditioning and that many learning situations represent a mixture of instrumental and classical conditioning. Studies of human associative learning reveal some complicating factors that make it difficult to study simple associations in isolation. For example, organisms are perfectly capable of learning by observation—they do not need to directly receive rewards or punishments for learning to take place. In addition, research on paired-associated learning and illusory correlation demonstrates that people's prior knowledge can influence what is learned and the speed of learning. The importance of prior knowledge in learning will be a theme that continues throughout this book.

Content and Meaningful Learning

Although learning simple associations is a fundamental form of adaptation, one can still ask about the learning that is richer in content or more meaningful. People master complex sets of material when they learn calculus, computer programming, or literary criticism. Children must acquire language and must learn how the words of the language map onto actions, objects, and events in their world. Clearly, there is more to becoming an art expert than is captured by paired-associate learning. Cognitive psychologists should be able to say something useful about complex learning.

We looked at three recent cognitive psychology textbooks and noted that "learning" was not a chapter in two of them and was combined with memory in the third book. If learning is so important, what's going on here? The answer, we believe, is that meaningful learning is embedded in a variety of content areas. In the three textbooks we alluded to, complex learning is integrated into chapters on concept formation, comprehension and inference, language, and problem solving. We have also found it natural to discuss complex learning in particular content areas. So our discussion of complex learning will be scattered through many of the remaining chapters of this book.

The question about meaningful learning, however, also raises the issue of what appears to be a huge discontinuity between simple associative learning and

A DEBATE
Models of Conditioning and Causal Induction

Earlier we noted that Rescorla's work on contingency learning in rats is paralleled by studies with humans of illusory correlation and contingency learning. Learning about causes is fundamental to much of human reasoning, so it is important to understand how it works (and doesn't work). Recently a great deal of attention has been devoted to similarities between the learning of causal relations by humans and conditioning in animals. The discussion and debate has centered around two related issues. One concerns the extent to which the main empirical findings in the two domains are the same (see Young, 1995, for a review). For example, both humans and animals show blocking effects but Shanks (1985) found that humans also show backward blocking. In backward blocking two cues (e.g., A and B) are paired with some outcome, followed by a period where one cue does not appear (e.g., B) and the other (e.g., A) is followed by the outcome. This additional period produces a weakened association between cue B and the outcome. This is called backward blocking because the usual blocking paradigm reverses the order of the these two training stages. For a time it was thought that animals do not show backward blocking effects and that this represented a fundamental difference between human and animal contingency learning. However, Miller and Matute (1996) noted that the typical animal conditioning study uses biologically important stimuli such as food, water, or pain (e.g., shocks, illness) whereas the typical human study uses weaker outcomes (e.g., information about outcomes, points, etc.). They reasoned that biological salience may be a critical factor determining the pattern of results obtained. When they tested rats on stimuli that were weaker in biological salience they were able to demonstrate reliable backward blocking (see

(Continued)

complex meaningful learning. Do they have anything to do with each other? We think that the answer lies, in part, on the level of description we adopt. We doubt that discovering the neural basis of habituation will take us very far toward understanding how children learn to read. And obviously, classical conditioning is very different from language learning. At the same time, there are theoretical issues and challenges that apply directly to both types of learning. The learnability problem in classical conditioning (figuring out what goes with what) is paralleled by learnability problems in language acquisition; in both cases, if learning is to succeed, it

A DEBATE
Models of Conditioning and Causal Induction *(Continued)*

also Denniston, Miller, & Matute, 1996). In short, it is important to control for biological significance in comparing human and animal findings.

A closely related issue is just what form of theory or model best accounts for these empirical regularities. Early work in conditioning provided strong support for an associative learning model developed by Rescorla and Wagner (1972). This success and the parallels between animal and human data suggest that associative learning models should be able to account for human contingency learning and causal induction. In contrast, models of human contingency learning have focused on statistical relations between causes and effects and distinctions between "true causes" and "enabling conditions" (e.g., a lighted match may be seen as the cause of a fire while the presence of oxygen is merely an enabling condition). Researchers studying human causal induction have been encouraged by the same parallels we have noted to argue that their models apply to animal conditioning studies.

Currently, there is much debate and a corresponding flurry of research designed to contrast the predictions of (updated forms of) associative learning models with predictions of (updated forms of) more cognitively oriented statistical and causal learning models. A sampling of this debate can be found in the edited volume on this topic by Shanks, Holyoak, and Medin (1996) and recent articles by, for example, Cheng, 1997; Larkin, Aitken, and Dickinson, 1998; and Lopez, Shanks, Almaraz, and Fernandez, 1998. Although it is too early to judge the outcome of this debate, there has been a clear beneficial effect to theories in both areas of having interactions across the animal conditioning and human contingency learning literatures.

must be guided or constrained. We believe that there are levels of description that will allow researchers to discover useful learning principles across a range of types of learning.

A final reason to expect meaningful learning to have something to do with simple learning is that simple learning is not simple. The most extreme efforts to get rid of meaning by using nonsense syllables only succeeded in showing how ingenious people can be in organizing highly impoverished situations. Learning is not an isolated process but rather consists of relating what is new to what is already known.

Summary

Even within the narrow range of situations we have examined, there is reason to believe that a variety of underlying learning mechanisms may be determining performance. Nonetheless, there certain generalizations that seem to extend across diverse tasks. For our purposes, the most obvious generalization is that "equipotentiality," the idea that any stimulus is equally easily associated with any other stimulus or response, does not hold; that is, organisms seem to come prepared or biased to form certain kinds of associations and not others. Given the complexity of figuring out which of a large set of potential factors should be linked to some event, commitments favoring some possibilities over others are necessary if we are going to be able to learn the "right" things (where "right" is defined in terms of the adaptation of organisms to their environment).

One can view learning as a gamble on nature's part, a gamble that organisms will be able to learn quickly enough to profit from learning and that the right things will be learned. We reviewed material on fixed-action patterns, critical periods, and other forms of constrained learning to illustrate the continuum of flexibility of learning. When environments are highly stable, nature may not gamble at all (as we saw for fixed-action patterns) or hedge the bets by providing various forms of guidance or constraints. Although constraints connote taking away opportunities, the other side of the coin is that constraints enable learning. The same biophysical constraints that prevent a crab from flying or even walking straight allow it to move about effectively in its environment.

Although individual species have diverse adaptations to their environments, they have enough in common to foster hope for making broad generalizations concerning learning. We saw this in our discussion of basic learning where principles from conditioning and instrumental learning in animals found application in human learning, including the aversion learning associated with chemotherapy. These developments have led to a renewed interest in fundamental principles of learning and memory.

We also noted, however, that it is important to distinguish between learning and performance and that rewards and punishments do not automatically and directly strengthen response tendencies. For example, Levine's studies showed that people may not learn a simple concept if they are evaluating a set of more complex hypotheses. Finally, we noted that even simple contingency learning may be affected by illusory correlations, that reflect ideas or theories about what is likely to go with what.

We are now ready to consider the information processing associated with complex cognition in greater detail. The next chapters, on attention and perception, describe work on how organisms take in information and make sense of it.

Key Terms

autoshaping

blocking

classical conditioning

compensatory response model

conditioned response

conditioned stimulus

credit assignment

critical periods

extinction

fixed-action patterns

habituation

illusory correlation

imprinting

instrumental learning

learning

learning-performance distinction

operant behaviors

reinforcement

releasers

respondent behaviors

unconditioned response

unconditioned stimulus

unusualness heuristic

Recommended Readings

The field of ethology provides an important perspective on both human and animal behavior. An excellent overview of this work is provided by Alcock (1989). Ilene Bernstein's (1978) work on chemotherapy and learned food aversions in children is both interesting and of great practical significance (and see Tyc et al., 1997 for a more recent overview). Similarly, Shepard Siegel's research on conditioning and drug tolerance underlines the relevance of basic learning processes to contemporary problems. Articles by Maier, Watkins, and Fleshner (1994) and Kiecolt-Glaser et al., (1998) discuss the intriguing possibilities associated with the idea that the immune system may be conditioned. Rozin, Wrzesniewski, and Brynes (1998) describe some intriguing observations on evaluative conditioning and disgust reactions. Rescorla's (1988) paper is a very accessible summary of modern developments in Pavlovian conditioning (see also Hollis, 1997).

The article by Ball and Hulse (1998) provides an overview of the issues that can be addressed by studies of birdsong. The review papers by Estes (1969) and Bandura (1982) raise a number of important issues about the control of human behavior by reinforcement. The paper by Miller and Matute (1996) offers a nice methodological analysis of comparisons of human and animal contingency learning. Finally, the Shanks, Holyoak, and Medin (1996) edited volume reviews work on causal and contingency learning drawn from both animal and human learning research.

Chapter 3

Perception

The Problem of Perception

Visual Perception
Low-Level Vision
Localization

High-Level Vision
Feature Detection Theories
Structural Theories
Template Matching and Alignment
Face Recognition and Visual Subsystems

Levels and the Integration of Information in Perceptual Context Effects
The Word Superiority Effect

Summary

Key Terms

Recommended Readings

You can see a lot just by looking.

—*Yogi Berra*

THE PROBLEM OF PERCEPTION _____

Perception of the world around us is one of the most striking aspects of conscious experience. Opening our eyes reveals a complex world of objects, colors, and movement that we perceive without obvious effort. Sounds reach our ears. We feel objects touching us, the warmth of nearby surfaces and the position of our limbs in space. We are able to detect a variety of odors in the surrounding world as well. Perhaps even more amazing, even though this information comes in through different sense organs, we end up with a sense of a coherent world.

Perception is an example of an adage in cognitive psychology that what is easy for people to do is difficult for computers, and what is easy for computers to do is hard for people. After all, computer programs have been developed that can beat the world's best chess players, but there are no computers that have anything close to the perceptual abilities of your average 5-year-old child.

Why is perception so difficult? A central problem is that there is considerable ambiguity in the world that the perceptual system must resolve. For example, in vision, light reflecting off surfaces in the world reaches our eyes and strikes the *retina*. The retina is located at the rear of the eye and is made up of light-sensitive cells that turn photons (the physical packets of light) into electrical signals that can be processed by the brain. The retina is a two-dimensional surface; thus, we are immediately left with the problem of reconstructing the three-dimensional world outside from the patterns of light on these two dimensions. This reconstruction is difficult, because there are an unlimited set of objects that can produce the same image on the retina. Figure 3.1 shows three different bars, each of which would yield the same image on the retina. Of course, our perceptual experience does not have these ambiguities, so the perceptual system resolves them before the point that we are aware of the visual world.

Perception is far too big a topic to cover completely in a single chapter. Instead, we will sketch some important issues in visual perception. Bear in mind that psychologists have also studied other perceptual systems (or *modalities*), and many

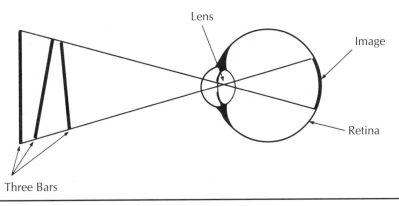

Figure 3.1   Three different bars that project the same image on the retina.

of the same issues that we will discuss for vision arise for these other types of perception. For example, there is quite a bit of other work on audition (i.e., hearing) such as work on music perception (Krumhansl, 1992; Palmer, 1997) and speech perception (see Chapter 9). There is also work on perception of odors, perception of body position in space, perception of touch and perception of heat.

As we will see, vision is a prime example of how the cognitive system deals with a substantial amount of information. Be on the lookout for ways that the visual system seems specifically adapted to the world. Through evolution, the human perceptual system has developed in a way that is well suited to people's goals. One thing in particular that will be important in the present discussion is the way that the perceptual system uses simplifying rules to process information quickly.

VISUAL PERCEPTION

What are the goals of vision? We need to have a sense of the three-dimensional structure of the outside world. We need to know *what* objects are out there. We need to know *where* those objects are located, so we can navigate around them and pick them up. We need to know *how* the objects are acting. Are they moving toward us or away from us? It is vitally important to know whether some object is rushing toward us or away from us and whether the object is a loved one or an automobile. The perceptual system must also deliver information in such a way that relevant knowledge from memory can make contact with it. As we shall see, vision does not involve a passive one-way flow of information from the eye to higher level processes. Rather, perception is an active process in which different levels of analysis interact to determine what we perceive and understand.

At a coarse level, we can divide vision into low-level and high-level vision, as shown in Figure 3.2 (see Marr, 1982). Low-level vision involves extracting preliminary information from the pattern of light that hits the retina. For example, objects in the world often have sharp borders. Thus, the visual system tries to find discontinuities in the pattern of light that might signal edges which may be the borders of objects. In contrast, high-level vision is concerned with the perception of larger-scale elements of the world like whole objects or faces. We begin with a discussion of low-level vision, focusing on the way the visual system uses a variety of cues to construct an initial representation of the visual world. Then, we will turn to high-level vision.

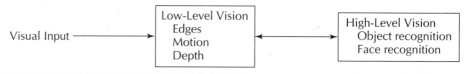

Figure 3.2   An overview of vision, separating processing into low-level and high-level vision.

Low-Level Vision

The goal of vision is to enable people to interact with their three-dimensional environment. Along the way, the visual system will form internal representations of the visual world. It is important to bear in mind, however, that the end goal of vision is *not* simply to form some internal representation of what is out there in the visual world, but rather to extract useful information that will allow people to interact with the environment. James J. Gibson (1950) pointed out that perceptual systems are designed to serve a person's goals, and so the visual system seeks out information that will help an individual achieve his or her goals. The sensitivity to goals may help constrain the way information about the visual world is interpreted. Constraints like these are critical, because there are many possible patterns in the outside world that are consistent with any pattern of light that strikes the retina.

Low-level vision helps serve people's goals by extracting information that determines features of the objects in the world, where they are located, and how they are moving. In the following sections, we will discuss the detection of edges as an example of information relevant to what objects are. We will examine segregation of objects and the localization of objects in depth as examples of information relevant to where objects are. Finally, we will describe research on motion perception as an example of information relevant to how objects are acting in space.

Edge Detection

To get an idea of the complexity of visual information processing, one has only to explore any one step in detail. For example, how do we know where an object begins or ends? Intuitively it seems obvious. Objects have clear boundaries, and so if we just find the edges of objects we will be able to find the objects in the world. It turns out that the detection of edges is considerably more difficult than one might first imagine.

The first question that needs to be addressed in edge detection is how to separate coarse edges (which may signal boundaries of objects) from the fine details of an object (which may delineate parts of the object). Consider, for example, the F made of Bs in Figure 3.3. The F is a large object with thick lines. The Bs that make it up are smaller and have narrower lines. In vision research, edges that are thick

```
B B B B B B B B
B
B
B
B B B B B B
B
B
B
B
B
```

Figure 3.3   Type of stimulus employed by Navon (1977) to look at processing of coarse and fine detail information.

like the ones in the F are said to be detectable on the basis of *low spatial frequency* information. Spatial frequency is the number of lines of a uniform thickness that can fit into a particular unit of distance. The thicker the lines, the fewer that can be placed in a given space, and hence the lower the spatial frequency. Thus, the low spatial frequency information in an image consists of very coarse features of objects like thick lines and overall shape.

In contrast, edges like the ones that make up the narrow Bs in Figure 3.3 require attention to *high spatial frequency* information to be detected. Think of high spatial frequency information as thin lines and fine detail information in images. One easy way to distinguish between high and low spatial frequency information is to squint. Squinting filters out the high spatial frequency information. If you squint, and you can still recognize the object you are looking at, chances are you are using low spatial frequency information to do so. For example, if you hold Figure 3.3 at arm's length from your face, you can probably see both the F (based on low spatial frequency information) and also the Bs (based on high spatial frequency information). If you squint, you will easily make out the F, but the individual Bs will probably be hard to detect (because the high spatial frequency information has been filtered out).

The visual system seems to have different spatial frequency analyzers that process information independently (Graham, 1992). Indeed, it has been proposed that observed differences in the functions of the right and left hemispheres of the brain may occur because the right hemisphere prefers to process relatively lower spatial frequency information than does the left (Ivry & Robertson, 1998). Regardless of possible hemispheric differences, the presence of independent spatial frequency channels means that the process of edge detection can take place at different levels of resolution (i.e., for both coarse and fine detail information). There is some evidence, however, suggesting that processing of scenes typically starts with global (or coarse) information and gradually incorporates local (or fine detail) information. In a classic study, Navon (1977) used objects like the F made of Bs shown in Figure 3.3. Navon found evidence for what he called *global precedence,* in that the letter F was more accessible early in processing than was the letter B. Global precedence is not always observed. Later work demonstrated that display size (visual angle) is an important mediating factor, and with larger viewing angles local precedence can be observed, at least for letter stimuli (Kinchla & Wolf, 1979).

An innovative set of studies by Oliva and Schyns (1997) suggests that scene processing need not go from coarse to fine. Instead, the visual system may focus on the output of particular spatial frequency channels when that output is useful for the task at hand. As a demonstration of this point, Oliva and Schyns used specially generated *hybrid* stimuli. In the training phase of their study, half of the subjects were shown images like the top one in Figure 3.4. This item contains low spatial frequency information from a picture of a city (squint and you'll see it) and high spatial frequency noise (that is, a random pattern of high spatial frequency information). The other half of the participants saw similar pictures, except that the meaningful picture was captured in the high spatial frequency information, and low frequency noise was added. People were given a brief exposure to these pictures and were asked to name them (e.g., "city"). After seeing these pictures, they were shown an

Figure 3.4   Examples of the hybrid stimuli used by Schyns and Oliva (1997). The top picture mixes the low-frequency (coarse) components of a highway scene with the high-frequency (fine) components of a city scene. The bottom picture has the low-frequency components of a city scene and the high-frequency components of a highway scene.

Source: Schyns & Oliva, 1994.

additional set of hybrid images in which the high and low spatial frequency parts of the images contained different pictures. In Figure 3.4, for example, the bottom image has a low spatial frequency picture of a city and a high spatial frequency picture of a bridge. People were simply asked to name the object in the picture.

If people always process visual scenes going from coarse information to fine information in perception, then they should always name the hybrid picture consistent with the low spatial frequency information. In accordance with this idea, people who saw the images that had content only at low spatial frequencies in the training phase primarily named the hybrid pictures with the object appearing in low spatial

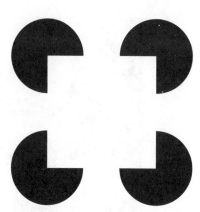

Figure 3.5   An example of an illusory contour: The visual system interprets this display as a white square lying on top of four black circles.

frequency information. In contrast, people who saw the images that had content only at high spatial frequencies named the hybrid pictures with the object appearing in the high spatial frequency information. Further, most participants reported seeing only one scene in the hybrids, and were surprised to find out that the hybrids actually contained information about two different scenes. These results suggest that people can select the output of different spatial frequency channels independently and that they do not have to go from coarse processing to fine processing. While it is not obligatory to go from coarse to fine processing, it seems to be the case that people *typically* process visual information in this way (e.g., Goldstone, 1994; Goldstone & Medin, 1994; Sanocki, 1993; Schyns & Oliva, 1994).

Even within a particular level of resolution, edge detection is not straightforward. Edges are defined by differences in brightness between regions, but these differences are not guaranteed to be sharp and instead may fade more or less continuously. One thing the visual system does during edge detection is to enhance the differences between light and dark regions in order to make edges stand out better. For this reason, the bright part of an edge may appear brighter than it really is, and the dark part may appear darker. This enhancement of edges can even occur in places where there are no actual edges in the image. Figure 3.5 shows an example of an illusory contour. Because of the orientation of the open Pac-Man shapes, it appears as if there is a white square on top of four dark circles. Because the visual system interprets this image as a white square on top, the square looks brighter than the surrounding white background, even though there is no actual edge present in the figure.

In sum, the visual system uses spatial frequency analyzers to determine what information is likely to be an edge. Thick edges can be detected using low-spatial frequency information. Thin edges require high spatial frequency information. Edges themselves often manifest themselves in a fairly rapid change from light to dark in an image. The visual system enhances differences between light and dark, which can lead to perceptual illusions.

Figure 3.6   **Reversible Figure-Ground Pattern**   This image can be seen as either a pair of silhouetted faces or a white vase.

Localization

To locate objects in our environment, we first have to segregate objects from one another and from the background. Associated with this task is the further problem of determining the position and movement of objects in the world. Essentially, to know where an object is in the world, we must first know that it is an object, and thus we must segregate the visual information about each object from that of other objects and the background. Second, we must determine how far the object is from us. Finally, if the object is moving, we need to get a sense of the direction and speed of that motion so that we can predict the object's location in the future. Because segregation, fixing distance, and determining movement are all important for determining where an object is, it should not be surprising that they are closely related, a claim that is supported by physiological evidence that these three functions are handled by the same part of the nervous system (Livingstone & Hubel, 1988).

Segregation

Much of the early work on object segregation was done by a group of researchers known as the Gestalt psychologists, who focused on the perception of whole objects and proposed a number of principles for how the perceptual system organizes objects. For example, they were very interested in **figure-ground relations.** In an image, the figure is the main object (or objects) that is the focus of the percept, and everything else is background. *Figure* is determined by regions of contrast that are connected and cohesive. *Figure-ground* is not completely determined by the stimulus alone as can be seen by reversible figures that allow more than one organization. As an example, Figure 3.6 can be seen either as a vase or as two profile faces.

The Gestalt psychologists also identified principles of grouping for organizing figures. For example, the closer two figures are to each other, the more likely it is that they will be grouped perceptually. Thus, the stimuli in Figure 3.7a are seen as

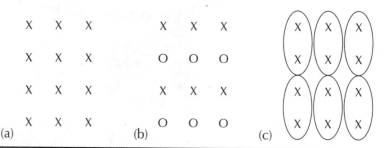

(a)   (b)   (c)

Figure 3.7	**Grouping by Proximity, Similarity, and Common Region** In (a) the pattern will tend to be organized as three columns. In (b) it will be grouped into three rows. In (c) it will be grouped into three columns, and within each column, the items in each region will be grouped.

organized into three vertical columns. This **proximity principle** trades off with similarity and membership in a common region. In Figure 3.7b, for example, the stimuli are grouped by similarity, as the same spatial layout now appears as four horizontal rows rather than three vertical columns. In Figure 3.7c, the objects are grouped by membership in a common region (Palmer, 1992).

The perceptual system also seems to prefer contours that continue smoothly along their course. For example, Figure 3.8a is seen as comprised of the parts shown in Figure 3.8b rather than the parts shown in Figure 3.8c. Organization by **good continuation** does not even require that contours be continuous. Figure 3.8d is seen as a single rod and a rectangle rather than as two rods and a rectangle or as a single, irregular object. These assumptions made by the perceptual system tend to serve us well. In situations like those shown in Figure 3.8d, there is an excellent chance that a single rod and a rectangular shape are really present.

Distance

The visual system uses many different kinds of information to determine where objects are located. The retinal image gives information on where things are relative to each other horizontally and vertically, so the key problem is determining their distance in depth. In this section, we describe a number of cues used to derive the

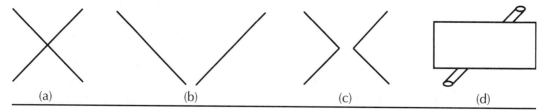

(a)   (b)   (c)   (d)

Figure 3.8	**Good Continuation** The line segments in (a) tend to be decomposed into the two lines in (b) rather than into the two lines shown in (c). The lines do not even have to be literally continuous. The figure in (d) is seen as a single rod and rectangle.

distance of objects. Although perceiving an object's depth may seem effortless, it is a remarkable achievement given that the retinal image is flat and has no depth at all. It is also a remarkable achievement, because the visual system seamlessly integrates a number of different pieces of information to determine the distance to an object. We do not have the conscious experience of combining these sources of information. Instead, the visual system does it for us automatically.

MONOCULAR CUES   Anyone who has spent time looking at artwork will already be familiar with many of the cues to depth, because artists have long exploited these cues to give a sense of depth in their paintings. Some of the cues to depth require information coming from only a single eye. Three straightforward examples are interposition, linear perspective, and relative size (see Figure 3.9). Interposition refers to the observation that when one object interrupts the contour of a second object, the first object is perceived to be in front of the second one (as for the boxes in Figure 3.9a). Linear perspective is the observation that when straight lines gradually converge (e.g., as in the road in Figure 3.9b), they are perceived as parallel, with the converging points seen as more distant. Relative size refers to the observation that people tend to perceive the smaller of two identical (or similar) objects as being farther away than the larger object (as in the ants in Figure 3.9c).

Although shadows might seem to be a source of confusion in perception, our visual system can use information from cast shadows to determine the apparent position of an object and its shape (Figure 3.10). The sphere on the left occupies the same relative position in both the top and bottom versions, but the shadow leads one to see the bottom sphere as farther off the "ground" than the top sphere. The perceived shape of the objects is affected by shading for the right-side figures; the top figure is seen as a flat disk, whereas the bottom figure appears as a vertically oriented oval shape. At the same time, however, colors, textures, and shapes of shadows are physically constrained in natural situations in ways that the human perceptual system seems to ignore. For example, Cavanagh and Leclerc (1989) report that the only requirements for perceiving depth through shadow are that shadow regions are

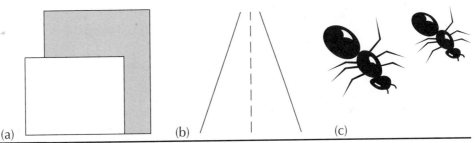

(a)   (b)   (c)

Figure 3.9   An example of three monocular cues to depth. Occlusion, shown in (a), occurs when one object is in front of another. Linear perspective, shown in (b), occurs when lines appear to recede into the distance. Relative size, shown in (c), occurs when two objects of the same size differ in depth. The further object casts a smaller image on the retina and so is assumed to be further away.

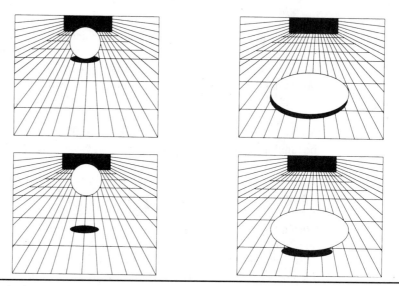

Figure 3.10   Cast shadows can influence the apparent position of an object and its shape.

Source: Cavanaugh & Leclerc, 1989.

darker than surrounding nonshadow regions and that there are consistent contrast differences along shadow borders. It did not seem to matter much at all whether the shape of the shadow corresponds with the shape of its source object.

We should note in passing that another remarkable property of the perceptual system is **size constancy.** That is, we tend to perceive an object as being the same size, even though its size on our retina decreases, the farther away it is from us. For example, a pen on the desk will appear to be the same size whether you put it at the front of the desk or at the back, even though the image of the pen on the retina is smaller when the pen is far away than when it is close. At extremes of distance, size constancy may break down; from an airplane, cars on the ground may appear to be the size of ants (this effect is enhanced by the unfamiliar overhead perspective provided by an airplane). There is evidence that size constancy is present even in 6-month-old infants (McKenzie, Tootell, & Day, 1980).

TEXTURE GRADIENTS   So far we have described cues that allow the perceptual system to infer depth. The fact that we are not aware of these inferences has led to the idea, which can be traced back at least as far as Helmholtz before 1900, that these inferences are unconscious. Consistent with this view, Gibson (e.g., 1950, 1986) claimed that people do not infer depth, but rather perceive it directly. His idea is that the perceptual system does not combine information from multiple cues; instead, perception involves a direct sensitivity to higher-order **invariants.** Invariants refer to properties of the pattern of light that hits the retina that remain unchanged despite various transformations in the world or object. That is, there is information directly in the stimulus.

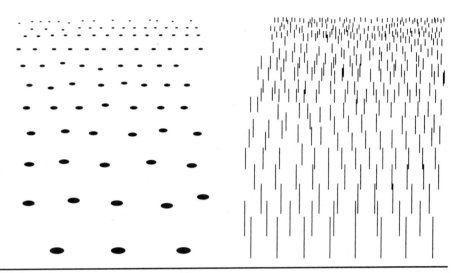

Figure 3.11   Two examples of texture gradients.

Source: Gibson, 1950.

As one example, Gibson pointed out that **texture gradients** are a powerful source of information. A texture gradient arises when we view a surface in perspective. The elements that make up the surface appear to be packed closer and closer together as the surface recedes. Two-dimensional figures embodying this property are seen as having depth (Figure 3.11). Gibson argued that size constancy is also directly perceived as a higher-order invariant. There is a constant ratio between the retinal size of an object and the retinal size of its adjacent textural elements.

Gibson's ideas about direct perception are controversial, especially his argument that invariants negate the need for any sort of internal, mental representations (for criticisms, see, e.g., Fodor & Pylyshyn, 1981). Nonetheless, Gibson's work has been very influential, because it focused attention on the information that is available to the perceptual system. Gibson's criticisms of research restricted to two-dimensional stable stimuli have served to reinforce the study of the perception of objects and events in the world.

MOTION PARALLAX   So far, in discussing distance perception, we have considered only situations in which both the observer and the observed scene remain stationary. Of course, in real life we are often moving about, and motion provides an important source of information about the spatial arrangement of objects around us. As we move our heads from left to right, for example, the images projected by objects in our environment move across the retina from right to left. Relative motion or **motion parallax** provides a very effective depth cue. Nearby objects appear to move more quickly than objects farther away. You can often see this when driving a car on a scenic freeway in the evening. The trees whiz by you. The mountains move more slowly than the trees. The moon does not appear to move at all, giving rise to the illusion that it is following you.

STEREOPSIS   In the 18th century, the bishop George Berkeley (1975) argued that the visual system could not possibly use information about the distance between the eyes, because it would take too long to work out the geometric calculations. What Berkeley had not counted on was the brain's ability to use this information implicitly, without awareness that it is being used. One important cue—**stereopsis**—arises from the fact that our two eyes are set a few inches apart, and hence get slightly different views of the world. As Figure 3.12 illustrates, when we fixate on an object, our eyes converge slightly so that the axes or lines of vision meet at a point in the visual world. Any neighboring point in the visual field will then project to a point on each retina some distance from the center of vision. As in the example in Figure 3.12 (compare points A and B and their associated retinal locus), the retinal distance generally is not the same for both eyes but varies with the depth of the fixated point. In the example of Figure 3.12, the a_2 to b_2 distance is greater than the a_1 to b_1 distance. This means that information about **retinal disparity** can potentially be used to determine how far away the fixated point or object is. (You may recall from geometry or trigonometry that information about the length of one side of a triangle and its two adjacent angles can be used to determine the lengths of the two other sides. In short, depth or distance can be determined by triangulation.) While it would probably take a long time to calculate these geometric relations consciously (as Berkeley suggested), Marr and Poggio (1979) presented a procedure that could match the images from the eyes quickly and could calculate the depth of objects by finding corresponding elements in pairs of scenes.

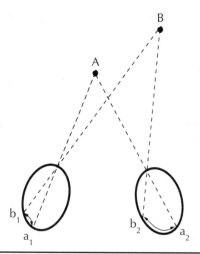

Figure 3.12   **Retinal Disparity**   Two points, A and B, at different distances from the observer, present somewhat different retinal images. The distance between the images on one eye, a_1b_1, is different (disparate) from the distance between them on the other, a_2b_2. This disparity is a powerful cue for depth.

Source: Hochberg, 1978.

AN APPLICATION

Perception and Consciousness

The centrality of visual perception to our conscious experience may seem so obvious that it does not need to be mentioned. Indeed, when we speculate on what it would be like to be blind, part of the power of this exercise comes from the belief that a substantial part of our conscious experience would be wiped away. Because of the importance of perception in conscious experience, researchers exploring the nature of consciousness have turned to perceptual phenomena for insight.

In one prominent discussion, Dennett and Kinsbourne (1992) use apparent motion as a lever for discussing consciousness. For now, let us just consider a simple study. Two dots flash on a computer screen one after another. The first flashes at the center of the screen. The second flashes in one of eight locations around the first soon after the first disappears. People's conscious experience of this situation is that the dot moves from the first location to the second. Furthermore, if the first and second dots are different colors, people report that the dot changes color somewhere along the route from the first to the second.

This conscious experience is something of a puzzle. It is not possible to know either which direction the dot is going to move or what color it is going to change into until *after* the second dot has appeared. Nonetheless, people's conscious experience is still one of the dot moving from the first location to the second. Thus, conscious experience is filling in a number of details after all of the events have already occurred. This idea conflicts with our commonsense intuition that our conscious experience gives us a readout of events as they occur. Phenomena like this are a puzzle for understanding consciousness, and further research will have to be done to understand it.

SUMMARY   The visual system uses a variety of sources of information to determine depth. Monocular cues like size constancy, linear perspective, and texture gradients make use of the way light reflects off objects as a function of distance. Motion cues, like motion parallax, make use of differences in patterns of motion as a function of distance to estimate the distance to an object. Finally, binocular cues make use of information about the distance between the eyes to estimate distance. Normally, only specialists such as vision scientists and artists are aware of these cues; our conscious experience is just of seeing things in depth. The computations that the nervous system performs take place outside our conscious awareness.

The use of all of these cues is an excellent example of how well adapted the visual system is to the environment. All of the properties used by the visual system

AN ENIGMA
Change Blindness

A central aspect of our visual experience is its stability. If I look at a picture of a person, the picture seems to remain in a single location in space. Thus, it may come as a surprise that our eyes are constantly moving when we look at an image. In particular, our eyes make jumping movements called *saccades* and then stop to fixate on different aspects of a scene. A longstanding puzzle in vision has been to understand how the visual system integrates the information from one fixation with information from a second fixation following a saccade (e.g., Irwin, 1991).

A possible solution to this problem may come from recent studies demonstrating **change blindness.** Change blindness is the phenomenon that the visual information accessible to conscious experience is transient. As an example of this phenomenon, Rensink, O'Regan, and Clark (1997) showed people a scene for 240ms followed by a blank screen for 80ms followed by the a version of the same scene for another 240ms. This second version of the scene was identical to the first except for one change. The two scenes were flashed back and forth (with an intervening blank screen for 80ms) until the person was able to identify the change in the

(Continued)

are ones that make use of physical regularities in the world. Presumably, the match between the visual system and the environment is a result of an extended evolutionary history that enabled the development of a visual system that can exploit regularities in the world to give rise to an accurate sense of the depth of objects in space. This ability to use so many cues to depth is a testament to the power of evolution to shape our cognitive abilities.

Motion

A challenge to the problem of localizing things is that some of them may move. Our earlier example of motion parallax cues assumed that the objects were stable and the observer was moving. We must also be able to perceive objects as they move. In addition, we care about whether things are moving toward us or away from us (for obvious reasons). So how do we perceive motion?

ILLUSORY MOTION   It may occur to you that we could perceive motion by the motion of images across the retina. However, the perception of motion cannot be equated with movement of an image across the retina. First of all, when we move in our environment, the retinal images also move, and we need to distinguish self-motion

AN ENIGMA
Change Blindness *(Continued)*

pictures. The blank screen was used to ensure that there was no longer any afterimage from the first picture when the second one was presented.

The changes between pictures included objects that were present in one picture and absent in the other, changes in color of objects, and changes in the location of objects. When these changes were not central to the action taking place in the scene, people took an average of almost 11 seconds to identify the differences. When the changes were important for the action in the scene, the changes were noticed on average in about 4.5 seconds, which is short, but still not immediate. Grimes (1996) obtained similar results with a slightly different technique (see also Simons & Levin, 1998).

Thus, in change blindness, people are not aware of substantial changes in the visual world. Presumably, they are not aware of these changes, because no enduring representation of the visual world is kept. Instead, what is accessible to consciousness is the information from the current fixation. Thus, we may not have to integrate much information from one fixation to another, because most of the information available in the world is lost. We will discuss the implications of change blindness for memory in Chapter 8.

from the motion of objects. Second, as we will discuss further below, our eyes are constantly in motion searching the visual world. Finally, motion across the retina is not necessary for us to perceive motion. Recall, for example, Roger Shepard's work on apparent motion (discussed in Chapter 1). The rapid alternation of two isolated stimulus events is often not perceived as two isolated stimulus events but rather as continuous motion and transformation between the two images. The simplest case of apparent motion involves flashing a light in darkness and shortly thereafter flashing another light near the location of the first. When there is a short time interval between flashes, the perception is of a single light in motion. Only for long interflash intervals do the lights appear as isolated flashes. Apparent motion is responsible for our seeing movies as involving action and motion rather than as a series of rapidly presented still photographs.

REAL MOTION   Even when an image does move across the retina, the problem of motion perception remains complex. As we just noted, movement across the retina could arise because the eyes—rather than the object—are moving. The visual system must integrate information from the motor system in order to "correct" for eye movements in determining real motion. It is therefore remarkable that the visual system is quite sensitive to real motion (Nakayama, 1985).

Motion does provide a rich source of information. When the perceiver is moving forward (as when a pilot is landing an airplane), the image is constantly expanding across the retina as the objects get closer. (Try standing this book up on the table and then moving closer to it. The edges of the book get closer and closer to the edge of what you can see as the image of the book expands.) The rate of this expansion is determined by the perceiver's velocity. The direction of motion of any given point on the image helps determine the direction of motion. Visual motion also may provide information about the shapes and boundaries of objects (see Spelke, 1990, for a discussion of research and Ullman, 1979, for a formal treatment of shape from motion).

Summary   This ends our survey of the multifaceted problems involved in localization. Figuring out where an object is requires a combination of determining what aspects of the visual world are objects (segregation), figuring out how far away the objects are, and figuring out how they are moving. Each of these aspects of perception is actually the combination of a number of different cues. In general, in the discussion of low-level vision, we have examined ways that the visual system uses multiple sources of information to determine simple properties of the visual world. Equally challenging or perhaps more so is the problem of identifying what something is. When we identify an object, we can access a body of knowledge that is relevant to interacting with that object. For example, it may be important to know whether some elongated object is a piece of rope or a snake. The problem of object recognition involves high-level vision, to which we now turn.

HIGH-LEVEL VISION

So far, we have touched on only a small part of the early vision problem and have said next to nothing about higher-level processes that give rise to object and scene perception. Both Marr (1982) and Johnson-Laird (1988) provide very readable discussions and descriptions linking lower-level and higher-level vision (see Hildreth & Ullman, 1989, for a general review of computational vision).

In this section, our attention will focus on one of the most central and difficult problems in perception: how we identify objects in the world based on visual properties like their shape. We will consider a number of ideas concerning how recognition is accomplished. Each of these ideas makes a different proposal for the way information about visual objects is represented.

Feature Detection Theories

Feature-based models have enjoyed long-standing popularity. The key idea of featural models is that all objects are composed of separable, distinct parts referred to as **features.** It seems intuitively natural to explain similarity between objects in terms of properties that they share. A pencil is similar to a pen because both are about the same size and shape and both can be used for writing. Furthermore, features provide a vocabulary for constructing objects. Just as the 26 letters of the English alphabet can be used to compose more than 100,000 words, a small set of visual features may be sufficient to describe a large number of objects.

There is even physiological evidence for features. In a now classic study, Lettvin, Maturana, McCulloch, and Pitts (1959) used microelectronic recording techniques and determined that frog visual systems have four distinct kinds of feature detectors: edge detectors, which respond strongly to the border between light and dark regions; feature movement contrast detectors, which respond when an edge moves; convex edge or "bug detectors," which respond when a small, circular, dark spot moves across a frog's field of vision; and dimming detectors, which react when overall illumination is reduced.

The feature detectors in a frog's visual system seem to be innate. In contrast, it appears that people undergo perceptual learning allowing them to create new visual features (see Goldstone, 1998, and Schyns, Goldstone, & Thibaut, 1998, for a discussion of this issue).

According to featural models, recognizing an object involves decomposing a complex stimulus into its features and then matching the features against the features in the representations of objects in long-term memory. Just as each letter of the alphabet has a unique set of features, objects may also have a unique set of features. As an abstract example, if all dogs have features x, y, and z and no other objects have those three features, then when the perceptual system detects features x, y, and z, it should conclude that the object is a dog.

How could we tell that one object has a feature that another one does not? Treisman and Gormican (1988) studied this issue using a visual search task. In one experiment, people either looked for a tilted line segment against a background of vertical line segments or searched for a vertical line segment against a background of tilted line segments (Figure 3.13a). The former task is much easier than the latter one: A tilted segment against a background of vertical segments seems to pop out of the background, whereas the reverse task requires effortful search. Treisman and Gormican interpret these results as indicating that the vertical line acts as a standard and that any departure from the standard (e.g., the tilted line) is coded as having an extra feature that the standard lacks. This extra feature is readily detected against a background of vertical lines. The standard vertical line does not stand out against a background of tilted lines because the standard has no extra feature. (Here's an analogy: Round numbers often act as standards of comparison. For example, the number 100 might be a standard. In this case, 99 might be thought of as 100 minus 1, so that it has an extra feature that the standard is missing.) Treisman and Gormican suggest that search asymmetries can be used to discover which stimulus of a pair is used as a reference value in early visual coding and which stimulus can be thought of as having an extra feature.

Attractive as featural models are, they are incomplete as theories of object recognition. Feature models typically ignore spatial relationships among features. Featural descriptions may include spatial components, but they ignore spatial relations.

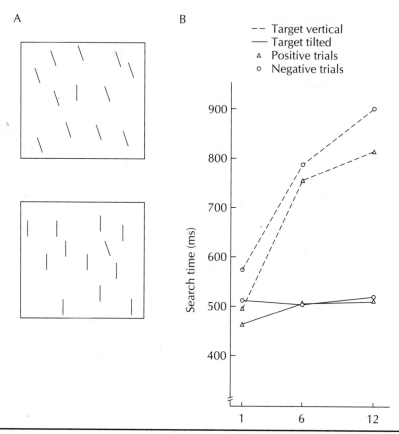

Figure 3.13   Examples of displays testing search for targets defined by (A) line orientation and (B) corresponding search latencies.

Source: Treisman & Gormican, 1988.

Describing T as a letter with a horizontal line segment (—) and a vertical line segment (|) does not distinguish between a T and a +. In short, featural models face what could be termed an anagram problem; that is, if letters are features of words, then what distinguishes *atom* from *moat* from *otma* from *mtao?* (See Markman, 1999, for a discussion of this issue.)

Featural models also seem to presuppose that objects have already been identified and isolated in complex scenes because otherwise the perceptual system would get lost trying to compose features from different objects into a single, coherent object. Even spatial segregation would not help very much—a cup of coffee with a spoon in it is not a single object. But if objects are already isolated before a featural analysis is applied, how is this segregation accomplished? So it seems that, at best, featural models can address only part of the problem of object recognition or that feature detectors are only one aspect of an object recognition system.

Structural Theories

As we discussed, a key limitation of featural models is that they do not take spatial relationships into account. One class of theories that focuses explicitly on spatial relationships is **structural description** theories. Structural descriptions include both features that describe parts of objects as well as spatial relationships that describe how the parts connect (Sutherland, 1968; Palmer, 1977; Waltz, 1975). Returning to the example of a T described above, the structural description would contain the features horizontal line (—) and vertical line (|) as well as the relation that the top end of the vertical line connects to the center of the horizontal line. The description of a + would have the same two features, but the relation would now connect them at their midpoints.

Experiments by Steve Reed (1974) provide a nice demonstration of the need for structural analysis. Participants were shown patterns and then were asked to decide whether a second pattern was a part (subset) of the first one. Figure 3.14 shows some of the patterns used, along with possible parts. Note that some of the subsets involve natural parts (e.g., 3D) whereas others do not (3A). Reed found that people were much faster at identifying subsets that would correspond with a structural description than subsets that would not. For example, it took an average of 1.47 seconds to verify that 3D was a subset of 3 compared with 2.08 seconds for 3A. In addition, people made more than twice as many errors on 3A as on 3D. This study demonstrates that people are good at breaking objects up into components that must be related to each other. It does not specify how these relationships are understood.

A major advantage of structural description theories is that they are able to account for how we can recognize a large number of objects without having to assume that we know about a massive number of features. To see how this works, we will consider Biederman's (1987) recognition-by-components theory of object recognition. He suggests that our representations of objects are based on 36 basic shapes called **geons.** Geons are simple three-dimensional shapes like cylinders, cones, blocks, and wedges (see Figure 3.15 for examples). Structural descriptions of complex objects are built up from these components using spatial relations. In this way, a small number of geons combined with spatial relations can be used to describe millions of different objects.

In order for a theory based on geons to work, there must be some way to extract information about geons from images using lower-level feature information. The reason that Biederman selected the geons he did was that these basic shapes can be recognized based on "nonaccidental" relationships between contours in the image to determine part decomposition. Nonaccidental properties are cues that predict the parts of objects. They are called nonaccidental because they are unlikely to appear in an image by accident. For example, if an image has two parallel lines in it, this probably reflects that there are parallel lines in the object (rather than that the object happened to be oriented in a way where two lines in an image just happened to be parallel). Furthermore, if two lines in an object are parallel they are often part of the same object. Other cues or nonaccidental properties include smooth continuation, cotermination, and types of symmetry (Figure 3.16). The key idea is that some

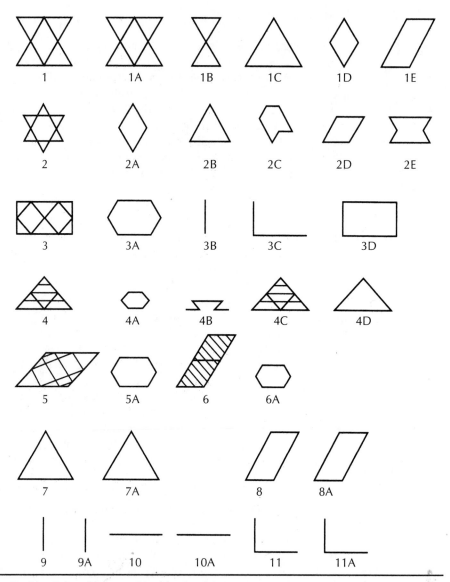

Figure 3.14   **Positive Pairs of Patterns Used by Reed (1974)**   A pattern is positive if it is a part or subset of the pattern it is paired with. For example, 1A, 1B, 1C, 1D, and 1E are each subsets of pattern 1.

patterns are better predictors than others and that the perceptual system is tuned to these informative aspects of scenes.

The recognition-by-components theory has some nice properties. It explains how objects can be recognized using only a limited number of basic elements whose presence can be extracted from lower-level elements of the visual image. In addition,

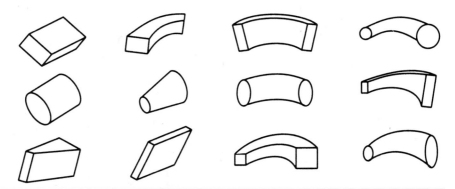

| Figure 3.15 | **Possible Set of Geons for Natural Objects**   Cylinders, cones, blocks, and wedges may all be features of complex objects. |

Source: Biederman, 1987.

the theory itself has been implemented in a computer model, which demonstrates that it is actually capable of forming the basis of an object recognition system (Hummel & Biederman, 1992). Nonetheless, the theory also has limitations (Ullman, 1989, 1996). For one, the decomposition of an object into geons may not be refined enough to distinguish between objects that have more or less the same parts (e.g., dog versus wolf or cat). Second, some objects (e.g., a loaf of bread) are difficult to decompose into parts that both characterize the object and are applicable to a variety of other objects (see also Kurbat, 1994). One could, of course, use more units and smaller ones, but the cost of adding more units is that the structural descriptions become much more complex (more geons in objects and more relations among geons to be coded). Remember, though, that an important appeal of the recognition-by-components theory is that object representations are based on a limited set of geons. Adding a lot of new geons would thus reduce the appeal of the recognition-by-components theory.

It has proven difficult to provide good evidence for specific structural description theories like recognition-by-components. For example, Biederman and Ju (1988) found that outlines of objects could be recognized at least as fast as full-color pictures. This result indicates that information about the texture and color of objects does not add much information that is necessary for object recognition. This finding is certainly consistent with the geon theory's focus on shape, but it does not favor this theory over other structural description theories that have been developed (e.g., Marr, 1982).

Similarly, Biederman (1987) described studies in which people identified line drawings with some line segment information removed. For example, the left-most column of Figure 3.17 shows some line drawings. In the middle column, line segment information is removed from between vertices (that is, at places where two or more line segments come together). In the right-most column, the information is removed at the vertices. Biederman suggested that the vertices contain information about the relations between geons, and he predicted that when line segments were removed

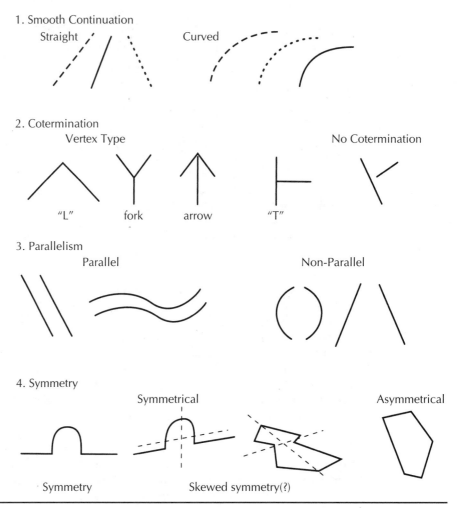

1. Smooth Continuation

Straight   Curved

2. Cotermination

Vertex Type   No Cotermination

"L"   fork   arrow   "T"

3. Parallelism

Parallel   Non-Parallel

4. Symmetry

Symmetrical   Asymmetrical

Symmetry   Skewed symmetry(?)

Figure 3.16   **Contrasts in Four Viewpoint-Invariant Relations**   Smooth continuation, cotermination, parallelism, and symmetry are nonaccidental, informative properties; whereas noncotermination, nonparallel segments, and asymmetrical patterns are not informative with respect to geon determination. In the case of parallelism and symmetry, biases toward parallel and symmetrical percepts when images are not exactly parallel or symmetrical are seen.

Source: Biederman, 1990.

from the vertices (as in the right-most column) that people would have more difficulty recognizing the objects than when the segment information was removed from between vertices (as in the middle column). The data were consistent with this prediction. As for the Biederman and Ju data just described, this finding is consistent with the recognition-by-components theory, but it is also consistent with many other theories of high-level vision that suggest that vertices contain important information for recognizing objects (e.g., Marr, 1982; Waltz, 1975).

Figure 3.17 **Sample Items From a Study Described by Biederman (1987)** The line drawings on the left have line-segment information removed from them. The objects are easier to identify if the segment information is removed from between vertices (as in the middle column) than if it is removed from the vertices themselves (as in the right-most column).

Source: Biederman, 1987.

A second problem with providing evidence for a specific structural description theory is that as models become more complex, it becomes harder to see exactly why they succeed or fail. For example, the recognition-by-components theory could be roughly correct but may fail to account for some observations because the objects have not been described in terms of the right set of geons. In this case, we need a different analysis of geons, not a new theory. A related issue is that the visual system may employ multiple recognition mechanisms, and the recognition-by-components theory could be correct as far as it goes but fall short by not including other mechanisms (see Tarr, 1995). In this case, experimental evidence inconsistent with recognition-by-components should lead researchers to modify the theory, not abandon it. In sum, while recognition-by-components provides an interesting way of explaining object recognition, it is likely to be difficult to find experiments that will support one structural description theory over others.

Template Matching and Alignment

The feature theory and the structural description theory both assume that people's representations of visual objects consist of lists of language-like elements that describe the image. The template-matching approach to recognition assumes that the representations of images are actually two-dimensional arrays of picture elements (or pixels). The optical scanners that banks use to read account numbers from checks use this kind of **template matching.** A template is just a copy of an image. Matching a template involves finding corresponding elements between the current visual image and the template and determining how well they match up. Figure 3.18 gives a simple example of matching a test instance against either the J template or the T template. If we look at cells that are filled in one pattern or the other, the instance matches the J template in 11 cells and mismatches in 2 cells; it also matches the T

Test Instance

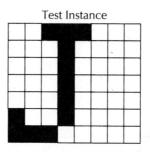

J Concept

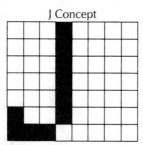

T Concept

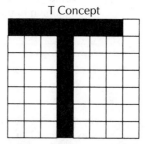

Figure 3.18   **Template Matching**   If decisions are based on number of matching cells, then the test instance would be classified as a J.

Source: Smith & Medin, 1981.

template in 8 cells and mismatches in 10 cells. Therefore, the instance more closely matches the J template is classified as a J.

This template matching approach may seem too simple to be a viable candidate to explain how people recognize objects. After all, if we made the J larger or rotated it a little, it would no longer match the template for the J in memory and would not be correctly classified. In contrast, people have no trouble at all recognizing objects that differ in size. They can even recognize objects that have been rotated, though it may take a little longer than it does when the object is oriented in a familiar way. Further, when objects in a three-dimensional world are rotated in depth, that can have a significant impact on the image of the object on the retina. In addition, occluding objects can hide key aspects of an object in the world, decreasing the match of the object to a template.

Ullman (1989, 1996) has tried to address many of the criticisms of template theories. Object recognition is assumed to consist of two stages: using a set of transformations to *align* the object presented with object templates or models stored in memory and then searching through these models to find the "best match" (most similar model) to the object. (See Ullman, 1996, for a detailed description of this approach and Tarr, 1995, for related relevant observations.) The key idea is that objects may be represented using multiple descriptions that correspond to viewing an object from different perspectives.

A virtue of template models is that they implicitly include information about part relations and structure. This implicit information does not, however, lead to computational complexity problems, as it can be demonstrated that aligning an image with a template requires matching only three independent points. Furthermore, templates can be quite useful for identifying objects that do not have obvious parts. Like the structural description theories, the template theories can be difficult to evaluate. Distinguishing between structural description and template theories is the subject of the debate box in this chapter.

Face Recognition and Visual Subsystems

One of the most striking observations from the neuropsychology of vision is **prosopagnosia,** the selective impairment of face recognition. People affected with this form of brain damage may not be able to recognize the faces of family members or even photographs of themselves. These same people can recognize nonface objects such as eyeglasses. One possibility is that our brain has a system dedicated to face recognition. However, Farah and her colleagues (Farah, 1992; Farah, Wilson, Drain, & Tanaka, 1998) have argued that there are two visual subsystems: one used to recognize objects by decomposing them into their parts or features and the other, more holistic in character, used to recognize objects with little or no part decomposition.

Let us consider this proposal in a bit more detail. When we talk about faces, we often break the face down into parts such as eyes, a nose, a mouth, and hair. Just because we talk about faces that way does not mean that we use these parts to actually recognize faces. What Farah and her colleagues are suggesting is that many

A DEBATE
Structural Descriptions and Templates

Quite a bit of recent research has tried to distinguish between structural description theories and template theories of object recognition. Much of this research has centered on a core distinction between the theories. Structural description theories assume that representations are **object centered.** That is, the description lists a set of parts of the object and the relations between those parts. The structural description is not influenced by the relative orientation of the object to the observer (unless the orientation makes it difficult to extract the features or geons from the image). In contrast, template theories are **viewer centered.** The representation of a current image is an array that shows the object as it appears to the viewer at that time. Aligning the image to stored arrays requires transforming it in some way. For example, the image could be rotated or stretched.

One way to distinguish between these theories would be to demonstrate that people are storing different views of objects in memory and that processing depended on the view to which the current stimulus is compared. A number of findings of this type have been obtained (e.g., Diwadkar & MacNamara, 1997; Tarr, Bulthoff, Zabinski, & Blanz, 1997). One early set of studies capitalized on findings in mental rotation (Tarr & Pinker, 1989). The classic mental rotation studies demonstrate that it

(Continued)

common objects (like eyeglasses and houses) are broken down into parts when they are recognized, but that faces are not. Instead, people are sensitive to other kinds of information such as the configurations of the parts that take into account more global aspects of the face (Rhodes, 1988). While nobody has yet successfully characterized the global or *holistic* properties people use to recognize faces, they have provided evidence that people are using properties more global than the individual parts when recognizing faces.

As one example, Tanaka and Sengco (1997) taught people to identify each of a set of faces with a different name (e.g., one face might go with the name Bill and another with the name John). Then, people were shown parts of a face and a name and were asked whether that part went with the face that had been given that name (e.g., "Is this Bill's nose?"). These recognition questions were asked in one of three ways: (1) the part was shown in isolation, (2) the part was shown along with the rest of the face it had been seen with, or (3) the part was shown along with the rest of the face it had been seen with, but the eyes of the face were moved further apart or closer

A DEBATE
Structural Descriptions and Templates *(Continued)*

takes longer to verify that two objects are the same if one is rotated to a different orientation than the other (Shepard & Cooper, 1982, see Chapter 8). In Tarr and Pinker's study, people had to say whether a line drawing was the same or a mirror reflection of a standard they saw at the beginning of the experiment. First, in a long practice block, people were only shown items at three orientations (0°, 120°, or 210°). After this practice block, people were shown figures at a number of different orientations. On these trials, people's responses were faster the closer the orientation of the test item was to the orientation of the nearest practice item. This finding suggests that people had three different views of the objects in memory (one each at 0°, 120°, or 210°), and they were using these views to identify new objects.

Findings like this provide impressive demonstrations that viewer-centered information is used in object recognition. Nonetheless, template models, which are often assumed to be viewer centered, cannot explain data like those of Reed (1974), demonstrating that people have strong preferences about the component parts of line drawings (see also Hinton, 1979, for a discussion of the role of structure in mental imagery). Thus, current research is looking for a way to combine viewer-centered and object-centered information in models of object recognition.

together than they had been when studied originally. As it turns out, when the eyes of a face are moved closer together or further apart, the face looks very different. In this study, people were best at recognizing parts of faces within a face they had seen before, worst at recognizing parts in isolation, and in the middle when the parts were presented in a face where the distance between the eyes had been changed. If people use the individual parts to recognize faces, then changing the distance between the eyes should not affect recognition judgments for other parts like the nose or mouth. Because these judgments were affected by changing the distance between the eyes, it suggests that people are using information more global than the individual parts to recognize faces.

Interestingly, no difference between these conditions was observed when the faces were inverted (that is, turned upside-down) or when pictures of houses were used instead of pictures of faces. As we will discuss in Chapter 8, inverted faces are often quite difficult to recognize, suggesting that the holistic properties used to recognize normal faces are disrupted by turning them over. Taken together, the results of this study indicate that people are not identifying individual parts of faces when recognizing them, but instead are using more global or holistic properties of faces to recognize them.

Summary

Currently, researchers are looking for models of object recognition that will be able to perform accurately across a wide range of conditions. We described three main theories of object recognition: feature theories, structural theories, and template theories. It is not the case that we have a number of successful models and that we are trying to decide which model gives the best account of human object perception. That is to say, we are not yet blessed with even one clearly successful model. But bear in mind that the approaches that we have been discussing are not mutually exclusive. Biederman's recognition-by-components theory employs features to construct geons, and geons can be viewed as higher-level features. Similarly, Ullman's alignment approach relies on features in segmenting objects and picking points to align. Clearly, object recognition is an exceedingly difficult problem, and it is nothing short of amazing that we do it effortlessly.

All of the proposed systems for object recognition use information that comes from low and high-level vision. So far, however, we have paid little attention to the question of how different sources and levels of information are combined. We turn now to a specific computational model that is concerned with integrating different levels of information in recognition. The model will serve to illustrate one particular way in which low-level and high-level information is combined.

LEVELS AND THE INTEGRATION OF INFORMATION IN PERCEPTUAL CONTEXT EFFECTS

So far, we have described perception as if it proceeded in a single direction from the retinal array to complex percepts. Notice in Figure 3.2, however, that the boxes for low-level vision and high-level vision are connected by arrows that go in both directions. These arrows reflect that the perception of some unit of information depends not only on lower-level input but also on the surrounding context. Processing information starting with low-level information and working to high-level information is often called **bottom-up** processing. There are also **top-down** influences on perception, in which context influences how things are perceived.

An example of the use of top-down information is shown in Figure 3.19. Here, an inkblot obscures part of the last letter in the word. The top string of letters forms a word only if the last letter is seen as a P, while the bottom string forms a word only if the last letter is seen as an R. Thus, people should be more likely to interpret the last letter consistently with what would make the string of letters a word. As examples like this demonstrate, the perceptual system integrates a variety of sources of information in developing an interpretation of a visual stimulus.

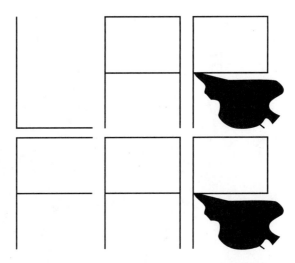

Figure 3.19   An example of a top-down influence on perception. The right-most letter has a blotch on it. It will be interpreted as a P in the context of the string LA? and as an R in the context of the string FA?.

The Word Superiority Effect

In order to make the influence of top-down information more concrete, we will begin with a discussion of the *word superiority effect* (Reicher, 1969), which is a striking example of a top-down influence on perception. Then, we will present a model that can explain this phenomenon. A sample procedure for demonstrating the word superiority effect involves brief exposure to a string of letters followed by a probe of one position. A participant must say which of two letters appeared in that position. For example, the stimulus might be the nonword ZORK, and the probe in the fourth position might ask whether D or K was presented. On another trial, the stimulus might be the word WORK with exactly the same probe. Reicher found that people were more accurate identifying the letter that appeared if the string of letters formed a word than if it formed a nonword. This finding was obtained even if the two options (in this example, D and K) would both produce a word given the string of letters presented. Intuitively, you might have thought that letters in words are identified first, and then that words are recognized next. The word superiority effect argues against this intuition.

This phenomenon can be explained using a connectionist model employing **interactive activation** (McClelland & Rumelhart, 1981). The model, sketched in Figure 3.20, contains three levels: the feature level, the letter level and the word level. At each level, there are *nodes* (the circles in Figure 3.20) that stand for particular features, letters, or words. Nodes have levels of *activation*. The activation of a node corresponds to the extent to which the system believes the item that the node corresponds to is present. There are also connections between the nodes (the lines in Figure 3.20 that allow activation to spread from one node to another). Connections can be *excitatory*, in which

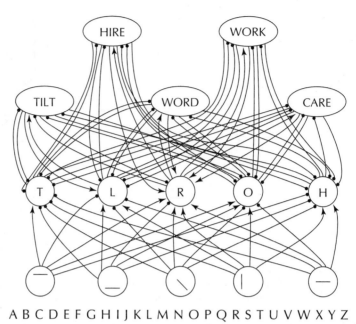

ABCDEFGHIJKLMNOPQRSTUVWXYZ

Figure 3.20   A few of the neighbors of the node for the letter R in the third position in a word and their interconnections. Lines ending in arrows are excitatory or positive, and lines ending in dots are inhibitory. For example, R in the third position inhibits any other letter in the third position, and WORD inhibits WORK, CARE, HIRE, and TILT (and other words). The block alphabet used for these stimulations is shown below the network.

case when one node is highly active, it increases the activation of the node to which it is connected. Excitatory connections are represented by lines that terminate with arrows in Figure 3.20. Connections can also be *inhibitory,* in which case when one node is highly active, it reduces the level of activation of the node to which it is connected. Inhibitory connections are illustrated in Figure 3.20 by lines that terminate with circles.

In the interactive activation model, nodes at the feature level have excitatory connections to nodes at the word level that are consistent with the presence of that feature. For example, a diagonal segment has an excitatory connection to the node for the letter R, but an inhibitory connection to the letter L. Thus, when the diagonal feature is presented (and thus is active) it makes the node for the letter R more active, but the node for L less active. Likewise, the node for the letter T in the first position in the word has an excitatory connection to the word TILT, but an inhibitory connection to the word HIRE. Nodes for letters and words have inhibitory connections to other words and nodes at the same level. These connections reflect that a given letter is either a T or an L, but not both, and that a word is either WORD or WORK, but not both. Finally, activation flows along connections in both directions. Thus, if the node corresponding to the letter T in the first position is active, it tends to excite the word TILT. Likewise, when the word TILT is active, it tends to excite the node representing a T in the first position.

Processing begins in this model by activating the features present in a word shown to the system. Activation then flows to the letters connected to those features.

Next, activation flows from the letters to the word nodes. After some of the word nodes are activated as well, activation from the word nodes flows back to the letter nodes (hence the interactive activation in the name of the model). The patterns of excitation and inhibition represent a set of constraints to be satisfied or sources of information to be integrated. What emerges are the most plausible candidate letters (and word), given all the information that is present. The process seems fairly chaotic, but the patterns of activation stabilize in a fairly short time. This activation of the nodes corresponds to the interpretation made of the input.

To illustrate how the interactive activation model works, consider the stimulus of the printed group of four letters, WOR(?), where the question mark indicates that some of the featural information is occluded (as in the example in Figure 3.19) and that the fourth letter is consistent with both the letter R and the letter K. By providing specific quantitative values (parameters) for the strengths of excitation and inhibition, one can generate specific activation values, as shown in Figure 3.21. At the word level, consider what happens to the activation of the candidates WORK, WORD, WEAK, and WEAR. Note that WORK is the only word consistent with all the available information. The interpretation WORD is consistent with most of the information, and its activation initially rises because of the excitatory input from the W, O, and R letter units. Eventually, however, the activation of WORD falls below its resting level, because it has inhibitory connections to WORK, and the node for WORK becomes highly active. The activation of WORK steadily increases. WEAR and WEAK are never very strongly activated because they receive little activation from the letter level. Note that WEAK eventually is slightly more active than WEAR. This is because WORK becomes highly activated and feeds back to the letter level to reinforce K rather than R in the final position.

At the letter level, the inhibition from the featural level prevents the letter D from being activated. Note that although both K and R are consistent with the features available in the fourth position, K quickly becomes more activated. This is because of positive feedback from WORK at the word level. Since WORR is not a word, it does not receive positive feedback from the word level. Although we have oversimplified the model, you nonetheless can get a fair idea of how interactive activation works to integrate information.

The interactive activation model successfully predicts a variety of phenomena concerning context effects on letter and word perception. For example, the interactive activation model is consistent with the word superiority effect because without the word-level feedback, processing might converge on some letter outside the choice set (e.g., R). In that event, the participant would have to guess (between D and K). These and other observations provide good support for the ideas embodied in the interactive activation model. The original interactive activation model directly built letters and words into the network. In more complex network models, it is possible for new words and higher-level features to be learned from experience (see, e.g., Seidenberg & McClelland, 1989).

Summary

The current consensus views object recognition as involving the integration of multiple sources of information, with top-down context exerting an important influence

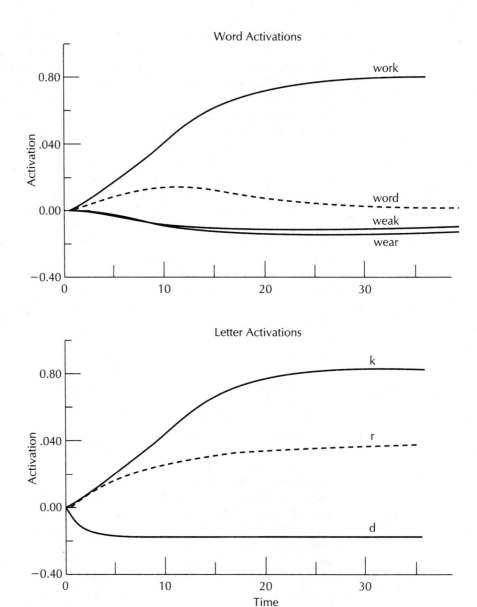

Figure 3.21   The time course of activations of selected nodes at the word and letter levels after extraction of the features. Time is based on number of cycles of activation.

Source: McClelland & Rumelhart, 1981.

on perception. The interactive activation model is an example of how sources of information may be combined. The word-superiority effect demonstrates that knowing letters influences the perception of words, and that recognizing a word influences the perception of letters. The interactive-activation model uses the spread of activation through a connectionist network to account for this effect. Although connectionist models are far from the only way to integrate information (e.g., Massaro, 1987; Massaro & Friedman, 1990), it is clear that perception is an active, dynamic process that is sensitive to context.

Summary

This concludes our discussion of visual perception. We have covered a lot of ground, so it is worth reviewing the main points. First, perception involves taking in information about the physical world that will help the organism achieve its goals. Because the physics of the world has not changed since the dawn of time, the perceptual system has had a long evolutionary history to adapt to it. Thus, we have many mechanisms that are tailored specifically to the world. Adaptations of this type in vision include sensitivity to texture gradients, and to differential patterns of movement of objects that can signal how far away the object is. Complex adaptations to the structure of the environment are evident in other perceptual modalities as well.

A second key aspect of vision is that there is significant ambiguity in the signals that reach the eyes. Despite this ambiguity, our perceptual experiences are not ambiguous, but rather reflect a particular interpretation of the world generated by the visual system. This interpretation is influenced both by qualities of the stimuli that reach the eyes (bottom-up information) and by information about what the stimuli are, which is derived from higher-level vision processes (top-down information). Indeed, one reason why perception has been so difficult to understand is that both lower-level and higher-level vision interact in complex ways so that it is impossible to completely separate out individual components of the process.

Finally, significant work remains to be done to understand how we take the low-level information from vision about edges, locations, depth, and movement, and combine that information to allow us to perceive complete objects and to identify those objects. The visual system seems to use many different kinds of representations of the world. We use structural descriptions to represent the parts of objects and the relationships between those parts. We also use more holistic kinds of representation, particularly for complex perceptual tasks like face perception that require the recognition of individual faces, each of which may differ only subtly. This complexity makes it clear that Yogi Berra was right in saying we can see a lot by looking—just how we do so remains a challenging puzzle.

Key Terms

bottom-up processing	prosopagnosia
change blindness	proximity principle
features	retinal disparity
figure-ground relations	size constancy
geons	stereopsis
good continuation	structural descriptions
interactive activation	template matching
invariants	texture gradients
motion parallax	top-down processing
object centered representation	viewer centered representation

Recommended Readings

The area of perception has not been uncontroversial. J. J. Gibson's (1986) ecological approach to perception includes an attack on the idea of computations and internal representations in favor of "direct perception." Fodor and Pylyshyn (1981) offer a thoughtful critique of direct perception. Although the current consensus is that perception requires internal representations and processing mechanisms, the Gibsonian approach remains as a plausible dissenting view.

The Gestalt psychologists uncovered many important principles of perceptual organization. Excellent reviews of this work can be found in the classic work of Goldmeier (1972) and Wertheimer (1950).

A good general introduction to computational vision and its goals is provided by Poggio (1984); Hildreth and Ullman (1989) offer a comprehensive overview. An excellent review of theories of object recognition is presented in Ullman (1996). Sekular and Blake (1994) give a nice introduction to the concept of spatial frequency analyzers. Farah (1990) reviews the various types of agnosias that can occur after different brain injuries. Farah, O'Reilly, and Vecera (1993) report an interesting analysis of prosopagnosia; they develop a neural net model and then "lesion" it to account for the effects of brain damage.

There has long been a relationship between the study of perception and the study of consciousness. Recently, there has been a surge of interest in consciousness. For reviews of philosophical approaches to consciousness, see Dennett (1991) and Chalmers (1996). In addition, there are journals that publish empirical research devoted to consciousness such as *Consciousness and Cognition.*

Chapter 4

Attention

Introduction

Initial Observations in Perceptual Attention
Sensory Stores
Evidence for Capacity Limitations
Focused Attention

Capacity and Attention
Bottleneck Theories
Late Selection
Capacity Theories

Feature Integration Theory

Attention in Complex Tasks
Capacity and Automaticity

Central Executive Functions
Dual-Task Interference

Attention and the Brain

Summary

Key Terms

Recommended Readings

What holds attention determines action.
—William James

INTRODUCTION

The word *attention* seems to have many different meanings. When we talk about attending to a lecture, we mean something like *concentration*. When we talk about attending to a particular conversation in a crowded room, we mean *selection*. When we talk about being able to attend to only so many things at one time, we are referring to *limits in capacity*. When we talk about no longer having to attend to skills that we perform well, we are referring to *automaticity* (and perhaps that *conscious* monitoring of the skill is no longer required). Despite our use of the same word to describe each of these situations, it is not clear that they are really the same. Indeed, the difficulty in trying to learn about the cognitive psychology of attention is that many seemingly different situations have all been studied under the heading of attention.

What do these aspects of attention have in common? Each of them recognizes that people cannot do an infinite number of different things at the same time. We cannot listen to a lecture on attention and also think about the great party we attended on Friday night. We cannot process all of the information about every conversation taking place at a party simultaneously, let alone all of the sights, sounds, smells, and tastes there. We all may be able to walk and chew gum, but without a lot of practice, it would be difficult to read one paragraph and take dictation about another. With a lot of practice, however, we do get better at doing different things at the same time. When first learning to drive, it is hard to change stations on the radio (or even to sneeze) for fear of driving off the road. After years of practice, however, it is possible to drive, wipe the nose of a sneezing 4-year-old, and still maintain a conversation on a cellular phone. The goal of cognitive theories of attention is to explain the types of limitations people have in processing information and how people learn to deal with those limitations.

In order to provide an overview of research on attention, it is important to start with some distinctions. Much research on attention has focused on *perceptual attention*. Perceptual attention involves situations in which the goal of the task is to process information about some kind of sensory stimulus like the identity, color, or size of a visually presented object. These tasks examine issues like whether people are able to select one perceptual item rather than another, or whether attention can be divided across perceptual items. A second stream of research focuses on attention involved in *complex actions* that take place over a longer period of time like doing addition or driving a car. It is unlikely that conclusions drawn from studies of perceptual tasks will hold for more complex actions as well. Finally, both types of attention relate to the idea that there is some kind of centralized process that directs what is attended to and what is not.

This chapter provides a sampling of ongoing research on attention. We will begin with a discussion of perceptual attention. This work was initially organized around the notion of attention as a limited resource, although more recent investigations have begun to stress the role of attention in the coordination and control of action. Indeed, one might want to reverse the quotation from William James at the beginning of the chapter and say that action determines attention. After discussing studies of perceptual attention, we turn to the influence of attention on more complex actions. In this section, we also explore what happens as cognitive skills become more practiced. Then, we will discuss the idea of a centralized executive or processor that controls attention. Finally, we will briefly examine the relationship between attention and the brain.

INITIAL OBSERVATIONS IN PERCEPTUAL ATTENTION _____

Sensory Stores

When we perceive the world, at what point do we start to limit the amount of information that we process? There seems to be a wealth of information available about the immediate sensory environment, and this information seems to persist. For example, everyone is familiar with the rich but transient memory that lasts for a second or so after the glimpse of a scene (as from the window of a moving train). As another example, we can often figure out what time it is after hearing the chime of a clock. We have a memory for the first few chimes, even if we do not notice that the clock is chiming until after the second or third tone. In these cases, we can typically provide a good deal of information about a scene if interrogated immediately, but after even a few seconds filled with new sensory input, the ability to recall information is almost entirely gone.

It is possible that the perceptual system places severe limits immediately on what information is taken in. Consistent with this hypothesis, some of the earliest psychological experiments (e.g., Cattell, 1886) used a full report technique in which subjects are given a single brief look at an array of letters and then are asked to report as many of the letters as they can. In this task, subjects typically reported no more than four or five of the presented letters. One possibility is that this limited **span of apprehension** results from an inability to identify more than a few letters at a time (apprehension is just an old jargon term for "perception"). An alternative hypothesis is that the initial sensory store has a high capacity, but that the process of transferring information from the sensory store to short-term memory limits what can be reported. On this view, reporting letters takes some time, and by the time some of the letters are reported, the memory of other letters has faded from the sensory store.

A complete explanation for the span of apprehension results was not provided until 1960, when a doctoral student at Harvard University, George Sperling, devised an ingenious **partial report technique.** As illustrated in Table 4.1, subjects were shown a display of letters for a fraction of a second and then heard a tone indicating which row they were to report. (They had practiced so that they knew which tone went with which row.) To estimate how many letters the subject must have seen and had available in memory at the end of the display, Sperling reasoned as follows: Suppose that (on the average) a subject proves able to report three letters from any row of the display in Table 4.1. Since the row to be reported is not signaled until after the display goes off, we can infer that the subject must have perceived three-fourths (9) of the 12 letters presented.

Table 4.1   **Sperling's Partial Report Technique**

Present variable-size letter arrays for 50 milliseconds	Immediately following offset of array, present signaling tone telling subject which row to report	Subject tries to report letters from the appropriate (signaled) row
A D J E ——— High tone (top row) X P S B ——— Medium tone (middle row) M L B H ——— Low tone (bottom row)		**?**
(1)	(2)	(3)

Source: From "The information available in brief visual presentations," by G. Sperling, 1960, *Psychological Monographs, 74.*

Figure 4.1 shows full report performance along with the estimated number of letters seen according to the partial report results. Under the whole report procedure, there is no increase in the number of letters reported when the display size doubles from 6 to 12. This demonstrates the standard limited span of apprehension result. Sperling even found this pattern of results when the display was on for a full second. The estimates from partial report trials show no such leveling off: As the display size increases beyond 6 letters, the estimated number of letters perceived continues to increase. In short, when more than 4 or 5 letters are presented, observers apparently perceive more letters than they can give in a whole report, a result consistent with the idea of a rapidly fading sensory store and a limited short-term memory. This visual persistence associated with the sensory store is apparently quite brief; when the tone cue is delayed by just half a second, estimated performance from partial report is no better than whole report results. Evidently, much of the information in a brief visual experience never enters memory storage in a form that can survive even the short time needed to give a full report.

These results and a large body of subsequent research provide strong evidence for the idea of a sensory store. This store is assumed to record sensory experiences automatically, to persist beyond their duration, and to have a very large information capacity. Although we have concentrated on the visual sensory store (often called **iconic memory**), much research (e.g., Crowder, 1982; Crowder & Morton, 1969) has also examined the auditory sensory store (referred to as **echoic memory**). Echoic memory is what allows you to play back the first few chimes of a clock in order to determine what time it is.

Evidence for Capacity Limitations

Studies of early sensory stores suggest that the limitation on the amount of information we process does not seem to be set by the information available from our sensory stores. Instead, these processing limitations must appear later. If a large amount of

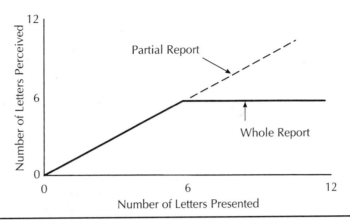

Figure 4.1   **Results From Sperling's Partial-Peport Technique**

Source: Sperling, 1960.

information is available in the sensory store, how much of this information (and what kind of information) can be processed before attentional limitations are observed?

This question has been addressed using visual search tasks. S. Sternberg (1966) laid out a logic for using search tasks as a powerful method for understanding information processing, and search techniques continue to be used widely to study attention. Let's take a closer look at the method and logic of these studies. On each trial, subjects are shown a visual display with varying numbers of elements in it and are told to search for a particular target. For example, the display might have four letters, BKST, and the subject might be asked to search for the target letter T. On some trials, the target is present in the display (as in this example), and on some trials it is missing. The subject presses one button if the target is present and a second button if it is absent. The experimenter measures the accuracy of the response and how long it took to respond. The response times are typically measured in milliseconds (ms), which are thousandths of a second.

The power of this method comes from examining what happens when the number of elements in the display is varied. Imagine that the cognitive system was able to process the entire display in parallel with unlimited capacity. Then, no matter how many elements in the display, the amount of time it would take people to respond would be the same. That is, they would be just as fast to respond that the target was present or absent if there were 4 elements in the display as they would if there were 8 or 12 elements in the display.

If there is some limitation in capacity to process information, then the expected pattern of data is different. First, let's consider the simple case where people look at one element in the display at a time and compare it to the target. On trials when the target is *not* in the display, people must search through all of the elements in order to determine that the target is missing. In this case, it would take longer to respond to displays with many elements than to displays with few elements. Imagine that it takes 320ms for people to formulate and execute the motor movements necessary to press a button. If it takes 20ms to compare each item in the display to the target, then it would take 320 + (4 × 20) = 400ms for people to respond that the target was absent for displays with 4 elements (including the amount of time to form and make the response), and it would take 320 + (8 × 20) = 480ms to respond that the target was absent for displays with 8 elements.

On trials when the target is present, the expected pattern is slightly different. Here, people can stop searching as soon as they find the target. Thus, on average they will only have to look at half of the items. Thus, for displays with 4 elements, on average subjects will look at only 2 of them, yielding an average response time of 320 + (2 × 20) = 360ms. Likewise, for displays with 8 elements, on average subjects will look at only 4 of them, yielding an average response time of 320 + (4 × 20) = 400ms. If these predicted response times for both target-present and target-absent trials are plotted on a graph, the slope of the increase in time for target-present trials is only half that for target-absent trials. (It is worth taking a moment to work through this logic if it is not already clear.)

This technique distinguishes between the case of unlimited capacity parallel search and limited capacity search. Unfortunately, it does not distinguish between serial search and parallel search. Townsend (1971) pointed out that a parallel search with limited capacity can give rise to the same pattern of response times as the limited capacity serial search just described. Thinking about attention using the **spotlight metaphor** may help. Imagine a spotlight with a limited amount of power that can be narrowly or broadly focused. When it is narrowly focused (i.e., on a small number of items), the illumination in the target area is strong, and the search can proceed rapidly. When it is broadly focused (i.e., on a large number of items), then a large area is covered but with much weaker illumination in any one spot, slowing down the search. In brief, it is difficult to distinguish between a serial process and a limited capacity parallel process, but both of these limited capacity processes can be readily distinguished from an unlimited capacity parallel search.

Studies using search tasks demonstrate that some visual information can be processed in parallel without apparent capacity limits. For example, Figure 4.2 shows a display like that used by Anne Treisman (1988). When the target and distractor (nontarget) elements differ in some simple feature such as color or orientation, and the distractors are homogeneous (i.e., they all have the same value of the feature), response times do not increase with display size on either target-present or target-absent trials (see the left side of Figure 4.2A and 4.2B). The results are the same when distractors do not differ from each other along irrelevant dimensions (right side of Figure 4.2A and 4.2B). These results suggest that the early stages of visual processing allow selection on the basis of simple features to be performed in parallel when the distractors differ from each other along the relevant dimension (as in Figure 4.2A middle, where the distractors differ in color).

Despite these impressive demonstrations of unlimited capacity search, more complex searches show evidence of limited capacity search (middle portion of Figure 4.2B). When the distractors are heterogeneous within a single dimension (i.e., they have many values along the dimension), reaction time increases with display size and does so about twice as fast for target-absent trials as for target-present trials. As we discussed, this pattern is consistent with the idea that each element must be examined serially or by a limited capacity parallel process, but is inconsistent with

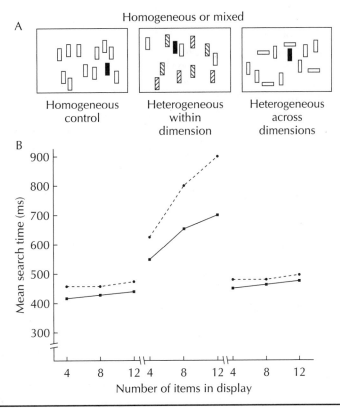

Figure 4.2 Example of displays used in search tasks where the distractor items vary in their heterogeneity. Targets could vary in color and orientation (here we use variations in shading to represent color differences). In the homogeneous condition, all distractors were the same and differed from the target in either color or orientation. In the heterogeneous within-dimensions condition, the distractors had different values along the relevant dimension, color. In the third condition, distractors were heterogeneous but along irrelevant dimensions. Display size indicates the number of elements in each display. Solid lines show performance on target-present trials, and dashed lines show performance on target-absent trials.

Source: Treisman, 1988.

a parallel unlimited capacity search. In sum, it appears that simple features can be processed in parallel, but that finer discriminations require more focused, limited capacity (either serial or parallel) processes.

Focused Attention

If fine perceptual discriminations require focused limited capacity processes, then there have to be mechanisms to focus attention on particular perceptual elements at the expense of others. For example, imagine that you are at a crowded party in a friend's apartment. You are having a conversation with someone who is standing just to your left, and you are talking about a football game that was on television that day. While having this conversation, you are likely to be oblivious to other conversations going on in the same room. Nonetheless, you are not incapable of processing other auditory information. If a fighter jet flew over the apartment and broke the sound barrier, you would hear the sonic boom, and would likely be startled by it. In addition, if someone in a nearby conversation mentioned your name, you would probably notice, and might even process the next few lines of their conversation before switching back to your own.

Even this simple example raises a number of questions about people's ability to focus attention. Clearly, focusing attention does not mean that all other input is suppressed. Salient stimuli, like a loud sonic boom, or more prosaically the sound of broken glass, will typically cause people to attend to them. Most salient stimuli are often extreme along a key dimension, however. For example, salient noises are typically loud. Thus, it would not be difficult to assume that very loud sounds (or bright lights) command attention by virtue of their extremeness. Recognizing your name is more problematic to explain. If you are able to recognize your name in a conversation that you were not previously attending to, does that mean that you were actually following several conversations at once? Was the information about the other conversation only processed once your name was mentioned? In that case, how would you know your name had been spoken? More generally, what are the limits on a person's ability, on the one hand, to select the most relevant input to attend to in such a situation, and, on the other hand, to be aware of a significant event occurring outside his or her momentary focus of attention? This last question makes clear the fundamental problem: We need to focus attention to process relevant information adequately (because processing capacity is limited), but we also need to ensure that no critical information is excluded.

Studies that examine selective attention typically present information to more than one *channel* and assess people's ability to track the information on only one (or a small number) of those channels. The notion of a channel is somewhat vague. In vision, channels are conceived of as different locations in space or perhaps objects (more on this issue below). In audition, channels are also often locations in space. People are quite good at localizing sounds in the space around them, because they are sensitive to time and loudness differences between the sounds that reach each ear. Further, people can selectively attend to sounds coming from specific locations.

One experimental procedure that relies on people's ability to localize sounds in space is the **dichotic listening experiment.** In this type of experiment, the individual who is being studied listens to a tape-recorded message with earphones. The earphones are set up so that a different message is sent to each ear. To examine people's ability to attend selectively, subjects are asked to follow only one of the inputs (e.g., the one coming to the left ear). Then, by testing the person afterward, one can determine whether both messages were actually heard or whether the irrelevant messages were ignored, and only the relevant ones were heard. For the experiment to be informative, the subject must be attending to the relevant input. Typically, attention is ensured by having the subject *shadow* (that is, repeat aloud) the message coming in over one of the earphones.

Some pioneering experiments by E. C. Cherry (1953) showed that an individual is typically able to tell whether a voice was present on the unattended channel, and, if a voice was present, something about the physical attributes of the nonattended message, but not much about its meaningful content. For example, the subject is generally unable to tell even the language in which the nonattended message was spoken. In a classic study, Neville Moray (1959) had subjects shadow a message in one ear, while the same voice read words in the other ear. Despite the fact that the same word list was repeated as many as 35 times to the nonattended ear, in a later memory test people did not recognize that these words had been presented.

Even in the absence of special instructions, it appears that an individual typically attends to only one channel at a time. For example, imagine you were in a dichotic listening test, and you heard the sequence {6, 2, 9} to the left ear, and the sequence {4, 7, 5} to the right ear. If you were asked immediately afterward to repeat the digits, you would probably group together those heard over each channel saying {6, 2, 9, 4, 7, 5} rather than alternating your report across ears (e.g., {6, 4, 2, 7, 9, 5}), even though that would allow you to order the numbers by the time that they were heard. Studies of this type motivated a number of theories of selective attention in perception. We will describe some of these theories in the next section.

Summary

In perceptual tasks, a substantial amount of information appears to enter the sensory store. It can be difficult to estimate the amount of information that makes it into the sensory store, because the process of reporting information from the store can reduce the overall amount of information that can be reported. Studies using search tasks demonstrate that there are significant capacity limits after the sensory stores. These limits are a method used by the cognitive system to overcome potential complexity in processing. If we had to process too much information, processing would take too much time. Processing only selected information avoids this problem. In the next section, we will focus on different proposals about how the amount of information processed by the cognitive system is limited.

CAPACITY AND ATTENTION

Theories of selective attention are concerned both with how people attend to information on some channels at the expense of others, and also with how much information is processed on unattended channels. In this section, we begin by describing bottleneck theories of attention. These theories assume that all inputs are processed completely up to some particular stage, but only attended channels are processed more fully than that. Different theories disagree on how much processing is done before the attentional bottleneck. Next, we contrast bottleneck theories with capacity theories, which assume that information processing requires cognitive resources, and that limited resources can be allocated across the cognitive tasks that need to be performed.

Bottleneck Theories

British psychologist Donald Broadbent (1958) used findings from dichotic listening experiments to formulate a filter or **bottleneck model** of attention. According to this theory, an individual's mental apparatus includes a central processing system that receives inputs from sensory channels and compares them with items stored in the memory system to determine their meaning. Overload of the central processor is prevented by means of a selective filter interposed between the central processor and the outside world that sifts incoming stimuli by letting through those that have certain properties and excluding others. In the example of a person listening to a conversation at a party, the filter mechanism would be set to screen out all incoming auditory stimuli that did not have the properties of speech sounds. Of the sounds that pass this first filter, those having certain properties (say, those characterizing the voice of the person with whom the individual is conversing) are admitted to the input channel to which the central processor is attending, thus enabling the individual to follow the conversation.

An important characteristic of this filter is that it is flexible—one can readily shift attention to another conversation. However, the filter can use only lower-level auditory characteristics (e.g., loudness) rather than what is said (i.e., the message's semantic [meaning-related] properties) as a basis for selection, because selection occurs prior to a stimulus being fully analyzed. The bottleneck is produced by the fact that the filter cannot shift back and forth across sensory channels fast enough to follow two conversations at once, for example.

The original conception of a filter proved oversimplified; for instance, subjects shadowing one channel in a dichotic listening experiment nonetheless notice their names with some frequency (about 30% of the time) if the name occurs in the unattended channel (Moray, 1959). This observation is consistent with a system that is sensitive to high-priority events that are not currently the subject of attention; one's name is a pretty good clue that the associated information will prove relevant. It has been necessary to amplify the model to incorporate several stages, as illustrated in Figure 4.3. At the first stage, the incoming sensory information is analyzed for its physical characteristics (pitch, speech versus nonspeech properties, origin in space, etc.). If required by demands of the task, a decision or response can be made on the basis of this analysis—for example, determining who is speaking. At the next stage, stimuli are checked against a list of high-priority messages maintained in the permanent memory system, such as danger signals or the vocal pattern of an individual's name. If the stimulus is not flagged at the permanent priority check, it is then matched against a list of current priorities. In the case of the conversation, a high current priority would be set for auditory inputs of the voice of the other person in the conversation and low priority for voices of the other people or for nonspeech sounds. Stimuli passing this stage of the filter system receive further processing, leading to the comprehension of the meaning of the message, whereas those of low priority are ignored and typically receive no further processing.

Figure 4.3 (Treisman, 1960, 1964) describes *attenuation theory,* which allows for the possibility that the analysis of a message's content occurs fairly early

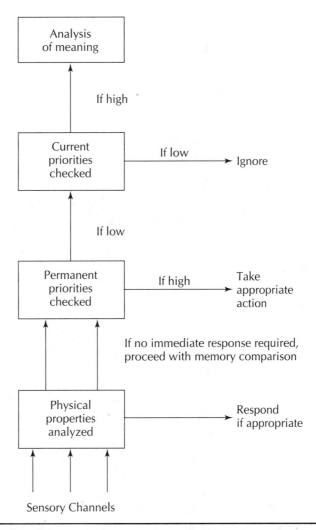

Figure 4.3   **Filtering Model Sensitive to Priorities**   Unlike Broadbent's model, the filter model allows certain stable, high-priority kinds of information (e.g., one's own name) to be checked even without directed attention.

in processing in that the check for high-priority items involves the permanent memory system. Also, it should be emphasized that the system is not thought to operate in a passive, mechanical fashion. The early stage of analysis of physical properties may operate almost automatically, but the priorities at the higher levels are continually shifted in accord with the individual's purposes and expectations.

The role of expectations can be seen in an experiment of the following kind: Suppose that in a dichotic listening situation the subject is asked to shadow a message coming into the left ear:

Give me liberty and shut the door

while into the right ear comes a second simultaneous message:

Please leave quietly or give me death

If the subject had been actively attending to the words of a speech by Patrick Henry and had been generating expectations about its content, then following the passage "Give me liberty," current priorities would be high for words constituting the appropriate continuation and low for words that would not. Consequently, the subject would very likely report, "Give me liberty or give me death," even though the task was to report only what was heard over the left earphone. Individuals' well-established habit of adjusting priorities so as to make sense out of what they hear leads them to extract the meaningful and, in this case, familiar message from the garbled input, in spite of instructions to pay attention only to words coming over a particular channel.

Late Selection

So far, we have described what can be called an **early selection theory** of attention. On this view, only a minimal amount of processing is done to stimuli before one channel is selected, and selection occurs before information enters short-term memory. Sperling's partial report studies described earlier in this chapter suggest that there is quite a bit of information available in the sensory store. Further, studies of visual search suggest that these simple characteristics can be processed in parallel for a number of stimuli. Thus, we might expect that somewhat more processing is done even on unattended stimuli.

Compatible with these results are theories suggesting that attentional limitations occur later in processing after stimuli have already been recognized. Deutsch and Deutsch (1963) and Norman (1968) proposed models in which information is processed in parallel nonselectively until the results are placed in short-term memory (where they are subject to rapid loss). In brief, this view assumes that the bottlenecks of attention are the limitations of short-term memory (see Chapter 5 for more discussion of short-term memory). Not all the information sent to short-term memory can be stored, and what is not rehearsed or elaborated is likely to be forgotten. It has not proven easy to contrast these **late selection theories** with the early selection theories presented in the previous section. Tasks that prevent attention switching between channels, such as shadowing, may impose an additional load on short-term memory. Therefore, both types of theories seem consistent with poor memory for nonshadowed information, even at short retention intervals (see Kahneman & Treisman, 1984, and Pashler, 1998, for reviews).

Capacity Theories

Bottleneck theories are focused primarily on how much processing of stimuli is done before a channel is selected. A second approach to attention focuses instead on how tasks and strategies can be used to allocate attention. This view uses the metaphor that

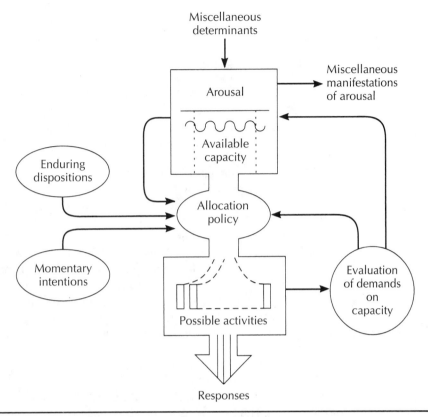

| **Figure 4.4** | **Capacity models of attention** The key idea is that attention is of limited capacity but may be allocated in a somewhat flexible manner according to task demands. |

Source: Kahneman, 1973.

attention is a limited resource that can be allocated across tasks that need to be performed. Figure 4.4 illustrates a version of this theory proposed by Daniel Kahneman (1973), which suggests that our inability to perform two tasks at once may not derive from a bottleneck at any particular stage of processing, but rather from a nonspecific depletion of a limited pool of resources. On this view, attention is a resource that can be allocated to a task. The amount of processing that can be done on a particular task is proportional to the resources devoted to it. Thus, whereas bottleneck theories assume that stimuli are only processed up to a certain point, resource theories assume that information can be processed until the available processing resources are all being used. Thus, on the resource view, two tasks that do not demand too much cognitive effort should not interfere with each other. Furthermore, because resources can be allocated, if one task is more important than another, then resources can be devoted to the more important task at the expense of the less important one. Bottleneck theories do not permit this selective processing of information.

The distinction between bottleneck and capacity theories is somewhat blurred by *multiple resource theories* (e.g., Navon, 1984; C. D. Wickens, 1984).

AN ENIGMA
Attentional Blink and Repetition Blindness

Many observations in the study of attention seem to accord with our intuitions. People generally cannot do too many things at once (which your mother told you when you were a child). Many low-level aspects of perception happen without effort (just open your eyes), but more complex visual tasks like searching for specific objects (like Waldo in the "Where's Waldo" books) are effortful. Nonetheless, there are some intriguing findings in the attention literature that do not seem at all consistent with our common-sense beliefs. Two counterintuitive phenomena that are of great interest to researchers these days are the attentional blink and repetition blindness (e.g., Broadbent & Broadbent, 1987; Kanwisher, 1987; Shapiro, 1994). Both of these phenomena can be observed using a technique called **rapid serial visual presentation** in which a sequence of stimuli such as pictures, words, letters, or digits are presented quickly. For example, if the stimuli are letters, they might be presented for 15ms with 75ms between items. For more complex stimuli like words, the presentation times are longer.

In the **attentional blink,** people perform two tasks. For example, they might be asked to press a button when they see a white letter in a sequence in which the rest of the letters are black. Let's call this white letter the *target.* The second task often involves detecting some other aspect of the item, such as recognizing that the letter T appeared in a sequence. Let's call the object of the second task the *probe.* The probe always appears after the presentation of the target. In these studies, people are quite good at detecting the probe when it is the next letter that follows the target. Interestingly, if the probe is between the 2nd and 6th letter presented after the target (in the interval between 100ms and 450ms after the

(Continued)

The idea behind this type of theory is that there are multiple pools, each of which has limited resources that can be allocated. For example, there might be a pool of resources for processing visual information and a separate pool for processing auditory information. In this case, visual resources could not be spent on auditory tasks (and vice versa). Whether or not two tasks interfere with each other, on this view, depends on how much they draw on the same resource pools. Just what constitutes a resource pool? One idea is that pools are different for different modalities. There is some evidence that auditory and visual tasks can be performed together more readily than two auditory tasks or two visual tasks (C. D. Wickens, 1980), which is consistent with the idea that there are separate resource pools for vision and audition.

AN ENIGMA
Attentional Blink and Repetition Blindness *(Continued)*

target), then people have difficulty detecting it. This finding is interesting both because it seems strange to have a window in which the second task is difficult and also because this window does not follow the target immediately, but instead it starts about 100ms after the presentation of the target. That is why the phenomenon is called the attentional blink.

Repetition blindness also involves rapid serial visual presentation. In this case, people are shown lists of items like words or letters in which one item is repeated. The experimenter varies the number of items between the first and second appearance of the repeated item, and people are asked to identify which item was repeated. The finding of repetition blindness is that people have difficulty identifying the repeated word or letter. This finding is interesting, because there are many situations in real life in which we encounter sequences that have repeated items like written and spoken sentences. This phenomenon may explain why it is is often difficult to detect typographical errors in which the same word appears twice in a row (as with the word "is" in this sentence). In general, repetition blindness may cause some problems with processing in tasks in which the same item is repeated.

There are some similarities between the attentional blink and repetition blindness. Both of them involve an inability to detect one item after the presentation of the first. Nonetheless, these phenomena do appear to be different (see Chun, 1997, for a discussion of differences between the two). At this time, there is no generally accepted explanation for either the attentional blink or repetition blindness. Because they are counterintuitive and fall outside of the explanatory abilities of current theories of attention, they remain the source of much current research.

The bottleneck and resource theories have different implications for how one should think about attention as well as different answers to the questions of whether and how attentional limitations can be overcome for particular tasks. Pashler (1998) suggests a model of perceptual attention within each modality in which there is both a bottleneck *and* a capacity allocation mechanism. On this model, the processing of some stimuli may be blocked early, but analysis of information from those channels that pass the gate is subject to limitations based on the amount of available processing resources. Another critical assumption of this view is that different modalities (e.g., vision and audition) may have different attentional mechanisms, as evidenced by the fact that people can attend to objects in one region of space, but to sounds coming from a different region of space. Many details of this theory remain to be worked out, but it provides an avenue for reconciling bottleneck and capacity theories of attention.

Summary

An important metaphor used to conceptualize attention is as a bottleneck. On this view, stimuli are processed up to some point, after which they are only processed if they pass the bottleneck. Theories adopting this metaphor have argued about whether the bottleneck is early (so that only low-level properties of unattended stimuli are processed) or late (so that many properties of unattended stimuli are processed). An alternative way to conceptualize attention is as a resource. Resource theories assume that unattended stimuli are processed to the extent that there are available processing resources that have not been allocated to other (presumably more important) tasks. While the distinction between resource and bottleneck theories can be blurry, these metaphors have been helpful for developing new theories and experimental tests of attention (see Fernandez-Duque & Johnson, 1999, for a discussion of these and other metaphors for attention).

FEATURE INTEGRATION THEORY

To this point, we have thought only about the kind of attention that limits the perceptual information that is processed. It has been proposed that another function of attention (or perhaps another kind of attention) is to bind perceptual features together into coherent representations of objects (Treisman & Gelade, 1980). For example, when we perceive a green triangle, it is quite clear that the triangle we see has a green color. Although it seems obvious to us that we perceive these combinations of features as coherent objects, this is not a trivial point, because different aspects of vision are actually processed by different neural pathways. Thus, at some point this information must be brought back together to form representations of objects. The idea is that attention is required to create these unified object representations.

One basis for the proposal that attention influences the creation of object representations is data from various search tasks. For example, people find it easy to search for green things (triangles or circles) against a background of red things or to search for circles (red or green) against a background of triangles (red or green). These data are consistent with the idea that if we focus only on a single dimension (like color) it is easy to distinguish between distinct values (like red or green). In contrast to this ease, it is difficult to search for green circles against a background of green triangles and red circles (that is, to search for the *conjunction* of the properties *circle* and *green*).

As we discussed earlier, search time can be used as an index of the difficulty of search. When people search for a single feature (e.g., green things), their search time does not increase with display size (i.e., with the number of objects in the display), suggesting that people can search all of the members of a set of objects for the presence of a value of a single dimension in parallel with unlimited capacity. In contrast, when people search for conjunctions (e.g., green circles where there are green and circle distractors), their search time increases with display size, suggesting a limited capacity (serial or parallel) search.

Why do we have to search serially for a conjunction of features? To answer this question, we have to think about what it means for a conjunction of features to be part of the same object. In vision, a pair of features are part of the same object if those features both occupy the same location in space at the same time. For example, a green triangle is the co-occurrence of green and a triangular shape in the same location in space. Thus, we must combine information about *what* is in the world (a triangle, a green thing) and *where* it is located. Although our perceptual experience is that we see both what something is and where it is located simultaneously, the brain separates these two kinds of information early in processing. There is good neuropsychological evidence that the **what system** and the **where system** of the brain are functionally and neuroanatomically separable, parallel systems (see e.g., Ellis & Young, 1988; Ungerleider & Mishkin, 1982), and even spatial attention may have functionally distinct subsystems (Posner, 1988). Note that these observations raise problems for the idea that there is an early selection based on location, followed by later processing of the contents of information at that location (Kramer, Weber, & Watson, 1997). "What" and "where" appear to operate in parallel rather than sequentially, and these sources of information may be coordinated only at a later stage of processing.

Feature integration theory is based on the idea that attention is required to take the information from many different dimensions and coordinate (or integrate) it in a way that we can recognize that all of this information occurred at the same location. On this view, there are distinct subsystems that operate in parallel early in perceptual processing to represent low-level properties of objects. Thus, simple features like color (e.g., green) should be easily detectable, even if one is uncertain about what object the feature appeared in or where it appeared. In contrast, conjunctions of features are more difficult to process. The information about each feature (color, shape, size, etc.) contains information about where in space it was located. Forming a representation of an object in space requires finding the various features that all occurred at the same location. Thus, color information is not directly linked to shape information; rather, color and shape are indirectly linked through common spatial information. For example, when a blue triangle is presented at a location, *blue* and *triangle* are directly linked with that location, and this common location is used to integrate *blue* and *triangle* into *blue triangle*.

An early observation consistent with the importance of location was provided by Snyder (1972). He showed people displays with many colored letters and asked people to report the identity of a letter in a particular color (e.g., to say which letter appeared in red). Often, they would report the identity of a neighboring letter in the display, even though the instructions said nothing about location. For example, they would report seeing a red N, when in fact they had seen a red T and a green N. Of importance, people actually reported seeing a red N, even though there was no red N in the display. This finding suggests that going from color to shape requires people to compute a spatial address, and that they sometimes make small errors in this computation. In further support for this proposal, Treisman and Gelade (1980) found that performance on detecting conjunctively defined targets was completely at chance on

A DEBATE
Objects or Locations?

Studies of visual attention typically involve search for some target object in an array. Some studies have explored the effects of having people shift their attention prior to the presentation of the array. For example, subjects might be asked to fix their gaze on a point at the center of a screen, and press one button if a T is present in an array and another button if it is not present. Prior to the presentation of the array, a small box might appear somewhere on the screen. People are typically faster to respond that the target appears at the same location as the box than if it appears in a different location. Further, studies have shown that when the object does not appear in the cued location, people's responses are faster when the object appears close to the cued location than when it appears far away (Downing & Pinker, 1985; W. A. Johnston & Dark, 1986).

This result is consistent with the metaphor that attention is a spotlight focused on a particular location in space. There is something odd about directing attention to locations, though, because a major goal of vision is to identify objects in the world. Thus, it would seem to be a better idea to allocate attention to specific objects. In fact, studies like the one just described do not provide any evidence to tell whether people are attending to locations or to objects, because the studies involve objects in fixed locations (Egeth & Yantis, 1997).

(Continued)

trials if subjects had poor information about *where* the target appeared (in some conditions, people were asked to say both whether a target was present and, if so, where). In contrast, for simple feature detection, people perform considerably above chance, even if they do not know where the target appeared.

As usual, as research progresses, things tend to get more complicated. It might have occurred to you that a person should be able to ignore all red things in looking for a green circle, because red and green are processed in distinct ways in early vision. As it turns out, the speed with which one can conduct a search for a conjunctive target depends on how distinctive each single feature is from possible distractors (Duncan & Humphreys, 1989), so it is easier to search for a red object in the midst of a set of green distractors than to search for it in the midst of a set of pink distractors. Consequently, modifications and alternatives to the feature integration theory have been advanced (see e.g., Cave & Wolfe, 1990; G. W. Humphreys & Muller, 1993; Treisman & Sato, 1990; Wolfe, 1994).

To summarize, computing representations of coherent objects requires some way of combining information about the various properties of objects. Feature

A DEBATE

Objects or Locations? *(Continued)*

Several ingenious studies have provided evidence suggesting that people may be primarily allocating attention to objects in the world rather than locations (although they can allocate attention to locations). As one example, Egly, Driver, and Rafal (1994) showed people pairs of rectangles. The rectangles were spaced so that the opposite ends of the same rectangle were the same distance from each other as were adjacent ends of different rectangles. On each trial, one end of one rectangle brightened. This served as a cue to draw people's attention. Subjects were instructed to respond when one end of a rectangle was filled in, and on 80% of trials, the target appeared at the cued location. On the remaining trials, the cue appeared either on the opposite end of the same rectangle that was cued (the same-object condition) or on the adjacent end of the other rectangle (the different-object condition). Note that these latter two targets are equally far away from the cue, but they differ in which object they are part of. Not surprisingly, people were fastest to respond when the target appeared in the same location as the cue. When the target appeared in a different location from the cue, the results supported the idea that attention is allocated to objects. Specifically, people were faster to respond in the same-object condition than in the different-object condition.

(Continued)

integration theory proposes that there is no single representation of an object, but rather a collection of features that are all indexed to a common location in space. The perception of an object requires bringing together the various features that are all indexed to the same location. It requires attention to coordinate the representations of individual features, which can influence performance on tasks (like search tasks) that require consideration of many different features of an object at the same time.

ATTENTION IN COMPLEX TASKS

At the beginning of this chapter, we mentioned various meanings of the word *attention*. The perceptual attention studies described so far provided evidence for attention as selection, and for attention as limits in capacity. This work focused on perceptual tasks in which people were asked to search for objects or features in an array. As the tasks that people carry out become more complex, it is important to worry about how different tasks and different perceptual modalities can be

A DEBATE

Objects or Locations? *(Continued)*

Other studies have addressed this issue by having the objects move. In one study, Kahneman, Treisman, and Gibbs (1992) presented people with displays like the one in Figure 4.5. The task was to name the letter presented in the target field as rapidly as possible. A preview field is shown where objects appear with letters inside them and then a linking display is shown where letters are removed and the objects move into a new position. The critical variable is the relation between the preview and the target fields. On same-object target trials, the same letter appears within the same object as during the preview. On different-object target trials, a previously presented letter appears within a new object. The actual distance a letter moves is the same for both of these types of trials. Finally, on no-match trials, a new letter appears within an old object. The first two conditions set up potential priming or facilitation conditions, and the no-match trials serve as a control. Kahneman et al. (1992) found that same-object trials led to faster response times than the other two conditions, which did not differ from each other. In short, this speedup or *priming* appeared to be object based. If priming were location based, there would be no reason to expect any difference between same-object and different-object trials.

These data cast doubt on a simple spotlight model of attention. However, these studies do not prove that people are incapable of focusing attention on locations, and indeed it appears that people can attend both to locations and to objects (Egeth & Yantis, 1997). Further, it is possible that object-based attention is implemented by first determining an object's location and then allocating attention to that location (see Kramer, Weber, & Watson, 1997, for discussion and evidence bearing on this point). Finally, it has been shown that the degree to which people attend to objects is influenced by the task people believe they are about to perform or even on the task that they just performed (Watson & Kramer, 1999). Still, an object-based theory of attention does seem consistent with the idea that a central goal of vision is to identify objects.

(Continued)

A DEBATE
Objects or Locations? *(Continued)*

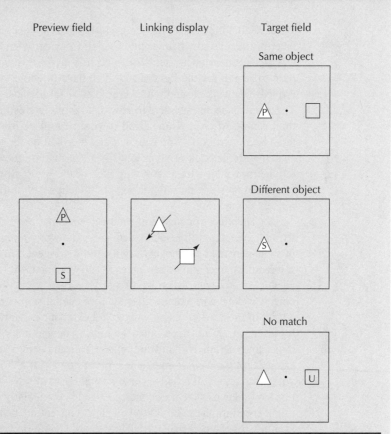

Figure 4.5	Example of displays used in the Kahneman et al. experiment. A preview field is shown, and then a linking display appears where the letters are absent and the objects move into new positions. The target field can have: (1) the same letter appear within the same object (same object), (2) a previously seen letter appear in a different object (different object), or (3) a new letter appear (no match). Note that the spatial distance of a letter between the preview and target fields is the same in the same-object and different-object conditions.

Source: Kahneman, Triesman, & Gibbs, 1992.

coordinated. An important line of research in this vein focuses on the influence of learning on attention. In particular, how does learning decrease the amount of attention required to carry out cognitive tasks? Let's turn to this work now.

Capacity and Automaticity

We have all noticed that practicing a task makes it feel as though it requires less mental effort than it did when we first tried it. Consider what happens when you move to a new apartment or house. When you first arrive, every action requires effort. You have to search for the light switch. You have to decide where to put new mail that arrived. You walk around with a crumpled sheet of paper looking for a waste basket. These mundane chores seem to crowd out more interesting things you might want to think about. After you have lived in your new place for a few months, all of those tasks become routine. You can pick up your mail on the way inside, flip on the light switch with the back of your hand, drop the mail on the table in the hall, and throw out the junk mail with a satisfying flick of the wrist, all without breaking your concentration on some pressing problem. Somehow, all of these tasks became less cognitively demanding.

There is strong experimental evidence that practice does produce **automaticity** and a reduction in resource demands. The word *automaticity* has been the source of some debate in psychology. By the most stringent criterion, a process is automatic if it requires no cognitive resources to carry out and if it runs to completion once it is begun. For example, when we fix our gaze on a scene, the detection of the edges of objects is done without any effort and we cannot stop ourselves from detecting these edges. In most of the cases where we talk about cognitive tasks being automatized, however, we do not mean that they have become automatic by this definition, but rather that there is a significant reduction in the perceived difficulty of the task. For example, in the well-worn example of driving a car, although we improve at the task with practice, it still requires some mental effort to drive a car. That is why conversation slows down as the traffic increases and in particularly difficult circumstances, you might even turn the radio off to be able to concentrate better. In normal driving, however, it is possible to make decisions about what to do next (e.g., to turn or to pass a car) well in advance of when the decision must be carried out, and so this planning can be integrated with other activities currently being pursued.

Cognitive research has demonstrated that whether practice leads to a reduction in attentional demands depends on the type of practice and on the structure of the task. To illustrate what we mean by task structure, we will return to search tasks like the one we described earlier in which people are asked to say whether a target (e.g., the letter T) appeared in a display (e.g., the letters BKQR). In the search tasks we will describe now, the display will be shown briefly, so people are no longer looking at the letters at the time that they make the response, but the logic of the search task is the same as what we described above (Sternberg, 1966).

Research with these kinds of search tasks suggests that the time required to say that a target was in the display increases about 35–40ms for each item in the display. Recall that this pattern of data is consistent with the idea that there is a serial search or a limited capacity parallel search (in this case through memory). What would happen if people were able to practice the task? It turns out that the effects of practice depend on whether the task is set up with **consistent mapping** or with **varied mapping.** Under consistent mapping, if an item is a target on one trial, it never appears in the display unless it is a target. Items that are in the display, but are not the target are called *distractors*. In the example above, if this were a consistent mapping task, the letter T would only appear in a display on trials when T is the target, but not when some other letter is the target (i.e., it would never be a distractor). In this case, we say that the target set and the distractor set do not overlap. In contrast, under varied mapping, the target set and the distractor set overlap. Thus, a given letter may appear on some trials as a target and on other trials as a distractor.

When people are given a lot of practice with a search task, consistent mapping and varied mapping yield different results. Consider a representative study by Kristofferson (1972) in which participants were trained on either consistent mapping or varied mapping for 30 days. Like Sternberg, Kristofferson found that reaction time to respond that a target was in the display increased with the number of letters in the display when the varied mapping procedure was used. Thus, people were still performing some kind of serial search (or limited capacity parallel search) even after considerable practice. That is not to say that practice had no beneficial effect. Reaction time did decrease across the 30 days of practice, so people were getting faster to perform the task overall. While people got faster overall, the lines relating reaction times to display size did not change their slope from one session to the next, so even by the end of the study, each additional letter in the display increased response time about 36ms. This result suggests that practice did not increase the amount of search time per item under varied mapping.

A different pattern of improvement was noted under the consistent mapping condition. In addition to an overall speedup, practice produced a change in the relation between display size and search times. The difference in reaction time to a display with four elements versus a display with only one early in training was more than twice the difference observed late in training; that is, the search time per item decreased substantially with practice. Thus, it appears that practice speeds up memory search in the consistent mapping case, but not in the varied mapping case.

The difference between consistent and varied mapping was systematically explored by Schneider and Shiffrin (1977). One experiment involved a visual search task in which participants were first given a set of targets to search for. This set of targets was called the memory set, because the subject had to remember which items to search for. On each trial, a display frame was presented in which 1, 2, or 4 items were presented in a 2 × 2 grid. The display frame was preceded and followed by masking frames consisting of a 2 × 2 grid of masks, where the masks were just dots that outlined a rectangle about the size of a letter. Figure 4.6 shows the procedure for two sample trials. The critical frame appears in position c, which is then followed by a mask d. Both (A) and (B) show positive trials; J is in the display for the varied mapping trial in (A) and 8 is in the display for the consistent mapping trial in (B).

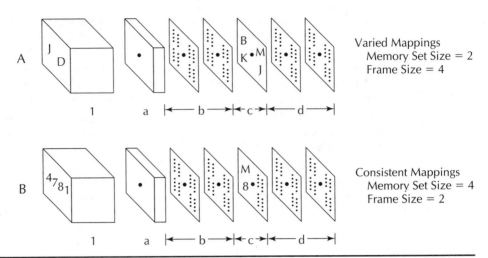

Figure 4.6   Two examples of a positive trial in the single-frame search paradigm of Experiment 2: (a) varied mapping with memory set = (J, D) and (b) consistent mapping with memory set = (4, 7, 8, 1). (1: presentation of memory set; a: fixation dot goes on for 0.5 s when subject starts trial; b: two frames of masks; c: target frame; d: two postmask frames. Frame time = 160ms for each of the five frames.)

Source: Schneider & Shiffrin, 1977.

As Figure 4.7 indicates, under consistent mapping conditions the reaction time functions were nearly flat across the range of memory set sizes and frame sizes. Thus, in the consistent mapping conditions, people exhibited a pattern of search consistent with an unlimited capacity parallel search. Consistent with this interpretation, participants in the consistent mapping condition reported that after practice, the targets seemed to "pop out" and the search became effortless. Schneider and Shiffrin argued that search tends to become increasingly automatized in procedures involving consistent mapping.

Schneider and Shiffrin did not argue that automaticity comes without any costs. If consistently mapped stimuli automatically attract attention, they may interfere with processing when the task is changed. To test this idea, Shiffrin and Schneider (1977) first trained people in a consistent mapping condition until their search times were about the same regardless of the size of the display frame. Then, they switched people from a consistent mapping task to a varied mapping task, so that items that were always targets previously sometimes appeared as distractors. In this condition, there were times when an object that was in the current memory set appeared in a display frame along with a distractor that came from the previous consistently mapped memory set. On these trials, there was a 22% drop in the probability of the correct target being detected. This result suggests that the item that had previously been consistently mapped drew attention away from the other items in the display frame, and thus people did not recognize the presence of a member of the current memory set in the display frame. In this case, the cost of automaticity is a reduction in flexibility of

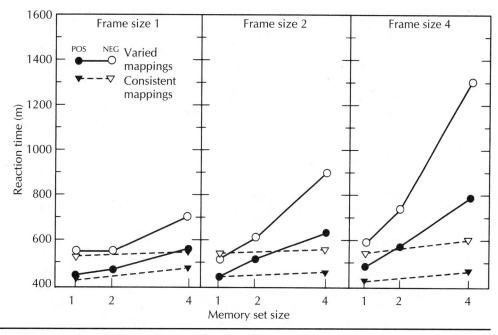

Figure 4.7   Mean reaction times for correct responses as a function of memory set size for both varied and consistent search conditions from Experiment 2 of the Schneider and Shiffrin experiment.

Source: Schneider & Shiffrin, 1977.

cognitive processing. By automatically focusing on the item that had been consistently mapped before, people were unable to flexibly attend to items from a new memory set.

Schneider and Shiffrin take these data to suggest that consistent mapping is required for the development of automaticity. This conclusion has been challenged, however. In one paper, Hirst, Spelke, Reaves, Caharack, and Neisser (1980) argued that people could learn to perform two complex comprehension tasks simultaneously without either task being automatized. They trained people to read while taking dictation (in the form of short sentences). Because neither task has the sort of "consistent mapping" used by Schneider and Shiffrin, there should be no opportunity for "automaticity" to develop. After considerable practice, however, participants could write short sentences while reading aloud, as well as answer complex comprehension questions about what they had read. Hirst et al. argued that their subjects were not alternating between tasks, but had "restructured" them so that both tasks could be performed simultaneously.

It is not entirely clear what restructuring means. Pashler (1998) reviews studies like this, and suggests that people may become more adept at capacity sharing. At any given moment, a person has some amount of cognitive effort they can use to perform a task. Many complex tasks do not require constant cognitive work, but rather they require bursts of difficult cognitive work. For example taking dictation may require storing information about what was said (a difficult cognitive activity) followed by typing (which may not require much attentional monitoring). As people become more skilled at complex tasks, they may require less monitoring of a task, and so the short bursts of activity associated with different tasks can be coordinated in a way that permits fluent performance of multiple tasks when they are performed simultaneously. For example, people might be able to interleave the process of reading a passage into the task of taking dictation by performing the complex parts of the reading task during the times when less effortful aspects of the dictation task are being performed. On this view, the Hirst et al. results involve capacity sharing.

Not all cases of automaticity reflect capacity sharing. In particular, there is good evidence that the automaticity achieved under conditions of consistent mapping involves a shift from carrying out a task in an effortful way to retrieving the correct response from memory. One prominent theory of automaticity that rests on this principle is Logan's (1988) instance theory of automaticity. Normally, a task has some algorithm or procedure that can produce correct performance, but this algorithm may take considerable time to carry out. For example, you can multiply 39 times 39 to arrive at the answer 1,521. Having done so, if you are immediately asked what 39 times 39 is, you do not have to perform the computation again if you remember the result you just computed. Logan views task performance as a race between the algorithm or procedure and the memory for stored instances of the appropriate answer or response. Consistent mapping (39 times 39 is always 1,521) ensures that the retrieved instances will be useful, and performance improves with practice as one accumulates more stored instances. Notice that this process works best for consistently mapped items, because every instance retrieved from memory will suggest the same response when items are consistently mapped. Logan developed a quantitative model for this presumed race process and demonstrated that it accounted for reaction time speedups with practice as well as the decreased variability of reaction times (see Cheng, 1985, for further arguments concerning changes in operations versus changes in their speed and Rickard, 1997, for a discussion of differences between race models and shifts from one operation to another).

According to the instance theory, automatic processes are not completely involuntary, but rather can be controlled. One may not be able to control responding on the basis of automatic processes perfectly, however, because they tend to be fast and to allow less time for the act of control to take place. Automatic processes may also be controlled by manipulating retrieval cues to make access to stored examples easier or more difficult. One challenge for the instance theory of automaticity is to specify just what an instance is and to describe how generalization from prior experience occurs (see Palmeri, 1997, for a discussion of this issue). Some differences between the current situation and past ones clearly matter, while others do not. If you have been asked what 39 times 39 is in a written format, you could presumably retrieve the answer when the same question is asked orally, and so the modality in which arithmetic problems are learned may not matter to the development of automaticity. In contrast, if you are driving down the street and notice that a stop sign has been installed at an intersection where none had been before, then a new action is required. Theoretical and empirical work must focus on what constitutes an instance (see Lassaline & Logan, 1993, for some relevant evidence).

The studies in this section demonstrate that practice at a task decreases the cognitive resources necessary for it to be completed. When the task is structured so that there is a consistent mapping between stimulus and response, then people may gradually shift from slow effortful processes (like the procedure for multiplying large numbers) to faster processes (like retrieving responses from memory). More effortful tasks that become less effortful may be restructured in a different way. Practice may allow an individual to coordinate the bursts of cognitive activity needed to carry out more than one task simultaneously.

CENTRAL EXECUTIVE FUNCTIONS

One aspect of attention that we have not discussed much so far is the central executive type of attention. It may seem strange that we have not addressed this issue so far, because most of the colloquial uses of the term *attention* refer to our ability to select one task rather than another. When we talk about "paying attention to a cognitive psychology lecture," we really mean that we are selecting a particular task to carry out rather than some number of other things we might do (such as day-dreaming).

As a means for exploring the role of attention in determining what actions will be carried out, Alan Allport (1989) has argued for addressing the Marr's computational level question (see Chapter 1 of this book) of what function attention serves. Allport suggests that attention is critically involved in selection for action. Consider what is involved in reaching for either a stationary or moving object in a scene where many objects may be present. For the grasp to be successful, one must determine where the object is relative to oneself. Information about the position and size of other objects in the scene must not be allowed to interfere with the relevant information. In short, selective processing is needed to map just those aspects of the scene to the goal object onto appropriate control parameters for action (or potential action).

As Allport notes, selection cannot consist simply of a split into two pools, relevant and irrelevant. Action may be complex and rely on multiple sources of information; frequently two or more categories of action must be coordinated. When conditions for two actions conflict, one or both must be modified to allow their continued execution, or one action may take priority over the other.

Dual-Task Interference

Some recent work by Pashler (1989, 1991, 1994a; see Pashler, 1998 for a review) suggests that the response selection phase, when people are asked to perform two tasks at once, represents a genuine central bottleneck rather than capacity sharing. Recall from our discussion earlier that capacity sharing occurs when people are able to interleave the cognitive processing demands of two tasks performed at the same time. In contrast, actions may need to be performed sequentially.

This claim can be assessed using the Psychological Refractory Period (PRP) task. This task involves having people carry out two tasks, both of which are typically quite easy. For example, participants might hear a tone and see a letter on a computer screen. Their job is to press one of two keys with their left hand, depending on whether the tone was high or low, and then to press either of a different pair of keys with the right hand, depending on what letter was presented visually. The tone and letter stimuli may appear simultaneously or may precede or follow each other. Often, however, people are asked to respond in one task (e.g., to the tone) before the other (e.g., to the letter). The standard finding is that the response time to the second stimulus becomes slower than it would have been if it were presented alone when the interval between stimuli is small (Welford, 1952).

What is the cause of the slowing of the second response? Pashler (1998) suggests that the PRP task can be used to explore this issue. Figure 4.8 shows the standard finding. The idea here is that there are cognitive and motor processes that can take place before and after the central processor is involved. The reason that responses to the second stimulus (called S2) are longer than they would be alone is that some amount of processing of the second stimulus must be delayed until after the central executive finishes processing stimulus 1 (called S1). Pashler assumes that selecting a response requires the central executive system. This account derives support from the finding that tasks that affect the difficulty of processing stimulus 1 (such as making the stimulus harder to process perceptually) increase the time required to respond to stimulus 2 (as shown in the middle part of Figure 4.8). In contrast, increasing the difficulty of processing stimulus 2 does not increase the time required to respond to stimulus 2. As illustrated in the bottom part of Figure 4.8, this counterintuitive finding arises because the additional time required to process stimulus 2 takes place at the same time as the response selection is going on for stimulus 1. As long as the additional time to respond to stimulus 2 is shorter than the time required to select a response to stimulus 1, the overall time to respond to stimulus 2 will not increase. Pashler (1998) provides evidence consistent with this interpretation.

Why should there be a bottleneck at the response selection stage of processing? One possibility is that many different tasks may involve the same motor systems. For example, imagine you are sitting at your desk and must answer the phone with one hand and jot down something in a note pad with the other hand. Both of these actions may involve complex motor movements. It may be difficult to plan both of these movements at the same time without interference, and so the cognitive system may follow a general rule or guideline of planning one action at a time to avoid error. Indeed, we all know of instances (such as learning to pat your head while rubbing your stomach) in which it is difficult to do independent things with different body parts.

Attention is needed for the coordination and control of action. A system must also be able to assign priorities in the case of conflicts and, as we argued at the beginning of this chapter, to be interruptible when unanticipated events of importance arise. The response to these various demands appears to involve functionally separable but partially overlapping attention subsystems. For our purposes, this analysis

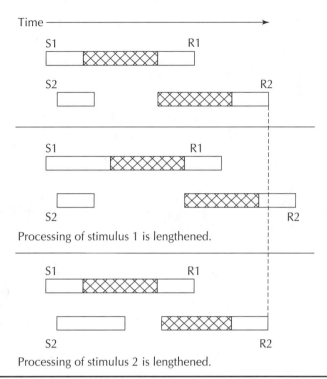

Figure 4.8   Timing of responses in the psychological refractory period (PRP) task. Time moves along the horizontal in this figure. The hatched area of each task represents the part requiring central executive control. The top panel demonstrates the standard finding that responses to a second stimulus are longer in the PRP task than they would be without the competing task. The middle panel demonstrates that increasing the difficulty of the first task affects the amount of time it takes to respond to the second stimulus. The bottom panel demonstrates that increasing the difficulty of the second task does not affect the amount of time required to respond to the second stimulus, because the increased time to process this stimulus can occur in parallel with the response selection for the first stimulus.

casts a very different light on attention. From a capacity framework, we are led to focus on the limitations of information processing, and we might wonder how much more effective we might be if we did not have these limitations. From the perspective of multiple goals and the need to coordinate and control action, attention becomes a positive enabler of intelligent action. If we were unable to select information or if we were able to select information in only an all-or-none fashion without further segregation, we would be unable to think or act. Potential interference between tasks and the need to prioritize and coordinate tasks means that one cannot always do two things at once as well as one could do either thing in isolation, but we believe that attention should be thought of as enabling organisms to properly organize relevant information and not solely as a limitation.

AN APPLICATION
Attention Deficit Disorder

What would happen if you were unable to pay attention to a single task? Chances are, solving problems or reading would be very difficult. You might find particular aspects of a task so inviting that you might lose track of what you were trying to do and your mind might wander off into something else. According to the Diagnostic and Statistical Manual IV (DSM-IV) published by the American Psychiatric Association, a deficit in sustained attention to tasks is characteristic of Attention Deficit/Hyperactivity Disorder (ADHD). This disorder (which may reflect a cluster of related subdisorders) is becoming increasingly frequently diagnosed in children in the United States (Swanson, Lerner, & Williams, 1995).

ADHD has been associated with abnormal processing in the frontal lobes of the brain (Swanson et al., 1997). This interpretation is also supported by the observation that the most widely prescribed drug for the disease—the stimulant methylphenidate (or ritalin)—appears to increase activity in the frontal lobes of the brain. Children with ADHD seem to have difficulty focusing attention and also have difficulty inhibiting competing activities.

As evidence for diffuse attention in ADHD, Ceci and Tishman (1984) had normal and ADHD children study a series of pictures of familiar objects. On the wall of the room where the study took place were a number of brightly colored posters. Normal children were better at recalling the objects in the pictures than were the ADHD children. This finding was not due to an overall greater ability to remember things, however, as the ADHD children were *better* able to recall the objects on the posters than were the normal children. This result suggests that ADHD children had more difficulty focusing on the specific task that was presented. Similar results are reported by Milich and Lorch (1994), who studied normal and

(Continued)

ATTENTION AND THE BRAIN

At the beginning of this chapter, we discussed that there are many different aspects of cognition that are all called attention. It seems unlikely that there will be a single theory that will encompass everything for which we use the term *attention*. This conclusion is supported by research in cognitive neuroscience (see Parasuraman, 1998, for a review of this work).

One way to see the variety of different kinds of attention is in the patterns of attention problems that can occur as the result of brain damage. One unfortunate but

AN APPLICATION

Attention Deficit Disorder *(Continued)*

ADHD children watching television in the presence of toys. When there were no toys present, both groups of children watched the TV program for the same overall amount of time in a 23-minute session, but the ADHD children looked away from the TV more times than did the normal children. When toys were present, ADHD children watched the TV for less time overall than did the normal children. Because the children were informed in advance that they would be given a test about the programs, there was an implied demand that they should watch the TV show. Thus, this study provides additional evidence that ADHD children have more difficulty focusing and sustaining attention than do normal children, particularly in the presence of interesting distractors.

Finally, there is evidence that ADHD children have difficulty inhibiting inappropriate responses. For example, ADHD children given a Stroop task have much more difficulty in the case where the color words mismatch the colors of ink than do normal children, suggesting that they are having trouble keeping themselves from focusing on the color word (Barkley, 1997a). This finding reflects a general aspect of ADHD that Barkley reports, in which potentially distracting aspects of a task (like the color words in the Stroop task, discussed in Chapter 1) are more likely to disrupt the performance of an ADHD child than are distractions not relevant to a task (like background noise).

In sum, ADHD is a disorder that is marked by difficulty in sustaining attention. Thus, the system of executive attention seems to have broken down in this case. ADHD seems to be mediated by problems in the frontal lobes, although more work is necessary to better understand the neurophysiology responsible for this disorder.

dramatic example of a breakdown is unilateral *neglect,* a deficit associated with damage to the brain in which patients fail to attend to information on one side of space. For example, patients with lesions (i.e., damage) to the right hemisphere of the brain may ignore (i.e., neglect) the left side of visual space (e.g., leaving food on the left side of their plates). Figure 4.9 shows performance of a patient with damage to the right hemisphere on clock drawing and line cancellation tasks (from a study by Grabowecky, Robertson, & Treisman, 1993). The patient largely ignores the left visual field for both drawing and noticing lines.

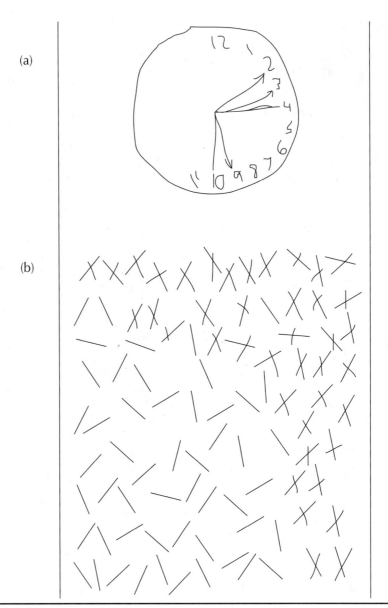

Figure 4.9   Examples of performance of a patient with unilateral neglect on (a) the clock drawing task and (b) Albert's line cancellation test (Albert, 1973).

Source: Grabowecky, Robertson, & Triesman, 1993.

A different pattern of breakdown is seen in Balint's syndrome. In this disorder, patients seem unable to attend to more than one object at a time. For example, if they are presented with a display showing two circles, they will only report seeing one of them. Interestingly, Balint's syndrome patients will report seeing both circles if the circles are connected by a line so that they form a single object (see Driver & Baylis, 1998, and Ivry and Robertson, 1998, for discussions of Balint's syndrome).

As a final example, Alzheimer's Disease patients (who have a number of cognitive deficits) seem to have particular difficulty shifting attention (Parasuraman & Greenwood, 1998). For example, they have trouble moving their eyes in a direction away from an object flashed on a computer screen. They also have trouble attending to a second location after being given a cue to attend to an initial location. In contrast, Alzheimer's Disease patients perform normally on other tasks. For example, when cued to attend to a particular location, these patients respond faster to a target item presented in that location than to a target item presented in a different location, just as do normal individuals.

These examples suggest that not all aspects of attention (here largely perceptual attention) break down together. Instead, patients may have some aspects of attention that are spared while others break down. There are many other disorders of attention that we have not discussed here (including Attention Deficit/Hyperactivity Disorder, discussed in the box An Application on pages 144–145). In addition, cognitive neuroscientists are beginning to use brain imaging techniques like EEG, PET, and fMRI to study attention. These studies promise to help determine which aspects of attention reflect common underlying processes.

Summary

As discussed at the outset, the word *attention* seems to refer to many things. Psychologists have not yet decided whether all of the phenomena described by *attention* refer to a single underlying construct. However, all of these aspects of cognitive processing do serve a similar function. All of them deal with paring down the amount of information the cognitive system must deal with to a manageable level. In perception, attention serves to focus on a subset of the potentially limitless amount of information available in the environment. In the generation of object representations, attention helps to bind together features of a common object. At the level of action, attention allows us to carry out a number of tasks with out having those tasks interfere with each other. Human attention appears to be accomplished through overlapping but partially independent subsystems that operate on different types and levels of information. As we have seen in this chapter and the previous one, just how these sources of information are integrated to provide a unitary perceptual experience is a matter of great current research interest. Attention and perception are exquisitely adapted to allow us to move about in, act in, and make sense of our environment.

Key Terms

attentional blink	bottleneck model
automaticity	consistent mapping

dichotic listening experiment

early selection theory

echoic memory

feature integration theory

iconic memory

late selection theory

partial report technique

rapid serial visual presentation

repetition blindness

span of apprehension

spotlight metaphor

varied mapping

what system

where system

Recommended Readings

Although we have learned quite a bit about attention, William James's (1890) book continues to inspire and influence attention researchers. Research on attention got a large boost from human factors research associated with the Second World War. One practical problem was that of radar experts, who had to maintain attention in order to detect infrequent (but important) targets. Broadbent's (1958) comprehensive and interesting book had its roots in that tradition.

There is a great current interest in the neuropsychology of attention. Desimone and Duncan (1995), Posner and Raichle (1995) and the chapters in Parasuraman (1998) offer detailed reviews of this literature. The general topic of attention is given an intensive overview by Pashler (1998), who examines both perceptual attention and central executive functions. The volume edited by Dagenback and Carr (1994) provides a good survey of the role of inhibitory processes in cognition. The book by Barkley (1997b) provides a detailed treatment of current thinking on Attention Deficit/Hyperactivity Disorder. Important contributions to attention often appear in the *Attention and Performance* series of edited volumes published by Academic Press.

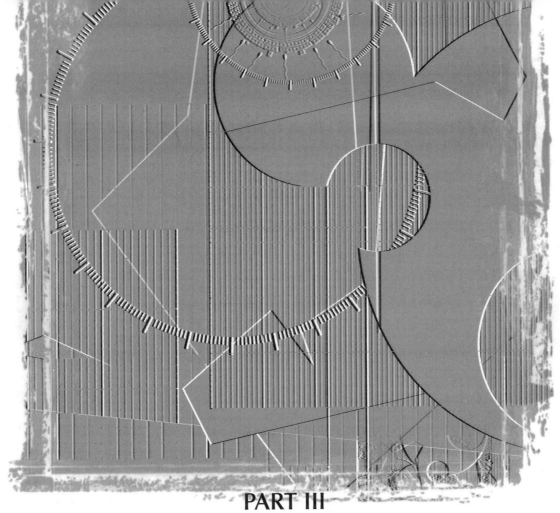

PART III
MEMORY

Chapter 5
Memory: Remembering New Information

Chapter 6
Memory Systems and Knowledge

Chapter 7
Remembering New Information:
Beyond Basic Effects

Chapter 8
Spatial Knowledge, Imagery, and Visual Memory

Chapter 5

Memory: Remembering New Information

Introduction
Centrality of Memory
Uses of Memory

Short-Term Memory
Introduction
Characteristics of Short-Term Memory
Working Memory
Summary

Long-Term Memory
Introduction
Encoding
Retrieval
Encoding-Retrieval Interactions
Forgetting
Summary

Models of Memory for New Information
General Approach
Simple Association Models
The SAM Model

Summary

Key Terms

Recommended Readings

I distinctly remember forgetting that.

—*Clara Barton*

INTRODUCTION

Centrality of Memory

The importance of memory frequently goes unnoticed. Often we think of memory as a repository in which names, dates, and the like can be kept until they are needed. Close analysis, however, shows memory to be a far more pervasive aspect of mental activity.

To appreciate the centrality of memory to mental life, we need only imagine what it would be like to be deprived of our memory for a time—or even more dramatic, to observe someone who has had this unhappy experience. Consider the following tragic case of a brain-injured man whose ability to store new information was virtually lost following surgery (Milner, 1966, pp. 112–115):

> This young man (H. M.) [...] had had no obvious memory disturbance before his operations, having, for example, passed his high school examinations without difficulty. . . . The patient was drowsy for the first few postoperative days but then, as he became more alert, a severe memory impairment was apparent. He could no longer recognize the hospital staff . . . he did not remember and could not relearn the way to the bathroom, and he seemed to retain nothing of the day-to-day happenings in the hospital.
>
> [...] Ten months after the operation the family moved to a new house which was situated only a few blocks away from their old one, on the same street. When examined . . . nearly a year later, H. M. had not yet learned the new address, nor could he be trusted to find his way home alone, because he would go to the old house. Six years ago the family moved again, and H. M. is still unsure of his present address, although he seems to know that he has moved. . . .

One gets some idea of what such an amnesic state must be like from H. M.'s own comments. Between tests he would suddenly look up and say, rather anxiously,

> Right now, I'm wondering. Have I done or said anything amiss? You see, at this moment everything looks clear to me, but what happened just before? That's what worries me. It's like waking from a dream; I just don't remember.

Memory plays a critical role in psychology. It is inextricably involved in every cognitive task from the simplest to the most difficult—from the memorization of a person's name to understanding speech to formulating and following personal goals. In fact, memory influences are discussed in almost all chapters of this book. Before discussing memory in detail, it is useful to consider some of the different functions that memory may serve.

Uses of Memory

It is common to view memory as something that allows one to store and retrieve facts: What is the capital of Oregon? What did you have for dinner last night? Furthermore, we tend to equate having a "good memory" with the ability to retrieve obscure or detailed facts.

Clearly, we do store and remember facts, but our memory is not used simply for the recollection of facts we have learned. Even in situations in which some fact is being queried, we often do not (or cannot) retrieve the exact fact but rather retrieve relevant information that may allow us to answer the question. For example, what about questions like:

1. What is the telephone number of the president of the United States?

We do not have to search through all our knowledge concerning the president to realize that we do not know this phone number.

To further complicate the picture, consider the following question:

2. How many windows are there in your current residence?

Most people can answer this question correctly, but they do not do so by directly retrieving this information (unless they have recently washed or painted their windows). Instead, people typically employ mental imagery and may imagine themselves walking through their house or apartment and counting the windows. In brief, our old knowledge is often used to derive some new knowledge.

Finally, consider questions like the following:

3. Did Julius Caesar have toes?

4. Do elephants eat more in a day than lions?

Both questions could be readily answered, but again not on the basis of fact retrieval alone. In the case of Caesar, our answer is based on a plausible inference from our knowledge that most people have toes. Similarly, the answer that elephants eat more than lions may derive from the general rule that there is a positive correlation (though not a perfect one) between size and how much an animal eats.

These examples suggest that there is a lot more to memory than retrieving facts. Indeed, our memory is needed in all acts of interpreting objects and events. Even to understand the questions we have just been considering requires access to (stored) knowledge about English grammar and the meanings of the associated words.

These observations provide clues to some of the central functions that memory serves. First, we cannot store every fact or conclusion that follows from the facts we already know—there are just too many of them. Our memory system is organized as a natural inference system that allows us to store a few facts and derive others as needed. We will take a closer look at such inferences in Chapter 6. A second major function of memory is to relate new events to prior knowledge in order to understand them. Just how this is done is addressed in Chapters 6, 7, and 8. A third general function of memory is to deliver relevant knowledge when it is needed. Even with our heavy reliance on inference, we have stored a tremendous number of facts and other bits of knowledge in memory. Just how we access that knowledge is a fundamental question. If we see a black widow spider, we need to access the knowledge that it is possibly poisonous. It will not help us to retrieve the fact that Thanksgiving is on a Thursday or that spiders spin complex webs. Furthermore, we need to access this knowledge quickly—and for this to happen, memory must be organized. The amazing thing is that memory is used so automatically that much of the time we are scarcely aware of how crucial it is for nearly everything we do. Our understanding of memory needs to include not only its failures (where did I park my car *today*?) but also its countless successes.

Although our knowledge is used in many ways, it is also true that one of the ways is the usual sense of remembering or recollection—to store and retrieve new information. The systematic study of such memory began over a hundred years ago, when Ebbinghaus (1885) used himself as a subject for an extensive study of what is remembered over time. In this chapter we examine this memory for new information. Even here, we will see that the use of prior knowledge has a major influence on the acquisition of new knowledge. We begin by investigating how information may be retained over very short periods, the study of short-term memory. We then examine a variety of findings on how information is retained (and forgotten) over longer periods, the study of long-term memory. Finally, with this background, we can discuss some explanations or models for remembering new information.

SHORT-TERM MEMORY

Introduction

Suppose that someone tells you the combination to a bicycle lock or the code to operate a burglar alarm, and you cannot write it down. How would you try to keep from forgetting it? A common (and useful) strategy is to keep repeating the numbers over and over to yourself. The idea is that by repeating the numbers you are keeping them active and available. The mechanism that keeps information active and available is what psychologists call **short-term memory** (also called *primary memory*). It is helpful to think of two ways in which this type of short-term memory may be useful. First, if you attend carefully to some information, such as the lock combination, it is registered in this short-term memory, making the information available for further processing, for more permanent storage, or both. Second, if you recall some information from permanent memory into short-term memory (e.g., the birth date of a sibling), it is available for further processing (e.g., figuring out the age of your sibling). As we have repeatedly mentioned, much of the information in the world is incomplete and requires augmentation by memory. Short-term memory is a crucial link in this augmentation, keeping available the information from the world to be augmented by memory. Short-term memory allows different information to be compared and integrated. In addition, it helps deal with the complexity problem (i.e., of knowing what information may be relevant) by keeping available recent information. Although any information is potentially relevant to a task (e.g., solving a problem, understanding a story), recent information is more likely to be relevant.

Short-term memory is biased toward keeping recent information available. However, if information in short-term memory is to be available immediately,

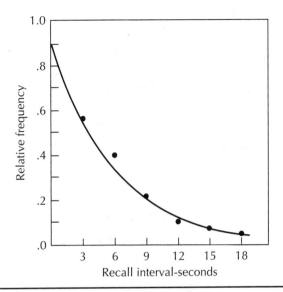

Figure 5.1   Proportion recalled in short-term memory task as a function of delay during which subjects are counting backward by 3.

Source: Peterson, L. R., & Peterson, M. J., 1959.

short-term memory needs to be limited. We can see the effects of these limitations in the forgetting that occurs and the errors people make.

Characteristics of Short-Term Memory

Short-Term Forgetting and Rehearsal

Events occurring both during and immediately following an experience are critically important determiners of short-term forgetting. Consider the following classic experiment by Peterson and Peterson (1959; also see J. Brown, 1958). The experimenter would say a three-letter consonant group (e.g., *BKF*) and then immediately say a three-digit number (e.g., 397). The subject then counted backward by threes (or fours) from this digit (i.e., 397, 394, 391, etc.). This counting task keeps the subject from being able to subvocally repeat the consonants. At the end of a preset interval (3, 6, 9, 12, 15, or 18 seconds), the subject was asked to recall the consonant group. The proportion of correct recalls for each interval is presented in Figure 5.1. As can be seen, the proportion of items recalled decreased sharply over the interval. If subjects cannot rehearse the items, they do not remember them for more than a matter of seconds.

In or out of the laboratory, it is universally observed that one can maintain memory for a few letters, numbers, or words just seen or heard almost indefinitely if one rehearses them repeatedly. By simply repeating the items over and over (termed

maintenance rehearsal or *primary rehearsal*), one in effect imprints the items anew in short-term memory on each repetition, much as one can prevent an old clock from running down by winding it at intervals.

People can forget items that were in short-term memory even if there is no explicit interfering task. In many memory theories (e.g., Atkinson & Shiffrin, 1968), it is assumed that short-term memory has an extremely small capacity, limited to a few items at a time. Consequently, if a person is presented with additional items immediately after seeing or hearing some to-be-remembered information, these new items may enter short-term memory and, in effect, crowd out some of the earlier information the person is trying to retain. Rehearsal may take place, but only of the items still in short-term memory.

Coding in Short-Term Memory

How is information in short-term memory coded? Some of the processes involved are brought out nicely in a simple experimental situation developed by Conrad (1964). On any one trial, the subject views a series of items, typically a string of four to six consonants that appear one after another on a display screen at a relatively rapid rate. Following a retention interval during which the subject reads aloud a series of rapidly presented random digits, a recall signal tells the subject to report as many of the letters as possible.

To find out how the visually displayed letters are stored in short-term memory, we may examine the nature of the errors made in recall. A subject who makes errors in recalling a string of letters is most likely to replace a letter that was shown on a particular trial with another letter that *sounds like* the one presented (for example, *T* with *V*), suggesting that there is an acoustic, not visual, code. If the subject is prevented from pronouncing the letters as they appear (for example, by being required to say something else), these acoustic confusion errors do not appear at the time of recall. A striking consequence of preventing the formation of acoustic memory codes in this way is that memory for the letters is greatly reduced.

Conrad's experiment shows that information may be coded (or recoded) into acoustic codes in short-term memory. For some time, such coding was thought to be a necessary characteristic of short-term memory. However, further research has now shown that other codings of information are also prevalent in short-term memory (for example, visual codes, which are discussed in Chapter 8). In addition to acoustic and visual codes, the semantic (meaning-related) aspects of items affect short-term memory. A clear demonstration of semantic effects may be seen in a clever paradigm pioneered by Delos Wickens and his colleagues (Wickens, 1972) called **release from PI** (proactive interference). The procedure is as follows. Subjects are given a triad of category members (e.g., flowers such as rose, tulip, daisy) to remember, but a distractor task is given so that subjects cannot rehearse the items. Recall is then requested. This test is followed by another triad from the same category (e.g., three new types of flowers) with the same procedure. A third triad is then presented with the same procedure. Recall of the second triad is lower than recall of the first, and recall of the third triad is lower than recall of the second, a phenomenon known as

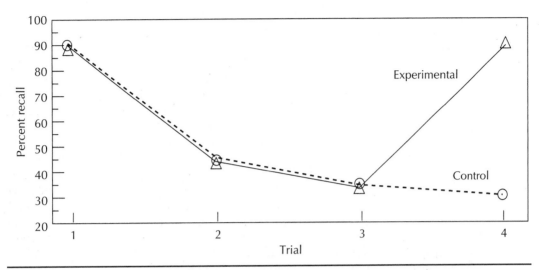

Figure 5.2 **Illustration of Typical Results Obtained in Release From PI Studies** For the first three trials, subjects have to recall three-word triads from the same category but are not allowed to rehearse the items. On the fourth trial, the triad is either from the same category yet again (control) or from a new category (experimental).

proactive interference (discussed later in this chapter). The interest, however, is in the recall of a fourth triad, which is either from the same category or from a new category. As shown in Figure 5.2, when the triad is from a new category, recall increases back to the level achieved for the first triad. When the triad is from the same category as the first three triads, its recall is even lower than the third triad recall. Clearly, knowledge about the category is affecting the recall, which is evidence for some type of semantic coding.

Limitations and Chunking

Consider again the example involving a lock combination. If it was a long combination and the numbers were 10, 20, 30, 40, 50, 60, 70, and 80, would it be easier to remember than 50, 30, 60, 20, 80, 10, 40, and 70? Almost everyone would agree that the first combination would be easier to remember. As another example, compare your ability to remember the following:

A string of 10 letters: R, P, L, B, V, Q, M, S, D, G

A set of 52 letters: I pledge allegiance to the flag of the United States of America.

Although the words include 52 letters, most people find them much easier to remember than the string of 10 letters. Why?

The answer for both of these examples is fairly obvious. In the first case, you can simply remember (i.e., keep in short-term memory) the idea that the numbers went from 10 to 80 in increments of 10 rather than remember the exact order in which the numbers occurred. In the second case, you need remember only that the sequence is the opening to the Pledge of Allegiance, rather than remembering the exact letters and their order. The coding you use to store these easy-to-remember groups of information is called **chunking.** A *chunk* refers to any meaningful group of information. Rather than storing each piece of information in the chunk in short-term memory, you can store the idea that the chunk occurred. When you need to retrieve the information, you can remember that the chunk occurred (because this idea is in short-term memory) and then you can bring the constituents of the chunk from more permanent memory. For example, if you were asked to recall the set of words in the second example, you would use the chunk "first sentence of Pledge of Allegiance" to retrieve the sentence from memory. If you were asked to recall the letters in that set of words, you would first retrieve the words and then, for each word, spell out the letters (again using information from more permanent memory).

The idea of chunking was outlined by George Miller (1956) in a famous paper ("The magical number seven plus or minus two"). He pointed out that a large number of seemingly disparate findings could be reconciled if we computed memory limitations not in terms of some physical unit, such as letters, but rather in terms of a psychological unit, chunks. Counting this way, he identified the short-term memory span to be about seven (or five to nine) chunks. Although the exact limits are controversial, the idea that people chunk information is widely accepted. This chunking allows us to keep track of much more information and have it available for processing. This ability becomes even more important as we deal with complex situations for which a great deal of information may be relevant.

In addition, it is important to realize that chunking is a function of our prior knowledge. What is meaningful depends on what we know, as well as what we are currently experiencing. For example, consider these two sequences of letters and try to remember them (adapted from Bower & Springston, 1970):

F BIV IPG NPC BS vs. FBI VIP GNP CBS

Our knowledge does not provide chunks to be readily used for most of the first letter sets but does for the last four letter sets.

Finally, keep in mind that the examples in this section were chosen to illustrate chunking that everyone would be able to understand. However, the chunking often occurs with each person's own organization scheme. So, given a set of 14 numbers to remember, one person might note that the first 7 are similar to a good friend's phone number, the next 3 are her dorm room number, and the final 4 are the year her dog was born. Another person would have a very different chunking of the same numbers.

Working Memory

We have been concentrating on memory effects of briefly remembered information as if short-term memory was simply a "storage device." That is, we have been concerned with how information is coded, retained, and accessed, but not with the actual *use* of this information in any complex task. Baddeley and Hitch (1974) began a series of experiments addressing the question, "What is short-term memory for?" In some clever studies, they showed that short-term memory should not be thought of as just a holding pen for a small set of chunks of information. This work led to the most influential current theory of short-term memory, which focuses on the use of the information as well as its storage. To emphasize the importance of this use, they call this mechanism **working memory.** Working memory refers to a brain and cognitive system that provides temporary storage and manipulation of information that is necessary for a variety of complex cognitive tasks.

The evidence for a working memory comes from a variety of sources but can be illustrated by the following study (Logie, Zucco, & Baddeley, 1990), which shows that the verbal memory and visual memory for items are not part of a single storage system. This study employed a dual-task paradigm in which people are asked to do two things at the same time. The logic of a dual-task study is that if carrying out two tasks at the same time hurts the performance of one or both tasks, then these tasks probably tap a similar limited capacity (such as a short-term store). Of greatest interest for us in this study was performance on a simple recognition memory span test, presented either as a verbal span of letters or a visual span of a simple 2 x 2 array. In each case, subjects were presented with one array followed by a second one (2 seconds later) in which one letter or cell was changed between the two presentations. Subjects had to say which letter or cell had changed. These tasks are quite easy, and subjects could normally perform them without error. In the experiment, however, subjects were asked to perform one of two secondary tasks at the same time as the memory task. One of the secondary tasks was a visual task involving a visually presented array of letters, and the other was a simple arithmetic task in which they kept a running sum of a set of single digits. The logic of this study was that if the visual memory span task involved a different store than the verbal letter span task (i.e., if it involved a visual store of some type), it would be more interfered with by a visual secondary task. The opposite would be true for the verbal span task: It would be more interfered with by a secondary task that involved verbal material (such as maintaining a running sum of numbers). As predicted, the visual secondary task selectively interfered with the visual memory task, and the verbal secondary task selectively interfered with the verbal memory task.

Some further evidence for the distinction between verbal and visual representations in working memory is provided by a very different type of study in which the brain activity of different regions of the brain is examined using positron emission tomography (PET), a methodology briefly described in Chapter 1. In this procedure, subjects are injected with a nontoxic radioactive substance that provides information about where the most active brain regions are. (When a brain region is involved in cognitive processing, its metabolic requirements increase, so there is an increased blood flow to this region, leading to more of the radioactive substance, which can be monitored.) Verbal and visual tasks led to very different patterns of brain activity, supporting the idea that they may involve different types of representations (Jonides, Reuter-Lorenz et al., 1996).

These results (and others) suggest that there are at least two separate parts to working memory: one for verbal information and one for visual information. However, there are many ways that each part could work, plus there is a need to coordinate them in some way. Baddeley has proposed a particular theory that tries to incorporate the known behavioral and neuropsychological data.

The Working Memory Theory

The current conception of working memory (Baddeley, 1986, 1996; Baddeley & Hitch, 1994) assumes three components: a control process and two highly specialized subsystems. We have illustrated this theory in Figure 5.3 in a way we hope will make it easy to remember. As discussed in Chapter 4, there is a *central executive* that controls attention and coordinates the activities of the other parts. The two specialized

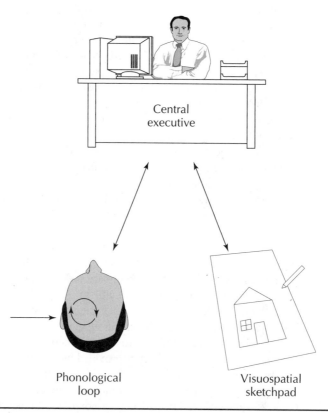

Central
executive

Phonological
loop

Visuospatial
sketchpad

Figure 5.3   **Working Memory Model**   The working memory is assumed to consist of a central executive and two subsystems, the phonological loop and the visuospatial sketchpad. The phonological loop holds acoustic information for about 2 seconds and contains a process for producing inner speech. The visuospatial sketchpad maintains and manipulates visual and spatial images. The central executive coordinates the two subsystems.

Source: Baddeley, 1986.

subsystems are the **phonological loop** and the **visuospatial sketchpad.** We first describe each of the subsystems and then discuss the functions of the central executive.

PHONOLOGICAL LOOP   The phonological loop is the subsystem that accounts for many of the results that we have been considering in this chapter. It is assumed to consist of two parts: a *phonological store,* which holds acoustic or speech-based information for about 2 seconds, and an *articulatory control process,* which is the process that produces the inner speech we all hear in ourselves. Thus, suppose you hear someone talking but are not paying close attention. If the person stops and asks you to repeat what was said, you could often repeat the last part of it, because your phonological store still has the last 2 seconds stored. The articulatory control process is what allows us to subvocally rehearse information to ourselves, helping to keep the information available by refreshing the phonological store. This reliance on the phonological store and inner speech is what leads to the acoustic errors in recall that were discussed earlier in this chapter.

Try this exercise: You will be getting two short sets of words to remember. For each set, rehearse the words (i.e., repeat them silently over and over to yourself) so that you will remember them. You should try to do this at as comfortable a pace as you can, but still try to remember all of them. Rehearse them for 60 seconds, and keep track of how many times you rehearse them by making a mark each time you say the first word. Your rate of rehearsal per minute is the number of marks multiplied by the number of words in the set. The first set to rehearse is: *sun, book, cat.* Rehearse these words before you go any further. The second set of words to rehearse is: *jar, sit, fan, road, tune, heat.* Now rehearse this second set of words. Most of us rehearse the second set much faster than the first. Why? The rehearsal of verbal material relies upon the property of the phonological store for keeping about 2 seconds of material available. So, when there is more material to rehearse, the articulatory control process tries to get a full cycle of rehearsal in about 2 seconds. The more material, the faster the rate.

In case that demonstration did not work for you, there are related experimental results examining how differences in rehearsal rates affect the memory for the materials. For example, Baddeley, Thomson, and Buchanan (1975) compared immediate memory for short lists of two-syllable words that usually are pronounced quickly (e.g., bishop) or slowly (e.g., harpoon). The memory performance was higher for the words that could be more quickly pronounced. The phonological loop view would predict this difference because the faster a word can be pronounced (or subvocalized), the more words can be rehearsed before the test. (Cowan, 1994, discusses additional related effects.)

The phonological loop idea gives a very different interpretation of the immediate memory span than does the chunking view of Miller (1956). Miller, as discussed in the last section, argued that the span was due to how many chunks the information could be divided into, with people able to remember a certain number of chunks (around 7). According to the phonological loop view, it is not the number of chunks that is crucial, but rather how long it takes to rehearse the information. Thus, if the chunks are fast to rehearse then the memory span is greater than if the chunks are slower to rehearse (as shown by the Baddeley et al., 1975, paper just mentioned).

What is the function of the phonological loop? A first guess might be that it is crucial for language comprehension; that is, perhaps this subsystem helps to keep speech available so that we can better understand what is being said by making inferences and connecting words such as pronouns to their referents (see Chapter 9). However, some evidence casts doubt on this possibility. For example, a brain-damaged patient who has a memory span of only two items and has great difficulty maintaining verbal information nevertheless has been found to have normal language comprehension (Martin, 1993). Thus, the phonological loop must not be necessary for language comprehension.

Baddeley, Gathercole, and Papagno (1998) suggest that the main function of the phonological loop may be for acquiring language, especially learning new words. They believe that this subsystem evolved to help people maintain the phonological forms of new words while more permanent memory records were being constructed. For children, learning new words is a crucial part of language acquisition, and it often requires them to temporarily store novel phonological material. So, Baddeley and his colleagues argue that while we think about the phonological loop in adults as allowing this echoing back of recent words or aiding us in memory span tests, it may have come about for a very different purpose. As one type of evidence, they point out that phonological loop performance is often related to children's memory of nonwords (e.g., bleximus) but not to their learning of words. Baddeley et al. also speculate that the phonological loop might be helpful in learning syntax (see Chapter 9).

VISUOSPATIAL SKETCHPAD   Close your eyes. (Sorry; first read the rest of this paragraph and *then* close your eyes.) Picture a cone-shaped object. Now imagine rotating this object so that you can see around the cone, then its bottom, then its top.

The visuospatial sketchpad allows us to maintain and manipulate visual and spatial images (see Chapter 8 for further examples). The effects discussed earlier in this chapter suggest that this sketchpad operates separately from the phonological loop. To remind you of one effect, the use of the sketchpad is interfered with by visual tasks but not by verbal tasks; the phonological loop is interfered with by verbal tasks but not by visual tasks.

The phonological loop and visuospatial sketchpad are the two main subsystems that have been examined, but it may be that further distinctions are necessary. As one example, the research by Martha Farah and her colleagues (discussed more fully in Chapter 8) has shown that there are both visual and spatial representations being used, perhaps suggesting that the sketchpad needs to be further divided. Additional evidence for this distinction comes from research using the PET neuro-imaging technique, in which spatial and visual tasks led to very different patterns of brain activity (Smith & Jonides, 1997).

What is the function of the visuospatial sketchpad? Baddeley and Hitch (1994) suggest that it may be involved in planning and executing spatial tasks. Because the visual world around us changes quickly, it may be crucial to have a system that can keep track of recent visuospatial information. Even as we simply move through the world, we need to keep track of how the stationary objects change relative to our location. In addition, the world does not usually stand still for us, and we need to constantly update how the locations of moving objects are changing.

CENTRAL EXECUTIVE   There seems to be an important mechanism in cognitive systems that allows us to select among possible actions. At this time, however, the central executive is not yet well understood. Because working memory has more than one subsystem, something is needed that helps to allocate attention focused on the different subsystems and how they are coordinated. In addition, the output of these subsystems needs to be used (such as to verbalize the phonological loop to repeat back items in a memory span task). The central executive component is the part of working memory that performs those functions.

The importance of being able to coordinate these subsystems can be seen in an interesting line of research (cited in Baddeley & Hitch, 1994, p. 490). It appears that coordination may be affected in particular types of brain damage, such as Alzheimer's disease. They report work in which a task was chosen that primarily taps a particular subsystem: digit span for the phonological loop and tracking for the sketchpad. (Tracking requires people to be aware of the spatial location of an object over time as it moves.) They selected Alzheimer's patients whose performance on each task was as good as the performance of normal subjects. However, when the subjects had to perform the two tasks simultaneously, the Alzheimer's patients showed a much greater impairment than did the normal subjects. This result suggests a separate coordination process that may be selectively impaired in Alzheimer's patients. The evidence is only suggestive at this time, but it does show that there is much promise in combining cognitive theory and neuropsychological work (see Smith & Jonides, 1997, for discussion).

The Future of Working Memory

After reading this section on working memory, you may have a number of questions. Some of your questions may reflect the fact that there are many unanswered questions in this field. One question may be, "Why these two subsystems?" In fact, there is no commitment to these two subsystems. As the work described so far suggests, the visuospatial sketchpad is likely to consist of two very different subsystems, with visual and spatial representations. In addition, there are suggestions that there may need to be a much larger number of subsystems, such as ones to deal with the meaning of the stimuli (Schneider & Detweiler, 1987). Other interesting work has indicated that people can encode specific odor information (White, Hornung, et al., 1998), plus people who know sign language may encode signs in a special subsystem (Wilson & Emmorey, 1998). Baddeley acknowledges the possibility of further subsystems. However, more experimental evidence is needed before adding any new subsystem to ensure it is used across a variety of tasks. Much still remains to be learned about this working memory view, especially about the critical central executive component. (See Kimberg, Desposito, & Farah, 1997, for views that do not incorporate a central executive.)

Summary

In this section on short-term memory, we have discussed how it is important to have some information that is quickly available. One purpose of such information is to allow the information to be used in reasoning, comprehension, etc. A second purpose is to keep the information available for storage in a long-term memory. In addition, one can retrieve information from long-term memory and use it to augment information in short-term memory (and then use it for reasoning, comprehension, etc.).

An important characteristic of short-term memory is that it limits the amount of information that is quickly available. This limitation allows us to focus on what might be most relevant, but does so at the expense of losing some information. Chunking provides one means of using this limited short-term memory in a way to increase the limitation.

Much of the work in this area over the last 20 years has focused on the idea of working memory. Baddeley's view is that there is a central executive that coordinates the activities of two subsystems: the phonological loop and the visuospatial sketchpad. This section outlined each of these subsystems, the evidence for them, and recent work extending our understanding of each. As just mentioned, there is still much work to be done both in understanding the central executive and delineating the subsystems. Nonetheless, it seems that a simple view of short-term memory as a single unitary store is unable to account for many of these findings. Working memory is an intellectual descendant of short-term memory, incorporating many of its ideas but extending them to include multiple subsystems and a central executive. (Throughout the book, we will often use short-term memory and working memory interchangeably since, for those purposes, the important point is that there exists a mechanism that retains information for a short time.)

LONG-TERM MEMORY

Introduction

Items that enter a person's memory system and survive the critical first few seconds may be retained for very long periods. In fact, there is a real question whether memories, once established, are ever completely lost. But if **long-term memory** is permanent, why does it sometimes fail or even mislead us, as when our memory for an event changes over time? Why do nearly all of us often have difficulty in recalling names and dates or the details of lectures or textbook chapters?

Even a partial answer to the central question of the fallibility of memory is complex. We need to keep in mind two general themes. First, people are faced with figuring out which information from their huge store of knowledge might be relevant to any situation. Second, the information they are given is often incomplete and must be augmented. Together, these ideas lead to a conception of the human as an active— as opposed to passive—processor of information. The ability to remember will be

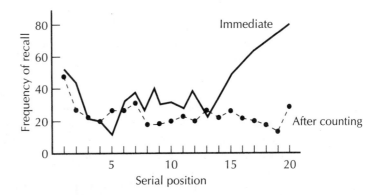

Figure 5.4   Serial position functions for free recall tests given immediately after the presentation of a 20-word list as compared to a test given after a 30-second delay, during which subjects were counting backward.

Source: Postman & Phillips, 1965.

affected by the processes that occur at the time the information is learned (i.e., how it is encoded and organized), as well as the processes that occur at the time the information is retrieved. Let's start with a simple example of remembering, which also illustrates active processing of the material being learned.

One technique that has proven useful in analyzing memory is known as **free recall.** In the simplest form of a free recall experiment, the subject is presented with a list of words and asked to reproduce from memory as many of the words as possible. Though the task sounds simple, even extremely intelligent and literate adults can typically remember only a relatively small number of words from a random list (for example, on the order of 10 to 20 out of a list of 50 words). The study of the factors responsible for this limitation has taught us much about memory.

For example, the probability of recalling an item depends on where it appeared in the list, a phenomenon referred to as the **serial position effect** (Figure 5.4). Items at the beginning and at the end of the list are more likely to be recalled than items in the middle of the list. The increased recall for items at the beginning of the list is referred to as the **primacy effect;** the increased recall for the last items is the **recency effect.** Why are these items better recalled?

Let us begin by examining the recency effect. Suppose we delay recall for half a minute or so while distracting the subjects by, for example, asking them to solve an arithmetic problem or to count out loud. After this delay, the recall of items at the end of the list suffers, but performance on the items in the beginning and middle positions remains unaffected (Figure 5.4). One interpretation of this finding is that the recency effect occurs because items at the end of a list are being recalled from short-term memory (or the phonological loop of working memory) and the arithmetic task presumably eliminates this advantage. Because recall of items in other positions is not similarly affected, they presumably are being recalled from long-term memory. This account of the recency effect has been generally accepted for a number of years and has intuitive appeal. Although there is still some debate about this interpretation (see Crowder, 1993), the best current explanation for the recency effect with immediate free recall is that people are recalling items from short-term memory.

What causes the primacy effect? One explanation relies on the idea discussed earlier that short-term memory is influential in determining what information is transferred into long-term memory but is limited in the number of items it can hold. By this account, subjects may actively rehearse items to try to remember them but can rehearse only a few items at a time. When the early part of the list is being encoded, items may be added without bumping out other items because the short-term memory limit has not been exceeded. Thus, items very early in the list generally will be retained longer in short-term memory, leading to more rehearsal and better long-term memory for these items. This robust finding is one illustration of how people may actively process material and how this active processing may affect their memory for the material. We now consider more complex cases of how information is encoded and retrieved, as well as the important relationship between encoding and retrieval.

Encoding

Everyone understands that what activities we engage in when an event occurs affect the probability that the event will be remembered. For example, quickly reading a section of text (such as this one) while thinking about some personal problem will lead to far worse memory for the text than concentrating and writing a summary of the text after reading it. **Encoding** refers to this initial processing of the item that leads to a representation of it in memory. In this section we consider four encoding influences on memory: levels of processing, memory for meaning, organization, and elaboration.

Levels of Processing

Craik and Lockhart (1972) proposed that an item could be processed in a number of different ways and that the resulting memory depended on how the item was processed. This approach, referred to as **levels of processing** or sometimes *depth of processing,* argued that we should be focusing not only on the material being learned but also on how the person encodes such information. They further argued that these different ways of processing information could be viewed as a continuum that ranges from the shallow analysis of physical characteristics of the item to the deeper level of meaning. These differences in encoding processes are crucial because they can have large effects on what is remembered.

As one example, Craik and Tulving (1975) presented subjects with a list of 60 concrete nouns about which the subjects had to answer one of three questions (see Table 5.1 for examples). The questions required subjects to examine the *case* (upper vs. lower) in which the word was typed, the sound of the word for a *rhyme*, or the

Table 5.1   **Study Conditions for a Levels-of-Processing Experiment***

		Response	
Condition	**Question**	**Yes**	**No**
Case	Is the word in capital letters?	TABLE	table
Rhyme	Does the word rhyme with *weight*?	crate	market
Sentence	Would the word fit the sentence:	friend	cloud
	"He met a _____ in the street"?		

*Typical questions and words presented. Subjects would see one of the two possible words (e.g., *crate* or *market*) and then be tested on their memory for the words that had been presented.
Source: Craik & Tulving, 1975.

meaning of the word to see if it fit in a *sentence*. For example, as in the table, the sentence condition would ask if the word fit in a particular sentence and then give the word for which half the time the answer would be yes and half the time no. These questions were chosen to induce increasingly deeper levels of processing by the Craik and Lockhart account. The questions were presented auditorily and were followed 2 seconds later by a brief (200 milliseconds, or 1/5 of a second) presentation of the word. Subjects then answered the question. Following this question-answering procedure for all 60 words, subjects were given a *recognition test* in which they had to identify which words they had seen in the list. More specifically, they were given 180 words and asked to check off the words about which they had been asked questions. The results are quite straightforward. The probability of recognizing a word increased substantially from the case condition (17%), to the rhyme condition (37%), to the sentence condition (65%). Thus, even though the word was presented for only a short time and the encoding manipulation was simple, there was a large difference in recognition memory.

The Craik and Tulving study used an **incidental learning** procedure in that the subjects were not aware that they would be required to remember the words for a later test. Does this levels analysis make the correct predictions even when subjects know about the later test? The answer is yes. As one example, Hyde and Jenkins (1969) presented words to subjects and asked them either to indicate the number of letters in the word (a low level of processing) or to rate the pleasantness of the items (requiring a deeper analysis of meaning). The subjects were then given a surprise free recall test. As in the Craik and Tulving study, the deeper analysis group (pleasantness) remembered substantially more, 68% versus 39%. In addition, two other groups were tested with the same tasks but were told before they rated the words that there would be a final recall test. These groups showed almost exactly the same difference as the groups not told about the final recall test (69% versus 43%). Knowledge about a final test appears to have little effect on memory, whereas the level to which the material is processed has a large effect.

Although many studies showed effects of processing on memory, the levels of processing approach was criticized by a number of researchers (e.g., Baddeley,

1978). One criticism is that the idea of different levels of processing was based on intuition and no independent measure of depth was provided. Thus, the interpretations of experiments had a circularity: Those types of processing that led to better memory were deeper, and deeper processing led to better memory. A second criticism, which we will discuss in detail shortly, is that what is better remembered often depends on how the memory is tested. Despite these criticisms, however, we believe that the levels-of-processing framework helped to focus researchers on the important question of how the processing of material affects memory.

Memory for Meaning

We have been considering how people may remember an unrelated set of words, but such remembering does not characterize many real-world uses of memory. We often do not need to remember a precise set of words, but rather their meaning.

The extent to which the goal of understanding affects what is remembered can be understood by the errors people make when tested for their memory of meaningful material. One type of error occurs because the act of comprehending sentences often includes plausible inferences, and the results of these inferences may be indistinguishable in memory from information actually given. For example, if a few minutes after you read the sentence "Three turtles rested on a floating log and a fish swam beneath it" you are asked whether you had read that the fish swam under the turtles, you are very likely to say yes. In fact, Bransford, Barclay, and Franks (1972) showed that when people were tested for exactly what they had read, they were generally unable to distinguish between the literal information and natural inferences based on the information. However, the subjects detected even small changes in sentences that altered the meaning. For example, if subjects saw the sentence above substituting "beside" for "on," they would know that they had not seen a sentence about a fish swimming under the turtles.

Organization

So far, we have focused on memory for single items or events. Often, however, our encoding of and memory for an item depends critically on other items that are present. In particular, if the items can be organized in some way, performance often increases.

An experiment by Bower, Clark, Lesgold, and Winzenz (1969) shows that organization improves memory. They presented groups of about 28 items either organized by their category (e.g., rare metals such as silver and gold; common metals such as lead and iron, etc.) or in a random order for four trials, with a recall test after each trial. They found that the grouped presentation led to much better performance. On the first trial, the grouped and random conditions recalled 65% and 18%, respectively. The grouped condition recalled 95% of the words on the second trial and all the words on the third and fourth trials. The performance of the random condition also improved with trials, but by the fourth trial recall was 63%, less than the grouped condition's performance on the first trial. Clearly, organization of the information at encoding can greatly improve memory performance. (Halpern, 1986, presents an interesting similar experiment involving memory for song titles with the organization by genre, such as Christmas songs.)

Elaborations

Often when we are presented with some information, we not only encode its meaning but also elaborate or explain it. For example, on seeing a woman at a door opening an umbrella, we may make a simple elaboration that she is doing so because she is about to go out, it is raining, and she does not want to get wet. These elaborations provide a means of integrating and retaining information to the extent that they help relate the current information to our knowledge.

The effect of such relevant elaborations is nicely illustrated in a study by Stein and Bransford (1979). Ten sentences were presented that had a simple idea (e.g., "The fat man read the sign"), an irrelevant elaboration (e.g., "The fat man read the sign that was two feet high"), or a relevant elaboration (e.g., "The fat man read the sign warning about thin ice"). After a short delay, subjects were given the simple idea sentences with the adjective (e.g., "fat") blanked out and asked to fill in the appropriate adjective. The adjective was recalled 42% of the time by subjects who had read the simple sentences, but 74% of the time by subjects who had read the sentences with relevant elaborations. Therefore, elaborations that help to integrate the materials with prior knowledge facilitate memory for the materials. (Also of interest, the subjects who read the irrelevant elaborations recalled the adjective only 22% of the time, a reliable decrease from the simple sentence condition.)

Elaboration has been recognized as an important part of our memory processes and examined in a variety of situations. For example, in many studies, as well as in life, older people recall much less than young adults, sometimes as little as half as much in laboratory experiments. Although there may be aspects of memory that get worse with age and that nothing can be done about, older people may be able to remember more with some memory aids, such as elaborations. Cherry, Park, Frieske, and Rowley (1993) tested this idea. With no elaborations, they replicated the usual finding of worse memory for older people. However, when older people (mean age of 68 years) were given elaborations at both encoding and retrieval, their recall was as high as that of young adults, who also had the elaborations at encoding and retrieval. (For other effects of elaborations, see Reder, 1979, for the role of elaborations in memory for prose, and Reder, Charney, & Morgan, 1986, for how elaborations might be used in teaching people computer skills from computer manuals.)

These elaborations can be viewed as helping to augment and interpret the information; that is, we take the incomplete information presented, augment it with further information from our memory, and interpret it. As we will see in Chapter 7, often it is easier to remember more if the information to be remembered fits together well. Thus, elaborations may greatly influence our memory. However, one should keep in mind that there is also a possible downside to interpreting and augmenting our knowledge with what we already know—the encoding of new information may be changed to conform to our prior knowledge.

Retrieval

Let us now assume that you have encoded information and want to remember it. Suppose you had just taken a vacation and someone asked you what you had done. How would you retrieve the various memories for the vacation? One possibility would be to start thinking about the vacation and tell the person about whatever events pop into your head. The problem with this approach is that less accessible events may not come to mind. Depending on what events are remembered, it is possible that an entire part of your vacation will not be recalled. A very different means of describing the vacation events would be to think about your vacation in chronological order and recall events in the order that they occurred. Although such an approach does not guarantee that all events will be remembered, it will often increase the number of events recalled.

As an experiment, time someone to see how many animals he or she can name in 1 minute. Then give him a minute to name states as fast as he can think of them. Although there are many more animals than there are states, chances are very good that the person will name more states than animals in the minute. It is easy to generate states rapidly because one can use a natural retrieval plan based on geographic location (e.g., Washington, Oregon, California, etc.). Of course, there are many ways of organizing the generation of animal names (e.g., farm animals, zoo animals), but they do not provide for a systematic order of recall and one often finds that names already recalled come to mind again. One person who was able to generate a large number of animal names in a minute imagined himself walking through a particular zoo and recalled the animals in each area as he (mentally) passed by.

In both of these examples, recall is much higher if the person has a **retrieval plan**—an organized set of cues to use to retrieve the information. One of the main difficulties in recalling information concerns developing an organized plan for retrieval. The plan needs to have two main characteristics. First, the various cues in the plan should be organized so that no cue is likely to be forgotten. In the states example, if you remembered the states by regions, you would be better off using adjacent regions such as Northeast, then Middle Atlantic, rather than jumping from Pacific Northwest to Southeast. Second, each cue in the plan should be able to lead to the recall of a number of items not recallable from other cues and also do so in as systematic a way as possible (so items are not recalled more than once or missed altogether). With an appropriate retrieval plan, the organized cues will guide retrieval and lead to more items being recalled.

M. D. Williams and Hollan (1981) examined a particularly interesting case of how people use retrieval plans by asking people to recall the names of their high school classmates. The subjects could, of course, quickly remember a number of people whom they knew well. After that, though, they developed various retrieval plans for remembering additional classmates. Although these plans were not as completely organized and systematic as the types of plans for remembering states, they did help in remembering people who would otherwise not be recalled. For example, one common strategy was to think of particular high school activities (e.g., baseball team, band, cheerleading) and then try to name people who participated. As long as many different activities are used, recall may be greatly improved. (Note that generating these activities might also benefit from a retrieval plan, such as athletic activities, musical activities, etc.) The point is that we do have strategies that we can use at retrieval to increase what we can remember.

Encoding-Retrieval Interactions

We have been considering how encoding and retrieval may affect memory for events. However, the picture is more complicated than that. It is useful to consider an analogy between human memory and a library. The remarkable fact about a large library is that one is normally able to obtain quickly almost any one of the millions of volumes stored in the stacks. The secret of this capability lies in the organization and retrieval systems. Books can usually be found regardless of the number of books stored because they are coded, books having the same codes are shelved together, and the codes are related to "pointers" filed in the card catalog. It is crucial that the same cues used for encoding information also be used for retrieving that information. One cannot get rapid access to a book if all one knows is that it has a green cover and was written by a person whose middle initial is E. Memory clearly differs from a library organization in many ways, but our ability to remember something critically depends on the cues at retrieval being similar to how the memory was encoded.

A major principle of memory is that recall or recognition of an event usually increases with the amount of the original context that is supplied at the time when retention is tested. If one thinks of a primary use of memory as retrieving relevant information, then the retrieval of information in a similar context to the current situation (as opposed to a different context) is a good guess as to its relevance.

This importance of context is nicely illustrated in the difference between recognition and recall. Recognition is generally believed to be easier and more accurate than recall. One reason is that the individual being tested is presented with more of the context of the original experience than would be the case on a recall test. Thus, if a student has read in a text assignment that John B. Watson was the founder of behaviorism and we wanted to test the student's knowledge of this fact, we might present the statement "The founder of behaviorism was John B. Watson" and ask the student to respond "true" or "false." Because nearly all of the elements that the individual was attending to at the time of the original learning are supplied as part of the test, conditions are optimal for retrieving the relevant long-term memory. We might, by contrast, ask, "Who founded behaviorism?" In that case, part of the original context is missing, and conditions are less favorable for reactivating the relevant memory.

Encoding Specificity

How can we be sure that this difference between recognition and recall reflects encoding-retrieval matching of context rather than simply the fact that recognition is easier than recall? The answer is quite simple: because it is possible to find situations in which recognition is worse than recall, and these situations occur when the match between encoding and retrieval contexts is greater for recall than for recognition. Much of the work in this area is due to the efforts of Endel Tulving and his colleagues. The methodology and ideas are quite complicated, so we start here with a simpler situation (based on a study by Light & Carter-Sobell, 1970). Suppose you were given a list of word pairs (e.g., *river bank*) and asked to remember the second word of each pair. Later you might be given one of two tests. In the recognition test, you would be given a word pair (e.g., *piggy bank*) and asked if you remember having seen the second word on the original list. In the cued recall test, you would be given a cue (e.g., *river*) and asked to recall the word from the original list that it had been paired with. On which test do you think you would do better? In fact, performance is usually higher on the cued recall test.

Clearly, the difficulty in the recognition test is that the word *bank* has two very different meanings. Even though you are being asked to recognize the word you saw before, if you encode it very differently (i.e., with a different meaning, such as *piggy bank*) you may be unable to remember having seen it earlier. The cued recall task, however, asks you to recall a word consistent with the meaning you encoded earlier. Thus, recognition may be harder than recall because the encoding is not consistent with recognition, but it is consistent with recall.

Tulving and his associates have conducted a large number of studies that show the same **encoding specificity effect** (i.e., that retrieval depends on matching the specific encoding), where the differences between the encodings are much more subtle. For example, the word *light* can be thought of as having a number of related meanings such as "a bulb" and "not dark." Tulving showed that if on a recognition test, subjects used a different sense of the word than they did in encoding, then recognition could be quite low. In fact, if a cued recall test used the same sense as at encoding, performance could be even higher than in the recognition test. Memory is not simply a matter of how well an item is encoded but also a matter of how well the study encoding matches the test.

Consider the example illustrated in Table 5.2 (which is a simplification of the design of Tulving & Thomson, 1973, Experiment 2). For the 24 critical items, subjects were shown the target word (e.g., LIGHT) in capital letters and a weakly associated word (e.g., *head*) in lowercase letters. There were four tasks that together comprised the experiment. First, as the study task, subjects were instructed that their task was to learn the words in capital letters but that they might find it useful to use the words in lowercase letters. Second, subjects participated in a free association task that included generating six words to a strong associate of each target word. For example, the word *dark* may have been given, for which a large proportion of subjects generated the word LIGHT (the target) as one of the six words. The purpose of this task was to get subjects to generate the target words, but in a different sense than the original target word (*light* as in "dark," not *light* as in "headlight"). Third, subjects were asked to look over the words that they had generated and mark any that had been target words in the first part of the experiment (i.e., a recognition test). Hence, the recognition was tested with the word encoded in a different sense than it had been at study. Finally, they were given a cued recall test in which the word studied with the target word was provided (e.g., *head*) and they were asked to generate the target word studied with this word.

Table 5.2   **Phases of an Encoding Specificity Experiment**

1. **Study list:** Learn target words in capital letters.

Cue	Target
head	LIGHT
grasp	BABY

2. **Free association:** Generate 6 words to each word presented.

Word	Possible generated responses
dark	light, black, room . . .
infant	sleeping, bottle, baby . . .

3. **Recognition:** Mark any generated words that were on the study list in capital letters.

4. **Recall:** Recall the words from the study list in capital letters, using these cues that they were studied with.

grasp _____

head _____

Results: Recognition—22% of the generated words that were on the study list were marked as having been on the study list.

Recall—59% of the study list words were recalled.

Source: Tulving & Thomson, 1973.

How does this experiment show recognition can be worse than recall? In the third task, recognition, when checking off the free associates that had been target words, the exact target word was often included, and subjects needed only to decide if it had been in the first part of the experiment. In the final cued recall task, the subjects needed to generate the target word given the word with which it had been studied. If recognition is easier than recall, one would expect higher performance in recognizing target words than in generating target words from the cues. However, contrary to this expectation, only 22% of the generated targets were recognized,

Table 5.3   **Studied Words Recalled Under Different Combinations of Encoding Condition and Retrieval Cue**

Retrieval Cue	Encoding Condition	
	Rhyme	Sentence
Rhyme	40%	29%
Sentence	10%	78%
Mean	25.0%	53.5%

Source: Fisher & Craik, 1977.

while 59% of the targets were recalled when cued by the words with which they had been studied (e.g., recall of LIGHT when cued by *head*). Thus, the context in the cued recall test matched the study encoding better than did the context of the recognition test, and performance was higher in the cued recall test. The match between encoding and retrieval context is crucial for understanding how well items are remembered—the encoding specificity effect.

Encoding-retrieval interactions are powerful enough to override some other types of memory effects. Remember that in our discussion of encoding effects we described a study by Craik and Tulving that showed semantic (meaning-related) processing of words (such as required in the "sentence" condition) led to better memory than did processing for a rhyme (Table 5.1). Fisher and Craik (1977) argue that the better memory for semantic processing may be because when no retrieval cue is specified, people are likely to use semantic cues. They conducted a study similar to that of Craik and Tulving in which some of the words were encoded by rhymes and some by meaning, but now some of the cues at test were rhymes. For example, they might be asked during study when shown the target word *crate*, "Does it rhyme with the following word: weight?" At test, they were given a number of different cues (including *weight*) and asked to recall as many of the target words as they could. The relevant data are presented in Table 5.3. When tested with rhyme cues, words learned under the rhyming condition were recalled better than words learned with the sentence encoding condition (40% to 29%). However, this result does not negate the importance of encoding condition. Encoding words by meaning often leads to better recall than encoding them by their sound. In fact, even in the Fisher and Craik study, although the sentence condition led to lower recall than did the rhyming condition when there was a rhyme cue, the sentence condition had much higher recall for sentence cues (78% to 10%), and so had a higher overall recall rate, as can be seen in Table 5.3. Nonetheless, it does show that the encoding-retrieval interactions can be quite strong and are important to an understanding of memory.

Context Change

The work just discussed shows that memory for an item is affected by the match of encodings at learning and retrieval. Other research has examined the effect on changing contexts, even when the same item is encoded and tested. *Context* refers to all the information that might be encoded aside from the item of interest. For example, we just discussed how the surrounding cues can affect the meaning encoded. The work on context examines the influence of even more peripheral factors and has focused on two types of context cues: external cues such as the physical environment and internal cues such as body states. Each research area has yielded evidence for the importance of context in remembering. **Context effects** refer to the improvement (or decrement) in memory of having information occur with the same (or different) context.

The research on environmental context shows that being in the same physical setting for the learning and testing of new material improves recall. The most dramatic example of this idea is the research of Godden and Baddeley (1975). They had scuba divers learn lists of words either on land or about 20 feet underwater and then tested them in one or the other setting. The recall was almost 50% better if the test occurred in the same setting as during learning. Less dramatically, Steven Smith (Smith, 1979, 1986; Smith, Glenberg, & Bjork, 1978) has shown that recall is facilitated if the test occurs in the same room as the learning. The effect has proven difficult to obtain when recognition is the measure, but recent results suggest that it can be reliably obtained under certain conditions (Murnane & Phelps, 1993).

In addition to the effects of external context, memory is influenced by major changes in internal context as well—how one feels inside can partially determine how items are encoded and retrieved. For example, a person who has too much to drink one night may have little memory of the evening's events the next day. Nonetheless, this memory failure is not permanent, and the individual may well recover this memory the next time he or she drinks too much. This influence of memory on matching internal contexts of alcohol or drug states is referred to as **state-dependent recall,** because the memory is influenced by one's internal state (though the effects tend to be small). This effect of internal context extends to one's mood as well. For example, Gordon Bower (1981), with a standard free recall paradigm, found that people sometimes recalled more if they were in the same mood (happy or sad) at study and test (see Blach, Myers, & Papotto, 1999, for a recent review). This research has important implications for therapy as well, since depressed patients will tend to recall more unpleasant memories.

Thus, a number of experimental results show the effects of external and internal context on memory. There is still much controversy over exactly when context effects occur (see Eich, 1995; S. M. Smith, 1994), suggesting that our understanding of context is incomplete. This difficulty should not obscure the fact that context can have large influences on memory or the consensus that an understanding of context is necessary for understanding memory. Memory is very sensitive to the subtle changes of how an item is encoded and retrieved.

Spacing Effect

Although the encoding specificity and context change experiments may appear to be contrived situations, the importance of matching conditions between study and test is evident in many situations. We present one illustration here that also allows us to discuss an interesting empirical finding, the **spacing effect.**

A DEBATE
Odor, Emotion, and Memory

We not only see and hear things—we also smell them. Odor is an important sensory property for many objects, and odors are often associated in memory to particularly emotion-laden events. Many of us have memories of the odor of favorite childhood foods or even the distinctive odor of a loved one (or loved automobile). In addition, odors can provide a very distinctive environmental context and may lead to context effects. That is, if a distinctive ambient odor is present during learning of a list, then memory of the items is higher if the odor is also present during test. How should we account for odor-based context effects?

One possibility is to think of the odor as a concept in memory that gets linked to items in the list. (This is similar to a number of explanations for context effects, and does provide a clear account for much of the data.) An alternative, however, is that odor, because of its emotion-related influences, might behave very differently than these other context effects. Odor may be particularly influential when emotion is involved.

(Continued)

The spacing effect refers to the common observation that memory is better for repeated information if the repetitions occur spaced over time than if they occur massed, one after the other. This effect is remarkably robust, found with a variety of materials, study conditions, types of tests, and situations outside the laboratory (see, e.g., Glenberg, 1976; Hintzman, 1976; S. M. Smith & Rothkopf, 1984). As one example, an early study by Melton and Shulman (cited in Melton, 1970) involved presenting subjects with lists of 48 words, 24 of which appeared twice in the list. The twice-presented items were repeated after either 0, 2, 4, 8, 20, or 40 intervening items. Different groups of subjects were shown the items at different rates of presentation before a free recall test. The data are presented in Figure 5.5. As the number of events between repetitions increased, the probability of recall increased.

What causes this spacing effect? Once again, attempts to decide among competing explanations have led to a deeper understanding of how it may depend on several different factors (see, e.g., Glenberg, 1979; Greene, 1989). One cause particularly relevant here is the effect of varying encodings and context. Suppose you are presented with a list of words to remember. When repetitions occur, the further apart they are the more likely you will encode the word differently (you can imagine what would happen with multiple-meaning words such as *bank,* but as we saw with encoding specificity, even the encodings of single-meaning words may change). A number of studies have shown that experimentally manipulating the encoding of

A DEBATE
Odor, Emotion, and Memory *(Continued)*

Herz (1998) tested these possibilities in a clever way. Students wrote autobiographical memories that were evoked by each of 16 words. (Note that this is an incidental learning technique that often leads to fairly good memory for the words.) The odor manipulation of context was whether the odor, a somewhat unpleasant odor of violet leaf, was present at study or not. The emotion-related manipulation was anxiety and relied on the fact that students are often anxious before an exam. Half the students participated in the study before they were to take an exam, whereas the other half had no exam scheduled that day. One week later, all students were tested on recall of the 16 words on a day they did not have an exam. Herz found that the recall of the groups depended on their combination of stress and odor. In particular, the group that had an exam the day of study remembered far more when an odor was present during study than when it was not (59% vs. 33%). The non-exam groups were little affected by the odor being present or not (46% vs. 41%). Thus, odor appears to be especially helpful in aiding memory when emotion (or in this case, anxiety) is involved.

items changes the spacing effect. For example, Madigan (1969) manipulated encodings by a technique similar to that used in encoding specificity (i.e., presenting the critical word with another word next to it to influence its encoding). He found (1) that different encodings led to better recall and (2) that the effect of the different encodings was larger on the massed items, which would usually be encoded in the same way otherwise.

Some later work suggests that the spacing effect may depend importantly on the repetition *reminding* the learner of the earlier presentation (see, e.g., Bellezza & Young, 1989). By this account, the learner then stores some information about the changes in the encoding and context from the prior presentation. At some later test, this reminding may provide additional information that might be retrieved and used in remembering that the particular word was presented. A finding consistent with this interpretation is that spacing effects occur only for items recognized on the second presentation (Bellezza, Winkler, & Andrasik, 1975). Whatever the future evidence about this particular explanation, the variations in the spaced presentations appear to be an important component of the spacing effect. Because the changes in encoding and context are greater with greater spacing, spaced presentations tend to be better remembered than massed presentations (Greene, 1989).

The spacing effect is not due simply to the encodings, however; it also depends critically on the retrieval conditions. As one simple example, Glenberg (1976) finds

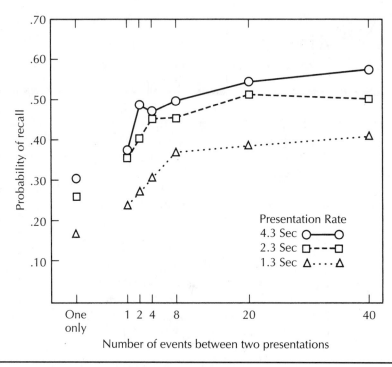

Source: Melton, 1970.

Figure 5.5   **Illustration of the Spacing Effect**   The figure shows the probability of recalling words occurring once or twice with varying number of other words between the two presentations. The three curves each represent data for different rates of visual presentation of the words. From data of Melton and Shulman.

that long spacings lead to worse memory than shorter spacings at short retention intervals. At short retention intervals, the test context is more similar to the learning context than at long intervals. Thus, the spacing effect depends on the change in encoding and context between presentations, as well as their relationship to the retrieval context.

Although most studies have examined spacing effects for short spacings and delays, the effects appear to work over a very long time. Bahrick, Bahrick, Bahrick, and Bahrick (1993) present an interesting case in which all four authors (members of a family) studied foreign language vocabulary for up to 4 years and then tested themselves over the next 5 years. The words were tested at 14-day intervals, 28-day intervals, or 56-day intervals (2, 4, or 8 weeks, respectively). The recall data for all the words are presented in Figure 5.6. As can be seen there, recall decreased with the delay between the final study period and the test, as would be expected. Most interesting, the greater the spacing between study intervals, the higher the recall, and this effect persisted (and even grew) at the end of 5 years. Even though the words were studied equally often, for the test after 5 years, those words studied every 56 days were recalled more than one and a half times as well as the ones studied every 14

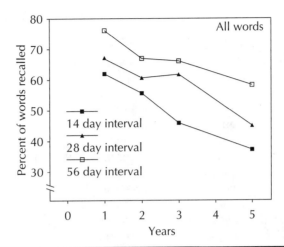

Figure 5.6   Recall of foreign language vocabulary words as a function of spacing at study for retention intervals of 1 to 5 years.

Source: Bahrick, Bahrick, Bahrick, & Bahrick, 1993.

days. The spacing effect is a very robust finding (and suggests that students will remember the information longer by spacing their study during a course).

Encoding and Retrieval in the Brain

Our discussion has focused on memory tasks with behavioral measures, such as recall or recognition. However, there has been a great deal of research over the last few years in cognitive neuroscience examining how the brain might accomplish various memory tasks. Let us just mention a couple of results.

First, can one tell by examining the activation in the brain during study which items are likely to be remembered well later? The answer appears to be yes, at least under some circumstances. In one study, Wagner, Schacter, et al. (1998) asked subjects in an fMRI machine to decide if each word during study was abstract or concrete. (Remember that fMRI, functional magnetic resonance imaging, is a technique for examining what regions of the brain are most active.) Later (outside of the machine), subjects were asked to decide whether a word had been seen earlier or not. The activation in particular regions predicted whether particular items are likely to be remembered well. (See Schacter, 1996, 1999, for very readable discussions.)

Second, can one get evidence about particular cognitive processes from looking at the brain activation? Yes, but it is important to realize that this involves lots of complex inferences, and we are just beginning to learn how to do it. It is amazing to imagine that we will be able to isolate how various processes occur in the brain. Increases in knowledge about brain function will have a significant impact on our understanding of cognitive processes (as well as provide new ideas for dealing with cognitive difficulties). However, the brain is enormously complex and there is much

AN APPLICATION

How to Study for Exams and Remember Names of People You Meet

Two very common questions asked of cognitive psychologists are: How can I better study for exams, and how can I better remember names of people when I first meet them? Let us use the principles we have examined in this chapter to suggest some answers.

How should you study for exams? As this chapter shows, there is much we know about effective study—it is important to encode the meaning of the material, organize it, and elaborate it. The most useful advice is that you need to be an active processor of the information, not just a passive reader of the text and notes. It is also useful to understand the type of test you will be getting so you can understand the cues that will be most helpful during the exam. For instance, if you are going to be asked definitions, then you need to be able to generate the definitions given the term, whereas if it is a multiple-choice test, you need to be able to recognize the correct definition for each term. Our best advice for the next step in studying is to space your practice. If you are going to study eight hours for an exam, you are much better studying one hour a night for eight nights than you are studying eight hours the day before. (This also works if you are going to study much smaller amounts of time as well.) Cramming for an exam will sometimes allow good test performance on an exam immediately after your study time, but if you want to retain the material for longer times, then spaced practice is far superior (see

(Continued)

to be learned about how to interpret brain activations. For example, one group of researchers conducted a study that suggested that they had isolated different regions for encoding and retrieval (Nyberg, Cabeza, & Tulving, 1996). However, Nolde, Johnson, and Raye (1998) examined these results along with a number of other studies and ended up with a very different interpretation in terms of whether the processes required to perform the task are simple or more complex.

We do not want to prejudge this current controversy, but rather use it as an illustration. There is a lot to learn. What has become clear is that the two areas of cognitive psychology and cognitive neuroscience advance through interaction. On the one hand, the brain measures suggest situations in which we might want to treat two phenomena as different (because they lead to activation of different brain areas), which in turn can lead to changes in cognitive theories. The advances in cognitive neuroscience provide a type of data that was previously unavailable, and as a result may address some questions that seemed unresolvable on the basis of previous experimental techniques. On the other hand, the brain is so complex that one needs to have ideas about what to look for before conducting research. For

AN APPLICATION

How to Study for Exams and Remember Names of People You Meet
(Continued)

the section on spacing effects). For no more overall effort, you can learn much more.

How should you remember names? There are many memory "tricks" for remembering names, such as thinking of a salient characteristic and pairing it with the name (e.g., bushy eyebrows Jones). Making rhymes may help as well. Two simple techniques may greatly improve your memory. First, pay attention. This may sound obvious, but a common problem is that people do not deeply encode the name when it is said, so remembering it is very difficult. Try to use the name immediately, such as in saying, "Well, Jim, it is good to meet you. Your last name, Upplestart, is very unusual." Second, space your practice. An effective way of learning in these cases is to have an expanding spaced practice (Landauer & Bjork, 1978). For example, you might say the name immediately after hearing it, then again a minute later, then 5 minutes after that, then 20 minutes after that. In one study, this simple expanding practice scheme led to about a 33% improvement over a standard uniform spaced practice. Why does this expanding practice help? Landauer and Bjork suggest that the practice acts as a type of test and that it is most effective if done soon before one would have forgotten the material otherwise. With more repetitions, the time before forgetting increases, so the expanding practice leads to better memory.

example, the PET examination of working memory mentioned earlier in this chapter began with the Baddeley theory and asked whether there was neural evidence for it. This interaction between cognitive psychology and cognitive neuroscience is still in its early phases and promises some exciting advances in the near future.

Forgetting

Every student has had the experience of studying a lesson but being unable to remember some of the material at the time of a later test. We all have had experiences in which we know the answer to a question but the answer seems to have temporarily "slipped our minds." Why can we not remember things that we know we know?

Two main theoretical questions come to mind concerning these common incidents. First, what has happened to the missing items; that is, are they permanently lost or are they still in memory? Second, what caused the forgetting?

Not Remembering Versus Permanently Forgetting

Current thinking concerning the nature of forgetting is that once entered in long-term memory, items are not lost but rather may be retrievable only under some circumstances. Much of what seems to be lost under some circumstances is retrievable under other circumstances.

One of the observations suggesting that "forgotten" information may not be lost is fascinating, although not very convincing. In the course of some neurosurgery, various parts of the brain may be stimulated, in part to ensure that areas serving vital functions will not be destroyed. Brain surgery often requires only local anesthetics, so patients are conscious during these surgeries (but they are not in pain). There have been reports in which these patients offer a "long-forgotten" memory in response to a particular stimulation. For instance, in response to an electrode in the temporal lobe, one patient mentioned, "There was a piano over there and someone playing. I could hear the song you know" (Penfield, 1959, p. 172). Although such reports suggest memories may be permanent, most researchers are skeptical because these reports are rare and the memories cannot be verified.

The difficulty with assessing whether real-life events that cannot be remembered are truly lost has led to studies of forgetting in laboratory experiments. These studies ask whether information that seems to be forgotten might be retrievable using other cues or under other circumstances. This research clearly shows that retrieval failure cannot be equated with loss from memory (also see the discussion of recovered memories in Chapter 7).

One of the many kinds of experiments leading to the idea that memory is permanent has to do with the possibility of intentional forgetting. When we are dealing with a mechanical or electromagnetic memory, as in the case of a tape recorder, we know that we can erase items from the memory of the device just as easily as we can enter them, but we don't seem similarly able to erase material from our own memories at will. Some researchers have investigated the problem of **intentional forgetting** with special experiments (see, e.g., Bjork, 1972; H. M. Johnson, 1994, presents a review). For instance, subjects were shown a number of lists of items to remember, but on some trials, partway through the list a signal would inform the subjects that they should try to forget everything preceding this signal. The results showed that whether the items to be forgotten were forgotten or remembered depended on the memory measure. The items preceding the "forget" signal proved not to take up short-term memory capacity; the items following the signal were remembered as well as if they had been presented alone. Also, if the subjects were later given an unexpected recall test for the full list, they were unlikely to remember any of the items preceding a "forget" signal. If, however, the subjects were given a recognition test, they were perfectly able to recognize the "forget" items as belonging to the list. From the capacity and recall results, we would have believed that the items preceding the "forget" signal were lost from memory storage. However, from the recognition test it is clear that these items were not lost.

Sometimes when it appears that forgetting is complete, more indirect and sensitive measures may reveal that something from the original memory remains. For example, even unrecognized information from an earlier learning session will sometimes show a **savings in relearning.** Nelson, Fehling, and Moore-Glascock (1979) presented subjects with a series of digit-word pairs such as *27-hates*. A month later, subjects were tested on their recognition memory for these pairs. For pairs that were not remembered, the digits and words were presented again, either with the original pairing or switched (i.e., the digits were paired with different words). Despite the fact that the subjects had been unable to recognize the original pairing, pairs that were presented again were learned better, with performance of 57% correct on such pairs as opposed to 22% for the switched pairs. If the earlier memory were truly lost, such savings would not occur.

Burtt (1941) provides another more dramatic example of this savings. In this study, conducted during the 1920s and 1930s, Greek passages were read to a toddler aged 15 months. Three short passages were read once a day for 3 months, then another three passages were read once a day for 3 months, and so on, until the child was 3 years old. He was then tested at ages 8.5, 14, and 18 years. For these tests, Burtt measured the time it took the child to learn new passages versus these old passages (one-third of the old passages were tested at each test age). The old passages were learned considerably faster than were the new ones for the first test at 8.5, somewhat faster at 14, and only a little bit faster at 18. The details of the materials and statistics are not provided (a not uncommon occurrence in some older articles), so we should perhaps be a little skeptical of this particular finding. However, based on much research, savings in relearning shows that some observed forgetting may not be due to permanent memory loss.

Overall, there is much evidence that forgetting is sometimes due to retrieval difficulty. Might it also be possible that some memories are permanently forgotten? Yes, though clearly this is a difficult point to prove. There is no direct evidence with humans, but Schacter (1996) reviews a variety of recent research consistent with the idea that memories that are not used may be essentially lost.

Causes of Forgetting

Three main hypotheses have been proposed for how forgetting occurs: *decay, interference,* and *overwriting.* One of the earliest hypotheses about the causes of forgetting was the "law of disuse," according to which items that are not recalled or studied for a period of time tend to lose strength in memory as a result of an automatic process of decay. Anecdotally, if you have not thought of an event for a while, it often seems that the longer this period has been, the less likely you are to be able to remember the event. In the laboratory, the evidence for this forgetting with time is very easy to demonstrate and quite robust, going back to the earliest systematic study of memory (Ebbinghaus, 1885). Using himself as a subject, Ebbinghaus investigated the learning and remembering of many lists of nonsense syllables. When he varied the delay at which lists were tested, he found that his memory for the lists dropped off quickly, but then the drop-off slowed (not unlike the shape of the short-term memory delay graph shown in Figure 5.1, though the delays involved were much greater). No one argues that memory does not get worse with delay; the question is whether this decrement in performance reflects the effect of decay or some other cause.

It has been very difficult to find support for the **memory decay hypothesis** because in real life any period of time during which decay for memory might be occurring is filled with activities that might in themselves influence forgetting. How can one be sure whether it is the time that is leading to decay or whether the other activities are affecting memory? One possibility is to compare the effects of time when it is filled with many activities versus when it is filled with far fewer activities, such as when one is asleep. In a classic experiment, Jenkins and Dallenbach (1924) contrasted memory after varying numbers of hours of waking or sleep. Memory for the earlier lists was much worse when the subjects were awake than when they were asleep. The result of less forgetting during sleep casts doubt on the theory that disuse leads to decay, but it does not definitively rule out the theory. For example, perhaps the lower rate of metabolism when sleeping might influence the rate of decay from memory.

An alternative explanation for forgetting is that the earlier items are more difficult to retrieve because of interference from later material. This forgetting caused by later learning is called **retroactive interference,** and has been the subject of much research. In a typical experiment, one group of subjects learns certain material such as a list of vocabulary words—call it List A—and then, after an interval, is tested for recall. A second group of subjects learns List A, then learns List B (consisting of different words), and then after the same interval is tested for recall of List A. The experimental design, then, takes the form:

Group	Original Learning	Interpolated Learning	Test
Experimental	List A	List B	List A
Control	List A	Rest	List A

The typical finding is that recall of List A is poorer for the experimental than for the control group.

Somewhat surprisingly, however, it also proves to be the case that earlier learning may interfere with memory for related material learned later. The process is termed **proactive interference,** as was used in the release-from-PI studies discussed earlier. One can examine this interference with the following design:

Group	Prior Learning	Learning	Test
Experimental	List B	List A	List A
Control	None	List A	List A

Again, the typical finding is that recall of List A is poorer for the experimental group than for the control group.

At first thought, it may seem strange that forgetting of material can be influenced by learning that went on earlier. At least a partial explanation of these interference effects is that the more items a cue is stored with, the less effective it is in retrieving any particular item (see, e.g., Watkins, 1975). For example, suppose that you are trying to remember what you ate for dinner two months ago when you had dinner with a friend. If this was your only dinner with this friend, the friend is a useful part of the retrieval cue. But if you have dinner with this friend a couple of times a week, then all the dinners the friend has had with you (including ones more than two months ago) make it much harder to retrieve that particular dinner. The experimental group has more items learned with the context "cue," so performance is lower. This proactive interference is important in short-term remembering as well, as seen in the release-from-PI paradigm (Figure 5.2), and causes some of the drop-off in recall seen in the Peterson and Peterson paradigm (Figure 5.1).

The third hypothesis for forgetting is overwriting—our memories may be changed by later events, so that the original memories cannot be retrieved because they do not exist. Suppose that there was an original event that was encoded and then a similar later event (e.g., memories for two roller-coaster rides). Overwriting refers to a case in which an originally encoded part is replaced with a related part of the later event. This assertion is quite controversial, and we consider it in more detail in Chapter 7 when we examine the effects of misleading questions in eyewitness testimony.

The fact that much of our forgetting appears to be due to interference does not mean that all of it is. Some theories include multiple sources of forgetting, such as decay and interference (see the ACT theory in Chapter 6). Finally, although we are focusing on forgetting, it is important to realize how well we remember most things that we need to remember.

Summary

This section has examined a large variety of results and ideas in long-term memory, so it may be helpful to recap what we have discussed. We began with a simple experiment, a study of a list of items followed by free recall, and examined the primacy effect (better memory for the first few items on the list) and the recency effect (better memory for the last few items on the list).

The encoding and retrieval of more meaningful material is often very active, and one's memory depends on how one processes the material. We considered a number of such active encoding influences including the level of processing, memory for meaning, the organization of material, and elaboration of the items. The important point of this work is that what one remembers is a function both of what was presented and how it was processed. Similarly, for a given type of encoding, how much one can retrieve often depends upon the types of retrieval plans or strategies used.

Besides the importance of active processing at encoding and retrieval, the match between encoding and retrieval is also important. This influence is best illustrated with the encoding specificity effects in which recognition with different study-test encodings leads to lower performance than cued recall with similar encodings. In addition, memory is better when the context at test matches the context at study.

The final issue discussed in this section was forgetting. Interference of similar materials is a common cause of forgetting. We distinguished between retroactive interference, in which new material leads to forgetting of earlier material, and proactive interference, in which old material leads to forgetting of newer material. Besides the large influence of interference, it also appears that some forgetting may be due to decay.

AN ENIGMA
Sleep Can Help Your Memory

Suppose that you were told that sleep would help your memory. Sounds great, and it appears that it may be true. The main idea behind the effect of sleep is *consolidation*. Consolidation refers to a gradual change in the system, such as encoding a new memory. The idea is that rather than thinking of the brain as immediately encoding a memory, the neural changes are made over a period of time. If something is done during that time to interfere with consolidation, then the memory's encoding may be disrupted. Sleep provides a time when the brain can consolidate the new memories without as much other activity to interfere. Stickgold (1998) presents an excellent review of much of this research.

Sleep is often characterized as consisting of five stages, including rapid-eye movement (REM) sleep, in which we dream, and slow-wave sleep (SWS), sometimes referred to as deep sleep. Sleep cycles through these stages every 90 minutes or so. There has been a long history of how sleep might affect memory and learning, with much focus on the role of dreams and REM sleep.

Studies with rats show that following training on complex tasks, there is an increase of REM sleep. In addition, depriving rats of REM sleep (as opposed to depriving them of other phases of sleep) leads to a decrement in learning. (They are deprived of such sleep by waking them during that stage.) One interpretation is that the extra REM sleep is allowing consolidation of what was learned.

Interestingly, human performance appears to be related to both REM and SWS stages of sleep. In Chapter 6, we discuss two different types of

(Continued)

MODELS OF MEMORY FOR NEW INFORMATION _____

General Approach

In this section, we examine some models of memory aimed at explaining the basic memory effects just reviewed. Memory models consist of hypotheses about the structure of memory and the processes that operate on this structure. Presumably it will ultimately be discovered that information entering memory is encoded somehow in entities within the brain. But for the present we know little about bases of particular memories in the brain. When we speak of *structure,* we mean that we are trying to form a picture of the way in which the contents of memory are organized.

AN ENIGMA
Sleep Can Help Your Memory *(Continued)*

memories. *Declarative* memories are what we often call "knowing that," such as facts, memory for episodes, etc. *Procedural* memories are what we call "knowing how." These might include knowledge about how to type, tie shoelaces, shoot a basketball, etc. The interesting result is that REM sleep appears to be related to the consolidation of procedural memories, whereas SWS appears to affect the consolidation of declarative memories. That is, deprivation of REM leads to poorer retention in procedural tasks, but not in declarative tasks, whereas the opposite is true in SWS deprivation. (This is a slightly idealized result, but it is clear that each type of sleep has a primary influence on a different type of task.)

How might consolidation work? One possibility suggested by McClelland, McNaughton, and O'Reilly (1995) is that new memories are temporarily stored and then repeatedly reactivated (like replaying a tape) so that the neural changes can be gradually made. This reactivation also serves to interleave the memories, leading to a type of spaced practice, as well as helping to integrate them.

This is very exciting work, not only because of the obvious importance of understanding the role of sleep in learning, but also because it gives researchers a way to examine some of the brain regions and neurochemistry that might be involved in memory. Does this mean you should listen to tapes in your sleep to learn? No, but it does suggest the importance of getting a good night's sleep when one is learning difficult new material.

The memory structure is the person's internal representation. Memory *processes* specify how the structure is used to store and retrieve information. The development of models can help us understand the ways in which information is stored, organized, and retrieved in the normal and impaired functioning of memory. In this section, we begin with some simple models to explain how models are used to make predictions and how they are tested. We then progress to a more complex model.

Simple Association Models

Consider the sketch of three successive types of association models of memory structure illustrated in Figure 5.7. All three models are attempts to understand what

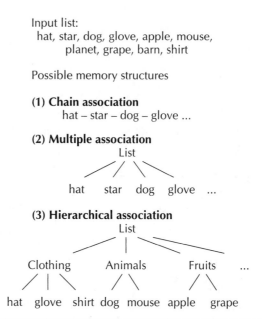

Input list:
hat, star, dog, glove, apple, mouse,
planet, grape, barn, shirt

Possible memory structures

(1) Chain association
hat – star – dog – glove ...

(2) Multiple association

(3) Hierarchical association

Figure 5.7   Three alternative association models for the memory structure underlying free recall of the list of words shown at the top.

Source: Estes, 1976.

happens when an individual is presented with a list of words such as the input list at the top (*hat, star, dog,* . . .) and is then expected to recall the words.

In the earliest form of association theory, the chain association model, successive items of the list are linked together by single associations or connections—*hat* with *star, star* with *dog,* and so on. In this scheme, the first word is associated with a symbol for the list (for example, the people might think of it as "the list of words I am about to see"). When they are asked to recall the list, they bring the symbol to mind, leading to recall of *hat,* which in turn leads to recall of *star,* and so on. However, the model predicts that if in the course of recalling the list, people failed to remember some item—say, the word *dog*—then they would be unable to remember any of the items that followed. This implication has been shown to be false by many experiments.

The next level of complexity is the *multiple association* model illustrated in the middle of Figure 5.7. Here it is assumed that each of the words on the list is associated with a common list symbol. This model does not run into the same problem as the first one if the individual omits a word during recall. Still, there is no way to predict from this model that words with similar meanings would tend to be grouped together during recall, which is an important property of performance in this task.

This last fact, however, can be accommodated by the third try, the *hierarchical association* model illustrated at the bottom. Here the individual words of the list are associated with category names (clothing, animals, fruit), which in turn are associated with the list symbol. Now when the individual thinks of the list symbol at the time of recall, he or she is likely to remember one of the category labels, which in turn leads to recall of the members of the category that appeared on the list, then another category label, and so on. This hierarchical association is one means of limiting complexity and is useful for reasoning about categories (as will be discussed in Chapter 10). In addition, this model predicts the clustering by categories in free recall that often occurs in these tasks. It is also consistent with many of the results on organization, such as the one discussed earlier in this chapter.

These associative models assume that the connection between items, the association, is simple, with no real meaning attached to it. These associations capture the powerful intuition that when we are thinking of one idea we may be very likely to think of some other specific idea (e.g., black may lead to white). Although these simple associative models have difficulty in accounting for some of the complexities of human memory, such as people's ability to deal with embedded sentences (e.g., see J. R. Anderson & Bower, 1973, Chapter 2), they have led to the development of more sophisticated models.

One of the earliest cognitive models of memory was that of Atkinson and Shiffrin (1968). Of particular interest here, they proposed a model in which short-term memory was used to keep items available and also to help transfer information into long-term memory. They made much more explicit the distinction between the structure of memory, such as the short- and long-term memories, and the processes of memory, which would direct the rehearsal of items or the transfer from short-term to long-term memory. Later models have built upon many of the ideas from this model to produce models capable of accounting for a wide variety of results. We end this chapter by describing one of these models, SAM, to show how much of what we have learned in this chapter might be incorporated into a model.

The SAM Model

Introduction

The **search of associative memory (SAM)** model has been developed by Richard Shiffrin and his colleagues to account for a large number of different memory effects (see Shiffrin & Raaijmakers, 1992, for an overview of this work). (Yes, this is the same Shiffrin of the Atkinson & Shiffrin model just mentioned.) The model begins with some basic assumptions that build on the results we have been examining in this chapter. First, short-term memory is viewed as a limited buffer that (1) is used to access knowledge from long-term memory and (2) affects what information is stored in long-term memory. Second, long-term memory is assumed to consist of a large set of interconnected concepts. These connections include hierarchical connections, as in the simple model just discussed, but include many other types of connections as well. For example, if two concepts often occur together then this co-occurrence is represented by interconnections between the concepts. Third, memory retrieval is assumed to be cue-dependent, meaning that what is retrieved depends on the cue used to probe the memory. Fourth, memory is assumed to be nonerasable, with forgetting due to retrieval failure. Fifth, context is considered to be a crucial determinant of memory retrieval. These general assumptions are not a model but rather provide some guiding principles for construction of a model. Although the SAM model is far more complicated than the simple associative models, it is able to account for a much greater number of memory effects.

Description of the Model

Memory is assumed to consist of a large number of interconnected feature sets called images. These images contain information about (1) the context in which the learning occurred; (2) the item, such as its meaning, name, and other facts; and (3) the relation to other images. To remember something, a person is assumed to gather a set of cues or probes in short-term memory and use them to activate associated images in long-term memory. These probes result in various images being activated to varying degrees as a function of their connections to the probe. With this overview, we now go into a little more detail.

SHORT-TERM MEMORY   The images stored in long-term memory are assumed, as in many explanations, to be encoded from short-term memory. In particular, short-term memory is assumed to be a limited buffer (e.g., four items). Suppose a person is given a list of words to learn, such as the list given in Figure 5.7 (*hat, star, dog, glove, apple,* ...). Table 5.4 shows what might be in the short-term memory buffer as each new word is encountered. (To help us keep track, we use Time1 to mean when the first word is presented, Time2 for the second word, etc.) At Time1, only the first word is in the buffer, along with the context of the study list. (Contextual information is always being encoded, but here we are labeling the particular contextual information as study context to mark it as the contextual information encoded dur-

Table 5.4   **Example of the Contents of Short-Term Memory for SAM: Given the Input List in Figure 5.7 (hat, star, dog, glove, apple...)**

Time	Contents of Short-Term Memory				
TIME 1	*<study context>*	hat			
TIME 2	*<study context>*	hat	star		
TIME 3	*<study context>*	hat	star	dog	
TIME 4	*<study context>*	hat	star	dog	glove
TIME 5	*<study context>*	hat	star	glove	apple

Note: This example assumes that the short-term memory can hold four words plus the study context and that the fifth word, *apple,* bumped an earlier word, *dog.* The longer an item is in short-term memory, the more strongly connected it becomes to the study context and to other items that are in short-term memory at the same time.

ing study.) The first few words are retained in short-term memory until its capacity is reached, at Time4. After this, new items put into short-term memory bump one of the old items out. For example, with a buffer of four items, capacity will not be reached until the word *apple* is read (Time5), meaning that *hat* will have been retained in the buffer during the presentation of three additional items, *star* for two, and so on. When *apple* enters the buffer, one of the items—say, *dog*—will be bumped out.

LONG-TERM MEMORY   The simple assumption in this model is that, in the absence of encoding strategies, storage in long-term memory depends on the time an item is in short-term memory. After reading the list, the person will have a set of interconnected images in long-term memory. Those items that were retained for a long time in short-term memory (e.g., *hat*) will be strongly connected to the study context. In addition, any pairs of items that were retained together in short-term memory will have strong interimage strengths (e.g., *hat star*). Thus, the longer an item is retained in short-term memory, the greater its association to the study context (and some images) and the more images to which it is associated.

MEMORY RETRIEVAL   The memory probes (cues) activate these images in long-term memory as a function of three factors: how strongly the image is associated to the context, how strongly the image is associated to other activated images, and how similar the image is to the probes. Finishing our example, if *star* is the probe item, it will lead to much activation for its image and also for the image of *hat* (as well as for other items it co-resided with in the buffer). As can be seen in Table 5.4, *star* co-resided in the buffer for a relatively long time with the study context and with *hat*, less so with *dog* and *glove,* and even less so with *apple*.

The most important point about memory retrieval is that context is crucial. If a word in the list is not strongly associated to the study context or if the test context is very different from the context at study, then memory for the list items will be very poor. The reason for this is that in these tasks, the goal is not just to remember any strongly encoded item, but to remember a strongly encoded item that occurred in *this* list. Thus, it must be strongly connected to the study context. Although there clearly are many cases in which one does not care where one learned some information (for example, answering the question "Who is the president?"), the research and models in this chapter address memory for items learned in a particular context. (The next chapter examines memory for other types of knowledge.)

SAM Model's Account of Some Memory Phenomena

The SAM model is able to accommodate a large number of memory effects. In this section, we illustrate how it accounts for a few important findings presented in this chapter.

First, primacy effects are accounted for by the short-term memory assumptions. As a reminder, primacy effects refer to the finding that the early words in a list are better remembered than the middle items in the list. By the SAM account (and similar to some other explanations that have been offered), the probability of recall is a function of context-to-image strength and interimage strength. The first few items on a list have an advantage in that they are retained in the buffer until its capacity is reached. Thus, if we assume a four-item buffer, the first item will be retained at least until the fifth item is read. It then has a chance of being bumped out with each new item. However, an item from the middle of the list immediately has a chance of being bumped by a new item (because the buffer is already full). There-fore, on average the early items have more time in short-term memory, leading to greater context-to-image strengths and interimage strengths. Although the SAM account is similar to other accounts of the primacy effect, it is important to note that the short-term memory assumptions are also being used in other ways to help account for a number of other effects.

Second, encoding specificity effects are accounted for because remembering in the SAM model is highly dependent on the context. As discussed earlier, encod-ing specificity effects refer to the finding that the retrieval depends on a match between the encoding and retrieval cues, including the context. In the experiments showing encoding specificity, subjects learned a target word in the context of anoth-er word to lead it to be encoded in a certain way, such as *head* LIGHT. Subjects then generated close associates to a number of words, such as *dark*. The recognition task involved checking off any of these associates that had been in the study part—this is a major change in context (e.g., *light* in the context of *dark* rather than the study context of *head*) and people do very poorly. Thus, retrieval of the study item (*head* LIGHT) is poor in recognition, because recognition is hurt by changes in the context from study to test or by changes in the encoding of the item (so the match of the item to its image is hurt). However, the cued recall reinstates much of the study context (*head* ___), so retrieval is high. This finding is predicted by SAM because the acti-vation of images requires a strong connection to all the probes (both the cues and the context).

Third, context effects are accounted for because context is included in all the probes. Therefore, a change in context will decrease the activation of the image.

Fourth, interference effects are accounted for because of a competition among similar images. That is, all images are activated as a function of their simi-larity to the cue, so they can be viewed as competing for retrieval. Thus, if an addi-tional image is strongly associated to the probes, it will decrease the probability of other images being remembered. Suppose you are interested in the probability of re-calling a particular item, given the context as a cue. The more items associated with the context, the less likely the particular item of interest will be remembered. This interference occurs both for items studied before the item of interest (i.e., proactive interference) and for items studied after (i.e., retroactive interference).

The SAM model is far more complicated than the simple models with which we began this section, but it accounts for far more results. We believe that the SAM model has two important strengths: First, it demonstrates that these simple assump-tions, when elaborated in clever (but reasonable) ways, can provide detailed quanti-tative accounts of a variety of memory data. Quantitative descriptions (or *fits*) of data are made by turning the assumptions of the model into equations, and then solving the equations in a manner that best predicts the data. As an example of how SAM

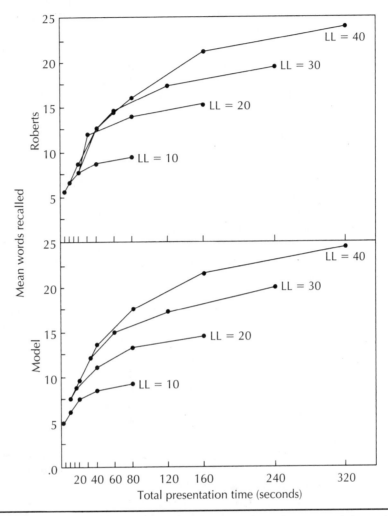

Figure 5.8   Example of a fit of the SAM model to some memory data. The top panel shows data from Roberts (1972) in which the recall was measured as a function of presentation time and list length (LL). The bottom panel shows the fit of the SAM model.

Source: Raaijmakers & Shiffrin, 1981.

can be used in this way, Figure 5.8 shows an instance of how well SAM can fit the data from a memory experiment (Roberts, 1972) that varied the length of the list and the presentation time. As you can see, the predictions of the model are quite close to those of the actual data.

A second important strength of SAM is that it provides a unified account of a wide variety of memory phenomena. We have mentioned only a few effects that it deals with, but research papers provide a large number of additional results that

SAM can model using the same set of assumptions (e.g., Shiffrin et al., 1990; see a review in Shiffrin & Raaijmakers, 1992). In addition, it has led to another model (REM, Shiffrin & Steyvers, 1997), which combines ideas from SAM along with ideas from other models. The goal of memory research is to provide an integrated understanding of how memory works. A model that provides a unified account of a large number of memory results is an important step toward this goal.

Summary

Memory has many functions. In this chapter, we addressed remembering new information. We considered both short-term and long-term memory with a focus on how each helps us deal with the problems of complexity and relevance. Short-term memory allows the augmentation of incomplete information, the integration of information, and the transfer of information to long-term memory. The evidence suggests that there may not be a unitary store, and the concept of working memory was introduced, consisting of a phonological store, a visuospatial sketchpad, and a central executive process to coordinate them.

Long-term memory depends critically on the encoding and retrieval processes used, as well as how the encoding and context at learning match the encoding and context at the time of retrieval. In addition, forgetting appears to be largely due to retrieval failure, but decay may also have an effect.

How can such effects be explained in a unified way? We examined one important current model of memory, SAM, which incorporates many of the ideas about short-term and long-term memory to account for a variety of memory effects such as primacy, encoding specificity, and interference.

We hope that you now have a better appreciation of how complex (and marvelous) your memory really is. Rather than being a storehouse of passively received information, memory involves the active interpretation of events, its augmentation with knowledge, and often its reorganization or elaboration. In addition, memory retrieval often provides relevant information and is sensitive to a variety of factors to increase the likelihood that retrieved information will be relevant.

Key Terms

chunking

context effects

encoding

encoding specificity effect

free recall

incidental learning

proactive interference

recency effect

release from PI

retrieval plan

retroactive interference

SAM

intentional forgetting

levels of processing

long-term memory

maintenance rehearsal

memory decay hypothesis

phonological loop

primacy effect

savings in relearning

serial position effect

short-term memory

spacing effect

state-dependent recall

visuospatial sketchpad

working memory

Recommended Readings

G. A. Miller (1956) has written the classic (and charming) paper on chunking. Baddeley (1990) provides a thorough and interesting review of short-term memory and working memory research and theory. The journal *Memory & Cognition* published a number of papers in 1993 (Volume 21, No. 2) concerning research on short-term memory and its future. A recent book by Miyake and Shah (1999) gives up-to-date conceptions of working memory.

Readers interested in levels of processing should look at Craik and Lockhart (1972) and Craik and Tulving (1975), as well as at criticisms, such as those of Baddeley (1978). The research and ideas on encoding specificity are reviewed in Tulving (1983). Bower (1981) discusses his work on mood and memory, and Eich (1995) reviews the work in this area. S. M. Smith (1994) gives a good overview of context effects in memory.

The Shiffrin and Raaijmakers (1992) chapter is a good overview of the work done in the SAM theory. Shiffrin and Steyvers (1997) provide an introduction to a model, REM, which incorporates aspects from a variety of recent models, including SAM.

Chapter 6

Memory Systems and Knowledge

Introduction

Semantic Knowledge
Characteristics of Semantic Memory
The Hierarchical Model
Evaluation of the Hierarchical Model

Episodic Memory
Are Episodic and Semantic Memory
    Distinct Memory Systems?

Procedural Memory

Implicit and Explicit Memory
Spared Learning in Amnesia
Implicit and Explicit Memory with
    Normal-Memory Adults
Evaluation of the Implicit-Explicit Distinction

Two Models of Memory
Introduction
The ACT Theory
A Parallel Distributed Processing
    Model of Memory

Summary

Key Terms

Recommended Readings

Appendix: Learning in a Parallel Distributed
    Processing Model

I hear and I forget.
I see and I believe.
I do and I understand.

—*Confucius*

INTRODUCTION

It is amazing to think about the variety of things that are stored in memory. We know lots of factual information. For example, we know what a *chair* is, what a *table* is, what *trust* is. We remember things that happened to us. For example, we may recall what we ate for breakfast this morning, the first time we went on a date or the dialog from a movie we saw. We can perform a variety of skills. For example, we may be able to type, to ride a bicycle, to fly a kite or to solve addition problems. While it is clear that we remember facts, events in our life and skills, these types of memory seem different. For example, one of the authors had a young daughter who was visiting Lincoln's house in Springfield, Illinois, and volunteered that "Lincoln had freed the Native Americans when they were slaves in Egypt." This knowledge (though factually inaccurate) can be described using language. In contrast, if you are asked to describe how to perform a skill like shooting a free throw or tying a knot, it can be difficult to put the actions into words. Rather than describing these skills, it always seems easier to demonstrate them and perhaps to physically show someone how to carry them out by guiding their hands or bodies.

In order to capture the unique characteristics of these types of memory, psychologists have made distinctions among different memory systems. In this chapter, we describe a few central distinctions that have been made by memory theorists. These distinctions are based on observations from experiments as well as on the patterns of memory loss that occur as a result of brain damage. Thus, we will discuss both behavioral evidence and the relationship between memory and the brain in this chapter. Finally, many of these distinctions among memory systems have been incorporated into computational models (i.e., computer-based simulations) of memory. At the end of this chapter, we describe two representative models of memory in order to provide insight into the ways psychologists have constructed models of memory.

SEMANTIC KNOWLEDGE

Characteristics of Semantic Memory

Most of the time, when we think about memory, we are interested in **episodic memory,** which is the memory for specific events or episodes in our life. For example, we may remember a birthday party we had or a conversation with someone. We will discuss episodic memory in the next section of this chapter. First, we focus on **semantic memory,** which consists of our ability to store and retrieve facts such as categories (e.g., dog, cat), and types of events (e.g., going to a movie). Semantic memory has three important characteristics. First, it is organized by content. That is, similar concepts are more likely to call each other to mind than are unrelated concepts. For example, in the classic studies of Meyer and Schvaneveldt (1971) people were given a **lexical decision task,** which involves seeing a letter string (e.g., DOCTOR) and classifying it as a word or a nonword. They were faster to make a lexical decision if a semantically related word (e.g., *nurse*) were shown just prior to the letter string than if an unrelated word (e.g., *butter*) were shown. They argued that the semantically similar word *primed* the target word (*doctor*), making it easier to retrieve. Findings of this type demonstrate that semantic memory is organized by content. It is useful to organize semantic memory around content, because it allows us to retrieve information from memory that is likely to be relevant to a current situation. For example, if we are in a hospital, and we see a nurse, we are probably more likely to encounter a doctor than a school bus.

A second characteristic of semantic memory is that it permits us to make *inferences* about properties of concepts. Consider the following two questions:

Is a robin a bird?

Is a robin made of molecules?

When answering the first question, most of us feel like we already know the answer, and were just retrieving the stored information. Answering the second question requires a more indirect approach. Rather than simply retrieving the answer, we must make an inference. Perhaps we reason that a robin is a bird, that birds are animals, that animals are physical objects, and that physical objects consist of molecules. This example suggests that our concepts are nested, so that more specific concepts are members of more general supersets. By organizing concepts in this way, we can infer that properties of more general categories (like animal or physical object) are also true of more specific categories connected to them (like bird or robin). Thus, much of the power of memory comes not just from our ability to retrieve stored information, but from the fact that we can use this information to compute or infer new information that we may never have learned.

A final aspect of semantic memory is that the information in it is not tied directly to information about the source of the knowledge. That is, when we think about the concept "table," we do not feel as though we are reasoning about a particular table that we encountered in the past, but rather that we are reasoning about the concept of a table in general. Thus, information about the concepts we know appears to be independent of the information we know about events in our life (i.e., episodic memory).

The Hierarchical Model

One of the most influential early views of long-term memory, the **hierarchical model** of Collins and Quillian (1969, 1972) assumes that a person's relatively permanent accumulation of knowledge about the meaning of words is organized in a hierarchical network of associations. Network models are successors to simple associationist models (such as the ones discussed in Chapter 5).

Networks, as illustrated in Figure 6.1, consist of nodes and links. You may recall that we saw a network model in Chapter 3 when we discussed interactive activation. The **nodes,** shown as ovals in Figure 6.1, correspond to concepts or ideas. Although these nodes are often designated by a word, the node does not represent the word from a language, but rather the concept referred to by the word. For

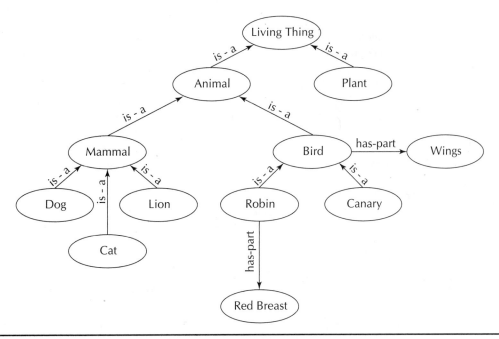

Figure 6.1 Hierarchical memory structure for meanings of familiar words belonging to the familiar categories. If an individual is presented with an example of a particular word such as *robin,* it is assumed that a message travels upward along the associated paths, activating first the memory representation of the category label "bird," then the representation of "animal," and so on.

example, the English word *table* and the Spanish word *mesa* both refer to the same underlying concept. The **links** that connect two or more nodes (shown as lines in Figure 6.1), designate relations between the concepts denoted by the nodes. Links have two key properties. First, they are *labeled* with the relation they designate. In Figure 6.1, there are two relations shown, the "is-a" relation and the "has-part" relation. Second, they are *directed,* so that they point from the first element in the relation to the second. For example, in Figure 6.1, the "is-a" relations point from the more subordinate category (e.g., robin) to the more superordinate category (e.g., bird).

A key assumption is that concepts are *hierarchically organized* in a network. That is, more general concepts are connected to more specific concepts through *class inclusion* links labeled "is-a" (as in the sentence *a robin "is a" bird*). For example, as illustrated in Figure 6.1, a concept such as *living thing* is represented by a high-level node in the network. This concept is directly related to the subordinate categories *animal* and *plant.* Similarly, the concept *animal* is associated with *mammal, bird,* and so on, and the concept *mammal* with *dog, cat, lion,* and so on. However, the labels on the links between the subordinates and their superordinates indicate the nature of the relationship, not just that they are associated. Thus, the relationship between wings and bird is not an "is-a" relation, but rather a "has-part" relation, which specifies that birds have wings as a part.

Whenever assumptions are made about how information is represented, it is also necessary to determine how that information is processed. Without knowing about both the representations and the processes, it is not possible to know what predictions the representation makes for people's behavior (Palmer, 1978). Early proposals for networks of this kind suggested that *activation tags* are passed from one node to another along the links, traveling in the direction that the links point (Collins & Quillian, 1972; Quillian, 1968). The activation tags are like hikers through the network who mark each node they visit. For example, to verify that the sentence "Canaries have wings" is true, one activation tag would start at *canary,* and a second at *wings.* The tag from *wings* cannot go anywhere in the network in Figure 6.1, because it has no links that point away from it. However, the tag from *canary* can go to *bird* (following an "is-a" link) and to *wings* (following the has-part link). It is then possible to verify that the sentence "Canaries have wings" is true, because canaries are birds (as specified by the "is-a" relation) and birds have wings (as specified by the "has-part" relation). Thus, network models can account for how information in semantic memory can be inferred.

It is more difficult to determine that a sentence is false using a network model. For example, to verify the sentence "Cats have wings" activation tags begin at the *cat* node and the *wings* node. In this case, there is no path from cat to wings. Since the only way to tell whether there is a path between nodes is to actually find one, presumably the system waits some amount of time, and if no path is found, it responds that the sentence is false.

Is the hierarchical model a good model of the inner workings of semantic memory? One way that psychologists have examined models of semantic memory is to analyze people's *reaction time* when asked to answer a question or verify a sentence. Suppose, for example, that you are asked on one occasion to say true or false to indicate the truth of the sentence "A robin is a bird" and on another occasion to say true or false to indicate the truth of the sentence "A robin is an animal." Given the network in Figure 6.1, the first of these sentences ought to be verified more quickly than the second because the pathway through the memory network from the word *robin* to the category label *bird* is shorter than the pathway from *robin* to the category label *animal.* Experiments confirming this prediction gave a major boost to the idea of a hierarchical network model (Collins & Quillian, 1969; Landauer & Freedman, 1968).

Evaluation of the Hierarchical Model

When models fail to make the correct predictions, it is often possible to understand the reason for their failure and try to improve subsequent models. The Collins and Quillian work generated much further research, and a number of incorrect predictions were found (though see Collins & Quillian, 1972, for some counterarguments). One problem may be illustrated quite easily. People are faster to verify that a robin is a bird than they are to verify that a penguin is a bird. This difference is an example of the **typicality effect:** Instances that are more typical of a category are verified more quickly than atypical instances of that category. The Collins and Quillian model fails to predict this result, because all concepts are connected directly to their superordinates by "is-a" links. Thus, this model predicts that there will be no typicality effects. One way to fix the hierarchical model is to use links of different strengths, with stronger links being traversed more quickly (Collins & Loftus, 1975). With this change, typicality effects are accounted for by having different link strengths. For example, if the *robin-bird* link is much stronger than the *penguin-bird* link, the model is consistent with the observed typicality effect.

A second problem for the Collins and Quillian model is that the basic hierarchical effect (i.e., that *robin-bird* is verified more quickly than *robin-animal*) sometimes reverses. For example, "A chicken is a bird" takes longer to verify than "A chicken is an animal." This violates the presumed hierarchy, and one would need to explain why the hierarchy works for *robin* but not for *chicken*. The only solution to this problem in this type of network is to allow another path between *chicken* and *animal* that can be traversed more quickly than the *chicken-bird* path, but such a change would violate the hierarchical nature of the model.

A third problem for this model concerns the description of how false responses are made. Although Collins and Quillian noted that there were a few possible ways that subjects might decide a sentence was false, their model did not allow easy descriptions of these possibilities. Because the simple view is that one responds "false" if the category label is not found in the upward search across "is-a" links, the only variable that should make a difference is how far down in the hierarchy the first term is. The problem is that there are systematic differences among false sentences that this model cannot account for. For example, people need more time to respond "false" to "A bat is a bird" than to "A bat is a plant." Intuitively, although a bat is not a bird, it has many similarities to birds, such as having wings and flying. When trying to decide if a bat is a bird, hierarchical knowledge (i.e., that a bat is a mammal and birds are not mammals) suggests a "false" response. However, this response is slowed down by the many similarities between bats and birds, because often items that are similar do belong to the same category. In general, false responses in which the subject and category are related or have similarities (such as *wings* and *flying* for *bat* and *bird*) often lead to longer reaction times (Smith, Shoben, & Rips, 1974). This difference is called the *relatedness effect*. In contrast to this result, the hierarchical model predicts that people use only hierarchical knowledge and that similarities do not matter.

All three of these failures can be viewed as stemming from the same assumptions: Superordinate information is equally available for all concepts and is the only information used to make category judgments. A number of theories have departed from both assumptions (e.g., Collins & Loftus, 1975), and we will later see a theory that includes these changes and can account for results that the hierarchical model cannot.

Many of the semantic memory models were investigated during the 1970s. Research on the representation of knowledge and its use has not ended. Rather, this research has become applied to many areas beyond what is usually referred to as memory research. As shown in later chapters, investigators in language, decision making, reasoning, and problem solving have also examined how semantic memory is used in their domains of interest.

EPISODIC MEMORY

As discussed in the previous section, semantic memory is our memory for facts about the world. Facts are not the only things we know, however. We also remember large numbers of autobiographical details. When sitting in the house where we grew up, we might remember events that occurred in different rooms. We remember birthday parties, discussions, and games. Some psychologists have suggested that these aspects of our lives are recorded in *episodic memory*. Most of the memory studies that we have discussed so far (for example, in Chapter 5), are concerned with episodic memory. When you are asked to recall the words from a list that you saw previously, you must do this by remembering the words that were associated with a particular context (a specific list at a particular time and place).

Episodic memory has characteristics that differ from those of semantic memory (see Tulving, 1983, for an extensive discussion of these differences). One important difference between them is that episodic memory has more temporal (i.e., time-related) organization than semantic memory. When we remember an event, we tend to recall the aspects of that event in series. For example, you may remember a trip to a football game starting with the drive there, then recall the tailgate party in the parking lot, followed by the game, and then the drive home.

Episodic memory also involves an association between a memory and its source. It is assumed for example, that people know which information about an event they actually saw or heard, and which parts they only found out about second hand. Indeed, the reason why people are able to testify in court as witnesses is that the law assumes people can report what they saw, and that their reports are likely to be correct. As we will see in Chapter 7, however, memory for source information is not always completely accurate.

Finally, a key difference between episodic and semantic memory is in the way the truth of an item in memory can be established. An item in semantic memory is determined to be true by consensus of a group. For example, a particular object with a flat top and four legs might be counted in the category of tables because members of the community agree that it is a table (see Medin, Lynch, Coley, & Atran, 1997, for a detailed discussion of this issue). In contrast, the individual determines the truth of a fact in episodic memory. If we believe that a particular episode occurred, then that seems to be enough to verify the truth of an episodic memory for that individual.

Are Episodic and Semantic Memory Distinct Memory Systems?

What evidence is there for the distinction between episodic and semantic memory? Some of the most important evidence for this distinction comes from the way memory breaks down in different kinds of amnesia. At the beginning of Chapter 5, we mentioned one amnesic patient, H. M., who had great difficulty learning new information. As we will see in this section, amnesia seems to lead to a dissociation between episodic and semantic memory. One explanation of H. M.'s condition, for example, is that he has an intact semantic memory, but his episodic memory system is grossly impaired (see Tulving, 1983, 1985, for reviews).

In this overview, we are interested primarily in characterizing the symptoms of a general type of amnesia. Permanent amnesia can be characterized by four symptoms: First, there is severe **anterograde amnesia,** meaning that new information cannot be learned. Second, there is some **retrograde amnesia,** the loss of memory for events before the trauma (e.g., operation, injury), though this is often patchy and variable. (It is interesting to note that television shows usually portray amnesic people very differently from this profile. The typical TV amnesic has profound retrograde amnesia but little if any anterograde amnesia.) Third, some amnesic patients, especially near the time of trauma, show considerable confabulation (mentioning "facts" that are not true) when faced with questions they are unable to answer. Finally, despite these significant memory deficits, other intellectual functions are often relatively intact.

Although we have presented this single characterization of amnesia, amnesias vary in many ways. It is clear that the memory deficits differ greatly and depend on the nature of the problem and the anatomical site of the damage (see e.g., Cohen & Eichenbaum, 1993). For present purposes, we will have to be satisfied with a brief look into anterograde and retrograde amnesia.

Anterograde Amnesia

The beginning of Chapter 5 included a long quotation from one of the many papers that documented the memory deficits of H. M. His amnesia is among the most severe of any documented case, with great anterograde and retrograde deficits as well as some short-term memory impairment. He is unable to remember people he has met many times since his operation. His performance is always very poor on new tasks that require him to consciously remember something. For example, although he can perform well on perceptual tasks, if they require him to find some figure in a complex picture, his performance deteriorates greatly because he is unable to remember the figure he is searching for. In addition, although he is able to learn short tactile (i.e., touch) mazes, his performance on longer mazes is abysmal. He showed no improvement at all over 215 learning trials of a maze and made more than 2,800 errors, whereas normals learn this maze with an average of 17 trials and 92 errors (Milner, 1965).

Although he has been studied for more than 35 years, H. M. shows little change. He has been able to learn a few significant facts after great amounts of repetition, such as the floor plan of the house he now lives in and the fact that his father has died (Corkin, Sullivan, Twitchell, & Grove, 1981). However, he is unable to keep track of most of what is going on in his world. Thus, H. M. has a profound deficit in his episodic memory.

Retrograde Amnesia

Retrograde amnesia refers to the inability to remember information from before the trauma. In general, retrograde amnesia occurs less frequently than anterograde and in most amnesic cases is completely limited to the few years before the trauma. One

AN APPLICATION
False Memories

In the late 1980s there began a great interest in the sudden recollection of memories from childhood. There were numerous reports of adults who had vivid memories of traumatic events from their childhood that they had forgotten. This question was of more than passing importance as some legal cases were decided on the basis of testimony given by adults who recovered memories of events that they believed occurred when they were children. Those who recovered memories of childhood trauma were united in their conviction that these events had really happened. This belief that the events occurred was based on the emotional and visual richness of the memories themselves.

On the basis of these events, cognitive psychologists have been particularly interested in whether it is possible to induce people into a state where they claim to have a memory for a past situation that has the vividness of other memories, but for which the original event did not occur. A pattern of data like this would not prove that reports of recovered memories are false, but it would demonstrate that simply having the vividness normally associated with memories is not a guarantee that a recollected event actually occurred.

A number of lines of research have addressed this issue. One proposal about episodic memory is that it keeps track of both the information recalled as well as its source (Johnson, Hashtroudi, & Lindsay, 1993). On this view, if a new piece of information were somehow associated with the wrong source, it would be erroneously classified as a memory from that source. In one study directed at this possibility, Garry, Manning, Loftus, and Sherman (1996) gave people a life events inventory in which they were asked about events that might have happened to them as children. In another session, the same subjects were asked to imagine that certain events (which were on the inventory) happened to them as children. Later, they were given the same life events inventory again. People's rating that an event had happened to them as children was more likely to increase if

(Continued)

group of amnesic patients, however, those with Korsakoff syndrome, show large retrograde deficits. These patients have usually developed this syndrome after severe and prolonged alcoholism (the cause of Korsakoff syndrome appears to be a thiamine deficiency resulting from poor diet, because alcoholics tend not to eat well, and because the metabolism of alcohol involves thiamine). At the onset of the syndrome, these people change dramatically. Although many have a history of violence,

AN APPLICATION

False Memories *(Continued)*

they imagined the event happening to them than if they did not imagine the event happening to them.

Studies like the one by Garry et al. are hard to interpret, because it is possible that imagining the event led people to remember something that actually did happen to them as a child. For this reason, it would be nice to have a technique for inducing false memories in the lab. Such a technique was devised by Roediger and McDermott (1995). They showed people lists of words in which all of the words on a list were associated with some other word that was not on the list. For example, the list associated with the word *sweet* included *sour, candy, sugar, bitter, good, taste, tooth, nice, honey, soda, chocolate, heart, cake, tart,* and *pie.* Subjects were shown the lists and were asked to recall the words on the list. In one study, although the word *sweet* was not on the list, it was recalled as being on the list 55% of the time. Subsequently, people were shown words from the list as well as distractors and were asked whether they recognized whether the words were on the list. The word was recognized as being on the list 81% of the time. In most cases, when the word was recognized, people reported that they remembered the word actually being on the list as opposed to simply believing it to be on the list without having an actual memory of having seen the word. Thus, this technique appears to induce false memories (that is, memories of things that did not happen) in a laboratory task.

In summary, studies of memory suggest that people can have the subjective experience of remembering an event that never actually occurred. This happens either when people mistakenly associate a memory with the wrong source, or when they have seen so many things consistent with the event that the event that did not happen is somehow represented as well. Finally, it is important to emphasize that these data do *not* indicate that recovered memories cannot happen. They simply demonstrate that reports of recovered memories must be treated with care. We will return to the issue of recovered memories again in Chapter 7.

---

they become passive, apathetic, and uninterested in alcohol (Butters, 1984). In addition, they have little ability to learn any new material (i.e., severe anterograde deficits) and experience difficulty recalling events from the past (i.e., retrograde deficit).

Cohen and Squire (1981) examined the retrograde deficits of several types of amnesic patients, including Korsakoff patients. The study of retrograde amnesia can be quite tricky because the experimenter has no control over what was learned by the patients and has no knowledge of the extent or conditions of learning. Nonetheless, a number of tests have been devised that appear to be good indicators of past memory. Cohen and Squire had seven different tests, including (1) television programs that had aired for only one year between 1963 and 1977, (2) photographs of people who had become famous between 1930 and 1979, and (3) famous public events from the 1930s to the 1970s. The Korsakoff patients averaged about 54 years of age in 1980, meaning that they were born around the mid-1920s. Although the other amnesic patients showed mild retrograde deficits limited to the few years before the trauma, the Korsakoff patients' retrograde amnesia was severe and extended back several decades to when the patients were quite young. In addition, the forgetting was slightly graded, with Korsakoff patients having more difficulty remembering recent events and faces than with remembering those in the distant past. This result has many possible explanations. For example, prior to the onset of Korsakoff syndrome, many of these patients had been drinking heavily, which is known to lead to some anterograde deficits. If new information was learned increasingly less well as drinking progressed, the graded effect may simply be due to learning less during the latter premorbid (i.e., before the disease onset) stages.

Butters and Cermak (1986; see also Butters, 1984) present some very interesting data to show that this possibility will not explain all of the graded effect. In particular, they describe some research on a patient, P. Z., who had been an eminent scientist at a university before he developed Korsakoff syndrome when he was 65. In addition to having written many research articles, chapters, and books on his specialty, he had also written an autobiography that had been finished a couple of years before the onset of Korsakoff syndrome. Butters and Cermak conducted tests on his knowledge of various types of information contained in his autobiography. For example, P. Z. had discussed a number of scientists in his book, and these names were given to him for identification. These scientists were categorized by whether they had achieved prominence before 1965 (17 years before the onset of P. Z.'s amnesia) or after 1965. Compared to another scientist of his age and in his specialty, P. Z. showed forgetting of all the scientists, but this difference was greater for scientists who had become famous after 1965. Even more dramatically, he was tested about more personal information in his autobiography, such as relatives, colleagues, or research assistants. As can be seen in Figure 6.2, he remembered those events from the distant past well but did not remember recent events at all. Because these test items were taken from his autobiography, we can be confident that they had been learned originally. The exact explanation for this temporal gradient is still uncertain.

Amnesia, Episodic, and Semantic Memory

It is clear that amnesia is largely a deficit in episodic memory either for the past (retrograde amnesia) or for new information (anterograde amnesia). However, the amnesia literature does not provide perfect support for the distinction between episodic and semantic memory. First, the retrograde amnesia of patients with Korsakoff syndrome includes both past autobiographical memories (episodic) and world knowledge (semantic). Second, the research on anterograde amnesia suggests that both

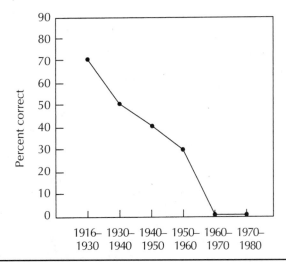

Figure 6.2   Retrograde amnesia for recall of information from P. Z.'s autobiography.

Source: Butters & Cermak, 1986.

new episodic and semantic memories are hard to acquire. Under near-optimal learning conditions, Glisky, Schacter, and Tulving (1986) were able to get amnesic patients to learn some computer-related vocabulary words. But many of the words were not new ones and had technical definitions related to their usual meaning (e.g., save). Even so, learning was very much slower than that of controls. Gabrieli, Cohen, and Corkin (1988) performed a number of sensitive experiments trying to detect semantic knowledge that might have been learned by H. M. since his amnesia but they found little learning.

Another intriguing finding that obscures the boundary between episodic and semantic memory is that words for concepts that are lost due to brain damage or aging seem to be those for concepts learned later in life rather than earlier (Hirsh & Ellis, 1994; Hodgson & Ellis, 1998). For example, Hodgson & Ellis (1998) showed line drawings of objects (e.g., a cat or a raccoon) to older adult subjects (age range 71–86 years). The likelihood that the older subjects would be able to name the objects was significantly related to estimates of the age at which these concepts are learned by children. For example, cats are learned before raccoons, and older adults were better able to name the picture of a cat than to name the picture of a raccoon. This finding was obtained even taking into account different frequencies with which different concepts are encountered. These results suggest that semantic memory may be organized in part around the other concepts and contexts that are available when a new concept is acquired. To the extent that context is important in the acquisition of concepts, the distinction between episodic and semantic memory is blurred (see also, J. R. Anderson & Ross, 1980; Hintzman, 1984; McKoon, Ratcliff, & Dell, 1986).

AN ENIGMA
Becoming Famous Overnight

How is episodic information used in tasks besides simply retrieving information about autobiographical events? One important use of episodic information is revealed in studies by Jacoby and his colleagues (Jacoby, Kelley, Brown, & Jasechko, 1989; Jacoby, Woloshyn, & Kelley, 1989). They asked subjects to read a list of unfamiliar names like Victoria Marsh or Adrian Farlow. Some of these names appeared on the list once, and other names appeared on the list four times. For example, they might see the name Victoria Marsh once and Adrian Farlow four times. The subjects were told that the names on this list were people who were not famous. After studying the list, subjects were shown another list. Some of the names on the list were people who were moderately famous (e.g., Roger Bannister), some were names that had appeared on the previous list, and some were new names. Finally, a similar test consisting of names of moderately famous people, names from the first list and new nonfamous names (e.g., Maureen Degnan) was given the next day.

How should people respond in this test? The people selected as famous were ones whose names might be familiar, though their accomplishments might not (Roger Bannister was the first person to run a four-minute mile). Thus, familiarity provides a good criterion for deciding that a

(Continued)

So where does this leave us? Our view, similar to the view outlined in Anderson and Ross (1980), is that by definition there is a clear content distinction between the two types of memories. That is, we can discuss the two different types of information as semantic and episodic with general agreement about each, but we do not believe that there is any convincing evidence of a functional distinction, with each type of information requiring different structures and processes to be involved in encoding and retrieving.

PROCEDURAL MEMORY

Both semantic memory and episodic memory have a number of characteristics in common. Both involve knowing that a particular fact is true or that a particular episode occurred. In addition, both types of memory are either highly verbal (i.e., they can be easily described) or they are easy to imagine. Because of these characteristics, both semantic and episodic memory have been called **declarative memory**

AN ENIGMA
Becoming Famous Overnight *(Continued)*

name is famous. One can reason that if a name seems familiar, it must be because the person is famous. Reading a name on a list will also make a name seem more familiar, but as long as subjects remember that the name was on the list, they will know that it is not famous.

In these studies, people rarely mistook nonfamous names that appeared on the list to be famous when the test was given immediately after reading the list. Indeed, they were more likely to say that a new non-famous name was famous than to say that one of the nonfamous names from the list was famous. This finding is not surprising, because people should be good at remembering names on a list they just read. A different pattern was obtained the following day. On this test, people were much more likely to say that a name that appeared on the list the previous day was famous than to say that a new nonfamous name was famous. Fur-thermore, this effect was stronger for names read just once on the list than for names read four times. This latter finding suggests that people forgot where they had encountered names from the list, particularly those names only presented once. They misinterpreted the familiarity of those names and assumed that the names must denote famous people. Thus, by losing the source of the information, subjects turned nonfamous peo-ple into famous ones overnight!

(Cohen, 1984; Cohen & Eichenbaum, 1993; see also Schacter, 1992; Squire, Knowlton, & Musen, 1993, for somewhat different proposals). Declarative memory is often contrasted with **procedural memory,** which involves knowing *how* to carry out different activities such as getting dressed, reading a word, driving a car, or per-forming surgery. These memories are not verbalizable, but rather involve knowledge about the actual doing. For example, in tying your shoelaces, you do not think about the sequence; you just do it. To see this distinction, ask yourself whether you begin by putting the left part of the lace under the right or the right under the left. To answer this question, most people need to imagine themselves tying the shoelaces. Even though at one time you were taught explicitly how to start and continue the tying, the procedure has become so well learned that it no longer requires accessing this earlier declarative knowledge. It may seem strange at first to think about phy-sical skills as involving a type of memory, but part of the point here is that these procedural memories have very different characteristics from declarative memories.

As this discussion implies, a key difference between procedural and declar-ative memory is that procedural memories are not easily talked about. Another cen-tral difference between procedural and declarative memory is the amount of time that it takes for the information to enter into memory. Episodic memory, which is one type of declarative memory, involves a single exposure to the item. We may remember a birthday party we had as a child despite the fact that the party occurred only once (though we may have thought about it many times over the years, which may have strengthened the memory and made it easier to recall later). In contrast, skills take considerable time to acquire. For example, when you first learn to swim, each stroke is effortful and often poorly carried out. Over the course of weeks, or months, the strokes become less effortful and more fluidly carried out. This time course is characteristic of the development of procedural memory.

Evidence for the distinction between procedural and declarative memory also comes from the study of brain-damaged patients. For example, despite the fact that H. M. could not learn lists of words, and could not acquire new facts about his life, he was able to learn complex skills. One classic example is mirror tracing. In mirror tracing, subjects are asked to trace a figure that they can only see in a mirror. Thus, they must learn that to move right in the image, they must actually move their hands to the left. Though H. M. could not remember performing this task after repeated exposures, his performance improved dramatically (Milner, 1965). It is worth thinking about why H. M. could learn mirror tracing, but could not learn to solve a maze. Presumably, mirror tracing involves learning what motor movements to make in the apparatus in order to move left or right. In contrast, learning the maze would require recognizing the maze itself and the locations within the maze. The idea underlying procedural memory is that the ability to learn new motor movements may be independent of other forms of memory so that it may be spared even when the ability to learn new facts is impaired. Finally, evidence for this distinction comes from studies of consolidation of memories through sleep. Recall from the Enigma box in Chapter 5 that REM sleep seems to help retention of procedural tasks, while slow wave sleep (SWS) aids retention of declarative memories (Stickgold, 1998).

IMPLICIT AND EXPLICIT MEMORY

What does it mean to remember something? Most of the time, we think of remembering as an ability to intentionally recall something. Using declarative memory, you might remember the seven digits of a friend's phone number or recall the plot of the movie you watched last week. When recalling something like a phone number, not only is the recollection intentional, but there is also a conscious experience of the information remembered. This kind of explicit conscious recollection is so obvious a part of remembering that it is easy to think that it is the only way to observe people's memory. To be more specific, **explicit memory** tasks refer to cases in which people are asked to recollect (e.g., recall or recognize) an event from a certain time and place and they are aware of the recollection.

Explicit memory can be contrasted with **implicit memory,** which refers to cases in which some previous experience affects performance without necessarily being associated with any direct (or conscious) recollection of the experience. For example, reading a briefly presented word does not require remembering having seen the word earlier on a list, but if you read words faster that you had seen recently, we could infer that the particular experience was retained in memory. These tasks are also called *indirect* or *incidental* tasks. Most memory research since the early work of Ebbinghaus in the late 1800s has used explicit memory tasks such as recall or recognition (although Ebbinghaus also used savings in relearning, a type of implicit memory task discussed in Chapter 5). But memory has a number of functions, only one of which is the direct access and recollection of an experience. To be clear at the outset, implicit and explicit memory differ in whether there is a direct recollection or conscious experience associated with the memory.

After years of emphasizing recollection, many memory researchers have begun to investigate implicit tasks and how the type of memory tested by these tasks might be related to memory tested by more explicit tasks. Many of the analyses of implicit memory can be considered together as types of **repetition priming**—a previous exposure to a stimulus affects its subsequent processing. For example, suppose you were asked to name the first three fruits that come to mind. Now, further suppose that before that task you were shown a list of words, one of which was *banana*. It might not surprise most people that the probability of generating *banana* when asked for three fruits would be much higher than if you had not seen *banana* in the previous list. Less obvious is the fact that this increased probability can occur even if a person no longer remembers having seen *banana* on the list. One reason for the interest in the distinction between implicit and explicit memory is the possibility that they may be separate memory systems. In order to address this possibility, we will first turn to work on memory in amnesic patients.

Spared Learning in Amnesia

As we discussed earlier, patients with anterograde amnesia have great difficulty learning new information. Although they may show severe impairments in their ability to remember new information that they are queried about, their learning on some tasks is not impaired at all. Specifically, learning tends to be spared on tasks that do not require direct recollection of an earlier experience. Such effects clearly are crucial to our understanding of amnesia, as well as our conceptions of memory.

One place this can be seen is in H. M.'s performance on mirror tracing studies described earlier. These implicit tasks are a good example of spared procedural memory in amnesics. Implicit memory has also been found in perceptual tasks and in verbal tasks. To illustrate this spared learning in perceptual tasks, Cohen and Squire (1980) had amnesic patients and normal controls learn to read mirror-reversed words such as shown in Figure 6.3. Look at the figure and try to read the word triads (sets of three words). This task is difficult at first, but people improve with practice and become quite proficient (see, e.g., Kolers, 1975). Each person was shown triads of words and had to read 50 of these triads on each of three days and then once more about three months later. Amnesic patients showed improvement in this skill at about the same rate as normals. This improvement can be seen in the left

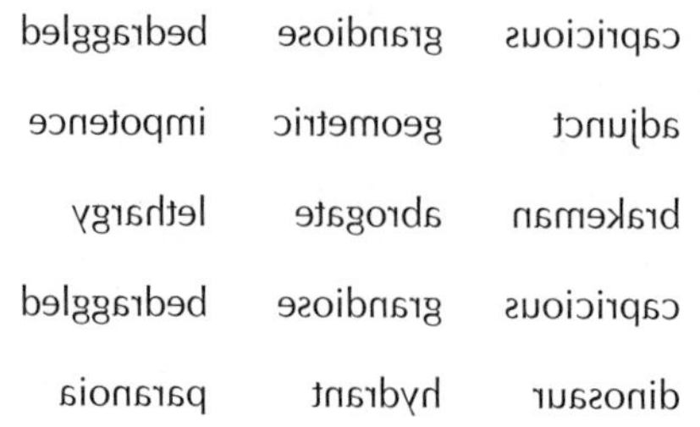

capricious	grandiose	bedraggled
adjunct	geometric	impotence
brakeman	abrogate	lethargy
capricious	grandiose	bedraggled
dinosaur	hydrant	paranoia

Figure 6.3   Examples of mirror-reversed word triads. Try to read them and note how you improve with practice. The fourth line is read even more quickly, because it is a repetition of the first line, an example of repetition priming.

Source: Cohen & Eichenbaum, 1993.

panels in Figure 6.4. The three different graphs represent three different types of amnesics, but the differences among the types is minor compared to the main point—all amnesics are improving at this reading task and doing so at about the same rate as normal control subjects. The graphs on the right side of the figure show the reading time for *repeated* word triads. The performance of all amnesics is improving, and their mean time for repeated triads is faster than their corresponding time for nonrepeated triads (left side of figure), suggesting that something about the particular triads is being retained. This improvement, at about the same rate as the normals, occurred even though their recognition performance for words they had seen before was far worse than the recognition performance of the normals. Other studies with different perceptual and cognitive tasks have found similar sparing of learning, although the amnesic patients often learn at a slightly slower rate than normals (e.g., Knowlton, Squire, & Gluck, 1994).

In addition to the findings with learning new skills, amnesic patients often show repetition priming effects even though they may be unable to explicitly remember the earlier experience. For example, Graf, Squire, and Mandler (1984) presented amnesic patients and control subjects with a list of words twice and then tested the subjects in a variety of memory tasks. The words were chosen so that the first three letters of each word (e.g., *mar—* for the word *market*) occurred in a number of words that were not on the list (e.g., *marry, marble, marsh*). Although their experiments involved several different tests, we consider here the cued recall and word completion tests. In the cued recall test subjects were given the first three letters (e.g., *mar—*) and were asked to recall a word from the earlier list that began with the same three letters. In the word completion task, they were given the first three letters and were told to make these into words by writing the first English word "that comes to mind." Thus, the subjects received exactly the same cues, and the only difference was in the instructions. In both tasks, the dependent measure was how often the words from the list were given as responses.

The results of the cued recall and word completion tests are shown in Figure 6.5. As expected, amnesic subjects were worse on the cued recall test, as can be seen in the left two bars. But on the word completion test (the right two bars), the

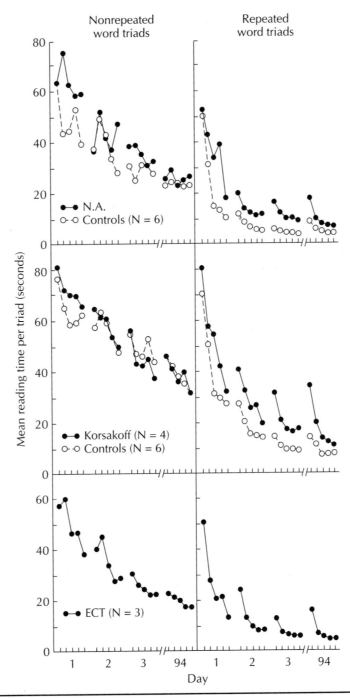

Nonrepeated word triads

Repeated word triads

Mean reading time per triad (seconds)

●—● N.A.
○--○ Controls (N = 6)

●—● Korsakoff (N = 4)
○--○ Controls (N = 6)

●—● ECT (N = 3)

Day

Figure 6.4 Mean reading time for mirror-reversed word triads across practice on 3 days (and a final day 3 months later) for three different types of amnesics. The left-hand graphs show how the general skill of reading mirror-reversed text improves with practice and indicates that the amnesics improved at about the same rate as normal controls. The right panels are reading time of word triads that were repeated in each block. The faster times for the right-hand panel indicates that both amnesics and controls retained usable information about those triads. Again, the improvement for amnesics and controls was about the same.

Source: Cohen & Squire, 1980.

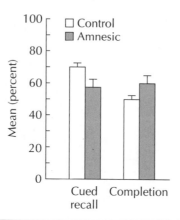

Figure 6.5   Performance by amnesics and controls on an explicit cued recall task (*left*) and an implicit word stem completion task (*right*). The amnesics had lower cued recall but performed equally to the controls on word stem completion.

Source: Data from Graf, Squire, & Mandler, 1984.

amnesic subjects performed at least as well as control subjects. Thus, these repetition priming effects also show preserved learning in amnesia. Notably, the amnesic performance on word completion was almost exactly the same as in cued recall (57.2% vs. 57.6%). Control subjects were much more likely to give the study word to the cue when asked to do so. There are many other results consistent with this general picture, including a variety of different priming effects, such as with spared learning of auditory priming (e.g., Schacter, Church, & Treadwell, 1994). Although it is an open question as to whether these repetition priming and skill learning effects are due to the same processes, both suggest that some learning may be spared in amnesia.

One additional complexity in the study of implicit memory is worth exploring briefly. Findings like increased likelihood of completing a stem (e.g., *mar—*) with a word that appeared on a previous list seems consistent with the idea that the initial presentation of the list is somehow increasing the activation of existing elements in memory. We will discuss this account in more detail below. However, a study by Musen and Squire (1991) suggests that amnesic patients can learn novel associations too. They had amnesics (and normal controls) read a list consisting of words and nonwords (which were created by changing one letter in each syllable of a real word, such as changing *market* to *narbet*). After reading the first list, each subject read a second list containing some new words and nonwords, and some words and nonwords that appeared on the first list. Both amnesic and normal subjects were faster to read both repeated words *and* repeated nonwords. If amnesics improved only for known words, this finding could be interpreted as an increase in the activation of representations of existing words. Because reading of nonwords also was speeded, the amnesics must have learned something about words that they did not know previously. This finding suggests that amnesic patients can show implicit memory even for items that were not known prior to the experiment.

There are many more studies with many more tasks, but we hope the point is clear. Amnesic memory is greatly impaired when an earlier experience is *explicitly* queried (such as in recognition: "Did you see this?") but does not appear to be impaired when the experience is *implicitly* queried, such as by examining priming effects.

Implicit and Explicit Memory with Normal-Memory Adults

The difference between implicit and explicit memory task performance is not only true for amnesics. A (very, very) large number of studies have shown that different manipulations may have very different effects on implicit and explicit tasks. This idea and its theoretical implications have been a dominant force in memory research for the past 15 years. To illustrate the ideas here, we have chosen just a few well-known results.

In one of the first studies in this area, Jacoby and Dallas (1981) examined the effect of a presentation of the word on its subsequent recognition (an explicit task because it requires remembering the word) and perceptual identification, the ability to identify a word presented for a very short time (an implicit task because it does not require recollecting any specific experience). They presented a list of 60 words and asked questions that forced subjects to consider the meaning, rhyming, or particular letters in the word (as in the Craik & Tulving, 1975, study discussed in Chapter 5). Following this study list, subjects were presented with 80 words, 60 that had been presented on the study list and 20 that had not. Half the subjects were given a perceptual identification test for each word, in which the word was presented for 35 milliseconds (about $\frac{1}{30}$th of a second). The other half of the subjects received the 80 words one at a time and had to respond whether they had seen the word on the study list. Jacoby and Dallas found a repetition priming effect on perceptual identification. Words presented on the list were identified correctly 80% of the time, while words that were not presented on the list were identified correctly 65% of the time.

By itself, that result may not seem surprising. Perhaps subjects simply were more likely to guess a word from the list if they were unsure of what they had seen in the brief perceptual identification trial; that is, perhaps this implicit measure is also being influenced by recollection. A problem for this explanation is that Jacoby and Dallas found that manipulating the question asked at study (meaning, rhyme, or letter) affected recognition but had *no* effect on perceptual identification. These data are presented in Figure 6.6. As can be seen in the top bars, questions about meaning led to much better later recognition than did questions about rhyme, which in turn led to better recognition than did questions about whether a particular letter was present. But, as can be seen in the lower bars in this figure, this manipulation had no effect at all on the perceptual identification task, with the probability of reporting the correct word being about the same for the three study conditions. Thus, the repetition priming effect on perceptual identification was not due to subjects' explicit guesses of words on the list, because they would have guessed much better in the meaning condition than the rhyme condition and better in the rhyme condition than the letter condition. Somehow, the prior experience had an effect on perceptual

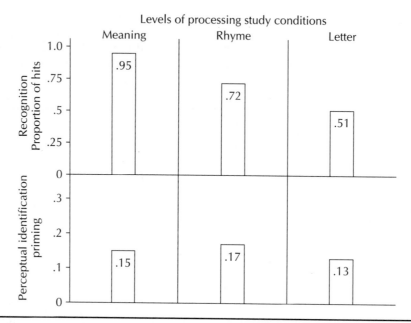

Figure 6.6   Performance on two test tasks for three different levels of processing manipulations at study. The top panels show that the recognition performance was affected by the study manipulations. The bottom panels show that the study manipulations did not affect perceptual identification performance.

Source: Jacoby & Dallas, 1981.

identification that did not depend on the variables that influenced its effect on an explicit memory task.

Some researchers have argued that implicit tasks may reflect sensitivity to a temporary activation of the concept. So, if you see a word on a list, it may activate its corresponding concept for a short time, leading to a facilitation in implicit tasks. Such a view would argue that levels of processing manipulations have no effect because implicit tasks are simply sensitive to whether the concept is active, not the strength of the activation. This activation view cannot be all there is to the implicit memory tasks, however. First, effects on implicit tasks can be quite long-lived, with some effects showing only small decreases over a week or more (see, e.g., Tulving, Schacter, & Stark, 1982). Second, other experimental variables, such as the physical similarity between the study and test presentations, affect implicit measures but not explicit measures (e.g., Rajaram & Roediger, 1993). If the presentation of an item activated the concept, it is difficult to see why manipulations of the physical characteristics of the words would affect implicit memory measures. Finally, the finding of Musen and Squire described above, where implicit memory can be found for novel items argues that implicit memory cannot simply be an activation of existing items in memory.

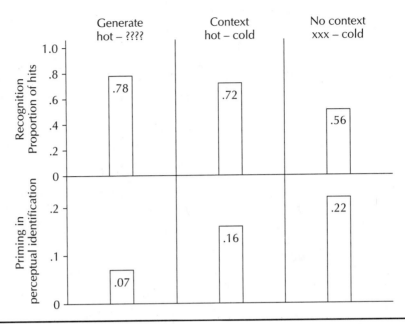

| | Generate
hot – ???? | Context
hot – cold | No context
xxx – cold |

Figure 6.7   Performance on two tasks for three different study conditions: Generate, Context, and No Context. The top panels show that recognition performance decreased from generate to no context. The bottom panels show that perceptual identification performance increased from generate to no Context.

Source: Data from Jacoby, 1983.

So far, we have discussed findings where one manipulation affects one type of test, while another manipulation affects the other type of test. In fact, the same manipulation can have *opposite* effects on explicit and implicit tests, as shown by a well-known study by Jacoby (1983). He manipulated the study conditions under which subjects studied words before the tests. In one condition, "Generate," subjects were given a word and asked to generate its antonym (e.g., *hot—????*). In a second condition, "Context," subjects read the word in the context of its antonym (*hot—COLD*). The third condition was a control, "No Context," condition in which subjects read the word alone (e.g., *xxx—COLD*). At test, subjects were given either an explicit recognition test, in which they had to select words they had studied, or an implicit perceptual identification test (as in the Jacoby & Dallas, 1981, study described earlier). The results are shown in Figure 6.7 and demonstrate clearly that the study manipulation had very different effects on the explicit and implicit tests. More specifically, recognition performance was highest in the Generate condition (a finding known as the *generation effect;* Slamecka & Graf, 1978) and lowest in the No Context condition. However for the perceptual identification test, performance was highest in the No Context condition and lowest in the Generate condition.

A DEBATE
How Many Memory Systems Are There?

In this chapter, we have described different types of memory as if they were independent systems of memory. Part of the reason for this organization is that many memory theorists have thought about these systems as being functionally separate. Many theorists seem to accept the distinction between procedural and declarative memory as a good description of the organization of memory. As mentioned, however, the proposal that semantic and episodic memory are distinct systems is not accepted by all. In addition, the distinction between implicit and explicit memory remains controversial. Let's examine this in more detail.

One criticism of studies supporting the implicit-explicit distinction comes from Ratcliff and McKoon (1995a, 1995b, 1997), who have argued that implicit memory tasks like stem completion and speeded object recognition are not tapping a different kind of memory from explicit tasks like recognition and recall. Instead, when people see an item in a study list, they are biased to respond "yes" to that item in later memory tasks. Whether this facilitates performance depends on the response required by the later memory task. They demonstrate this point through a number of studies in which they present study objects that are similar to ones that will appear on the test, but require a different response. For example, they might show the word *absent* on a study list and then give the stem *abst—* on the test. The stem has elements that appeared in the study list, but is inconsistent with the stem. Given trials of this kind, subjects are much slower to respond than they are to stems for which no word was available. From data like this, Ratcliff and McKoon argue that implicit memory does not simply facilitate processing.

(Continued)

Evaluation of the Implicit-Explicit Distinction

Research on implicit and explicit memory is one of the staples of memory research in cognitive psychology. Beginning with the observation that amnesic patients have spared learning for some types of tests, much research has been conducted on both amnesic patients and people with normal memories. What have we learned from this work on implicit and explicit memory? The research on implicit-explicit measures and their relations has provided new findings that are challenging current theories. Although new findings will eventually lead to better theories, in the course of doing

A DEBATE

How Many Memory Systems Are There? *(Continued)*

Other theorists suggest that implicit memory phenomena should be explained by the similarity in processing of stimuli at study and at test (e.g., Roediger, 1990; Roediger & Blaxton, 1987; Roediger & McDermott, 1993; Roediger, Srinivas, & Weldon, 1989). This view is called **transfer appropriate processing** and is related to the idea of encoding specificity discussed in Chapter 5 (Morris, Bransford, & Franks, 1977). Roediger adds the idea that explicit and implicit tasks typically use different processes. In particular, explicit tasks usually rely on the meaning of the material and can be referred to as *conceptually driven,* whereas implicit tasks more often rely on the match between perceptual operations at study and test and so can be referred to as *data-driven* (see also Jacoby, 1983). Thus, recall or recognition may emphasize meaning, which is why a level of processing effect is found in explicit tasks. Perceptual identification is not affected by that variable, but is affected by the physical similarity of items at study and test because of its perceptual emphasis.

There is some evidence against the transfer-appropriate processing view of the implicit-explicit distinction. Careful studies have found sparing of implicit memory in amnesics on tasks that tap both conceptually driven and data driven processing (Vaidya, Gabrieli, Keane, & Monti, 1995). The data from these studies are better described by models positing a distinction between implicit and explicit memory than between perceptual and conceptual processing. Further advances in cognitive neuroscience will provide information about the way these types of memory are mediated in the brain which will clarify remaining questions like the extent to which performance on implicit tasks simply reflects a bias to respond positively to stimuli seen in the past.

so they also lead to disagreements. These disagreements reflect differences of opinion about the importance of different types of evidence and what it means to argue that memory systems are distinct (see A Debate box).

Important memory distinctions are not going to be decided on the basis of a single study. Rather, what has developed over the past 20 years is an appreciation of how different sources of evidence may all be used together to help understand and refine the important distinctions. Thus, memory researchers incorporate results from a variety of sources including (1) neuropsychological studies of amnesia (some of which we discussed here), (2) studies using psychophysiological measures (such as brain blood flow) and from brain imaging studies, (3) other neurosciences involving models of animal memory (in which the hippocampus has been suggested as important for declarative memories), and (4) evolutionary arguments (see, e.g., Sherry & Schacter, 1987).

There is no current consensus, partly because so much of the work is new and has not been fully assimilated and confirmed. Our current opinion is that the evidence suggests that there are multiple memory systems. The distinction between procedural and declarative memory has particularly good support. However, there are three points that should be noted: First, there is a danger in allowing each new finding of a difference in performance between two memory tasks to be used as evidence for a new memory system (Roediger & McDermott, 1993). Rather, the criteria for establishing a new memory system should be quite stringent to avoid unnecessary proliferation. Second, the analysis of different systems requires a careful cognitive analysis as well. A clear lesson from cognitive neuroscience is that the complexities of the brain require researchers to begin with useful cognitive distinctions (e.g., Jonides et al., 1996; McClelland, McNaughton, & O'Reilly, 1995; Schacter, 1992). Third, the single system proponents have not given up, and new possibilities are still being proposed (e.g., Bower, 1997; Ratcliff & McKoon, 1997; Shiffrin, 1997).

TWO MODELS OF MEMORY

Introduction

All of this discussion about memory systems can seem rather fuzzy. It would be nice to have models of memory that were specified to the point where we understood their specific predictions for particular experimental tasks. Psychologists are sensitive to this need for clearly defined models, and a number of them have been proposed. In the remainder of this chapter, we will describe two very different types of models that are designed to account for many of the phenomena described in this chapter and Chapter 5. The first one, a network model called ACT, extends the network metaphor of the hierarchical model and provides an account of various types of memory phenomena. The second, a PDP or connectionist model, also provides an account of many memory phenomena but in a very different way. (Also see Hintzman, 1988, for another approach to modeling memory.)

The ACT Theory

The network model we will consider here combines the storage and retrieval of episodic and semantic knowledge. The **ACT (adaptive control of thought)** theory of John R. Anderson (1976; revised as ACT*, pronounced "act-star," in 1983, and as ACT-R in 1991) is an attempt to account for a wide variety of phenomena and data

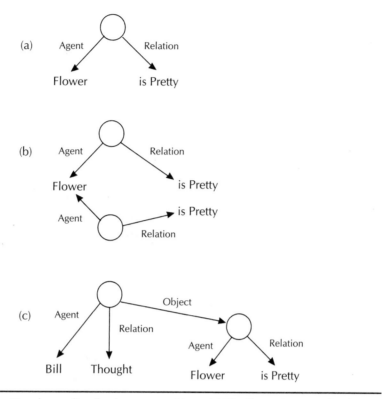

Figure 6.8   ACT propositional encoding for three propositions: (a) The flower is pretty. (b) The flower is pretty and red. (c) Bill thinks that the flower is pretty.

in memory, learning, language, problem solving, and reasoning within the same framework. Although this ambitious project can be dealt with only briefly here, Anderson's view of memory has been influential and has helped psychologists to understand the interrelations among memory phenomena.

Representation in the Model

Anderson conceptualizes memory as a network of nodes and links, but the nodes (concepts) and links (relations) are organized into propositions. **Propositions** can be thought of as the smallest unit of meaning about which one can reasonably assert truth or falsity. For example, one cannot find the word *pretty* either true or false without knowing what *pretty* is being asserted about. In contrast, "The flower is pretty" is a proposition, because it makes sense to say that it is either true or false. Thus, propositions can be viewed as encoding a fact. Figure 6.8a shows how ACT would represent this fact. The labels on the links specify the "role" or semantic relation of the node in the proposition. Note that a sentence can have multiple propositions. For instance, "The flower is pretty and red" contains two propositions, one claiming the flower is pretty and one claiming the flower is red, as depicted in Figure 6.8b. Both

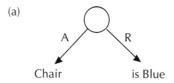

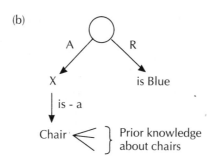

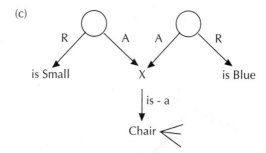

Figure 6.9 **The Type-Token Distinction** Panel (a) shows the simplified representation with no distinction made between types and tokens. Panel (b) shows how the distinction is represented. X is a token, a specific chair that is blue. The *chair* node is the type node, encoding knowledge about chairs in general. Panel (c) shows how new information about the token, X, is represented off the token node. To simplify the figure, the semantic relations on the links have been abbreviated, with *A* for agent and *R* for relation.

propositions have the same agent because the information in the two propositions (pretty and red) is being claimed about the same particular flower. Each proposition can be said to be true or false, which allows for the possibility that the flower might be pretty but not red. In addition, propositions can be embedded to express complex ideas, so the simple proposition "the flower is pretty" can be embedded within a more complex sentence, such as "Bill thinks that the flower is pretty," as shown in Figure 6.8c. In fact, people are able to understand very complex embedding of propositions, such as "The two lawyers argued about whether the witness had meant to say that Bill thinks that the flower is pretty." We do not present the representation of this sentence.

The idea that memory consists of propositions is important when one realizes that Anderson is trying to account not only for semantic knowledge but for new episodic knowledge as well. The claim is that people encode the meaning of new information, not the exact wording; thus, it is important to have a memory organized around the meanings. Indeed, people often do forget the exact wording of sentences and remember the meaning or gist of new information (Bransford, Barclay, & Franks, 1972).

Because memory is assumed to consist of propositions, another representational issue arises. Concepts in the hierarchical network described above were general concepts (e.g., the idea of a chair), but the information contained in a proposition like "the chair is blue" is often about a particular chair. If you were representing the meaning of the sentence "The chair is blue," you would not want to attach the meaning to the general concept of chairs as shown in Figure 6.9a. This representation would actually mean that chairs in general are blue, when all we really mean to say is that a particular chair is blue. To keep track of the distinction between a specific chair and chairs in general, ACT makes use of a **type-token distinction.** Philosophers of mind have used the word *type* to refer to general concepts, and the word *token* to refer to specific instances of that concept (like a particular chair that happens to be blue). In a network model like ACT, a token of a chair can be represented using an arbitrary label as in Figure 6.9b. Here, the symbol X is used to stand for a particular chair that is blue. We know it is a chair, because this symbol is connected to the concept *chair* using an "is-a" link. Knowledge about chairs in general is attached to the *chair* node. Knowledge about the token X is attached directly to that symbol. Figure 6.9c shows a second fact also connected to X.

A final aspect of the network representation used by ACT is that links differ in strength. Frequently encountered relations are represented by stronger links than infrequently encountered information. As we will see in the next section, this difference in strength will influence the way information is processed in the network.

Processing in the Model

The representations in ACT are much more complex than are those in the hierarchical model. The processing of information in the network also differs from that in the hierarchical model. In the hierarchical model, activation tags were sent from one node to another along the directed links, marking each node they visited until an intersection was found. In ACT, as well as other network models that followed the hierarchical model (e.g., Collins & Loftus, 1975), each node has a level of *activation*. The activation of a node corresponds to the degree to which it is accessible in working memory (see Chapter 5). In ACT, working memory is just the set of nodes in the network with some level of activation. The limitation on working memory is the maximum amount of activation that can exist in the network at any time (Anderson, Reder, & Lebiere, 1996).

When a sentence is being processed, the nodes corresponding to concepts in that sentence are given some activation. Activation then *spreads* through the network along the links. The stronger the link between two nodes, the more activation that one node gives another. This **spreading activation** is similar to the interactive activation discussed in Chapter 4. An analogy may help make this idea clearer. Activation spread can be viewed as information being broadcast (e.g., yelled) to all close neighbors, who in turn broadcast it to their neighbors, and so on. If a node is connected to many nodes that have some activation, then it will receive some activation from all of those nodes. Thus, the activation that arrives at a node is a function of both the number of activated concepts it is linked to and also the strength of the links to those nodes. In order to limit the total activation that flows in the network, each node also has a decay rate. At each time step, some of the activation in each node fades or dissipates so that if a node ceases to get activation from neighboring nodes, it will eventually return to a state of zero activation, where it falls out of working memory.

A final important point about processing is that the activation that spreads from any concept is divided among the links from the concept, with the strongest links (i.e., those encoding more frequently occurring relations to that concept) receiving more activation. As we will see, the division of activation among the outgoing links will turn out to have an important influence on the predictions of the ACT model.

It is instructive to consider how this process works for a simple recognition question (i.e., "Have you seen this sentence? [...]"). When a sentence is given for recognition, the concepts contained in the sentence are activated, and activation spreads from these concepts to the neighboring concepts through the links in the network. Recognition occurs when the activation from the concepts leads to an intersection (i.e., the appropriate proposition or propositions are activated) and the level of activation is above some threshold. This intersection is evaluated as indicating that the concepts were studied in the same sentence, and the answer "yes" can be given to the recognition question.

Evidence Consistent With ACT

What is the evidence for a spreading activation search? The results of Meyer and Schvaneveldt's (1971) research discussed earlier, in which *doctor* primed *nurse*, are consistent with models that use spreading activation like ACT-R as well as extensions of the hierarchical model (Collins & Loftus, 1975). Essentially, the presentation of a priming word will spread activation to neighboring concepts, which will ease the retrieval of those semantically similar words. Ratcliff and McKoon (1988, 1994) argued against spreading activation, but additional arguments in favor of spreading activation have been presented by McNamara (1992, 1994).

This discussion of activation and its spread is rather abstract, but an example should help to make the ideas clearer. Suppose you had learned a number of sentences about a doctor and a number of sentences about a lawyer, and you were queried about whether you had learned the sentence "The lawyer fought the doctor." Figure 6.10 provides a schematic of this portion of the assumed propositional network. The concepts *lawyer, fought,* and *doctor* would be activated. The activation would spread from these concepts and, given their connectedness, it is likely that an intersection would occur in which the proposition that includes all three of them

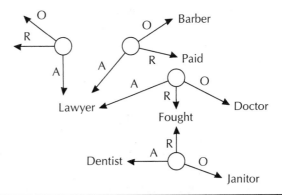

Figure 6.10   ACT propositional encoding for the sentence "The lawyer fought the doctor," as well as for a number of other sentences that include the concepts "lawyer," "fought," and "doctor." The fan off each concept is the number of other propositions in which it occurs, so the fans of lawyer, fought, and doctor are 3, 2, and 1, respectively. To simplify the figure, the semantic relations on the links have been abbreviated, with *A* for agent, *R* for relation, and *O* for object.

would be activated. The time to the intersection would depend on how long it took for the activation at the intersection of these three concepts to rise above some threshold, which in turn would depend on how much activation spread from each concept down the relevant links. The amount of activation that spreads down a link (1) increases, the stronger (more frequently used) the link, and (2) decreases, the more links from the concept with which the activation needs to be shared.

Because ACT assumes that frequency affects the strength of the links, which in turn affects the speed with which knowledge is accessible, it predicts the well-researched finding that more frequently occurring information is accessed more quickly than less frequently occurring information (e.g., see Anderson, 1976, pp. 283–290). ACT also provides an account of how memories may interfere with one another, which may make some information inaccessible (as discussed in Chapter 5). This interference stems from an examination of the **fan effect.** Recall that we pointed out that the amount of activation leaving a node is divided among all of the links exiting that node. The number of exiting links is called the *fan* of the concept, because a picture of many exiting links resembles the structure of a fan. The more links emanating from a concept, the more divided the activation, and thus the longer it will take other nodes in the network to reach high levels of activation. Assuming that retrieval requires a node to reach a threshold level of activation, this will slow down the retrieval of concepts attached to nodes with a high fan. (Although we discuss this interference in terms of time to retrieve information, interference also includes cases in which the asked-for information is not found within a reasonable time and the person decides he or she cannot remember.)

The fan effect is an important prediction of ACT, and Anderson and his colleagues have provided a great deal of empirical support for it (see Anderson, 1976, 1983, for reviews). A typical experiment varies the fan from the different concepts in each sentence. Using Figure 6.10 as an example, concepts are included in one, two, or three other learned sentences, such as *doctor, fought,* and *lawyer,* respectively. The results show that the time to recognize a sentence increases with the number of other sentences learned about the different concepts. Thus, it takes longer to recognize sentences that include concepts that are also included in many other sentences.

We have considered the ACT model as applied to learning episodic information, but an important aspect of the model is that the same representation and retrieval principles are used for explaining memory for knowledge about semantic information, such as concepts (Anderson & Ross, 1980) or historical knowledge (C. H. Lewis & Anderson, 1976). The main problems with the hierarchical model of semantic information arose from having all category information equally available and using only superordinate information to make category judgments. ACT addresses both of these problems: Having links that vary in strength allows some category knowledge to be accessed more quickly than others, and the use of a network, not a hierarchy, with spreading activation and the evaluation of intersections, means that nonhierarchical information will affect category judgments. For example, the typicality effect (i.e., that *robin-bird* is verified more quickly than *penguin-bird*) comes about because the high frequency of typical instances (e.g., robin) leads the propositions containing them and the category (e.g., bird) to be activated much more quickly than propositions containing atypical instances (e.g., penguin). The hierarchy from the Collins and Quillian model is included (with "is-a" labeled links), but much nonhierarchical information is incorporated as well.

A brief discussion of a study by Lewis and Anderson illustrates the power of the ACT theory to incorporate both semantic and episodic information. In this study, subjects learned episodic fantasy facts about well-known historical figures, such as "George Washington wrote *Tom Sawyer.*" The fan, or number of these facts, learned about each historical figure varied from zero to four, as shown in Table 6.1. In the examples in the table, there is only one new fantasy fact about George Washington (fan of 1) and four new fantasy facts about Napoleon Bonaparte (fan of 4). At a later test, the dependent variable is the time to verify well-known historical facts (e.g., "George Washington crossed the Delaware"). The results were that reaction time to verify semantic information increased with each additional fantasy fact learned about the individual. Thus, the more episodic facts one learned about the individual, the more interference in retrieving well-learned semantic knowledge.

This last result has an interesting implication. Everything else equal, the more you learn about a concept, the longer it should take you to retrieve any particular fact about that concept because the fan has increased. Yet often it seems that when we know much about a topic we have quick access to a large number of facts. There may be many reasons for the increase in accessibility of concepts in an area of expertise, and one important influence is likely to be the way we use our memory in real-world situations. Often, we are not concerned with verbatim recognition of a particular fact, but rather whether a particular fact is true or not (or if we believe it is true). If you learn that "A dax is a bird" and "A dax flies," and you were asked if a dax has wings, you would respond "yes." You would not care whether you had learned that a dax has wings as long as it is a likely inference from what you do

Table 6.1   **Examples of Material Used in the Lewis and Anderson (1976) Experiment**   The numbers before the test facts indicate the number of study sentences that included this famous person.

Examples of artificial facts studied:
George Washington wrote Tom Sawyer.
Napoleon Bonaparte was from India.
Napoleon Bonaparte was a singer.
Napoleon Bonaparte is a liberal senator.
Napoleon Bonaparte had a ranch.
Examples of test probes:
  Actual facts
    0 Fidel Castro is Cuban.
    1 George Washington crossed the Delaware.
    4 Napoleon Bonaparte was an emperor.
  Fantasy facts
    1 George Washington wrote Tom Sawyer.
    4 Napoleon Bonaparte was from India.
  False
    0 Fidel Castro was a Texan politician.
    1 George Washington is a swimmer.
    4 Napoleon Bonaparte was a humorist.

Source: Lewis, C. H., & Anderson, 1976.

know. Reder (1982) has proposed that memory judgments are often made along the lines of these plausible inferences rather than by retrieving the exact information queried.

Reder and Ross (1983) provide evidence that, if responses are based on plausibility, as opposed to the strict recognition of the sentence, then the more facts known about a concept, the faster the response. In their study, subjects learned a number of sentences about some person and some activity (e.g., Steven, moving):

Steven called to have a phone installed.

Steven read and signed the lease.

Steven unpacked all of his boxes.

Subjects were then queried about a sentence that was related to these activities, such as "Steven mailed out change-of-address cards" or new sentences about Steven that were unrelated to moving. (During the experiment, the subjects had learned about two other people who had mailed change-of-address cards.) In one condition, subjects were required to make strict recognition judgments about whether they had studied the exact sentence. As in the previous fan effect research, the more facts they learned about the queried concepts, the longer the time to respond that they had seen that exact sentence (e.g., "Steven read and signed the lease"). In another condition, subjects were presented with these same test sentences but now had to respond whether this test sentence was plausible, given the other facts they knew about this person. In this condition, the more facts they had learned about the queried concepts, the faster the response. This result is important in showing that people can often base their judgments on plausible inferences. In real-world use, one is rarely concerned with whether a literal fact has been learned at a particular time but rather whether the information is likely to be true. Under these circumstances, the number of relevant facts may aid rather than hinder the judgment.

The ACT theory has focused researchers on a variety of questions, such as the use of strict recognition versus plausibility judgments. According to this theory, the same representation used to make one type of judgment has to be suitable for predicting effects in the other type of judgment. Using a single representation for both judgments greatly constrains possible explanations. (See Reder & Ross, 1983, for one way to account for these results within the ACT framework.)

We have been focusing on ACT's claims about factual, or declarative, memory, but how might it deal with the distinction between procedural and declarative memory? The ACT model makes a fundamental distinction between procedural and declarative representations. The theory represents the two types of memories differently and independently, although any particular task may use both. The network representation is the declarative representation. Anderson views this representation, along with the spreading activation, as a method for activating relevant information. The procedural part of memory, however, is the part that takes this possibly relevant information and makes use of it. The details of the procedural memory in ACT, a representation called *productions,* are discussed in more detail in Chapter 13 when we discuss expertise and creativity.

General Points

Part of the reason for providing such detail on ACT is that this theory provides possible answers to two important questions about the flexibility of memory related to our themes of relevance and complexity: (1) How do we determine what knowledge is relevant? (2) Once we have determined relevance, how do we find the exact information we are looking for?

First, given all that one knows, how is the relevant knowledge retrieved? Spreading activation can be viewed as a mechanism for focusing on information that is likely to be relevant. That is, when one uses a concept, often the most relevant knowledge is knowledge closely related to the concept. Spreading activation makes this knowledge more accessible. In ACT, knowledge that is closely related to the activated information (i.e., frequent, low fan, or both) is available more quickly. Thus, this model claims that the relevant knowledge in a particular situation is likely to be the knowledge that has been related to it in the past. (Also, see Anderson, 1990a, for a model that builds upon this claim.)

Second, this model gives an interesting partial answer to the question, How do we retrieve the specific information we are looking for? The answer is that we may not always retrieve the information, but instead, we may infer the right information given what we do retrieve. Rather than viewing the use of memory as retrieving exactly the information queried, this model takes the view that other information may be relevant as well and that sometimes one may respond without having the exact information queried. For example, people may answer that a bat is not a bird, not because they know that it is not a bird but because they retrieve various items of information suggesting that it may not be or that it may be more similar to some mammals, or both. Similarly, with episodic materials, they may answer a query about a particular event by retrieving other knowledge about that event or related events. In short, remembering is not simply retrieving stored facts, but rather memory may be used in a variety of ways in the service of accessing relevant knowledge quickly.

A Parallel Distributed Processing Model of Memory

In this section, we will consider **parallel distributed processing (PDP),** a very different approach to modeling memory that combines episodic and semantic memory into the same system (McClelland & Rumelhart, 1986a). In the ACT model just described, each concept exists as a separate node in a network. Adding a new concept is straightforward. A new node can be added to the network, and links between that concept and related concepts can be added. In contrast, in a simple PDP model, the same set of nodes is used to represent all of the concepts in memory. Thus, adding new concepts will not only add this new information, but will also change what is known about other concepts. At such an abstract level this may sound like doublespeak, but the McClelland and Rumelhart proposal is quite specific in how prior experiences can affect memory and the results of memory retrievals. We discuss these models in detail, because they are widely used in cognitive psychology.

In this section, we first give a general overview of the way PDP models work. The section after that provides more details of the mechanism of these models in the form of an example. Finally, we have included an appendix to this chapter that provides a more specific description of the mathematics underlying connectionist models.

General Description of the Model

Parallel distributed processing (PDP) models were inspired by examinations of the structure of the brain. The brain has lots of cells called neurons that send electrical signals to each other. No particular neuron seems to be all that important to cognitive activity. For example, you lose neurons all the time, but that does not significantly impair your cognitive performance. Neurons in the cortex of the brain (the outer folded area of the brain) are organized into layers, and the neurons in a particular layer often seem to have a common function. Furthermore, most of the brain is active in processing information most of the time, so the same areas of the brain (and presumably the same neurons) are involved in processing in many different contexts. Finally, as discussed in Chapter 1, when an electrical signal is sent down a neuron, it leads to the release of chemicals that influence neighboring neurons. There are two important aspects of these connection between neurons that are captured in connectionist models. First, connections have a *valence,* which determines how the activation of one neuron affects the activation of another. In particular, the connection may

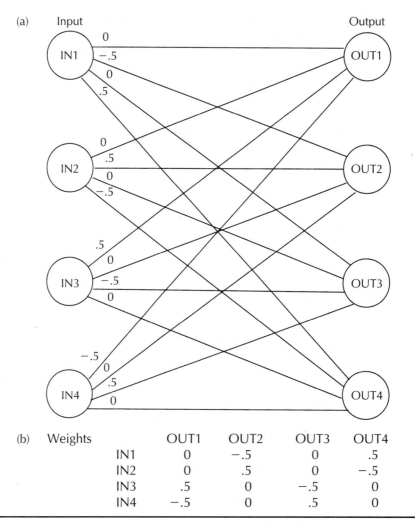

(a)   Input   Output

(b)   Weights

Weights	OUT1	OUT2	OUT3	OUT4
IN1	0	−.5	0	.5
IN2	0	.5	0	−.5
IN3	.5	0	−.5	0
IN4	−.5	0	.5	0

Figure 6.11   A simple example of a PDP network with four input elements and four output elements. (a) This network perfectly responds to the PAIR1 and PAIR2 associations given in the text. The input-output weight is indicated by the number on the line connecting them. (b) The matrix provides another way of showing the weights on the input-output connections of the network. For example, the weight of the connection between IN1 and OUT2 is -.5.

be *excitatory,* in which case the firing of one neuron makes the other one more likely to send its own signal, or it may be *inhibitory,* in which case the firing of one neuron makes the other one less likely to send its own signal. Second, connections have a *strength* that determines the degree to which the activation of one neuron affects the activation of another. In the brain, connections can be made stronger or weaker through learning.

While PDP models do not attempt to model the precise way that brains carry out computations, they do take these observations as a metaphor that guides the way the models are put together. A simple PDP model is illustrated in Figure 6.11 (this model is related to Cohen et al.'s model of the Stroop effect discussed in Chapter 1). By now, you should be familiar with the idea that there are nodes (the circles) and links (the lines). In a PDP model, the nodes are analogous to neurons (and hence will sometimes be called *units* in this discussion). The nodes are organized into layers. In this example, there is an *input layer* on the left and an *output layer* on the right. In a PDP model, each unit can have a level of activation. Activation of a unit in the input layer can affect the activation of a unit in the output layer by having activation spread across the links between layers. These links can vary in their valence (whether they are excitatory or inhibitory) and in their strength, just as the valence and strength connections between neurons in the brain can vary.

Just as no individual neuron in the brain matters crucially to processing, so too no individual unit in a PDP model is crucial. Unlike the ACT model, where nodes represented specific concepts, in a PDP model, it is the *pattern* of activity across the units in a layer that represents a concept. For example, the pattern of activation $(+1 \; -1 \; -1 \; +1)$ on the input units might represent "DOG" and the pattern $(-1 \; -1 \; +1 \; +1)$ on the output units might represent "BARK." (A pattern of activation on a particular set of units is said to represent a concept when that pattern is consistently interpreted as meaning that concept.) Following the convention in many PDP models, we will use the value of $+1$ to talk about a unit that is very active and a value of -1 to talk about a unit that is very inactive (a value of 0 is often used for values that are unknown). We must make clear that this example is highly simplified. In many actual connectionist models, the input and output patterns may have hundreds of input and output units.

The goal of processing in a PDP model is to associate some pattern of activity in the input layer with some other pattern of activity in the output layer. For example, we can construct a network that could respond with the pattern for the sound an animal makes (e.g., BARK) given the pattern for the name of the animal (DOG). The weights of the links between the input units and the output units can be adjusted to allow this association to be made. We discuss the procedure for adjusting the weights to learn an association in the appendix to this chapter.

If all we could do was to store the association between one input and one output, this model would not be very useful. We would have to have a different network for every association between concepts, which would not be very efficient. The power of PDP models is that it is possible to store many different associations between inputs and outputs in the same network. Thus, the same set of input nodes might participate in patterns of activation for the names DOG, CAT, and GOAT, while the same set of output units might participate in patterns of activation for the associated noises BARK, MEOW, and MEH.

Because a number of associations are stored in the same network, it is possible for different associations to interfere with each other. In particular, if the pattern of activity for one concept is similar to the pattern of activity for another (we will be more specific about what we mean by *similarity* below), then the model will have

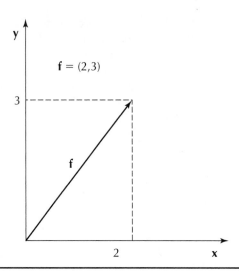

Figure 6.12   The geometry of a simple two dimensional vector. This vector, *f*, points to the point (2,3).

difficulty telling these concepts apart. In this case, the model may confuse one concept for another. This pattern of performance seems reasonable, because people are more likely to confuse one item for another when they are similar than when they are dissimilar.

So far, we have established that PDP models are based on an analogy to the structure of the brain. The individual units do not carry much information, but the pattern of activity across a layer of units represents information. Somehow, the weights on the links between layers can be set to learn associations between a number of different input and output patterns. In order to explore PDP models more deeply, it is necessary to provide a little more detail about how they process information.

A More Detailed Look at Processing

Because PDP models have had such a profound effect on cognitive psychology over the past 15 years, we think it is important to discuss them in some detail. A warning in advance, however. The concepts in this section are difficult and sometimes technical, but these details are necessary to understand the way these models work.

At a general level, it is helpful to think of a pattern of activation as defining a vector in space. A vector is a line that can be described using a list of numbers like the coordinates in the Cartesian coordinate plane you probably learned in algebra. For example, the dark arrow in Figure 6.12 is a vector that points from the origin (where the x and y axes meet) to the point (2,3). Vectors like this can be described by a list of numbers that specify the coordinates of the end of the vector. This vector (which is labeled **f**) can be described by the values (2,3). Each value of the vector represents its position relative to a certain dimension. The vector **f** is a vector in a 2-dimensional space, and the values in the list correspond to the locations of the vectors along the x and y dimensions respectively.

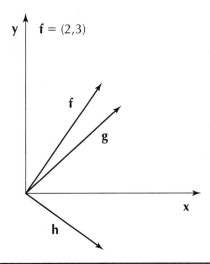

Figure 6.13 **Similar and dissimilar vectors** The vector **g** points in a direction similar to the direction of the vector **f**. In contrast, the vector **h** is orthogonal to the vector **f**. Vectors **f** and **g** should be used to represent similar concepts, while the vectors **f** and **h** should be used to represent independent concepts.

Notice that the list of values for the vector **f** is like the list of values for the pattern DOG (-1 $+1$ $+1$ -1) and the pattern BARK ($+1$ $+1$ -1 -1). The difference is that these patterns have four values (they are 4-dimensional vectors). It may be hard to imagine, but you could think of these vectors as pointing to locations in a 4-dimensional space.

This geometric view of vectors is helpful, because it tells us when two patterns are similar. In particular, two vectors are similar when they point in a similar direction. For example, in Figure 6.13, the vectors **f** and **g** point in a similar direction. Similar vectors represent similar concepts. In contrast, the vectors **f** and **h** point in independent (or orthogonal) directions. Two directions are independent when moving in one direction means you are not moving at all in the other. For example, North and East are orthogonal, because if you walk due North, you are not walking at all East. However, Northeast is not orthogonal to North, because if you walk Northeast, you are moving somewhat in a northerly direction. In a normal (Euclidean) space, lines that are 90° apart are orthogonal. In a PDP model, orthogonal vectors are used to represent independent (i.e., dissimilar) concepts.

All that a PDP model is doing is finding a set of numerical weights on the connections between input and output units so that a particular input pattern (say $[-1 \ -1 \ -1 \ -1]$) will lead to a desired pattern on the output units (say $[-1 \ -1 \ +1 \ +1]$). The actual equations that create the **connection weights** that cause the desired output pattern given a particular input are shown in the appendix. Once these weights are established, though, patterns that are similar to this input vector in (4-dimensional) space will yield patterns on the output units that are like the desired output pattern. Input patterns that are orthogonal to the learned pattern on the input units will not yield any output pattern at all.

After a first association is learned, a second association between a different input pattern and some other output pattern can be learned in the same network by adding together the connection weights that associate the first input and output (say patterns for DOG and BARK) to connection weights that associate the second input and output (say patterns for CAT and MEOW). If it turned out that the patterns that stand for DOG and CAT are orthogonal (or nearly orthogonal) both the associations for DOG-BARK and CAT-MEOW can be learned. Only when the vectors for DOG and CAT point in nearly the same direction will it be difficult to learn associations for both of them, because then they will interfere with each other.

The important thing to remember is that the geometry of vectors is very important for understanding how PDP models work. The list of activations on the input units corresponds to a vector in a space with N dimensions (where N is the number of input units). Vectors that point in a similar direction to this input vector will be treated similarly by the network. Vectors that point in dissimilar (i.e., orthogonal) directions to this input vector will be treated differently. In the next section we will give a simple example that demonstrates the mathematics that makes use of the connection weights.

A Simplified Example

We present a simplified example, borrowed from McClelland, Rumelhart, and Hinton (1986). Although the area of research on PDP models is growing quickly and many more recent models exist, for the beginner this model may show the points more clearly. Even for this model, we will make some simplifying assumptions. First, we will assume that the stimuli can be represented as vectors with only four values. Second, we will assume that the network is quite simple, with the four-value input leading to a four-value output. The input vector will represent the stimulus, and the output vector will represent the system's response to the input. Each of the four input units is connected to each of the four output units, as shown in Figure 6.11a. Figure 6.11b shows the weights of the simple network in matrix form. The matrix is set up so that a given value in the matrix corresponds to the strength of the connection between the input unit denoted by the row and the output unit denoted by the column. If the value is positive, the connection is excitatory (because higher activation on the input unit leads to higher activation on the output unit), and if the value is negative, the connection is inhibitory (because higher activation on the input unit leads to lower activation on the output unit). Finally, the larger the value in the matrix, the stronger the connection between that input and output unit. (The chapter appendix explains how these weights were computed.)

This network was trained on two different arbitrary associations with the following input-output pairings (i.e., given an input vector, the goal is to produce the corresponding output vector):

	Input Vector	*Output Vector*
PAIR1	(+1 −1 −1 +1)	(−1 −1 +1 +1)
PAIR2	(−1 +1 −1 +1)	(−1 +1 +1 −1)

We are specifically setting up this example so that the two input vectors are orthogonal. (There is a way of checking whether vectors are orthogonal, but for now, let's just take it on faith.) Because the input vectors are orthogonal, we will be able to store associations for both of these input vectors in the same connection matrix without having them interfere with each other.

Assuming we have this network, how is it used? To determine the value of the output vector, we multiply the value of the input element by its weight and add all the values for a given output element. (It may be helpful for you to refer to the figure.) For example, using PAIR1, let's first determine the value for output unit 1, OUT1. As you can see, it has connection weights to each of the input units, the lines in Figure 6.11a between IN1 and OUT1, IN2 and OUT1, etc. In Figure 6.11b, these are the numbers in the column under the heading OUT1. OUT1 gets an activation of +1 from the first input element (IN1) times the weight between IN1 and OUT1 of 0, so it is 0; OUT1 also gets −1 times 0 from IN2, −1 times .5 from IN3, and +1 times −.5 from IN4. Thus, the value at OUT1 is:

$$OUT1 = (+1 \times 0) + (-1 \times 0) + (-1 \times .5) + (+1 \times -.5) = -1$$

The second element, OUT2, gets an activation of +1 from IN1 times the IN1 to OUT2 weight of −.5, plus −1 from IN2 times the IN2 to OUT2 weight of .5, plus −1 from IN3 times 0, and +1 from IN4 times 0, with the sum being −.5 + (−.5) = −1. Using this same method, the output for the remaining two elements of the output vector is as desired, −1 and +1. Thus, this set of weights does encode the PAIR1 association; that is, given the input (+1 −1 −1 +1), the network responds with (−1 −1 +1 +1).

This example shows that these weights will transform the input vector of PAIR1 to the appropriate output vector. However, memory systems usually encode more than one stimulus. The power of the PDP approach is that the same weights can be used to encode multiple associations. For example, the simple network we have presented was constructed by also having it learn the association PAIR2 previously given. Referring again to Figure 6.11, the input (−1 +1 −1 +1) leads to the desired output (−1 +1 +1 −1). To do one calculation here:

$$OUT1 = (-1 \times 0) + (+1 \times 0) + (-1 \times .5) + (+1 \times -.5) = -1$$

This example can be used to illustrate four points about the PDP approach: (a) its distributed nature, (b) the encoding of specific and general information, (c) the use of partial information, and (d) the effects of learning.

DISTRIBUTED REPRESENTATION   First, this example shows the knowledge is distributed (hence the *D* in PDP) in two ways: (1) the knowledge does not reside in any single location but is encoded throughout the network in the weights; (2) the same sets of weights can be used to encode multiple pieces of knowledge. As we shall see, distributed representations facilitate generalization and the use of partial information.

GENERAL AND SPECIFIC INFORMATION   As we mentioned, a basic problem in memory is how one deals with both remembering specific information and learning abstractions. For instance, as we meet new people, we may want to remember each person, but at the same time use these people to learn more about people in general and also about specific categories of people. Many theories would assume that specific and abstract learning would require separate connections. In the PDP approach, however, the same set of weights can lead to remembering specific information and learning abstractions.

If we look at the two input and output vectors in PAIR1 and PAIR2, we see that certain values are the same. In particular, IN3 (-1) and IN4 ($+1$) occur in both pairs, as do OUT1 (-1) and OUT3 ($+1$). What would happen if we gave the network an input that was just these similar values on IN3 and IN4? That is, what if we gave the network the input (0 0 -1 $+1$)? (Remember that 0 reflects an unknown value.) Given this input, the output (-1 0 $+1$ 0) is obtained. That is, given the values shared by the two input units, the values that the output vectors have in common is generated. One can think of the input (0 0 -1 $+1$) as a general pattern that captures common aspects of the two inputs. Thus, although this general pattern was never before presented, the network has captured the regularities of the two patterns.

PARTIAL INFORMATION   An important feature of our memory is that we may use partial information about an event or association to retrieve further information. You may have learned to associate the appearance of a dog with its name, but if you see just the face of the dog, you can often recall its name. As we noted in Chapter 5, the more of the encoding context one has at retrieval, the better, but an exact match is not usually needed to retrieve some information. The PDP models allow use of partial inputs to retrieve partial outputs.

For example, again using Figure 6.11, suppose one just had the first three elements of the input for PAIR1, ($+1$ -1 -1 0). The output would not be the exact association learned, (-1 -1 $+1$ $+1$), but a similar output ($-.5$ -1 $+.5$ $+1$). Thus, partial input allows one to retrieve some relevant information but often not exactly the encoded information. How close to the original output one gets depends on how much of the input is unknown and how much that unknown input could be made up for by the regularities already encoded into the network.

LEARNING MORE IN THE SAME NETWORK   How do these systems learn additional information? The learning details are described in the chapter appendix, but we provide a characterization of one general learning procedure here. The output activation values are a function of the input values times the weights (what the system knew before the input). These output values are then compared to some target values. (Learning requires some feedback. This feedback about performance may come from an outside source, such as a teacher or parent, or the system itself may notice discrepancies between the output and target values.) The error, the difference between the output and target values, is used to change the weights, with more change being made to weights that led to greater error or that were from high input values.

We chose the particular network in Figure 6.11 to illustrate how two different associations could be perfectly stored together in the same network. We did this by selecting input vectors that were orthogonal. Perfect remembering is not usually

After learning

$$(\ 1 \quad 1 \quad 1 \quad -1) \rightarrow (\ 1 \quad 1 \quad 1 \quad 1)$$

	OUT1	OUT1	OUT2	OUT3
IN1	0	−.25	.83	.75
IN2	0	.75	.83	−.25
IN3	.5	.25	.33	.25
IN4	−.5	−.25	.99	−.25

Figure 6.14   New matrix values for input-output connections after learning PAIR3.

the case in PDP models. Rather, as more information is stored, it begins to affect the retrieval of earlier information. For instance, suppose we had the network in Figure 6.11 also learn another pattern pair:

PAIR3: input (+1 +1 +1 −1) and output (+1 +1 +1 +1)

This new input vector is not orthogonal to either the input vectors in PAIR 1 or PAIR 2. The new weights (again, see the chapter appendix for learning details), in matrix form, are given in Figure 6.14. Given the input (+1 +1 +1 −1), this network would give the output (+1 +1 +1 +1). However, the earlier pair outputs would suffer: PAIR1 output would be (−1 −1.5 +.66 +.5) instead of the earlier (−1 −1 +1 +1), and PAIR2 would be (−1 +.5 +.66 −1.5) instead of (−1 +1 +1 −1). Because this new input vector was not orthogonal to the ones already learned, the changes to the weights made to accommodate the new pair were inconsistent with some of the weights needed to generate the earlier pairs. This interference problem (an instance of retroactive interference) can be quite severe in some PDP models, and is more severe than any interference that people show (McCloskey & Cohen, 1989; Ratcliff, 1990; French, 1999).

General Properties

The PDP model views retrieval as bringing to bear relevant knowledge, which can come from multiple sources. Because all the memories are encoded together in the same set of weights, every memory influences the "remembering" of every other memory. The advantages of interactive memory structures come from the need for flexibility and multiple purposes. In the future, we may see only partial inputs and need to "remember" the rest, or we may see new items and have to "remember" similar old items and respond in similar ways. The PDP approach argues that these needs are met by storing new experiences in the same set of weights.

Remembering is often thought of as a retrieval of a memory trace, but such a view is inappropriate when there is no separate memory trace to retrieve. Rather, PDP models take the view that one should think about the circumstances of remembering—one is given some cue or partial information about the memory and must reproduce the rest of it. For example, you may be asked, "Do you remember what

John said about Mary's bike?" You use the cue to probe memory for some episode in which this cue is incorporated. Similarly, PDP models would claim that all remembering is a matter of taking some partial information and reproducing the information that was stored with it. Remembering, then, is a type of pattern completion in which the original pattern must be reproduced from some subset of it. The PDP models can be quite good at such pattern completions. In fact, weight adjustments could be made to perfectly reproduce a pattern, except that the same weights also have to reproduce all the other patterns experienced before. Thus, instead of a memory trace, the PDP model encodes new information as an adjustment in these weights, with the extent of the change depending on how well the old weights did in reproducing the pattern. If the new pattern was "consistent" with much of your previous knowledge, it could be well reproduced with little adjustment of the weights, whereas if it was very different, greater adjustments might be required. Thus, memory can be viewed as incorporating weights that provide a compromise between recalling old information and adjusting for recall of new information.

McClelland and Rumelhart (1986a) argue that such a model allows learning generalizations and remembering specific instances. The generalizations occur naturally. Because the same set of weights is used to encode all the different instances, those units that tend to participate in multiple instances of a given type will mutually activate each other, forming a generalization of those instances. This point can be seen with the example above where two values were common to the two input vectors, and presenting only those two values yielded the pattern on the output vectors associated with those two input values. This same explanation works in considering the related distinction of semantic and episodic memories. This model incorporates both in the same way. The model encodes each episodic memory as an adjustment to the weights. The semantic memory is claimed to arise from the fact that many of the episodic memories have similar subpatterns of activation that will be repeated. For example, experiencing different dogs in different contexts would lead to some units being activated in all of these cases (which together would represent the pattern for "dog") as well as some specific subpatterns that would be activated as a function of some specific properties of the dog (e.g., color brown) or context (e.g., met in park).

Returning again to the different ways in which forgetting can occur (decay, interference, overwriting), what ways does the PDP model use? Interference and overwriting are most important. Because there are no specific symbols or locations for memories, there is no mechanism for memories to decay. The interference and overwriting explanations are hard to tease apart here. The change in weights can be viewed as overwriting the influence of one memory with that of another, but the original memory is not really lost. Rather, the change in weights can be viewed as a type of interference, with the encoding of each memory affecting the retrieval of the other.

Finally, how does this model incorporate the implicit-explicit (or procedural-declarative) distinction? The PDP model of McClelland and Rumelhart (1986a, 1986b) is not committed to such a distinction. They argue that this distinction is plausible, but the data do not rule out other possible interpretations. For example, they suggest that perhaps differences in how much the weights between connections change during learning could account for a procedural-declarative distinction. By this account, procedural tasks would be sensitive to small weight changes because they are modifications of previously existing memories. Declarative memories, by contrast, would involve large weight changes because they require the learning of a new pattern of activation. McClelland and Rumelhart (1986b) further speculate that the spared learning in amnesic patients could reflect an ability to make small weight changes, whereas the loss of conscious recollection could reflect a loss of the ability to make large weight changes. These ideas have yet to be fully evaluated. An alternative possibility is to consider the PDP model to be a model of something like procedural memory, in which small changes are made to previously learned interconnections (also see Schacter, 1989). Because new PDP modeling techniques continue to be developed, and the nature of the memory distinctions described in this chapter is still being elucidated, it is not yet clear how (or whether) PDP models will be able to provide a global account of memory systems (though see McClelland et al., 1995, for an interesting discussion of these issues).

Evaluation of PDP Models

The development of PDP models has increased greatly in recent years. The model we described only stores associations between inputs and outputs. Indeed, there are now PDP approaches that capture more complex kinds of information that might be needed for reasoning or making analogies (see Hummel & Holyoak, 1997).

On the positive side, PDP models of memory incorporate rather simple processing assumptions to perform complex tasks. Each unit is quite simple, but when configured appropriately, the models can be very powerful. In addition, they provide an alternative view to the idea that cognition is a type of symbolic computation.

On the negative side, it is still unclear whether these models are consistent with certain memory phenomena. For instance, McCloskey and Cohen (1989) argue that interference effects are problematic for PDP models in that when the models adjust the weights to try to reproduce the new pattern, they may lead to very poor memory of the earlier patterns. Using the same weights to capture multiple memories has the advantage of leading to generalizations, but the flip side is that it leads to interference. McCloskey and Cohen argue that such interference can be catastrophic in that the earlier memories are essentially lost (also see Ratcliff, 1990, for some related criticisms of the learning algorithms). Not surprisingly, there have been attempts to address these problems (e.g., see French, 1999; Kruschke, 1992; Robins, 1995; and Sloman & Rumelhart, 1992, for some possible solutions). This area of research has attracted many investigators, and the next few years should see substantial development and clarification of advantages and disadvantages.

Summary of Memory Models

We have examined two models that encode episodic and semantic information together. In both ACT and PDP models, episodic and semantic memory are merged together. ACT has a single network memory in which all information is encoded.

PDP models have a set of input units connected to a set of output units. Both episodic and semantic information can be represented on these units.

An advantage of having a single memory as opposed to a separate episodic and semantic memory is that the model suggests how semantic information might be acquired. Models proposing a single system generally have semantic information result from the accumulation of similar episodes. The PDP model argues that they arise naturally as the aspects of input vectors that are similar from episode to episode. Dissimilar aspects of episodes will interfere with each other. (The ACT theory is less clear about this, but an interference explanation is one possibility here as well.) The point is not that incorporating both types of knowledge in one memory is correct, but rather that implementing a memory model has required theorists to deal with a number of issues that have not been dealt with by other investigators arguing for multiple systems who have not implemented their proposals in a computational model.

Summary

In this chapter, we have explored a number of distinctions that memory theorists have made to describe different kinds of memory. Many of these distinctions were motivated by patterns of deficits observed in brain-damaged patients. Further, the memory systems could also be separated using different manipulations in experiments on normal people.

We described a number of important distinctions in memory. First, there is a distinction between semantic memory, which is memory for facts, and episodic memory, which is memory for episodes in someone's life. Second, there was a distinction between these kinds of declarative memories, and procedural memory, which is memory for skills. Finally, a distinction was made between explicit memory, which involves conscious access to recollected information, and implicit memory, which involves tasks that are influenced by prior exposure to some items, without conscious access to that information. The distinction between implicit and explicit memory is motivated by extensive studies of amnesic patients.

In order to make the discussion of memory more concrete, we then examined two models that incorporate both semantic and episodic information: ACT and a PDP model. An important idea in these models is that our knowledge allows us to make inferences beyond the specific information we have encoded. By organizing our knowledge, we greatly increase our ability to apply this knowledge to new situations. Intuitively, we might think that it would be best if we could use all the knowledge that is relevant. However, it should be noted that the use of relevant knowledge might have a cost as well. If our memory made all relevant knowledge available to be used, it would be difficult to recollect a single experience without being influenced by other knowledge. In many models there is a trade-off between retrieval of specific information and the use of more general knowledge.

In addition to the general knowledge issues that arise from this chapter, we have also investigated a number of disparate models. An examination of models can sometimes be frustrating to the beginner. We think it important to answer directly two common complaints. First, if the goal of models is to simplify, doesn't it seem as if the models are getting very complex? Second, if people cannot agree on the correct model, where is the progress?

Yes, models are becoming more complex, and they are likely to continue to become even more so. However, memory is quite complex, and it may take a complex model to give a reasonable account. Despite their increasing complexity, our understanding of the important characteristics of models has increased as well. Although many current models require the use of computers for figuring out their predictions, extensive analyses of these models provide a clear idea of which characteristics are affecting which aspects of the predictions.

It is important not to confuse disagreement with lack of progress. Throughout the chapter, we have described very different models that attempt to account for roughly the same set of results. This competition among models leads to new tests, which may lead to new findings, which may lead to an even better understanding of memory. Disagreements about the types of memory distinctions are fuel for progress.

Key Terms

adaptive control of thought (ACT)	nodes
anterograde amnesia	parallel distributed processing (PDP)
connection weights	procedural memory
declarative memory	propositions
episodic memory	repetition priming
explicit memory	retrograde amnesia
fan effect	semantic memory
hierarchical model	spreading activation
implicit memory	transfer appropriate processing
lexical decision task	type-token distinction
links	typicality effect

Recommended Readings

The early work on semantic memory models is well reviewed in E. E. Smith (1978; also see Smith, Shoben, & Rips, 1974). Smith and Medin (1981) discuss much of this work in the context of research on concepts and categories.

An overview of memory systems is given by Squire, Knowlton, and Musen (1993). Research on episodic memory is described in a book by Tulving (1983). Research on people's memory for source information is reviewed by Johnson, Hashtroudi, and Lindsay (1993). Finally, the distinction between procedural and declarative knowledge is discussed in depth by Cohen and Eichenbaum (1993). Research on implicit memory is reviewed in the contributions in the edited volume by Reder (1996). A review of neuropsychological evidence bearing on memory is given by Gabrieli (1998).

The ACT theory is presented in great detail in the original monographs (J. R. Anderson, 1976, 1983), which also contain references to the many experimental studies examining this theory, and is updated in Anderson (1990a) and Anderson and Lebiere (1998).

The PDP work has had an enormous influence on psychological research over the past 15 years. Many seminal papers in this line of research are contained in a two-volume set called *Parallel Distributed Processing* (McClelland & Rumelhart, 1986c; Rumelhart & McClelland, 1986b). McClelland et al. (1995) provides both an overview of a number of recent PDP models and a proposal linking PDP modeling with cognitive neuroscience. A nice introduction to PDP models including computer code you can use yourself is given by James Anderson (1995). Elman, Bates, Johnson, Karmiloff-Smith, Parisi, and Plunkett (1996) apply these techniques to the study of cognitive development.

Appendix: Learning in a Parallel Distributed Processing Model _____

In this appendix, we present an example of the learning processes in a PDP model by showing how it can learn the weights used in the example given in the chapter. As in the chapter, we assume that each of the four input values (IN1, IN2, IN3, IN4) is connected to each of the four output values (OUT1, OUT2, OUT3, OUT4). The weight on each connection (e.g., IN1–OUT2 as the weight between IN1 and OUT2) is what changes with learning. To simplify the illustration, we will assume a very simple weight-change method.

To begin, let us assume all weights are zero. We want to teach the pattern association PAIR1, that when $(+1\ -1\ -1\ +1)$ is given as input, $(-1\ -1\ +1\ +1)$ should be the output. To determine the value of each output, we multiply the value of the input element by the weight between the input and output and add all the values for a given output element. In this case, because all the weights are zero, the output from this input (or, in fact, any input) is (0 0 0 0).

For any single input, it is easy to change the weights to get a particular output. However, we want the knowledge about each output value to come from multiple sources, so that if any one source cannot contribute (e.g., because of missing input), the others can at least partially make up for it. That is the reason for a more complicated weighting scheme—to distribute the knowledge.

Let us go back to our example now. If we were to present the same input again, we would want the system to respond with something closer to the desired pattern. The learning of the system is in terms of the weight changes. The idea behind the weight change is simple, although the details can get complex. The basic idea is that we compare the output value with the expected value or target (in this case, $[-1\ -1\ +1\ +1]$) and the difference is the "error." Learning then consists of changing weights to reduce this error. The method used is to assume that each weight between an input and output element contributed to that error. However, knowing each weight contributed does not tell you how to change them. A common method for determining weight changes is to assume that weights from large input values contributed more to the error than weights from lower input values. Thus, the change made to each weight is determined by the size of the error and the input activation.

For instance, OUT1 was expected to be -1 but was 0, so the error can be calculated as the target (-1) minus output (0), or -1. The rule used (referred to as the delta rule) is to multiply the error (-1) by the activation value of the input element and then multiply it by some learning parameter, which for purposes of illustration we will set to .33. (The learning parameter is important in the mathematics for keeping the change from being too large, but we will not explain it further here.) Thus, by this scheme, the weight on IN1–OUT1 would be changed by the error (-1) multiplied by the input value (1) multiplied by the learning parameter (.33),

$$-1 \times 1 \times .33 = -.33$$

In Figure 6.A1, we have calculated the weight changes for each input-output connection. The errors were all equal except for sign, and the inputs were all equal

Want association   Input (1 −1 −1 1)

                              Output (−1 −1 1 1)

Start with 0 weights

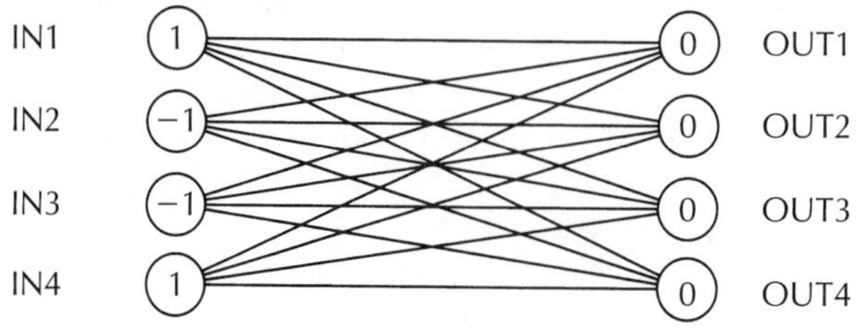

	Target (T)	−1	−1	1	1
Output (O)		0	0	0	0
Error (T-0)		−1	−1	1	1
(×Learning parameter .33)		−.33	−.33	.33	.33

Weight changes	OUT1	OUT2	OUT3	OUT4
IN1	−.33	−.33	.33	.33
IN2	.33	.33	−.33	−.33
IN3	.33	.33	−.33	−.33
In4	−.33	−.33	.33	.33

Figure 6.A1   The first pass at learning the PAIR1 association presented in the chapter. The network starts with all 0 weights and gets the output (0 0 0 0). The middle part of the figure shows the determination of error, and the bottom part shows the weight changes made.

except for sign, so the weight changes in this example are all equal except for sign. Since the original matrix of connections was all 0, this weight change matrix added to the original matrix leads to a new matrix that is equal to the weight changes. In general, the new weight is equal to the old weight plus the product of the error and input activation values (and the learning rate). The smaller the error (or input activation), the smaller the change to the weight.

Figure 6.A1 shows the set of weights after the first presentation. If the same stimulus (+1 −1 −1 +1) is presented again, the activation for the output vector is (−1.32 −1.32 +1.32 +1.32), a much closer fit to the desired pattern of (−1 −1 +1 +1) (Figure 6.A2). The error is (+.32 +.32 −.32 −.32), and the weight changes are made again (input x error x learning parameter), with the resulting weight changes

Using weights in bottom of Figure 6A.1 for Pair 1

Input   (1 −1 −1 1)

Output   (−1.32 −1.32   1.32 1.32)

Target (T)	−1	−1	1	1
Output (O)	−1.32	−1.32	1.02	1.02
Error (T-0)	.32	.32	−.32	−.32
(×.33)	.10	.10	−.10	−.10

Weight changes				
	.10	.10	−.10	−.10
	−.10	−.10	.10	.10
	−.10	−.10	.10	.10
	.10	.10	−.10	−.10

New Weights				
	−.23	−.23	.23	.23
	.23	.23	−.23	−.23
	.23	.23	−.23	−.23
	−.23	−.23	.23	.23

Figure 6.A2   Continuation of the example from Figure 6.A1 showing the error, the matrix of weight changes, and the new weights after the weight changes are added to the old weights (which are presented in Figure 6.A1).

given in Figure 6.A2. In the bottom of the figure, we show the result of adding these weight changes to the weights given in Figure 6.A1.

If the input is presented a third time, the output vector would be quite close, (−.92 −.92 +.92 +.92). As shown in Figure 6.A3, the weight changes made are getting smaller (+.02 or −.02). The matrix given at the bottom of Figure 6.A3 will take the input of (+1 −1 −1 +1) and give the desired output (−1 −1 +1 +1). Thus, the weights have "learned" the association of these two patterns.

This example shows that this simplified scheme will work in converging on the correct output with practice. One might wonder how the same system would learn the other pattern association given in the chapter, PAIR2, that (−1 +1 −1 +1) leads to an output of (−1 +1 +1 −1). We use exactly the same procedure as when learning the first association. If (−1 +1 −1 +1) is given as input to the matrix, the output is (0 0 0 0). (The weight changes encoding PAIR1 have no effect on the output of PAIR2 because the two input vectors are orthogonal. As was shown earlier in the chapter with two examples involving PAIR3, if the input vectors are correlated, weight changes to encode one input-output pair do affect the output when the other input vector is presented.) Thus the error from the target of (−1 +1 +1 −1) is (−1 +1 +1 −1), and we determine weight changes for each input-output connection.

Using weights in bottom of Figure 6A.2

Input   (1 − 1 −1 1)
Output   (−.92 −.92 .92 .92)

	Target (T)	Output (O)	Error (T-0)	(×.33)
Target (T)	−1	−1	1	1
Output (O)	− .92	− .92	.92	.92
Error (T-0)	− .08	− .08	.08	.08
(×.33)	− .02	− .02	.02	.02

Weight changes			
.02	.02	.02	.02
.02	.02	.02	.02
.02	.02	.02	.02
.02	.02	.02	.02

New Weights			
−.25	−.25	.25	.25
.25	.25	−.25	−.25
.25	.25	−.25	−.25
−.25	−.25	.25	.25

Figure 6.A3   Continuation of the example from Figure 6.A2 showing the error, the matrix of weight changes, and the new weights after the weight changes are added to the old weights (which are presented in Figure 6.A2).

These weight changes are given in the middle of Figure 6.A4. When they are added to the matrix learned from the first pattern, the resulting matrix has changed dramatically. In fact, the matrix is quite close to the one given in Figure 6.11, which perfectly associates both pairs of patterns. It would take a couple of additional weight changes to get to the exact matrix, but we will leave that to the interested reader.

Learning a new association pair $(-1\ \ 1\ -1\ \ 1) \rightarrow (-1\ \ 1\ \ 1\ -1)$

Input	$(-1$	1	-1	$1)$
Output	$(\ 0$	0	0	$0)$

Target (T)	-1	1	1	-1
Output (O)	0	0	0	0
Error (T-0)	-1	1	1	-1
($\times$.33)	$-.33$	$.33$	$.33$	$-.33$

Weight changes				
	$.33$	$-.33$	$-.33$	$.33$
	$-.33$	$.33$	$.33$	$-.33$
	$.33$	$-.33$	$-.33$	$.33$
	$-.33$	$.33$	$.33$	$-.33$

New weights				
	$.08$	$-.58$	$-.08$	$.58$
	$-.08$	$.58$	$.08$	$-.58$
	$.58$	$-.08$	$-.58$	$.08$
	$-.58$	$.08$	$.58$	$-.08$

Figure 6.A4   The effect of learning PAIR2 on the matrix from Figure 6.A3, showing the error from using the weights from PAIR1 for responding to PAIR2. The matrices encode the weight changes and the new weights. Compare to Figure 6.11 to see how the learning is converging on the matrix of weights presented there.

Chapter 7

Remembering New Information: Beyond Basic Effects

Introduction

Schemas: Understanding and Remembering Complex Situations
Introduction and Motivation
Understanding
Schemas
Scripts
Schema Activation
Problems With Schemas
Summary

Reconstructive Memory
Encoding-Retrieval Interactions Revisited
Schemas and Stereotypes
Summary

Memory in the World
Introduction
Eyewitness Testimony
Flashbulb Memories
Recovered Memories
Summary

Knowing Your Memory
Introduction
Strategies and Knowledge
Metamemory
Summary

Summary

Key Terms

Recommended Readings

> **Recollect,** *v. To recall with additions something not previously known.*
> —Ambrose Bierce, The Devil's Dictionary

INTRODUCTION _____

In the last two chapters, we have explored the structure of memory. Psychologists have managed to uncover the fundamental components of memory by creating experimental methods that differ in many ways from the situations people typically experience. Now it is time to put things back together again to understand how what we have learned about memory relates to more common situations. For example, how we remember complex events like visiting a doctor's office or going to a birthday party. How does our understanding of memory change the way we think about expert testimony in trials (which is based on episodic memory)? Is it possible for people to recover memories of traumatic situations they appear to have forgotten? Although we do not promise to give definitive answers to these questions, we will discuss these questions from a memory point of view and give you, we hope, a better understanding of such issues.

In this chapter, we go beyond basic memory effects to examine memory in more complex and real-world situations. The last two chapters have addressed fundamental issues in memory. Chapter 5 distinguished between short-term and long-term memory, examined forgetting, and discussed a particular model, SAM, to account for many memory effects with simple materials. Chapter 6 extended these ideas to consider how we represent knowledge, examined a network and PDP model, and investigated recent work on implicit and explicit memory.

Although these studies in simple situations provide much information about memory, how it works, and how it is used in a variety of tasks, much of what we experience and remember is more complex. A theme throughout this book is that we use our knowledge to help us deal with the complexity of the world. So far, however, we have not considered the impact of knowledge on what we encode and retrieve from memory. To this end, we start by exploring how prior knowledge influences the way we encode and remember complex situations. We then consider how we may reconstruct things we have seen in the past when we do not remember all of the details immediately. The next part of the chapter considers three problems of memory in the everyday world: eyewitness testimony, recovered memories (in which information about traumatic events is remembered after a long period where it was not recalled at all), and flashbulb memories (in which we feel that we have a snapshot of an important event). Finally, we explore what people know about their memories and how they might improve their memory. We consider individual differences in memory, including a discussion of strategies and knowledge effects, as well as examining some expert memorizers (mnemonists).

We have two basic goals in this chapter. First, we hope to show how your new understanding of memory allows a deeper analysis of some important problems. Second, we hope to show that although there are some new issues that arise with more complex situations, there is also much continuity with the work on more basic memory issues.

SCHEMAS: UNDERSTANDING AND REMEMBERING COMPLEX SITUATIONS

Introduction and Motivation

Let's consider two real-world situations and what you might experience. First, you go to a restaurant to eat. The event is complex and involves a number of subparts such as entering, ordering, being served, eating, and paying. Even without intending to do so, you would usually encode all of these main points plus many other aspects of the event. Second, you are watching a TV program that has children in a schoolroom. You encode information about the room, the arrangement of desks, the people, and the social relationships (among many other things). What are you doing and how are you doing it?

A crucial point to note is that in both cases, the encoding is not focused on remembering the situations, but on understanding them. Let's compare this to the situations we discussed in Chapter 5. When given a simple list of words to remember, the person has the goal of remembering the words on the list, not getting some overall understanding of the list. However, in many real-world situations, the goal of the encoding is not to remember exactly what happened, but to understand what is happening so that one can act appropriately. If you order a tuna sandwich and get a burrito, you do not just want to remember this happened but you want to know this is not what you ordered and that you can ask to return it and get a tuna sandwich. The memory you have for this eating experience is a byproduct of your understanding. If you process the situation deeply to understand it, you will remember it well (barring too many similar interfering events). This is similar to the incidental learning results discussed in Chapter 5—you do not need to intend to remember something to remember it well; rather you need to process it deeply. Even with simple materials, active processing of the material, such as organizing, elaborating, and processing for meaning, will lead to better memory.

We have tried to make two points with this discussion. First, the encoding of more complex situations is often focused on understanding the situation. Second, although this seems very different from memory work presented in Chapters 5 and 6, it really is not. Even in that work, active processing for meaning helped memory; however there was often no overall understanding that could be derived from the materials. In this section, we examine cases in which we understand more complex situations.

Our ability to understand sentences, texts, events, and the like relies critically upon our knowledge. What we learn or understand depends on what we already know. Knowledge not only allows us to verify whether specific facts are known, but also allows us to make new inferences that are crucial for our understanding. For example, although we may never have thought about a robin as having a heart, it is easy for us to use our knowledge (of robins as birds, as living things, as well as of the size of robins) to understand a sentence such as "It was as small as a robin's heart."

To appreciate the role that knowledge plays in understanding and how this knowledge may be represented, it is first important to be clear as to why understanding is a very complex process. Even reading a simple passage involves far more than understanding the information that is explicitly conveyed. Read the following few sentences (adapted from Charniak, 1973):

> Jane heard the jingling of the ice cream truck.
>
> She ran to get her piggy bank and started to shake it.
>
> Finally some money came out.

This passage appears to be quite straightforward, but it is easy to show that in understanding this passage readers generate a number of inferences that might be wrong at least some of the time. How old is Jane? Why did she get the money? Did she turn her piggy bank upside down? Was the money that came out in the form of coins or bills? How big was the piggy bank? None of this information is explicitly stated, but we would be quite surprised to find that Jane was 87, owned a piggy bank the size of a car, and shook out a handful of thousand-dollar bills in order to make an offer to purchase the truck.

This passage illustrates a number of important points about comprehension. First, the meaning of these sentences is not simply the words in the sentences but also the knowledge that you bring to bear to understand these sentences. In this case, you used your knowledge about ice cream trucks and selling to understand the sentences. Put more generally, *meaning is a function of both the input and activated knowledge.* Second, meaning does not come through some passive assimilation of the meaning of the sentences because the meaning of the sentences is partly in the reader. Thus, *comprehension is an active, not passive process,* with the reader constructing the meaning from the input and his or her activated knowledge. Third, and perhaps less obvious, *understanding consists of constructing an integrated representation.* That is, we understand this passage when we are able to figure out how all this information fits together to make sense. Finally, *memory for events is fallible in systematically predictable ways.* Thus, while people are prone to make errors in what they can recall about events, we can use our knowledge of the structure of memory to make guesses about what they will and will not remember.

Imagine that the preceding passage included, after the first sentence, the additional sentence "She had thrown away yesterday's paper." Even though the rest of the sentences fit together nicely as before, most readers would feel that they did not fully understand the story, not because they could not understand this additional sentence by itself but rather because they do not know how this sentence fits with the others. Suppose, however, the readers knew that the preceding day's paper included a coupon entitling the person to a free ice cream cone. This additional knowledge would allow the readers to integrate the new sentence with their understanding of the other sentences. Thus, understanding consists of integrating presented information with previously acquired knowledge to construct a unified representation. The meaning consists not just of the presented information but also of the activated knowledge, including any inferences needed to connect this structure.

However, it is not only the knowledge a person has that is important. As we have often seen, we possess so much knowledge that a crucial consideration is how the relevance of information is determined. That is, how do we get to the right information without getting lost in a sea of irrelevant possibilities? It is not total knowledge that is crucial but rather the knowledge that the reader *brings to bear* in understanding. The remainder of this section will further illustrate the themes that (1) information in the world is incomplete and ambiguous and that (2) completing this information by using our knowledge to generate inferences introduces the problem of computational complexity yet again. Given that so much knowledge is potentially relevant, how do we come to use the appropriate information?

Before beginning an examination of the particulars of the knowledge structures that underlie our understanding, we give two further examples to help you see the influence of knowledge in understanding. Read over and think about the following paragraph from Bransford and Johnson (1972):

> The procedure is actually quite simple. First you arrange things into different groups. Of course one pile may be sufficient depending on how much there is to do. If you have to go somewhere else, due to lack of facilities, that is the next step; otherwise you are pretty well set. It is important not to overdo things. That is, it is better to do too few things at once than too many. In the short run this may not seem important but complications can easily arise. It is difficult to foresee any end to the necessity for this task in the immediate future, but then one never can tell. After the procedure is completed one arranges the materials into different groups again. They can be put into their appropriate places. Eventually they will be used once more and the whole cycle will then have to be repeated.

Do you understand this passage? As one indication of your understanding, how well do you think you would be able to remember this passage an hour from now? Probably not very well. But suppose that in addition to the paragraph you were given a title for it. This seems like a pretty minor change that ought not to affect things very much, but in fact it does. The title of this passage is "Washing Clothes." Now go back and reread the paragraph. It seems obvious that you would now remember it much better. Although you knew about laundry the first time you read the passage, this knowledge was not activated and did not influence your understanding of the passage. The title serves to activate such knowledge and makes the passage sensible and easier to remember. When this contrast (title vs. no title) was tested in an experiment, the group receiving the title ahead of time recalled twice as much.

The idea that activated knowledge affects understanding is not limited to contrasts between cases in which we have relevant activated knowledge and cases in which we do not. Rather, the *particular* knowledge that is activated can influence our understanding. Consider the story in Table 7.1 (from R. C. Anderson, Reynolds, Schallert, & Goetz, 1977). Most people would interpret this story as one in which Rocky is a prisoner. If, however, people read this story with knowledge activated about wrestling (e.g., just having watched a wrestling match), then they might read this as a passage about wrestling. In one experiment, physical education majors were much more likely to interpret this passage as about wrestling and remember those facts consistent with that interpretation. When asked questions about the passage,

Table 7.1   **Wrestling/Prisoner Story**

> Rocky slowly got up from the mat, planning his escape. He hesitated a moment and thought. Things were not going well. What bothered him most was being held, especially since the charge against him had been weak. He considered his present situation. The lock that held him was strong but he thought he could break it. He knew, however, that his timing would have to be perfect. Rocky was aware that it was because of his early roughness that he had been penalized so severely—much too severely from his point of view. The situation was becoming frustrating; the pressure had been grinding on him for too long. He was being ridden unmercifully. Rocky was getting angry now. He felt he was ready to make his move. He knew that his success or failure would depend on what he did in the next few seconds.

Source: Anderson, R. C., Reynolds, Schallert, & Goetz, 1977.

64% of physical education majors answered with the wrestling answer, while only 28% of music majors answered with the wrestling answer. The activated knowledge we bring to bear in understanding has a large effect on our understanding. What is this activated knowledge? We turn to that now.

Understanding

How are we to understand understanding? First, as we hope is clear by now, understanding is not simply a matter of decoding some input but rather requires actively supplementing the input with knowledge. The sentences about Jane and the ice cream truck illustrate the extent to which world knowledge may be used in understanding.

Second, the knowledge that is often brought to bear in understanding is not just a relevant fact or two but more of a body of knowledge. For example, in understanding the earlier passage about ice cream, it was not enough to have one or two facts about ice cream; rather, a whole set of facts about ice cream trucks, money, and children was needed. To understand something requires fitting it into some integrated representation. Furthermore, the information in the world is often incomplete, and other knowledge must be accessed and integrated to form some unified representation. In many cases, such as the ice cream passage, the amount of knowledge needed to make sense of the input is great. The need for large amounts of relevant knowledge greatly complicates the computational complexity problem. By this we mean that if knowledge is a set of richly interconnected separate small units (e.g., propositions), then determining which units are relevant and which connected ones are not is going to be impossibly difficult.

We have seen that understanding requires the careful integration of new input with a potentially vast amount of prior knowledge. The amazing thing is, however, that we don't find ourselves sitting around mulling over thousands of interpretations and inferences every time someone says something to us. Quite the opposite. In fact, the realization that little effort is involved in understanding complex situations is an important clue to the nature of comprehension processes; that is, certain units of knowledge and inferences are often used together. It appears our comprehension system has learned to access and use them as a whole. This large unit of knowledge is called a *schema* (the plural of *schema* is *schemata,* but we'll refer to them as *schemas* for simplicity).

Before explaining more about schemas, let us mention one of the earliest studies on this topic, examining the schemas people have for stories. Bartlett (1932) conducted experiments that were much like the game of "telephone" that you might have played at parties in which one person starts off by whispering some saying in the next person's ear, who repeats in into another person's ear, and this continues until the last person says it aloud. Even without a smart aleck who decides to spice things up, the saying usually gets quite changed by the time it has gone through a number of people. Why? Part of the answer may be that the whispering is not always clear, but even so the important point is that people are not randomly interpreting the message they hear but doing so by using the knowledge they have. Bartlett had subjects use this method (which he called the *method of serial reproductions*) to tell a short story from an unfamiliar culture; that is, the first subject would read the story, tell it to the next person, and so on. By the final subject, the story had lost many of the details, as might be expected, but also had become more coherent (at least by Western standards). Many of the strange mystical events were reinterpreted and "explained" according to the readers' expectations. People were using their knowledge of stories and trying to fit what they were hearing to this general idea.

Schemas

The term schema is used to refer to a wide variety of different constructs, but almost all of them have several points in common (also see Rumelhart & Ortony, 1977). Simply put, a **schema** *is a general knowledge structure used for understanding.* Let us look at these ideas in some greater detail.

First, a schema is knowledge. It does not refer to information in the world but rather to one's knowledge about the world. Second, a schema is general. It does not encode information about one particular situation but rather about a particular *type* of situation. Third, a schema is structured; that is, a schema does not just consist of some set of facts but also includes how these facts are related. This structure is part of what allows a schema to be used for inferring additional information. Fourth, a schema is used in comprehension. The structure of the schema is such that it includes how the knowledge is related in this type of situation, but it does not include information about any exact situation.

An example may help to clarify this idea. Figure 7.1 has a simple version of an ice cream–buying schema. Such a schema would contain all your knowledge about ice cream buying, though the figure presents just a small subset of this knowledge. A schema is often viewed as consisting of a **frame** that includes **slots** for particular information. An ice cream–buying frame would have slots for the buyer, what

ICE CREAM BUYING SCHEMA

Buyer:	person
Item-purchased:	{ice cream cone, ice cream sundae, . . .}
Flavor:	{vanilla, chocolate, . . .}
Seller:	{store employee, street vendor, . . .}
Cost:	some small mount of money

Specific example of ice cream buying schema being used
Representing: John went to the ice cream store and left with a chocolate cone.

Buyer:	John
Item-purchased:	ice cream cone
Flavor:	chocolate
Seller:	store employee
Cost:	some small amount of money

Figure 7.1   **Ice Cream–Buying Schema**
Note: On the left are the frame slots and on the right are the values that can be put in the slots. A bracket { } means that one of those values is used.

kind of ice cream was purchased (e.g., both the form and the flavor), the seller, and the amount paid. Understanding consists of filling in these slots. Although your schema would include knowledge that someone buys some type of ice cream, the schema is general and would not contain the particular person or the particular ice cream. That is, the schema would include the expectation that purchasing ice cream involves an exchange in which one person pays money to another person to receive some quantity and type of ice cream.

You would use this schema to understand a particular ice cream–buying event. Your understanding of a particular event would usually include information about who bought the ice cream and which flavor they chose. The bottom part of Figure 7.1 gives an example of what might be stored using the ice cream schema for the particular event "John went to the ice cream store and left with a chocolate cone." As you can see, the frame is the same, but the values of the slot have been filled in by the details of the particular event. For example, the buyer slot is now filled in as John. Thus, you would understand this event by finding the appropriate frame and filling in the values pertaining to this event. Note that you do not have to try to figure out exactly what information might be relevant or what knowledge should be brought to bear. The relevant information fits into the slots, and the schema is a unit of structured knowledge that is brought to bear to understand what happened in this event.

A frame also contains *default assumptions* concerning slot values. If a text fails to mention some piece of information, the default value may be assumed. For example, if we read, "John went to the ice cream store and left with a chocolate cone," we assume that John paid for it (a default value) rather than stole it and that chocolate was the flavor of ice cream he selected (instantiating or filling in the slot for type) and not the color of some cone-shaped object. Finally, slots contain restrictions about what information can fill them. For example, in the ice cream–buying schema, it is not permissible to have the buyer slot filled in by "chocolate-vanilla swirl" or to have the ice cream flavor be "Jane."

The idea of a schema is complex and puts a very different perspective on knowledge, understanding, and remembering. Previously in our discussion, the difficulty in understanding seemed to be figuring out what relevant knowledge to bring to bear and how to have some control over the inferences. Now the difficulty is knowing what schema to use. As we saw in the washing clothes passage, the determination of the appropriate schema is not always simple.

Schemas can occur at various levels of abstraction and can be embedded. For instance, if you have a schema for ice cream buying, this schema may include much knowledge that comes from your schema about buying in general (e.g., what money is) and some that is applicable only to ice cream buying (e.g., what the truck bells signal and the menu, often with pictures, of the different ice creams available).

What are the advantages of schemas? They help us understand and remember. Schemas allow us to treat the knowledge about events as connected rather than independent. This organization provides information about how facts fit together and supports inferences about things not stated directly. Once a schema is selected, we need only to figure out which information relates to which slots in order to understand a new situation. In addition, schemas *generate expectations* about what is likely to be true. These expectations are invaluable for helping us to understand later events and to notice if something unusual is present. The power of these schemas arises because they include information about how all the different aspects of the situation are related. Thus, they can be used for predicting what is likely to be true and what will occur.

Although the examples we have been considering make the case that knowledge and understanding might benefit from such large knowledge structures, is there any evidence that people have and use such knowledge structures? We clearly would not be spending so much time explaining them if they were not important parts of cognition. We will see these ideas used in later chapters as well (most notably Chapter 13, Expertise and Creativity), but for now let us examine some examples of their use. We first look at two simple cases and then consider a particular type of schema for stereotyped events.

In one study, Brewer and Treyens (1981) examined whether college students have schemas for particular types of rooms that they use for perceiving and remembering the room. Their experiment was simple: Subjects for an experiment were told that the graduate student experimenter needed to make sure that the previous subject was finished, and they were asked to wait in his office. Thirty-five seconds later, they were ushered into another room and then tested on their memory for the office they had waited in. There was much evidence in their recall and recognition judgments that their general knowledge about graduate student offices had been used to remember the particular office. For example, based on prior work, the researchers knew that college students had a strong expectation that graduate student offices had many books, so they set up the experimental office without any books. Despite this anomaly, 30% of the subjects recalled that books had been present. People's general knowledge of different types of locations (such as a graduate student office) affects how they remember a particular location of one of those types.

Research also suggests that what people remember about an event is information that violates expectations relevant to a schema rather than information irrelevant to it (e.g., Mandler, 1982). As one example consider the pictures in Figure 7.2 used in a study by Markman and Gentner (1997). In the top picture, there is a lot going on. There is a man painting a portrait of a woman. There is also a cigarette dropping ash in a trash can, which may cause a fire. If the top picture is compared to the middle picture, this highlights the event of taking a picture (with the inconsistency that a woman is having her picture painted in one case and a man is having his picture taken in the other), and the burning cigarette is irrelevant. In contrast, if the top picture is compared to the bottom picture, then the schema of causing a fire is highlighted (with the inconsistency that a cigarette is causing the burning in one case and a candle in the other), and the picture-taking aspect is irrelevant. Consistent with the idea that people focus on inconsistent information rather than irrelevant information, people asked to rate the similarity of the top picture and the middle picture were better able to remember the top picture on a later test when given the woman in the dress as a cue than when given the cigarette as a cue. In contrast, people who rated the similarity of the top picture to the bottom picture showed the reverse pattern, and were better able to remember the top picture given the cigarette as a cue than given the woman in the dress.

Schemas have become a common part of theorizing in almost every area of psychology. One of the authors did a computer search for "schema" on a subset of the available sources (PsycInfo 1967–1999) and found 3,139 entries. For example, a useful concept in work in personality and social psychology is that of self-schema, the knowledge that one has about oneself. Other areas in which schemas were being used were music, depression, religion-as-schema, perspectives on organizational changes, and love schemas (really). We do not have space to detail all these uses, so instead we turn to a particular type of schema that has to do with stereotypical sequences of events—scripts.

Scripts

Consider the following passage, adapted from the work on scripts by Schank and Abelson (1977):

> John was hungry.
>
> He went into a restaurant and ordered a sandwich.
>
> He paid his bill and left.

Almost all readers find these sentences easy to understand. Although these sentences contain only 18 words, they allow you to make a large number of inferences with varying degrees of certainty. Did John eat his sandwich? From whom did he order a sandwich? What was the bill for? Many of these questions seem silly because the answer is so obvious, but in fact none of these answers is stated in the sentences.

A **script** is a knowledge structure containing the sequence of events that usually occurs in a particular stereotyped situation. Thus, scripts are a type of schema

Figure 7.2   **Inconsistent and Irrelevant Information in Schemas.**   These pictures, based on Markman and Gentner (1997), demonstrate how information can be inconsistent with or irrelevant to a schema. When the top picture is compared to the middle picture, the woman in the top scene is inconsistent (because a man is having his picture taken in the middle scene) and the cigarette is irrelevant (because there is no corresponding element in the middle scene). When the top picture is compared to the bottom picture, the woman in the top scene is now irrelevant (because there is nothing corresponding to her in the top scene) and the cigarette is inconsistent (because there is a candle causing the fire in the bottom scene).

Table 7.2   **Subjects' Responses of Ordered Actions in "Going to a Restaurant"**

Open door
Enter
Give reservation name
Wait to be seated
Go to table
BE SEATED
Order drinks
Put napkins on lap
LOOK AT MENU
Discuss menu
ORDER MEAL
Talk
Drink water
Eat salad or soup
Meal arrives
EAT FOOD
Finish meal
Order dessert
Eat dessert
Ask for bill
Bill arrives
PAY BILL
Leave tip
Get coats
LEAVE

Note: Items in all capital letters were mentioned by most subjects; items in italics by fewer subjects, and items in regular lower-case letters by the fewest subjects.

Source: Bower, Black, & Turner, 1979

for mundane or routine events. They have slots and requirements as to what can fill these slots. In addition, the scripts are structured, with the events causally linked to one another. This causal linking allows us to make inferences to understand events and to make predictions about future events.

To make this idea concrete, Table 7.2 gives a number of actions in the script for restaurants (from subjects' responses in Bower, Black, & Turner, 1979, to be described soon). When a script is being used for understanding, it is presumed that there are some entry conditions that were true (e.g., that the customer is hungry and has money for the restaurant script) and that a successful conclusion of the script results in a different state of affairs (e.g., that the customer is not hungry and has less money). The actions can be broken down into what are referred to as *scenes*, such as entering, ordering, eating, and exiting. Within each scene, there are a number of actions that are presumed to occur in that particular order. Thus, the ordering scene is not just a set of actions, but a set of ordered actions. Although the actions may look like a simple sequence, it is important to remember that the actions are causally linked so that changes in one may lead to changes in another. For example,

John was hungry and ordered a hamburger.

It was burned.

He would not pay.

In addition to all the usual inferencing (e.g., pay what?), this passage introduces a deviation in the usual script routine: The food was badly prepared. Because we understand that the payment at the end of the meal is directly linked to the food, it is easy for us to understand that the food preparation can affect the payment.

Although it may seem that this knowledge and its use are straightforward, the process is actually quite complicated. The causal connections between all the parts of the script have to be present to allow us to understand not only the normal script actions but any of a large number of possible problems or unusual events that can occur. For each of these events, we can often quickly understand its implications for other script actions (such as how the burning of the hamburger affects the payment). Programming computers to make such inferences, even for a relatively small number of possibilities, is difficult and painstaking (see Lenat & Guha, 1990).

Because of the highly structured nature of the knowledge, scripts allow us to generate predictions about what is going to happen (see Charniak & McDermott, 1985, for a discussion of this issue). The slot values are highly correlated, such that knowing the value in one slot allows you to predict the values of other slots. If you went to a restaurant with red-and-white checkered tablecloths, you would be more likely to expect a candle on the table in a Chianti wine bottle than if there were no tablecloths. If the tablecloth and candle were present, would you expect Chinese or Italian food? In fact, the number of inferences one can make from just a small sampling of what the restaurant is like is quite large. We use this information to help fill in gaps in what we read or observe, as well as to predict what is likely to occur.

Again, one may reasonably ask whether there is any evidence for the "psychological reality" of scripts. Do people have and use such knowledge structures? The evidence generally supports the claim that people really do have scripts. Bower et al. (1979) conducted a number of studies examining people's knowledge and use of scripts, such as going to a restaurant, attending a lecture, grocery shopping, or visiting a doctor. Given these labels, they found that people had no trouble generating a series of ordered actions and that there was good agreement about what the actions were (see Table 7.2 for an example) and what the main scenes were (similar to the all-capital-letter entries in Table 7.2). These scripts were also used for remembering particular events. For example, in one experiment the subjects read about events, such as John going to see a doctor.

The Doctor

John was feeling bad today so he decided to go see the family doctor. He checked in with the doctor's receptionist, and then looked through several medical magazines that were on the table by his chair. Finally the nurse came and asked him to take off his clothes. The doctor was very nice to him. He eventually prescribed some pills for John. John left the doctor's office and headed home. [We never said the scripts were interesting.]

There were 18 such short passages, each of which contained six script actions. Twenty minutes later, the subjects were given the script titles and asked to recall the passage as exactly as they could. They were able to recall about three of the stated script actions per passage. Of particular interest, they recalled on average almost one script action *that did not occur in the passage*. For example, a person recalling this passage might recall that John lay on the examining table or that he had his temperature taken. Clearly, these are reasonable inferences given the passage, but that is the point. Only because of our knowledge of doctor visits are such inferences reasonable.

Whether people make use of the ordering of the actions was also tested directly. Subjects were presented with 10 lists of actions, including some scripts. The actions within the scripts were either in their usual order, or 4 of the 12 actions were out of order (e.g., for attending a lecture, the action "close notebook" might be near the beginning). Subjects were asked to recall the actions in the order they had been presented. Script actions that were presented in their usual order were recalled in their exact order 50% of the time, while misordered actions were recalled in their exact order only 18% of the time. Thus, people use their knowledge of the order of script actions for remembering particular event sequences.

People appear to have scripts of a large number of stereotyped events, though some appear to be more stereotyped than others. For example, consider the script for a doctor's appointment. The scenes might include arriving, waiting in a waiting room, entering an examination room, being examined, paying, and leaving. Note, however, that the exact events that occur within each scene and the order of the events seem far less stereotyped than in the restaurant script. For example, one does not necessarily receive or pay the bill before leaving a doctor's office. This observation, as well as others, led to further investigation of the exact nature of the knowledge used in understanding stereotyped events (e.g., Schank, 1982). Despite controversies concerning the details of how schemas are organized, most researchers would agree that people's understanding and memory for these events are influenced by some type of general knowledge structures. Researchers continue to work on issues about how scripts affect memory for different types of actions, such as script-relevant and script-irrelevant actions (e.g., Erdfelder & Bredenkamp, 1998).

Schema Activation

Although we have focused on the effects of activated schemas, a crucial first step is to activate the appropriate schema. If one uses a restaurant script to understand a home-cooked meal, many of the inferences and predictions will be inappropriate. This problem is the usual complexity problem, with a focus on schemas: Given all the knowledge one possesses, how is the relevant schema determined?

Although this issue is far from resolved, several possible ways in which schemas are activated have been proposed. First, certain key words (or objects, if one is not reading or listening) may help to *trigger* the appropriate schema. In the case of the restaurant script, these key words may include *restaurant, out to dinner, waiter, chef*, and so on. Second, in addition to the words that are distinctively associated with restaurants, other words may provide at least some support for this schema being appropriate (e.g., *hungry*). Third, events often occur in a context that can also provide support for the relevance of particular schemas. If you knew John was in town for a convention and was hungry, *restaurant* would become more activated than if he were sitting home and was hungry. As in the memory retrieval work discussed previously, it may be reasonable to conceive of this activation as coming from multiple sources, with some sources more strongly associated and thus contributing more activation and more support.

Problems With Schemas

You will have noticed that our discussion of schemas has been full of examples and general description but short on details that would necessarily be part of a computational model. The reason for our vagueness is that it is not entirely clear just how to implement the desired properties of schemas. For example, it is straightforward to have slots with default values but exceedingly difficult to implement the idea that the values in some slots constrain the acceptable values in other slots. One needs to be able to do this to capture situations like the example of Chinese versus Italian restaurants discussed earlier where clusters of properties tend to co-occur.

This kind of observation is what motivated David Rumelhart and his associates to implement schemas within a PDP or connectionist model (e.g., Rumelhart, Smolensky, McClelland, & Hinton, 1986). Connectionist models have the advantage that they tend to be sensitive to properties that co-occur. Further, recent advances in connectionist models have explored ways to account for knowledge like causal information that also often appears in schemas (Hummel & Holyoak, 1997).

A variety of perplexing puzzles associated with the use of schemas still remains. Sometimes, for example, situations may involve a mixture of schemas. One wouldn't want to disrobe when one meets one's physician in a restaurant nor would one want to stand in front of the cash register waiting to pay for one's meal in the event of a fire. Although the notion of schemas represents a powerful approach to constraining relevant knowledge, there are still some subtle mysteries to be solved. As of this writing, there is no implemented system that handles the relevance problem with anything like people's gracefulness and flexibility.

Summary

In this section, we have examined how people might encode and remember much more complex situations. The major claim is that people bring to bear large knowledge structures, schemas, to understand these situations. Memory for the situation derives from the schema and how it is used for encoding. The schema is an important concept throughout psychology—so much of our knowledge is embedded in general knowledge structures that are used for understanding and remembering events, people, problems, etc. We then examined scripts, a specific type of schema for a causally linked sequence of events in a stereotyped situation, and some psychological evidence for them.

A main point from the motivation for schemas is that many situations must be augmented with knowledge. These large knowledge structures provide a way in which our relevant knowledge can be brought to bear to help with the problem of too little information and too many possibilities. It is important to bear in mind, however, that the purpose of using knowledge to interpret a new situation is to allow us to function effectively in that situation, not necessarily to remember it with perfect accuracy. Thus, schemas may also create situations in which we misremember something that came from our prior knowledge as actually being a part of the event itself. We turn to this issue in the next section.

RECONSTRUCTIVE MEMORY

Encoding-Retrieval Interactions Revisited

All of us have had experiences where we "remembered" some event only to find that we had remembered it incorrectly, perhaps combining two similar events in our memory. A common mistake is to believe something happened during one time (e.g., a date or party) only to realize later that it had happened at a different time (such as a different date or party). For example, suppose you remember a date with dinner at Restaurant X and then Movie Y, only to later find out those were different dates (maybe with the same person). How do such misrememberings come about?

This is a puzzle if one thinks of remembering as "activating" or "retrieving" an encoded event, as we have in the earlier chapters. There clearly is no trace of an earlier event that has both Restaurant X and Movie Y in it, so how did you remember it that way? The problem is in thinking of remembering as a simple process of retrieving an encoded event. Our memories are imperfect (due to interference and decay, as discussed in Chapter 5) so we cannot always retrieve a complete encoding of what we are trying to remember. Especially for complex situations, we may have various parts or fragments that we then actively put together in order to remember what happened.

So, in remembering that date, you might have remembered that you had dinner and a movie, then probed memory further with those cues (and information about the person you were dating) and retrieved additional information about a dinner and a movie, so put them together in the same date. This may lead to problems in some cases, but often it will lead to fairly good remembering. For example, if you had just gone to one restaurant and one movie with this person, you probably will recall it accurately. **Reconstructive memory** refers to integrating different sources of information in remembering.

Table 7.3　　　　**Burglar/Home Buyer Story**

> The two boys ran until they came to the driveway. "See, I told you today was good for skipping school," said Mark. "Mom is never home on Thursday," he added. Tall hedges hid the house from the road so the pair strolled across the finely landscaped yard. "I never knew your place was so big," said Pete. "Yeah, but it's nicer now than it used to be since Dad had the new stone siding put on and added the fireplace."
>
> There were front and back doors and a side door which led to the garage which was empty except for three parked 10-speed bikes. They went in the side door, Mark explaining that it was always open in case his younger sisters got home earlier than their mother.
>
> Pete wanted to see the house so Mark started with the living room. It, like the rest of the downstairs, was newly painted. Mark turned on the stereo, the noise of which worried Pete. "Don't worry, the nearest house is a quarter of a mile away," Mark shouted. Pete felt more comfortable observing that no houses could be seen in any direction beyond the huge yard.

(Continued)

A particularly intriguing example of this is the recollection of Watergate lawyer John Dean, which was an important factor in the resignation of President Richard Nixon. His conversations with Nixon were important events in his life and you might expect that he remembered them quite well. However, when testifying, he would sometimes confuse details from two different visits, though the recordings of the meetings showed he did remember the main points (see Neisser, 1981, for more details and an interesting analysis).

Let's consider this idea from the perspective of encoding and retrieval discussed in Chapter 5. You encode some information about an event. At retrieval, you have some cues and use those to probe for the event. If the encoded information is still highly available (perhaps because it was meaningfully encoded, not too similar to other events, and fairly recent), then you will probably remember it very well. If, however, the encoded information is less available (perhaps because it was not as deeply encoded, is similar to many other events, and is not fairly recent), then you may not retrieve all of it (or even any of it). If it is a complex event, such as a date, you may retrieve parts and then put the parts together into a whole. How well this reconstruction works depends on whether there are constraints within the parts that might alert you to an accurate or inaccurate reconstruction. For example, if you remember a dinner and movie but they are with different people, then they are probably not parts of the same date. The difficulty is when you do not remember enough about the events to know whether they are from the same date or not—you might remember events involving the same person, but not remember time of year or clothing you were wearing that might help you decide whether the remembered situations came from the same date or different ones.

Table 7.3   *(Continued)*

The dining room, with all the china, silver, and cut glass, was no place to play so the boys moved into the kitchen where they made sandwiches. Mark said they wouldn't go to the basement because it had been damp and musty ever since the new plumbing had been installed.

"This is where my Dad keeps his famous paintings and his coin collection," Mark said as they peered into the den. Mark bragged that he could get spending money whenever he needed it since he'd discovered that his Dad kept a lot in the desk drawer.

There were three upstairs bedrooms. Mark showed Pete his mother's closet which was filled with furs and the locked box which held her jewels. His sisters' room was un-interesting except for the color TV which Mark carried to his room. Mark bragged that the bathroom in the hall was his since one had been added to his sisters' room for their use. The big highlight in his room, though, was a leak in the ceiling where the old roof had finally rotted.

Source: Pichert & Anderson, 1977.

The basic problem we have been examining is that we may retrieve only par-tial information and we want to integrate them into a remembering of a single event. In addition, as will be seen in the next section, sometimes we use our knowledge to augment what we remember, leading to other types of misrememberings. This issue is seen best in the context of schema-related retrieval.

Schemas and Stereotypes

When remembering schema-related knowledge, we often use the schema to help us remember the event. Suppose you were asked to remember your visit to a particular restaurant you had gone to once. You might use general knowledge about restaurants to help you remember the sequence of events or exactly what your group ordered. For example, you know that there are different types of restaurants, so you might first try to remember if it was a seafood restaurant, a Chinese restaurant, etc. Depending on the type of restaurant, you might use your knowledge to probe about the décor or likely specialties or other information you know about restaurants of that type. As you retrieve information from memory about this particular restaurant, you can use your restaurant schema to probe still further (for example, who paid for the meal?). The point is that the schemas you bring to bear for understanding an event can also be used in helping you to retrieve the memory of that event. We have seen how the schema can influence what is stored. The schema can also influence what is retrieved.

Let's examine a simple demonstration from R. C. Anderson and Pichert (1978). Read the story in Table 7.3 from the perspective of a burglar. Now, just to yourself, try to recall as much as you can. When you are done, imagine that you are a prospective homebuyer. Can you remember anything else about the original story? Most people find they can. The experimental results were clear—the perspective one took had a large influence on recall. In particular, one can divide the passage into ideas that are relevant to a burglar (e.g., the coin collection), ideas that are relevant to a home buyer (e.g., huge yard), plus ones that are not particularly relevant to either. The ideas that are relevant to the perspective used by the person reading the passage are much more likely to be recalled than are the ideas relevant to the other perspective (64% vs. 46%). This difference shows, as have other results presented here, that the knowledge we use for understanding affects what we understand and remember. More interesting, for our present purposes, the subjects then were told to take the other perspective and asked to recall again. The main result is that they were able to recall about 10% more when they used the other perspective (e.g., switching from the burglar to homebuyer perspective).

Why does this happen? As you might guess, the effects come about because people use their knowledge of what might be of interest to burglars or homebuyers to guide their retrieval. A coin collection may be remembered by people taking a burglar's perspective, because they are interested in valuable, portable objects. However, a coin collection would be of little interest to a homebuyer, since presumably the owners would take that with them when they sold the house. Prospective homebuyers would be thinking of characteristics of the structure and property that might make it desirable (or undesirable) as a place to live. When Anderson and Pichert asked the subjects in their experiment what happened when they got the new perspective, many of them said that new facts that they had not remembered before just popped into their heads.

The point here, again, is that remembering is not always simply retrieving a trace. Sometimes we remember different sets of partial information, or fragments, and put them together. Other times, remembering involves reconstructing the original event, using some information from the event and some other knowledge we might have of events of that kind. There was no simple memory representation of the story in Table 7.3 that could be found and reported. Rather, what was recalled depended on both the stored representation and the schema used to guide retrieval.

In the burglar–home buyer experiments, it seems that the perspective was providing additional memory cues to help "find" parts of the memory for the story, but often when we reconstruct an event, we mix up what we remember with what we believe should be true. Vicente and Brewer (1993) point out some embarrassing (to psychologists) cases in which research results are misremembered to fit into our schema. For example, there is a famous set of studies by deGroot (1965) that have been replicated by Chase and Simon (1973) and are discussed in some detail in Chapter 13. The results show that chess experts can remember many more pieces on a chessboard after a quick glance than can less expert players. When a group of cognitive psychologists were queried about deGroot's findings, most of them remembered the main result but also remembered a particular control condition that was not there. (The control condition is having chess pieces put randomly on a board, in which case one finds that there is no effect of chess expertise, ruling out a differential general memory explanation.) This control condition was included in the Chase and Simon replication but was remembered as being in the original because it is important for the interpretability of the result. Thus, the knowledge used as to what the results meant led them (us) to "remember" the control condition as having been there because it should have been.

As another example, the effects of stereotypes may be heightened by these reconstructive properties. Suppose you have a strong stereotype about a group of people and are asked to remember an event involving someone from this group. In addition to any effect on encoding that the stereotype has (which might be considerable), the stereotype also guides retrieval of the event. If you thought such people were mean, you would be more likely to retrieve behavior exhibiting the meanness of this individual than if you thought they were nice. Just as understanding and encoding should not be taken as simply storing the presented information, remembering cannot be thought of as simply accessing the memory trace. We are active processors who interpret the world when understanding and interpret our knowledge when remembering.

Summary

Remembering is often reconstruction, rather than simple retrieval of the exact, complete information you want to know. We examined two different cases. First, you may remember fragments and put them together into a single remembering. Second, you may augment a remembered fragment with knowledge, such as from a schema. In both these cases, you are trying to remember a particular event by using what you retrieve and what you know. It is important to realize, however, that while sometimes you know you are combining fragments or filling in partial information, there are also times when you do not. This can lead to situations in which a reconstructed memory is not actually experienced as a reconstruction.

MEMORY IN THE WORLD _____

Introduction

The goal in the earlier memory chapters was to provide a better understanding of some fundamental issues about how information is encoded, retrieved, and used. To best illustrate these effects, it is often useful to conduct laboratory experiments with control over many extraneous factors. However, this sometimes makes it difficult for the student to see how these ideas might work under more realistic (natural) situations in which we have to remember more complex material. In this chapter, we have been expanding beyond these basic effects to show how memory might work in a broader way. In this section, we investigate research on eyewitness testimony, flashbulb memories, and repressed memories. This work allows us to judge the truthfulness of the opening quotation, which suggests that our recollections may often contain false information.

Eyewitness Testimony

Suppose you were an eyewitness to a crime or an accident. When you are asked to remember the event, you "find" the queried information and tell exactly what you saw. Right? Wrong, at least some of the time. As we have seen in the last two chapters, remembering can be quite complex and affected by many things. Here we examine a particular situation in which a person's memory is critical—eyewitness testimony.

Eyewitnesses are an integral part of our justice system. In the United States each year, more than 75,000 suspects are identified by eyewitnesses (Wells, Luus, & Windschitl, 1994). In many cases, eyewitnesses are the main evidence available. Although the need for accurate eyewitness testimony is great, we have already discussed much in this book that suggests why memory for witnessed events may not necessarily be accurate. For example, the event of interest may have been brief, the witness may not have been attending to it, and the arousal and emotion of the moment may have made the encoding and memory of the event more difficult to retrieve. Although it is clear that eyewitness testimony can be inaccurate, there is also much evidence that it is often correct. Our purpose in this section is not to explore all eyewitness testimony but rather to examine a particular situation that has implications for both eyewitness testimony and our understanding of memory—misleading questions and the effects they have on people's memory.

Misleading Information

Imagine the following situation. You are watching a red sports car driving down a side street, and it then pulls up to a stop sign. After waiting, the car then turns right and shortly thereafter knocks down a pedestrian who is crossing the street at the crosswalk. A few days later, the driver's lawyer asks you, "Did another car pass the red sports car while it was stopped at the yield sign?" You answer the question. Then, the lawyer asks that if your memory is so good, was there a stop sign or a yield sign at the corner? You mistakenly say there was a yield sign. The lawyer's misleading question (i.e., presupposing a yield sign when there really was a stop sign) has probably affected your response. (We say "probably" only because it is possible that you would have answered yield sign even without the misleading question.)

So, what does this imaginary scenario show? Misleading information can be suggested after the event (which is called *postevent*) that can affect what answers a person gives to later questions. More dramatically, the testimony of a witness might be changed by inserting misleading information into earlier questions. Is this imaginary scenario likely? Unfortunately, it probably is.

This scenario was taken from an experiment by Loftus, Burns, and Miller (1978). We describe here a typical manipulation. They showed subjects a series of slides depicting such an accident, with half the people being shown the red sports car stopped at a stop sign and half the people being shown the same car stopped at a yield sign. As part of a 20-question test, half of each group was later asked a question like our example (with misleading information that contradicted the slide they had seen), and half were asked a question that did not mention a sign at all: "Did any car pass the red sports car when it was stopped at the intersection?" Thus, half the subjects had a question that was misleading, and the other half of the subjects did not. They were given a recognition test in which two slides were presented side by side and they had to say which slide they had seen earlier. The critical slide pair was one in which the red sports car was stopped at a stop sign in one slide and a yield sign in the other slide, as shown in Figure 7.3. If they had been given misleading information, would people choose the slide with the misleading information? The answer is yes. The group given no misleading information in the questions chose correctly about 85% of the time; the group getting misleading information chose correctly only 38% of the time. The misleading information had a large effect on people's response. This result, that the misled group chooses the misleading suggestion more often than does the control group, is called the **misinformation effect.**

This effect appears to have important implications for eyewitness testimony, but why is it important for our understanding of memory? One clue may be seen in the title of this Loftus et al. (1978) paper, which was "Semantic integration of verbal information into a visual memory." That is, the researchers were arguing that the memory for the original event was changed by having the postevent misleading questions integrated with it. This brings up a basic question about memory, which we briefly addressed in Chapter 5; "Can earlier memories be overwritten?" Many theories of memory, such as the SAM theory discussed in Chapter 5, assume that long-term memories are not alterable, though the retrieval of the memory for any event can be interfered with by other memories. However, some theories, such as the PDP model discussed in Chapter 6, do allow for such changes. What is the evidence?

Figure 7.3   **Two Slides in a Recognition Test**   The task is to pick which of these two slides had been seen earlier, the one with the stop sign or the one with the yield sign. Some subjects have received misleading information to try to confuse them about what they had seen. For example, if they had seen the stop sign, they might have been asked a question in which it was presupposed that they had seen a yield sign.

Source: Loftus, Miller, & Burns, 1978.

This research on misleading information, which was pioneered by Elizabeth Loftus, has led to a great deal of interest and investigation. Over 20 years later, there is no controversy about the basic effect: Presenting misleading postevent information can affect people's responses and increase the probability that they will respond with the misleading suggestion. This effect occurs whether people are asked misleading questions or if they later read a narrative about the crime in which the misleading information is substituted (e.g., McCloskey & Zaragoza, 1985; Zaragoza & Lane, 1994). Although the effect is agreed upon, there is a lot of controversy over its explanation.

EXPLANATIONS FOR THE MISINFORMATION EFFECT   The explanations can be grouped in many ways, but for our purposes we can consider three types: overwriting, source confusions, and misinformation acceptance. First, *overwriting* explanations assume, as one might guess from the name, that the misleading information alters the original trace with the misleading information (sometimes called by the graphic name of "destructive updating").

Second, the misleading information may not impair the original memory, but instead may provide some competing information that can be retrieved and used at times as if it were the original memory, *because the source of the memory is not clear.* This explanation requires some explanation. For a number of years, Marcia Johnson has conducted fascinating research on how people distinguish true memories from imagined memories (e.g., Johnson & Raye, 1981). This research has also led to a more general consideration of how people distinguish the sources of memories. Sometimes you may explicitly remember where some information came from, but often you infer the source by cues in the memory itself (for example, a memory that is rich in visual perceptual detail is more likely to have been seen). Lindsay and Johnson (1989) argue that part of the difficulty in correctly answering questions following postevent misleading suggestions is that the memory for the misleading suggestion may be incorrectly inferred as having been seen. If this is true, then people who retrieve this memory might respond as if it were the original memory. This is referred to as a *source confusion*.

Third, there may be no fundamental memory problem with being given misleading information; rather, it may just be that people use the misleading information because they do not know better and *they assume the misleading information is true.* Suppose they did not remember what sign was there, but the misleading question mentioned a yield sign. When asked to choose between a slide with a stop sign and one with a yield sign, why wouldn't they choose the yield sign? Although various possibilities of this type exist, we will collectively call them *misinformation acceptance.* The point is that one can well know that the answer is based on the postevent information, not the original memory, and yet believe it is the correct answer.

Let us make clear the distinction between these last two explanations, because they are easy to confuse. The source-confusion explanation is that you believe that the postevent suggestion was actually seen. The misinformation-acceptance explanation claims that you understand that the postevent suggestion was given as a

Table 7.4   **The Original and Modified Test Procedure of McCloskey and Zaragoza (1985)**

Condition	Slides	Narrative	Original test	Modified test
Control	Hammer	Tool	Hammer vs. Screwdriver	Hammer vs. Wrench
Misled	Hammer	Screwdriver	Hammer vs. Screwdriver	Hammer vs. Wrench

Source: McCloskey & Zaragoza, 1985.

postevent, but you do not remember the original seen event so you give the postevent answer because you believe it to be the correct one.

EVIDENCE FOR EXPLANATIONS OF THE MISINFORMATION EFFECT   We have just presented three very different explanations for the misinformation effect. Which is correct? As often happens when a complex question is explored, the result turns out to be more complex than was initially conceived. Instead of simply giving the answer, we go through some relevant findings and explain their implications.

McCloskey and Zaragoza (1985) argued for the misinformation acceptance hypothesis in the following way: The advantage of the control group may not be because they remember the original event any better. Rather, the advantage may occur because when the misinformed group subjects do not remember the original event they may sometimes remember the misleading question, and in those cases they will choose the misleading answer. For example, suppose people saw a series of slides depicting a theft, in which a maintenance worker steals $20 and a calculator from an office and slips the calculator in his toolbox under his hammer. They then might read a narrative of the theft in which the calculator would be described as being put under a tool (control condition) or screwdriver (misled condition). The full design for the experiment is given in Table 7.4. As can be seen there, in the Loftus et al. (1978) design, one would then contrast the misled (screwdriver) and original (hammer) possibilities. By the earlier results, the hammer would be chosen less often in the misled condition than in the control condition, which would be interpreted as a type of overwriting.

McCloskey and Zaragoza suggest that one can get that difference without any overwriting from the misleading information. If subjects in the control condition do not remember the original event well, they have to guess between the two options. However, if subjects in the misled condition do not remember the original event well, but do remember the misleading information, then they will answer with the misleading information (screwdriver). Thus, even if the misled and control conditions had equal memory for the original item (hammer), the misled condition might be expected to choose the misled item more often.

How could one test whether the memory for the original item is impaired in the misled condition? The modified procedure suggested by McCloskey and Zaragoza is to contrast the original (hammer) with a new item (wrench). The logic of the test is the following: If misleading people truly impairs their memory for the original event so that it cannot be retrieved, then they should think both of these possibilities are unfamiliar and guess wrench as often as hammer. If, however, the misleading narrative has not affected their memory for the original event, then they should guess the hammer as often in the misled condition as in the control condition. That is, even though they might go with the misled option of the screwdriver if it were available, when it is not one of the choices, they will show that they remember the original event as well as the group not given misleading information. (We have been discussing this study in terms of particular items to make the explanation simpler, but there were several different items and all the choices were counterbalanced.)

McCloskey and Zaragoza (1985) conducted six different experiments using both the Loftus procedure and their modified procedure. The Loftus procedure led to a replication of the earlier Loftus results, the misinformation effect: People in the misled condition, when asked to choose between hammer and screwdriver, chose the misleading option (screwdriver) 35% more often than did people in the control condition. This result appears to support the overwriting hypothesis. However, in the modified procedure, when people had to choose between hammer and wrench, there was no evidence that memory for the original event had been impaired. Subjects in the misled condition chose the tool they had seen in the slide (hammer) as often as did subjects in the control condition. McCloskey and Zaragoza argue that this finding supports the misinformation acceptance explanation and that there is no evidence for overwriting.

Although other findings also suggest that much of the misleading information effect may be due to such aware uses of misleading information (see Lindsay, 1993), there is also evidence of source confusions. For example, Lindsay (1990) provided the misleading information in a narrative immediately after the event but tested subjects' memories 48 hours later with a series of cued recall questions (see Table 7.5). He told the subjects right before the test that the narrative had been false, so if they remembered the answer as coming from the narrative then they should not give that answer. Thus, if subjects remembered that the information came from the narrative, rather than assuming it was true (which the misinformation acceptance explanation claims), they should now assume it was false. (This general approach, called the *logic-of-opposition* procedure, is adapted from Larry Jacoby's work, e.g., Jacoby, Woloshyn, & Kelley, 1989.) Despite this instruction, Lindsay found that subjects often recalled information from the narrative. Further, even if people are asked directly whether some information was from the slide or the questions following the slides, they sometimes mistake the source. Thus, it appears that source confusions do occur as well.

Is there any evidence for overwriting? The research area remains controversial, with some researchers believing that the evidence for overwriting is clear (e.g., Belli, Lindsay, Gales, & McCarthy, 1994; Loftus, 1994; Tversky & Tulchin, 1989), while others argue that there is no evidence yet for such a claim (e.g., Zaragoza & McCloskey, 1989). Some evidence suggests that the memory for details for the original event is impaired by the misleading information (e.g., Belli et al., 1994; Lindsay,

Table 7.5 **Procedure of Lindsay (1990): Logic of Opposition**

1. View slide sequence.
2. Read narrative with misleading information.
3. Wait 48 hours.
4. Cued recall test: Subjects were told that the test questions had been selected so that any answer mentioned in the narrative was wrong and should not be reported. Thus, if subjects remembered an answer as coming from the narrative, then they knew it was not the correct answer.

Source: Lindsay, 1990.

1990). However, it should not surprise us, given the discussion of interference in Chapter 5, that having a second encoding of an event may interfere with remembering the original encoding. The question is whether this impairment is evidence of overwriting. Ayers and Reder (1998) present an excellent review of the misinformation effect and account for the effect in terms of a network model (similar to the ACT model presented in Chapter 6). They argue that the data can be well understood in terms of standard memory phenomenon, such as interference, as examined in Chapter 5.

Although there is still controversy over the overwriting explanation, there is clear evidence that sometimes the misinformation effect may be due to (or partially due to) misinformation acceptance and source confusions. In any case, there is general agreement that exposing eyewitnesses to misleading postevent information can severely compromise the accuracy of their testimony.

Flashbulb Memories

Do you have some memory of an event that was very important to you that you can vividly remember? Maybe you can remember all the people who were there, what everyone was wearing, who said what, and how you felt. Many of us can recall some particular important event and feel that it is almost like some photograph that was taken at the time. Perhaps there was some major personal event (a first date, a college admission, a wedding) or some historical event (the fall of the Berlin wall, the space shuttle *Challenger* explosion) that stands out for you. These memories "feel" very different from the memory we might have of what we ate for dinner last night or the last book we read. Are they any different?

Brown and Kulik (1977) began the study of what they called **flashbulb memories.** They asked 80 people if they could recall the circumstances when they first heard about some important event (e.g., the assassination of President John F. Kennedy in November 1963) and, if so, to recall it. All but one of the participants could recall the assassination, even though the event had occurred 13 years before. How many other events can you so clearly remember from 13 years ago? Brown and Kulik argued that these flashbulb memories were special—that they involved a special biological mechanism that we have developed through evolution so that highly

AN APPLICATION
Improving Eyewitness Testimony: The Line-up

Eyewitness testimony is crucial in many legal situations. Given what we have discussed over the last few chapters (and especially the misinformation effect), you might guess that such testimony may sometimes be inaccurate. It is—mistaken eyewitness identification is the most frequent cause of convictions of innocent people. The testimony is particularly compelling when the witness has high confidence in his or her report and this confidence is conveyed to the juror. Because of the importance of this issue in legal situations, it has been a source of much examination. Here we examine one issue of practical importance—line-ups.

In a line-up, as you have seen in the movies, a witness is asked to pick out the person he or she saw commit the crime out of a group of similar-looking people (sometimes this is done with photographs). If the witness picks out the person suspected by the police, this is viewed as strong evidence against the person. An interesting practice, that is not prohibited in U.S. cases, is that the person running the line-up may give feedback to the witness about the choice (such as, "Yes, that is who we thought." or "Are you sure it is that one?").

Although we can probably all see the problem in questioning the witness' choice, giving positive feedback about the choice has its own, perhaps less obvious problems (see Wells & Bradfield, 1999). First, in experimental analogs to this situation, the witness given positive feedback about the identification subsequently had higher confidence in the identification than a witness not given such feedback. Given that the confidence of the witness may affect the jury's evaluation, this is an important influence. Second, the feedback affects other aspects of the witness' recall, such as how good the viewing conditions were. Witnesses who are told

(Continued)

consequential surprising events are very well remembered. Why? Presumably because such events may be crucial for our survival. (Remember, that is why the mechanism developed; that does not mean that every current use of it is crucial for our survival.) Because of this special mechanism, these memories were assumed to undergo little forgetting and include both the focal event and the surrounding circumstances; that is, these flashbulb memories were assumed to have an exceptional amount of detail.

Since then, a number of other studies have looked at people's memory for various events, and a controversy has arisen about whether some special mechanism is needed to account for this finding. The argument for such a mechanism is simple:

AN APPLICATION

Improving Eyewitness Testimony: The Line-up *(Continued)*

they were correct in their identification judge the viewing conditions for the crime as better than witnesses not given the feedback. In a real-world case, it may be that people who are correct do have better viewing conditions, but this result occurred in an experiment in which everyone had the same viewing conditions (the crime was presented on videotape) and people were randomly assigned to be given the feedback or not.

Why might this happen? Given what we have discussed about the misinformation effect and reconstructive memory, perhaps it is not too surprising that information given about an identification could have such effects. Wells and Bradfield (1999) suggest that the confidence judgments are partly inferred by the witnesses based on their accurate identification (some reasoning, though not necessarily conscious, like, "Given I was correct, I must have had a good look at the person."). As in many cases, people are reconstructing an episode based on different sets of partial information.

What can be done? Wells and Bradfield suggest that one partial solution would be to have line-ups done with the person operating the line-up being unaware of which person is the suspect. This is a standard technique for good research design and ensures that the person will also not give any subtle cues to the witnesses (unintentional or intentional). Even then, however, the witnesses may find out later that they chose the person the police suspected. Fortunately, if people are told to think about their confidence and the viewing conditions *before* they find out if their choice was correct or not, then the feedback has much less influence on their later confidence. These changes, which were being considered for inclusion in a Justice Department report in 1999, show how psychological research on memory can be applied to real-world situations.

The memory for these events seems so much better than we would expect for memories that old, so the usual memory mechanisms would not account for them (see McCloskey, 1992, for an analysis of the arguments in this debate).

Is that true? There are two parts to the question: First, are flashbulb memories really as accurate as this argument assumes? Second, is this accuracy really so much greater than what we might expect for nonflashbulb memories? To answer the second question first, we really do not know. There have been some interesting attempts to examine our memory for past events in our lives (e.g., Brewer, 1988), but we do not have the right control condition against which to compare flashbulb memories. However, we do know that there is forgetting of memories for events, so if flashbulb memories show almost no forgetting, that might be enough to argue for a special memory mechanism.

Are flashbulb memories as accurate as they seem? Notice that in the Brown and Kulik (1977) study we simply do not know if the memories were recalled correctly or not—we have no independent assessment of the accuracy. Neisser and Harsch (1992) provide such an assessment (also see McCloskey, Wible, & Cohen, 1988). The morning after the space shuttle *Challenger* exploded in January 1986, these researchers gave a group of undergraduates at Emory University a questionnaire about the explosion and how they had heard about it. Not surprisingly, most of the students remembered exactly what they had been doing, who told them, and other facts. Two and a half years later, the researchers contacted the students and asked them to participate in a study. During this study, they were again asked about their memory for how they heard about the *Challenger* explosion. (Interestingly, only about 25% had remembered filling out the questionnaire earlier.) Here is the recall of one participant (Neisser & Harsch, 1992, p. 9):

> When I first heard about the explosion I was sitting in my freshman dorm room with my roommate and we were watching TV. It came on a news flash and we were both totally shocked. I was really upset and I went upstairs to talk to a friend of mine and then I called my parents.

This is a very reasonable recall *except* that her recall the day after the *Challenger* exploded had been that she had found out in a class, felt sad, and then watched TV to get the details. In fact, there were many cases of inaccuracies in their flashbulb memories.

Rather than just state this result, a little more information may make this point more clearly. The researchers scored each recall against the original (day after) recall. To come up with some accuracy score, they assumed, based on past research, that the three most important parts of the original memories were the location, the activity (e.g., watching TV, playing ball), and the informant (i.e., who had told them). Of secondary importance were the time of the day and the other people who may have been present. They gave each recall a score between 0 and 7, with 2 points awarded for each important part and 1 point for the parts of secondary importance. Thus, a score of 7 indicates that the person had recalled the circumstances when they heard about the *Challenger* almost perfectly 2½ years later. Only 3 of 44 participants received a score of 7. The mean score was only 2.95 out of 7, and 50% of the participants scored 2 or less. In addition, of the people who thought they remembered the circumstances, there was almost no relation between accuracy of recall and their confidence in the recall. For example, the 13 people with the highest confidence in their recall (5 on a 5-point scale) had a mean accuracy that was almost the same as the mean accuracy for the less confident participants. Thus, there is good evidence that flashbulb memories are not necessarily accurate. In addition, these results demonstrate that confidence is a poor measure of the accuracy of a memory. This point cannot be overemphasized. In many cases, a person's confidence in a memory is taken as strong evidence that the memory is accurate ("I know what I saw!"), but these data suggest that confidence and accuracy are not strongly related.

Many researchers argue that we do not need to posit a special mechanism to account for flashbulb memories. What does cause some events to be so well remembered? (Remember, although they may not always be accurate, by definition they appear to be very vivid, almost photographic memories.) It appears that a number of different usual memory mechanisms may help such memories to stand out (e.g., Brewer, 1992). First, because of the importance of the event and the emotional content, such memories are much more likely to be thought about and talked about. Notice that this is a type of rehearsal at a much later time. This displaced rehearsal tends to improve memory of the event for two reasons that we discussed in Chapter 5: Rehearsing and spaced practice both increase the probability that the information is remembered. Second, the events encoded in these memories tend to be very unusual. As discussed in Chapter 5, interference is a function of the similarity of the events. Very unusual events tend to be quite distinctive and thus suffer less interference from other events. An alternative is that the strong emotional tone of the memory can affect its memorability, though it is also possible that such memories are unusual so that the gain in memorability is a function of the distinctiveness again.

Not all researchers agree with the "nothing special" conclusion, and the reason for the disagreement addresses what is meant by "flashbulb memories." Conway et al. (1994) question whether the results showing that flashbulb memories are forgotten really concerned flashbulb memories. In particular, they dispute whether the *Challenger* explosion was likely to lead to a true flashbulb memory. Their argument is that, while the explosion was certainly newsworthy and sad, it was not consequential for most of us; that is, it had less effect on our lives than many of the other events for which we may have flashbulbs, such as our personal big events or events such as the John F. Kennedy assassination, which for many people felt like a terrible blow and a change in the country's future. Flashbulb memories require the event to be surprising and consequential.

Conway et al. (1994) addressed this idea by taking an important event that would be consequential for some people, but not for others, and showed that the first group had flashbulb memories while the second group did not. They chose Margaret Thatcher's unexpected resignation as prime minister of the United Kingdom in November 1990. This event had immense consequences for many people living in the United Kingdom, because for 11 years she had been the dominant figure in politics and had changed the country greatly. The researchers examined subjects' memories for the circumstances under which the news was heard, both for people in the United Kingdom and for people in the United States and Denmark. (The reason that there are eight authors on the paper is that they represent researchers in different parts of the world who tested people in their area.) The 369 people were tested within 2 weeks of the event and again 11 months later. The scoring was similar to that of Neisser and Harsch (1992), but all five of the aspects were scored on the two-point scale (rather than considering two of them to be more minor), and an 11-month-old memory was considered flashbulb if the score was 9 or 10 out of 10. The results are quite striking. Unlike the Neisser and Harsch results, the U.K. residents showed a very high accuracy, with 86% classified as flashbulb memories, compared to 29% for non-U.K. participants. The researchers argue that a special mechanism is indicated and that the combination of high consequentiality and high emotion may serve to integrate the flashbulb memories better to make them less vulnerable to forgetting. It is, of course, difficult to compare these data directly to those of Neisser and Harsch, because the situations vary along a number of dimensions. These data do suggest that further work is needed to assess the mechanisms underlying flashbulb memories.

Although there is still controversy, our reading is that while flashbulb memories may feel different than other memories, there is no evidence that they are. The large difference in the Conway et al. study is impressive, but it is hard to know whether it implies a qualitatively different mechanism (see, for example, arguments by Finkenauer et al., 1998). In many cases, it appears that usual memory mechanisms generally provide a good account of such vivid memories. However, the idea that there could be a special mechanism to keep us aware of highly consequential events seems quite adaptive, and we do not think the question has been definitively answered yet.

Recovered Memories

Here is a news story that is becoming more and more common: An adult remembers some horrific event that has been forgotten for many years. Often these events involve extended abuse by a parent or family friend. In one case, a woman remembered seeing her abusive father rape and kill her young schoolgirl friend. She had forgotten the incident for 20 years. After remembering, she eventually went to the police who prosecuted and convicted this man based mainly on her evidence, though the conviction was later overturned (see Loftus & Ketchum, 1994; Terr, 1994).

There are many other recent cases of people recovering long-lost memories, including a few highly publicized cases involving celebrities. In some of these cases, the abuse was sufficient that, if true, the law was clearly broken. However, the statute of limitations had run out. A number of states have since passed laws allowing such cases to still be prosecuted by dating the time from when the memory is recovered. (The reasoning is that the criminal should not benefit from having traumatized the witness.)

This controversy is an emotionally wrenching one. The accusers are often torn between their beliefs in their memories and their feelings for the person they are accusing, such as a parent. The accused people often claim that such events never happened and appear to be devastated by the accusation, with their lives ruined. What do we know about memory that might inform this controversy?

Before beginning to look at what we know, let us be clear what the debate is about. There is no doubt that the incidence of child abuse is shockingly high and distressing. No one, on either side of the argument, believes otherwise, and no one wants to see guilty abusers go unpunished. Then again, no one wants innocent people to be wrongfully accused and punished. For the purposes of this section, we need to consider this as a discussion of the memory issues, not the more emotional issues that often lurk behind the discussion. How can we tell whether these memories are accurate recollections of the past?

The simple answer to our question is that we cannot tell (unless there is corroborating evidence). To explain this quandary, let us go back and examine more closely what the claims are.

Why does it seem so strange to have forgotten a memory for a long time and then to "recover it"? After all, we forget things all the time and, at least some of the time, remember them later. Besides the long period during which the memory is forgotten, the most obvious strange part is that these memories are *so* important. This is not like forgetting your high school classmate's name or what you wore to a school dance. How can we forget such memories as watching a classmate get murdered or being abused over an extended period? These seem like precisely the sorts of events that ought to trigger flashbulb memories.

The standard answer is *repression*. The idea of repression was first introduced by Freud more than 100 years ago: People push very painful memories into their unconscious so that they do not have to think about them. However, these repressed memories still may influence attitudes and behaviors, and therapists may use the client's behaviors as clues to such repressed memories. This idea is one accepted by many therapists but still controversial (see Conway, 1997; Loftus, 1993; Terr, 1994, for discussions of evidence). For our purposes here, let us agree that there might be some means, repression or otherwise, that could make people forget very traumatic experiences. Even if we grant this, how are such memories recovered and why should we believe they are accurate, given the forgetting that most memories undergo after such long periods?

Terr (1994) provides arguments for both these points. First, recovery of such memories usually occurs when a person is now able to deal with the painful memory. The memory is usually triggered by some perceptual cue, such as the expression on the face of a child leading to a memory of a similar facial expression on a child in a witnessed murder. Second, Terr argues that such traumatic memories usually undergo little forgetting, much as flashbulb memories. Although we have seen that there is some reason to doubt the accuracy of flashbulb memories, Terr draws upon her own work with children who have undergone traumatic events (such as snipers or bus hijackings) to claim that the memories are usually very well remembered. She argues that when the memories are recovered, they appear to be preserved and that is why people feel so confident about their recollections once the memories have been recovered. Of course, as we discussed above, people's confidence in a memory is not necessarily related to the accuracy of that memory.

Opponents disagree, not with the fact that any particular memory might be accurate, but with the assertion that recovered memories have been preserved. They argue that there is simply no evidence that this is true. First, there is lots of evidence that people sometimes do misremember. As we saw in the section on misleading information, although researchers disagree about whether memory traces are changed, there is no disagreement that people may recall inaccurately. (Also see the An Application box in Chapter 6 for a laboratory paradigm that can lead to false memories.) Therapists, in an effort to help their clients, may lead them to incorrectly remember events by making misleading suggestions or forcing them to reconstruct events from images or small bits of recall that they have had (Loftus, 1993). Second, there is much evidence that confidence is not always a good predictor of recall accuracy, as seen in the previous section with the Neisser and Harsch (1992) data on memories from the *Challenger* explosion. These skeptics of recovered memories cannot know whether a particular memory is accurate, but they do claim that one cannot be sure it is.

One complaint by people who believe that recovered memories are accurate is that the research evidence is not very germane. Showing that people can be misled into misremembering the type of sign on a road is hardly the same as misremembering an extended period of abuse. The subjects in the misleading information experiments are under no stress, and the tests examine minor details of the situation. Although there is no research that looks directly at such traumatic cases, Loftus (1993, 1997; Loftus & Ketchum, 1994) points to a few indications that neither the trauma nor the centrality of an event makes it invulnerable to forgetting. First, she cites work showing that people can be misled into believing that they had been awakened in the middle of the night by a loud noise. Sometimes this misleading is so successful that even when the people are informed they were misled, they argue that it really happened. Second, she cites some research in which people were misled into believing a number of different events from their childhood that never really happened, such as that they had been lost in a mall as a young child and had been found only after much searching. Still, being lost in the mall is not the same as continued abuse (though research ethics limit how close one can get). In addition, there appear to be some, not yet well-understood, limits on the types of false memories that people will be misled about. For example, Pezdek, Finger, and Hodge (1997) were able to mislead people about being lost in the mall, but not about having received a rectal enema.

Loftus also points to two specific cases in which traumatic events were "remembered" even though they had never happened. One, a person who had confessed to many satanic rituals and abuses involving his children was misled into believing he had orchestrated a sexual encounter between his son and daughter, though neither of them nor him had mentioned such a thing. (This was a check by one of the investigators to see if his confessions might not be accurate.) Two, a playground sniping incident, a very traumatic event, was well remembered even by the students who had not been in school that day. It is difficult to argue that either of these cases provides strong evidence, but they are suggestive that memories of traumatic events can be very inaccurate.

Can people really misremember such important information? Sure, the details might not be exactly correct, but if they remember being abused as children, might they really just be wrong? There does seem to be evidence that even misremembering the parts may lead to a very inaccurate memory. As we saw earlier, the source for particular memories may not be part of the memory, but inferred from information in the memory. The work by Marcia Johnson, cited there, shows how people can get confused about what they experienced and what they thought about. Again, this does not show any particular recovered memory is false, but it does show that there are ways in which people may remember something happened and yet be wrong. We sometimes remember some of what happened and piece together or *reconstruct* the rest (as discussed earlier in this chapter), and such reconstructed memories can be inaccurate.

So, here is where we find ourselves. The believers in recovered memories argue that the laboratory research is simply irrelevant and that it is implausible that someone could make up a whole history of abuse that did not occur. The skeptics argue that it is more implausible to believe that a recovered memory must be true just because of the feeling attached to it, without independent corroboration (which is often, though not always, lacking).

What do we know? Let's consider four points. First, it is clear that many people have had a highly emotional event in which they feel they are recovering what happened long ago after not having remembered it for many years. Schooler, Bendiksen, and Ambadar (1997) describe it as a very emotional sudden onrush, much like an insight.

Second, it seems clear that one can construct false memories for events that never happened. Given the research we have already presented on misleading suggestions and flashbulb memories, we see no reason to believe that recovered memories are protected against forgetting. Some of the recovered memories are likely to be false, especially if they have been recovered after what Loftus (1994) calls "memory work." By this term, she is referring to the variety of techniques, such as age regression under hypnosis, suggestive questioning, and sexualized dream interpretation, which may be used in therapy to help a person recover memory. In fact, recently there have been some successful lawsuits against therapists by patients claiming that the therapist implanted false memories in them. Although it is difficult to know whether any particular recovered memory is true, it seems unlikely that they are all accurate.

Third, in some cases the recovered memories may be true. There is still much controversy about this, and especially whether one can forget multiple episodes of abuse that extended over years, but this is our best current interpretation of the work (and there are tons of papers on this issue). The most convincing is work by Schooler et al. (1997). In four different cases, they were able to corroborate at least partially the earlier events. Note, however, that although they corroborated that the abuse events had happened, it is very hard to ensure that the memories had truly been forgotten in the interim period (and in some cases there was evidence of some memory for them before the recovery). Still, these memories were believed by the people to be recovered after many years and the abuse events remembered did occur.

Fourth, to reiterate a point made above, confidence does not appear to be that useful for deciding whether a memory is accurate. This is not a matter of people lying—it is perhaps principally this strong confidence in the memory that makes it so difficult to believe that it might not be true. However, as we have seen over the last three chapters, memory is not simply a passive recording of what happened. People are active interpreters of the world, with the encoding of any event influenced by context, our goals, our prior knowledge, and our expectations. When remembering an event, people are influenced by these factors again, plus they may reconstruct a full event from partial information. With active encoding and reconstructive remembering, there are many chances for memories to differ from the actual events. In

A DEBATE
Does Hypnosis Help Remembering?

A debate has been going on for a number of years about whether hypnosis helps people to remember. This issue has generated much interest recently because of the use of hypnosis in therapies that lead to recovered memories (though this is just one of many techniques that are used). Does hypnosis lead to remembering such long-ago memories?

Lynn, Lock, Myers, and Payne (1997) present a review of a variety of research on the use of hypnosis for improving what one can remember. Two main findings are especially pertinent. First, there is no evidence that hypnosis leads to more accurate recall. In some studies, hypnotized participants do recall more, but they recall more of both items that were on the list and items that were not on the list. Overall, their memory was no more accurate than nonhypnotized participants (there are standard measures for taking into account the mix of accurate and inaccurate recalls). In addition, in many studies hypnotized participants do no better than nonhypnotized participants, and sometimes not as well as nonhypnotized participants who are given extra encouragement to try their best on the test.

(Continued)

addition, confidence in memory does not seem to be sufficient to ensure it is true, as we saw earlier with flashbulb memories.

It is clear that there is much we do not know about recovered memories. The research in this area addresses some basic questions about how our memories work, while at the same time investigating issues of significance to many people (and our legal system). Although many papers have gotten mired down in the emotions of the writers, there are signs that the discussions and research are beginning to address more substantive issues. One example is debate about scientific issues related to this topics, such as whether traumatic memories may have special consequences in different brain regions (e.g., Nadel & Jacobs, 1998). A second example is the formation of teams of clinicians and researchers to more fully explore the issues together. This is an area of very active research. Although it is clear that much more research is needed before we understand these types of memories, some progress has been made.

Summary

In this section, we have examined memory in much more complex situations than the laboratory research presented in Chapter 5. In each case, however, the ideas

A DEBATE
Does Hypnosis Help Remembering? *(Continued)*

Second, hypnotized participants have great overconfidence in their recall compared to nonhypnotized participants. Many people believe their memory for materials learned during an experiment is better than it actually is, but hypnotized participants show even greater overconfidence. In addition, this confidence in recall occurs regardless of the accuracy of the information recalled.

So, what do these findings mean for using hypnosis for recovering memories? First, although it is possible that hypnotism may lead people to remember things they may not have otherwise, one must also be aware that a greater proportion of these "memories" may not be accurate. Thus, it may be a useful technique if there is an independent way to corroborate the retrieved information, but one needs to be wary of relying upon uncorroborated information retrieved under hypnosis. Second, one cannot use the rememberers' confidence in their recall as a strong predictor of accuracy.

were strongly influenced by the basic laboratory work. We have seen how real-world memories may be influenced at encoding by the way in which they are processed and the prior knowledge brought to bear. The retrieval may be also influenced by these factors, plus we may reconstruct the full event from partial information.

In trying to analyze a complex real-world situation, it is often frustrating how many different factors are varying simultaneously and how many possible explanations exist. The research on eyewitness testimony and flashbulb memories provides good illustrations of how one may analytically address such situations and arrive at a much better understanding of what is going on. The work on recovered memories is still quite new, and it is difficult to see what the final resolution will be. It is interesting to note how it involves aspects of ideas from both the flashbulb memories (in terms of the consequentiality) and the research on eyewitness testimony. In addition, there have been suggestions for how standard memory effects (e.g., encoding specificity and directed forgetting, both discussed in Chapter 5) might have a role in the forgetting and recovery of memories (see Schooler et al., 1997). We hope that the understanding of memory and memory research that you have gotten in these chapters will help you to understand later findings as well.

KNOWING YOUR MEMORY

Introduction

We end our discussion of memory with two questions: First, how can you improve your memory? All of us would like to remember more (and more easily). We will examine how encoding strategies and knowledge affects what you remember. In addition, we consider some implications of these ideas and briefly discuss some fabulous rememberers. Second, what do you know about how your memory works (before you read these chapters)? As we will see, everyone has some idea of how their memory works and it affects a variety of real-world behaviors, such as whether we believe someone or how much we study for exams.

Strategies and Knowledge

For the most part, research on memory is concerned with processes that are believed to be common to all normal individuals, at least beyond the very earliest stages of development. Indeed, one of the important results to come out of much of the work that we have been discussing in the past two chapters is that there is not much difference between people in their basic memory abilities. People may know different things, which may lead them to recall different aspects of a scene (based on the schemas they possess), but the basic mechanisms of memory appear to be similar across individuals.

Despite this similarity in general processes, we all know people who are particularly good (or bad) at remembering. Perhaps you have had the experience of going with someone to a movie, lecture, or athletic event and finding later in discussing this event that the other person's memory for exactly what happened is much more (or less) accurate than your own. The question then arises, "If we all have essentially the same basic machinery, why do people differ in their abilities to remember?" Three common answers might be that (1) some people are more motivated to learn, (2) some people are just better at remembering things, and (3) some people are just more interested in that sort of thing. As in many commonsense answers, there may be some truth to these assertions, but they do not really serve to explain the differences. Although we believe that the commonalities of human memory are much more striking than the differences, an examination of these differences helps to point out some important issues that might not be noticed during study of the common aspects. The growing weight of evidence favors the idea that a great part of the individual differences we see in memory performance is a consequence of the strategies used and of differences in prior knowledge. First, we briefly discuss what strategies you might use for remembering, and then consider how knowledge may influence your remembering.

In Chapter 5 we examined the influences of encoding and retrieval plans on memory. Based on that research, there are a number of steps you can take to improve your memory. In encoding the information, you want to make sure to actively process it for meaning, integrate it with what you know, and store it in such a way that it can be accessed by the retrieval cues you are likely to have. When trying to retrieve the information, it is important that you think about the retrieval cues and, if you are not successful at first, develop additional retrieval plans to probe your memory. Let us expand a little on these strategies for better remembering.

The first step toward effective remembering is always carefully attending to the material at the time of original presentation. If you do not actively process the information when you first get it, it is unlikely that you will remember it for long. You can think about what the information means, relate it to other knowledge you have, elaborate upon it, and organize the information into higher-order units or chunks. Then, be sure to rehearse the information to ensure it is better remembered.

Further, we have noted that effective rehearsal is not simply a matter of rote repetition but rather of noticing potential retrieval cues and integrating them with the items to be remembered. Still more effective is the procedure of forming a retrieval plan—that is, thinking in advance of the situation in which recall may be needed. A talk that is to be given in class or at a dinner meeting would be remembered best if practiced in the classroom or at the table, with audiences actually present. That is not ordinarily feasible, but one may provide a substitute by imagining the classroom situation or the dinner meeting and the cues that are likely to be present in that situation while rehearsing the material of the talk.

When you are trying to retrieve the information, the retrieval plan you set up should help you to remember. If you are still not successful, you can try to generate additional cues based on your general knowledge of the type of thing you are trying to remember. We have all had cases in which we have relied upon simple methods for remembering, such as using the alphabet to try to think of someone's name. All of these steps will help in improving your memory, but they do involve effort.

Though one can use various strategies to improve memory, what we remember depends greatly upon what we already know. Earlier in this chapter, we discussed schemas and the role they have in encoding and retrieving information. Perhaps the largest source of individual differences in memory performance is knowledge differences in a particular domain. It is much easier to remember something if we have a framework in which to embed that new knowledge. For example, when we (the authors) read a technical journal article in our research areas, we often remember the authors, the year of publication, the journal in which the article was published, and the gist of the findings for a long time. Yet when we read novels, we barely remember the main characters long enough to finish the book.

There is clear evidence that the ability to acquire new facts about some domain depends a great deal on what one already knows. For example, Spilich, Vesonder, Chiesi, and Voss (1979) found that people who knew more about baseball were much better able to remember descriptions of baseball games. The researchers read a description of a half-inning of baseball to people and later examined their memory. For the 98 game-relevant facts, the people with more baseball knowledge recalled twice as many (24 vs. 12). For the facts that were not relevant to the game, the groups showed no difference in recall. Thus, having prior knowledge allows one to understand (and remember) the relevant information better. Such an effect may not be surprising if you have ever sat through a game of a sport you did not understand well. As discussed earlier, this previous knowledge allows one to interpret new information more easily to make it meaningful, to incorporate it into what one already knows, and to retrieve it easily by using prior retrieval schemes. Knowledge has a large influence on what you remember, though we have also gone over some simple strategies you can use to increase what you remember (and we will mention some more in the next section).

Extraordinary Memories

There may be upper limits on the amount of information that can be stored in the human memory system, but there is no reason to believe that the limits are ever approached. Rather, we see case after case in which new efforts to improve encoding and retrieval lead to increases in what had seemed to be the upper limits for particular situations.

Consider the simple memory span test that appears in nearly all intelligence scales and is commonly used by neurologists to check on memory functioning. The examiner simply reads a list of random digits aloud at a rate of about one per second, and at the end of a sequence the person being studied is asked to recall them in order. For normal adults, the average **memory span** is about seven digits. Thus, if presented with the sequence 3, 2, 9, 4, 6, 7, 1, most students would be able to recall the sequence correctly, but if one additional digit—say 5—was added, many would fail (see the discussion in Chapter 5 on short-term memory). But if the same individuals thought to group the digits into subgroups of chunks of two or three adjacent elements, say 329 467 15, most would be able to remember eight digits without difficulty. More dramatically, mentally retarded children who ordinarily score very low on the test have been brought up to nearly normal levels when they were encouraged to use this technique of chunking.

An extreme example of the role of strategies and knowledge comes from a study showing that an individual was able to achieve a memory span of more than 80 digits (Chase & Ericsson, 1981)! The person, a runner, organized the digits into chunks that would correspond to running times for different distances. For example, the sequence 2141034084750 might be broken into chunks corresponding to running a marathon (2 hours, 14 minutes), a 100-yard dash (10.3 seconds), a mile (4 minutes, 8 seconds), and 10 miles (47 minutes, 50 seconds). Although it might be tempting to believe that this person has some unique ability, Chase and Ericsson showed that another person taught this same strategy was able to get up to a span of 40 (before the study was stopped) and improved at about the same rate as the original subject. How were they able to do this? In fact, this ability made use of a number of principles we discussed in Chapter 5. The subjects quickly chunked the numbers to access long-term memory (for running times) and could provide a hierarchical structure for organizing these chunks (see Ericsson & Kintsch, 1995, for a recent discussion of these ideas).

Mnemonists, people who are able to remember great amounts of information, have long provided entertainment with their extraordinary feats of memory. For example, Lucas (the ex–New York Knickerbocker forward, for basketball fans) memorized the first column of names and phone numbers on a few hundred pages of the Manhattan telephone book! Most mnemonists use well-known methods, called **mnemonics,** to perform their feats (many of these are described in popular books, such as Bellezza, 1982; Lorayne & Lucas, 1974).

Mnemonics have often been promoted as useful learning techniques, especially when the material to be learned involves much memorization, such as foreign language vocabulary. There is a large variety of different mnemonics that can be used in different situations. As many people know, it is sometimes useful to imagine some strange or bizarre image that includes whatever you want to remember. For example, to remember to call the vet to make an appointment for your dog, you might imagine your dog dialing the telephone (although in this case a note in some often used location might be even more helpful). Einstein and McDaniel (1987) review a great deal of the large literature on such effects. Although such bizarre images do not always improve memory, they do under a wide variety of conditions (see Richardson, 1998, for a full discussion of current work).

Suppose you want to remember an ordered set of items, such as the planets or the parts of a speech. A mnemonic technique for remembering such ordered sets is the **method of loci.** With this technique, you imagine moving along a familiar path (e.g., from your dormitory room to the chemistry building) and "depositing" to-be-remembered items at each of the landmarks you cross. Then you recall the items later by mentally traversing the path again. For example, suppose you wanted to remember the order of the planets. If your path goes by at least nine buildings, you could remember a planet with each of the buildings, such as Mercury with the closest building to your dorm (perhaps by imaging the Roman god in front of the building or even the name in a sign in front of the building), Venus to the next closest, Earth to the yet next closest, etc. Then, to remember the order of the planets, you mentally work along the path, stopping at each building, and recalling the planet associated with that building. In Chapter 5, when discussing retrieval plans, we mentioned one person who could remember a large number of animal names by imagining himself walking through a zoo he frequented. Although mnemonics can be very helpful in memorizing information, there is also a cost involved. In particular, the techniques only work well when you have spent much time learning and practicing them. Mnemonists spend a great deal of time and mental effort to learn to use these mnemonic techniques so well (though see the An Enigma box for another type of mnemonist).

Metamemory

Even before you read the last three chapters, you knew a lot about how memory works. You have lived with your memory for quite a while, plus you have many experiences seeing how other people's memories work. Interestingly, one's knowledge of memory greatly influences behaviors and decisions. As one example, suppose you are a juror and the trial hinges on the testimony of the defendant who

AN ENIGMA
An Amazing Rememberer

Although strategies play an important role in remembering, some memory differences between people do not seem explainable by different strategies. Luria (1968) describes an unusual mnemonist, whom he refers to as S. S was a journalist who annoyed his editor by never taking notes of the lengthy assignments he was given. In response to the editor's command to repeat the assignment, S did so flawlessly, apparently unaware that his memory was anything out of the ordinary. Once he had been examined in the laboratory, the remarkableness of his memory was quite apparent. S could repeat back lists of 70 words in a memory span test (longer lists were not tried). In addition, he could produce these lists in reverse order as easily as in the order given and could rapidly produce the successor or predecessor of any word in the list. Finally, and amazingly, he could recall lists that had been presented 16 years earlier (he was studied periodically over a very long time), even though by then he had become a professional mnemonist and had memorized many thousands of lists.

How did he do it? S converted every item to a visual image. (In fact, he appeared to have to a fantastic extent an ability we all have, called *synesthesia,* to experience stimuli in one sense by using a different sense. For example, certain colors look hot and certain sounds feel smooth.) Every word, number, or sound would lead to a rich image. Thus, his ability

(Continued)

claims not to be able to remember what was said in a conversation. If the conversation occurred 10 years ago and the point was a minor one, then you might well believe the defendant. On the other hand if the conversation was very recent and concerned a very major and unusual discussion, then you might doubt that the defendant would have forgotten that conversation.

As another example, suppose you are studying for a test. How do you decide when you have learned the material well enough? If you stop too early, you may do poorly. If you study much longer than you need to, then you have lost other opportunities for spending your time (such as studying for other classes?). The point is that your knowledge about what you will be able to remember has a major influence on your behaviors.

Over the last decade there has been a great deal of attention paid to **metamemory**—that is, people's ability to know how likely they are to be able to remember something or how effective some strategy may be. Although we have all had cases in which we greatly misestimated when we were ready for an exam, metamemory often is fairly accurate. For example, T. O. Nelson, Dunlosky, Graf,

AN ENIGMA

An Amazing Rememberer *(Continued)*

to encode new information was quite unusual, but he was faced with the difficulty of organizing his images in some reasonable way to encode the order in which items appeared. Even in his case, strategies were important, and he used the method of loci to organize these images. When he became a professional mnemonist, the strategies became even more important because people would give him extremely difficult lists to memorize. He developed his own method, a combination of several mnemonic techniques, for taking advantage of his imagery ability.

In fact, his memory was so image oriented that he was often unable to use simple logical organization. For example, when given the following table of numbers to remember,

1 2 3 4

2 3 4 5

3 4 5 6

4 5 6 7 and so on

he did not notice that each line's first number was the next whole number and that the rest of the numbers in the line were immediate successors. Rather, he just remembered the table in the same way he would have if the numbers had been in a totally random order.

and Narens (1994) studied people who were learning new words in a foreign language, Swahili. The learners' judgments about how well they had learned each word were used to allocate study time for future study trials and improve their learning. In other work examining what children know about their memories, third graders understand that their memory is vulnerable to suggestions from others, such as their parents or siblings, though first graders do not (O'Sullivan, Howe, & Marche, 1996).

How are judgments of metamemory made? The evidence suggests that we do not have direct knowledge of how well we know something, rather we make an inference based upon some aspect of our remembering. This answer might seem strange, but imagine again that you are studying for an exam. How would you decide when you knew the material? For many of us, once we could answer the questions quickly we would assume that the information was well learned. Note that this is not exact information about how much we know, but an inference based upon how quickly we retrieve answers. As we have seen throughout the last three chapters, there are many factors that could influence our remembering of materials, and our speed in remembering is only a rough index to how well we know the material (and even a rougher index to how well we will remember during the exam). For example, if you study the same fact several times in a row, your answer to a question for that fact would be very fast, so you would infer that you know that fact very well. However, as we discussed in presenting spacing effects in Chapter 5, such massed studying does not usually lead to good remembering with a later test. Your metamemory may sometimes lead you astray, but it does not usually. As we pointed out, people know much about how their memory works.

Summary

In this section, we have focused on what you know about your memory and how you can improve it. The strategy and knowledge people bring to a task have a large influence on what they remember. Memory is not a passive recording of the world but an active process in which one interprets the world as a basis of what one knows. The work on mnemonists indicates that many of the exceptional memory abilities are based on strategies that can be learned (with much hard work) by many of us. We ended the section by considering metamemory, what people know about how their memory works. Although this research area is fairly new, it is an exciting one. Our knowledge of how our memory works influences many of our judgments and actions.

Summary

 This chapter had a variety of topics, but they all had in common that the situations went beyond the memory effects we had concentrated on in the previous chapters. We began this chapter by noting that much of our memory outside the laboratory results not from some intention to remember, but rather from our efforts to act and understand the world. To address this issue, we considered how larger knowledge structures might be used in understanding and remembering information. These schemas provide a way in which our relevant knowledge can be brought to bear to help with the problem of too little information and too many possibilities. We examined the general idea of schemas and the more specific event schemas, scripts. The work continues on how best to think about the structure of the schemas, their activation, and their learning.

 The next section examined reconstructive memory and questioned the idea that remembering is simply retrieving a fully encoded event. Rather, we may reconstruct the event from pieces of partial information that we retrieve. What we remember is often integrated with other retrievals or augmented with more general knowledge to give a complete and coherent remembering.

 Next, we discussed three types of memory effects that occur outside the laboratory: flashbulb memories, eyewitness testimony, and recovered memories. Most people have the phenomenological experience of a flashbulb memory, but the research suggests that there may not be a special mechanism for such memories (although there is still some controversy). Eyewitness testimony and recovered memories have received much recent attention in the press. We tried to present the evidence used by both sides in each debate, as well as our opinions about the weight of this evidence. The research on the misinformation effect in eyewitness testimony does seem to have progressed, so that the main controversy is over whether the earlier trace is changed or not. The research on recovered memory is much more recent and not yet clearly understood. The issue is an emotional one for the people involved, and the issues are difficult ones on which to do ethical studies, so we think it is not likely to be resolved in the near future.

We ended the chapter by considering how to improve our memories and what people know about their memories. Many individual differences in memory are due to effects of knowledge and strategy. People who know more about a topic can better remember new information about that topic. People who use more effective memory strategies can better remember new information, in some cases leading to incredible feats of memory. The final part of this section considered metamemory, what people know about their memories, and how this knowledge influences their behaviors.

Memory is involved in just about every cognitive process and is important in many, many real-world activities. Thus, our choice of topics for this chapter was just meant to illustrate the importance of memory beyond the laboratory. We believe that this examination shows how an understanding of memory may help in understanding more complex situations.

Key Terms

flashbulb memory	mnemonics
frame	reconstructive memory
memory span	schema
metamemory	script
method of loci	slot
misinformation effect	

Recommended Readings

The early ideas on schemas and scripts are given in Rumelhart and Ortony (1977) and Schank and Abelson (1977). There are so many papers on these topics, it is hard to recommend a few, though Schank (1982) provides an interesting revision of script theory. Schemas are very popular within most fields of psychology, so particular papers relating schemas to another research topic are best accessed via computer search. Although we touched on the role of schemas and scripts in text comprehension, we did not examine text comprehension more widely. Kintsch (1988) provides a combined symbolic-PDP model of text comprehension, as well as a large number of references to the field (also see Kintsch & van Dijk, 1978). Kintsch (1994) reviews some of his work and shows how it can be used to help design texts for readers with different levels of knowledge.

The second section of the chapter examined eyewitness testimony, flashbulb memories, and recovered memories, each of which has an extensive literature. For the misinformation effect in eyewitness testimony, Ayers and Reder (1998) provide an excellent critical review, and H. M. Johnson and Seifert (1994) give a somewhat different look at how people may get misled. A very interesting overview of children's testimony is given by Ceci and Bruck (1993). The best places to begin looking at the flashbulb memory research are the books by Winograd and Neisser (1992) and Conway (1995), plus the original Brown and Kulik (1977) paper is worth reading. For recovered memories, the early views are given in books by Loftus and Ketcham (1994) and Terr (1994), who present strong cases for the opposing sides. A more recent book edited by Conway (1997) gives a variety of opinions.

Ericsson and Kintsch (1995) present a very interesting idea of how people might use their short- and long-term memories during expertise. Those interested in memory expertise might look at one of the popular books, such as Bellezza (1982) or Lorayne and Lucas (1974). The book by Luria (1968) is a short and wonderful examination of a particular mnemonist. See Bellezza (1996) for a review of mnemonic devices and an evaluation. There is much work coming out these days on metamemory, with an earlier review by T. O. Nelson & Narens (1990) and edited books by Metcalfe and Shiamura (1994) and Reder (1996), which ties this work to the implicit memory ideas discussed in Chapter 6. A short, very readable overview is given in Schwartz, Benjamin, and Bjork (1997).

Finally, Schacter (1996, 1999) provides interesting presentations of many of these ideas for a general audience and ties many of these issues to the cognitive neuroscience findings.

Chapter 8

Spatial Knowledge, Imagery, and Visual Memory

Introduction

Representations
Relations Between Representations and Referents
Analog Representations
Summary

Spatial Knowledge
Maps and Navigation
Spatial Representations From Descriptions
Hierarchical Representations of Space
The Brain and Spatial Cognition
Summary

Imagery
Evidence for Use of Visual Imagery
Representation of Images
Summary

Visual Memory
Remembering Details
Memory for Pictures
The Picture-Superiority Effect
Memory for Faces
Summary

Summary

Key Terms

Recommended Readings

One picture is worth more than ten thousand words.
—*Chinese proverb*

INTRODUCTION

Suppose you are sitting in your living room at night and all of a sudden the power goes out. You could probably navigate around furniture or other obstacles that are in their usual places. The ability to mentally keep track of the environment and spatial relations among objects is necessary for any sort of navigation in the world. You could probably also describe what your furniture looks like. In both of these cases, you are accessing knowledge that you learned from visual experience in the world. Memory is clearly essential for many tasks, and much of what we learn is from our visual experience. The purpose of this chapter is to explore how spatial and visual knowledge is represented and the different ways in which we can use this knowledge.

In our discussion of perception in Chapter 3, we noted that organisms must develop representations of the three-dimensional world from two-dimensional projections on the retina. That is, organisms do not perceive the world directly but rather must figure out the connection between events associated with their perceptual system and events in the world. Informally, we could say that people construct an internal model of the world.

Our mental representations of our environment are typically so good that we are not even aware that they are representations—under "normal" conditions our representations mirror the world quite closely. But try a simple experiment (which you very likely performed in childhood) that creates "abnormal" conditions. Press on the corner of your eyeball with your eyes open. The scene in front of you seems to move (this is easiest to do with one eye closed), even though you "know" that it did not. But if you just move your eyes back and forth normally, the scene does not shift. The brain is able to take active movement into account in developing a representation but has no mechanism for dealing with the passive movement associated with pressure on the eyeball.

The point of this example is that we *represent* our environment, and when we successfully make our way around a darkened room, we are relying on previously stored representations of the layout of the room. A fundamental question concerns the form of mental representations of the environment and objects in it. A good deal of the research associated with this question has focused on imagery or mental images. Are images "pictures in the head" and, if so, what properties do they have? What is the relation between imagery and perception? Finally, are images fundamentally different from the mental representations of abstract propositions expressed through language?

Chapters 5 and 6 focused on basic ideas concerning memory for new simple events and for factual knowledge. However, most of the work in those chapters examined knowledge that was gained from reading or verbal communication. Our evolutionary history suggests that we had to learn how to successfully move about in the world long before we developed any language skills. Therefore, it seems likely that understanding how we develop and use knowledge about our environment provides basic clues into the nature of human intelligence. Although the information-processing tradition has found computers to be a useful metaphor for understanding intelligence, that metaphor may pay insufficient attention to the close link between organisms and their environment. Computers don't have to worry about the environment—the programmer puts information directly into the machine. Researchers in artificial intelligence are still in the very early stages of interfacing computers with an environment as they attempt to build robots capable of moving about in the world. As we shall see, useful representations are a crucial prerequisite for intelligent action.

In this chapter, we describe work on spatial and visual knowledge from the perspective of asking questions about mental representations. We first take a closer look at the notion of a mental representation and then provide a sampling of ongoing research on spatial knowledge, imagery, and visual memory.

REPRESENTATIONS

Relations Between Representations and Referents

We have already suggested that an internal model of the three-dimensional environment makes it easier to move and act appropriately than does a two-dimensional retinal pattern. A **representation** of the outside world is an internal model that is linked to external objects and events and that preserves information that is important for the organism. Representations are analogous to the data structures used by computers to store information that is used by programs. What form do these representations take? Some motion pictures about the nervous system, for example, seem to suggest that the internal representation is essentially a tiny replica of the item in the outside world being represented (the *external referent*). In many cases, the films also include a tiny person (a *homunculus*) whose function is to perceive the internal representation! Of course, the films do not indicate how the perceptual system of the tiny person works, though perhaps the homunculus also has representations (in which case we really need to study the psychology of homunculi).

Roger Shepard (1981, p. 290) has argued that a representation need not be literally similar to its referent, any more than a lock must resemble a key. In his words,

> Just as the essential thing about a lock and its key is the unique functional relation between them whereby the lock is normally (i.e., from the outside) operated only by its corresponding key, the essential thing about a perceptual representation and its object is the unique functional relation between them whereby the percept is normally (except while dreaming or hallucinating) elicited only by its corresponding object.

To use another example, we often use a map to navigate between one part of the country and another. The fact that major highways are colored red while minor roads are black or gray tells us nothing about the color of the actual roads. Major highways with many lanes are drawn thicker on maps than two-lane highways. Representing more lanes with thicker lines is a natural convention, but we recognize that it is simply a convention. One could use the opposite coding scheme, and people could adjust accordingly. Whatever the coding scheme, certain crucial information such as spatial relationships and type of roads must be preserved. But the map is not literally a likeness of the country. The two keys to representation are that the information important to the organism is preserved and that the cognitive system have some mechanism for extracting the information in the representation and using it (Markman, 1999; Palmer, 1978).

Analog Representations

To say that representations of referents must preserve relevant information does little to restrict the form that representations must take. Researchers such as Roger Shepard and Stephen Kosslyn, have argued that mental representations of objects and spatial relationships are *analog* in character. An **analog representation** mimics the structure of the referent in a more or less direct manner. Immediately, this definition runs into difficulty because we have not said what we mean by structure or a direct manner. In the case of space, one can propose that two relevant structural properties are that space is continuous and that spatial relationships are salient (e.g., that the nose is above the mouth on a face).

But what do we mean by "more or less direct manner"? We mean that the representation has properties that bear the same relationships as the properties of the external referent. For example, the map in Figure 8.1 might be an analog representation for the relative spatial locations of cities. In the external referent for this map, city A is closer to city B than it is to city C. Because a two-dimensional map is being used for this representation, it is a natural property of distances that once points A, B, and C are placed on the map in the configuration they have in Figure 8.1, that point A is closer to point B than it is to point C. Because distances in a two-dimensional map must have the same relationships as the distances between cities, the map is an analog representation. Of course, this map has a lot of information that corresponds to the external

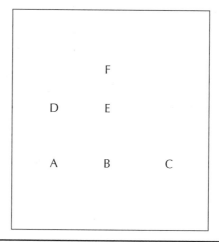

Figure 8.1   A simple map (analog representation) of the relative location of six cities.

referent in an analog fashion. The map is probably drawn to scale (e.g., 1 inch on the map may correspond to 100 miles). Also, the relative directions are preserved by the map. City F is directly north of city E, and on the map F is directly above E, and so on.

This same information could be represented as a series of languagelike propositions, as discussed in presenting the ACT model in Chapter 6. **Propositional representations** are assertions that have a truth value (e.g., city F is north of city E)—they are abstract and not tied to any particular sensory modality. Table 8.1 shows two different ways of using propositions to represent the information in Figure 8.1. The

Table 8.1   **Two Sets of Propositions Representing Some of the Same Information Represented in Figure 8.1**

F as a Reference Point	*Route Information*
E is 10 miles south of F	(A, B) 10 miles east
	(B, A) 10 miles west
B is 30 miles south of F	(A, C) 20 miles east
	(C, A) 20 miles west
D is 10 miles south and 10 miles west of F	(A, D) 20 miles north
	(D, A) 20 miles south
A is 30 miles south and 10 miles west of F	(A, E) 10 miles east, 20 miles north
	(E, A) 10 miles west, 20 miles south
C is 30 miles south and 10 miles east of F	(A, F) 10 miles east, 30 miles north
	(F, A) 10 miles west, 30 miles south
	(B, C) 10 miles east
	(C, B) 10 miles west
	(B, D) 10 miles west, 30 miles north
	(D, B) 10 miles east, 30 miles south
	(B, E) 20 miles north
	(E, B) 20 miles south
	(B, F) 30 miles north
	(F, B) 30 miles south
	(C, D) 20 miles west, 20 miles north
	(D, C) 20 miles east, 20 miles south
	(C, E) 10 miles west, 20 miles north
	(E, C) 10 miles east, 20 miles south
	(C, F) 10 miles east, 30 miles north
	(F, C) 10 miles west, 30 miles south
	(D, E) 10 miles west
	(E, D) 10 miles east
	(D, F) 10 miles north, 10 miles east
	(F, D) 10 miles south, 10 miles west
	(E, F) 10 miles north
	(F, E) 10 miles south

Source: McCloskey & Zaragoza, 1985.

representation form on the left encodes city locations relative to some reference point, in this case city F (any reference point would do). This representation makes some information easy to determine. For example, one can directly look up (retrieve) the fact that A is 30 miles south and 10 miles west of F. Other information is less easy to come by. For example, what are the relative positions of C and D? To answer this question, one would need to retrieve the facts that D is 10 miles south and 10 miles west of F and that C is 30 miles south and 10 miles east of F and then combine these facts with some rules (e.g., if D is X miles south of F and C is Y miles south of F, then C is Y minus X miles south of D) to come up with the answer.

The propositional representation on the right side of Table 8.1 allows one to directly retrieve information about how to get from C to D (or from D to C). The cost is that many propositions have to be encoded. For six cities, we require 30 propositions; for seven cities, 42 propositions; and for only 40 cities, 1,560 propositions. And even with all these propositions, we have not exhausted all the information about spatial relationships. For example, the route information does not tell us that the most direct route from A to C requires that we pass through B. Again, we could develop a procedure for deriving this information.

The general point is that particular types of representations allow us to access some types of information easily and other types of information with greater difficulty. Analog representations are good for configural (spatial relationship) information, and they allow for easy integration of new information. Adding a new city to the analog representation in Figure 8.1 is simple and does not require that a large set of new propositions be encoded (as does a route representation).

Propositions *can* represent spatial relations, so there has been much debate on the need for analog representations (J. R. Anderson, 1978; Kosslyn & Pomerantz, 1977; Minsky, 1975; Palmer, 1978; Pylyshyn, 1981; Shepard, 1981; see Barsalou, 1994, for an overview). Our reading is that most researchers now agree that people have both analog and propositional representations. For example, the ACT model described in Chapter 6 that encodes much information as propositions also contains analog representations for capturing visuospatial information. The argument as to why general purpose representations, such as propositions, may be poor choices for biological organisms is best summarized by Shepard (1981, p. 288):

> Such a general purpose system will not be suited to the rapid prediction of and preparation for external developments in a three-dimensional, Euclidean world. [...] The more nearly the constraints prevailing in the world have been "hard-wired" into the system, the greater will be the effectiveness of the system in that particular world.

Summary

In this section, we have distinguished between analog representations (such as maps) and propositional representations. Each type of representation has advantages for some types of processing. Although there has been much debate over whether analog representations are needed to account for human abilities, most researchers accept the need for such representations. (See Barsalou, 1999, for a strong argument for the primacy of such representations.) We have belabored the subject of representation because it is crucial to understanding the basis of much of the ongoing research on spatial knowledge and imagery. The issue of representation sounds a bit esoteric, but it is central to the problem of how organisms are able to act intelligently in their environment. We turn now to related empirical work, beginning with spatial knowledge.

SPATIAL KNOWLEDGE

Maps and Navigation

Our mental representations include information about spatial relationships and about how to navigate in our environment. Let us begin with two simple examples from Thorndyke and Hayes-Roth (1982): "Point to the Statue of Liberty from where you are sitting. Now point to your favorite local restaurant from where you are sitting." These two cases are accomplished by most people in very different ways. For the first case, we remember that the Statue of Liberty is in New York City, where New York City is relative to our town, and what direction we are facing. For the local restaurant case, we may simply remember how we get there and point in that direction. These examples illustrate two of the main types of knowledge we have about space: **survey knowledge,** a bird's-eye view often learned from maps, and **route knowledge,** gained from navigating through the environment. Researchers are interested in characterizing these types of knowledge and in understanding when and how they might be learned. What sorts of experiences lead to survey as opposed to route knowledge? We can begin by noting that the different types of knowledge are useful for different spatial tasks.

Survey knowledge is very useful for making judgments involving global spatial relations, such as distance judgments between two points. Survey knowledge allows fast scanning and measuring. It can often be acquired quite easily. However, if knowledge is acquired from maps, some judgments, such as those involving orientation, may be difficult. For example, Thorndyke and Hayes-Roth (1982) tested people on their spatial knowledge of the floor of a large, irregularly-shaped office building. Simplifying the results, subjects just shown the floor plan were able to perform many tasks quite well, such as estimating distances, but had great difficulty with orientation tasks, such as pointing to one location while standing in another.

Route knowledge may require more time to learn but does allow people to perform well on tasks that are difficult if the knowledge is learned only from maps. Direct experience with the routes appears to lead to a more orientation-free representation, so that people can use their knowledge of the route very flexibly (see, e.g., Presson, DeLange, & Hazelrigg, 1989). If the environment is irregular (e.g., the streets are winding and cross at unusual angles), the knowledge acquired through navigation may distort the overall view (Byrne, 1982; B. Tversky, 1981). However, if the environment is regular (i.e., a city with a grid of streets, a building with a simple layout), experience in navigation is often sufficient for learning survey knowledge as well. An interesting proposal is that this greater navigational experience may lead to a different type of survey knowledge than that acquired from maps in which the full layout may be seen from a navigational perspective (Thorndyke & Hayes-Roth, 1982) or in a more integrated model-like way (Presson et al., 1989).

For both theoretical and practical reasons, how navigational experience affects the representation of space is of great interest and is under much current investigation. Recent theoretical work has examined learning differences that arise not just from different experiences but from different goals of the learner (e.g., Taylor, Naylor, & Chechile, 1999). They explored the differences in the spatial representations people formed depending on whether they had the goal of learning the overall layout of a building or routes between different locations. As active processors of information, the particular goals people have in learning spatial knowledge can have large effects on the representation. For example, people were much more accurate at estimating distances between points in a building when they started with the goal of developing a layout representation than when they started with the goal of learning routes. Applied research has also focused on the role of experience in learning spatial representations. As one example, an important area of research builds upon the great improvements in virtual-reality environments to address how people may navigate and explore such spaces (e.g., Ruddle, Payne, & Jones, 1999).

Spatial Representations From Descriptions

Although much of our spatial knowledge derives from our experiences in the environment, we also receive spatial information via descriptions. Spatial representations are often important in text comprehension. Readers do not simply remember descriptive sentences but rather spontaneously construct spatial mental models of scenes being described (e.g., B. Tversky, 1991). For example, suppose you are on a street corner and you walk north one block, turn left and walk a block, turn left again and walk one block, and then turn left one final time and walk a block. If you developed a spatial representation as you were reading, you should know that you are back at your original starting point.

Further research suggests that spatial representations are organized around landmarks (important locations) and are independent of the perspective from which a text is written (e.g., Ferguson & Hegarty, 1994; Taylor & Tversky, 1992). How was this generalization established? Let's take a closer look at one of the Taylor and Tversky experiments. In their first study, people were given either survey or route descriptions of four different settings, one of which is shown in Figure 8.2. The descriptions were fairly lengthy, and we'll give you only enough to illustrate the difference:

> *Survey Description of Resort Area.* The resort area is bordered by four major landmarks: the National Forest, Matilda Bay, Bay Rd., and the Forest Highway. The eastern border is made up of the National Forest. The National Forest has facilities for camping, hiking, and rock climbing. The southern border is made up of Matilda Bay. . . .

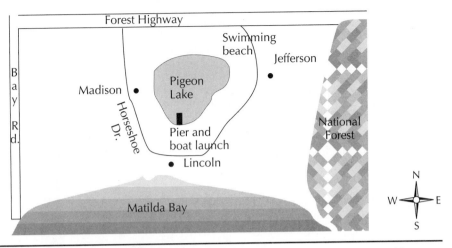

Figure 8.2   Map of the resort area associated with the survey and route descriptions used by Taylor and Tversky (1992) in their Experiment 1. People who read the text were not shown the map.

Route Description of Resort Area. To reach the Pigeon Lake region, drive south along Bay Rd. until you reach, on your left, the point where Forest Highway dead-ends into Bay Rd. From this intersection you can see in the distance that Bay Rd. continues to Matilda Bay and its many recreational areas. You turn left and travel about 40 miles. . . .

It is important to remember that at no point did the people reading the descriptions see any map. For each of the descriptions, a series of tests was given to assess comprehension. The test questions were verbatim, paraphrased, or required an inference from the spatial information given in the text. For example, a verbatim, nonspatial test probe might be: "The National Forest has facilities for camping, hiking, and rock climbing," a statement that appeared in both the survey and route descriptions. The key questions concerned location inferences. An example of a survey inference is: "Horseshoe Dr. runs along the southern shore of Pigeon Lake," which did not appear in either description. A corresponding route inference might be: "Driving from the boat launch up toward Madison, you see Pigeon Lake on your right." Of course, there were also statements that were false.

The reaction times and accuracy at verifying the different types of questions are shown in Figure 8.3. The first thing to note is that people were pretty accurate. Error rates never exceeded 20% in any condition. Second, people were fastest and most accurate for verbatim (and paraphrase) statements that did not involve any spatial information (types 1 and 2 in the figure). Third, for verbatim items that did involve spatial information, each group was faster and more accurate in responding to the exact information they had read (types 5 and 6). This result is not very surprising, since the verbatim route statements were actually inferences for people who read the survey descriptions and vice versa. Fourth, and the most important result, is what happens when subjects have to respond to inference questions, that is questions

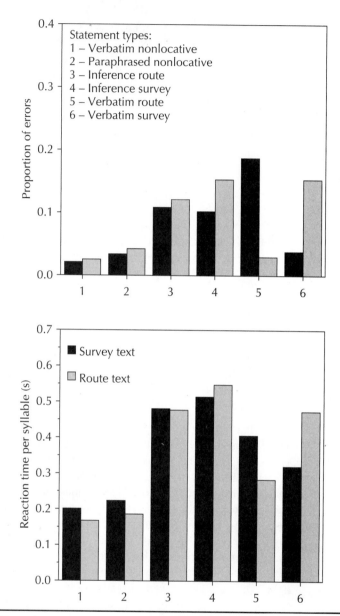

Figure 8.3   **Results of Experiment 1 of Taylor and Tversky (1992)**   The top graph shows error rates for the different types of test statements for the people who read route and survey descriptions, and the bottom graph shows reaction times for the two groups on these statements.

that ask about information that was not directly provided in the text (types 3 and 4 in the figure). Here, there was no interaction between how the group learned the information and how it was tested (route versus survey)—there were no reliable differences in reaction time or errors. If the route and survey groups had different forms of spatial knowledge, one would have expected that the survey group would be faster than the route group on survey inference questions and that the route group would be faster than the survey group on route inference questions (just as they were for the verbatim route and survey information). But as Figure 8.3 shows, there is no evidence for such an interaction. These and other studies support the idea that spatial representations of the reader can be independent of the perspective given in the text. Often people construct an integrated mental model of the space whether given route or survey knowledge. (See Bryant & Tversky, 1999, for some further ideas of what can influence the perspectives taken.)

Hierarchical Representations of Space

It is tempting to view our representations of spatial layouts like maps. However, there is evidence that our representations of space are influenced by nonspatial knowledge. Answer the following question: Is Seattle north or south of Montreal? Most people believe Seattle is south of Montreal, although in fact it is north of it. In this case, most of us do not know the latitudes of both cities or their relative latitudes, but we do know that Canada is generally north of the United States, that Seattle is in the United States (i.e., that the United States is *superordinate* to Seattle), and that Montreal is in Canada (i.e., that Canada is *superordinate* to Montreal). We then make the reasonable inference that Montreal is north of Seattle. This type of plausible reasoning will usually lead to the right answer, but not always, especially given irregular boundary lines. (Try your friends on "Which is farther east: Reno or Los Angeles?" Again, Nevada is east of California, but L.A. is east of Reno.) These errors suggest that people use hierarchically organized information (Reno is in Nevada, Nevada is east of California) to answer questions about spatial relationships.

Stevens and Coupe (1978) provide further experimental evidence of the use of superordinates (Nevada is superordinate to Reno) in making spatial judgments by showing systematic distortions with this type of material. In addition, they found that even after learning from simple new maps such distortions occur. For example, in one study subjects learned one of the maps shown in Figure 8.4, then had to judge, from memory, the relative positions of x and y. Performance was much better when superordinate information was congruent with the question. For example, subjects were more accurate at saying that x was west of y when the superordinate was east-west (left side of Figure 8.4) and more accurate at saying that x was south of y when the superordinate was north-south (right side of Figure 8.4). Thus, it appears that the superordinate units are used to make spatial judgments.

A number of other studies show that such nonspatial influences do not depend on having some unambiguous hierarchical structure. For example, Hirtle and Jonides (1985) conducted some studies on residents of Ann Arbor, Michigan, involving various locations in Ann Arbor. They found that each of the residents had a hierarchical representation that was used for making spatial judgments, though the particular hierarchy differed from person to person. McNamara (1986), using a layout of objects in a simple rectangular space, found that people tend to organize such a layout hierarchically

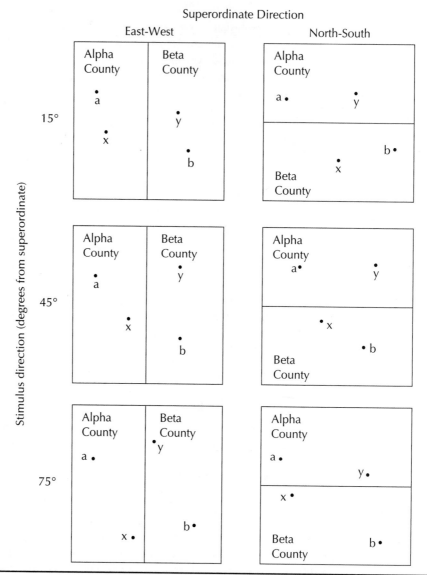

Figure 8.4   **Prototypical Stimuli From Experiment by Stevens and Coupe (1978)**   After a short study period, the map was taken away and participants were asked to indicate the relative direction between pairs of cities, including the x-y pair.

Source: Stevens & Coupe, 1978.

and that the organization is evidenced in spatial judgments about the layout. For example, if they thought of two buildings as being in the downtown area, they might underestimate the distance between the two buildings and overestimate the distance between one of these buildings and a building not in the downtown area. (For further reading, a very interesting paper by B. Tversky, 1981, provides some demonstrations of heuristics that people employ in remembering maps that lead to other types of systematic distortions, such as misremembering that two streets cross at right angles when they do not.)

Thus, evidence suggests that a simple spatial map view of spatial knowledge is not correct. Rather, learners organize the spatial information to include nonspatial knowledge as well. Note that this effect occurs for knowledge learned both by survey and routes. Clearly people do have extensive knowledge about the spatial layout of an area, which may be stored in an analog fashion. However, additional knowledge about relations, such as hierarchies of locations, is also used in making spatial judgments. Thus, many researchers believe people may have a dual representation of spatial knowledge, including both distance (analog) and nondistance (often propositional) information (e.g., Curiel & Radvansky, 1998; McNamara, Halpin, & Hardy, 1992).

The Brain and Spatial Cognition

This dual representation idea also has some support from cognitive neuroscience. For example, Stephen Kosslyn (1987) suggests that the human brain has at least two distinct kinds of representations for spatial relations. One type is categorical in nature and determines relations such as "inside of" or "above." The second form of representation specifies distances in a continuous or analog form. In support of Kosslyn's theory, Hellige and Michimata (1989) report evidence that the left hemisphere of the brain is specialized for categorical information and the right for metric information concerning space (see Kosslyn, 1994, for other arguments and evidence on this point, and Ivry & Robertson, 1998, for an alternative interpretation of this evidence). In addition to the behavioral and neuropsychological evidence for this dual representation, computational models of spatial cognition that use the dual representations are able to simulate a variety of findings in this area (e.g., Baker, Chabris, & Kosslyn, 1999).

The importance of spatial cognition to our normal lives is underlined by studies of people who have suffered brain injury and have impaired spatial cognition. A particularly striking phenomenon is **spatial neglect,** which we described in Chapter 3. Patients appear behaviorally unaware of objects or events on the neglected side—as if part of their world effectively ceased to exist (see, e.g., Chedru, 1976). In some patients, unilateral neglect includes or may be confined to their own limbs and body surface (Bisiach, Perani, Vallar, & Berti, 1986). For example, in putting on a shirt, such a patient may not put the arm on the neglected side through the shirt sleeve. Even more striking, when their attention is called to a neglected limb, such patients may deny that it is theirs and express puzzlement concerning how it got there. The study of such patients has provided some important clues to how space is normally represented (see Bisiach, 1996, for an overview).

Summary

Our spatial knowledge is crucial for our navigation in the world. In this section, we have examined how people represent and use spatial knowledge in a variety of tasks.

We began by distinguishing between survey and route knowledge, and the different tasks for which each might be most useful. The work on spatial descriptions from texts suggests that people often represent the space being described in an internal model and use the model to both understand and reason about further information in the text. The knowledge gained from maps and surveys, however, is not just metric, distance information, but also knowledge of other relationships (such as hierarchies). Both types of knowledge are used in making spatial judgments, and the work in cognitive neuroscience supports such a distinction. In addition, spatial representations play a crucial role in a variety of more abstract tasks such as understanding of graphs and diagrams (e.g., Novick, Hurley, & Francis, 1999; Tversky, 1995).

IMAGERY

Try these three examples. First, imagine a capital letter *F,* and then imagine it rotated clockwise 90 degrees (quarter-turn). Next, picture what your high school looked like, or picture the face of a good friend or the Statue of Liberty. Finally, imagine yourself walking from one friend's house to another's, or imagine giving someone directions for getting from the grocery store to your school. Almost all people experience visual images in performing these, and many other, tasks. In this section, we examine various results and ideas about how such images occur and are used. In addition, we examine the relation between imagery and perception.

As we just described in the last section, our knowledge about space is used in accomplishing many goals. However, this knowledge can be used even when we are not in the space or when we do not have a map available. Imagine being in a room with objects. Shut your eyes and take two steps forward. You are easily able to compute where you now are in relation to many of the objects. As in all memory tasks, you are augmenting the incomplete information available by bringing relevant knowledge to bear. Furthermore, what knowledge you bring to bear and how it is represented will have a large impact on the complexity of processing and your ability to accomplish your goals. Images are one form of representation that appears to preserve much about the spatial relations among objects, making it easy to know the relative positions of the objects even as we move.

By its nature, imagery is a totally internal event. As discussed in Chapter 1, psychology went through a long period in which internal events were not studied. No one doubted that people could have mental images, but there was much doubt about whether these images were psychologically relevant. For example, imagine a robin. Do robins have beaks? Do robins lay eggs? It may seem that you answer the first question by inspecting your image and that you answer the second by the use of some other knowledge in your memory. Nonetheless, it is possible that even the first question was answered by your use of other knowledge. You presumably know either that robins have beaks or that robins are birds and birds have beaks. If you are able to answer the question without the image, what is the evidence that you in fact used the image to answer it? Let's take a closer look at this question.

Evidence for Use of Visual Imagery

A great deal of evidence exists for the importance of images in performing various tasks. A full discussion of such evidence and its implications would be a book in itself (see, e.g., Kosslyn, 1983, 1994; Richardson, 1980). A brief discussion of several different types of evidence may provide you with an appreciation of the case for visual imagery.

Selective Interference

The earliest pieces of evidence in the modern work on imagery relied on the idea of *selective interference.* In these studies (see, e.g., Brooks, 1968), subjects would be asked to perform some task while imaging or not imaging. If imaging led to a decrease in task performance, the argument goes, there is evidence that imagery is using related processes. Most important, however, is the idea that the influences would be selective. That is, interference should be greater between tasks using the hypothesized same processes than on tasks thought to use different processes. The work by S. J. Segal and Fusella (1970) provides a clear example. Before each trial, the subject was asked either to form a visual image of a common object (e.g., a tree), to form an auditory image of a common sound (e.g., a typewriter sound), or to form no image. Then the subject was presented with a very weak visual signal (a small blue arrow), a very weak auditory signal (a chord from a harmonica), or no signal. The subject's task was to say whether there had been a visual signal, an auditory signal, or no signal. The results were quite clear. First, imaging led to worse detection performance than not imaging. Second, and most important, the two types of imagery selectively interfered with detection of their corresponding signals. That is, visual imaging led to worse performance on detecting visual signals, and auditory imaging led to worse performance on detecting auditory signals. Not only were subjects less likely to detect a signal in these cases but also, when no signal was presented, they were more likely to report a signal of the type they had been imaging (i.e., a false alarm). Thus, these results show that imagery can selectively interfere with the detection of signals.

Manipulation of Mental Images

Some of the best known evidence for the use of visual images are the studies of **mental rotation** conducted by Shepard and his associates (see, e.g., L. A. Cooper & Shepard, 1973, 1978; Shepard & Cooper, 1982; Shepard & Metzler, 1971). In these studies, subjects are presented with an object and asked whether another object is merely a rotation of the first. Figure 8.5 provides examples of the objects used. The forms in A and B can be rotated into correspondence, but the forms in C cannot be aligned through rotation. Therefore, the correct answer would be "yes" for A and B and "no" for C. Most people are able to do this task accurately, but the time to make the decision can be taken as an indication of the difficulty of the task. Data from a typical experiment are also shown in the figure. The larger the required rotation, the longer it took to answer the question. In fact, the increase in time was extremely

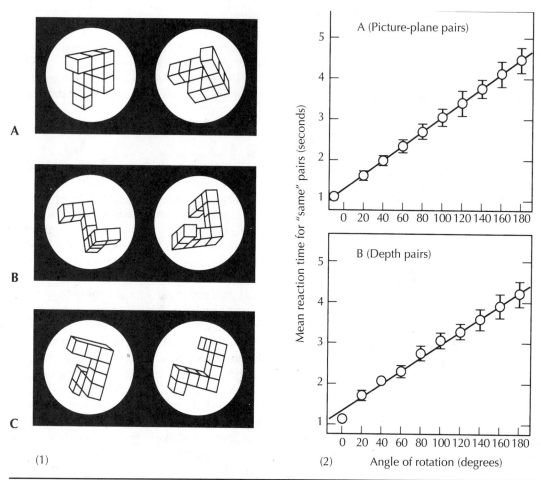

Figure 8.5

(1) Examples of pairs of perspective line drawings presented to the subjects: (A) a "same" pair, which differs by an 80-degree rotation in the picture plane; (B) a "same" pair, which differs by an 80-degree rotation in depth; and (C) a "different" pair, which cannot be brought into congruence by any rotation.
(2) Mean reaction times to two perspective line drawings portraying objects of the same three-dimensional shape. Times are plotted as a function of angular difference in portrayed orientation: (A) for pairs differing by a rotation in picture plane only and (B) for pairs differing by a rotation in depth. The vertical bars around each circle indicate a conservative estimate of the standard error of that mean.

Source: Shepard & Metzler, 1971.

systematic; the increase from 0 to 60 degrees was the same as between 60 and 120 degrees, which in turn was the same as between 120 and 180 degrees.

These results were interpreted as strong support for an analog representation underlying visual imagery. If the representation were analog, then one would expect these results, just as it would take longer to rotate the actual object for larger angles.

However, if the underlying image were propositional, there is no reason why such a systematic relation between angle and reaction time would occur. The findings led to a number of challenges (see Anderson, 1978, and Kosslyn, 1994, for discussions). For example, Just and Carpenter (1976) suggested that the linear reaction time effects are artifacts of eye movements, not due to the use of images. In particular, they found that when patterns in a mental rotation task are presented simultaneously, participants move their eyes back and forth between the patterns and do so more with increasing angular disparity. How could one test their suggestion? One possibility is to present the two objects one after the other, instead of simultaneously. Even under these circumstances, reaction time continues to be a linear function of degree of rotation (e.g., L. A. Cooper, 1975, 1976; Cooper & Shepard, 1973). Thus, the mental rotation results do not appear to be due to eye movements.

Although there is still some controversy, many researchers believe that the mental rotation findings provide good evidence for the use of imagery. This linear function suggests that mental rotation takes place at a fixed rate, like the movement of the hands on a clock. These results are consistent with the idea of an analog internal representation—to see if the objects are the same, the image of one is rotated in a rigid way at a fixed rate, just as you might do with real objects.

Pictorial Properties of Mental Images

A variety of other results show that mental processing of images is very similar to what would happen with physical objects. Stephen Kosslyn has demonstrated that people's scanning of mental images shows effects similar to scanning physical scenes or maps (Kosslyn, 1973; Kosslyn, Ball, & Reiser, 1978). For example, in one study (Kosslyn et al., 1978) subjects learned a simple map in which seven locations were marked by objects. The test trials began with the naming of one of the objects. Subjects were asked to image the entire map and focus on the location of the named object. Another object was then named. If the object was not on the map, subjects pressed one button. If the object was one of those marking a location on the map, subjects scanned to it and pressed another button when they reached it. (The instructions were to image a black speck moving in the shortest straight line from the first object to the second.) The results showed that longer distances took longer to scan, just as it might be if one moved one's eyes across a scene or map from one location to the next.

Further parallels between images and the manipulation of physical objects come from another clever set of studies by Kosslyn (1975, 1976) examining the effect of image size. This research begins with the observation that the smaller an object, the harder it is to see any attribute of it. Is the same true of images? In these studies, subjects were told to image objects at different sizes. After they had an image, subjects were asked whether the object had some physical attribute (e.g., ears, a beak). Kosslyn found that the smaller the image, the longer it took to verify that this attribute was present (when it was) and to decide that it was not present (when it was not).

These and other studies providing support for imagery have received some sound methodological criticisms (Intons-Peterson, 1983; Intons-Peterson & White, 1981; Mitchell & Richman, 1980). For example, these critics have argued that subjects might well have figured out what effect the experiment was examining, which may

have influenced the results. (It is standard practice in experiments to not let the subjects know the exact issues being examined so that such knowledge will not affect
their performance.) Although some studies did suffer from methodological problems,
on the whole, the main findings appear to survive (see Finke, 1985, for a balanced
review, and Barsalou, Solomon, & Wu, 1999, for some recent results and discussion).

Representation of Images

How Equivalent Are Imagery and Perception?

The findings just reviewed make a good case that images are analog representations
and that they can interfere with perception. However, it is not clear how these
images correspond to the representation one has of visually perceived objects.
Some researchers believe that there are major differences between our representations from imaging and from perception. Chambers and Reisberg (1985) argued
that perceptual stimuli must be interpreted, but images are already interpretations.
In support of their position, they produced strong evidence that visual stimuli and
images behave differently. In one experiment, they presented participants with
ambiguous stimuli such as the one shown in Figure 8.6. Take a quick look at the figure and see what it depicts. If you look at the figure for a while, you will be able to
interpret it differently. Chambers and Reisberg showed this figure for 5 seconds,
asked people to form a clear mental image of it, and then removed it. This brief presentation did not give people time to reinterpret the figure. None of the 15 participants was able to come up with a second interpretation by using just their mental
image of the figure. When, however, the participants were asked to draw the figure
(from memory) and then reinterpret it, all 15 were able to see the second interpretation! (If you have not yet seen both possibilities, it may help to know that one
interpretation is a rabbit—the left side is its ears—and the other a duck—the left
side is its bill.)

Finke, Pinker, and Farah (1989), however, were able to demonstrate some
ability of people to reinterpret visual images. For example, participants asked to
imagine the letter *D* on its side and placed on top of the letter *J* spontaneously report
"seeing" an umbrella. Therefore, mental images can, under some circumstances, be
given new interpretations; reinterpretation does not constitute a qualitative difference between imagery and perception.

M. A. Peterson, Kihlstrom, Rose, and Glisky (1992) conducted a systematic
series of studies on reinterpretations of mental images. They find a consistent pattern
of reversals (even for the duck-rabbit figure) that suggests that mental images can
indeed be ambiguous. Peterson et al. distinguish between reversals that involve feature reinterpretations (e.g., thinking of the curve in a *J* as the handle of an umbrella)
and those that require a shift in reference frame (e.g. the front of the rabbit figure as
the back of the duck figure). Although they observed both types of reversal, changes
in reference frame were harder than feature reinterpretations. This difference may
explain why Finke et al. (1989) were more successful than Chambers and Reisberg

Figure 8.6   Ambiguous figure from Chambers and Reisberg's experiment (1985).

Source: Chambers & Reisberg, 1985.

in observing reversals (though the debate continues; see Rouw, Kosslyn, & Hamel, 1997, and Reisberg, 1998).

Are Visual Images Visual?

It seems clear from the studies we have reviewed that images encode analog spatial information. The results are consistent with either of two very different ideas about the nature of this representation. One possibility is that these visual images are really spatial representations. On this view, the knowledge we use to generate and use images is abstract and not tied to any specific modality. It is more like knowledge about the general layout of an object or scene, rather than just the type of information we could get by looking at the scene. The contrasting idea is that these visual images are truly visual representations; that is, the visual images are tied to the visual modality, and we have encoded knowledge about the literal appearance of the objects or scenes. On this view, a visual image requires some of the same representations and brain systems usually engaged when that same object is seen.

This distinction addresses the question of whether visual imaging involves the visual system. In addition to its centrality in research on visual imagery, the question has important implications for a number of theories of cognition (see Farah, 1988, for some examples). The results from research on this issue have been somewhat mixed. In favor of spatial representation, one impressive argument is that congenitally blind subjects show a number of imagery effects. For example, Kerr (1983) conducted research patterned after Kosslyn's scanning and size experiments just discussed. In one study, similar to the Kosslyn, Ball, and Reiser (1978) scanning study, she had blind and sighted subjects learn a simple layout of seven different geometric figures on a board. Following learning (the figures were raised so that blind subjects could learn by feeling them), subjects were read the name of an object and asked to imagine the board and "focus" on the named object. They were then given the name of another object and asked to imagine a raised dot going from the first to the second object. When the dot reached the second object, they were to push a button. The results revealed that both blind and sighted subjects showed the usual increase in response time with distance.

AN APPLICATION
Athletic Practice for a Couch Potato

Wouldn't it be great if you could improve some athletic skill, such as free-throw shooting in basketball, from the comfort of your easy chair? Well you can, at least a little. A common technique in sports is to mentally rehearse the activity, and the evidence suggests that it really helps.

Given the enthusiasm many people have for sports, and the money involved in professional sports, there is always interest in techniques that might improve performance. In addition to sports, some tasks are danger-ous or expensive to practice, so improvement that can come through men-tal rehearsal would be important. There is enough interest in this topic that in 1995 a special issue of the *Journal of Applied Psychology* was devoted to the relation between imagery and physical actions.

Driskell, Copper, and Moran (1994) provide a careful analysis of a large number of studies on mental practice to try to understand whether it does improve performance and, if so, how it might best be used. In their review, *mental practice* "refers to the cognitive rehearsal of a task in the absence of overt physical movements." This would include mentally going through the preparation and shooting of a free-throw, but would not include many other techniques, such as "psyching-up" or relaxation. How would you test if men-tal practice helps? In these studies, there are usually three groups who go through different practices and then are all tested at the end on the task of interest (e.g., shooting free throws). The mental practice group is told to see themselves performing the task successfully from start to finish. The control group has no practice. The physical practice group has actual practice

(Continued)

Because the blind subjects have been blind from birth, it is assumed that they do not have visually based representations (though they can encode spatial information). Thus, finding that the scanning effects are similar for blind and sighted subjects sug-gests that there is no reason to believe a visual representation is necessary for imagery.

Although these findings seem problematic for the idea of visual representa-tions, other results provide strong support for such an idea. Martha Farah has mar-shaled several strong arguments in favor of visual representations (see also Finke, 1985). First, relying on neuropsychological studies of brain-damaged patients, she notes that when cortical lesions from brain damage lead to selective visual deficits, there are often parallel imagery deficits (Farah, 1988). For example, if cortical dam-age leads to central color blindness, the patients lose their ability to image in color. Second, she provides some interesting data combining reaction times and brain potential recordings that are consistent with visual representations (Farah, Peronnet,

AN APPLICATION

Athletic Practice for a Couch Potato *(Continued)*

(e.g., shooting free throws) for the same amount of time that the mental practice group practices. If the mental practice group does better than the control group, then this is evidence that mental practice helps. The physical practice group allows an assessment of how much mental practice helps relative to physical practice.

Across the 35 studies reviewed, the results were quite clear. Most importantly, mental practice did help—the mental practice group performed better than the control group. However, mental practice did not help as much as physical practice (sorry). The authors also found that the optimal duration for mental rehearsal is about 20 minutes, and they suggest that one continue this mental rehearsal every one or two weeks to maintain the benefit.

Why does mental practice help? We are not sure, but one possibility favored by Driskell et al. is that the practice allows one to gain better control of movements that have important symbolic or verbal components. For example, although the exact amount of force to apply when shooting a free throw can only be practiced by shooting a free throw, many other aspects of the free throw may be practiced mentally. For example, remembering to hold the ball a certain way, to spread your legs to shoulder width, to bend your knees, to take a short time to relax before shooting, and a variety of other physical actions may all be practiced in your mind. Then, when you are taking an actual free throw, those mentally practiced components will be easy to remember and do, and thus will help your shooting. Good luck.

Gonon, & Giard, 1988). This study used a procedure similar to the selective interference paradigm but looked for facilitation of imaging and detecting the same content. In particular, subjects were asked to form an image of a capital H or a capital T or not to form an image. They were then given a very brief (20 milliseconds) presentation of one of these letters or nothing, followed by a masking stimulus. The subjects' task was to report whether they had seen a letter or not. These researchers found that people were better at detecting a letter if they had been imaging the same letter; that is, if they were imaging H, they were more likely to detect H than T. Thus, the facilitation was specific to the content of the image, suggesting that at some point the visual and imaginal representations joined (or fed into the same process). In addition, event-related potentials were recorded by putting electrodes on various scalp areas of the subjects. These recordings from the visual cortex showed systematic effects of this match between the image and the stimulus (i.e., whether they were the same, H-H or T-T, or were different, H-T or T-H) less than 200 milliseconds after the stimulus was presented. This finding provides strong support for the idea that the representation of the image involves the visual cortex and is truly visual.

Converging support for visual rather than abstract imagery comes from a study using the positron emission tomography (PET) recording procedure described in Chapter 1. Roland and Friberg (1985) measured blood flow while people performed either an auditory (imagining a tune) or a visual (walking through one's neighborhood) imagery task. They found an increase in blood flow to the visual cortex during visual imagery but not during auditory imagery, and the reverse pattern for blood flow in the auditory cortex.

Summing up, we have evidence for both spatial and visual representation of images. Farah, Hammond, Levine, and Calvanio (1988) suggest that the evidence is mixed because the representation is neither entirely visual nor entirely spatial. Rather, both spatial and visual representations of images exist, but which is used depends on the task. In addition to accounting for the number of mixed findings and some other general arguments, they describe two further pieces of relevant evidence. First, they note that there may well be two anatomically distinct cortical systems for dealing with visual representations. One system is involved in representing the appearance of objects, and the other with the location of the objects in space (the what and where systems discussed in Chapter 3).

A second piece of evidence in favor of this compromise solution comes from neuropsychology. Of most relevance, Farah, Hammond, et al. (1988) present results from a patient who suffered brain damage from an automobile accident. Although the patient does well in intelligence and simple visual acuity tests, he suffers from severe deficits in visual recognition. Not only is he unable to recognize a number of common objects and animals but also he often has trouble recognizing his wife and children. In various imagery tasks, he sometimes performed at normal levels and sometimes at far below normal levels. Most interesting, normal performance was found on all seven of the spatial imagery tasks for which he was tested. These tasks, such as the scanning and mental rotation tasks, clearly require spatial information but have sometimes been shown not to require visual representations (such as from the work with congenitally blind subjects). In contrast, on the four visual imagery tasks that require specifically visual representations (that is, asking about a visual property such as the color of objects), the patient performed much below normal. In summary, the evidence appears to favor the compromise view in which both spatial and visual representations exist, as also suggested for working memory models (as mentioned in Chapter 5, Smith & Jonides, 1997). This is not, however, an uninteresting compromise, and it may serve as inspiration for integrative models of visuospatial representation.

Summary

This section has reviewed the evidence for mental imagery and examined the nature of the representation. Most researchers believe that people use mental imagery for a wide variety of tasks. The evidence from paradigms, such as mental rotation, selective interference, and scanning, suggests that the images are analog representations.

There is still considerable debate about further details of these representations. We reviewed an ongoing controversy about whether the images could be reinterpreted, as one could reinterpret the representation of a visually perceived object. In addition, we examined evidence for whether these representations are visual or spatial. This latter controversy seems to have been settled by compromise—there is evidence for both visual and spatial representations.

VISUAL MEMORY

Many people feel that their memory for visually perceived objects, scenes, and faces is quite good. We can remember what our cars look like, the inside of a restaurant, and the faces of friends and acquaintances. We may not be able to remember the name of someone with whom we have been only briefly acquainted, but we are confident that we would at least know we had seen the person somewhere before. In this section, we examine some research on memory for visual stimuli.

Remembering Details

Our confidence in our visual memory abilities is generally not misplaced. Before examining the impressive memory we have, however, let us consider a potential problem illustrated by the following two examples. First, picture the front of a very familiar public building. How many windows does it have on the front? Many people are able to picture the building but, when trying to answer this question, find that their image of the building does not include any definite number of windows.

For the second example, draw the front of a penny. Most people find this hard to do but still might feel that they know what it looks like. Nickerson and Adams (1979) asked subjects (all American citizens) to perform this task. When asked to draw a penny, they omitted far more than half the features or located them in the wrong place. When asked to choose a drawing of the real penny from 15 possibilities, fewer than half the subjects picked the correct one. G. V. Jones (1990) performed some related experiments with British coins (and British subjects) and found similar results. In fact, slightly fewer than half the subjects even knew the number of edges on a 50-pence coin (seven).

These results are quite surprising. Think of the number of times most people have seen a penny—how can they not remember what it looks like? As Nickerson and Adams note, however, the details that are not remembered are almost always irrelevant to one's use of a penny. People don't mistake a penny for a quarter or a button because they cannot remember where the date is on the penny. Memory is being used to accomplish goals; details that are without function with respect to these goals often may not be remembered as well as goal-relevant details. Again, we are active processors of information—we cannot encode all the information about every object, so we tend to encode information that is relevant to our goals.

AN ENIGMA
Failure to Notice a Changed Person

Suppose you were giving directions to someone who stopped you on the street and had something block your view of the person for a second. When you can see the person again, it is a different person. Would you notice? Most people are sure they would. The correct answer is "maybe."

In the An Enigma box in Chapter 3, we discussed *change blindness,* the work showing that people are not good at detecting changes. Researchers have suggested that these failures show that the visual representations are quite impoverished and contain few details (see Irwin, 1996, and Simons & Levin, 1997, for reviews). However, all of this work has been done with photographs or videos. Would the failures occur if the change was made in the real world where the visual information is so rich and the person is actively engaged in processing the world? Although we have discussed a simpler case earlier, we felt the possibility that people might be insensitive to real world changes merited another examination.

Simons and Levin (1998) tested this possibility, essentially by conducting the study described in the first paragraph. More specifically, they had an experimenter (let's call him Experimenter 1) stop a pedestrian on the Cornell University campus and ask for directions to a nearby building (see panel *a* on page 318). After 10 to 15 seconds, two people came by carrying a door and rudely walked right between the pedestrian and Experimenter 1. As they did, Experimenter 1 quickly changed places with one of the door carriers, Experimenter 2 (see panel b), so that when the door was past the pedestrian, Experimenter 2 was now standing there asking for directions (see panel c). (The change took about one second.) The pedestrian and Experimenter 2 conversed for a few minutes more. The pedestrian was then told this was a Psychology experiment about the "things people pay attention to in the real world. Did you notice anything unusual at all when that door passed by a minute ago?" Only about half the people did. So even though the change was central to the scene, occurred instantaneously (was not gradual), and was in the middle of an ongoing event, people often did not notice. Why?

(Continued)

Memory for Pictures

Suppose that you are allowed to look through 612 color pictures of common settings. When you finish, after about an hour (averaging about 6 seconds per picture), you are then shown two pictures at a time and asked to pick out which of the two were in the 612 pictures you had already seen. One picture

AN ENIGMA
Failure to Notice a Changed Person *(Continued)*

One clue as to the difficulty can be seen with a further breakdown of the data. The younger subjects (20–30), who were about the same age as the experimenters, tended to notice much more often than the older (35–65) subjects. Simons and Levin suggested that this difference could be due to a well-known effect in which people pay more attention to people of their own group, in order to discriminate them, whereas they pay less attention to people out of their group, because they are satisfied just to categorize them (for example, "college student"). This idea is similar to the finding by Nickerson and Adams that we described earlier in which people do not remember the visual details of pennies, because they focus primarily on information needed to categorize the coins. They tested this idea by redoing the experiment with both experimenters dressed as construction workers (though dressed with different-colored clothes). The prediction was that these workers were now a different group than the younger subjects, so the subjects might now simply note that the person asking for directions was in a different group (e.g., construction worker) and therefore would not show a high rate of change detection. The prediction was confirmed—younger subjects detected the difference only 33% of the time.

So, people do not appear to store detailed visual representations of these events—rather they may categorize some of the people and objects and store those categorizations (such as construction worker). If the change involves a change in category, then it is likely to be detected. For example, people are often categorized by age, race, gender, and profession (if obvious), so that if the change was from male to female or construction worker to police officer, then it would be detected. A second important predictor of whether the change will be detected is whether there are any consequences for the goal of the perceiver. If the change has no effect on what the person is trying to do then it is much less likely to be detected (similar to the reason why the penny details are not noticed). If however, the change caused a change in what the person was trying to do, then it is likely to be detected. The main idea, however, is that we do not appear to store detailed visual representations of much of what we perceive.

is one of the 612, and the other picture is selected from the same general pool (i.e., it is of the same type). How well do you think you would be able to do this?

Shepard (1967) conducted this experiment and found that people were correct about 97% of the time. If they were not tested for 3 days, they were still 92% correct. In fact, 120 days later, they were still 58% correct.

Figure 8.7   Frames from a video of the Simons and Levin (1998) study. Panel a shows Experimenter 1 asking a pedestrian for directions. Panel b shows door carriers coming between the pedestrian and Experimenter 1, plus Experimenter 1 taking the door and changing places with Experimenter 2. Panel c shows Experimenter 2 continuing the conversation. Panel d shows the two experimenters for comparison.

Source: Simons & Levin, 1998.

Realize that we are not claiming that subjects are remembering all the details of these pictures. As we just saw from the study on pennies, memory for details is not always good. Many different types of knowledge could allow subjects to perform well in this picture memory experiment. For instance, they might remember one unusual detail from a picture. However, to do this well on recognition, they clearly are making use of some memory for the pictures seen. It is important to realize that these are distinctive real scenes, not abstract pictures of similar items, such as snowflakes. Even so, when we remember that they saw more than 600, one after the other, and for a very brief time each, such memory seems quite impressive.

The results of Standing (1973) show an even more impressive memory for pictures. He presented up to 10,000 pictures for 5 seconds each over several days. Two days later, he tested for memory by presenting two pictures and asking subjects to pick the old one. The correct picture was chosen 83% of the time. Clearly, much can be remembered from very short exposures to visual stimuli.

Performance on picture memory tasks changes in an interesting way as we age. Koustaal and Schacter (1997) tested college students and older adults (around 60–75 years old) for their memory of photographs. Older adults were more likely to say they recognize a new photograph that was similar to one of the photographs presented for study (for example, one boat when the earlier photograph was of a different boat). In one experiment, when they had been shown 18 objects from the same category (for example, 18 boats), both groups were good at positively recognizing the ones they had seen—81% accuracy for the younger subjects and 83% for the older subjects. Taken alone, this finding might suggest that both groups were equally good at recognizing pictures they had seen. However, when subjects were shown new examples from the same category (a new boat), the younger subjects incorrectly said they had seen these boats 35% of the time, but older adults claimed to have seen them 70% of the time. That now changes our interpretation of the earlier finding. Younger subjects seem to have enough information in their visual memories to adopt a pretty stringent criterion for saying the pictures were ones they had seen. That allowed them to distinguish reasonably accurately between pictures they had seen before and those they had not. In contrast, older adults appear to have less information about the pictures. Thus, they tend to say that many pictures of items from the same class they saw at study had been seen before. This strategy makes the older adults appear accurate when we look only at their performance on the studied pictures. However, when we take into account their performance on the new pictures from the same category, we can see that older people are setting a criterion for saying that a picture is old that also lets through a lot of pictures that were not shown at the study phase.

Younger adults can rely on their visual memory to help distinguish photographs, but the older adults appear to process the photographs less fully, relying on the gist of what was presented.

The Picture-Superiority Effect

A common intuition is that pictures are better remembered than words. This intuition is generally correct. As one example, in the Shepard (1967) study just mentioned,

A DEBATE
Are Faces Special?

Faces are important visual stimuli—accurate recognition of faces allows us to differentiate our mate from our nonmates, our friends from our enemies. This importance has led to suggestions that we may have evolved with special mechanisms for face recognition. Do we recognize faces in the same way as we do other objects, or are they special? This issue has been the source of some debate.

There are several pieces of evidence that strongly support a faces-are-special position (see Farah, Wilson, Drain, & Tanaka, 1998, for an excellent overview and discussion). First, there is evidence that the brain regions involved in face recognition are not the same as those involved in object recognition. For example, some patients with brain injuries show impairment of face recognition, but not impairment of recognizing objects of equal visual difficulty. Second, there are recordings from single brain cells in monkeys that respond to faces and not to other visual stimuli. Third, infants' preferences for faces can be seen very soon after birth, suggesting some innate mechanism. For example, when they are 30 minutes old, infants will watch a moving face longer than they will other equivalent objects. Fourth, changes in the orientation of faces interferes with recognition much more than it does for other visual stimuli. Try taking a photograph of someone you know well and turning it upside down—it is much harder to recognize. This change in usual orientation affects the recognition of most kinds of objects, but much more so for faces. This greater impairment for faces when the objects are inverted is called the *inversion effect*.

(Continued)

another group of subjects looked at words rather than pictures. Even though there were fewer words than pictures (540 vs. 612), words were not recognized as well (88% vs. 97%). Many studies in the last 25 years have carefully controlled various factors and still found better memory for pictures, using a variety of picture types and testing conditions. This memory advantage for pictures over words is called the **picture-superiority effect.** This difference is found even if the memory test involves simply the names of the pictures rather than the pictures themselves.

Much of the research has been connected to the ideas of Allan Paivio, which are reviewed in Paivio (1971). He proposed a **dual-coding hypothesis** that predated many of the arguments about propositional and analog representations—items could be stored in either a verbal code (similar to the propositional view), an imaginal code

A DEBATE

Are Faces Special? *(Continued)*

Although most researchers agree on the effects, there is debate about how to interpret them. We concentrate here on one argument concerning how to interpret the first and last point above to give a flavor for the controversy. Gauthier and Tarr (1997) suggest that the different data for faces may not be due to their being innately special, but rather to their being treated differently than many other objects in two ways. First, we simply have much more experience with faces than with other objects, so part of the specialness may be due to this much greater experience. Second, when recognizing faces we need to know exactly which face it is, whereas when recognizing many other objects we only need to know the category, such as whether it is a cup, not exactly which cup it is. Because we often do not need to distinguish objects at much more specific levels, we may not develop the detailed processing and representations for them that we do for faces. As evidence for their claim, Gauthier and Tarr constructed some new nonface objects, which they called *greebles*. They found that when subjects learned to discriminate very similar greebles over a large number of trials, they showed an inversion effect on the greebles. Thus, they argue that some of the evidence for faces may be due to extended experience discriminating similar stimuli.

Our reading of this literature is that although the debate is not over, faces do appear to be special. Our best guess at this time is that some of this specialness may indeed be due to our great deal of experience at distinguishing individual faces, but some is also likely to be due to mechanisms that have evolved because of our special need to be able to expertly recognize faces.

(similar to the analog view), or both. This dual-coding hypothesis helped to make sense of many earlier results and gave explanations for later findings. For example, he suggested that pictures are better remembered because they are more likely to be stored in two independent codes than are words. As a further indication of distinct codes, Schooler and Engstler-Schooler (1990) found that verbally describing pictures of faces can *interfere* with memory for them. If there were only a single code, then verbal descriptions should only help memory. Instead, it appears that there are two codes and that the more attention paid to one type of code (e.g., verbal) the less time available for the other (imaginal) code. Although other hypotheses have been suggested for this effect as well, a common assumption is that picture superiority is caused by a richer, more distinctive coding for pictures than for words (e.g., Weldon & Coyote, 1996).

Memory for Faces

Despite the fact that most faces have the same set of features (nose, eyes, etc.), our memory for faces is excellent. In one fascinating study, Bahrick, Bahrick, and Wittlinger (1975) tested the memory of people for their high school classmates. For all 392 subjects, the experimenters obtained their high school yearbooks. These subjects ranged in age from 17 (newly graduated) to 74 (not so newly graduated). Of interest here is the face recognition test. Ten pictures were randomly chosen from each yearbook and photocopied. Each picture was put on a card with four other pictures taken from other yearbooks (but chosen so that fashion changes over the years and differences in picture type could not be used as a clue). Subjects were then asked to pick the face of their classmate from the set of five. The correct choice was made 90% of the time, and this accuracy persisted even in groups that had graduated about 35 years earlier. The group that had graduated nearly 48 years earlier still chose the correct face 71% of the time. Our memory for faces is quite incredible, making prosopagnosia, the lost ability to recognize faces that is associated with certain types of brain damage, even more dramatic (see the discussion in Chapter 3 on Face Recognition).

Although this excellent memory for faces may seem to contradict the findings that people do not remember details, the two findings are really quite consistent. In particular, the details not remembered are those that are not relevant for the goal (e.g., of recognizing a penny). For faces, however, the goal is not to recognize that it is a face (as opposed to, for example, a car), but rather to recognize whose face it is. Thus, the goal in face recognition forces one to consider at least some details to distinguish all the different faces one knows.

Summary

Much of our knowledge of the world derives from our visual experience, so our memory for visually experienced environments and objects is an important part of what we know. We have only been able to give a brief overview of the wide variety of results on visual memory. At the risk of oversimplification, we mention two conclusions that we think are particularly important for understanding visual memory. First, the great detail and complexity of visually perceived environments and objects leads to very rich representations. Think of comparing what you might encode from hearing the word *airplane* versus seeing an airplane. Second, although we have rich encodings of visual stimuli, we do not store everything. We lose much of the detail and actively encode the information that is most relevant to our goals.

Summary

We have argued that spatial knowledge and mental representations of visual information are fundamental to cognition. We have further suggested that, despite the controversy between analog and propositional theories of representation, the evidence favors the idea that human cognition uses both analog and propositional representations. Our definition of an analog representation was that it mimics or parallels the structure of what is being represented in a more or less direct manner. Both the notion of structure and "more or less direct manner" allow for considerable leeway in how literally imagery mirrors perception. Any particular representation scheme allows a system to access some forms of knowledge easily and other forms of knowledge only with difficulty. Studies of visuospatial cognition suggest that what the human conceptual system accomplishes easily is consistent with representations having many analoglike properties.

We began the chapter by examining spatial representations, which are crucial for navigation in space. Different types of spatial knowledge were distinguished, survey versus route knowledge, and the types of tasks that each allowed easier performance on were discussed. Spatial knowledge is important not just in navigating, but also in understanding descriptions of space, such as might occur in text. Interestingly, both behavioral and neuroscience results indicate that many of our spatial judgments do not rely solely on analog representations of the space, but make use of other, more categorical knowledge as well.

Visual imagery is an experience people commonly report, but there has been much debate about whether it influences performance. The evidence for the use of imagery that has been amassed over the last 30 years is very compelling. The debate is now over how visual images are represented. One issue is whether visual images contain enough detailed information so that they can be reinterpreted. The results seem to indicate that they sometimes do, but there is still a question as to how the images differ from the representations of visually perceived objects. A second debate has centered on the question as to whether visual images are really visual or might be spatial. Here, the evidence suggests that both representations occur.

The final section examined a variety of results in visual memory. Rather than repeat them here, we repeat the conclusions. First, visual experience provides a richness of representation beyond what one might usually get from verbal communication. Second, despite this richness, many details are not represented, though in many cases that is not obvious to the person unless they are queried directly about it. Much of the information not represented is not central to our goals, so we may often not notice that it is missing.

On a broader level, the study of visuospatial cognition is important because other cognitive mechanisms may have evolved by modifying existing systems. Given that the spatial representation system is probably one of the oldest, one might expect that other cognitive systems show a "spatial bias." The representation of spatial relations does appear to be fairly ubiquitous in human thought. Many of the metaphors that we use to describe how we think and feel rely on spatial relations (feeling up, feeling down, feeling close to another person, "higher"-level thinking, placing a plan on the back burner, and so on; see Lakoff & Johnson, 1980). We also find it natural to discuss the similarity of entities such as color in terms of being "close to" or "far from" each other.

Finally, in our discussions of comprehension and reasoning, we will make frequent reference to "mental models," which centrally employ spatial representations.

To close our argument that spatial cognition may bias other forms of cognition, we offer another spatial metaphor: The apple may not fall far from the tree.

Key Terms

analog representation

dual-coding hypothesis

mental rotation

picture-superiority effect

propositional representation

representation

route knowledge

spatial neglect

survey knowledge

Recommended Readings

There is a large literature on the debate concerning analog versus propositional representations. For further discussion, see articles by Kosslyn and Shwartz (1977), Pylyshyn (1979, 1981), Anderson (1978), Shepard (1981), and Barsalou (1994). Kosslyn's (1983, 1994) books offer extensive overviews of the structure and function of images. Markman (1999) provides an overview of approaches to mental representation.

Spatial cognition is a topic that is receiving increasing attention. B. Tversky (1981) and Byrne (1982) report interesting limitations in memory for spatial information. H. A. Taylor et al. (1999) provide a recent analysis of what might lead to route versus survey knowledge. The phenomenon of spatial neglect is as intriguing as it is disturbing. Descriptions of neglect can be found in Chedru (1976) and Bisiach et al. (1986), and a brief review is given in Bisiach (1996).

Parallels between imagery and perception from a neuroscience perspective can be read about in Farah (1988) and Kosslyn and Koenig (1992), plus it is discussed in a general treatment of memory by Schacter (1996). Rouw et al. (1997) and Reisberg (1998) contain recent discussions of whether images are reinterpreted. Schooler, Ohlsson, and Brooks (1993) provide intriguing evidence that verbalization can interfere with solving insight problems.

The three boxes (mental rehearsal, change detection, and face recognition) each contains mention of a review article that can be used for gaining access to the relevant literature. There is also a journal, *Visual Cognition,* that often has articles addressing topics in this chapter.

PART IV
LANGUAGE AND UNDERSTANDING

Chapter 9
Language

Chapter 10
Concepts and Categories:
Representation and Use

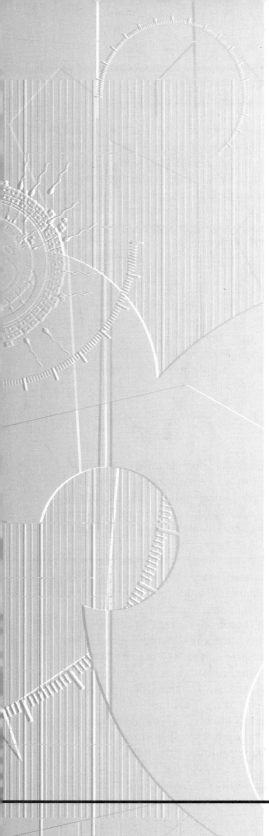

Chapter 9

Language

Introduction

Language and Communication
Principles of Communication
The Given-New Strategy
Presupposition and Assertion
Conversational Maxims
Summary

The Productivity of Human Languages
Productivity and Novelty
Ambiguity

Phonology
Phonological Rules
Speech Perception
Summary

Syntax
The Need for Structure
Structure
Phrase Structure
Transformations
The Psychological Reality of Syntax
Summary

Understanding Language
Heuristics and Strategies
Minimal Attachment

Text Comprehension

The Brain and Language

Summary

Key Terms

Recommended Readings

*Language is the armory of the human mind,
and at once it contains the trophies of its past
and the weapons of its future conquests.*
—*Samuel Taylor Coleridge*

INTRODUCTION

As you read this text, you may not be thinking about how truly amazing language is. Consider, however, that the authors of this chapter are not sitting in the room with you. Nonetheless, we can communicate our thoughts with you, teach you new things, and perhaps entertain you (or perhaps not). No other species that we know of is able to communicate using such a sophisticated system of symbols and structure that permits two individuals to converse about items that are not currently present and also permits the transmission of thoughts across space and time.

Before embarking on a discussion of the study of language, it is important to clarify one ambiguity. When we talk about language, sometimes we are referring to particular *languages*. For example, we might want to talk about the words or the grammar of English or French. Other times, when we talk about language, we are really talking about language *use*. In these cases, we are referring to the way people communicate with language (see Chiu, Krauss, & Lau, 1998, for a discussion of this issue). Psychologists have focused on both aspects of language. In this chapter, we begin with a discussion of the communicative uses of language. Then, we turn to the structure of languages. Finally, we will briefly explore what is known about language and the brain.

LANGUAGE AND COMMUNICATION

Talking about how language is used to communicate before describing the components of language may seem like putting the cart before the horse. After all, using language to communicate with someone clearly involves using words and putting them together to form sentences. However, it is hard to think about why the human language faculty would have evolved in the way it did without thinking about what language is for (Hauser, 1996).

Clark (1996) points out that the prototypical situation for human communication involves two people in face-to-face contact, speaking, involved in mutual conversation using a language both of them know. Of course, we communicate in many ways that do not satisfy all of these conditions. We communicate over the phone, where we are not in visual contact with the person we are talking to. We communicate using writing in letters, e-mail, and in chat rooms. We communicate in lectures, where one person speaks and an audience listens, without being able to engage in the conversation. There are even times when we manage to communicate with someone who speaks a different language, through some combination of gestures, smiles, and pidgin phrases that combine aspects of the languages spoken by each person. As you go through this chapter, keep this prototypical communication setting in mind. Many studies of language alter this prototypical situation, and as we discuss various studies, it is worth considering the influence of these changes on how people use language.

How is language used to communicate? Most of us have a sense of how conversations work. One person takes a turn, and then another person does. The first speaker may specify who should speak next (perhaps by asking a question of a particular participant), or another participant may just jump in at a natural break. This structure seems familiar, and is captured in the dialog in most books and movies. Sacks, Schegloff, and Jefferson (1974) specified a set of formal rules that would determine how turns are allocated in a conversation. Essentially, the current speaker takes a turn in the conversation. The speaker can pass the turn to someone else. If they do not pass it to someone else, then another participant can jump in at the end of the first speaker's turn. The first person to start speaking gets the next turn. If two people start at once, one person typically stops and allows the other to continue. If the speaker reaches a natural break, and nobody starts to talk, the speaker may continue.

This system of turn taking would appear to be a good description of how conversations take place. As Clark (1996) points out, however, this proposal misses a lot of what actually occurs in conversation. Participants in conversations typically give feedback to the speaker while the speaker is taking a turn (e.g., saying "uh-huh" or nodding). We rely on this type of feedback to keep coordinated. For example, if we talk on the phone and we go too long without hearing anything on the other end of the line, we begin to think that we have been cut off or that the other person is not listening. Thus, this feedback is crucial for coordinating a conversation. Furthermore, as soon as a participant in a conversation begins to lose the meaning of what the speaker is saying, he or she will typically jump in to get a correction. For example, if the speaker mentions an unfamiliar name, the participant will immediately ask for a clarification rather than waiting until the speaker has finished his or her turn.

The importance of this coordination in communication (which Clark, 1996, calls **joint action**) can be seen in a clever study by Schober and Clark (1989). They had pairs of people who could not see each other play a game in which they had to order a set of unfamiliar shapes in a grid by having a conversation. One person (the *director*) had the correct order, and he or she had to tell the other person (the *receiver*) how to generate that order. Both the director and receiver could converse freely so the receiver could ask for a clarification if necessary. Over the course of the task, the director and receiver would talk about the various shapes. By the end of the task, nearly all pairs of subjects were able to solve the task correctly. Afterward, another subject—called the *overhearer*—listened to the whole conversation between the original pair (which had been recorded) and tried to put the shapes in the proper order. On average, the overhearers placed fewer of the shapes in the correct order than did the receivers. Presumably, this occurred because the receiver (but not the overhearer) could ask for clarification when he or she did not know what shape was being described. This finding highlights that participants in a conversation coordinate rather than simply having one person speak and another one listen.

Principles of Communication

So far, we have suggested that communication is a joint action that involves a coordination among the participants in order to achieve understanding. Still, there must be some principles that people generally rely on in order to convey meanings. These communicative principles are often called the **pragmatics** of language. *Pragmatics* refers to the practical matter of making sure that people understand not just what is said but also what is meant. "Do you have a watch?" is not usually a question about possessions but rather about what time it is, and giving "yes" as an answer would miss the point. Interestingly, we are often unaware of the rules of communication that we commonly practice. Some basic principles of pragmatics have been identified, and we will briefly review them.

The Given-New Strategy

Haviland and Clark (1974) proposed that the organization of sentences supports a **given-new strategy.** Speakers or writers normally are trying to convey new information that is related in some way to what is already known. The listener (or reader) assumes that the speaker (or writer) knows and is able to gauge what the listener (or reader) does not know. Consider the following sentence: "The jokes that Horace tells are awful." The given information is that Horace tells jokes, and the new information is that the jokes are awful. The sentence presupposes that the reader knows who Horace is, and without that shared knowledge the sentence may seem strange.

Haviland and Clark (1974) demonstrated that the given-new principle influences people's comprehension of sentences. They presented subjects with pairs of sentences that either obeyed the given-new principle (as in a.) or violated it (as in b.).

   a. Last Christmas Eugene became absolutely smashed. This Christmas he got very drunk again.

   b. Last Christmas Eugene went to a lot of parties. This Christmas he got very drunk again.

They found that people are faster at comprehending the second sentence in a. than in b. In the second sentence, the word *again* presupposes that Eugene had gotten drunk before, an assumption that is directly stated only in the first pair of sentences. This example and others like it reveal that numerous strategies can be used to promote (see, e.g., Brennan & Clark, 1996; Clark & Schaefer, 1987a) or inhibit (Clark & Schaefer, 1987b; Schober & Clark, 1989) effective communication.

Presupposition and Assertion

The given-new strategy works well when a sentence includes a shared presupposition or background, followed by an assertion of new information. Because attention is directed at the new or asserted information, it may be possible to slip misleading information into the presupposition part of a sentence. Presuppositions are sometimes hard to deny (e.g., "When did you stop beating your spouse?"). Elizabeth Loftus has demonstrated that presuppositions can be manipulated to affect eyewitness testimony (we mentioned related evidence in Chapter 7). For example, Loftus and Palmer (1974) showed undergraduate students films depicting a traffic accident and then asked a variety of questions. In different films, two cars collided, and these collisions took place at speeds of 20, 30, or 40 miles per hour. The specific verb used to ask the question about speed was also varied to introduce different presuppositions. For example, some students might be asked, "About how fast were the cars going when they *hit* each other?" whereas others might be asked, "About how fast were the cars going when they *smashed* into each other?" (We added the italics.) The verb *smashed* seems to presuppose more speed than the verb *hit*. Loftus and Palmer found that the verbs used had a clear effect on estimated speeds. For the verb *hit*, the mean estimated speed was 34 miles per hour, and for *smashed* the mean estimated speed was 41 miles per hour. (Differences in actual speed had little effect.) The conclusion is that varying the presupposition associated with questions can affect the answers that are given, an observation that has clear implications for practical situations such as questioning witnesses.

Conversational Maxims

Making the right inferences from information that is presented may also depend on common conventions or rules. Grice (1975) proposed that cooperative communication requires adherence to a set of **conversational maxims.** He refers to these maxims as *quantity, quality, relation,* and *manner,* which can be approximately translated into *be informative, tell the truth, be relevant,* and *be clear.* It is important to note that while people are expected to operate as if they have these rules, it is unlikely that most people (who haven't studied language) know them explicitly.

Gricean maxims have two important influences on communication. First, they provide rules for formulating utterances. That is, in general, we strive to be informative, truthful, relevant, and clear. However, these rules also provide us with ways of communicating indirectly by explicitly violating the maxims. For example, if John says to Bill, "Can you close the door?" he is violating the maxim of quantity. Presumably he knows that Bill is capable of closing the door (assuming Bill is not a three-year-old). Thus, if Bill were to respond "Yes" to John's question, he would be violating the principle of relevance, because he would be answering a question that he is certain that John already knows the answer to. Instead, Bill is likely to interpret this question as an indirect speech act in which John is actually requesting that he close the door.

We often use indirect speech acts to say things we do not want to say overtly. Consider the following interaction:

PARENT: Where did you go?
TEENAGER: Out.
PARENT: What did you do?
TEENAGER: Nothing.

This exchange violates the principle of informativeness, but it does so obviously, so that it might be best read as an indirect speech act intending to convey "none of your business." In this case, violations of the Gricean maxims create polite ways of saying things that would be impolite if stated directly.

Using violations of the Gricean maxims to create and interpret indirect speech acts requires knowing something about what other participants in the conversation already know. This account would argue that people must be pretty good at keeping track of what other people know so that they can correctly interpret new utterances. However, there is some evidence that people are not optimal at keeping track of the information they would need to interpret statements correctly using the conversational maxims. For example, Keysar (1994, see also Keysar & Bly, 1995) found that people were not very successful at ignoring or discounting their own (privileged) knowledge in making judgments about what others would understand. The participants in his experiments were given information such as the following paragraph:

> Mark asked his office mate, June, to recommend a restaurant; his parents were in town and he wanted to take them to a good place. "I strongly recommend this new Italian place, called Venezia. I just had dinner there last night and it was marvelous. Let me know how you all enjoy it." That evening, Mark and his parents ate there; the food was unimpressive and the service was mediocre.

Then further information was given in one of the following two forms:

spoken
The next morning, Mark said to her: "You wanted to know about the restaurant, well, marvelous, just marvelous."

written
The next morning, Mark left a note on her desk: "You wanted to know about the restaurant, well, marvelous, just marvelous."

Participants were then asked to judge how June would interpret Mark's response. In the version where Mark speaks directly to June, one could imagine that he was either being polite or perhaps sarcastic and that Mark's intonation pattern would reveal which was which. For the written version, intonation information is missing, so it is reasonable to infer that June has no cues to Mark's possible sarcasm. Nonetheless, Keysar found that participants were just as likely to judge that June understood Mark to be sarcastic for the written version as for the spoken version. It appears that they were unable to ignore their knowledge, given in the first paragraph but unavailable to June, that Mark found the restaurant to be poor. It appears that conversational pragmatics may be tinged with some degree of egocentrism.

Summary

Language is used to communicate. When communicating in the typical face-to-face situation, people coordinate their conversation so that all participants understand the meaning of what is being discussed. One way that this coordination is achieved is through the use of typical strategies that participants can assume other people in the conversation will also know. For example, the Gricean maxims are rules that participants in a conversation can generally assume will apply to what is stated. Violations of these conversational rules can be used to communicate things indirectly that would be impolite to say directly.

The authors of this book are aware that researchers in this area would think we have barely scratched the surface of pragmatics, and they would be right. The question of how children learn principles of communications is intriguing, not to mention other issues, such as gender differences in patterns of turn taking in conversations. However, it is time to turn to the mechanisms that languages use to permit communication to occur. In the following sections we will focus on the sounds of language (*phonemes*) and the perception of those sounds, the meaning units of language (*morphemes*) and the structure of language (*syntax*). First, however, we will point out some important properties of natural language that will serve as a useful background to our survey of the mechanisms of language comprehension and production.

THE PRODUCTIVITY OF HUMAN LANGUAGE

The human language capacity is truly amazing. Many animals have communication systems (Hauser, 1996), but the range of topics that other animals can communicate about is fixed. For example, Cheney and Seyfarth (1990) describe communication among vervet monkeys in the wild. Vervets can call for help and can alert their group about predators in the air or on the ground. However, vervet monkeys do not have a general capacity to communicate about topics such as the weather or their feelings. In contrast, humans can discuss almost anything, even things that evolution could not have foreseen would be important to our species. In order for language to permit this rich range of discussion, it must have mechanisms that must allow novel topics to be put into language, and must allow new concepts to be transmitted through language from one person to another. We will discuss two properties that follow from this productivity in the following sections.

Productivity and Novelty

Language is productive in that units at one level of analysis allow the generation of many more units at the next level of analysis. For example, English has about 40 speech sounds that can be combined (according to certain rules) to generate many thousands of words. Rules for combining words make it possible to generate an unlimited number of sentences, so language is often characterized by novelty. When you hear or read the sentence, "The little green man had eaten too many four-leaf clovers," you understand the ideas being expressed, even though you doubtless have never seen this particular combination of words before. Of course, language does not permit all possible combinations of words—the sequence "four-leaf the too eat green many man little clovers had" is not a grammatical sentence, and thus it is hard to understand. A key aspect of this productivity is that it rules out the possibility that human language involves the use of a large set of memorized sentences.

Ambiguity

One consequence of the productivity of a language is ambiguity. To see this, let us first return to communication among vervet monkeys. Because they have a fixed set of topics about which they communicate, the utterances that monkeys make are not ambiguous. If one monkey makes an alarm call signaling a terrestrial predator (like a snake), the monkeys can immediately head for the nearest tree. The monkeys have different calls for different kinds of predators, so the call for terrestrial predator is qualitatively different from the call for an aerial predator (like an eagle). While there is some evidence that vervet monkeys consider the source of a call, and are less likely to respond to alarm calls made by young monkeys than by adults, the call itself signals the same thing regardless of who makes it (Cheney & Seyfarth, 1990).

As we discussed in the previous section, human languages are quite different from monkey calls, because they are productive. This productivity is evident at the level of speech sounds, words, and sentences. The way language implements this productivity is by re-using the components at a given level of language (e.g., sounds or words) in a variety of contexts. In each context, these components contribute something different to the intended meaning. Using the same component to mean something different across contexts is what creates ambiguity in language. The fascinating thing about language comprehension is that these ambiguities are rarely noticed.

As one example, although normal conversational speech seems perfectly intelligible most of the time, typical speech is actually not at all clear when presented word by word. For example, Pollack and Pickett (1964) surreptitiously recorded people's spontaneous conversations and then played single words cut out from these tape recordings to other people for identification. Single words were correctly identified less than half the time! This is ambiguity at the phonetic (speech sound) level.

As we will see in the next section, segmenting the stream of speech into individual words is very difficult. Speech does not provide natural breaks between words and is essentially continuous. Listening to a conversation carried out in a foreign tongue may give you a sense of the difficulty. And anyone spending much time around children will be able to come up with examples of incorrect segmentation. One well-known example is the passage in the United States pledge of allegiance "and to the republic for which it stands," which many children interpret as "and to the republic for Richard Stans."

Individual lexical items or words can also be ambiguous in their **semantics,** or meaning. For example, *saw* and *files* have very different meanings in the following two sentences:

1. Bill saw the files.

2. Bill files the saw.

Phrases can also be ambiguous. Consider the following sentence:

3. Visiting relatives can be a nuisance.

This sentence could refer to a type of relative, namely, those who are visiting, or to the act of visiting relatives.

In normal conversation, the context usually specifies the intended meaning, and almost always the ambiguities we have been describing go unnoticed. These ambiguities are, however, quite important when attention shifts to the questions of how languages are understood. How does the mind handle these ambiguities? Theories of language comprehension must address this issue.

We now turn to discussions of some key components of the language system. We begin with a discussion of speech sounds and the mechanisms of speech perception. Then, we will discuss the way that words can be organized into sentences and discuss the way the language comprehension system processes new spoken or written sentences. Finally, we will look more broadly at issues of comprehension of longer texts and discourses.

PHONOLOGY

At the base of spoken language are **phonemes,** which are the smallest significant sound units in language (they allow us to distinguish, for example, the difference between the words *lap* and *rap*). English has about 40 phonemes. Languages differ from one another to some extent in the particular phonemes they employ. For example, English considers the sounds for *r* and *l* to be different phonemes, but Japanese does not. By the same token, English does not distinguish between aspirated and unaspirated *p,* although other languages such as Hindi do. An aspirated *p* is accompanied by a slight puff of air, as when you say "puff." (You can verify this aspiration by placing your hand in front of your mouth to feel the puff or by holding up a match or candle to see the puff.) An unaspirated *p,* as in the word *spill* does not produce a puff. The French language does not aspirate *p* at all. One of the tasks of acquiring a language is to learn which sound units make a difference and which don't.

In this chapter, we begin with a discussion of phonological structure in the form of rules or operating principles. When we speak, we certainly have no awareness that we are applying or following "rules" for speech sounds, but a rule structure underlies the phonology of language. Most people can't state many of these rules, but their speech conforms to them. Following this discussion, we present a brief overview of research on speech perception.

Phonological Rules

Phonology is centrally concerned with the rules that determine what sound combinations are allowed in the language. Phonetics is the study of the sounds themselves,

AN APPLICATION

The Reacquisition of Phonological Distinctions

Because Japanese does not distinguish between *r* and *l,* when native speakers of Japanese speak English, they often substitute *r* for *l* and vice versa. All human infants have the capability of hearing and producing the distinction between all phonemes of all languages, but they gradually become insensitive to differences that are not part of the particular language they speak. For example, native speakers of English are not sensitive to the difference between aspirated *p* and unaspirated *p*.

For a long time, it was thought that once the people lost the ability to discriminate and produce a pair of phonemes that ability was lost forever. There is now research suggesting that these lost discriminations can be reacquired (Lively, Logan, & Pisoni, 1993; Lively, Pisoni, Yamada, Tohkura, & Yamada, 1994; Logan, Lively, & Pisoni, 1991). In one representative study (Lively et al., 1994), the subjects were native speakers of Japanese living in Kyoto (so that they did not have much exposure to English). The stimuli consisted of pairs of words that differed only in whether the word had *r* or *l* in one position. Words of this type are called *minimal pairs.* For example, the words *rap* and *lap* or *fur* and *full* are minimal pairs. Over the course of the experiment, subjects heard words spoken by five different speakers (all of whom were native speakers of English).

(Continued)

but we will treat phonetics and phonology as roughly synonymous. This statement contains the implication that rules are, in fact, determining pronunciations. An alternative possibility is that one simply memorizes the pronunciation of each of the basic meaning units of language, called **morphemes.** There are about 50,000 morphemes of English, but it is not possible to memorize their pronunciation, because how a morpheme is pronounced depends on the rest of the word it appears in. For example, in English the morpheme that indicates a noun is plural is the suffix *-s*. How that *-s* is pronounced depends on the word it appears in. The plural of *dog* is pronounced with a final [z], the plural of cat has a final [s], and the plural of fox has a final [iz]. So if one wants to maintain that pronunciations are simply memorized, one must assume that each combination of morphemes is memorized, which would involve many hundreds of thousands, if not millions, of distinct items.

Even if we grant that people could memorize the pronunciation of all combinations of morphemes, the strict memorization position fails to account for other regularities or generalizations. Consider how you would pronounce plurals of the following nonwords: *loap, fambish,* and *plur.* Almost everyone would apply the suffix [s]

AN APPLICATION

The Reacquisition of Phonological Distinctions *(Continued)*

On each trial, one written word appeared on the left side of the screen, and one appeared on the right. The subject heard a word over headphones that corresponded to one of the words on the screen, and they had to select the word they thought they heard. After each trial, they were given feedback. Subjects were given 40 minutes of training per session for fifteen sessions (over three weeks). After training, subjects were given posttests immediately, after three months, and after six months.

In a pretest, subjects were able to correctly identify 63% of the words they heard. Immediately after training, subjects were able to identify 77% of the words correctly. In a posttest given three months later, subjects were still at the same level of accuracy. After six months, performance did drop, but subjects were still significantly more accurate than they were in the pretest. These results suggest that a simple training regimen of repeated trials distinguishing between a pair of phonemes can be effective in allowing a person to reacquire a phoneme distinction that they had previously lost. An important finding in this work is that the training program must consist of words spoken by different speakers. In other studies that used only a single synthesized voice during training, no significant improvements were obtained in ability to distinguish among phonemes spoken by different speakers (Strange & Dittman, 1984).

to *loap,* [iz] to *fambish,* and [z] to *plur.* The strict memorization position cannot predict this consistency because you could not have previously memorized these novel strings. It appears that our pronunciation of words is principled, and the search for rules has the goal of describing these principles.

The fact that there are phonological regularities does not mean that we actually have some abstract rule that tells us how to pronounce words. For example, it might be that nonwords remind people of known words and that people pronounce the nonword by analogy with the known word (see, e.g., Glushko, 1979). *Loap* might remind one of *soap,* and *plur* of *blur.* We confess that nothing comes immediately to mind for *fambish* (perhaps *faddish* or *ambush?*). If no analogy is suggested, this procedure is not going to work. More important, our discussion has conveniently focused on words with the same final sound in them. However, the word *loap* is also similar to the word *loaf* (whose plural is *loaves*) and *loan* (whose plural is *loans*). Neither of these would suggest the right phoneme for the plural ending of *loap.* Perhaps we could restrict our analogies to favor similar word endings, but then we would be admitting that we need to constrain (or focus) our search more narrowly.

Thus, although the analogical mechanism is in principle a possibility, we suspect that the necessary guidance to ensure appropriate remindings would, in effect, build rules into the mechanism. (For a closer look at and analysis of this issue, see Treiman, Mullennix, Bijeljac-Babic, & Richmond-Welty, 1995.)

There is a way in which pronunciation could follow rules without the rules being represented at all. It could be that there are constraints associated with articulating morpheme combinations that may favor some realizations over others. That is, these pronunciation "rules" may just be a reflection of the way the articulatory system is set up. For example, it is difficult to add [s] or [z] to *fambish*. However, children often pluralize incorrectly. For example, a child may say *sock*[ziz] or *sock*[z] rather than *sock*[s]. Therefore, production or articulatory constraints are, at best, part of the story (and likely only a small part at that).

The distribution of English plural morphemes is, in fact, quite regular. For example, [iz] is used for words like *places, porches, cabbages, horses,* and *ambushes;* [s] for words like *soaps, lists, books,* and *graphs;* and [z] for words like *pies, plums, turns, holes,* and *lions.* The choice of suffix is governed by the last sound in the word. One can describe the regularity as follows.

[iz] if the noun ends with [s, z, č, ǰ, š, or ž]

[s] if the noun ends with [p, t, k, f, or θ]

otherwise [z]

The key observation is that there are regularities of pluralization that are captured in terms of phonological features present in the stem noun. Again, note that you need not be consciously aware of these rules in order to follow them. The general characterization of phonology in terms of systematic rules holds fairly uniformly across languages.

Still other observations demonstrate that other concerns like the grammatical structure or syntax of a sentence can influence how something is pronounced. Consider these sentences:

4. I am going to leave.

5. I am going to New York.

6. I'm gonna leave.

This is perfectly acceptable speech, but note that one cannot say:

7. *I'm gonna New York.

(The asterisk is a convention used in linguistics to indicate an unacceptable or nongrammatical sentence.)

Sentences 4 and 5 are essentially the same in their articulatory requirements. In sentence 4, however, the *to* is linked to *going* as part of the verb ("going to leave"), whereas in 5 *to* is separate from the verb because it begins a prepositional phrase ("to New York"). We can only contract *going to* to *gonna* when they are part of the same syntactic element in the sentence. When *going* and *to* play different roles, they cannot be contracted (which makes 7 ungrammatical). This observation further undermines the idea that how we say things is driven solely by articulatory constraints. It also makes clear that pronunciation is affected by aspects of language beyond those concerning speech sounds.

Speech Perception

In Chapter 3, we explored issues in visual perception. In this section, we consider speech perception. The ability to comprehend spoken speech is a fascinating ability, given the complexity of the sounds produced by the vocal tract. In normal speech, we produce as many as 250 words per minute, which is about 16–20 phonemes per second.

What makes the perception of speech particularly difficult is that speech does not consist of single phonemes separated by silent boundaries. Instead speech is continuous, with one phoneme flowing into the next. An important tool for analyzing speech structure is the sound spectrograph, which provides a visual representation of sound energy for different frequencies as a function of time. The left side of Figure 9.1 shows a spectrograph for the consonant-vowel combination [su] (i.e., Sue) produced by a male speaker of English. Although it looks as if there are two distinct segments corresponding to the consonant and to the vowel, more detailed analyses reveal a more complex picture. One can use computer-editing techniques to separate the two segments and play them individually to a listener. Upon hearing segment A, the listener will be able to identify the consonant [s]. However, the listener is also able to identify the vowel on the basis of segment A. That is, segment A contains information about both the consonant and the vowel that was spoken (Yeni-Komshian & Soli, 1981). This parallel transmission of information results from **coarticulation;** when the consonant is being pronounced, the articulators are already being shaped in preparation for the vowel sound. That is, the articulatory movements (the movements needed to produce speech) for the different sounds within a word overlap one another in time. Because of the coarticulation, individual phonetic segments do not correspond in a simple way to distinct acoustic (i.e., sound) segments in the speech signal.

It is worth underlining a principal implication of coarticulation: *There is no single invariant property in the acoustic signal that corresponds uniquely to a given phonetic segment of the language.* Instead, the acoustic signal associated with a phoneme changes with the context in which it is uttered. Consider the spectrogram of the consonant-vowel pair [šu] (i.e., shoe) on the right side of Figure 9.1. Note first that the speech sound for [š] has its concentration of energy at relatively lower frequencies than does the sound for [s]. (Compare the darkness of the spectrograms in the two A segments.) But the precise frequency composition of the sounds of [š] and [s] changes depending on which vowel follows the consonant during production. For example, for both [š] and [s], the energy of the speech sound is concentrated at a relatively higher-frequency region before [a] than before [u]. This means that the frequency region for [ša] will be very similar to the frequency region associated with [su]. In short, in order to identify whether a speaker produced [s] or [š], the listener must take into account the identity of the following vowel. Hence the perception of

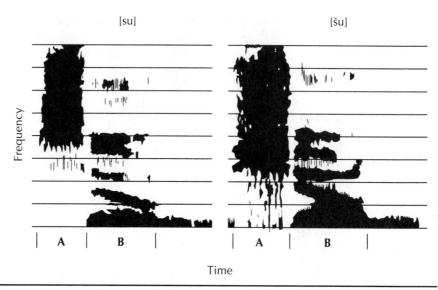

[su]   [šu]

Frequency

| A | B | | A | B |

Time

Figure 9.1   Spectrogram of [su] (Sue) and [šu] (shoe), produced by a male speaker of English. The darker the mark on the spectrogram, the more energy there is in the speech signal at that frequency at that time.

Miller, J. L., 1990.

phonemes is context-dependent (Diehl & Kluender, 1987; J. L. Miller, 1990). Speech perception entails the integration of multiple sources of information rather than the discrete identification of isolated segments of the acoustic signal.

A further complication is that there is more than one speaker in the world. The mapping of acoustic cues is highly variable from one speaker to the next. People's speech differs in pitch, quality of articulation, and, more broadly, style. In addition, people sound different, depending on whether they are excited or calm, shouting or whispering, talking to adults or children, and so on. Apparently, listeners are able to adjust and adjust quickly for these differences. With these observations in hand, we are ready to turn to speech perception.

Theories of Speech Perception

The fact that we can carry on a conversation is proof enough that speech perception is possible. But how, in general, is it done? Over the past few decades, two principal theories have been presented, referred to as the **motor theory** of speech perception and the **auditory theory** of speech perception. The motor theory is associated with Liberman and his colleagues at Haskins Laboratories (Liberman & Mattingly, 1985). It makes two claims: (1) There is a close link between the system responsible for perceiving speech and the system responsible for producing speech, which is why it is called a motor theory. This theory is consistent with proposals that perception and production systems for communication tend to evolve together (Hauser, 1996). The key idea is that we perceive speech by virtue of our tacit knowledge of how speech is produced, so that we naturally adjust for the lack of invariants in the speech signal associated with context and coarticulation effects. In other words, in perception, we determine which articulatory gesture the speaker has made and, by virtue of this, we are able to determine which phonetic segments have been produced. (2) Perception is innate. Our abilities to produce and perceive speech are inborn and species-specific. Given that humans are the only known organisms who produce speech and who would have knowledge about articulation, only humans should perceive speech as a structured sequence of phonemes. A shorthand description of the motor theory is that it claims that "speech is special."

The auditory theory is the logical antithesis of the motor theory. Its claims are: (1) that speech perception derives from general properties of the auditory system and (2) that speech perception is not species-specific. This claim follows from the observations that the human auditory system is similar to that of many other animals. The auditory theory is neutral with respect to which perceptual distinctions are innate or learned.

It is not clear how to provide critical tests that would distinguish between these two theories. Nonetheless, the contrast between these two orientations has provided a framework for an intriguing series of observations on speech perception. A sampling of research follows.

Recall that one consequence of coarticulation effects is that energy concentration at the higher frequencies of phonemes like [s] and [š] varies with the associated vowel context. Despite this, listeners have no difficulty recognizing which fricative, [s] or [š], has been produced. Mann and Repp (1980) showed that when context is carefully varied by employing synthesized speech sounds, the identification of [s] versus [š] varies systematically with the vowel context. This observation is compatible with the motor theory of speech perception because knowledge of constraints placed on speech by virtue of the way the speech system is physically constructed is assumed to guide perception of speech. These same findings pose a challenge to the auditory theory to specify properties of the auditory system that could give rise to context effects.

Another observation that was initially taken as favoring the motor theory is **categorical perception.** In the pronunciation of consonants such as [b] and [p], the closed lips are opened, releasing air, and the vocal chords begin vibrating. The time between release and vibration is known as **voice onset time.** In the case of the voiced consonant [b], the release and vibration are nearly simultaneous. For [p] the voicing is delayed. Lisker and Abramson (1970) performed experiments with computer-generated variations of voice onset time. They asked participants to identify whether a [b] or a [p] had been presented. Over most of the range of voice onset time, identification was unambiguous. That is, two categories could readily be distinguished, one corresponding to [b] and one corresponding to [p]. The main changes in identification were at a narrow category boundary in the neighborhood of a voice onset time of about 20–40 milliseconds.

Other studies focus on the ability of listeners to discriminate between two sounds varying in onset time. When two sounds fall on opposite sides of the category boundary (e.g., one [b] and one [p]), even small differences in voice onset time can be discriminated. In contrast, when both sounds fall on the same side of the category boundary (e.g., two different [b]'s), then even large differences in voice onset time cannot be discriminated well. Thus, it appears that a continuous variation in voice onset time is perceived in a largely all-or-none, or categorical, manner (Studdert-Kennedy, 1976). Categorical perception is consistent with motor theory (speech is special), even if it is not a necessary prediction of it. The challenge to auditory theory is to explain why perception should be categorical rather than continuous.

Recent evidence on categorical perception is more favorable to auditory theory. First, it is now clear that categorical perception is not unique to humans. Chinchillas have an auditory system similar to ours, and Kuhl and Miller (1978) found that identification functions for chinchillas showed the same sharp category boundaries that were noted for humans. In addition, there are both theory and data that suggest that categorical perception arises from rapid decay of auditory memory, not something special about speech (see, e.g., Fujisaki & Kawashima, 1970; Pisoni, 1973). Later evidence also suggests some ability to discriminate speech sounds within a category. These studies suggest that people perceive differences between speech sounds within a category, but after they categorize both sounds as members of the same category, these perceptual differences are forgotten (see Massaro, 1987). Overall, then, the observations on categorical perception seem consistent with the auditory theory.

Still other findings, however, are clearly inconsistent with any theory of speech perception that relies solely on auditory information. A particularly fascinating observation comes from a study by McGurk and MacDonald (1976). They developed a videotape showing a speaker mouthing /pa-pa/, but the sound they hear over the speaker is /na-na/. What should happen? One possibility is that they will just hear the input to the auditory system (in this case /na-na/). Another possibility is that they will be confused, because the visual and auditory input conflict. In fact, observers are not confused, but neither do they hear /pa-pa/ or even /na-na/. Instead, they report hearing an integration of the two, /ma-ma/. (Say each of these out loud, and try to identify the sense in which /ma-ma/ is a compromise between /pa-pa/ and /na-na/.) This has come to be known as the **McGurk effect**. Somehow the perceptual system integrates the information from the auditory and visual modalities to yield the unitary experience of a single speech sound. There is even evidence that infants have knowledge of the correspondences between articulatory movements on a speaker's face and the acoustic speech signal (Kuhl & Meltzoff, 1982). Obviously, the pure auditory theory cannot account for this observation. The auditory theory must be supplemented with some visual information and some means of integrating vision and audition (see, e.g., Massaro & Cohen, 1983).

The debate between the motor theory and the auditory theory has not been resolved, but many advances have been made in our understanding of speech perception. There are important observations that any theory must be able to address. The most salient is that speech perception involves the integration of a variety of sources of information, including information from both the auditory and visual modalities (as in the McGurk effect). It should be said that it is not entirely clear at what stage of processing these integration effects occur. One could argue for an early stage involving separate modules (visual vs. auditory; syntactic vs. phonological), followed by a later integration stage. Still, the remarkable thing is that integration takes place so smoothly that we are scarcely aware of it. Thus, while there are many potential ambiguities in speech, they are resolved by the workings of the speech perception system.

Summary

As this section demonstrates, even the speech sounds of language are complex. In order for human language to be able to discuss a nearly limitless range of topics, it is necessary to be able to create new words, and to embed those words in sentences. Thus, the speech system must be productive. Hence, it is governed by rules that determine aspects of word sounds such as the way that morphemes sound when added to novel words. The sounds of language are also affected by complex aspects of language like the structure of sentences.

The speech perception system is also quite complex. During speech, phonemes are produced at a high rate. The phonemes overlap so that there is no clean break in the speech signal between one phoneme and the next. Thus, people must use a variety of cues in order to decode the speech signal. Two of the prominent theories of speech perception are the motor and auditory theories. The motor theory assumes that people use their knowledge of speech production to comprehend speech. The auditory theory assumes that speech perception involves only an analysis of the information in the speech stream itself. These theories are being tested in ongoing research.

SYNTAX

The Need for Structure

In the section above on ambiguity, we pointed out that sentences are more than just arbitrary lists of words. In English, the order in which words appear strongly affects meaning. "John hit Bill" means something different from "Bill hit John." It is easy to see that these regularities cannot be correctly described by surface rules of the form "the actor always comes first and the acted upon comes second" because this rule would provide the wrong interpretation of the sentence "Bill was hit by John." Clearly, a deeper analysis of sentence structure that goes beyond word order is needed. **Syntax** is the grammatical structure that determines how words are combined to form sentences.

The need for structure is also revealed in the use of pronouns or pronominalization. Consider the following two sentences:

8. John thinks he passed the exam.

9. He thinks John passed the exam.

The standard reading of the first sentence is that he refers to John; that is, John thinks that John passed the exam. (Other readings are possible if, for example, the preceding sentence was "How did Bill do on the exam?") In the second sentence, however, *he* and *John* cannot refer to the same individual. Speakers of English clearly know this, but it is not obvious how to describe the rule or principle that is involved. One could offer the generalization that a pronoun that appears first in the sentence is not coreferential (does not refer to the same individual) with the proper noun that follows it. But this generalization is violated by sentences like:

10. After he studied very hard, John was able to pass the exam.

Yet another problem for surface-level analyses concerns the principles associated with converting a declarative sentence into a question. Consider sentences 11 and 12:

11. John is going to sleep.

12. Is John going to sleep?

It looks as if all one needs to do is move the helping verb *is* to the front of the sentence to create a question. Again, however, this simple rule of moving the first helping verb will not work. Consider the next pair of sentences:

13. John, who has become very tired, is going to sleep.

14. *Has John who become very tired is going to sleep?

Sentence 14 does not work. Although *is* can be moved, *has* cannot, suggesting that the principles of question construction require a deeper analysis of sentence structure. Perhaps we are guilty of belaboring the point, but we want to emphasize the fact that language use requires complex knowledge consisting of much more than simple rules based on word strings. Let's take a closer look at the sorts of structure associated with language use.

Structure

We will begin this section by reviewing some of the critical properties of syntactic structure. First, sentences are hierarchically organized; that is, sentences can be divided into their main parts and then further subdivided. Consider the following sentence:

15. The woman won the marathon.

It is natural to break this sentence into two parts, (the woman) and (won the marathon). The first chunk is known as a noun phrase and the second chunk as a verb phrase. The noun phrase can be broken down into an article, *the*, and a noun, *woman*. The verb phrase (won the marathon) can be subdivided into (won) and (the marathon); *won* is a verb, and *the marathon* is another noun phrase, which can be subdivided into an article and a noun. An easy way to represent this hierarchical structure is in terms of a tree diagram as in Figure 9.2.

Not only is a hierarchical structure intuitively natural but also we can show that the meaning of a sentence depends on the chunks or clusters that are constructed. Consider the sentence:

16. Susan saw a man eating shark.

The meaning of this sentence hinges crucially on whether one takes the chunks as (man) and (eating shark) versus (man eating) and (shark). The former

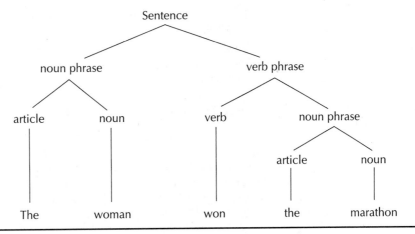

Figure 9.2   Tree structure of the sentence, "The woman won the marathon."

chunk supposes a restaurant scene; the latter, an ocean scene or an aquarium. In short, there is more to meaning than a string of words because how the string is chunked is important. Understanding a sentence involves figuring out the intended structure. The subtlety of our intuitions about grammar is quite remarkable, especially in light of the observation that people have great difficulty describing the "rules" of their language. Consider the following pair of sentences, both of which involve the word *that:*

17. The marathon that she won was exciting.

18. The marathon that allowed her to qualify for the Olympics was exciting.

The two sentences are similar in that they both link the word *that* with a relative clause. Note however, that the word *that* may be deleted from the first sentence without any loss of meaning, but *that* may not be omitted from the second sentence. The crucial difference seems to be that *marathon* is the object of the verb *won* in the first sentence but the subject of the verb *allowed* in the second sentence. The intuitions are obvious to any fluent speaker of English, but the underlying rules certainly are not.

Phrase Structure

The tree structure shown in Figure 9.2 illustrates what is referred to as the sentence's **phrase structure.** Phrase structure is the way that a sentence can be broken up into smaller components (or constituents). One major aspect of acquiring a language is learning its phrase structure rules. For example, English can be described in terms of rules. (The arrows here mean "can be written as or consisting of" and parentheses indicate a form which is optional):

Sentence $\longrightarrow$ noun phrase + verb phrase
Noun phrase $\longrightarrow$ (article) + (adjective) + noun
Noun phrase $\longrightarrow$ pronoun
Verb phrase $\longrightarrow$ verb + noun phrase
Verb phrase $\longrightarrow$ verb + prepositional phrase
Verb $\longrightarrow$ auxiliary + verb
Prepositional phrase $\longrightarrow$ preposition + noun phrase

If we add a list of words categorized as verbs, nouns, articles, adjectives, pronouns, prepositions, and auxiliaries, we have a procedure for generating sentences. The general goal of a set of syntactic rules is to be able, in principle, to generate all the acceptable sentences of a language and not generate any word strings that are not sentences. The rules we have just sketched are clearly inadequate. For example, they would not distinguish between

19. The man thought.

which is perfectly acceptable and

20. *The man solved.

which is not. The point is that some verbs (so-called *transitive* verbs, such as *solved*) require explicitly stated objects, whereas others (*intransitive* verbs, such as *thought*) do not.

Phrase structures are a considerable advance over viewing sentences solely in terms of a linear sequence of words. Chomsky (1957) has argued that phrase structure grammars are nonetheless inadequate as complete descriptions of natural language. One source of evidence for this claim is again the problem of ambiguity. Recall sentence 3 from earlier in this chapter:

3. Visiting relatives can be a nuisance.

This sentence could refer either to the act of visiting relatives or to relatives who are doing the visiting. But our chunking strategy will not solve the ambiguity in this case because in either event visiting modifies relatives (see Figure 9.3); that is, the ambiguity is at the level of underlying structure. Observations such as this suggest the need for further analysis and motivated Chomsky's description of **transformational grammars.**

Finally, it is important to note that much of the analysis of syntax comes from an examination of written sentences. Spoken language is not nearly as clean as written language. The next time you are in a big conversation, stop paying attention to the flow of the conversation for a moment, and just listen to the words and sentences people use while talking. There are numerous stops and starts in the conversation. Despite these disfluencies, syntax is still crucial to spoken language in conversation. For example, Clark (1996) points out that when people repair something they are saying, they will typically go back to the beginning of a grammatical unit. For example, they might say "Bob went into the . . . [uh] . . . into the garage." He suggests that this strategy makes it easier for listeners to follow the sentence.

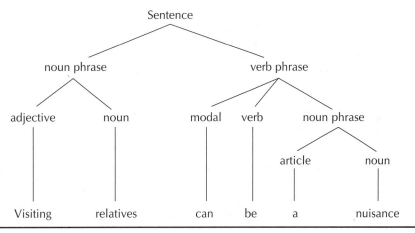

Figure 9.3   Tree structure of the sentence, "Visiting relatives can be a nuisance."

Transformations

How can one show the difference in meaning for the two readings of sentence 3? Figure 9.4 gives us a rough representation of the two readings. Both representations suggest that sentence 3 contains an unstated someone whose role is crucial to determining the intended meaning. One could think of an underlying word string like that shown in Figure 9.4 as providing the alternative meanings. Chomsky referred to this underlying structure as the **deep structure.** His idea was that different transformations are applied to deep structures to convert them into the sentences that get spoken or written. These spoken or written sentences are called the **surface structure.** These transformations differ as a function of whether the speaker wishes to make an assertion, ask a question, and so on.

An example of a transformation from deep structure to surface structure is *wh*-question formation. A *wh*-question is one that asks *who, where, which, why, what,* or *how* (*how* is included even though it does not start with *wh*). According to a transformational analysis, one formulates a question by moving a constituent from its normal "deep structure" syntactic position to the sentence-initial position; this movement is the transformation. In this analysis, when a question word appears at the beginning of a sentence, there is a gap or missing constituent within the sentence. Thus, if one converts sentence 15 to the question, "What did the woman win?" there is a gap corresponding to the object of the verb after the word *win.* You might wonder what evidence would support such a claim. The answer is that this analysis predicts that certain word strings should be judged to be ungrammatical. Specifically, filling the gap while retaining the question form should yield an ungrammatical sentence. It does, as the following example shows:

21. *What did the woman win the marathon?

(a)

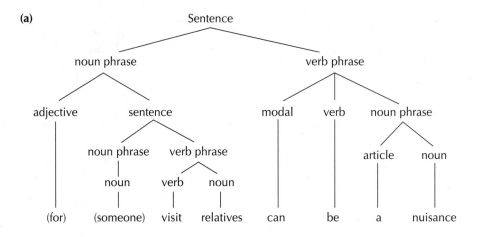

(b)

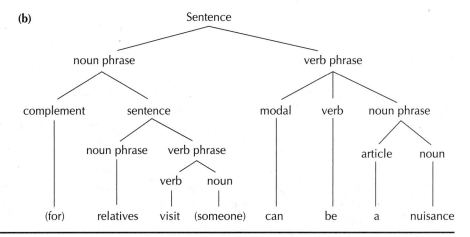

Figure 9.4   Two readings of the sentence "Visiting relatives can be a nuisance." In (a) doing the visiting is problematic whereas in (b) being visited is.

Our description of syntax in general and transformations in particular is vastly oversimplified. Some of the strongest evidence for rules comes from intuitions and evidence concerning the order in which rules apply, as in the joint application of case (e.g., *he* versus *him*) and questions. Overall, there is excellent psychological evidence for the distinction between surface and deep structure (Fodor, Bever, & Garrett, 1974).

More recently, transformational grammar theory has been substantially altered. One major trend has been to assign more structure or information about roles to individual lexical items (words). For instance, it is assumed that part of the semantic function of verbs is to include information about whether they take a direct or indirect object (e.g., *solved* requires an object). The net effect of assigning more structure or information to the *lexicon* (mental dictionary) is that the syntactic rules can involve less structure and consequently can be simplified. In fact, a prominent model of syntax, Chomsky's (1981, 1988) **government and binding theory,** has only one transformation. One of the goals of Chomsky's theory is to reduce differences between languages to differences in a small number of aspects or *parameters,* for which there are only a small number of alternative values. In this conceptualization, the problem of language acquisition (more properly, acquiring syntax) reduces to discovering the parameter settings that distinguish one language from another.

We are unable to go into the complexities of government and binding theory or any of its main alternatives (Bresnan, 1978; Gadzar, Klein, Pullum, & Sag, 1985; see Wasow, 1989, for a review; and Pinker, 1994, for a very readable description of Chomsky's theory). As we shall see in the next section of this chapter, there is good psychological support for the idea of transformation, and we now discuss some of this evidence.

The Psychological Reality of Syntax

A variety of evidence has been collected that bears on theories of syntax. For example, there is evidence for the psychological reality of grammatical categories like noun and verb. One piece of evidence comes from a clever study by Kim, Pinker, Prince, and Prasada (1991). The study looked at how people create past tense forms of verbs that are derived from nouns. For most verbs, creating the past tense in English requires adding the *-ed* suffix (e.g., "John kissed Janet."). Some verbs are *irregular,* and are given their past tense form in a different way (e.g., "The Titanic sank into the ocean."). Kim et al. looked at verbs that came from nouns, but sounded like verbs that already exist (and have an irregular past tense ending). For example, consider:

> When guests come, I hide the dirty dishes by putting them in boxes or in an empty sink.

> Bob and Margaret were early so I quickly boxed the dishes and (sinked/sank) the glasses.

People typically preferred the first option (sinked) as a completion to this sentence, even though the past tense has to be transformed from a verb that is normally associated with an irregular ending. Kim et al. suggest people recognize that this verb is derived from a noun, and so they will not use the irregular ending.

Other evidence focuses on the reality of rules that break sentences into smaller components. Consider, for example, an experiment by Caplan (1972). In his studies, people read sentences and then were presented with a word. Their task was to indicate whether the probe word had appeared in the sentence. Caplan carefully constructed pairs of sentences that had the same word at equal distance from the end of the sentence, but in one case the word fell before a clause boundary and in the other case the critical word fell after a clause boundary. For example, consider the following pair of sentences Caplan used:

a. Now that the artists are working in oil, prints are rare.

b. Now that the artists are working fewer hours, oil prints are rare.

The critical probe word is *oil,* and one may see that the words following *oil* are the same. (In fact, in one of his studies, the sentences were tape recorded, and Caplan spliced the end of the b. sentences into the a. sentences so that the auditory input was identical.) In sentence a, *oil* appears as part of the first clause, whereas in the second it appears in the final clause. If clauses are a natural unit of processing, then one might expect that reaction times to say that *oil* was in the sentence should be slower for the first sentence than for the second sentence. And this is what Caplan found. These data cannot be explained in terms of word order or position per se; instead, one needs to appeal to syntactic structures such as phrases.

Summary

Another way that languages permit an unbounded number of thoughts to be expressed is by having rules that govern the way words are combined to form sentences. This syntactic structure allows words to be combined in novel ways to express new thoughts. Current approaches to syntax assume that people have some deep structure they want to express. This deep structure is transformed using syntactic rules into a surface structure which can then be spoken or written. There is now considerable psychological evidence that this view of syntax is a reasonable way to characterize human language.

UNDERSTANDING LANGUAGE

The structural principles of language ought to have quite a bit to do with how we generate and understand sentences. In producing sentences, people presumably map from their intended underlying meaning onto some surface structure that is uttered or written as a string of words. In understanding sentences, the process is reversed; that is, listeners or readers must be able to break a string of words into appropriate chunks and apply rules and strategies to try to derive the appropriate meaning. The fact that we normally have little difficulty understanding sentences conceals the considerable underlying complexity of sentence comprehension. Let's take a closer look.

First of all, it seems clear that we try to understand sentences "on-line" as we hear or read them; that is, we do not wait until the end of a sentence, encode that sentence as a single chunk, and then send the sentence off to some pattern recognition device or sentence analyzer. Rather, comprehension processes start with the first word and (for English sentences) continue. Presumably our language comprehension device (we'll abbreviate it as LCD) looks up the meaning of the first word of the sentence in the mental dictionary or lexicon and attempts to determine the role it plays in the sentence. For example, the word *the* is an article or determiner that suggests the presence of a noun phrase and allows one to predict that the next word is likely to be an adjective or noun rather than a verb.

Suppose that *the* is followed by *bank*. The LCD would identify *bank* as a noun but would face difficulty determining whether the correct meaning involved a financial institution, a piggybank, or the border of a river. Presumably the ambiguity will be resolved later in the sentence, but the LCD must either select a meaning and backtrack if it is wrong or keep each of the candidate meanings active as possibilities. If the next word is an auxiliary such as *is* or *was*, the LCD should determine that the first two words, *the bank*, represent a noun phrase and that a verb phrase is beginning. If the fourth word is *overflowing*, the LCD is justified in believing that *bank* refers to riverbank, but the LCD must also be able to deal with sentences like:

22. The bank is overflowing with customers.

In certain respects, sentence comprehension is like the game charades, in which one person acts out an intended meaning and the others try to determine it from nonverbal clues. Because meaning can be only indirectly conveyed through signs or symbols, the LCD must make its guesses from the clues left by the speaker or writer in generating strings of words from an underlying intended meaning.

The LCD presumably uses both syntactic and semantic (meaning) information. For example, we can understand a sentence like "watered girl flowers" even though the word order is ungrammatical. Or consider the following sentence:

23. John wrote letters to the customers on his list.

Presumably the LCD does not understand this sentence as meaning that there are a group of customers who are literally standing on a (necessarily) large list owned by John. Instead, it ought to assume that the list contains names of customers. The correct interpretation depends on world knowledge about customers and lists. If we substitute the word *island* for *list*, a different reading is appropriate. The point is that syntax alone cannot determine the interpretation of a sentence. Thus, people must be able to bring real-world knowledge to bear when understanding sentences.

Heuristics and Strategies

As we have been emphasizing throughout this book, one way to understand how a system works is to try to identify constraints or strategies that make some tasks easy and natural and others difficult and unnatural. Language researchers have followed this approach in their efforts to understand how the LCD works.

There is evidence, for example, that the LCD is biased to expect active rather than passive sentences. For example, Slobin (1966) gave children and adults active sentences like "The dog is chasing the cat" or passive sentences like "The cat is chased by the dog" and then immediately showed one of two pictures—in this instance, a dog chasing a cat or a cat chasing a dog. The task was to decide whether the sentence described the action. Both adults and children were faster with active sentences than with passive sentences. This suggests that the LCD assumes that the first noun refers to the actor and that it needs to revise this hypothesis when it meets a passive sentence.

AN ENIGMA
Questions, Answers, and Self-Fulfilling Prophecies

An interesting facet of verb meaning is that verbs carry information about who or what caused an event to happen. For verbs that describe actions (such as *hit,* or *poke*), the subject is typically seen as causing the situation. For example, in the sentence "Mary poked Sam," Mary (rather than Sam) is assumed to have caused the poking. In contrast, for verbs that describe states (such as *like* or *revere*), the object is seen as causing the situation. For example, in the sentence "Mary likes Sam," it is assumed that some quality of Sam caused Mary to like him (see Au, 1986, for an extensive discussion of this issue).

While these inferences of what caused a situation are quite robust, people are typically unaware that they come from the way that a sentence is stated. This tacit inference of causality can have a significant impact on situations in which a person must determine the cause of an ambiguous situation.

As one example, Semin and DePoot (1997a, 1997b) have explored a variant of the *self-fulfilling prophecy* (Merton, 1948). A self-fulfilling prophecy occurs when people's beliefs about what will happen in the future lead them to take actions that ultimately cause that future event to take place. In this study, people played the role of an investigator in a rape case who was about to question the victim. The participants were given choices of questions to ask the victim. Before starting this mock interview, some participants were given information that predisposed them to think that the victim was telling the truth and that the alleged assailant was guilty. Others were given information that predisposed them to think that the victim was untrustworthy and that the alleged assailant was not likely to have committed the crime.

(Continued)

Sentences that lack the clues that help the LCD should be harder than average to understand, and sentences that remove ambiguous cues should be easier to understand. Consider the following two sentences:

24. John went to school and he played tennis.

25. The princess kissed the frog whom the king knighted.

Sentence 24 would be easier to understand if *he* were omitted because the LCD must consider the possibility that *he* refers to someone other than John. Sentence 25 becomes more difficult when *whom,* which is a clue to a second proposition, is removed:

AN ENIGMA

Questions, Answers, and Self-Fulfilling Prophecies *(Continued)*

In this case, it would be a self-fulfilling prophecy if this initial belief caused them to ask questions in a way that helped confirm their initial belief. That is what happened. People predisposed to think the victim was telling the truth preferred questions in which the assailant was the subject of action verbs (e.g., "Did Peter dance with you?"), and thus the assailant would be the implicit causer of the actions. People predisposed to think the victim was untrustworthy preferred questions in which the victim was the subject of the action verbs (e.g., "Did you dance with Peter?"), and thus the victim would be the implicit causer of the actions. Regardless of which version of the question was selected, the answer given was the same (e.g., "Yes."). In the end, participants generally concluded that the interview supported their initial belief.

This result is a self-fulfilling prophecy, because when the alleged assailant is the subject of the question, the answer is likely to be taken as evidence that he was in fact guilty (even by a third party listening to the question). In contrast, when the victim is the subject of the question, the answer is likely to be taken as evidence that the alleged assailant is not guilty (even by a third party). Thus, the phrasing of the question helps determine how the answer to that question will be interpreted.

This effect is particularly striking because of its subtlety. People who ask questions typically are not aware that they select verbs in a way that is influenced by their prior beliefs. Thus, when they receive responses that appear to confirm their beliefs, they interpret these responses as independent evidence for their belief, even though this interpretation was caused by the way they asked the question. These results have important implications for interrogation and examination in legal settings.

26. The princess kissed the frog the king knighted.

These conjectures have been confirmed in comprehension tests with adult subjects (see, e.g., Bever, 1970; Wanner & Maratsos, 1978).

Minimal Attachment

An important aspect of understanding a new sentence is parsing it. Parsing involves determining the grammatical form of the sentence. In Figures 9.2 and 9.3, we

(a)

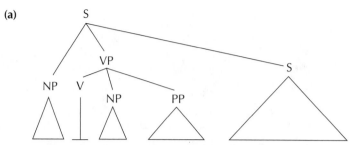

The spy saw the cop with binoculars but the cop didn't see him.

(b)

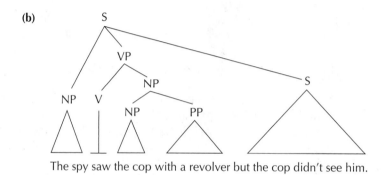

The spy saw the cop with a revolver but the cop didn't see him.

Figure 9.5   Minimal (a) and nonminimal (b) attachments for propositional phrases. In (a) the spy has the binoculars, and in (b) the cop has the revolver.

Source: Rayner, Carlson, & Frazier, 1983.

showed the structure of some English sentences. These graphs are often called *parse trees*. The trees have *nodes* in them that correspond to words or syntactic categories like verb phrase (VP) or noun phrase (NP). How are these trees constructed during language comprehension?

The idea underlying parsing is that the language comprehension system must be able to take a sentence and determine the correct parse tree for that sentence. By breaking the sentence down into its syntactic components, it is then possible to construct a meaning for the sentence. Strategies for parsing sentences must take into account the fact that sentences are heard and read one word at a time, and that language comprehension begins as soon as the first word is presented.

One strategy for comprehending sentences, called **minimal attachment,** begins by making a guess about the right parse tree for the first few words of the sentence. Then, this process attempts to attach each new word or phrase to an existing node in the current parse tree wherever possible (see Frazier, 1979). This abstract description can be clarified by a concrete example. Figure 9.5 illustrates two sentences, only one of which allows for minimal attachment. Let's start with the first sentence at the point where the words *with binoculars* are presented. At this point, the LCD assumes the sentence begins with the noun phrase *The spy*. Then, a verb phrase begins that encompasses the verb (*saw*) and a noun phrase denoting the object of the verb (*the cop*). When *with binoculars* is presented, minimal attachment suggests that this phrase should also modify the verb phrase. As it turns out, this choice makes sense, because *with binoculars* specifies the manner in which the action (seeing) took place.

In contrast, the second sentence cannot be understood using minimal attachment. In this sentence, the words *with a revolver* appear instead of *with binoculars*. Using minimal attachment, we could try to attach *with a revolver* to the verb phrase as we did in the previous sentence. However, the spy probably did not use a revolver to see the cop, and so this way of parsing the sentence does not make sense. Instead, as shown in Figure 9.5b, the phrase *with a revolver* is best seen as describing *the cop,* and so the parser needs to create a new noun phrase (NP) node that indicates that *the cop with the revolver* is the object of the verb.

This analysis suggests that the second sentence should be more difficult to parse in the *binocular-revolver* area than the first because of the initial bias simply to attach the prepositional phrase to the verb phrase. Rayner, Carlson, and Frazier (1983) recorded eye movements of people while they read sentences like these. Reading times proved to be longer in the *revolver-binocular* area for the sentence in which the correct interpretation violated minimal attachment (as the second sentence does). The Rayner et al. results are therefore consistent with the idea that the LCD follows the minimal attachment strategy. (The robustness of this effect is uncertain. See, for example, Osterhout & Swinney, 1993, for data that fail to support minimal attachment.)

Garden path sentences are another important phenomenon that give us insight into the parsing device. A garden path sentence is one that starts out as if it will have one syntactic structure, but then turns out to have a second. Consider a sentence like the well-known example:

27. The horse raced past the barn fell.

This garden path sentence seems to throw off the LCD totally when it arrives at the word *fell.* The sentence seems ungrammatical because the LCD has initially taken *raced* to be the main verb. The correct interpretation, though, is that the horse that was raced past the barn fell down. The observation that the LCD is fooled by garden path sentences reinforces the idea that sentence processing is incremental and that the LCD makes certain commitments that it sometimes has to retract later. Keep in mind, however, that garden path sentences are fairly rare and that the LCD makes the right guesses most of the time (see Garnsey, Pearlmutter, Myers, & Lotocky, 1997; and Trueswell & Kim, 1998, for insights into how garden path sentences are processed).

To summarize, it is important to recognize that language comprehension takes place over time. That is, a complete sentence is not presented all at once where it can be analyzed for its syntactic structure. Instead, sentences are encountered one word at a time (either through reading or through hearing). Because there are often many possible syntactic structures consistent with the fragment of the sentence encountered so far, the LCD uses heuristics to determine which syntactic structure is most likely to be the correct one. In cases like garden path sentences, these initial guesses are incorrect, and the sentence must be parsed again. Thus, garden path sentences are a valuable tool for learning about the heuristics used by the LCD.

TEXT COMPREHENSION

In the previous sections of this chapter, we have discussed some of the key components of language, including phonology, and syntax. As we discussed at the beginning of the chapter, however, language is used to communicate. Thus, we must now begin to put the components of language together to understand how a thought transmitted from one person can be comprehended by another. Many psychologists interested in comprehension have focused on text comprehension. Text comprehension is explored, because the same text can be presented to many different individuals. In contrast, it is difficult to create precisely the same conversational situation across people. In addition, by using text, there are a number of aspects of natural speech, such as gestures and intonation patterns that do not have to be considered.

Let us begin with a simple case. Suppose you wanted to build a computer program that would translate a sentence in Russian into English. What would you do? This question was addressed by a number of research projects in the early 1960s, when the United States government hoped that computers would help them better understand what the Soviets were thinking. One answer, which seemed promising, was to access the definition of every Russian word in a sentence and then translate the words into their best English match. This system, though it may sound simple, requires a great deal of work to try to get the right meanings of words and the right grammatical constraints. To test this idea and evaluate the output, the researchers had English sentences translated into Russian and then translated back into English. An often-quoted illustration of the inherent problems in such a task is the following: "The spirit is willing but the flesh is weak" was translated into Russian and then translated back into English as "The vodka is good but the meat is rotten." Most readers would agree that it does not capture the meaning of the original sentence, which leads to the question: What *is* the meaning?

The meaning of a sentence is not simply a combination of the definitions of the words. To begin with, many words have multiple meanings, so at the very least the meaning of a sentence includes some decisions about the appropriate meaning of the words. For example, "Mary went to the ball" could mean that Mary walked over to retrieve some playing ball, but when read in isolation it is usually interpreted to mean that Mary attended a formal dance.

The active nature of understanding even a simple sentence involves much more than resolving the ambiguity of words with multiple meanings. Our understanding includes many inferences that go beyond the information given. For example, suppose you were asked the meaning of "Mary kicked the ball." Here there is little doubt that the intended meaning of ball is the spherical object, and certainly most readers would understand this sentence to mean that some female had used a fast movement of her foot to propel a spherical object. But understanding goes beyond these observations. Readers would be quite surprised to learn that the ball was twice the size of Mary. Thus, understanding the sentence seems to have included an inference about the ball's size (though one should be careful about using intuition in the absence of empirical support). For example, it might have involved forming a mental image of the event (Glenberg, Kruley, & Langston, 1994). Why might this be so?

It is always possible to suggest an alternative explanation of a single example. Perhaps the meaning of ball includes information about its usual size. However, consider the following sentences, focusing on the word *caught*.

a. The python caught the mouse.

b. John caught the mouse.

Note that the sense of *caught* and the inferences about how the catching was done change in these two sentences. Although it is natural to assume that the python caught the mouse in its mouth, the same inference is very unlikely for John! We might also assume that the python intends to eat the mouse but John does not. (Brewer, 1977, shows that people often misremember the python sentence as having included eating.) Thus, the inferences made about the word *caught* do not depend simply on its meaning (as the alternative explanation for the earlier example proposed) but upon what it is that is doing the catching. In addition, the meaning of caught changes again when sentence b is changed to:

c. John caught the ball.

Now, the physical actions involved in catching are quite different (although most readers would still not make the inference that catching led to eating).

What does all this show? The basic point is that one cannot view understanding as some passive process in which the presented information is taken in and understood. Repeatedly throughout this book, we have seen that people must go beyond the information given in order to understand a situation. In the case of text comprehension, we are trying to understand complex events, texts, arguments, and so on that consist of many simple events, sentences, and utterances. However, it would be inefficient if every aspect of every event had to be described in painstaking detail. Instead, we are able to draw inferences from what is said to fill in details about what is not stated directly.

How can one tell when an inference is drawn? Gail McKoon and Roger Ratcliff have employed a variety of techniques (or converging operations) that generally agree with each other with respect to conclusions about when different inferences are made. One technique is to present a paragraph for comprehension and then give a speeded word recognition test in which the task is to indicate as quickly as possible whether a word appeared in the paragraph. If a word has been inferred, people should be slower to indicate that it did not appear in the paragraph. For example, participants might be given the sentence "The director and the cameraman were ready to shoot close-ups when suddenly the actress fell from the fourteenth story" and then probed with the word *dead*. A control sentence might use many of the same words but not include death as a predictable inference. For the preceding sentence, a control sentence might be "Suddenly the director fell upon the cameraman, demanding

A DEBATE
Inference During Comprehension

Just which kinds of inferences are drawn during reasoning and when these inferences are drawn are a topic that has been studied systematically. Pure forward chaining or backward chaining systems are each impractical. If we made every possible inference at the time a sentence was presented (pure forward chaining), comprehension would be unacceptably slow. If we made no inferences at the time a sentence was presented (pure backward chaining), then we would end up paying the price later when inferences were required to integrate new information that is presented. Instead, people seem to use a combination of forward and backward chaining inference. Thus, research has focused on which inferences get made immediately (forward chaining) and which are made only later (backward chaining).

Graesser, Millis, and Zwaan (1997) suggest that there are five general kinds of inferences people might make when comprehending a sentence: (1) general motives, (2) specific actions required to satisfy a goal, (3) reasons why something occurred, (4) consequences of an action, and (5) properties of objects or events. They suggest that different theories of inference differ in which types of inferences are likely to be made. McKoon and Ratcliff (1992) promote a minimal inference hypothesis in which the

(Continued)

close-ups of the actress on the fourteenth floor." Using these materials and others like them, McKoon and Ratcliff (1986) found evidence that these predictable but not explicitly described events are encoded into memory only minimally. Responses to probes like "dead" were slow only on an immediate test, as if the inference had been only partially activated or considered only briefly. McKoon and Ratcliff suggest that the sort of minimal coding that took place would be roughly that "something bad" happened. (We know from other experiments by McKoon and Ratcliff that their procedures are sensitive enough to detect the influence of inferences when they are drawn.) It makes sense for an inference system to be somewhat conservative about its guesses because otherwise we might often be forced to retract inferences. For example, the next sentence in the story involving the actress might have been "Miraculously, an awning broke her fall and she survived."

So far, we have considered only half of the inference and prediction problem. A simple sentence like "John caught the mouse" is consistent with any number of inferences. Without some control over which inferences are and are not made, a

A DEBATE

Inference During Comprehension *(Continued)*

only inferences that are made at the time a sentence is presented are those required in order to make sense of the discourse, as well as those that are easily accessible at the time the sentence is presented. On this view, the reasons why something occurred (number 3 from the list above) are most likely to be generated.

Graesser, Singer, and Trabasso (1994) favor a constructionist view of inference in which comprehension involves understanding why events occur. Like the minimalist hypothesis, this view assumes that reasons for actions (3) will be inferred. However, it further suggests that general motives (1) are likely to be inferred. In addition, the consequences of actions (4) are sometimes inferred, but only when the consequence involves the satisfaction of some general goal of a character (i.e., when the consequence is related to one of the character's motives).

At present, the debate over which types of inferences are made has not been resolved. The answer to this question is important, however. Research on artificial intelligence has often stumbled, because it is not clear how to integrate new information with background knowledge. If we understood more about what kinds of inferences people make immediately and what kinds of inferences are made only when needed, it would be a great benefit in the development of intelligent computer systems.

single sentence could leave us lost in thought for days (some early artificial intelligence systems that generated inferences were susceptible to this problem). There are two general strategies for making inferences. The first, called *forward chaining* inference involves a process like the one we have been discussing where inferences are drawn at the time that the sentence is read. This process has the advantage that the inferences will be available immediately later, but the disadvantage that the language comprehension device may require a long time to process the inferences at the time the sentence is read. An alternative strategy is called *backward chaining* inference. This strategy involves doing very little work at the time the sentence is presented, and then drawing inferences when more information is needed later. This strategy has the advantage of requiring little effort at the time the sentence is presented, but the disadvantage that substantial time may be required later when new sentences have been presented. The relative use of forward and backward chaining inference in comprehension has been of considerable interest, and is discussed in the A Debate box.

In summary, text comprehension involves more than just determining the meaning of individual sentences. People coordinate the information presented directly in language with their background knowledge in order to understand the meaning of what is said. This coordination involves sophisticated inference processes that act during comprehension to go beyond the information given.

THE BRAIN AND LANGUAGE

It has long been known that certain areas of the brain are extraordinarily important for the processing of language. Damage to these areas can lead to aphasia, a disorder in which language processing is disrupted. In the early 19th century, neurologists like Franz Joseph Gall were suggesting that the brain was not uniform, but rather that specific areas had specific functions. At around this time, Jean-Baptiste Bouillard published a report on selective loss of speech functions with brain damage. In the late 19th century, the neurologist Paul Broca made a similar observation, and he further claimed that the left hemisphere (i.e., side) of the brain was specialized for language. To complete this historical overview, another 19th century neurologist Carl Wernicke distinguished between two different kinds of aphasia, which he called motor and sensory aphasia and suggested possible brain regions associated with them. A more detailed historical overview is presented by Benson and Ardila (1996).

Much evidence on the relationship between language and the brain has come from studies of patients with lesions (i.e., damaged areas) caused by strokes, accidents, or gunshots. It is generally agreed that, for most people, language processing is associated with the left hemisphere of the brain. Damage to the lower parts of the frontal lobe of the left hemisphere (called Broca's area, see Figure 9.6) often leads to impairments in language production. The speech of Broca's aphasics is slow and

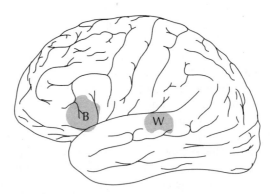

Figure 9.6   Side view of the left hemisphere of the brain indicating Broca's (B) and Wernicke's (W) areas.

Source: Goodglass & Geschwind, 1976.

halting, and grammatical function words, like *be, of,* and *the,* are frequently omitted. For this reason, Broca's aphasics are often said to have telegraphic speech. **Broca's aphasia** is also associated with comprehension problems for sentences whose meaning cannot be deduced from the content words and therefore require grammatical analysis. For this reason, Broca's aphasia has sometimes been considered a breakdown in the grammar system.

In contrast, damage to a region of the brain called Wernicke's area (see Figure 9.6) produces a strikingly different syndrome. Consider the following example taken from Goodglass and Geschwind (1976). The patient is asked to describe a scene where two children are stealing cookies while the mother's back is turned:

> Well this is . . . mother is away here working her work out o'here to get her better, but when she's looking, the two boys looking in the other part. One their small tile into her time here. She's working another time because she's getting, too. . . .

Patients with **Wernicke's aphasia** speak fluently and grammatically, but what they say makes little sense. Their speech is filled with neologisms (made-up words) and word substitutions. In addition, they have difficulty in naming objects (unlike Broca's patients) and in comprehending speech (Gardner, 1974).

The exact functions of Broca's and Wernicke's areas remain unclear, and brain damage to nearby areas produces a variety of other impairments that researchers are trying to understand (see Benson & Ardila, 1996; Pinker, 1994; Zurif, 1990, for discussions). In each case, general intelligence seems fairly well preserved. An interesting hypothesis about the difference between Broca's and Wernicke's aphasia was put forward by Blumstein (1997). She suggests that Broca's and Wernicke's aphasics differ not in the relative sparing of the grammar system, but rather in the degree to which words in the mental lexicon (i.e., the mental dictionary) are able to be activated: for Broca's aphasics, words in the mental lexicon are not strongly activated, while for Wernicke's aphasics the activation is so strong that related words are often mistakenly activated as well. In part, the evidence for this position comes from studies of lexical priming. A well-known finding (discussed in Chapter 6) is that normal people are faster to state that a string of letters is a word (i.e., to perform a lexical decision) when the string is preceded by a semantically similar word (i.e., they are faster to respond to DOCTOR when it is preceded by NURSE) than when it is preceded by a string of asterisks (Meyer & Schvanevelt, 1971). Broca's aphasics, who can answer correctly that the words *doctor* and *nurse* are semantically related, do not show this facilitation. In contrast, Wernicke's aphasics, who cannot correctly answer that the words *doctor* and *nurse* are semantically related, do show this facilitation. This suggests that the difference between these syndromes may reflect differences in activity in the mental lexicon rather than differences in preservation of the grammar system.

Finally, studies of the brain and language suggest that language is not simply a component of general intelligence. In particular, in a rare form of mental retardation called **Williams syndrome,** general cognitive abilities are severely impaired, but language ability is relatively preserved. The syndrome is associated with a defective gene that is involved in the regulation of calcium and affects brain development.

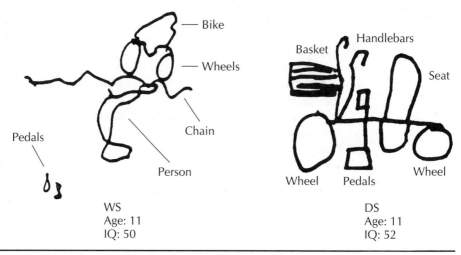

WS
Age: 11
IQ: 50

DS
Age: 11
IQ: 52

Figure 9.7   Drawing of a bicycle by a child with Williams syndrome (left side). For purposes of comparison, the drawing on the right is by a child with another form of mental retardation, Down's syndrome. The latter group does not display the language sophistication seen in Williams syndrome children.

Source: Bellugi, Bihrle, Jernigan, Trauner, & Doherty, 1990.

Children with Williams syndrome are severely retarded and not competent at a variety of ordinary tasks like drawing and addition (Figure 9.7). These same children are excellent grammarians. They speak and understand complex sentences and show normal levels of grammatical development. Oddly, they seem to have a penchant for unusual words. For example, Susan Carey (personal communication, October 1995) described a child with Williams syndrome who had a great interest in but little conceptual understanding of vampires. When Carey asked the child *why* vampires bite people's necks, the child replied "Well, you see, vampires have an inordinate fondness for necks." Asked to name animals, children with Williams syndrome might cite the vulture, unicorn, and koala rather than the usual dog, cat, and cow (Bellugi, Bihrle, Jernigan, Trauner, & Doherty, 1991).

This section provides a cursory review of research on the relationship between language and the brain. Most of the research described here has focused on studies of patients with particular forms of brain damage. There has not yet been extensive research on language and the brain in normal people using neuroimaging techniques, largely because it is difficult to develop the appropriate methodologies. With the extensive development of new brain-imaging methods, however, additional data on brain function in language processing is beginning to become available.

Summary

At the risk of being overly repetitive, the core aspect of language is that it allows people to communicate about a seemingly limitless range of topics. The difficulty in determining how language works is that we must explore a range of different levels of analysis. At one extreme, we need to understand the phonological rules that govern how speech sounds combine to form words. At the other extreme, we need to understand the social conventions people use to put together their utterances (such as the Gricean rules) that provide expectations about what will be stated. In between, we need to determine the nature of the syntax that allows words to be combined into sentences, as well as the complex machinations of the language comprehension device that permits sentences to be parsed and inferences to be drawn that go beyond the specific information stated in a sentence.

At the heart of all of these aspects of language is productivity. Each level at which languages can be analyzed reveals rules that permit that level to handle an incredible amount of information with a limited number of constituents. A small number of speech sounds can be used to form thousands of words. These words can be combined through syntax to form an infinite number of sentences. Sentences are coordinated with background knowledge to create rich representations of situations. Finally, participants in a conversation can coordinate their conversation in order to ensure that their representations of the current situation are sufficiently alike to allow the conversation to continue.

A spirit of excitement pervades the study of language. The more we look at phonology or syntax, the greater is our appreciation of the subtle complexities. Our experience is somewhat akin to that of a biology student taking a first look at a drop of water under a microscope. In both cases, the closer view reveals teeming life and structures that otherwise would be outside our awareness.

Key Terms

auditory theory	morpheme
Broca's aphasia	phoneme
categorical perception	phonology
coarticulation	phrase structure
conversational maxims	pragmatics
deep structure	semantics
garden path sentence	surface structure
given-new strategy	syntax
government and binding theory	transformational grammar
Gricean maxims	voice onset time
joint action	Wernicke's aphasia
McGurk effect	Williams syndrome
minimal attachment	
motor theory	

Recommended Readings

Clark (1996) provides an excellent introduction to the use of language for communication, and the chapters in the edited volume by Fussell and Kreuz (1998) are also useful. Chomsky and Halle's (1991) classic book is still an excellent source for understanding the sound patterns of language, and Levelt (1991) provides a fascinating overview of research on speech. Fodor, Bever, and Garrett's book (1974) is an excellent source for the study of language, especially with respect to syntactic processing. The collection of chapters on language in the book edited by Osherson and Lasnik (1990) provides a more recent review. Jackendoff's (1994) book offers a nice overview of phonology, syntax, and brain-language relationships. Hauser (1996) gives a detailed treatment of the evolution of communication systems. Benson and Ardila (1996) describe a variety of language disorders caused by brain damage, and current issues of the journal *Brain and Language* are an excellent source for ongoing research on aphasia.

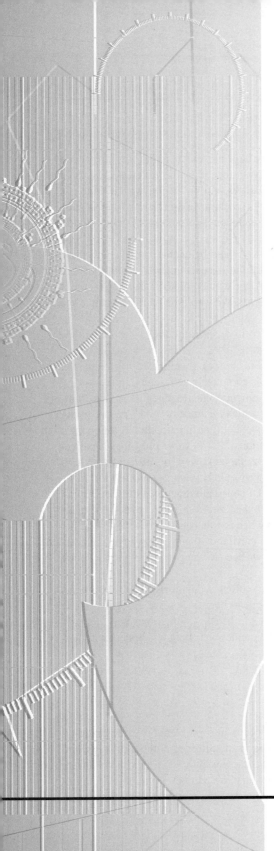

Chapter 10

Concepts and Categories:
Representation and Use

Introduction
Why Categorize?
Computational Complexity
Functions of Concepts
Concepts and Misconceptions
Summary

Structure of Natural Object Categories
The Classical View
The Probabilistic View
Between-Category Structure
Does Similarity Explain Categorization?
Concepts as Organized by Theories
Putting Similarity in Its Place
Are There Kinds of Categories?
Summary

Use of Categories in Reasoning
Goals and Ad Hoc Categories
Conceptual Combination
Categories and Induction

Summary

Key Terms

Recommended Readings

*Mind and world in short have evolved together,
and in consequence are something of a mutual fit.*
—William James

INTRODUCTION

Why Categorize?

A basic cognitive function is to categorize. We have names for groups of things such as dogs, cats, cars, computers, birds, birthdays, and balloons. Likewise, we have names for properties (tall, tepid, tense) as well as actions (walk, waver, wallow). Furthermore, we can combine single words to create an unlimited number of new categories, like green-garbed grumpy golfers and camel-carted carpets. But why do we need categories?

The answer is that without categories we would be unable to make any sense of our experience or to profit from it. If each thing we encountered was unique and totally unlike anything else we had ever known, we would not know how to react to it or make any useful predictions about its properties. We would be literally lost in a sea of new experiences, helpless to employ any of our prior knowledge to navigate it. Imagine a clinical psychologist unwilling to form or use any diagnostic categories, who argues that every individual is unique and requires a totally individualized plan of treatment. The concept of unique treatments for every individual seems reasonable, even commendable, but when implemented it is completely self-defeating. Following Kendall (1975), suppose we have available treatment A and treatment B (and presumably more). What is our rationale for selecting which treatment to give? We are trying to predict which treatment will be more effective, but if each individual is unique, we have no basis whatsoever for making predictions! If we knew only that a patient seemed to be more similar to people who had responded well to treatment A than to those who had responded well to treatment B, we would have some rationale for thinking that treatment A would be more effective. Of course, to draw on our experience in this way is to categorize. Even before medicine had any sort of effective set of treatments, a major conceptual advance was made when people began to reject the idea that every instance of illness was unique. It seems inevitable, then, that to have any basis for providing (and even tailoring) a treatment, we need to categorize, even if we do not necessarily use formal diagnostic categories.

The need to categorize is not specific to clinical diagnosis but rather applies wherever relevant knowledge might be brought to bear. When we recognize some entity as a dog, our knowledge about dogs (e.g., that they sometimes bark, usually like to be petted, and so on) allows us to make predictions about and understand their actions. Categorization is pervasive.

Computational Complexity

It is easy to show that categorization quickly runs into problems of computational complexity. That is, we could categorize things in an unlimited number of ways, and we necessarily employ a minuscule subset of these possibilities. Suppose we have a set of n things (where n stands for some number). We can determine that the number of ways of assigning those things to categories increases very rapidly with n.

With two objects a and b, we can set up two categorization schemes: (a) (b) and (ab), where the parentheses define category boundaries. If we double the number of objects, we can have 15 distinct category structures: (a)(b)(c)(d), (ab)(c)(d), (a)(bc)(d), (a)(b)(cd), (ac)(b)(d), (ad)(b)(c), (a)(bd)(c), (abc)(d), (a)(bcd), (acd)(b), (abd)(c), (ab)(cd), (ad)(bc), (ac)(bd), and (abcd). By the time we get up to 10 objects, there are more than 100,000 possibilities!

The fact that there are so many possibilities makes it natural to ask why we have the categories we have rather than others. One possible answer is that our categories mirror the structure of the world. Perhaps the world comes organized into natural "clusters," and our concepts mirror those natural groupings or categories. An alternative possibility is that we have the categories we have because we are the sort of creatures we are. Another way of putting it is that the categories we have represent a solution for a set of problems (e.g., coping with ignorance, making predictions) and that perhaps we can better understand human concepts by asking what problems they address and what functions they serve (see Malt, 1995, for a cross-cultural perspective on these questions). In the following sections, we will review these functions, describe a body of research on category learning, and then return to the question of why we have the categories we have.

Functions of Concepts

So far, we have described concepts at a relatively informal level. When we try to be more precise, we see that concepts serve a number of distinct roles. In this discussion, we will often mention both *concepts* and *categories*. These terms have sometimes been used interchangeably in the literature on categorization. In this chapter, we use **concept** to refer to a mental representation and **category** to refer to the set of entities or examples picked out by the concept. Some researchers suggest that categories have independent existence in the world (independent of the organisms that conceive of them). We do not endorse this view because we believe that in many cases (if not all) categories are constructed by the human mind as it relates to the world. As we'll see, our categories have to be linked to the world if they are to prove useful.

Classification

A central function of concepts is to allow us to treat discriminably different things as equivalent. We use the word *things* here, because category members may be physical objects, living things, properties, actions, or even abstract ideas such as "democracy." Deciding that two (or more) items are members of the same category is the process of *classification*. As we will see, classification is one of the most widely studied functions of categories in psychology.

Understanding and Explanation

Classification allows intelligent organisms to break apart their experience into meaningful chunks and to construct an interpretation of it. A major facet of this understanding is bringing old knowledge to bear on the current situation. For example, a person on a hike in the mountains who recognizes an animal as a rattlesnake will interpret the situation as dangerous. Concepts also support *explanations;* understanding why a friend reacted to a stick with alarm is explained with the knowledge that he or she initially classified it as a rattlesnake.

Prediction

A key aspect of classification is that it allows one to make *predictions* concerning the future, predictions that can be used to select plans and actions. For example, after we identify an animal as a rattlesnake, we can act to avoid it.

Reasoning

Concepts support *reasoning*. One does not need to store every fact and possibility if inferences can be derived from information that is stored. From the knowledge that all animals breathe, that reptiles are animals, and rattlesnakes are reptiles, one may reason (deductively) that rattlesnakes must also breathe, even though one may never have directly stored that fact. Furthermore, people can combine concepts to describe novel situations and to envision future states of affairs. You probably have never thought about or seen a *paper bee*. We asked a few people about this novel concept, and most of them came up with the idea that a paper bee is a bee made out of paper. Furthermore, everyone who arrives at this interpretation also envisions that such a bee would not be alive and could not breathe. To get an idea of how complex conceptual combination is, try to figure out the concept *paper committee*. Though it was natural to interpret paper bee as a bee *made of* paper, it seems more natural to interpret paper committee as a committee *concerned with* paper (or perhaps one that *exists* on paper, but not in reality) and certainly not one made out of paper.

Communication

To the extent that people share knowledge and index it in terms of the same categories, they will be able to communicate with each other. Communication allows learning on the basis of indirect experience. When an expert tells us to avoid sudden movements in the presence of rattlesnakes, we can follow this advice the very first time we are confronted with a rattlesnake.

Summary

One can readily see that concepts function in multiple ways and are essential to mental life. Understanding, explanation, and prediction are at the core of intelligent behavior. As we shall see, there is also a moral for researchers: the various conceptual functions may interact with and influence each other; for example, the reasoning and communication functions may affect categorization (e.g. Ross, 1997; Markman & Makin, 1998). Before turning to the question of how categories are structured, we focus on an important consequence of categorization.

Concepts and Misconceptions

While categories are clearly crucial for human cognitive activity, our ability to use categories sometimes causes problems. We may form the wrong categories or categories that are too broad for our purposes. Furthermore, the very nature of our categories virtually ensures that important information may be lost or that inappropriate inferences will be made. On the one hand, our categories are a sign that some set of items should be treated equivalently in some way. On the other hand, we cannot treat the items from a common category exactly the same in every way. After all, both pit bulls and poodles are dogs, but one might not want to interact with them identically. Nonetheless, we may end up treating members of a category as being very similar simply because of their common category membership.

As an example, Tajfel and Wilkes (1963) showed people four short lines labeled "A" and four long lines labeled "B" and asked them to estimate the lengths of the lines. A control group was given the same task without the category labels (Figure 10.1). Relative to the control group, people given labels rated the short lines as more similar in length than did people in the control group and they also rated the short lines as more different from the long lines than people in the control group. In other words the labels made the examples within a category more similar and the differences across categories more distinctive.

Consequences of categorization are also evident in the important domain of social categorization. When people are brought into laboratories and divided into groups based on an arbitrary dimension (e.g., whether they overestimated or underestimated the number of dots in a picture), in-group favoritism results. What do we

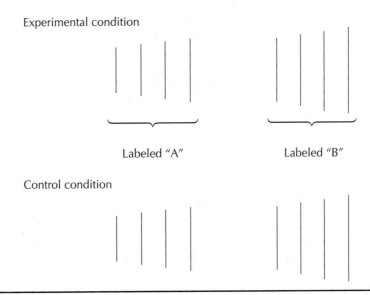

Figure 10.1   Stimuli like those used in the Tajfel and Wilkes (1963) study.

mean by in-group favoritism? It is easiest to answer this by looking at an experiment, such as the one reported by Howard and Rothbart (1980). They created an arbitrary method for dividing people into groups. Howard and Rothbart showed people a page full of dots, and asked them to estimate how many dots were there. Then, they arbitrarily told people that they had overestimated or underestimated the number of dots. Further, they told people that there were groups of people who tended to overestimate and underestimate dots and that these people often had other characteristics in common. Then, each person was told favorable and unfavorable information about members of their group (the *in-group*) and the other group (the *out-group*). Despite the fact that this division into groups was arbitrary, people showed significantly better memory for negative behaviors of the out-group than for negative behaviors of the in-group. Thus, these categories influenced people's perceptions in a way that favored the in-group.

What about more socially relevant categories? Hirschfeld (1994, 1996) has shown that the development of children's understanding of race involves much more than a passive accumulation of information in the environment. Instead, it appears their thinking about race is organized by theories and beliefs about innate potential. For example, in one of his studies, Hirschfeld asked children to judge what the offspring of racially mixed couples would look like. Two groups of children (7- to 8-year-olds and 11- to 12-year-olds) from a suburban middle-class school (where there were few minority children) were shown pictures one at a time of four couples, consisting of a black male and a black female, a white male and a white female, a black male and a white female, or a white male and a black female. Each child then was shown pictures of three infants representing a white infant, a black infant, and an infant intermediate between the white and black infants in terms of skin color, hair color, and hair texture. Finally, each child was asked which of the infants was the child of the couple. The normatively correct answer for the mixed race couple is the infant depicted as intermediate.

All children judged that the black couple would have a black infant and the white couple a white infant. Of greatest interest are the judgments for the racially mixed couples. Younger children showed no clear preference among the three choices. Strikingly, however, older children overwhelmingly chose the black baby for both mixed race pairs. Furthermore, in a comparison condition involving skin and hair color of animals, older children make the normatively correct choice of intermediate color. These results suggest that by early adolescence children have learned the culturally dominant model of social potential—in our culture, children of black-white mixed couples are treated as black. (Regardless of whether one thinks this is sensible, it appears to be a fact.) Interestingly, when Hirschfeld gave the same task to children from an integrated inner-city school, both younger and older children tended to pick the infant depicted as intermediate. This pattern held for both children who identify as white and as black, suggesting that the results are driven by cultural environment rather than the children's racial status per se. In short, race is a salient social category that is susceptible to systematic misperceptions and cultural influences.

The results just described are somewhat sobering and certainly do not leave the impression that categorization is necessarily a good thing. The process of categorization leads only too naturally to stereotypes and misperceptions of other groups (see

Devine, 1989; Tajfel, 1981, for examples). Perhaps knowledge of the fact of the human propensity for forming stereotypes can moderate or weaken our reliance on them. On a more optimistic note, there is evidence that stereotypes may yield to more concrete, specific information. Locksley, Borgida, Brekke, and Hepburn (1980) asked people to rate the assertiveness of target individuals who were described in one of three ways: (1) name only (conveying gender information), (2) name plus a descriptive paragraph irrelevant to assertiveness, or (3) name plus a descriptive paragraph relevant to assertiveness. In the first two conditions, male targets were rated as more assertive than female targets, but in the third females were rated as being as assertive as males; that is, when relevant information was provided, it was used and gender information was not used. In some cases, it seems, stereotypes are treated as default values that are employed only when no other information is available. Of course, what would be most helpful is a general theory about the conditions under which perceivers attend to and process information at the level of individuals versus categories. Both social psychologists and cognitive psychologists are keenly interested in this issue (e.g. Barsalou, Huttenlocher & Lamberts, 1998; Fiske, Neuberg, Beattie, & Milberg, 1987; Fiske, Lin, & Neuberg, 1999).

In short, categorization is necessary for all the reasons listed at the beginning of this chapter. But the benefits of categorization may come at some cost. Specifically, categorizing a set of objects can lead us to treat the members of the category as more similar to each other than they really are. In the case of social categories the result may be stereotyping.

Summary

In this section we noted that it is necessary to categorize in order to access relevant knowledge and make appropriate predictions and inferences. There are virtually an unlimited number of different ways in which we may categorize things and an important question is why we have the categories we have and not other ones. Part of the answer to that question is likely to be based on the different functions that categories serve (i.e. classification, understanding and explanation, prediction, reasoning, and communication). Finally we noted that for all of its benefits, categorization can both exaggerate (between category) differences and inappropriately minimize (within category) differences. We now turn our attention to the structural underpinnings of categories, beginning with natural object categories such as bird, fish, and tree.

STRUCTURE OF NATURAL OBJECT CATEGORIES ⸻

Almost all theories about the structure of categories assume that, roughly speaking, similar things tend to belong to the same category and that dissimilar things tend to be in different categories. For example, robins and sparrows both belong to the category *bird* and are more similar to each other than they are to squirrels or pumpkins. *Similarity* is a pretty vague term, but most commonly it is defined in terms of shared properties or attributes. If you are asked to justify why you think robins and sparrows are more similar to each other than either is to squirrels you are likely to appeal to specific attributes or properties. For example, you might note that robins and sparrows are similar in that they are living, animate, have feathers, wings, and hollow bones, and can sing, fly, build nests, and lay eggs. Squirrels have only some of these properties, and pumpkins have fewer still. Although alternative theories assume concepts are structured in terms of shared properties, theories differ greatly in their organizational principles. Let's take a look at the main views concerning category structure.

The Classical View

The **classical view** assumes that concepts have defining features that act like criteria for determining category membership. For example, a triangle is a closed geometric form of three sides with the sum of the interior angles equaling 180 degrees. Each of these properties is necessary for an entity to be a triangle, and together these properties are sufficient to define *triangle*. According to the classical view, concepts have rigid boundaries in that a given example either does or does not meet the definition. All members of a category are equally good examples of it, and learning involves discovering these defining features.

Most of us have the initial intuition that our concepts conform to the classical view and have defining features. But think a bit more about a concept like chair or furniture. What makes a chair a chair? We might start by saying that a chair is something an individual can sit on, but that definition does not exclude sofas, benches, or even rocks. Next one might add the proviso that chairs must have four legs, but that would exclude beanbag chairs. The more we think about it, the trickier it becomes. For example, we might start to worry about the difference between stools and chairs and ultimately decide either that we do not know exactly what a chair is or that we may be unable to describe it.

There has, in fact, been a fair amount of research done on people's knowledge about object categories like bird, chair, and furniture. Not only do people fail to come up with defining features but also they do not necessarily agree with each other (or even with themselves when asked at different times) on whether something is an example of a category (Bellezza, 1984; McCloskey & Glucksberg, 1978). For example, is a rug considered furniture? A parquet floor? A telephone?

Philosophers and scientists also have worried about whether naturally occurring things like plants and animals (so-called natural kinds) have defining features. And the current consensus is that most natural concepts do not fit the classical view. Even the concept of species is not well defined (see Sokal, 1974). For example, a species might be defined as an interbreeding population. But in some species, the males of one group are fertile with the females of the other, but the females of the first group are not fertile with the males of the other. Although some concepts like triangle may be well defined, many concepts do not appear to be, and for this reason cognitive psychologists have pretty much abandoned the classical view.

The Probabilistic View

The major alternative to the classical view is the **probabilistic view.** It argues that concepts are organized around properties that may be typical or characteristic of category members. For example, most people's concept of bird may include the properties of building nests, flying, and having hollow bones, even though not all birds have these properties (e.g., ostriches, penguins).

The probabilistic view has major implications for how we think about categories. First, if categories are organized around characteristic properties, some members may have more of these properties than other members. In this sense, some members may be better examples or more typical of a concept than others, as we noted in Chapter 6. For example, people judge a robin to be a better example of a bird than an ostrich is and can answer category membership questions more rapidly for good examples than for poor examples (see, e.g., E. E. Smith, Shoben, & Rips, 1974; Rips, 1989; Medin & Heit, 1999, for reviews). A second implication is that category boundaries may be fuzzy. Nonmembers of a category may have almost as many characteristic properties of a category as do certain members. For example, whales have a lot of the characteristic properties of fish, and yet they are mammals. Third, learning about a category cannot be equated with determining what the defining features are because there may not be any.

Features and Typicality

In some pioneering work aimed at clarifying the structural basis of fuzzy categories, Rosch and Mervis (1975) had subjects list properties of exemplars for a variety of concepts such as bird, fruit, and tool. They found that the listed properties for some category members occurred frequently in other members, whereas other members had properties that occurred less frequently. Most importantly, the more frequently a category member's properties appeared within a category, the higher was its rated **typicality** for that category. Typicality is a measure of how good or common an item is as a member of a given category. The correlation between number of characteristic properties possessed and typicality rating was very high and positive. For example, robins have characteristic bird properties of flying, singing, eating worms, and building nests in trees, and they are rated to be very typical birds. Penguins have none of these properties, and they are rated as very atypical birds. In short, the Rosch and Mervis work relating typicality to number of characteristic properties put the probabilistic view on fairly firm footing.

Although typicality effects are robust and problematic for the classical view, the underlying basis for typicality effects may vary with both the kind of category being studied and with the population being studied. Barsalou (1985) showed that the internal structure of taxonomic categories is based primarily on the central tendency (or the average member) of a category. In contrast, the internal structure of goal-derived categories such as "things to wear in the snow" is determined by some ideal (or the best possible member) associated with the category. The best example of snow clothing, a down jacket, was not the example that was most like other category

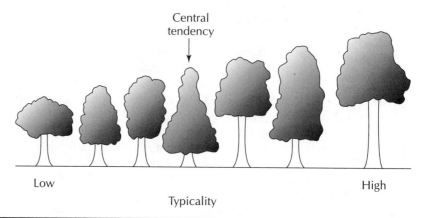

Figure 10.2   Typicality and central tendency illustrated for different kinds of trees varying in height. If typicality is based on central tendency, then trees of average height should be rated as the most typical. Tree experts, however, rate the tallest trees as most typical.

members; instead it was the example with the maximum value of the goal-related dimension of providing warmth.

One might hypothesize that ideals will only come into play when the category of interest lacks the natural similarity structure that characterizes common taxonomic categories such as bird, fish, and tree. However, recent evidence undermines this conjecture. Lynch, Coley, and Medin (2000) found that, for tree experts, the internal structure of the category *tree* was organized around the ideals of weediness and height (see Figure 10.2). The best examples of *tree* were not trees of average height but trees of extraordinary height (and free of "weedy" characteristics like having weak limbs, growing where they aren't wanted, and being susceptible to disease).

It might occur to you that "best example" isn't the same thing as "most typical." However, Lynch et al. used exactly the same instructions employed by Rosch and Mervis (1975) in their original investigation of typicality effects. Moreover, Lynch et al. also ran undergraduate participants, and they showed no effects of ideals (their responses were mainly based on familiarity). In short, the differences in goodness of example effects appear to depend on expertise, not the wording of the instructions.

Atran (1998) reports a similar finding in studies comparing goodness of example effects for the category *bird* among University of Michigan undergraduates and Itzá Maya adults living in the rainforests of Guatemala. Undergraduates based typicality on overall similarity (central tendency) just as Rosch and Mervis (1975) had observed. The Itzá Maya, in contrast, based typicality on ideals—the best example of bird was the wild turkey which is culturally significant, prized for its meat, and strikingly beautiful. In short, ideals may play an important role in the internal organization of categories. There remains the question of why undergraduates differed from the Itzá Maya in the basis for their judgments. The fact that Lynch et al. (2000) found that U.S. tree experts based typicality on ideals suggests that it's not just that the Itzá have a different notion of what typicality means. One speculation is that the

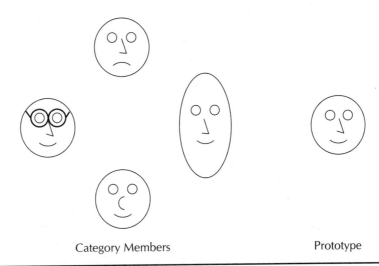

Category Members   Prototype

Figure 10.3   Example of family resemblance. Each of the category members shares features with the other category members, but none of them are identical. The prototype on the right is the central tendency of these category members.

internal structure of categories is determined not only by classification processes but also by other conceptual functions (e.g., those mentioned at the beginning of this chapter). Undergraduates may know little about birds or trees and their interactions with them may not go beyond categorization (if that). Tree experts and Itzá Maya presumably have extended and complex interactions with trees and birds, respectively, and ideals have more opportunity to come into play. Perhaps similarity is a useful way to structure concepts used primarily for classification whereas ideals may be better for concepts used for a broader range of conceptual functions. (See Ross, 1997; Markman, Yamauchi, & Makin, 1997; and Solomon, Medin, & Lynch, 1999, for different ways of developing this argument.)

Mental Representations of Fuzzy Categories

If categories are not represented in terms of definitions, what form do our mental representations take? The term *probabilistic view* seems to imply that people organize categories via statistical reasoning. Actually, there is a more natural interpretation of fuzzy categories that has been referred to as a **family resemblance** principle. Many people in an extended family might share features such as a distinctive chin, certain expressions, or a high forehead. For example, Figure 10.3 sketches a hypothetical family. In this example, the faces all share many properties, though no two faces are identical. The general idea is that category members resemble each other in the way that family members do.

A simple summary representation for such a family resemblance structure would be an example that possessed all the characteristic features of a category. The best example is referred to as the **prototype.** For example, the prototype (based on usual or modal values) for the faces of the category members in Figure 10.3 is shown on the right of the figure.

In a prototype model of categorization, classifying a new example is done by comparing the new item to the prototype. If the candidate example is similar enough to the prototype for a category, it is classified as a member of that category. The general notion is that, based on experience with examples of a category, people abstract out the central tendency or prototype that becomes the summary mental representation for the category. Note that no individual category member need have all the properties that are represented in the prototype. In that sense, a prototype is like a stereotype, which also may be true of no individual.

Laboratory studies of categorization using artificially constructed categories have been used to evaluate prototype theory. In these studies the experimenter creates the stimuli using salient properties and then assigns the stimuli to categories to create different kinds of category structures. For example, the stimuli might be geometric shapes varying in shape, size, and color, and fuzzy categories can be constructed by making sure that there is no simple rule that determines category membership. For example, one category might have examples that are usually large, usually red, and usually circular but there would be exceptions to each of these generalizations.

Normally many variables relevant to human category learning tend to be correlated with each other, and it is hard to determine which variables really are important. For instance, typical examples tend to be more frequent, and people's ability to classify typical examples quickly may be related to typicality, frequency, or both factors. The general rationale for laboratory studies with artificially created categories is that one can isolate some variable or set of variables of interest by breaking these natural correlations. Experiments with artificial categories reveal a number of salient phenomena associated with fuzzy categories, and several of these are consistent with prototype theories. For example, one observes typicality effects in learning and on transfer tests using both correctness and reaction time as the dependent measure (see, e.g., Rosch & Mervis, 1975). A striking result, readily obtained, is that the prototype for a category may be classified more accurately during transfer tests than are the previously seen examples that were used during original category learning (see, e.g., Homa & Vosburgh, 1976; Medin & Schaffer, 1978; Peterson, Meagher, Chait, & Gillie, 1973).

Typicality effects and excellent classification of prototypes are consistent with the idea that people are learning these fuzzy categories by forming prototypes. More detailed analyses, however, show problems with prototypes as mental representations. As we noted earlier, prototype theory implies that the only information abstracted from categories is the central tendency. A prototype representation discards information concerning category size, the variability of the examples, and correlations of attributes. The evidence suggests that people can use all three of these types of information (Estes, 1986; Flannagan, Fried, & Holyoak, 1986; Fried & Holyoak, 1984; Medin, Altom, Edelson, & Freko, 1982; Medin & Schaffer, 1978).

These same issues arise for real-world categories. For example, people seem to know that small birds are more likely to sing than large birds—a prototype does not capture this awareness of correlational information (Malt & Smith, 1983). In addition, how well an item belongs to a concept depends on the context in which it is presented (Roth & Shoben, 1983). For example, a harmonica is a typical musical instrument in the context of a campfire but atypical in the context of a concert hall. People seem to adjust their expectations in a manner sensitive to different settings. In short, prototype representations seem to discard too much information that can be shown to be relevant to human categorization.

Let's look at one further problem of prototype models in detail: predictions concerning category learning. To our knowledge, every model for category learning has some constraints or biases associated with it in the sense of predicting that some kinds of classification problems should be easier to master than others. One way to evaluate alternative learning models is to see if the problems they predict should be easy or difficult to acquire are, in fact, easier or more difficult for people to learn.

One constraint of interest is known as **linear separability.** Categories are linearly separable if one can categorize the examples perfectly by adding up the evidence from individual features. It is easiest to see what this means with a concrete example. Prototype models imply that categories must be linearly separable to be learnable. One way to conceptualize the process of classifying examples on the basis of similarity to prototype is that it involves a summing of evidence against a criterion. For example, if an instance has enough features characteristic of birds, it will be classified as a bird. More technically, there must be some weighted, additive combination of properties (some similarity function) that will be higher for all category members than for any nonmembers. If this is true, then the categories are linearly separable. All bird examples must be more similar to the bird prototype than to alternative prototypes, and all nonbirds must be more similar to their respective prototypes than to the bird prototype. If a bat were more similar to the bird prototype than to the mammal prototype, it would be incorrectly classified and the categories would not be linearly separable.

Figure 10.4 gives a more intuitive description of linear separability for examples that have values on two dimensions. In each graph category, members in

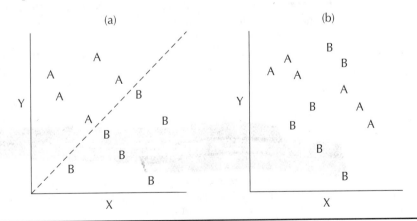

Figure 10.4 Two-dimensional example of two categories that are linearly separable (a) and are not linearly separable (b).

categories A and B are denoted respectively by the letters *A* and *B*. The position of each letter corresponds to its value on the X and Y dimensions (if it helps to be more concrete, think of these dimensions as the size and ferocity of animals). The categories are linearly separable if there is a straight line that perfectly partitions the categories (Figure 10.4a). If no straight line will partition the categories (Figure 10.4b), there is no way to construct prototypes such that all examples are closer to their own category prototype than to the prototype for the contrasting category. A number of neural network learning models favor categories that are linearly separable because, in effect, they add up the evidence favoring a classification decision (Minsky & Papert, 1988).

If linear separability acts as a constraint on human categorization, people should find it easier to learn categories that are linearly separable than categories that are not linearly separable. Studies employing a variety of stimulus materials, categories, subject populations, and instructions have failed to find any evidence that whether the categories are linearly separable influences the ease with which people learn categories (see, e.g., Kemler-Nelson, 1984; Medin & Schwanenflugel, 1981; see Smith, Murray, & Minda, 1997, for a dissenting opinion). This generalization has one striking exception: For social categories, there is strong evidence that linear separability does matter (Wattenmaker, 1995).

Wattenmaker suggests that social categories may be more compatible with a summing of evidence because (1) people may have a set of schemas or thematic structures that facilitate the integration of information across dimensions (e.g., the characteristic features knowledgeable, competent, hard working, and composed can readily be integrated if the category *scientist* is activated), and (2) people show considerable flexibility in relating features of examples to more abstract underlying properties (e.g., the characteristic features relaxed, thoughtful, and friendly could be seen as consistent with the abstract trait *intelligent,* but they may also be seen as consistent with the trait *kind*). Even with this salient exception of social categories, the sort of domain-general linear separability constraint implied by prototype models does not appear to hold. Overall, then, prototype models appear to have a number of serious limitations. An alternative approach, which is also consistent with the probabilistic view, assumes that much more information about specific examples is preserved. This approach appropriately falls under the general heading of exemplar theories.

Exemplar Theories

Exemplar theories provide an alternative way of representing probabilistic or fuzzy categories. **Exemplar models** assume that people initially learn some examples of different concepts and then classify a new instance on the basis of how similar it is to the previously learned examples. The idea is that a new example reminds the person of similar old examples and that people assume that similar items will belong to the same category. For example, you might classify one animal as a rodent because it reminds you of a mouse (which you know is a rodent) but classify some other animal as a rodent because it reminds you of a squirrel (which you also know is a rodent). As another example, suppose you are asked whether large birds are more or less likely to fly than small birds. You probably will answer "less likely," based on retrieving examples from memory and noting that the only nonflying birds you can think of are large (e.g., penguin, ostrich).

The exemplar models that have received the most attention (Brooks, 1978; Hintzman, 1986; Medin & Schaffer, 1978; Nosofsky, 1986) assume that examples that are most similar to the item to be classified have the greatest influence on categorization. This could arise because the likelihood of retrieving an example from memory depends on its similarity to the item. The idea that retrieval is similarity-based and context-sensitive is in accord with much of the memory literature (see, e.g., Tulving, 1983; Chapter 5). Surprisingly, exemplar models can even account for the observation that the prototype may be more accurately classified on a transfer test than examples seen during original learning. The reason is as follows: The prototype will tend to be similar to many examples from its own category and not very similar to examples from alternative categories. Therefore, the prototype should reliably remind the learner of examples from the correct category. In contrast, some of the examples seen during training may not be highly similar to some of the other examples from their own category and may actually be similar to examples from other categories. In this case, the example may remind the learner of examples from alternative categories. It is important to bear in mind that exemplar models do not assume that people are necessarily able to retrieve individual examples one at a time without confusing them. Instead, the idea is that a test example will tend to activate a number of similar stored representations.

Quite a few experiments have contrasted the predictions of exemplar and prototype models. In head-to-head competition, exemplar models have been substantially more successful than prototype models (Barsalou & Medin, 1986; Estes, 1986, 1994; Lamberts, 1995; Medin & Coley, 1998; Nosofsky, 1988a, 1988b, 1991; Nosofsky & Palmeri, 1997) even for natural language categories (Storms, De Boeck, & Ruts, 2000). See Homa, 1984, and Smith & Minda, 1998, for opposing views.

Why should exemplar models fare better than prototype models? One of the main functions of classification is to allow one to make inferences and predictions on the basis of partial information (see J. R. Anderson, 1990a, 1990b). Here we are using classification loosely to refer to any means by which prior (relevant) knowledge is brought to bear, ranging from a formal classification rule to an idiosyncratic reminding of a previous case (which, of course, is in the spirit of exemplar models; see also Kolodner, 1993). Relative to prototype models, exemplar models tend to be conservative about discarding information that facilitates predictions. For instance, sensitivity to correlations of properties within a category enables finer predictions: From noting that a bird is large, one can predict that it cannot sing. In short, exemplar models better allow predictions and inferences than prototype models.

Exemplar models do seem to preserve more information than prototype models. Because the prototype is an average exemplar, it loses information about the specific category members that were seen. Although the exemplar model stores the category members, that does not mean that it will ever be possible to retrieve that single exemplar, because activating one exemplar is likely to activate others that are similar to it. Generally speaking, however, exemplar models preserve more information

AN APPLICATION
Exemplar Similarity in Medical Diagnosis

Medical diagnosis is an important categorization task. Therefore, one ought to expect that models of categorization would be relevant to medicine and that questions about prototypes versus exemplars might apply to medicine. Brooks, Norman, and Allen (1991) demonstrated that exemplar similarity influences medical diagnosis and not just performance on tasks set up in psychology laboratories. They ran experiments with medical residents and general practitioners involving diagnoses of dermatological (skin) problems. The materials they used were color slides of dermatological lesions from the slide libraries of two practicing and teaching dermatologists. Slides were selected from a range of diagnostic categories to construct examples for a study phase (30 slides) and a test phase (60 slides). The test phase slides included some examples from the study phase, some selected to be very similar to a study example, and some that were not very similar but involved the same category. Not surprisingly, the physicians were more accurate on old examples that they had studied than for new examples. Of greatest interest is the fact that physicians were

(Continued)

than prototype models—information that people seem to be able to use. This does not prove that exemplar models are correct, but it suggests that learning depends more on examples than prototype models have assumed (Medin & Ross, 1989).

In short, exemplar models appear to have a number of effective characteristics, and future generations of models will likely embody these characteristics, directly or indirectly. For example, recent models of category learning that combine searching for rules with memory for examples have proven successful, at least for artificial categories (e.g. Nosofsky, Palmeri, & McKinley, 1994; Erickson & Kruschke, 1998; see also Ashby, Alfonso-Reese, Turken, & Waldron, 1998, for another dual-process approach to categorization). Instance-based ideas have also been incorporated into artificial intelligence categorization models (see, e.g., Kibler & Aha, 1987; Stanfill & Waltz, 1986). Finally, we note that there have been formal proofs that classifying on the basis of the single most similar example (a "nearest neighbor" principle) is not far from the optimal classification (Cover & Hart, 1967).

Although exemplar models have the virtue that they discard very little information that is potentially relevant to later judgments, the exemplar notion is incomplete as a theory of categories. Items are assumed to be placed in the category with the exemplars they are most similar to, but exemplar theories do not explain how concepts are created in the first place; that is, there are no constraints on what can be

AN APPLICATION

Exemplar Similarity in Medical Diagnosis *(Continued)*

more accurate on a new example highly similar to an old example than they were on a new, less similar example involving the same category.

This finding is surprising because both the residents and the general practitioners had considerable prior experience with dermatological diagnosis. One estimate is that about 6% of the cases general practitioners see involve dermatology. The physicians in the study by Brooks et al. had between 5 and 49 years of postgraduate experience. Nonetheless, the effect of specific example similarity did not diminish as a function of experience. It also appeared on both an immediate test and after a two-week delay between the study phase and the test phase. The effect was on the order of 10% to 20%, which is not only statistically reliable but clinically significant. This result is important because it suggests that if you need to see a doctor, the diagnosis may depend partially on the sorts of cases the doctor has seen recently. In summary, categorization processes studied in the laboratory are relevant to real world applications and a better understanding of these processes may have important application to medical diagnosis and training.

a concept. Furthermore, the only explanation for why a new example should be placed into a category is "because it is similar to an old example"—a very limited form of explanation. In addition, these models focus on how people learn to classify objects to the exclusion of other functions like prediction, reasoning, or communication. As we shall see, these three problems are also true for probabilistic view theories.

Summary

The proposals about types of category representations are summarized in Figure 10.5. Despite the strong intuition that categories are organized around defining features, the classical view of concepts does not account for a variety of observations (e.g., fuzzy categories, typicality effects) and the consensus favors the idea that concepts are structured more probabilistically. For this reason, various probabilistic views of categorization have been developed. The two most prominent theories of this type are the prototype and exemplar models. The prototype model assumes that category representations consist of a central tendency or average member of a category. The exemplar model assumes that people store individual exemplars of categories, and then classify new instances with respect to their similarity to these stored exemplars. In general, it appears that people's categorization shows a context-sensitivity that is

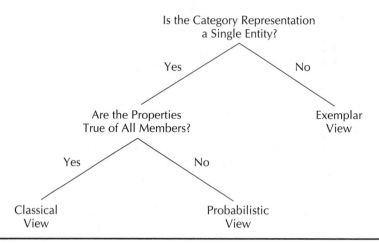

Figure 10.5   Summary of the types of category representations.

better described by exemplar models than prototype models. So far, however, we have focused mainly on the categorization functions of concepts. It is not clear how probabilistic view models will address other conceptual functions such as conceptual combination (see Kamp & Partee, 1995; Osherson & Smith, 1982, 1997; Fodor & Lepore, 1996, for discussion).

The discussion to this point has focused exclusively on the way information about individual categories is represented (or *within-category structure*). It is almost meaningless to talk about within-category structure without also worrying about how different categories are organized with respect to each other (or *between-category structure*). For example, when we say that examples within a category tend to be similar to each other we mean that they are more similar than pairs of examples that come from different categories. We turn now to some ideas concerning between-category structure before worrying again about why we have the categories we have and not others.

Between-Category Structure

Most things have membership in numerous categories. In this section we consider two types of between-category structure: a hierarchical, taxonomic structure and structures such as social categories that provide multiple, overlapping contrasts with, at best, a weak hierarchical structure.

Hierarchical Structure and the Basic Level

Often categories are organized *taxonomically* at different levels of abstraction. At each level, an example belongs to one of a set of mutually exclusive categories (as

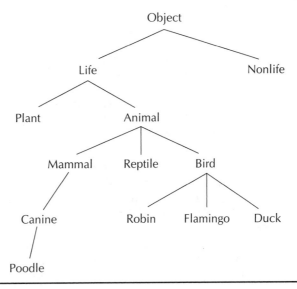

Figure 10.6   Part of a simple taxonomic structure.

we saw in our discussion of models of semantic knowledge in Chapter 6). A poodle is also a canine, a mammal, an animal, a living thing, and an object (Figure 10.6). A poodle is a mammal and not a reptile, an animal and not a plant, and so on.

An important observation about categories is that people are not confused about which label to use when asked about an object. For example, if you were looking at a four-legged furry animal that had just fetched a ball, you would be more likely to call it a *dog* than an *animal* or a *golden retriever.* This middle level of abstraction, which seems to provide the label that we would use as a default is called the **basic level,** and it appears to be psychologically privileged. For example, basic level concepts are the first to be learned, the natural level at which objects are named, and the highest level in which the instances all share the same parts and overall shape (Rosch, Mervis, Gray, Johnson, & Bayes Braem, 1976). The basic level resides at a middle level of abstraction. More abstract categories (like animal) are called *superordinates,* and more specific categories (like golden retriever) are called *subordinates.* There is some evidence that as one becomes more expert in an area, what was previously the subordinate level becomes the basic level. For example, dog might be a basic-level category for most people, but poodle might be at the basic-level for dog trainers (Tanaka & Taylor, 1991; see also Johnson & Mervis, 1997, 1998).

If we could understand just why the basic level is basic, we might gain further insight into what types of categories are natural or cohesive. One possibility is that the basic level is the highest level at which entities tend to share parts (B. Tversky & Hemenway, 1984; see Markman & Wisniewski, 1997, for a related idea). Another idea is that levels higher than the basic level have different purposes. For example, superordinate categories may serve to organize scenes (Murphy & Wisniewski, 1989; see

AN ENIGMA
Will the True Basic Level Please Stand Up?

The idea of a basic level did not originate in cognitive psychology—it began with anthropological studies examining categorization in different cultures. The lion's share of this work was done in enthnobiology. The general question was whether people in different cultures organize biological categories in similar ways (that is, whether there are universal principles of biological categorization). The general answer proved to be "yes" but cross-cultural agreement in people's categorization of plants and animals appears to especially strong at one level in taxonomic hierarchies, the basic level (Atran, 1990; Berlin, 1992; Berlin, Breedlove, & Raven, 1973; see Malt, 1995, for a review). But herein lies a yet-unresolved puzzle. The level that the cross-cultural studies of biological categorization suggest is basic corresponds more or less to the genus level (e.g., maple) in scientific taxonomy. Rosch et al., however, found that, for Berkeley undergraduates, examples of this level acted like subordinates. Rather than maple, oak, trout, and cardinal being basic, Rosch et al. (1976) found that tree, fish, and bird met their criteria for basicness.

Why do ethnobiological and psychological measures of the basic level disagree? One possibility is that the Berkeley undergraduates in Rosch's studies knew little about biological categories, especially relative to the people studied in cross-cultural investigations. In other words, maybe the difference is a difference in expertise (as in the findings of Tanaka and Taylor described earlier which suggest that the basic level may become more specific with expertise). A second possibility grows out of the fact that exactly comparable measures of basicness were not used; different measures may pick out different levels as privileged. Ethnobiological studies tend to use naming or linguistic criteria for basicness, whereas Rosch et al. relied more heavily on feature listings and perceptual tests. Interestingly, the clearest changes with expertise in the Tanaka and Taylor studies involved naming preferences. Until this puzzle is resolved we have to admit that we do not know exactly what makes the basic level basic.

More recently some direct cross-cultural comparisons have been done using comparable measures. Coley, Medin, and Atran, 1997 (see also Atran, Estin, Coley, & Medin, 1997), compared U.S. undergraduates

(Continued)

also Wisniewski, Imai, & Casey, 1996), and superordinate category members may tend to share common functions more than perceptual similarities (see, e.g., Rosch et al., 1976; Murphy & Smith, 1982).

AN ENIGMA
Will the True Basic Level Please Stand Up? *(Continued)*

and Itzá Maya adults of Guatemala using *inductive confidence* (reasoning from being told that one member has some novel property to all members having that property) as a measure of basicness. They assumed that if the basic level is the most abstract level at which category members share many properties, then inductive confidence should drop abruptly for categories above the basic level. For example, if U.S. undergraduates know that birds share many properties, then they might be confident that a property true of robins will be true of all birds. But since there are many fewer properties that all members of the category animals share, they presumably would not be at all confident that a property true of robins would be true of all animals. The Itzá Maya are members of a more traditional society and they rely on the rainforest for their livelihood. They might show a greater differentiation of the category bird (see larger differences among birds), and they might believe that a property true of a specific bird would not necessarily be true of all birds. This is the prediction one would make from the point of view that people in traditional societies tend to be biological experts, relative to U.S. undergraduates. Surprisingly, both the Itzá Maya and U.S. undergraduates consistently privileged the same level and this corresponded to the level of genus (robin, trout, and oak rather than bird, fish, and tree), consistent with expectations derived from anthropology.

These results raise a number of new puzzles that can only be answered by future research. Why do undergraduates show a different privileged level for induction versus other tasks such as speeded categorization or feature listing? One possibility draws on the distinction between knowledge and expectations. Undergraduates might be hard-pressed to list features that distinguish elms from oaks but they might nonetheless expect them to have lots of differences. It may be that the inductive confidence task gets at expectations rather than knowledge. Another question is how people from traditional cultures would perform on Rosch's perceptual tasks. Would they be fastest at the level of categorizing examples into bird, fish and tree or robin, trout, and oak? The Tanaka and Taylor studies with bird and dog experts suggest that the Itzá Maya might be fastest at the genus level, because the Itzá are almost certainly biological experts. Cross-cultural comparisons are needed to address this question.

Nonhierarchical Categories

Many of the categories that we use do not fit into a taxonomic hierarchy. This is particularly true in the domain of socially-relevant concepts. One can be a mother, a psychologist, a Democrat, a golf player, and a Mexican-American all at the same time, and no single category is either superordinate or subordinate with respect to the others. If there is no clear hierarchy, then by definition there is no basic level. Given that people tend to use categories to understand their experience, one can think of the various categorization schemes as competing for attention. We already know from the memory literature that it is implausible to think that to understand some behavior, people access all the potentially relevant categories they have and reason with them. So what does determine which categories people access and use? Two factors that influence category access are the frequency and recency with which a category has been used. For example, in one study (Srull & Wyer, 1979, Experiment 1), people first performed a sentence construction task that was designed to activate concepts associated with hostility. Then, in an ostensibly separate experiment, the participants were asked to form impressions of people based on reading a description of behaviors. The behaviors were ambiguous with respect to hostility. Ratings of the descriptions with respect to hostility increased directly with the number of times hostility-related concepts had been activated on the presumably unrelated sentence construction task. The Srull and Wyer study illustrates the point that category accessibility has an important influence on how social information is encoded and interpreted (see also Smith, Fazio, & Cejka, 1996).

Is there a notion of privilege for nonhierarchical categories? Some social categories, such as those marking race, age, and gender, may be accessed automatically (e.g. Bargh, 1994; Greenwald & Banaji, 1995) independent of any intentions on the part of people. There is even some intriguing evidence that the activation of one social category leads to the inhibition of competing social categories (Macrae, Bodenhausen, & Milne, 1995). Although the structural differences between hierarchical and nonhierarchical categories are important, there is little or no work that has directly compared them.

Summary

The idea of a privileged or basic level is a very important principle of categorization. Originally it was interpreted as indicating that the world is organized into natural chunks that more or less impose themselves on minds. Evidence that the basic level changes with expertise suggests that privilege depends on the interaction of goals, activities, and experience with objects and events in the world.

So far all of our discussion of within- and between-category structure has explicitly or implicitly assumed that similarity relations determine categorization (the classical view can be seen as a special case where only defining features contribute to similarity). We turn now to a closer examination of similarity. As we shall see, the notion of similarity can be a bit slippery. It is a very important construct but one must be very careful about how it is used.

Does Similarity Explain Categorization?

Similarity is a very intuitive explanation for how people categorize—we put things into the same category because they are similar. But similarity is very difficult to pin

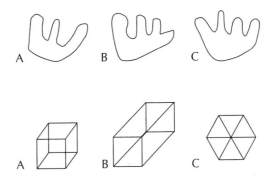

Figure 10.7   Sample of stimuli used by Medin, Goldstone, and Gentner (1993). For each set, people either saw A and B or B and C. The task was to list common and distinctive properties.

down. One problem with using similarity to define categories is that similarity is too variable. An example of the context-dependent nature of similarity is shown in Figure 10.7 (taken from Medin, Goldstone, & Gentner, 1993). People were either shown stimulus A and B together or stimulus B and C from sets of three like those shown in the figure. For each pair, people were asked to list common (shared) and distinctive features. Medin et al. (1993) found that the properties ascribed to stimulus B depended on whether it was paired with A or C. For example, for the top set, B was described as having three prongs when it was paired with A but four prongs when it was paired with C. For the bottom set, B was seen as three-dimensional when paired with A but two-dimensional when paired with C. Such observations suggest that similarity is heavily influenced by context.

Formal models of similarity allow similarity to be quite flexible. For example, Tversky's (1977) influential contrast model defines similarity as depending on common and distinctive features weighted for salience or importance. According to this model, similarity relationships depend heavily on the particular weights given to individual properties or features. A zebra and a barber pole could be seen as more similar than a zebra and a horse if the feature striped is given sufficient weight. This would not necessarily be a problem if the weights were stable. However, Tversky and others have convincingly shown that the relative weighting of a feature (as well as the relative importance of matching and mismatching features) varies with the stimulus context, experimental task (Gati & Tversky, 1984; Tversky, 1977), and probably even the concept under consideration (Ortony, Vondruska, Foss, & Jones, 1985). For example, a person from Maine and a person from Florida will seem less similar when they meet in Washington, DC, than when they meet in Tokyo.

Once we recognize that similarity is dynamic and depends on some (not well understood) processing principles, earlier work on the structure of fuzzy categories can be seen in a somewhat different light. Recall that the Rosch and Mervis (1975) studies asked subjects to list attributes or properties of examples and categories. It would be a mistake to assume that people had the ability to read and report their mental representations of concepts in a perfectly accurate manner. Indeed, Keil

(1979, 1981) pointed out that examples like robin and squirrel share many important properties that almost never show up in attribute listings (e.g., has a heart, breathes, sleeps, is an organism, is an object with boundaries, is a physical object, is a thing, can be thought about, and so on). In fact, Keil argued that knowledge about just these sorts of properties serves to organize children's conceptual and semantic development. For present purposes, the point is that attribute listings provide a biased sample of people's conceptual knowledge.

To take things a step further, one could argue that without constraints on what is to count as a feature, any two things may be arbitrarily similar or dissimilar. Thus, as Murphy and Medin (1985) suggested, the number of properties that plums and lawn mowers have in common could be infinite: Both weigh less than 1,000 kg, both are found on the earth, both are found in our solar system, both cannot hear well, both have parts, both are not worn by elephants, both are used by people, both can be dropped, and so on (see also Goodman, 1972; Watanabe, 1969). Now consider again the status of attribute listings. They represent a biased subset of stored or readily inferred knowledge. The correlation of attribute listings with typicality judgments is a product of such knowledge and a variety of processes that operate on it. Without a theory of that knowledge and those processes that use it, it simply is not clear what these correlations indicate about mental representations.

If similarity is so flexible, how can it provide the basis for determining categories? One possibility is that children are not as flexible about similarity as adults. Linda Smith (1989) has proposed that there is a developmental increase in the tendency of children to weight dimensions differentially, with the youngest children biased toward responding in terms of overall similarity. If flexibility arises only after most perceptual categories are learned, then similarity might be stable enough to support the initial development of many categories. A closely related idea is that children rapidly learn what types of similarity matter in particular contexts.

In part, the question may be just how flexible similarity is. For example, the object recognition theories reviewed in Chapter 4 certainly assume that similarity is stable enough to be useful. In particular, structural approaches to similarity such as geon theory may be more constrained than featural approaches (because it is the combination of geons and their relations that is important rather than some flexible weighting of individual features) and consequently may provide more stability (e.g., Medin et al., 1993; Goldstone, 1994a).

Even if similarity can be constrained, it still may not explain categorization. We believe that similarity is properly viewed as a general guideline or heuristic for categorization but that it does not provide the backbone of conceptual structure. Things that look alike do tend to belong to the same category. (But there are exceptions: Mannequins may look enough like people for us to confuse them with the real thing, but only briefly.) Furthermore, things that look alike superficially often tend to be alike in other, deeper ways (e.g., structure and function tend to be correlated). Overall similarity is a good but fallible guideline to category membership. When additional information (or a closer look) suggests that overall similarity is misleading, it is readily abandoned.

Figure 10.8 Sample triplet of stimuli from Gelman and Markman (1986). The task was to decide whether the bottom figure had a property true of the perceptually more similar choice (top right) or a property true of the example that belonged to the same category (top left).

A nice illustration of the fact that even young children are not strongly constrained by overall similarity comes from a set of experiments by Gelman and Markman (1986). They pitted category membership against perceptual similarity in an inductive reasoning task (an example is shown in Figure 10.8). Young children were first shown pictures of two animals and taught that different novel properties were true of them. Then they were asked which property was also true of a new (pictured) example that was perceptually similar to one alternative but belonged to the category of the other alternative, from which it differed perceptually. For example, children might be taught that a flamingo feeds its baby mashed-up food and that a bat feeds its baby milk, and then asked what a blackbird feeds its baby (see Figure 10.8). The blackbird was perceptually more similar to the bat than to the flamingo, but even 4-year-olds made inferences on the basis of category membership rather than similarity. That is, they thought that the blackbird would feed its baby mashed-up food. Therefore, even for young children, similarity acts as a general guideline that can be overridden by other forms of knowledge.

But similarity is not a notion to be lightly dismissed. Even if similarity is not some bedrock principle for *explaining* categorization it may nonetheless play an extremely important role. One way to summarize the upshot of current research is to say that similarity affects categorization *and* categorization affects similarity as well. There is increasing evidence that the features or building blocks of categories are not hard-wired into the nervous system but rather can be modified by experience (e.g. Gauthier & Tarr, 1997; Goldstone, 1994b; Oliva & Schyns, 1997; Schyns & Rodet, 1997; Schyns, Goldstone, & Thibaut, 1998). There is also abundant evidence that the relative weight given to different kinds of features varies with their relevance to a given categorization task. For example, in Chapter 4, we discussed that people can attend either to fine detail information or coarse information when processing an image. Schyns and Oliva (1999) extended this finding by demonstrating that people could learn to preferentially attend to either a coarse spatial scale or a fine spatial scale in a speeded categorization task. These results suggest that categorization and (perceptual) similarity are closely intertwined, so much so that one could as well say that categorization causes similarity as the converse.

Summary

It does not seem that similarity, at least in the form that it takes in current theories, is going to be adequate to explain categorization. As we have seen, similarity may be the outcome or by-product rather than the cause of categorization. To use a rough analogy, winning basketball teams have in common scoring more points than their opponents, but one must turn to more basic principles to explain why they score more points. Similar things may share properties and be in the same category, but similarity may not explain *why* they are in the same category. We will explore the process by which similarity is determined in Chapter 11. Now, we will focus on the idea that concepts are organized around theories. In the next section, we will briefly summarize some of the current work on the role of knowledge structures and theories in categorization and then turn to a way of relating similarity and knowledge-based categorization principles.

Concepts as Organized by Theories

A number of researchers have argued that the organization of concepts is knowledge-based (rather than similarity-based) and driven by intuitive theories about the world (see, e.g., Carey, 1985; Gopnik & Meltzoff, 1997; Keil, 1986, 1989, 1995; Murphy & Medin, 1985; Rips & Collins, 1993; Schank, Collins, & Hunter, 1986; Waldmann, Holyoak, & Fratianne, 1995; Wattenmaker, 1995; see Komatsu, 1992; Murphy, 1993; Medin & Heit, 1999, for general reviews). Murphy and Medin suggested that the relation between a concept and an example is analogous to the relation between theory and data; that is, classification is not based simply on a direct matching of properties of the concept with those in the example, but rather requires that the example have the right "explanatory relationship" to the theory organizing the concept. Classification may be more like an inference process than like a similarity judgment. We may induce that a man is drunk because we see him jump into a pool fully clothed. If so, our determination is probably not because the property "jumps into pools while clothed" is directly listed with the concept *drunk*. Rather, it is because part of our concept of drunk involves a theory of impaired judgment that serves to explain the man's behavior.

One of the more promising aspects of the theory-based approach is that it begins to address the question of why we have the categories we have or why categories are sensible. In fact, coherence may be achieved in the absence of any obvious source of similarity among examples. Consider the category comprised of children, money, photo albums, and pets. Out of context, the category seems odd. But if we are told that the category represents "things to take out of one's house in case of a fire," the category becomes sensible (Barsalou, 1983). In addition, one could readily make judgments about whether new examples (e.g., personal papers, magazines) belonged to the category, judgments that would not be based on overall similarity to category members.

Susan Carey (1982, 1985) has shown that children's biological theories guide their conceptual development. In one study, 6-year-old children rated a toy monkey to be more similar to people than is a worm, but they also judged that the worm was more likely to have a spleen than was the toy monkey (a spleen was described as "a green thing inside people"). Although worms may be less similar to people than are toy monkeys, they are more similar in some respects, namely, common biological functions. And Carey's work shows that children's biological theories help them determine which respects are relevant. Thus, the 6-year-old children's rudimentary biological knowledge influences the structure of their concept of animal (see also Au & Romo, 1999; Coley, 1995; Gelman, 1996; Hatano & Inagaki, 1994; Inagaki, 1997; Keil, 1989; Simons & Keil, 1995, for other studies on the development of biological knowledge).

The idea that concepts might be knowledge-based rather than similarity-based suggests a natural way in which concepts may change—namely, through the addition of new knowledge and theoretical principles. We have a different set of categories for mental disorders now than we had 100 years ago, in part because our knowledge base has become more refined. Often knowledge of diseases develops from information about patterns of symptoms to a specification of underlying causes. For example, the advanced stages of syphilis were treated as a mental disorder until the causes and consequences of this venereal disease were better understood.

Putting Similarity in Its Place

How are theories and similarity related? Clearly, theories may affect similarity (Wisniewski & Medin, 1994). For example, people can now recognize that the fact that the planets revolve around the sun is similar to the fact that when something is dropped it falls down and not up, because both involve gravity. Interestingly, similarity may also act as a constraint on theories. The impact of perceptual similarity on the development of causal explanations is evident in the structure of people's everyday theories. Frazer's (1959) cross-cultural analysis of belief systems pointed to the widespread character of two principles; homeopathy and contagion. The principle of **homeopathy** is that causes and effects tend to be similar. One manifestation of this principle is homeopathic medicine, in which the cure (and the cause) are seen to resemble the symptoms. In the Azande culture, for example, the cure for ringworm is to apply fowl's excrement because the excrement looks like the ringworm. Shweder (1977) has provided strong support for the claim that resemblance is a fundamental conceptual tool of everyday thinking in all cultures, not just so-called primitive cultures. In our culture, people reject acceptable foods just because they are shaped into a form that represents a disgusting object (Rozin, Millman, & Nemeroff, 1986). We will spare you a concrete example.

Contagion is the principle that a cause must have some form of contact to transmit its effect. In general, the nearer two events are in time and space, the more likely they are to be perceived as causally related (see, e.g., Dickinson, Shanks, & Evenden, 1984; Michotte, 1963). Of course, even children recognize that the timing relations may be rather subtle. If children are exposed to a ball that hits a second ball and there is a delay before the second ball moves away, then they will not interpret the collision of the balls as causing the movement (Leslie, 1988), though the collision will be seen as causing the second ball to move if it starts to move right after the collision. People also tend to assume that causes and effects should be of similar magnitude. Einhorn and Hogarth (1986) pointed out that the germ theory of disease initially met with great resistance because people could not imagine how such tiny organisms could have such devastating effects.

It is important to recognize that homeopathy and contagion often point us in the right direction. Immunization can be seen as a form of homeopathic medicine that has an underlying theoretical principle supporting it. Our reading of these observations, however, is not that specific theoretical (causal) principles are constraining similarity but rather that similarity (homeopathy and contagion) acts as a constraint on the search for causal explanations. Even in classical conditioning studies, the similarity of the conditioned stimulus and the unconditioned stimulus can have a major influence on the rate of conditioning (Testa, 1974).

One way of integrating similarity and explanation is in terms of a notion of **psychological essentialism** (Gelman, Coley, & Gottfried, 1994; Keil, 1989; Medin & Ortony, 1989; Wattenmaker, Nakamura, & Medin, 1988). The main ideas are as follows: People act as if things (e.g., objects) have essences or underlying natures that make them the thing that they are. Essentialism seems to be an idea present in many cultures (e.g. Atran, 1990; Walker, 1992). For biological categories in our culture, people might identify essence with genetic structure. The essence constrains or generates (often external) properties that may vary in their centrality. For example, people in our culture believe that the categories male and female are genetically determined, but to pick someone out as male or female we rely on characteristics such as hair length, height, facial hair, and clothing that represent a mixture of secondary sexual characteristics and cultural conventions. Although these characteristics are less reliable than genetic evidence, they are far from arbitrary. Not only do they have some validity in a statistical sense but also they are tied to our biological and cultural conceptions of male and female.

Note that psychological essentialism refers not to how the world really is but rather to how people approach the world. Wastebaskets presumably have no true essence, although we may act as if they do. Both social and psychodiagnostic categories are at least partially culture-specific and, therefore, may represent constructions rather than discoveries about the world (see also Morey & McNamara, 1987).

Why should people act as if things had essences? Possibly the reason is that it may be a good strategy for learning about the world. Recall that categorization faces computational complexity problems and that organisms face a strong need to make correct and useful predictions and inferences on the basis of their categorization schemes. One could say that people adopt an essentialist strategy or heuristic, namely, the generalization that things that look alike tend to share deeper properties (similarities) because it's typically an effective strategy. That is, our perceptual and conceptual systems appear to have evolved such that the essentialist heuristic is very often correct (Atran, 1990; Medin & Wattenmaker, 1987; Shepard, 1987). This is true even for human artifacts such as cars, computers, and camping stoves because structure and function tend to be correlated. Surface characteristics that are perceptually obvious or readily produced on feature-listing tasks may not so much constitute the core of a concept as point toward it. This observation suggests that classifying on the basis of similarity will be relatively effective much of the time, but that similarity will yield to knowledge of deeper principles. Thus, in the work of Gelman and Markman (1986) discussed earlier (Figure 10.8), category membership was more important than perceptual similarity in determining inductive inferences. Gelman and Wellman (1991) showed that even young children seem to use notions of essence in reasoning about biological kinds (see also Gelman & Hirschfeld, 1999). Susan Gelman has systematically traced the development of essentialism and its role in conceptual and linguistic development (see Gelman, 1998, for a review).

We have presented one way of relating similarity to knowledge structures and theories. Still, it would be misleading to state that there is any strong consensus on this general issue. Indeed, in the area of machine learning, a great deal of attention has been directed at the question of how to integrate similarity-based and explanation-based learning (see, e.g., Ellman, 1989; Flann & Dietterich, 1989; Rajamoney & DeJong, 1987; Wisniewski & Medin, 1994). Note that research on theories shares with the work on perceptual learning the idea that similarity has an important role to play but that role is governed by the consequences of other processes that work to constrain similarity.

Are There Kinds of Categories?

Almost all of our discussion has been focused on object concepts and their structure. But what about abstract concepts such as *democracy* or *dilemma,* adjective concepts such as *daring,* or verb concepts such as *dance?* Do the generalizations concerning object concepts apply equally to these other kinds of concepts or are there different principles involved when one moves beyond object concepts? One motivation for an interest in kinds of categories is that a number of researchers, especially in the area of cognitive development have suggested that cognition is organized in terms of distinct domains, each characterized by (usually) innate constraints or skeletal principles of development. For example, naïve psychology (theories about people), naïve biology (theories about livings things), and naïve physics (theories about the physical world) may constitute distinct domains with somewhat different principles of conceptual development (see Hirschfeld & Gelman, 1994, for examples).

It is transparently obvious that there are different kinds of categories, at least in the everyday sense of *different* and *kinds.* But to answer the sorts of questions we have raised, one must have some specific criteria in mind for what counts as a different kind. One might imagine that categories might differ in structure (as in our

A DEBATE
Category Specific Deficits

Studies of patients with brain damage often provide clues to normal brain functioning. One striking observation is that patients may show selective, **category-specific deficits** where they lose their ability to recognize and name category members from a particular domain of concepts. Nelson (1946) reported a patient who was unable to recognize a telephone, a hat, or a car but could identify people and other living things. Other researchers have noted the opposite deficit where people lose their ability to identify living kinds but retain the ability to categorize nonliving kinds.

Category-specific deficits seem consistent with ideas about domain-specific cognition but their interpretation has proven to be a matter of some controversy. On one side is the idea that living kinds and nonliving kinds are represented in anatomically and functionally distinct systems (Sartori & Job, 1988). An alternative view is that these deficit patterns can be accounted for by the fact that different kinds of information are needed to identify different kinds of objects (Warrington & Shallice, 1984). For example, sensory information may be relatively more important for recognizing living kinds and functional information more important for identifying nonliving kinds (e.g., artifacts). Although the evidence appear to be more consistent with the kinds of information view (see Damasio, Grabowski, Tranel, & Hichwa, 1996; Forde & Humpheys, 1999, for reviews), the issue continues to be hotly debated (see Caramazza & Shelton, 1998, for a vigorous defense of the domain specificity view of category specific deficits).

distinction between hierarchical and nonhierarchical categories), in the processing principles associated with them, or in principles that are tied to specific contents. The latter idea is tied to the notion of domain-specificity; the idea is that by looking only at principles that apply to all categories, we may be missing important principles that apply only to an important subset of categories (e.g., psychology vs. biology vs. physics).

Some of the candidate distinctions among kinds of categories, such as Barsalou's contrast between taxonomic and goal-derived categories have already been mentioned. We have space only to give a few examples of other contrasts. One distinction receiving increasing research interest is that between nouns and verbs, which may differ in structure (e.g., Macnamara, 1972; Gentner, 1981). One proposal is that nouns refer to clusters of correlated properties that create bounded chunks of perceptual experience. Verbs generally focus on relations among these entities involving things such as causal relations, activity, or change of state. Since relations require objects, nouns may be conceptually simpler than verbs and more constrained by perceptual experience. If so, then we might expect more cross-linguistic variability in verbs than nouns and that syntactic structure should play a greater role in verb learning than in noun learning. There is evidence for both of these claims (e.g., Bowerman, 1996; Choi & Bowerman, 1991; Levinson, 1994; Naigles, 1990; Pinker, 1994). Be aware, however, that the distinction between nouns and verbs is more subtle than we have implied. For example, motion may be associated with both nouns and verbs (e.g., runner); nonetheless, there is a bias for nouns to be associated with motion intrinsic to an object and verbs to be associated with motions involving relations between objects (Kersten, 1998a, 1998b).

Even more attention has been directed at the idea of domain-specificity. Much of the work on essentialism has been conducted in the context of exploring children's naïve biology (see also Au, 1994; Carey, 1995; Gopnik & Wellman, 1994; Spelke, Phillips, & Woodward, 1995). Although is it difficult to give a precise definition of a domain, the notion of domain-specificity has served to organize a great deal of research on conceptual development. For example, there has been a strong focus on the question of whether and when young children distinguish between psychology and biology. Carey (1985) argues that young children understand biological concepts in terms of a naïve psychology where human beings are the prototypical psychological entity. Only later on do they reorganize their knowledge into a less humanocentric, biological form where human beings are simply one animal among many. Others (e.g., Keil, 1989) have argued that young children do have biologically specific theories, though not as elaborate as those of adults. The issue is not a matter of idle debate because understanding how children's biological knowledge develops is highly relevant to science education as well as children's health-related behaviors (e.g., Au & Romo, 1996).

Summary

Research on object concepts has received disproportionate attention in the psychology of concepts. This work suggests that people may use similarity and theories as organizing principles for their categories, though neither type of information is sufficient by itself to account for people's behavior with concepts. Indeed, in many cases, both similarity and theories are related, as theories may help determine what people consider similar, and physical similarity may influence the development of theories.

Other kinds of concepts (besides object concepts) may have different structure and different processing principles (e.g., mechanisms by which they are learned). In addition, it appears to be a useful research strategy to analyze conceptual development in terms of different domains. Overall, then, there is a trend to organize categorization principles in terms of specific kinds of concepts (see Medin, Lynch, & Solomon, 2000, for a general review).

USE OF CATEGORIES IN REASONING

So much attention has been paid to structural aspects of categories that only modest attention has been given to the question of how categories may be used in reasoning. The promising results from the few studies that have been done suggest that this question is worthy of much more attention.

Goals and Ad Hoc Categories

Earlier we mentioned Barsalou's work on goal-derived categories (1985, 1987, 1989). In particular he has studied the organization of categories constructed in the service of goals, which we will refer to as **ad hoc categories.** "Things to take on a camping trip" and "foods to eat while on a diet" are two such ad hoc categories. Barsalou has found that ad hoc categories show the same typicality or goodness-of-example effects that are seen with more established categories. As we noted before, however, the basis for these effects is not overall similarity of examples to each other or to a prototype, but rather similarity to an ideal. For example, typicality ratings for the category of things to eat on a diet is determined by how closely examples conform to the ideal of zero calories. If goal-dervied categories are used repeatedly and consistently, they may become more stable in memory. In short Barsalou's work suggests that goals and the reasoning processes associated with them can affect category structure.

Conceptual Combination

As we mentioned at the beginning of this chapter, concepts provide "building blocks" or "mental tokens" that enable the construction of new concepts from old ones. For example, people use their knowledge of chocolate and rash to interpret *chocolate rash* as a rash caused by chocolate, even though they may never have seen the term chocolate rash before. **Conceptual combination** allows us to produce a virtually unlimited set of new concepts. Given that we hear novel combinations of concepts all the time, an important question is how people are able to understand them.

To our knowledge, a complete theory of how people combine concepts does not exist. Basically, we know that the most straightforward ideas are incomplete. One idea is that adjective-noun combinations are understood by constructing modified prototypes, the selective modification model of Smith & Osherson (1984). For example, according to their model, to understand the term *brown apple,* the apple prototype would be retrieved, the dimension of color would receive extra attention, and the prototypical value of red would be replaced with brown. In effect, one would be constructing a new prototype, brown apple, and the typicality of examples could be judged with respect to this constructed prototype. This modification model accounts for a number of phenomena associated with typicality judgments for combined adjective-noun concepts (Smith, Osherson, Rips, & Keane, 1988).

But conceptual combination is more complex than the modification model (or any other current model) implies. One problem is that the typicality of combined concepts cannot be predicted from the typicality of constituents. As an illustrative example, consider the concept *spoon*. People rate small spoons as more typical spoons than large spoons, and metal spoons as more typical spoons than wooden spoons. If the concept spoon is represented by a prototypic spoon, then a small metal spoon should be the most typical spoon, followed by small wooden and large metal spoons, and large wooden spoons should be the least typical. Instead, people find large wooden spoons to be more typical spoons than either small wooden spoons or large metal spoons (Medin & Shoben, 1988). One way for a prototype model to handle these results is to argue that people have separate prototypes for small spoons and large spoons. But this strategy creates new problems. Obviously one cannot have a separate prototype for every adjective-noun combination, because there are simply too many possible combinations. One might suggest that there are distinct subtypes for concepts like spoon, but one would need a theory describing how and when subtypes are created.

Another problem is that combined concepts may have properties that do not appear as properties of either constituent concept (Hampton, 1987, 1996; Murphy, 1988; see also Storms, De Boeck, Van Mechelen, & Ruts, 1998). For example, a salient property of the concept *pet bird* is that they live in cages, but this property is very atypical of either pets or birds by themselves.

A third problem is that people may complicate analyses by using a variety of strategies for comprehending combined concepts (Wisniewski, 1996, 1997; Wisniewski & Gentner, 1991). Consider, for example novel noun-noun combinations. When the two nouns are easily compared (because they have similar kinds of properties and are said to be "alignable") the combination is typically interpreted by extending a salient property of the modifying noun to the main noun. For example, a "zebra horse" might be understood as a horse with stripes. When the nouns are less comparable the most likely result is an integration where some relationship is found that meaningfully links the two concepts. For example, a "zebra house" typically is understood as a house for zebras rather than as a house with stripes. Models of conceptual combination that rely on a single process cannot account for these results (see Wisniewski & Love, 1998). So far, it seems that conceptual combination is as difficult as it is important (see Gagné & Shoben, 1997; Gerrig & Murphy, 1992; and Hampton, 1993, for other approaches to conceptual combination).

Categories and Induction

Finally, we note that categories play an important role in inductive reasoning. **Induction,** the use of some knowledge to draw inferences or expectations about other, more general situations, will be an important part of Chapter 11, but we include a sample here to illustrate the combined influence of similarity to examples and category membership in reasoning. Osherson, Smith, Wilkie, Lopez, and Shafir (1990) developed a formal model of category-based induction (see also Rips, 1975). The main idea is that judgments are based on both similarity to examples and knowledge of category membership. The model is formulated in terms of "argument strength," going from a premise or premises to the conclusion (candidate inference). For example, a premise might be "robins have property x" and the conclusion "sparrows also have property x" or "all birds have property x." We are using "have property x" to illustrate that properties were chosen so that participants in experiments would have no knowledge of whether these properties are true (e.g., "birds have sesamoid bones"). The task of the participants was to judge which argument form is stronger. For example, from the premise that robins have some property, people judge the argument with the conclusion that sparrows also have the property to be stronger than the argument with the conclusion that all birds have the property.

Argument strength is assumed to depend on two factors: the similarity of premise categories to the conclusion category and the similarity of the premise categories to examples of the lowest level category that the premise and conclusion categories share. For example, the strength of "robins have x" for the conclusion, "all birds have x," is based on the similarity of robins to bird (assumed to be perfect, because robins are birds) and the similarity of robins to other birds. The net confidence is assumed to be based on some weighting of these two factors. Similarly, the strength of "ostriches have x" for the conclusion, "all birds have x," is a function of the similarity of ostriches to bird (again, assumed to be perfect) and the similarity of ostriches to other birds. It follows directly that "robins have x" should be stronger than "ostriches have x" for the conclusion that all birds have x, because ostriches are less similar to other birds than are robins. In short, the model predicts typicality effects in reasoning (robins are more typical than ostriches).

Many of the predictions of the Osherson et al. model make intuitive sense, but a few predictions are quite surprising. The model predicts that going from the premise "bears have x" to the conclusion that "all mammals have x" will be stronger than going from "bears have x" to the conclusion "rabbits have x," even though rabbits are mammals. Note that whatever is true of all mammals must also be true of rabbits. The reason for this prediction by the model is that going from bears to rabbits involves weighting separately the similarity of bears to rabbits (which may be low), whereas going from bears to mammals is based on the overall similarity of bears to other mammals (which should be fairly high because bears are typical mammals). The results agree with this counterintuitive prediction.

Another prediction of the model makes intuitive sense but the associated results depend very much on who the research participants are. The prediction concerns premise *diversity*. Consider the following arguments: "Suppose we discover two new diseases, A and B. So far we know that Disease A affects the white pine and the weeping willow and that Disease B affects the paper birch and the river birch. Which disease is more likely to affect all trees, A or B? The Osherson et al. model predicts that people will say A for the same reasons it predicts typicality effects. The two trees associated with Disease A are very different from each other and together they represent the category "tree" better (trees that the white pine isn't similar to the weeping willow may be similar to). You, the reader, probably would make the same judgment, perhaps because you think that Disease B might be specific to birches. Surprisingly, however, when items like this (the items are different, because the plants and animals are different in Guatemala) are given to Itzá Maya adults, they do *not* pick the more diverse premises (Atran, 1998). And, in case you were starting to wonder about the reasoning processes of people in traditional societies, it also is the case that U.S. adults who know a lot about trees do not choose the disease associated with the more diverse pair consistently either (Coley, Medin, Proffitt, Lynch, & Atran, 1999). In fact, on the particular example given above tree maintenance workers overwhelming picked Disease B as more likely to affect all trees!

What accounts for these surprising results? The answer seems to be that both tree experts and Itzá Maya are reasoning about ecological relations and potential causal mechanisms. For example, a typical justification for choosing Disease B on the above item was that birches are very susceptible to disease and are very widely planted so there would be many opportunities for the disease to spread. Aside from suggesting that models of category-based reasoning need to make provision for people reasoning about potential mechanisms, these results point out that categorization and reasoning by novices in a domain may differ substantially from that of experts. If nothing else it should make cognitive psychologists more cautious about generalizing from results with undergraduate populations to all people.

Overall, the category-based induction model is quite successful. As we said at the beginning of this section, psychologists are just starting to explore the use of categories in reasoning (for extensions to nonblank properties, see Sloman, 1994; Smith, Shafir, & Osherson, 1993). The work on reasoning is part of a general trend to study how concepts are used and we can already see that this approach is delivering new insights into the nature of concepts.

Summary

Concepts serve to organize our mental life. Analyses of conceptual structure provide some important conclusions for our understanding of human cognition. Contrary to one's initial impression, many categories do not have defining properties but rather are fuzzy or probabilistic. These probabilistic categories may be organized around an average example (a prototype) or around specific examples seen during learning. The research we reviewed also suggests that things that are superficially similar tend to be similar in deeper ways, but similarity does not provide the basis for conceptual coherence. Concepts are often organized around theories and are knowledge-based rather than similarity-based.

Another important issue is that categories have many different functions. Much research on categorization has focused on how people learn to classify a set of items. However, people also use their categories to communicate, to reason, and to make predictions. Psychologists are now working on how category representations are used to serve these functions and also what people learn about categories in the process of using them.

What about the questions and problems with which we began this chapter? Why do we have the particular categories we have, out of the virtually unlimited number of possibilities? Are categories in the world to be discovered, or are they imposed on the world by our minds? We have suggested that perceptual similarity may serve as an initial classification strategy that is refined, deepened, and itself modified by knowledge and developing theories about the world. If our perceptual and conceptual systems suggested to us categorization schemes that did not serve our goals and did not allow for predictions and explanations, we would be poorly adapted. Therefore, it is tempting to say that categories are organized around our goals and that different organisms with different goals would have very different categorization schemes. Although this may be true, it is equally important to recognize the importance of our environment. If we lived in a very different world, we would need a different perceptual and conceptual system to pick out categories that would be useful in that world. As indicated in our opening quotation, we believe that William James was correct when he suggested that mind and world "are something of a mutual fit."

Key Terms

ad hoc categories	family resemblance
basic level	homeopathy
category	induction
category-specific deficits	linear separability
classical view	probabilistic view
concept	prototype
conceptual combination	psychological essentialism
contagion	typicality
exemplar models	

Recommended Readings

Because all three authors do research on categorization, we are tempted to say, "Read everything!" Fortunately, a number of reviews of the literature exist. For basic historical background, the edited volume by Rosch and Lloyd (1978) and the book by Smith and Medin (1981) are recommended. More recent analyses and overviews are provided by Estes (1994), Medin and Heit (1999), and the edited volumes by Hirschfeld and Gelman (1994), Lamberts and Shanks (1997), and Van Mechelen, Hampton, and Michalski (1993). A nice review of cross-cultural research on biological categorization is provided by Malt (1995) and the edited volume by Medin and Atran (1999) covers both cross-cultural and developmental research. Lillard (1998) argues that adult folk psychology differs across cultures—such a fact would have important implications for understanding the development of naïve or folk psychology. For analyses that focus on tests of or contrasts between particular models of categorization, see Anderson (1990a, 1990b), Erickson and Kruschke (1998), Estes (1994), Heit (1994), Hintzman (1986), Maddox and Ashby (1993), Murphy and Ross (1994), Nosofsky et al. (1994), Nosofsky and Palmeri (1997), Storms, De Boeck, and Ruts (2000), and Wisniewski and Medin (1994). A special issue of the journal *Cognition,* edited by Sloman and Rips (1998), is devoted to the topic of the role of similarity in cognition. Malt, Sloman, Gennari, Shi, and Wang (1999) offer a nice cross-cultural analysis of the relation between perceived similarity of containers and how they are named.

Finally, there is increasing interest in the use of categories in reasoning. A good place to start is Rips (1975), Osherson et al. (1990), Smith et al. (1993), and Sloman (1993, 1994, 1998); for developmental work, see Gelman and Markman (1986), Gelman and Wellman (1991), Gutheil and Gelman (1997), Keil (1989), and Lopez, Gelman, Gutheil, and Smith (1992); for cross-cultural work see Atran (1998), Choi, Nisbett, and Smith (1997), and Lopez, Atran, Coley, Medin, and Smith (1997).

PART V
THINKING

Chapter 11
Reasoning

Chapter 12
Problem Solving

Chapter 13
Expertise and Creativity

Chapter 14
Judgment and Decision Making

Chapter 11

Reasoning

Introduction

Logic and Reasoning
Validity and Truth
Deductive Versus Inductive Reasoning
Summary

The Psychology of Deduction
Conditional Reasoning
Conditional Reasoning in Hypothesis Testing:
   The Selection Task
Summary

The Psychology of Inductive Reasoning
Probabilistic Reasoning
Test Quality: A Case Study of Base Rates
Base Rate Neglect
Confusing Conditional Probabilities
Argument Structure and Relevance
Summary

The Importance of Content
Analogy and Similarity
An Example of Mapping
A Return to Similarity
Summary

Mental Models and Intuitive Theories
Intuitive Theories

Hypothesis Testing and Scientific Reasoning

Summary

Key Terms

Recommended Readings

Logic is the anatomy of thought.

—*John Locke*

*"Contrariwise," continued Tweedledee, "If it was so,
it might be; and if it were so, it would be;
but as it isn't, it ain't. That's logic."*

—*Lewis Carroll*

INTRODUCTION

In our exploration of cognition, two themes have come up repeatedly. On the one hand, the world presents us with more information at any moment than we can possibly deal with, and so we must find ways to limit the information that we process so that we do not get bogged down in thought. On the other hand, the world does not provide us with all of the information we need at any given moment. For example, if you hear a rustling noise late at night while you are sleeping, you get up and investigate, not because the rustling noise itself is problematic, but rather because it signals to us that someone or something is moving around the house. In this way, you are *reasoning:* that is, you are going beyond the information given to comprehend a situation. In this case, you are making an *inference* about what is true of the world.

People are quite skilled at going beyond the information given to comprehend the world around them. How is this ability to reason accomplished? People appear to reason using both general procedures that provide important information in many contexts as well as with knowledge about specific contexts. In this chapter, we will explore both general reasoning strategies as well as those based on specific knowledge. We will begin with a discussion of logic, which is a domain-general process for going beyond the information given. Then, we will briefly discuss induction, another general process of reasoning. Next, we will turn to types of specific knowledge people use when reasoning. Much of this discussion will focus on our ability to reason by analogy. Finally, we will bring both general and specific forms of reasoning together in a discussion of scientific reasoning.

LOGIC AND REASONING

Imagine a child walking to school. The day before, her friend told her that she would meet her at the corner, or in front of the mailbox. The child arrives at the corner, only to find her friend is not there. This situation is not a cause for consternation, however, for the child is likely to assume immediately that her friend is waiting in front of the mailbox.

This feat of reasoning is so straightforward, it seems hardly worth mentioning. However, it is an example of a simple logical inference. Given the knowledge that either one fact or another is true (either the friend will be at the corner *or* in front of the mailbox) and the evidence that one of those facts is not true (the friend is *not* at the corner), it can now be determined that the other fact is true (the friend must be in front of the mailbox). This reasoning strategy will work for any set of facts, regardless of what those facts are. We can write out this strategy as a **reasoning schema**—a template for doing logical reasoning—by substituting the specific facts with letters that correspond to any possible fact in the following way:

$$P \text{ OR } Q$$
$$NOT \text{ } P$$
$$\therefore Q$$

In this schema, the symbol $\therefore$ means *therefore*. The first two lines (before the $\therefore$) are called *premises*, and the statement after the $\therefore$ is called the *conclusion*. The schema tells us what to conclude given the premises. This schema will work no matter what facts are put into P and Q (try it).

A **logic** consists of a number of types of *operators* and *facts* and a set of *schemas* for combining the operators and facts in order to draw conclusions from a set of premises. In the example just given P and Q are facts. The facts may be true or false. There are also two operators: OR is an operator that is true when at least one of the facts it connects is true. For example, the statement P OR Q is true when P is true, when Q is true or when both P or Q are true. A statement involving the operator NOT is true only when the fact it operates on is false. Table 11.1 shows a truth table for some common logical operators.

The argument just described is a valid **deductive argument.** Deductive arguments are a special kind of argument, because the form of the argument guarantees that if the premises are true then the conclusion is also true. In the case of the young girl walking to school, she believes P OR Q to be true, and discovers that P is not true (i.e., she discovers NOT P). She immediately concludes that Q must be true, and happily continues on her way. When she reaches the mailbox, of course, one of two things might happen. She might discover (as expected) that her friend is waiting for her. In this case, the two premises of the argument are true, and the conclusion (Q) is also true. It is also possible that her friend is not in front of the mailbox. In this case, the conclusion (Q) is false. Because this schema is deductive, if the conclusion is false, then one of the premises must be false as well. Because she saw with her own eyes that her friend was not at the corner, she is likely to conclude that the premise P OR Q is false (and she will probably arrive at school and ask her friend why she said she would be at the corner or in front of the mailbox if that was not true).

You might have noticed that at the beginning of the previous paragraph, we described the argument above as a *valid* deductive argument. In a valid argument, the

Table 11.1 **A Truth Table for the Operators NOT, AND, and OR. The Table Presents the Truth Values of These Operators Given the Truth of the Facts P and Q.**

	P is True		P is False	
Operator	**Q is True**	**Q is False**	**Q is True**	**Q is False**
NOT P	FALSE	FALSE	TRUE	TRUE
P AND Q	TRUE	FALSE	FALSE	FALSE
P OR Q	TRUE	TRUE	TRUE	FALSE

truth of the premises guarantees the truth of the conclusion. It is possible to construct reasoning schemas that look like perfectly good arguments, but turn out not to be valid. For example, consider

A AND B

NOT A

∴ B

The operator AND is true only when both A and B are true. This reasoning schema is not valid.

To summarize what we have said so far, it is possible to reason using valid deductive reasoning schemas. A deductive schema is valid when it is set up such that when the premises of the argument are true the conclusion must also be true. Deductive reasoning like this is powerful, because it allows people to reason about the truth of statements regardless of what the statements are about. The valid schema given above can apply equally well to children walking to school and to scientific hypotheses.

Validity and Truth

One thing we have done so far is to distinguish between the validity of an argument and the truth of some statement. Validity refers to the structure of an argument; that is, it refers to the way the argument is set up. Truth, refers to whether a particular statement is true about the world.

Even though validity and truth are separate concepts, people sometimes have difficulty separating them and will evaluate arguments not only in terms of whether they are valid, but also on the basis of whether they are empirically true (that is, true about the world). Logical validity and empirical truth do not necessarily agree. Consider the following argument:

Premise 1: All doctors are professional people.

Premise 2: Some professional people are rich.

Conclusion: ∴ Some doctors are rich.

A moment's reflection will reveal that this argument form is not valid because it may be the case that all of the professional people who are rich are nondoctors (e.g., lawyers, engineers, etc.). The fact that the conclusion may be empirically true does not mean that the argument structure is a valid argument.

This case is a *content effect* in reasoning, because the meaning of the facts is affecting a judgment about the structure of the argument. It should not be surprising that there are content effects in reasoning. The point of being able to make inferences, to go beyond the information given, is to determine facts about the world that are likely to be true (or false). That is, we reason in service of determining truth. Thus, people are focused on determining what is true of the world, and the purpose of using deductive arguments is to help to determine truth. In the end, however, people may find truth more compelling than argument validity.

Another point to consider is that people expect arguments to be not only logically correct and empirically true but also relevant. Consider the following argument:

Premise 1: The picnic will be held outdoors OR

the picnic will be held at the gym.

Premise 2: The picnic will NOT be held outdoors.

Conclusion: ∴ The picnic will be held at the gym OR

cats have six legs.

It turns out that this conclusion is deductively valid because if X is true, then X OR Y must also be true, regardless of what Y is (see Table 11.1). The problem with the conclusion is that the number of legs cats have has nothing to do with the premises. Even if the conclusion was that "the picnic will be held at the gym or cats have four legs," we still would have a relevance problem. Typically, researchers supply the conclusions and ask participants to judge their validity; only rarely (see Johnson-Laird, 1983, for an exception) have psychologists studied which conclusions seem intuitively natural (and presumably relevant) to people.

In this section, we have seen that the split between domain-general forms of reasoning and the use of specific knowledge may not be as sharp as we assumed originally. In particular, the truth of a statement may influence the way people use an argument. Furthermore, people use some knowledge about the world to determine what conclusions are relevant. Before exploring how good people are at reasoning, we will first examine the differences between deductive reasoning and inductive reasoning.

Deductive Versus Inductive Reasoning

Deductive reasoning is special, because it allows us to assert the truth of a conclusion given the truth of the premises. Not all forms of reasoning are truth preserving in this way. Sometimes, we use arguments that expand on the premises such that if the premises are true, the conclusion is *probably* (but not *necessarily*) true. **Inductive reasoning** is concerned with certain beliefs supporting or being supported by (rather than being logically required by) other beliefs. Given that John has no alibi for where he was last night, that he possesses a crowbar, and that 15 television sets are found in his apartment, it is more likely that he broke into a local appliance store last night than it would be if he had an alibi, only one television set, and no crowbar. However, the conclusion that John robbed the appliance store is not deductively valid. In this case, the deductive form of the argument would look like this:

If John committed the robbery, then he has 15 television sets.

John has 15 television sets.

Therefore, John committed the robbery.

Put more abstractly, this schema has the form:

If P then Q

Q

∴ P

This form of argument is not valid. John's possession of the 15 television sets certainly makes us more likely to believe that John committed the robbery, but there may be other explanations. For example, John may be the apartment manager and may have purchased the television sets to furnish other apartments, or John may have a larcenous roommate, or John may run a television repair business from his apartment. Inductive reasoning goes beyond the information given by suggesting facts that might be true given a set of premises. Induction is always probabilistic rather than certain in character. The general point is that people employ both inductive and deductive reasoning to arrive at beliefs, and the same argument that is inductively strong or powerful may be deductively invalid.

The coexistence of induction and deduction in reasoning is important. Deductive schemas are truth preserving, because if the premises are true, the conclusion must be true. However, the truth of many premises we believe to be true is established using induction. Because induction is not truth preserving, we can never be absolutely certain of the truth of conclusions drawn from inductive arguments. Thus, we can never be certain of the truth of the premises in our deductive arguments. Thus, the cognitive system will always need to have other mechanisms for assessing the truth of beliefs, even those derived from valid deductive arguments.

Summary

Deductive reasoning is a domain-general way of going beyond the information given. Deductive reasoning derives its power from the fact that it is truth preserving so that the truth of the premises guarantees the truth of the conclusion. The validity of deductive arguments is determined by the form of the argument rather than by the content of the facts in the argument, and so it can be used in many contexts. Inductive arguments are not deductively valid. Instead, confidence in the conclusion is influenced by confidence in the premises as well as the relation between the premises and the conclusion.

THE PSYCHOLOGY OF DEDUCTION _____

In this section, we examine people's performance in deductive reasoning tasks. As we will see, people's performance on many deductive tasks is flawed. We will explore explanations for these shortcomings including problems integrating logical and empirical truth and processing limitations.

Conditional Reasoning

Conditional reasoning concerns what outcomes can be expected if certain conditions are met. In particular, the first premise of a conditional argument is a statement of the form "If P then Q." We will abbreviate this conditional statement as $P \rightarrow Q$, which is the notation typically used in logic. One other bit of terminology is also important. In the argument $P \rightarrow Q$, we will refer to P as the *antecedent* and Q as the *consequent*.

Modus Ponens and Modus Tollens

The best-known conditional argument form is referred to as **modus ponens.** It has the structure:

$$P \rightarrow Q$$
$$P$$
$$\therefore Q$$

This schema is also called "Affirming the antecedent" sometimes, because the second premise asserts the truth (i.e., affirms) the first part of the conditional (i.e., the antecedent). As an example of this schema, let P equal "John gets B or better on the final test" and Q equal "John passes the course." We can see that it follows from the first two premises that John passes the course.

A closely related form is **modus tollens** (or denying the consequent), which has the following structure:

$$P \rightarrow Q$$
$$NOT\ Q$$
$$\therefore NOT\ P$$

In this example involving John, the first premise, coupled with the observation that John did not pass the course, lets us conclude that he did not get a B or better on the final test. Both of these argument forms are valid or correct.

Modus ponens and modus tollens are the only two schemas involving conditionals that are valid deductive argument forms. There are two other argument forms that can be constructed using a conditional statement, but they are not valid. The first of these forms is **denying the antecedent** and has the form:

$$P \rightarrow Q$$
$$NOT\ P$$
$$\therefore NOT\ Q$$

This argument is not valid, because the fact Q might be true for some other reason. For example, if P is "It is raining" and Q is "The ground is wet" it is possible that the ground is wet even if it is not raining (perhaps because a sprinkler was on).

The other invalid form of conditional argument is **affirming the consequent,** and has the form:

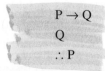

$$P \rightarrow Q$$
$$Q$$
$$\therefore P$$

This case is related to the invalid form denying the consequent. Again, the argument is invalid, because the fact Q could be true for many reasons, only one of which is the fact P.

While it may seem straightforward to recognize these invalid argument forms, consider the following argument:

> If it is sunny, the picnic will be held.
>
> It is not sunny.
>
> ∴ The picnic will not be held.

This argument form seems quite plausible. However, if we substitute P and Q for the facts, we will see that it is an example of denying the antecedent, which is an invalid form. Why does the argument seem plausible, then? Although you may not have realized it, the word *if* in English is ambiguous. Sometimes it refers to a simple conditional statement (as in many of the examples above). However, sometimes it means "if and only if," an interpretation known as the biconditional (because both P → Q and Q → P are true). The biconditional can be written using the symbol ↔, which highlights that the conditional goes both ways. When there is a biconditional, denying the antecedent is a valid form of argument. In this case,

$$P \leftrightarrow Q$$
$$NOT\ P$$
$$\therefore NOT\ Q$$

In order to get around this ambiguity in English, when talking about logic, the convention is to assume that *if* is conditional unless the biconditional is explicitly stated (by saying "if and only if" or sometimes by writing it as *iff*). By this standard, the preceding conditional argument form (about the picnic) is invalid, because it is denying the antecedent.

Unfortunately, natural language does not conform to this logic convention, and so determining which sense is meant in everyday conversation requires looking at the context. For example, the parent who says, "If you pick up your toys, I will read you a story" intends *if* to mean *if and only if,* whereas a sports fan who says, "If our quarterback is injured, then our team will lose" very likely has in mind a simple conditional. Given this ambiguity of *if,* it is not surprising that a fair proportion (more than 20%) of college students in reasoning tasks make the error of denying the antecedent (Marcus & Rips, 1979).

Modus ponens appears to be an intuitively correct and natural rule. College students are nearly always correct, regardless of the contents of P or Q and regardless even of whether they have meaningful contents (P and Q work just fine; see, e.g., Evans, 1977). Modus tollens is a different story. A third or more of the time, college students fail to agree that the conclusion is logically (necessarily) correct. It is not clear why modus tollens is so difficult. One speculation is that people often treat logical implication as reasoning from causes to effects. Modus tollens requires backward rather than forward reasoning, and it is probably easier to reason from causes to effects than from effects to causes. The fact that college students also have considerable difficulty avoiding the error of affirming the consequent is consistent with this suggestion. Consider again the example involving a quarterback. It is easy to imagine that an injury to a quarterback could lead to the loss of a game. Consequently, one may be tempted to conclude from the observation that the team lost that the quarterback was injured. But this conclusion does not follow as a deductive inference.

We might also expect modus tollens to be very susceptible to content effects (see Rips, 1990, for a review). Although modus tollens is difficult when presented abstractly, the following example seems natural enough:

If the horses had been to the waterhole, we would see their tracks.

We see no tracks.

Therefore, the horses have not been to the waterhole.

But wait, something is not right here! Our example heavily biases the reading of *if* as the biconditional if-and-only-if (see also Marcus & Rips, 1979, for examples of content influencing the interpretation of the conditional). To see this, change the argument form so that we affirm the consequent:

If the horses had been to the waterhole, we would see their tracks.

We see their tracks.

Therefore, they have been to the waterhole.

This argument seems virtually ironclad empirically, but it is not logically valid.

What makes this example tricky is that when conditional reasoning is embedded in a causal framework, whether or not there are compelling alternative explanations of Q may determine how natural it is to interpret if as a biconditional. For the above case it is hard to imagine how the horse tracks could have gotten there unless the horses made them. Let's try modifying the example, beginning with modus tollens:

If the horses had been to the waterhole, then the food we left out would be gone.

The food we left out is still here.

Therefore, the horses have not been to the waterhole.

This example seems reasonable and valid. Furthermore, we would not necessarily fall for affirming the antecedent when the argument form is changed to:

If the horses had been to the waterhole, then the food we left out would be gone.

The food we left is gone.

Therefore, the horses have been to the waterhole.

The reason we might not fall for this argument is that we could think of alternative reasons why the food might be gone. For example, other animals may have taken it.

Note that this discussion of content has nothing to do with the validity of the modus tollens argument form. These examples do serve to illustrate some of the difficulties associated with keeping argument contents distinct from argument form, especially when the conditional, *if,* is itself somewhat ambiguous. Although the if-then argument form is not to be equated with cause-effect relations, it appears that cause-effect relations influence whether *if* is interpreted as a biconditional and the difficulty of modus tollens.

Conditional Reasoning in Hypothesis Testing: The Selection Task

Consider the following example from Wason (see Wason & Johnson-Laird, 1972):

You are given the following four cards:

| E | F | 4 | 7 |

Each card has a letter on one side and a number on the other side. The task is to decide which cards must be selected to test the hypothesis that "If a card has a vowel on one side, it has an even number on the other side."

Before reading on, try the task: Which cards would you select?

What is the correct answer here? The rule "If a card has a vowel on one side, it has an even number on the other side" is a conditional statement in an unfamiliar domain. The cards that should be turned over are those corresponding to the two valid conditional reasoning schemas, modus ponens and modus tollens. In this case, P is "the card has a vowel on one side" and Q is "has an even number on the other side." The E should be turned over, because it is a vowel (and hence P is true), and so it is possible that there will be an odd number on the other side (NOT Q, which would make the rule false). The 7 (NOT Q) should also be turned over, because of the possibility that a vowel (P) would be on the other side, which would also falsify the rule. The typical college undergraduate given this task will correctly say that the E card should be turned over, but will typically miss the 7. Instead, college student subjects tend to say that the 4 should be turned over.

The E seems obvious, because an odd number on the other side would falsify the hypothesis suggested by the conditional. Presumably, the 4 is turned over, because even numbers are also mentioned in the conditional. However, if there is a vowel on the other side of the card, the hypothesis is supported, and if there is a consonant on the other side, then the rule simply fails to apply. Thus, no information relevant to falsifying the rule can be obtained from turning over the 4. In contrast, if the 7 is turned over, and there is a vowel on the other side, then the rule has been falsified.

Why do people fail on the Wason selection task? One idea is that the most natural way to link the hypothesis with the cards (or data) is to match terms in the hypothesis with states of affairs in the data (Evans, 1982). The hypothesis mentions vowels and even numbers, and the most common response is to select E and 4. If the matching hypothesis is correct, then if we change the wording of the hypothesis to "If a card has a vowel on one side, then it will not have an even number on the other side," we might expect performance to improve. Now the correct response is E and 4, and both vowels and even numbers are mentioned in the conditional. In fact, performance is considerably better on problems having the "if P, then not Q" format (Evans & Lynch, 1973; Manktelow & Evans, 1979; Wason & Evans, 1975).

Why should matching be important? In a general review of the literature, Evans (1982, 1983) suggests that two factors are involved. One is simply attention. The fact that terms are mentioned in the conditional statement draws attention to them. Why? Part of the answer may be that people are sensitive to Gricean principles or maxims for communication (as we discussed in Chapter 9) and they expect information to be relevant. If this analysis is correct, it suggests that the bias to attend to terms that are mentioned derives from the fact that most of the time information that is mentioned is relevant. A second factor suggested by Evans is that people do not necessarily determine all of the implications of a premise. For example, people apparently do not spontaneously convert "not an even number" into "odd number," or else the matching hypothesis would not have been supported in the Evans (1982) study. In short, the matching hypothesis appears to be at least part of the story about why the four-card problem is so hard.

The Wason and Johnson-Laird task is also very susceptible to content effects, though their interpretation is not always clear. Johnson-Laird, Legrenzi, and Legrenzi (1972) showed English adults a drawing of sealed and opened envelopes stamped with either a 4d or a 5d postage stamp (the d stands for an English penny) in a format analogous to the E, F, 4, 7 problem. Participants were asked which of the envelopes should be examined to test the rule "If a letter is sealed, then it has a 5d stamp on it." This problem uses concrete objects. Furthermore, there was an old English postal regulation that associated different postage rates with sealed envelopes than for unsealed envelopes. Thus, many English subjects were likely to be familiar with situations in which different postage would be placed on envelopes depending on whether they were sealed.

Which factor causes this content effect? Is it that the problem is concrete (involving envelopes and stamps instead of letters and numbers) or that the rule is familiar? Griggs and Cox (1982; Griggs, 1983) replicated the Johnson-Laird et al. experiment with college students in the United States and found no differences between the envelope condition and a control condition using abstract materials, suggesting that familiarity with the rule is more important than concreteness. This conclusion is further supported by the findings of Golding (1981), who demonstrated that English subjects old enough to remember the postal regulation performed well on the envelope task, whereas subjects too young to remember this regulation performed no better with the envelopes than with abstract materials.

This finding suggests that when people know a specific rule applicable to the domain, then they solve the selection task correctly. There is also evidence that people have other rules that are not specific to particular situations, but are not so general that they apply to any situation. One set of rules that has been studied in great detail are social schemas involving permission, obligation, or authorization (e.g., Cheng & Holyoak, 1985; Cheng, Holyoak, Nisbett, & Oliver, 1986). These social rules are called **pragmatic reasoning schemas,** because they are like the reasoning schemas described above, except that they are derived from pragmatic rules like permission. For example, people perform well when the rule is "anyone consuming Coca-Cola on these premises must be at least 100 years old" or even a completely unfamiliar rule such as "any lengths of red wool must be at least 6 meters long," as long as permission or authorization is involved (Wason & Green, 1984). Cheng and her associates have argued that conditional reasoning is organized around these sorts of pragmatic reasoning schemas rather than "syntactic logical rules." That is, reasoning skills are not completely abstract forms that are independent of content. Semantic contents, such as permission, are said to "trigger" particular reasoning schemas. Although it is clear that content yields powerful effects, the underlying basis for these effects remains controversial (see, e.g., Cheng & Holyoak, 1989; Cosmides, 1989; Gigerenzer & Hug, 1992; Klaczynski, Gelfund, & Reese, 1989; Oaksford & Chater, 1994; Rips, 1994; and Sperber, Cara, & Girotto, 1995, for further arguments and counterarguments).

An additional refinement is that the pattern of choices is sensitive to the implied point of view associated with permissions, obligations, and the like. For example, Manktelow and Over (1991) told British participants that a shop had promised customers, "If you spend more than 100 pounds, then you may take a free gift." Again there were four cards ("more than 100 pounds," "less than 100 pounds," "free gift," and "no free gift") with amounts spent on one side and status of gift on the other side. When the instructions implied that the shop may have not met its obligation, participants tended to select "more than 100 pounds" and "no free gift" cards. But when instructions implied that some customers may have taken more than they should have, choices shifted to "less than 100 pounds" and "free gift" cards. The pattern of responses is sensible and appropriate. More to the point, it underlines the fact that checking social obligations or contracts may be different in character from the original Wason and Johnson-Laird task. The fact that the correct answer in the Manktelow and Over study depends on the perspective taken (unlike the original four-card situation) shows that we are dealing with more than simple concreteness effects.

One final factor influencing performance in the selection task is whether the hypothesis or rule encourages a *unified* representation (in which the antecedent and consequent are thought of as part of a single object or event) rather than a *disjoint* representation (in which the antecedent and consequent are thought of as parts of different objects or events). In the standard version of the task, the relevant sources of information are on opposite sides of the cards, which Wason and Green (1984) argue should lead to disjoint representation. They offer the following rule as an example that encourages a unified representation: "If the figure on the card is a triangle, then it has been colored red." In fact, the representation is so unified that it's not clear how one could present shapes without revealing their colors. Wason and Green got around this problem by describing possible colors and shapes and asking their subjects to imagine the stimuli. An example of a rule that should lead to a disjoint representation would be "All the triangles have a red patch above them" or the alternative wording, "All of the cards that have a triangle on one half are red on the other half." They found that about 80% of their subjects solved the problem for the description that should lead to a unified representation compared with about 40% for problems that should lead to a disjoint representation.

Many of these phenomena may seem to you akin to Russian dolls; for each explanation, it seems that there is a deeper explanation inside it. Does a unified representation have anything to do with the matching hypothesis described by Evans? Are pragmatic reasoning schemas special, or are they just effective because they lead to unified representations? What is clear is that conditional reasoning tasks are underspecified in the sense that research participants bring a variety of types of knowledge to bear on them, including conversational rules, causal reasoning, and specific, relevant prior experiences.

Some researchers have taken these observations on content effects to mean that people have limited (or no) abstract reasoning abilities. Our reading of this literature is that content and logical form interact in terms of the way in which abstract forms are linked to (or embedded in) particular contents. This observation does not, however, mean that people cannot reason abstractly. For example, people are perfectly capable of reasoning from A $\rightarrow$ B and B $\rightarrow$ C that A $\rightarrow$ C. But when this reasoning structure is embedded in content, there are challenging issues concerning how one decides that an A, B, C, or implication has been instantiated and whether the B in the first term is really equivalent to the B in the second term. Consider this example taken from Lewis (1973):

If J. Edgar Hoover had been born in Russia, then he would have been a communist.

If J. Edgar Hoover had been a communist, then he would have been a traitor.

Therefore, if J. Edgar Hoover had been born in Russia, then he would have been a traitor.

This argument appears to have a valid structure, so why does the conclusion seem so strange? In this case, the "had been a communist" in the second premise is really a shorthand for "had been a communist living in the United States, and was director of the FBI." Thus, this argument really has the form *if A then B, if D then C; therefore if A then C.* This argument form is clearly not valid. In short, a central question is not so much whether people use reasoning schemas but how people take the information from a specific context and enter it appropriately into an abstract rule.

A DEBATE
Do People Have Abstract Reasoning Structures or Rules?

One reason for the fuss about whether people can reason abstractly is that analyses of other aspects of higher cognition often require an underlying abstract system for deduction that includes rules such as modus ponens (Rips, 1988). Research conducted from this perspective focuses on correct reasoning and treats errors and limitations in reasoning as secondary (see, e.g., Henle, 1962).

One view of reasoning that occupies a middle ground between abstract rules and specific situations is Johnson-Laird's (1983; Johnson-Laird & Byrne, 1989) *mental models* approach. He suggests that when people are presented with an abstract reasoning problem, they try to create a more specific model or image of the situation. For example, if a logic problem contained the statement "All artists are creative" they might imagine a number of people, where all of the imagined artists were creative (though there might be some creative people in the model that were not artists). By translating various logical statements into these models, Johnson-Laird argues that logic problems can be solved without actually having logical rules.

Rips (1986, 1990, 1994) has argued that mental models are also a form of logic, though perhaps one that does not follow all of the same rules as formal logic. Recall from our definition above that a logic has facts, operators, and schemas for drawing conclusions from premises. Rips suggests that mental models must have all of these properties in order to permit people to solve logic problems. The crucial issue in this debate,

(Continued)

Summary

People are clearly able to reason deductively. Certain inferences (like those that follow from modus ponens) seem to be made regardless of the content of the facts being reasoned about. Other inferences, like those that follow from modus tollens are much more difficult for people, particularly in abstract settings. When the situation is familiar, or when it follows a social schema, then people seem to reason in accord with principles of logic. It is important to keep in mind that the goal of reasoning is to establish what may be true about the world, and that the use of logical reasoning schemas is subservient to that goal. Deductive inference is a significant area of research in cognitive psychology, and our discussion here has only scratched the surface of the work being done. In some sense, the two sides

A DEBATE

Do People Have Abstract Reasoning Structures or Rules? *(Continued)*

however, is the status of rules. Rips has proposed a reasoning model in which formal rules of inference are directly represented (see also Braine, Reiser, & Rumain, 1984). The mental models approach uses procedures for constructing models that evaluate the validity of arguments but do not explicitly represent rules.

Finally, there is the suggestion described above that the rules used for reasoning are those important for particular domains like social reasoning (Cheng & Holyoak, 1985, 1989). Indeed, Cosmides (1989) suggests that humans are sensitive to rules for social reasoning, because we are adapted (through evolution) to be sensitive to aspects of our social world like dominance (which leads to a sensitivity to permission, because a subordinate must get permission to do something from a more dominant individual) and cheating.

Which view is correct? We know that under certain circumstances people can use rules directly. Logicians may use abstract rules for complex problems, and the rest of us may use them for simple problems. But there is also considerable support for the idea that people may reason by trying to think of concrete examples or the sort of mental symbol manipulation suggested by the mental models approach. Further, there is little question that people are quite sensitive to social rules like permission (though it is not clear what evolutionary niche would have helped make people sensitive to the difference between sealed and unsealed envelopes). Just which strategy people use is likely to vary across reasoning tasks and may also vary with the familiarity of the task.

of deduction, its centrality to cognition and its difficulty, are summarized by the quotations that began this chapter. In the following section, we turn our attention to research on the psychology of inductive reasoning.

THE PSYCHOLOGY OF INDUCTIVE REASONING

Abstractly speaking, inductive reasoning is concerned with how observations and beliefs support other beliefs. In certain respects, inductive reasoning runs in the direction opposite to deductive reasoning. The argument structure for inductive reasoning seems to be something like the following:

$$P \rightarrow Q$$
$$Q$$
$$\therefore P \text{ is more likely}$$

P can be a set of beliefs or a theory linked to certain expectations (Q) and if these expectations are satisfied (Q occurs), then we are more confident of P. For example, P may be the belief that all dogs bark and Q the observations of a particular dog that barks. Or P may be Einstein's theory of relativity, and Q may be the outcome of an experiment designed to test his theory. Inductive reasoning is inherently uncertain: One may always run into a variety of dog that does not bark, and some other prediction of Einstein's theory might turn out to be incorrect. We have already discussed category-based inductive reasoning in the chapter on concepts. In what follows, we focus on some general aspects of the relationship between inductive reasoning and reasoning about probabilities. Then, we will discuss a problem with focusing on general aspects of inductive reasoning.

Probabilistic Reasoning

Inductive reasoning involves using evidence to change our confidence in beliefs. There are many ways that we can phrase our level of certainty in a fact, but one way we often do it is using probabilities. When we hear on the radio that there is an 80% chance of thunderstorms, we are more likely to bring an umbrella to work than if we here there is a 20% chance of thunderstorms. Because of the common use of probabilities to talk about certainty, it is important to understand how people reason with and about probabilities (Budescu & Wallsten, 1995).

Let's start our discussion of probabilistic reasoning with an example. Suppose we are trying to diagnose a fairly rare but serious disease. A treatment exists for the disease, but it is both costly and risky. Therefore, it is important to make sure that the disease is present before giving the treatment. A new diagnostic test is developed that has the following two properties:

If the disease is present, 98% of the time the test will be positive.

If the disease is absent, only 1% of the time the test will be positive.

Suppose that we perform this diagnostic test on a patient and it turns out positive. How likely is it that the patient has the disease? Take a minute to come up with your own estimate.

In general, people have difficulty in reasoning about uncertain events like the one outlined here. We have given this problem to first-year medical school students, and the most common answer is that the odds are about 98 to 1 that the patient has the disease. As we shall see, the correct answer is that we cannot tell how likely it is that someone has the disease without knowing how common the disease is in the population being tested. We said that the disease was rare, and as we will see it is actually possible for positive tests to occur more often for people who do not have the disease than for those who do. In order to see this issue more clearly, we must take apart probabilities and think about base rates (that is the frequency of the event of interest in the population).

Test Quality: A Case Study of Base Rates

What is a probability? When a probability is calculated from a set of observations, the frequency of the event of interest (say a positive test) is divided by the total number of events that were sampled (where the event might be having a particular disease). Probabilities are useful, because they permit us to compare the relative likelihoods of different events. For example, we might be interested in the probability that a 9-year-old boy as opposed to a 9-year-old girl would wear glasses. Simply counting the number of boys and girls who have glasses is not appropriate, because there may be different numbers of boys and girls to begin with. Creating the probability by dividing the number of boys with glasses by the number of boys and the number of girls with glasses by the number of girls allows us to compare the boys and girls.

Notice, however, that when we create these probabilities (or proportions), we are losing all of the information about whether there are more boys overall or more girls. That is, we no longer know the base rate for boys in the population. More generally, the relative frequency of some event of interest in a population is called the **base rate.** In many problems that involve probabilities, base rate information has been removed or is provided in a separate place from information about other probabilities.

Let's pursue the disease example raised in the previous section further. To what extent does a positive result on a test for a disease mean that the person has that disease? Certainly, a positive result is likely to be stressful for a patient. To evaluate what the test means, however, two important pieces of information are required: The quality of the test and the prevalence of the disease in the population of patients given the test. Let's see why. The quality of a test depends on two factors: the likelihood of a true-positive test result and the likelihood of a false-positive test result. In this example, the true-positive rate (where the test was positive when the person did in fact have the disease) is 98% and the false-positive rate (where the test was positive but the person did not have the disease) is 1%. An easy way to think about test quality is in terms of the following table:

Test Results	Disease Present	Disease Absent
Positive	a	b
Negative	c	d

The table indicates the possible test results and the possible true state of affairs with respect to the disease. Cell *a* corresponds to patients who show a positive test result and have the disease, whereas cell *d* corresponds to patients who show a negative test and do not have the disease. The bigger *a* and *d* are, the better the test, because these are the cells that reflect when the test gives correct results. Now, the question is how many people actually have the disease when the test comes out positive. The total number of people who have the disease can be found by adding up the number of people in the Disease Present column ($a + c$), and so the proportion of positive tests among those with the disease is just the number of people who have the disease who test positively divided by the number of people who have the disease, or $a/(a + c)$. The false-positive rate (that is, the rate at which the test comes out positive, but the person does not actually have the disease) can be found by dividing the number of people who do not have the disease but test positively for the disease (b) by the total number of people who do not have the disease (in the Disease Absent column) or $b/(b + d)$. A third important quantity is the base rate of the disease in the whole population, which is just the number of people in the Disease Present column divided by the total number of people, or $(a + c)/(a + b + c + d)$. What we are really interested in, however, is the probability that the patient has the disease given a positive test result. The number of patients with a positive test result is found by adding together the Positive Test column ($a + b$), so the proportion of patients who test positively who actually have the disease is $a/(a + b)$. Similarly, the probability that a patient does not have the disease, given a negative test, is $d/(c + d)$.

We can use these equations to see how base rate influences the likelihood of having a disease, given a positive test. It will be useful to see the influence of different base rates on the effectiveness of a test. First, we will look at a disease that is relatively common (occurring in 50% of patients given a test) and then at a disease that is relatively rare (occurring in 1% of patients given a test). If the disease appears in half the population being tested, our table might look like this:

Test results	Disease Present	Disease Absent
Positive	98	1
Negative	2	99
Total	100	100

In this case the true-positive rate is 98%, the false-positive rate is 1%, the base rate 50%, and the probability of having the disease given a positive test is 98/99 or about 99% (because 98 of the 99 people who get a positive test actually have the disease). This corresponds to most people's intuitions concerning the answer to our initial problem. Indeed, in this case, the test would be quite a good one to use to diagnose the disease. Remember, though, we started this section by stating that the disease is fairly rare. Suppose only 1 in 100 patients has the disease (to stick with whole numbers, we will consider 10,000 cases in which 1/100 (that is 100) of them have the disease). Then our table would look like this:

Test results	Disease Present	Disease Absent
Positive	98	99
Negative	2	9,801
Total	100	9,900

Now for the same true- and false-positive test rates, the probability that the disease is present, given a positive test, is 98/(98 + 99) or a little less than 50%. Of course, a disease present in only 1/100 patients isn't even that rare. If the disease was present in only 1 in 10,000 patients tested, this probability would further shrink to less than 1%.

There is a simple, intuitive way to understand the influence of base rates on the probability that a disease is present when a positive test appears. Even if false-positive tests are rare, when one tests a large population of healthy people, the false-positive tests start to mount up. Because what matters is the relative number of true-positive and false-positive tests, when a disease is rare, the number of false-positive tests can overwhelm the number of true-positive tests. Thus, many (or even most) of the people who test positively for rare diseases may not actually have the disease.

Many screening tests have lower true-positive and higher false-positive rates than the present example. For diseases that are not very common among the population of people being tested, a positive test may raise the likelihood that a disease is present only from less than 1% to less than 10%. Therefore, it is absolutely essential to consider base rates in reasoning from diagnostic tests. As an example, when one reads about tests for drug use among athletes or in certain occupations (e.g., driving a bus), one needs to consider true-positive rates, false-positive rates, and base rates before jumping to any conclusions from a positive test. Unless the false-positive rate is zero, decisions can be made that unfairly harm innocent people. That is, when someone fails a drug test and protests his or her innocence, without knowing the base rates or the reliability of the test, it is possible that they are actually telling the truth!

Base Rate Neglect

It is time to get off our soapbox and ask whether people generally use base rate information. After all, if it is common for people to use base rates, then in the previous section we were preaching to the choir. Of course, the fact that most people shown the disease problem we described above fail to think about base rates suggests that people may not consider base rates in situations where they are needed. This point has been demonstrated by Tversky, Kahneman, and others who have noted that when base rate information is presented, it is frequently ignored. Consider the following problem taken from A. Tversky and Kahneman (1981, p. 63):

> A cab was involved in a hit-and-run accident: Two cab companies, the green and blue, operated in the city. You are given the following data:
>
> 1. 85% of the cabs in the city are green and 15% are blue.
>
> 2. A witness identified the cab as a blue cab. The court tested his ability to identify cabs under the appropriate visibility conditions. When the witness was presented with a sample of cabs (half of which were blue and half green) the witness made the correct identification in 80% of the cases and errors in 20% of the cases.

Question: What is the probability that the cab involved in the accident was blue rather than green?

In typical experiments, the most frequently given answer is .80, which corresponds to the reliability of the witness. The correct answer is actually 12/29 or .41 rather than .80 because of the low base rate of blue cabs. (To figure out where this fraction came from, just make up a table like we did in the previous section.) This finding suggests that the base rate information simply was ignored. Given that so many situations involve combining prior information with new information, it is not surprising that the use of base rate information has been extensively studied. In general, it appears that base rate information is more likely to be used when it is made salient (Fischhoff, Slovic, & Lichtenstein, 1979), when there is a clear conceptual relationship or causal linkage between the base rate information and the problem outcome (see, e.g., Bar-Hillel & Fischhoff, 1981; Gigerenzer, Hell, & Blank, 1988), and when the base rate information is conveyed through experience with examples rather than presented in summary form (Manis, Dovalina, Avis, & Cardoze, 1980; Koehler, 1996; Medin & Edelson, 1988). To give but one example, Gigerenzer et al. found that base rate information was used effectively on the following problem:

> In the 1978/79 season of the West German soccer "Bundesliga," Team A won 10 out of 34 games. We have selected some of the games that season randomly and checked their final results as well as their half-time results. For instance, on the 7th day of the season the half-time result was 2 : 1 in favor of Team A. What is your probability (estimate) that this game belongs to those 10 games won out of 34?

The base rate of winning was varied from a low of 7 to a high of 19 of the 34 games. Gigerenzer et al. observed that estimates of winning increased systematically as the base rate increased.

There are several important differences between the cab problem and the soccer problem. The most obvious is that the two pieces of information in the soccer problem are conceptually related in that both the base rate and the new information are directly linked to winning and losing. Of course, base rate information is relevant to both the soccer problem and the cab problem. However, the base rate is less salient in the cab problem, because the probabilities have divided the base rate information out, and so the actual base rates never appear directly. Differences between the use of frequencies and probabilities have been the source of a number of debates about research on reasoning (e.g., Kahneman & Tversky, 1996, and the reply by Gigerenzer, 1996; Koehler, 1996).

Confusing Conditional Probabilities

Conditional probabilities are probabilities that are true or present under specified conditions or circumstances. Consider the difference between:

The probability of A given that B is present.
The probability of B given that A is present.

If A is a symptom and B a disease, only the second provides the information that is crucial to diagnosis. It is fundamentally important to distinguish these two conditional probabilities because the former may be high at the same time that the latter is very small. For example, the probability of being tall, given that you are a professional basketball player, is very much higher than the probability of your being a professional basketball player, given that you are tall. Eddy (1982) documents the tendency of health professionals to confuse these two and to treat the first as if it was the second. He analyzed the use of mammography to decide whether to perform a breast biopsy to determine if a mass is malignant and showed that these conditional probabilities are sometimes confused even in technical medical journals. These confusions can lead to a very inefficient decision strategy. For example, along with the usual recommended biopsy if the mammography is positive, some medical articles include the advice that biopsy should be used when the mammography is negative, "just to make sure." Of course, if the biopsy is to be performed regardless of the outcome of the mammography, there is no point to the X-ray. Furthermore, a biopsy involves a significant surgical procedure! In general, a person who bases the decision on the probability of a symptom given a disease (rather than the reverse) is not only ignoring base rates but also neglecting the possibility of any false-positive tests (positive result in the absence of the disease).

People often experience considerable difficulty when they are asked to reason explicitly with information that is probabilistic in character. Gigerenzer (1994) argues that people are better able to attend to frequencies than to probabilities. Probabilities are relatively recent mathematical invention that allow people to focus on the relative likelihood of some event without having to consider the base rate. Because the base rate has been removed from a probability, perhaps we should be less surprised than we are that people neglect base rates when thinking about probabilities.

Argument Structure and Relevance

So far in our discussion of inductive reasoning, we have focused on probabilities, which can serve as a way of representing the strength of our belief in an inductive argument. Equally important, though, is determining which beliefs should be strengthened (or weakened) on the basis of an inductive argument based on a new piece of evidence. For example, suppose someone believes that zebras are striped and also that the moon is made of cheese. We could think of this belief as "zebras are striped AND the moon is made of cheese." If the person now sees a zebra and notices that it is striped, how should his beliefs change? Intuitively, we think this should increase the person's confidence that zebras are striped, but not his confidence that the moon is made of cheese. However, it is not clear what would keep the person from simply increasing his confidence in the belief "zebras are striped

AND the moon is made of cheese." Thus, a key problem is understanding which facts are relevant to a particular piece of evidence.

Another problem involves determining the best way to phrase a conclusion. To see this, we will take an example from Goodman (1965). When an object is described as being green, we mean that its color is green, and, unless some action is taken on that object, it will remain green forever. Consider now the property *grue*. Grue is a special property that applies to objects if they are currently green, but on some specific date in the future (say, January 1, 2050), they will spontaneously turn blue. Now consider the following pair of arguments:

1. All emeralds so far observed have been green; therefore,

   the first emerald to be observed after January 1, 2050, will be green.

2. All emeralds so far observed have been grue; therefore,

   the first emerald to be observed after January 1, 2050, will be grue.

Argument 1 predicts that the first emerald observed after January 1, 2050, will be green, whereas argument 2 predicts that it will be grue (that is, blue). Notice that both arguments have an equal amount of empirical support. That is, both of them predict that every emerald seen to date will appear to be green. Nonetheless, people find the first argument more compelling than the second (Sternberg, 1982; see also Osherson, Smith, & Shafir, 1986). It seems that inductive strength depends on more than just the way the argument is set up.

One could argue for favoring the concept *green* over the concept *grue* because the concept green is simpler than the concept grue. But as Goodman (1955) notes, simplicity is relative to the vocabulary available to describe a situation. Suppose we have as our basic concepts *grue* and *bleen. Bleen* means that before January 1, 2050, an object is blue, and after January 1, 2050, the object is green. Relative to this system, the concept green will be defined as an object that is grue before January 1, 2050, and bleen after January 1, 2050—a fairly complex concept!

Again the point is that argument structure is an incomplete measure of inductive power. Whether a concept seems natural (green vs. grue) is tied to our theories about categories, objects, and their properties. For example, there is nothing odd about the concept of *leaf* that specifies that a leaf can be green in the summer and brown (or yellow or red or purple for that matter) in the fall (see Tetewsky & Sternberg, 1986). Similarly, there is clear evidence that people's certainty about an inductive argument depends crucially on the properties and categories in question. For example, people are more confident that having a particular color will be true of all examples of a species than they are that having a particular weight will be true of all examples of that species (Nisbett, Krantz, Jepson, & Kunda, 1983). Perceived variability will presumably vary with specific contents; 1-pound boxes of chocolate vary more in color than in weight, whereas bags of oranges would vary more in weight than in color. In short, inductive strength is at least partly determined by specific contents and not just abstract argument forms.

Summary

Probability is an important way that people represent their confidence in the truth of beliefs. Research on people's ability to reason probabilistically suggests that they do not always use the information needed to reach the correct conclusions. For example, people often neglect information about the base rates of events, and they often confuse the probability that an effect will occur given a cause with the probability of a particular cause given an observed effect. Finally, while reasoning about probability is an important part of induction, it is clear that people make use of their knowledge about the specific content of domains in order to change their confidence in beliefs given evidence. We now turn to this central issue in more detail.

THE IMPORTANCE OF CONTENT

We have determined that the structure of inductive arguments does not give us enough information to know how to increase (or decrease) our confidence in a fact given some evidence. Thus, unlike deductive arguments (where we could rely on the structure of the argument to determine the truth of a conclusion given the truth of its premises) we need something beyond structure in inductive argument. The missing ingredient is the content of the information in the argument. In the first example above, we somehow know that seeing stripes on a zebra is relevant to zebras, but not to the moon. We also know that color is a property that is unlikely to change spontaneously without something occurring to (or inside of) an object to cause its color to change.

It is one thing to assert that content is important to reasoning. It is quite another to understand how content is important. In the rest of this chapter, we will explore some ways that content helps us go beyond the information given. We will start by talking about the role of similarity and analogy in inference. Then, we will explore mental models, which are detailed representations of the way the physical world works. Finally, we will examine scientific reasoning, which brings together aspects of both domain-general inference processes as well as the use of analogy and mental models.

Analogy and Similarity

One important way that we can go beyond the information given is to recognize that a current situation is in some way like a previous situation. In this way, we can establish parallels between the new situation and old ones and thus bring prior knowledge to bear on new circumstances. When the previous situation used is very different from the current one, we are performing **analogical reasoning.** When the previous situation is quite like the current one, we are performing similarity-based reasoning. Reasoning by similarity can often be done using the following argument:

> Object 1 has properties A and B.
> Object 2 has properties A, B, and also C.
> Therefore, it is likely that object 1 also has property C.

In general, the more properties that object 1 and object 2 share, the more likely it is that some new property (C in the preceding example) will be shared (as described in Chapter 10; see also Osherson, Smith, Wilkie, Lopez, & Shafir, 1990; Lassaline, 1996). Similarity-based induction is anything but ironclad. For example, suppose we have two cars that are alike in many ways (e.g., same style, same manufacturer). We still might not be confident that if one car is red, the other car is also red. For induction to work, the basis for similarity and the new property must be relevant to each other.

Theories of analogy have focused on how the corresponding elements between two items can be determined. As we will see, research on analogy has been applied to similarity as well, and may provide a way of determining which properties in a comparison are most relevant for reasoning. We begin with a discussion of analogy.

Analogy

When we think of two things as being analogous, we typically mean that they share some kind of deep similarity. For example, saying that the atom is like the solar system is an analogy, because these domains are not similar on the surface (a planet does not look like an electron nor the sun like a nucleus). Theories of analogy have gone beyond this simple characterization to define what these deep similarities are. In particular, analogy is thought to involve relational or structural similarity, which is the similarity in the relationships that hold among the features in an object (Hesse, 1966). Relations are parts of the representation of some item that bind together two or more aspects of that situation. For example, in the statement John is *taller* than Bill, *taller* is a relation, because it describes the relationship between John and Bill. Relations can be contrasted with attributes, which are aspects of the representation of an item that describe properties of an object. For example, John is *tall* or Bill is *heavy* would be descriptions of attributes.

Current theories of analogy have focused on how this relational similarity might be determined. An important theory of analogy is Dedre Gentner's (1983, 1989) **structure mapping theory.** This theory suggests that analogies consist of the match between two domains. One domain (called the *base*) is the one the person typically knows the most about, and the other (called the *target*) is often less familiar. In an analogy, one tries to find similar relations in the representations of the base and target. Aspects of the base and target domain are matched when they are related by the same relation in each domain.

To illustrate structure mapping theory, consider the analogy "an atom is like the solar system" shown in Figure 11.1. The top part of the figure shows the representation of the solar system. The representation consists of a graph with nodes and links. In this graph, there are three kinds of nodes: *objects* (shown in rounded rectangles), *attributes* (shown in bold rounded rectangles), and *relations* (shown in ovals). The links connect the attributes and relations to the properties they describe. For example, the relation *attracts* in the top representation in Figure 11.1 relates *Sun* and *Planet* and represents

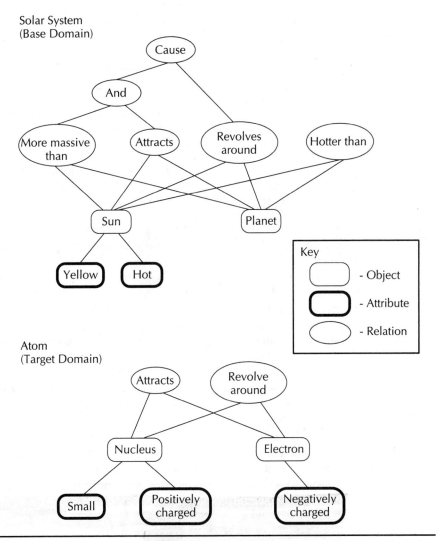

Figure 11.1   Partial depiction of the analogy between the solar system and hydrogen atom, showing a person's presumed initial knowledge of the solar system. When the domains are matched, the *attracts* relation and the *revolves around* relation in the base and target will be placed in correspondence. This match will lead the sun to be matched to the nucleus and the planet to the electron. The causal structure from the base can then be carried over to the target as an analogical inference.

the idea that the Sun attracts the Planet. Some of the relations in this figure are *higher-order relations,* which are relations that relate other relations. For example, the *cause* relation is a higher order relation, because it connects the set of relations representing that the sun is both more massive than the planet and attracts the planet to the idea that the planets revolve around the sun. At the bottom of the figure is a representation of the atom. This representation also has attributes and relations.

Given these domains, how is an analogy found? According to Gentner's structure-mapping theory, interpreting an analogy involves the following steps:

1. Setting up correspondences between the two domains.

2. Focusing on the matching relations rather than the matching attributes.

3. Focusing on **systematicity:** that is, systems of relations that are governed by higher order relations (that is relations on relations) rather than isolated relational matches.

4. Carrying relations from the base domain (solar system) to the target domain (atom) in order to extend knowledge about the target. (This process is called *analogical inference*.)

In this example, at the first stage all matches would be found between attributes and relations. When a match between a relation or an attribute is found, any objects related or described are also matched (which allows the sun and nucleus to be matched as well as the planet and electron). Step 2 suggests that the relational matches (such as *Attracts* and *Revolve around*) will be more important than the attributes. Step 3 focuses on systems of relations. In the base domain, the causal relation is at the top of a relational system. Finally, step 4 allows analogy to go beyond the information given by carrying information over from the base to the target. In particular, when there is a partial match between a system of relations in the base (like the causal system) and relations in the target (the *attracts* and *revolve around* relations are partial matches), then the rest of the system can be carried from base to target (Clement & Gentner, 1991; Markman, 1997; Spellman & Holyoak, 1996).

As discussed above, carrying over these relations is an analogical inference. In the present example, this inference posits that there is a difference in mass between the nucleus and electron that causes the revolution of electrons around the nucleus. This example shows both the power and the danger of analogical inference. Inference is powerful, because it permits one domain to be extended by virtue of its similarity to another. Analogical inference is also dangerous, because it may suggest inferences that are factually incorrect (as in this case).

Gentner's structure-mapping theory has been implemented as a computer program (Falkenhainer, Forbus, & Gentner, 1989) and has received a fair amount of empirical support. For example, people's judgments about the soundness of analogies is well predicted by relational similarity (Gentner, 1989; Gentner, Rattermann, & Forbus, 1993). There are alternative theories of analogy that disagree about some of the fine details of the way analogies are processed, but there is a general consensus that relational structure is at the core of interpreting analogies (Holyoak & Thagard, 1989, 1995; Hummel & Holyoak, 1997; Keane, Ledgeway, & Duff, 1994). In short, work on reasoning by analogy suggests that inductions are guided by systems of relations rather than simply by number of similarities or overall similarity. This bias serves people well, because it typically directs people toward underlying causal relations (like the causal relation in the solar system example in Figure 11.1).

An Example of Mapping

The ability to find correspondences between two different situations emerges fairly early. To explore this development researchers have asked the critical question, "Where is Snoopy"? In particular, Judy DeLoache (1995) has examined how children use correspondences between a scale-model of a room and a full-sized room to find a hidden toy. In her studies, there is a full-sized room and a dollhouse room with similar furniture in a similar configuration. Then, an experimenter hides a small ("Little Snoopy") doll in the small room and asks the child where they would expect to find a large doll ("Big Snoopy") in the large room. The experimenter explains to the child participating in the study that the two dolls like to do the same things in their rooms and that wherever Little Snoopy hides in his little room, Big Snoopy likes to hide in his big room. Then the experimenter hides the miniature Snoopy somewhere in the small room (e.g., behind the couch) and tells the child that she is going to hide Big Snoopy in the same place in the full-sized room. On other trials, the child is shown where the large doll is hiding in the large room and is asked to find the small doll in the miniature room.

Sounds easy, right? Well, it is easy for 3-year-olds and they are almost always correct. For 2½-year-olds, however, it is a completely different story—they almost always fail. Furthermore, their failure does not stem from forgetting where Little Snoopy was hidden; they readily find Little Snoopy in the miniature room after failing to find Big Snoopy in the full-sized room.

What is the problem for the 2½-year-olds? DeLoache suggests that the critical factor is that young children have difficulty representing that one room is a model of the other. In particular, children have trouble representing the relationships between the rooms. This interpretation sounds very abstract, but DeLoache has provided a very clever test of it. In a follow-up study, children were told about an "incredible shrinking machine" (an oscilloscope with flashing green lights) that could make big rooms small and small rooms big. The experimenter hid Big Snoopy and then took the child into the room with the shrinking machine, which was turned on to convert the large room into the small room. Although one might expect that this elaborate procedure would only confuse the children, DeLoache predicted that it would help performance because the shrinking or expanding operation should remove the need to have a higher order representation linking the two rooms. And this is precisely what she found! The 2½-year-olds were now successful 76% of the time, a level comparable to that for 3-year-olds (see also DeLoache, Miller, & Rosengren, 1997). This study underlines the point that the child's representation of the relation between the scale-model room and the full-sized room is crucial to successful performance.

A Return to Similarity

Analogy focuses attention on information that is likely to be important for reasoning. Systems of relations are more central than attributes or isolated relations. This view of the similarity between domains is different from the type of reasoning by

AN ENIGMA
Finding Differences of Similar Things

Applying structure mapping theory to ordinary similarity comparisons has an odd implication for the differences that can be found for pairs of similar objects. Structure mapping theory assumes that alignable differences are more important to similarity than are nonalignable differences, and it posits that alignable differences are determined by finding commonalities between two domains that lead to the detection of differences. Because similar objects typically have more correspondences than do dissimilar objects, this suggests that it ought to be easier to find differences for pairs of similar objects than for pairs of dissimilar objects.

This hypothesis was tested by Gentner and Markman (1994) who gave each subject a page with 40 word pairs on it. Half of the pairs were similar items (e.g., hotel/motel) and half were dissimilar items (e.g., kitten/magazine). Subjects were asked to list one difference for as many pairs as possible in five minutes. They were told that five minutes was not enough time to do all of the pairs, and so they should do the easy ones

(Continued)

similarity described earlier. We suggested that reasoning by similarity just meant that having some shared properties is an indicator that other properties of one object might also be shared by another.

There is no reason why the principles of analogical mapping developed in structure mapping theory could not be applied to comparisons of objects that are more similar than the domains typically compared in analogies. Indeed, current research in similarity has focused on parallels between similarity and analogy (Gentner & Markman, 1997; Medin, Goldstone, & Gentner, 1993). This work suggests that even comparisons of similar objects may involve structure mapping.

This work has two interesting implications. First, when reasoning by similarity, people will carry over those properties that are related to a match between base and target. In support of this prediction, Lassaline (1996) found that increasing the number of matching features between two similar objects did not greatly increase people's confidence that a new property of one object was also a property of the other. However, if the new property was causally related to one that matched between the objects, then people were quite confident that the new property was also true of the second object.

Second, the parallel between analogy and similarity helps suggest which differences between objects are likely to be most salient. In Figure 11.1, when the *revolve around* relation in the base is matched to the *revolve around* relation in the first followed by the hard ones. Consistent with the predictions of structure mapping theory, subjects listed a difference for more of the similar pairs (11.38 on average) than the dissimilar pairs (5.88 on average). At first glance, it might seem that this finding means that people picked the wrong pairs to list a difference for, and that if they had tried to list a difference for the dissimilar pairs, they might have been able to list a difference for more pairs. However, a second version of the study was done in which people got a page with either 40 similar pairs or 40 dissimilar pairs. In this study, people given the similar pairs listed a difference for more pairs than did people given the dissimilar pairs. Thus, it appears that it is actually easier for people to find differences for pairs of similar items than for pairs of dissimilar items. This pattern of available properties is sensible. It is better to be flooded with differences between similar items (because those differences are likely to be relevant for future reasoning) than to be overwhelmed by differences between dissimilar things (which are unlikely to be relevant).

target, it causes the sun to be matched to the nucleus (because both are at the center) and the planet to be matched to the electron (because both are revolving). These items are corresponding elements of the base and target domain that mismatch. Differences that consist of corresponding aspects of each object are called *alignable differences* (Markman & Gentner, 1993). Alignable differences are contrasted with *nonalignable differences,* which are aspects of one domain that have no correspondence in the other domain. For example, people asked to list the differences between a motorcycle and a car might say that "cars have larger engines than motorcycles," which is an alignable difference, or "cars have seatbelts and motorcycles don't," which is a nonalignable difference. Alignable differences are used by other cognitive processes that involve comparisons more often than are nonalignable differences (see Gentner & Markman, 1997, for examples).

Summary

Reasoning by analogy and similarity are powerful ways of using the knowledge from one domain to understand another. Analogy focuses on common relations between a base and a target domain. In addition to highlighting these relational similarities, analogy permits one domain to be extended by virtue of its similarity to another. The principles of analogy can also be applied to similarity comparisons. When applied to similarity, these principles suggest that people focus on differences that arise from the way objects are seen as similar (i.e., alignable differences) rather than differences involving aspects of one object that have no correspondence in the other (i.e., non-alignable differences).

MENTAL MODELS AND INTUITIVE THEORIES

Analogy is a general process by which people can take their knowledge of one domain and apply it to another in order to go beyond the information given. In Chapter 7, we discussed scripts and schemas, which also allow people to go beyond the information given. In a script, people have knowledge of a generalized event. When they recognize that a particular script is applicable, they can generate expectations about what will happen next, without having to wait for each next event to occur. People have a similar kind of knowledge structure that allows them to reason about physical objects in the world. This structure, called a **mental model,** contains causal information that can be used to understand how objects and physical processes work.

To begin, let's look at some general properties of mental models. First of all, mental models are actively constructed in the service of understanding and explaining experience. Second, they are often constructed spontaneously to understand situations and to make predictions (via mental simulation of these models) about the future. Third, mental models are often constrained by theories about the world rather than empirically derived through experience (see also Gentner & Stevens, 1983; Johnson-Laird, 1983).

Let's get more specific. Mental models often are used to describe the knowledge one has of how some object (i.e., a thermostat) works or how some situation is a function of a set of interacting processes and objects. For example, Nussbaum (1979) examined children's conception of the planet earth. The children had been told various facts about earth (e.g., Columbus sailed around it, space photographs, perceived flatness, sky) that they put together into some mental model to capture as many of the facts as possible. Some of these mental models are illustrated in Figure 11.2. For some children, this mental model consisted of a flat disk in the middle of water (panel a), which allows them to "understand" how Columbus was able to sail around the earth. To incorporate the pictures they had seen of a spherical earth taken from spaceships, the children might believe that there are two earths, the round one in photographs and their nice, safe, flat one at home (panel b); or they might believe that the picture was really of a disk, not a sphere (panel c). Some older children viewed the earth as a half-sphere, with the sky completing the sphere (panels d to f). These mental models would be used to understand observations and other information, as well as to reason about related phenomena. Thus, because of its focus on the workings of some particular object, system, or situation, a mental model can be a powerful reasoning tool (see also Samarapungavan, Vosniadou, & Brewer, 1996; Vosniadou & Brewer, 1987, 1994).

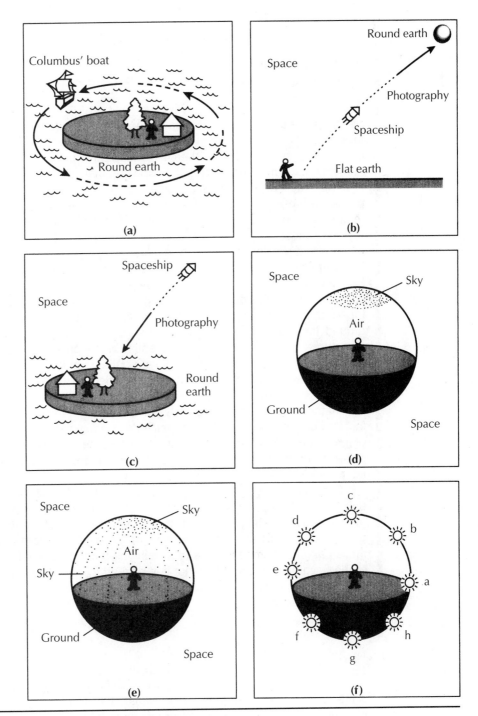

Figure 11.2   **Children's Conceptions of Earth**

Source: Nussbaum, 1979.

AN APPLICATION
Mental Models and Health Behavior

Mental models can have considerable practical importance to health professionals, because patients frequently develop models or beliefs about disease symptoms, causes, health threats, and treatments, and these models greatly influence their behavior when they are ill. A major difficulty in combating certain diseases is the high rate of patients not following physician-prescribed treatments or regimens, and, as we will see, a major reason for this nonadherence is the mental models that patients have of their diseases.

To illustrate this point, we describe a particular medical problem, hypertension. The National Health and Nutrition Examination Survey Phase 2 conducted from 1991 to 1994 estimated that 50 million Americans had hypertension or were taking medication for hypertension, and the World Health Organization documents that hypertension is prevalent around the world. Hypertension is largely asymptomatic (there are no symptoms to warn a person of potential blood pressure problems) so compliance is particularly important, and patient understanding is crucial.

We know quite a lot about the mental models associated with people's understanding of hypertension due to the important work by Meyer and Leventhal (e.g., Leventhal, Meyer, & Nerenz, 1980). First of all, despite the fact that patients were told that hypertension is asymptomatic, about 80% of patients indicate that they can detect some symptoms. For these patients, three general types of models have emerged from the extensive interviews.

One model, which Leventhal et al. (1980) refer to as the acute episodic model, appears to be derived from the representations or mental models of many other illnesses. Patients with this model believe that treatment will be short and lead to a cure of the disease. More than half of these patients claim to be able to specify the time and place for the onset of their hypertension and feel that it is caused by specific stress at home or work. A common focus of this group is on the speed of the heartbeat as an indication of hypertension.

(Continued)

Mental models can be used to guide behavior. For example, Kempton (1986) explored the way people think about the thermostat in their home. He found that people typically have one of two models about thermostats. Some people liken a thermostat to the accelerator in their car (by analogy). On this model, if you want the

AN APPLICATION
Mental Models and Health Behavior *(Continued)*

A second group of subjects, using a cyclic model, expects the symptoms to subside and then recur. They report random or repetitive symptoms and generally attribute the disease to their behavior in terms of drinking and diet. These patients often explain the disease in terms of arterial problems caused by excess blood or clogging of the veins.

The final model that emerged from these interviews was referred to as the chronic model. These patients view the disease as being due to the body's running down, either from age or hereditary factors. Because of this "cause," they expect the symptoms will be long lasting, if not permanent.

The beliefs about the causes affect the perception of symptoms assumed to co-vary with the illness (Pennebaker & Epstein, 1983). If patients view hypertension as a disease of the heart, they monitor their heart rate. If they believe the cause is emotional stress, they monitor changes in emotion. If they attribute the hypertension to arterial disease, they are sensitive to any feelings of numbness or coldness in their extremities.

These representations of hypertension are important because they affect whether people stick to physician-prescribed medication. Meyer, Leventhal, and Guttman (1980) examined how patients followed recommended treatments. The general finding was quite simple: If hypertensive patients believed that the treatment was affecting the symptoms they thought indicated hypertension (as previously described), more than half of them followed the treatment plan sufficiently to bring their blood pressure under control. If they did not believe that the treatment was affecting the "relevant" symptoms, only 24% followed the treatment and brought their blood pressure under control. For example, if a patient attends to heart rate as a symptom, when the heart rate is high, the patient is likely to take the medication (Pennebaker & Epstein, 1983). Medications for controlling high blood pressure do not necessarily decrease heart rate, and patients who focus on heart rate may discard their medication as ineffective. Similarly, patients who subscribe to the cyclic model may take their medications cyclically rather than in the continuous manner prescribed. In short, people's mental models of hypertension have a large influence on their health-related behaviors.

room to heat up fast, you should set the thermostat above the temperature where you want it, just as you press the gas pedal farther to get a car to accelerate faster. A second model is the switch model. This model of the thermostat (which is actually the correct one) is that when the temperature goes below some value (set by the user), a switch is thrown and the heat comes on. The heat stays on until the temperature goes above the value, at which point the switch is turned off and the heat goes off. (For air conditioning, the thermostat works the same way, except that the switch goes on when the temperature exceeds some value and off when it goes below that value). Kempton found that people who had the switch model of the thermostat set theirs infrequently, usually once in the morning and once at night. In contrast, people with the accelerator model were constantly fiddling with the thermometer to get the right temperature. These people would have to set the thermometer multiple times, because when it was set too high, it would eventually make the room warmer than the person wanted to be, and when the thermometer was set too low, the room would eventually get too cold. Because the thermostat was constantly being adjusted, people with the accelerator model of the thermostat tended to have higher heating bills than did those with the switch model.

Intuitive Theories

Where do mental models come from? We said earlier that mental models are not simply passive accumulations of expected events but rather are actively constructed theorylike structures. A dramatic demonstration of this phenomenon is provided by a study by Kaiser, McCloskey, and Proffitt (1986). They examined the development of beliefs about the physical world, which has been called **intuitive physics** (or sometimes naïve physics). They focused on developmental changes in intuitive theories of motion using the so-called curved tube problem (Figure 11.3). Grade school students and college students were shown a clear plastic tube in the shape of Figure 11.3A. The interior end of the tube was elevated so that a steel ball dropped into the elevated end would roll through at a moderate speed. Participants were asked to draw the path that the ball would take as it left the tube. The correct response is shown in Figure 11.3B, but a very common error is to draw the path indicated in Figure 11.3C. Another version of the problem substituted a "C-curve" for the full spiral, but again the correct answer remains the same. The most striking result concerns performance as a function of age, shown in Figure 11.4.

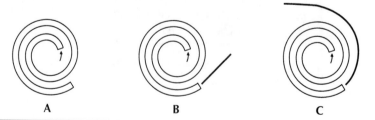

| | A | B | C |

Figure 11.3   The curved tube problem (A), its correct solution (B), and the most common incorrect response (C).

Source: Kaiser, McCloskey, & Proffitt, 1986.

Preschool and kindergarten children perform as well as college students, but the performance of third- through sixth-grade children is substantially worse than that of either older or younger participants. Other controls ruled out the possibility that the youngest children performed well simply because they could not draw curved lines.

Kaiser et al. suggested that grade school students are constructing theories of motion and that a precursor to the principle of inertia (that things in motion will stay in motion unless acted on by an outside force such as friction) is an idea about the persistence of motion. That is, the children act as if they have formed the generalization that an object tends to persist in moving the way in which it was moving. Empirically this is the case for the example of a bouncing ball (it continues to go both up and down for a while), and children may overgeneralize from situations like bouncing balls to the curved tube problem. Thus, the curvilinear motion error may arise as a by-product of the development of a general motion persistence principle that, although not completely correct, is very often useful in predicting and understanding motion. (See Cooke & Breedin, 1994, for an alternative interpretation, and Ranney, 1994, for a rebuttal.)

Yet to be explained is how incorrect theories of motion are replaced by correct expectations. Another look at Figure 11.4 will reveal that even college students

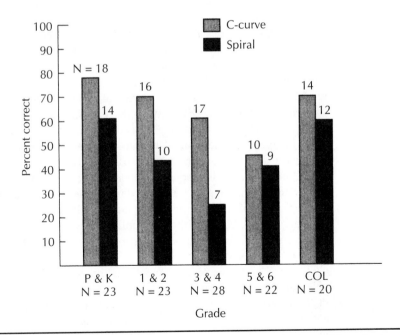

Figure 11.4   Proportion of correct predictions on the C-curve and spiral tube problems by age group (P = preschool, K = kindergarten, COL = college).

Source: Kaiser, McCloskey, & Proffitt, 1986.

are likely to make the error of expecting curvilinear motion, which suggests that the answer is that replacing useful but incorrect theories is not easy to do. Incorrect intuitive physics theories often persist in adults, even after they have taken college courses in physics (see, e.g., di Sessa, 1983; Gentner & Stevens, 1983; McCloskey, 1983). How naïve mental models are acquired and changed remains a fascinating problem. It also has obvious implications for education. The idea that learning involves a passive accumulation of information is clearly wrong, and understanding naïve mental models is fundamental to the goal of replacing initial naïve theories with more accurate explanations.

Some recent work has begun to explore how people use mental models to help them understand rules about the way the world works. In one set of studies, Schwartz and Black (1996) showed people a set of gears and asked them to predict the direction the gears would turn. There are two rules that determine the motions of a configuration of gears. First, adjacent gears always spin in opposite directions. Second, if a set of gears is arranged in a loop, then there must be an even number of gears in the loop, otherwise, there will be two adjacent gears both trying to move in the same direction, and the configuration will lock. Schwartz and Black found that when people are first reasoning about the motions of gears, they use a perceptual simulation of the motion of the gears and often make many hand motions to explore this motion. As they gain more experience in reasoning about gears, however, they eventually shift to using the rules. At this point, the perceptual simulations are no longer required (see also Schwartz & Black, 1999).

Just as theories in psychology can range from highly specific models to very broad conceptual frameworks, there is also some range in the scope of mental models. So far, we have considered mental models having a theorylike character. More generally, mental models can be thought of as constructed working models of the world used in the service of understanding. This broader definition suggests that mental models may be used in comprehending fairly specific situations. For example, suppose one reads that Bill is taller than John and that John is taller than Larry. One could construct a mental model representing these facts together and, by inspection, note that Bill must also be taller than Larry. In short, mental models may also serve to support reasoning. In this sense, Johnson-Laird's mental models approach to deductive reasoning (described in the A Debate box) can be thought of as a specific case of the general mental models framework (hence its name). (Note, however, that the application to deductive reasoning is somewhat atypical in that it is abstract rather than concrete and that it is missing the causal flavor of theories about the world.)

To summarize, people have mental models that allow them to reason about physical objects. These mental models contain causal information that allows people to reason about how an object acts. These mental models are related to general beliefs people have about the physics of the world. Like intuitive physics, mental models are often acquired by observing the actions of objects in the world. These observations may lead to models that are mistaken relative to the true physics of the world. Nonetheless, people's physical knowledge is adequate to allow them to predict the motion and behavior of objects.

HYPOTHESIS TESTING AND SCIENTIFIC REASONING _____

So far in this chapter, we have talked about reasoning both with general principles and also by using domain-specific knowledge. In this section, we will discuss scientific reasoning, which is an arena in which both types of reasoning come together. Science involves the generation and evaluation of hypotheses. Deanna Kuhn (1997) characterizes scientific reasoning as an attempt to achieve a coordination between theory and evidence, which is applicable both to science and to reasoning in everyday situations. To achieve this coordination, she argues that people must use *strategic, metastrategic,* and *metacognitive* ability. Strategic ability is knowing how to make inferences that will allow evidence to be used to support or refute a theory. Metastrategic ability allows people to determine what strategies should be employed at a given time. Finally, metacognitive ability involves understanding where knowledge comes from. For example, knowledge gained from reading someone's opinion should be separated from knowledge gained by observing the outcome of some experiment.

The reasoning techniques described in this chapter are strategies people have available for scientific reasoning. One strategy people may use is to generate a hypothesis by inductive argument. For example, after noticing that students who watch a lot of television get poor grades, one might hypothesize that television watching causes poor grades. This hypothesis can then be tested in an experiment. In addition, to the techniques described, college-educated adults also have strategies that facilitate drawing conclusions about whether one event caused another. For example, Spellman (1996) had people judge which of two fertilizers (red or blue) was effective in making plants bloom. People selectively focused on comparisons between cases where the red fertilizer was given or not, holding the presence of the blue fertilizer constant, and on comparisons between cases where the blue fertilizer was given or not holding the presence of the red fertilizer constant. Only this strategy allows people to disentangle the effects of the fertilizers from each other.

Given that people have a number of strategies they can use for scientific reasoning, it is important to know about their metastrategic ability. To what degree do people use the correct strategies when reasoning scientifically? Evidence bearing on this point comes from a simple but intriguing procedure presented by Wason (1960) who told subjects that the sequence 2, 4, 6 followed a rule and that their task was to discover this rule. The participants were allowed to generate sequences of three numbers; for any sequence, they would be told whether the example followed the rule. Very loosely, the situation is like a scientist trying to determine the "correct theory," and generating a sequence is like conducting an experiment. A common result was that a participant would hypothesize that the rule was "number ascending by 2" and provide test sequences such as 1, 3, 5; 101, 103, 105; 276, 278, 280; or 6.5, 8.5, 10.5. For each such sequence, the answer would be that it follows the rule, and often a participant would state with high confidence that he or she had discovered the rule. Note, however, that these test sequences all match the hypothesized rule. This ignores the procedure of producing a sequence inconsistent with the rule. For example, if a participant generated the sequence 10, 11, 14 and was told that it also followed the experimenter's rule, the hypothesis "numbers ascending by 2" would have to be rejected. Actually the rule that Wason had in mind was "any ascending sequence," which many participants failed to discover. The tendency to construct tests that are consistent with our hypothesis has been referred to as **confirmation bias.**

Other studies have used more realistic simulated research environments. For example, Mynatt, Doherty, and Tweney (1977) asked subjects to try to account for the motion of a particle that was "fired" from a position on a computer screen. The displays could be quite complex and featured a variety of objects occupying a variety of positions. The rule was that the particle stopped moving when it was near any gray figure (until fired again). Subjects were given an initial display and thereafter allowed to choose one of two displays to test their hypotheses. Again, subjects tended to select tests that were consistent with their hypotheses rather than those that might falsify it. This is further evidence of a confirmation bias.

An interesting perspective on confirmation bias is provided by Klayman and Ha (1987). They argue that what people term *confirmation bias* should instead be thought of as a **positive test strategy** and that it can be a very good heuristic under many realistic conditions. According to the positive test strategy, the focus is on testing direct implications of one's theory. Testing cases that are expected to show some properties of interest (the positive test strategy) is only clearly bad when the current hypothesis is a subset or special case of the correct hypothesis. To give a concrete example, suppose you have a new boss, and you think that it is OK to joke about Republicans and the economy with her. It is natural to test this hypothesis by telling jokes about Republicans and about the economy and finding out whether you were correct. Note that you are unlikely to find out whether it is all right to joke about religion, because that is not part of the hypothesis. Indeed, it might never occur to you to test the idea that you can joke about religion. In most realistic circumstances, argue Klayman and Ha, one would expect that hypotheses would either partially overlap with the correct state of affairs or not overlap at all. In both of these cases, the positive test strategy would provide useful information. The general point is that what looks like a poor strategy in a particular context (like the ones that appear in many experiments) may nonetheless be an effective strategy in broader contexts.

The idea of a confirmation bias suggests that people's theories may influence what tests they perform. That is, theories may influence metastrategic ability. Theories may also influence how evidence is interpreted. In one study, Koehler (1993) sent a survey to trained scientists who were either advocates or skeptics of parapsychological phenomena (e.g., ESP). The survey contained a description of a simulated research report along with data from the hypothetical study. The scientists were asked to evaluate the quality of the study. The scientists (of both types) evaluated studies that agreed with their prior beliefs as being of higher quality than studies that disagreed with their prior beliefs. Interestingly, subjects were asked both whether they felt that the outcome of the study influenced their evaluation of quality as well as whether they felt that the outcome of the study *should* have influenced their evaluation. The majority of subjects stated that the outcome of the study had not influenced their evaluation (even though it had), and the majority also stated that the outcome of the study should not have influenced their evaluation.

Other research demonstrates that people who are not trained in science are also resistant to data that contradict existing beliefs. Kuhn (1997) reports a study in which nonscientists were asked to determine the bases of ratings of TV shows on features such as length, presence of humor, day of the week aired, and presence of music. In this study, most subjects thought that humor would improve the ratings, but in the experimental materials it did not. Similar to the subjects in Spellman's study, the subjects in this study often examined pairs of shows that were similar in all respects except for the presence of humor. In this case, they found out that the ratings for these shows differing on humor were given the same rating. This outcome should have suggested that humor was not important to the ratings, but subjects persisted in believing that humor influenced the ratings and often gave elaborate reasons why no effect of humor was observed for the rating of that particular show. This finding, which is inconsistent with the results of Spellman's study, described above, demonstrates that people may have difficulty making a proper causal attribution when it conflicts with their prior knowledge.

The importance of prior beliefs on the judgment of evidence makes it worth considering how people should reason. In the study by Koehler (1993), described earlier, trained scientists clearly believed that prior beliefs should not influence their judgments of the quality of a new study. However, in real world environments, there are often things we believe strongly. If those beliefs are based on a lot of other evidence, then when a new result comes along that contradicts this prior belief, it makes sense to treat this new result skeptically. Only after we have significant evidence that our prior belief is incorrect does it really make sense to completely revise our theories about the world. Koehler (1993) makes a similar argument based on statistical principles. Thus, from a metacognitive standpoint, it is worth distinguishing between evidence that is consistent with prior beliefs and evidence that is not.

To the extent that prior beliefs are important in developing new studies and interpreting evidence, it is worth thinking about where these prior beliefs come from. Obviously, in many cases we have beliefs based on experience. If we have been through a situation before, then we are likely to know how to deal with that situation again in the future. In science, however, the current problem being explored will never be exactly the same as one solved before. Dunbar (1995, 1997) observed microbiologists at work and found that they often used analogies in order to generate ideas for new studies or to help them interpret the data from studies just completed. An interesting facet of these analogies was that the base and target domains were often very similar. For example, a scientist might draw an analogy from one kind of bacterium to another. This use of analogies from similar domains should not be that surprising. As we discussed above, analogies involve similarities in the relations in the domains. When making specific predictions about a complex domain like microbiology, only very similar things are likely to have the same relational structure as the object you are interested in. Thus, one bacterium provides a good analogy to another bacterium (but something more distant, such as an ameba, a giraffe, or a solar system, would probably not).

In sum, scientific reasoning bears many similarities to good thinking in general. People must develop explanations of the way the world works and then test those explanations against evidence from the world. Often people are better at generating tests that will provide information consistent with their hypotheses than tests that might disprove their hypotheses. This strategy can be problematic in some cases, but often works well in the real world. Furthermore, there is evidence that strongly held beliefs are resistant to evidence that contradicts those beliefs. Again, while this behavior can lead to problems, it is often better to be skeptical about new evidence than to constantly change beliefs radically on the basis of new evidence. Finally, analogy has been shown to be a significant source of new insights in science, though the base and target domains used in scientists' analogies are often quite similar.

Summary

We have only sampled from the literature on reasoning, and the pool on which our sample is based is itself probably not very representative of the variety of situations in which human reasoning is employed. There is far more to deductive reasoning than modus ponens, for example, and far more to scientific reasoning than confirmation bias.

We began this chapter by talking about strategies for reasoning that focus on the structure of arguments. Deductive inference derives its power from the fact that it is truth preserving, and so when the premises are true, the conclusion must be true.

While deductive inference is powerful, we can never really be assured of the truth of premises, because the evidence for most premises comes from inductive arguments. We discussed a number of strategies for inductive argument in this chapter such as probabilistic reasoning. Because inductive arguments can only influence our confidence in the truth of a statement, we are likely to have premises in deductive arguments whose truth is uncertain.

In order to gain more understanding of the role of content in inductive reasoning, we explored mental models, which are representations of causal information about the physical world. Mental models provide the kind of information about physical objects that scripts did for events. Thus, mental models provide a basis for reasoning about physical objects.

Finally, we put all of this together by examining research on scientific reasoning. Science involves using evidence to evaluate hypotheses about the world. Scientific reasoning employs many aspects of reasoning that are used all the time by most people. Where scientific reasoning differs from normal reasoning is that scientists must go out of their way to ensure that they create tests that will disconfirm their hypotheses, because there is a natural tendency toward confirmation. Further, they must realize that they are likely to try to resist data that are inconsistent with their beliefs. Nonetheless, it is clear that the capacity to reason like a scientist resides in all of us.

Key Terms

affirming the consequent

analogical reasoning

base rate

confirmation bias

deductive argument

denying the antecedent

inductive reasoning

intuitive physics

logic

mental models

modus ponens

modus tollens

positive test strategy

pragmatic reasoning schemas

reasoning schema

structure mapping theory

systematicity

valid argument

Recommended Readings

We admit to a modest prejudice. Prior to doing our review of this area, we thought that work on reasoning was a bit dry, if not dull. But we were very wrong! A central issue with respect to understanding the human mind concerns the extent to which logical truth and empirical truth can be separated. Do people have abstract rules that they use in reasoning? "Yes," according to Rips (1994; see also Smith, Langston, & Nisbett, 1992), and "No," according to the mental models approach associated with Johnson-Laird (1983; see also Johnson-Laird & Byrne, 1991). The pragmatic-reasoning-schemas view of Cheng and Holyoak (1985, 1989) is that rules may be tied to fairly abstract social schemas, whereas Cosmides (1989) argues strongly in favor of content-specific reasoning abilities. A firsthand reading of this paper will serve to convey some of the controversy and excitement linked with these distinct points of view.

Less drama but equal interest attaches to studies of inductive reasoning. Goodman's (1955) paper is a classic, and the psychological implications of Goodman's paper are examined by Tetewsky and Sternberg (1986). For contributions from analogy, see the papers by Gentner (1989), Holyoak and Thagard (1995), and Keane, Ledgeway, and Duff (1994). The extension of analogy to ordinary similarity is summarized by Gentner and Markman (1997). Finally, psychologists are, by necessity, interested in scientific reasoning. The Tweney et al. (1981) book provides a good introduction to research on scientific reasoning, and the Klayman (1988), Klayman and Ha (1987), and Koehler (1993) papers are important additions. Kuhn (1995) explores parallels between scientific reasoning and knowledge acquisition, particularly in development.

Chapter 12

Problem Solving

Introduction
Problems, Problems, Problems
What Is a Problem?
Types of Problems
Methods for Studying Problem Solving
Summary

Problem Solving as Representation and Search
Introduction
The Problem Space Analysis
Problem Solving as Search
Problem Solving as Representation
Summary of Problem Solving as Representation
 and Search

Reliance on Specific Relevant Knowledge
Introduction
The Influence of Related Problems
Summary

Summary

Key Terms

Recommended Readings

A man, viewed as a behaving system, is quite simple.
The apparent complexity of his behavior over time
is largely a reflection of the complexity of
the environment in which he finds himself.
—Herbert Simon, "The Sciences of the Artificial"

INTRODUCTION _____

Problems, Problems, Problems

Problem solving occurs throughout life. A young child may be trying to figure out how to stack blocks to make a tower that does not topple over. An older child may be trying to solve a mathematical word problem. Someone else may be attempting to figure out a perfect anniversary gift. An architect may be designing a house or a mathematician attempting to prove a theorem. Despite the diversity of these problems, the ways people go about solving them show a number of common characteristics. This chapter examines these commonalities and what they tell us about human thought and intelligence. We begin with what problems are and how psychologists study problem solving.

What Is a Problem?

Before proceeding to a discussion of how people solve problems, we first need to define what is meant by a problem. For our purposes, we can consider a person to have a problem when he or she wishes to attain some goal for which no simple, direct means is known. To elaborate, we consider a **problem** to have four aspects: *goal*, *givens*, *means of transforming conditions*, and *obstacles*. The *goal* is some state of knowledge toward which the problem solving is directed and for which at least some criterion can be applied to assess whether the problem has been solved. Using some of our examples, the goal might be to have a stack of blocks that does not topple or to have a properly designed house. The *givens* include the objects, conditions, and constraints that are provided with the problem, either explicitly or implicitly. A mathematical word problem explicitly provides the objects and initial conditions; the specifications for a house contain only some conditions (e.g., Tudor style), to which the architect may add.

Problems need to have some *means of transforming conditions,* of changing the initial states. This requirement excludes those situations for which no problem solving may be attempted. In our examples, we assume that the older child can understand the words in the word problem and has at least some relevant mathematical knowledge that might be applied, and that the mathematician and architect have some relevant knowledge for transforming the initial conditions. Finally, problems have some *obstacles*. A goal that can be attained simply by remembering an earlier solution with no change at all is not usually considered to be a problem. For example, suppose you were to find your way home from your friend's house a block away and had done so often in the past. Even though you can attain the goal, we exclude such cases from our discussion of problem solving. (We should point out, however, that one goal of learning in the cognitive system is to allow us to take problems whose solution had to be worked out and to turn them into problems with known solutions.)

In short, problem solving is taking place if a person is (1) trying to attain a goal, (2) starting from some set of conditions, the givens, (3) with some means of transforming these conditions, but (4) with no immediately available knowledge of a solution.

Types of Problems

Despite the idea that problems have common aspects, figuring out how to fix a flat bicycle tire seems very different from figuring out how to have an interesting career. Clearly, these two problems have many differences, such as their importance to the person, their time scale, and their difficulty. Just because two problems are different, however, does not mean that the problem solving is different in important ways. Rather, a crucial activity in understanding problem solving is to analyze which problem differences are important and which are not.

One distinction that has had considerable influence in the field is well-defined problems versus ill-defined problems (W. Reitman, 1965). **Well-defined problems** have completely specified initial conditions, goals, and means of transforming conditions. Many games and puzzles are well defined (though some tricky puzzles appear to be well defined but are not). For example, a maze puzzle is usually well defined. The initial condition is the starting point. The goal is some well-specified ending point, such as the exit of the maze. Thus, you will know when you have attained the goal. Finally, the means of transforming the conditions are by walking on any path in the maze. **Ill-defined problems** have some aspects that are not completely specified. The problem of having an interesting career is clearly ill defined. Even if you knew how to tell whether you would have an interesting career, you wouldn't know exactly how to transform the current situation to achieve this goal. Problems may differ on how well defined (or ill defined) they are, so it is best to consider this distinction as a continuum rather than a dichotomy.

Much of the early work on problem solving studied well-defined problems. However, this focus does not mean work on problem solving is irrelevant to how people solve ill-defined problems. For example, Voss and his colleagues (see Voss & Post, 1988, for an overview) have examined how people solve social science questions such as how to improve crop productivity in Russia (taking the role of the Russian minister of agriculture). Although this is a very ill defined problem, the results show many of the same processes that were discovered and analyzed in the research on well-defined problems. H. A. Simon (1973) has argued that a crucial part of problem solving is changing an ill-defined problem into a well-defined problem (or, often, a number of well-defined problems). For example, take the ill-defined problem of having an interesting career. You might first change that into a number of smaller (and less ill defined) problems, such as doing well in school so you can get a good job, and then further change each of these smaller problems into a number of still smaller well-defined problems, such as solving your six homework problems.

Methods for Studying Problem Solving

Before proceeding to a discussion of problem-solving results, it is useful to consider the methods used in problem-solving research. Many of the studies use measures of accuracy or latency (time to complete the problem). Unlike other research areas, however, the latency can be on the order of many seconds or even many minutes. If our goal is to understand the cognitive processes associated with problem solving, obtaining a single measure for the whole problem-solving episode is problematic. The number of possible explanations that could lead to the same accuracy level or latency is quite large. To reduce the number of possibilities, data are often obtained throughout the process of problem solving. Three methods that are often used in problem-solving research are (1) intermediate products, (2) verbal protocols, and (3) computer simulations.

Intermediate Products

Getting intermediate products simply means that instead of recording only the answer to the problem, we observe some of the work the subject does in getting the answer. If we are interested in how people solve puzzles, we collect information about the various moves they make in getting to the goal. If we are interested in mathematical problem solving, we collect and analyze the equations and other information the subject writes down in the course of problem solving. These intermediate products provide much finer constraints on possible explanations. That is, even if a number of theories are able to account for the answer given to a problem, only a few of those (perhaps only one) will be able to account for all the steps along the way to the final answer.

Verbal Protocols

The second method often used in problem-solving research is a **verbal protocol.** Although there are a number of possible ways to collect such data, the most common is to ask the subjects to "think aloud" as they go about solving the problems. That is, they are asked to say whatever they are thinking about but not to embellish or explain it for the experimenter's benefit. The idea behind this measure is straightforward: People's thoughts provide further information about the course of their problem solving. For example, B. H. Ross (1984) collected verbal protocols of people learning to use a text-editing program. One learner said, "How do I move a paragraph? Oh, yeah, the last time I moved a paragraph, I did. . . ." This comment suggests that the person was remembering what was done in the earlier task to figure out what to do in the current task.

As you might suspect, not all verbal protocols provide useful information. For example, one of the authors was watching *Sesame Street* with his preschool daughter when the addition problem of 5 plus 3 was presented. She closed her eyes, paused, and finally said, "Eight." He was quite impressed, given that she had never counted without her fingers before, and asked her if she knew how she had done that. She replied that she did: "I used the brain." True, but again not very informative. This difficulty of providing good protocols does not occur just with children. Many people find it hard to keep talking about what they are thinking, especially when the problem solving becomes tricky. It is common for subjects to be quiet in the crucial part of the problem solving. When these quiet subjects are then prompted as to what they are thinking, they sometimes reply, "I am thinking how to solve the problem." True, but not very informative.

A DEBATE
Can We Trust Verbal Protocols?

The use of verbal protocols has led to some debate. The debate centers around the veridicality and reactivity of protocols. *Veridicality* refers to whether the protocols reflect what the person is thinking. *Reactivity* refers to whether the protocol changes how the person does the task. If the goal is to use verbal protocols to better examine the underlying process, then the goal is thwarted by either nonveridical protocols or reactivity in protocols. What is the evidence?

Some means of soliciting protocols clearly lead to distortions. For example, asking subjects to think back to how they solved a problem (a mistake made by one of the authors in the example of his daughter's addition, mentioned in the text) or why they used a particular method requires the subjects to go beyond articulating their current thoughts. Whenever you ask someone to go back and explain what they did (and why), there is a risk that they will reconstruct an answer ("I probably was trying to . . ."), rather than remember. (Remember the discussion of reconstructive memory in Chapter 7—one cannot always know whether one is remembering or reconstructing). Certainly, many times the answer will be veridical, but sometimes it may not, and the experimenter has no way of distinguishing the veridical reports from the reconstructions.

This difficulty has led to some research on how best to collect protocols and the validity of these protocols (see Ericsson & Simon, 1993, for a good review and theoretical framework, and Chi, 1997, for a practical

(Continued)

The box, A Debate, provides some arguments about the use of verbal protocols. Despite the difficulties with collecting useful protocols, they have proven a vital source of information. Simply put, they provide information that is nearly impossible to gain from other current methods.

Computer Simulation

Verbal protocols may be used as direct evidence for some hypotheses or to generate new ideas that are then tested by other methods. However, a common goal in problem-solving research is to build a computer simulation that is meant to mimic the problem-solving process as revealed by the protocols.

Verbal protocols allow us to see the products of thought, not the processes that led to that thought. That is, we can see that a person thought of moving a

A DEBATE

Can We Trust Verbal Protocols? *(Continued)*

guide). Ericsson and Simon provide some guidelines for when protocols might be problematic and when they might not. A conservative interpretation of their proposals is that if the information is easily verbalizable and would be consciously available in the course of problem solving, then asking subjects to verbalize it should have little effect on their performance, except to often slow down their performance.

If researchers follow Ericsson and Simon's guidelines, are the protocols veridical and nonreactive? Often. Although they review and analyze many supportive cases, there are at least some instances in which there does seem to be some reactivity (such as Russo, Johnson, & Stephens, 1989; Schooler, Ohlsson, & Brooks, 1993). For example, in many cases having to give a protocol when making decisions leads people to consider information that is easy to verbalize, and perhaps even to make decisions that are easy to justify. Ericsson and Simon examine the studies that show reactivity and suggest why this might have occurred, but it is still not clear whether one can always anticipate whether reactivity will occur before the data are collected. This is still an issue in debate. However, most researchers believe that although they are not free of problems, verbal protocols have provided a great deal of insight into the problem-solving processes. A common strategy is to use verbal protocols for getting further ideas of the processes people are using, and then to follow up these studies with more traditional dependent measures.

certain piece in a puzzle or about performing a certain calculation, but we cannot see the full details of what led to considering that move or calculation. With computer simulations, researchers make hypotheses about what processes led to these products and try to incorporate them into a program. This programming has three advantages. First, it forces the researcher to be *explicit* about the processes. A program cannot just be told to "find some relevant information." Instead, the programmer must be clear about what would be considered relevant information, and by what process this information would be found. Second, creating a computer model allows a check of whether the posited processes will work together at all; that is, are they *internally consistent?* One process may end up undoing the work done by another or interfering in some unexpected way. Third, the simulation allows us to see whether the posited processes are *sufficient* to lead to the protocol behavior observed. When the simulation runs, does it lead to behavior similar to the protocols?

What can be said if a simulation meets all these goals? There is no way to ensure that the simulation is leading to the results for the same reason that the person is. There may be many ways to get a certain behavior, so finding one way does not *prove* that people do it that particular way. At the very least, the simulation provides one strong hypothesis that can be tested by later work. In addition, often the act of designing and experimenting with the simulation helps the researcher understand the ideas better and see other ways of testing them. An important aspect in designing (and assessing) these simulations is that they be *compatible* with what is already known about how people think. For example, if the simulation required keeping track of dozens of calculations at the same time, we would realize that this could not be how people would accomplish the task.

Summary

We began the chapter by defining a problem to be a situation in which a goal cannot be obtained directly. In our analysis, a problem has a set of givens, a goal, a means of transforming conditions, and obstacles. We distinguished between well-defined problems, in which aspects of the problem are well specified, and ill-defined problems in which they are not. We ended with a discussion of methods for studying problem solving that aim to learn more about the details of how problem solving occurs: intermediate products, verbal protocols, and computer simulations. Now that we have an idea of what a problem is and the methods used for examining problem solving, it is time to consider current conceptions of how people solve problems.

PROBLEM SOLVING AS REPRESENTATION AND SEARCH

Introduction

Consider the problem presented in Figure 12.1. This problem, which may be familiar to some of you, is called the Tower of Hanoi problem or the three-disk problem. As you can see, there are three pegs and three disks of different sizes stacked by size on the left peg. The problem is to get the disks stacked in the same arrangement on the right peg. To make this task a little more difficult than simply picking up the three disks and putting them down on the right peg, there are two rules. First, only one disk may be moved at a time (which obviously must be the top disk on a stack). The next disk may not be moved until the previous one has been put on a peg. Second, a disk may not be stacked on a smaller disk. Take a minute to try to solve this problem.

What do you need to do to solve this problem? First, you need to keep track of the current situation, that is, which disks are on which pegs. To start, all disks are on the left peg, but with each move, you need to know the new configuration.

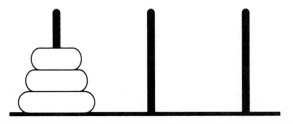

Figure 12.1   **Tower of Hanoi Problem**   The goal is to move the tower from the left peg to the right peg, moving only one disk at a time and never putting a disk on a smaller disk.

Second, for the updated configuration, you need to consider the possible moves and how they may help you reach the solution.

At a simplified level, these two aspects are what a theory of problem solving needs to explain. First, how are the problem and the various possible configurations represented? That is, how does a person take the (incomplete) information given in the problem, elaborate it, and represent it? Second, how is this representation operated on to allow the problem solver to consider the possible moves? Although the number of possible moves in the Tower of Hanoi problem is quite small, most problems have a large number of possibilities. In this section, we first consider a particular view of problem solving by Newell and Simon (1972) that has been very influential in both psychology and artificial intelligence. Then, using the ideas from this view, we examine both questions in more detail.

The Problem Space Analysis

Starting in the late 1950s, Allen Newell, Herbert Simon, and their colleagues began a long series of investigations on problem solving in both humans and computers (e.g., Newell, Shaw, & Simon, 1959). Much of their theory and evidence is presented in their gigantic 1972 book, *Human Problem Solving* (for an overview, see Simon, 1978). Newell and Simon were pioneers in the detailed use of verbal protocols and the use of computer simulations to model underlying cognitive processes. For the various tasks they described in their book, they collected extensive protocols, programmed simulations, and analyzed the underlying commonalities of problem-solving behavior. They consider problem solving in terms of an information-processing system (i.e., the problem solver) and the particular task environment (i.e., the problem). We briefly outline each of these influences and then describe how they interact.

Information-Processing System

Newell and Simon view problem solvers (whether people or machines) as systems that are processing information. In addition, they argue that a few key characteristics of the human information-processing system influence how it may solve problems. Very briefly, these characteristics concern the processing and storage limitations of

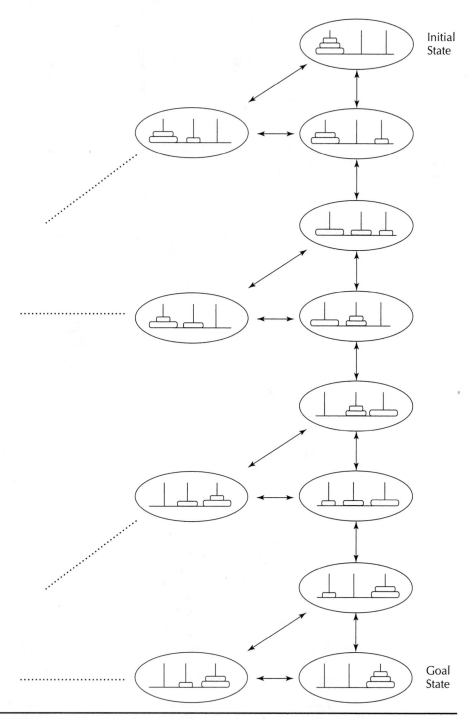

Initial
State

Goal
State

Figure 12.2   Partial Problem Space for Tower of Hanoi   Each three-peg drawing represents a state of the problem. The arrows indicate that one can move from one state to the next by applying a legal operator.

the problem solver. First, information is generally processed in a serial fashion. Second, we have a very limited-capacity short-term memory in which four to seven "chunks" (i.e., meaningful units) may be stored for immediate availability (see Chapter 5 for a discussion of chunks). Third, we have an essentially unlimited long-term memory in which other information may be stored, but it takes time to access and store information in long-term memory. For present purposes, it is sufficient to realize that the problem solver is limited in how much can be kept track of and processed at any one time, so that any problem solving will be affected by these limitations.

Task Environment

The *task environment* is the term Newell and Simon use for the problem. They use a different term to make it clear that they are talking about the objective entity presented, not how it is encoded by the problem solver. Before any problem can be solved, it must be represented in memory in some way. The task environment influences problem solving by influencing this representation, which is called the problem space.

Problem Space

The **problem space** is the problem solver's internal representation of the problem. It consists of states and operators. A **problem state** consists of knowledge that is available to the problem solver about the problem environment at a given time. Some states may represent information about the current situation, while others may represent past situations or guesses about what will happen in the future if a particular action is taken. A problem space is a collection of past, current, and future states that are linked by the operations required to get from one state to the next. These operations are the **problem operators,** and they describe the means of moving from one state to another. Because it is assumed that that cognitive operations are carried out serially, only one operator can be applied to a problem at a time. A graph can be drawn consisting of states connected by operators that lead from one state to the next. This graph is like a map of a space, where the locations are states and the avenues from one location to another are the operators. A solution to a problem, then, is a path that connects the initial state to the goal state. On this view, problem solving can be conceived as a search for a path through the state space that connects the initial state to the goal state.

   Before proceeding further, let us return to the Tower of Hanoi problem given in Figure 12.1 and examine part of its problem space, given in Figure 12.2. As we noted in discussing this problem, a problem solver needs to keep track of which disks are on which pegs. Thus, the states of knowledge in a problem space for this problem would include these facts, which we have depicted as a picture of the arrangement (note that there is no claim that people have such picturelike representations in their heads—see Chapter 8 for a discussion). The initial state would include the information that all three disks are on the left peg. The goal state would include the information that all three disks are on the right peg. The intermediate states would be all possible configurations of disks on pegs that could be produced by legal moves. The operators would be these legal moves. The only permissible means of moving from one state to another would be a move in which a disk from the top of a stack is picked up and put on a peg that contains no smaller disk. Because of the small number of disks and pegs, the total number of legal moves from any state is quite small, 27 in this problem. As may be seen in Figure 12.2, some states may be arrived at by multiple routes (i.e., through different sequences of moves), but there does exist a unique solution for solving this problem in the minimum number of moves (seven). The minimum solution is the path along the right side of the figure.

It is important to distinguish the complete problem space that could be constructed for a problem, which we shall call the *objective problem space,* from the representation used by the problem solver. All of the states in the problem space could be thought of by a human problem solver, but due to short-term memory limitations, only a small number would be at any one time. Thus, in solving this problem, a human problem solver might represent only a part of the full objective problem space.

Although the Tower of Hanoi has a simple problem space, for many problems the objective problem space can be very large. From the starting position in chess, for example, there are 20 possible first moves for the first player and then, for each of these, 20 possible moves for the second player. Thus the objective problem space would have an initial state plus 20 times 20 intermediate states (401 total states) just for the first move of each player.

Newell and Simon's framework transformed the idea of problem solving into one of representation and search. Although the representation of the problem precedes the search through this representation, until recently much of the research was concerned with how problem spaces are searched. In the next section we consider this search problem, and in the succeeding section we examine how problems are represented.

Problem Solving as Search

How might people search a problem space? We first need to distinguish between an algorithm and a heuristic. An **algorithm** is a systematic procedure that is guaranteed to lead to a solution. For example, if you are trying to find your way through a maze, you can easily get lost and find that you have returned to a dead end that you have visited before. However, an algorithm exists for finding your way out of a maze (if there are no unconnected walls). Put your left hand on a wall of the maze. Then walk, making sure never to remove your hand from the wall. This method will allow you to find your way out, since in the worst case you would eventually touch all the surfaces of the maze, including the ones on the exit path. This method may also take you down many dead ends. For any problem space, assuming there is a solution, an algorithm would be to consider all the possible moves from all states until one gets to the goal state. Although algorithms guarantee solutions, they can be extremely time-consuming. In the Tower of Hanoi problem space, examining every possible move may not be too cumbersome because the number of possible operators is small. However, for all the possible moves for a game of chess, the time involved is astronomical. For example, although white has only 20 opening moves, after white's third move, the number of possible board positions is 7.5 million; after black's third move, 225 million (Holding, 1985).

Some algorithms can be learned and used by people (e.g., rules for addition); however, in many cases there are simply too many possibilities. Exhaustively searching through very large problem spaces is not feasible, so some means is needed to reduce this complexity and guide the search. In the field of problem solving, **heuristics** are those methods that can be used to guide the search so that a complete search is not needed. Heuristics are general rules and guidelines that do not guarantee a solution, but they usually allow a good chance at a solution with much less effort than an algorithm. To the extent that individual differences in problem-solving ability are due to differences in search, the claim would be that these differences are largely due to differences in the ability to select and apply heuristics. How we overcome the complexities of search is an important component of problem-solving skill. We first consider a simple heuristic and then examine some alternatives that overcome some of its limitations.

Simple Search

Assume you are at some state in the problem space. How do you decide which possible states to proceed to next? One possibility is to choose a state randomly. Although at times there is no alternative but to choose randomly, a better alternative is usually available. One reasonable heuristic might be to look at all possible next states and choose to go on to the one that is "best," the one closest to the goal. Given that the goal of the problem is to reach the goal state, the determination of best should take this goal into account. The determination of what is best can vary, so there are a number of heuristics that could fit under this type.

One form of this heuristic is called **hill climbing.** The term refers to the following analogy: Suppose that you were blindfolded, put in some unfamiliar terrain, and told to find the highest point in the terrain without taking off your blindfold. How would you do it? A good method would be to move your foot around, feel the angle of the terrain in all directions, and then move in the direction with the steepest incline. When you get to a location where no direction leads to an incline, you stop. Using this method is reasonable, given the situation. When you take off your blindfold, however, you may see that you are on top of *a* hill, but higher hills may be elsewhere. That is, you may have ended up at a local maximum. Figure 12.3 illustrates these situations. In panel A, the blindfolded person would move steadily up the hill to the top, until no move led to higher ground. On taking off the blindfold, the climber would be at the highest point. In panel B, however, if the same strategy was followed, the person would be at the highest point of that hill, not of the highest hill. This is called a *local maximum* because it is the highest point on this (local) part of the terrain, but not the highest overall. If the climber had started at a different point (marked "Starting point 2"), then the same strategy would have succeeded in finding

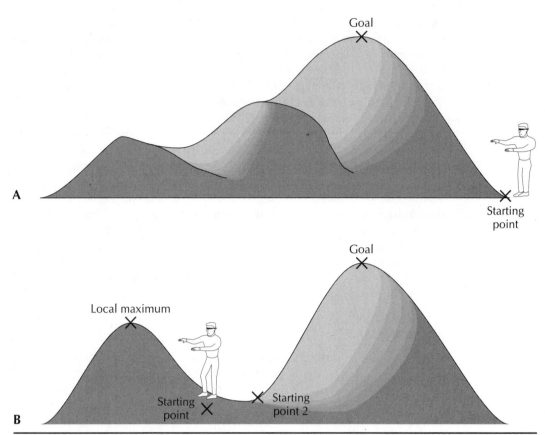

Figure 12.3   **Illustration of Hill-Climbing Heuristic**   The terrain represents the closeness to problem solution, with higher elevation being closer to the goal. Panel A shows a blindfolded person moving steadily up the hill by feeling the terrain. Panel B shows the problem of local maximum for this heuristic.

the highest overall point. Hill climbing can lead to the right answer, but success depends both upon the terrain and upon where one begins.

In a problem-solving setting, hill climbing means that you start with the givens and at each step you choose the operators to always move "up" toward the goal. First, you examine all possible operators to see all possible next states (moving your foot around). Then, each of these possible states is compared to the goal state (feeling the angle of the terrain). Finally, you choose the operator that takes you to the state that is closest to the goal state (moving in the direction with the steepest incline). For example, in the Tower of Hanoi problem you would make the move to the state that looks most like the goal state (e.g., has the disks on the goal peg). The decision about how to evaluate which state is closest to the goal can be quite complex in some settings because of multiple criteria—for instance, in chess, the evaluation function would include the value of the pieces and positional strengths.

Hill climbing takes into account the goal and chooses the next state that is closest to the goal. This method requires the problem solver to consider all possible next moves but may not lead to a solution (because of a local maximum). The main problem (but also the reason why it is a relatively easy heuristic to employ) is that one is selecting operators based only on the very local consideration of the next state.

Overcoming Problems with Simple Search

The difficulty with simple search heuristics is that not all problems can be solved by constantly moving toward the goal. Some problems require the problem solver to move away from the goal for a while. An example may illustrate this point. Imagine that you are in a restaurant in New York City and you find out that you need to go to San Francisco immediately. How would you solve this problem using the hill-climbing heuristic? At each step, you go in the direction that takes you closest to the goal. Thus, you would always move to the west. Even if we were to assume that you could get to your car (i.e., that it was parked directly west of the restaurant and that no walls blocked your exit), you would end up driving all the way to San Francisco unless you happened to drive through an airport on your way. Clearly, this heuristic fails to capture the full power of human problem solving, even in this fairly simple situation. No heuristic that bases its decision on a single step could solve such a problem reasonably.

The same difficulty occurs in a large number of other situations. As one further example, we may consider a case in which exploratory surgery is performed to help in diagnosis. Clearly such surgery in itself is a step away from the goal of curing the patient. Most patients feel worse, not better, immediately after such a procedure. Nonetheless, most people have no difficulty understanding that such a procedure can be crucial for attaining the goal of good health. Sometimes we must move away from the goal in order to attain it.

To be able to solve problems of this sort, the problem solver needs to plan beyond a single move ahead. The determination of what state to go to is not based simply on how that state relates to the goal, but rather how that state fits into some plan to reach the goal state. These planning heuristics require the problem solver to break the problem down in some way and try to find solutions for these subproblems. We concentrate here on a particular heuristic called **means-ends analysis** because of its importance in artificial intelligence (AI) systems and its frequent occurrence in human problem solving (Newell & Simon, 1972).

Means-Ends Analysis

The basic idea of means-ends analysis is quite simple. The first step is to compare the current state with the goal state and characterize this difference. Then use this difference to help decide what operator should be chosen. If more than one operator could be used, choose the one that removes the largest part of the difference first. This technique is then applied to the new difference (i.e., between the new state and the goal) and so on, until all the differences are reduced and the goal state is reached.

This presentation may be somewhat abstract, so let us return to the earlier example in which you are at a restaurant in New York City and find out that you need to go to San Francisco immediately. How would means-ends analysis proceed? You compare your current state to your goal state and determine that the difference is over 3,000 miles. You consider your operators for reducing mileage differences and determine that, for such a large difference, an airplane is the best operator. Given that airplanes usually leave from airports, not restaurants, you now produce the subgoal of reducing the difference between being at the restaurant and being at the airport. You might decide to reduce this difference by using a taxi, which produces a further difference to reduce between being inside the restaurant and having a taxi to get into outside. As you can see from this example, although the elimination of differences does produce other differences, by eliminating the largest difference first, often any further differences are relatively minor. Of course, possibly no taxi could be found or some other difference could not be reduced. Means-ends analysis is a heuristic, so one has to realize that it may not always succeed.

Although this means-ends analysis is a general technique, it does require that the problem solver know which operators can reduce which differences. The restaurant example was solvable only because we know which types of transportation can reduce which mileage differences. Even general techniques may not be able to help without some relevant domain knowledge. In summary, means-ends analysis is a useful planning heuristic. It is simple but quite powerful. In addition, it is a very general heuristic in that it can be applied at any level of abstraction or representation of the problem, and it has been widely used in computer simulations.

Working Backward

Another heuristic that can be helpful is **working backward,** in which one works from the goal back to the givens. In some situations the number of possible directions to go from the givens (i.e., operators to apply to the initial state) is quite large, and it is difficult to know which to choose. Rather than approach the problem that way, it may be better to start at the goal and ask what would need to be true for the goal to be true. Then one may take each of these "prior-to-the-goal" statements and ask again what would need to be true for each of these statements to be true. The intention is to keep working backward in that way until you are able to satisfy a set of these statements by the givens. Once that set of statements is true, you know that it implies that the next set is true, which, in turn, implies that the next set is true, and so on up to the goal.

Consider this simple example: Prove that the product of any two consecutive whole numbers (i.e., 1, 2, 3, . . .) is even. Just for fun, try it. If you start working forward from the givens, you may represent the problem as one number, n, and the next number, $n + 1$. The product would be $n \times (n + 1)$. There are ways to solve this example by working forward from these givens, but they are not obvious. Let us see how one might work backward from the goal. The goal is to prove the product is even. For a number to be even, it must be represented as $2w$, where w is a whole number. Thus, w must equal the product of the two numbers divided by 2. For this to be true, one of the numbers must be divisible by 2, meaning it must be even. Now the proof will be complete if you can show that the givens imply that one of the numbers must be even. But odd and even numbers alternate, so for any two consecutive numbers, one of them must be even. The proof is complete.

The basic point is that if the number of directions from the goal is small and the number from the givens is large, you may want to consider working backward from the goal. (Wickelgren, 1974, provides a detailed elaboration of this method and advice about when it may be useful.)

Summary of Problem Solving as Search

The difficulty with searching a problem space is that the number of possibilities is often far too large to try them all, so some shortcut or heuristic is needed. We distinguished between algorithms, systematic procedures that are guaranteed to lead to a solution, and heuristics, shortcuts that avoid a complete search but are not guaranteed to lead to a solution. In many cases, the use of algorithms is not practical, so heuristics must be used. We described a few heuristics in detail. In hill climbing, one chooses the operator at each step that will move closest towards the goal. In means-ends analysis, one checks the difference between the current state and goal, then applies the operator that eliminates the largest part of the difference. In working backwards, one begins at the goal and proceeds to work to the givens.

Although we have contrasted some different means of searching problem spaces, problem solving may make use of more than one heuristic. For example, it is quite common to work both forward and backward on a given problem, setting up statements that imply the goal and then working from the givens to these statements. Even within means-ends analysis, some subgoals may be solved by using a working backward, forward, or hill-climbing heuristic. The switch between different heuristics serves to reduce the computational complexity of search.

We hope this helps you to understand the quotation at the beginning of the chapter, in which Simon argues that people are simple systems whose behavior can look quite complex. These heuristics are meant to be fairly simple, widely applicable procedures. However, when they are applied to very complex situations, the problem solving may look very complicated.

Problem Solving as Representation

Some Examples

Try to solve the following problem (which is taken from Wickelgren, 1974). You are given a 5 x 5 checkerboard, as shown in Figure 12.4. Starting with the square that has the dot, try to draw a line through all the squares of the checkerboard. You may only go horizontally or vertically, you may not lift the pencil off the paper or go outside the checkerboard, and you may pass through each square only once. Show how to do this or prove that it is impossible.

If you are like most people, including the authors, you probably tried various solutions without success but were not sure whether the problem could be solved or

Figure 12.4   **The 5 x 5 Checkerboard Problem**   The goal is to start at the dot and draw a line through all the squares without picking up your pencil, without passing through a square more than once, and without using diagonal lines.

Source: Wickelgren, 1974.

whether you had not yet found the solution. In fact, there is a simple means of determining that this problem cannot be solved. However, this determination requires that you concentrate not on the visible checkerboard but rather on a more abstract representation of the board. First, note how many black and white squares there are (13 and 12, respectively). Second, note that any horizontal or vertical line passing through two squares will pass through one black square and one white square. Third, note that because you are starting on a white square, you will always have passed through at least as many white squares as black squares (i.e., the same or one more white). Fourth, note that if you are to pass through an odd number of squares (i.e., 25), you need to end on the same color on which you started. Since you start on a white square, you need to end on a white square. But since there are more black squares than white squares, you cannot pass through all the black squares while only passing through each white square once. Therefore, it is not possible to accomplish this goal. So, instead of using a spatial representation of the checkerboard and trying to figure out how to travel through the board, it is much easier to turn it into a more abstract representation on which you can perform simple mathematical operations.

A second problem is to play a game called *number scrabble* (Newell & Simon, 1972). The rules are quite simple. The numbers 1 to 9 are written on separate pieces of paper and laid face up on a table so that all the numbers can be seen. Two players alternate choosing numbers. A player wins who has exactly three numbers that total 15 (e.g., 9, 4, and 2). Try playing it against yourself or a friend for a while.

This game is often difficult for people playing for the first time. There is a lot to keep track of, and it is easy to fail to recognize that the opponent can win on the next draw. For example, once you and your opponent each have at least two numbers, you must keep track of which number still on the table can be combined with

4	3	8
9	5	1
2	7	6

Figure 12.5   **Number Scrabble Square for Isomorph to Tic-tac-toe**   This tic-tac-toe representation is equivalent to the number scrabble game described in the text but is much easier to do (if you know how to play tic-tac-toe).

any pair of numbers you have (and your opponent has) that add up to 15. You must ensure that you either select a number that adds up to 15 in your own hand, or one that keeps your opponent from winning. That is a lot of information to keep track of!

The game becomes much easier if a different problem representation is used. The key insight is that a magic square using the numbers 1–9 can be made in which every row, column, and diagonal adds up to the same number (in this case 15). If we lay out this magic square as in Figure 12.5, then you can see that this configuration looks like a tic-tac-toe board. If you just memorized this board, then you could think of the numbers as describing locations on the tic-tac-toe board. The numbers in your hand would be Xs, and the numbers in your opponents hand would be Os. All you are trying to do is to get numbers that add up to 15, which means that you are trying to complete a row, column, or diagonal, just as you would in tic-tac-toe. The game is much easier to play once you have transformed it from a difficult mathematical representation to a familiar spatial one.

The Importance of Representation

Newell and Simon argued for thinking of problem solving as representation and search. Although much of the early work on problem solving examined how people search a problem space to find a solution to a problem, the likelihood that one solves a problem also depends on the way in which the problem is represented. As Simon (1978, p. 276) points out: "The relative ease of solving a problem will depend on how successful the solver has been in representing critical features of the task environment in his problem space." Even much before the information-processing approach, the Gestalt psychologists (discussed in Chapter 3, Perception) had a theory of problem solving that focused almost exclusively on the representation. They believed that once a solver had the appropriate representation, the solution would come easily.

The point we wish to make clear is that *problem representation is crucial.* In the 5 x 5 checkerboard problem, the representation of the problem needs to have information about the alternating color of the board *and* information about the alternating color coverage of a horizontal or vertical line. Representing the board as just a 25-square grid is unlikely to enable anyone to solve the problem. (See Kaplan & Simon, 1990, for a detailed discussion as to how including these alternations in the representation can lead to insight in a different problem using a checkerboard.) In the number scrabble problem, the representation of the problem as tic-tac-toe makes the problem much, much easier.

In addition to the problems that we have presented, there are a number of other demonstrations in which a problem cannot be solved until it is thought about in the "right way." You almost surely have had the same type of experience in some course. You worked and worked to solve a problem to no avail but found that once you looked at it in a different way (i.e., re-represented the problem), its solution was obvious. The new representation of the problem allowed you to access and apply operators that were not available from the earlier representation. Our demonstrations are rather extreme examples to make a point, but even subtler variations in representation may have a large effect on problem solving. Much current research is focused on how people generate problem spaces and how the problem space affects performance.

Why Does Representation Matter?

The representation of the problem is the problem space, which consists of states and operators. The particular representation used makes a difference because different problem spaces may contain different information. The key difficulties in developing an effective representation are incomplete information and computational complexity. First, if crucial information is missing from the states, the problem may be impossible to solve. The problem is often incomplete, and information must be added from the problem solver's memory to arrive at an adequate representation. In the checkerboard problem, if information about the color of the squares is not included in your representation, you may be stuck with being able to say only that you have not come up with a solution.

Second, some representations may affect the operators by making it difficult to apply and evaluate possible moves. Keeping track of all the irrelevant information may make it too hard to process the relevant information well. The number scrabble problem is very complicated if all your representation consists of is three sets of numbers: the numbers you have chosen, the numbers your opponent has chosen, and the numbers remaining. You constantly have to check whether you or your opponent have any triples that add to 15 or any doubles that add to a number that can be made to 15 by the addition of one available digit. These calculations and bookkeeping chores are very difficult to do accurately in your head and in a reasonable amount of time. Even if you can keep track of all the necessary information of possible operators, this bookkeeping means that less time and effort are spent on planning the search through the space or on the strategy. Again, in number scrabble, once the relation to tic-tac-toe is understood, the player may concentrate on planning ahead to get two numbers each from two triplets so that the opponent will not be able to block both. This planning is possible if you have the states and operators efficiently represented but is much harder if you do not.

In short, some problem representations allow problem solvers to apply operators easily and traverse the problem space in an efficient way; other representations do not. Earlier we stressed that the objective problem space might have more states than the problem space used by the solver. Now we see that it may also have different states and operators. Although we have stressed the importance of representation, note that a good representation is crucial but not sufficient to solve a problem. In most cases a good representation does not immediately lead to a solution, but rather allows the problem solver to proceed with an efficient search of the problem space.

Other Examples of Representation Effects

The idea that the representation of the problem is crucial is easy to illustrate with simple puzzles; however, it is important to realize that these effects of representation extend to all of problem solving. We will see a number of examples in the section on expertise in the next chapter, but here we point out some effects of different types of representation on problem solving.

FUNCTIONAL FIXEDNESS   Consider the following task, presented by Duncker (1945). Subjects were asked to attach a candle to a wall to provide light. They were given a box of tacks, candles, and matches. The tacks were too small to go through the candle. How could the subjects accomplish the goal? Try to solve this problem yourself.

The problem can be solved by using the box as a platform. The solution, illustrated in Figure 12.6, is to empty the box of tacks, tack the box to the wall, melt the bottom of the candle a little and stick it to this box. Very few subjects solve this problem. It appears that most participants do not think of the box as a possible part of the solution but rather as a container for objects. **Functional fixedness** refers to this inability to use objects in ways other than they are typically used. (For later research see Glucksberg & Danks, 1968; Weisberg & Sulls, 1973.) The basic argument is that if the representation of the problem does not include the box, then a solution that requires the box will never be attained.

CONTENT EFFECTS IN PROBLEM SOLVING   The clearest examples of representation effects are cases in which two problems are formally equivalent but show large differences in difficulty (not unlike the content effects in reasoning that we discussed in Chapter 11). Such problems are called *problem isomorphs*. Thus, number scrabble and tic-tac-toe are problem isomorphs, though they are usually represented quite differently by most people. A large number of isomorphs have been constructed for the Tower of Hanoi problem (see Kotovsky, Hayes, & Simon, 1985, for detailed descriptions). For example, in some isomorphs, three different-sized monsters have different-sized balls, and the globes are exchanged according to certain rules. The full statement of this problem and the rules are given in Table 12.1. In fact, if one realizes that the monsters are like pegs and the balls like disks, one can see that the rules map exactly to the rules for the standard Tower of Hanoi problem. Formal equivalence is not psychological equivalence, however. The different isomorphs vary greatly in their ease of solution, with the one in Table 12.1 taking 8 times as long to

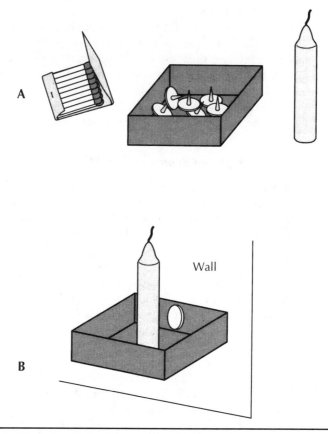

Figure 12.6   **Duncker's (1945) Candle Problem**   The subjects are asked to attach a candle to the wall and are given a box of tacks, candles, and matches, as shown in panel A. The solution is shown in panel B.

solve on the average as the peg-disk version (and another variant taking 16 times as long to solve). Kotovsky et al. (1985) provide evidence for a number of sources of difficulty. A primary source, as in the number scrabble problem, is the heavy processing load imposed by the operators in the more difficult problems.

Another source of content effects comes in how people interpret the problem situation, which may influence which operators they think are relevant. For example, Bassok, Wu, and Olseth (1995) had college students learn about solving permutation problems (which involve understanding the number of different ways that various sets of objects can be grouped together). For permutation problems, we can pair objects together arbitrarily. Caddies could be grouped with other caddies, or with golfers, or with golf carts. When people read a problem about one group of caddies being grouped with another, the problem gets interpreted only as looking at ways that pairs of people can be constructed. In contrast, when caddies are grouped with

Table 12.1   **A Monster Move Problem: Isomorph to Tower of Hanoi**

Three five-handed extraterrestrial monsters were holding three crystal globes. Because of the quantum-mechanical peculiarities of their neighborhood, both monsters and globes come in exactly three sizes with no others permitted: small, medium, and large. The small monster was holding the large globe, the medium-sized monster was holding the small globe, and the large monster was holding the medium-sized globe. Since this situation offended their keenly developed sense of symmetry, they proceeded to transfer globes from one monster to another so that each monster would have a globe proportionate to its own size.

Monster etiquette complicated the solution of the problem since it requires that:

1. Only one globe may be transferred at a time;

2. If a monster is holding two globes, only the larger of the two may be transferred; and,

3. A globe may not be transferred to a monster who is holding a larger globe.

By what sequence of transfers could the monsters have solved this problem?

Source: Kotovsky, Hayes, & Simon, 1985.

golfers, the problem is interpreted as *assigning* caddies to golfers. Finally, when caddies are grouped with golf carts, the problem is interpreted as assigning golf carts to caddies. People use this information about the role someone should be playing in the problem to decide how numbers in the word problem should be entered into the equations for permutations. The point of this work is that problem solving is sensitive both to mathematical relations, but also to the way the problem is stated. The way the problem is stated influences how the problem is represented.

Other Representations of Problems

We have concentrated on the representations of a few problems in order to make clear why representation is so important in problem solving, but we think it is important to make explicit that there are many more types of representations that are used in problem solving. In many domains, such as physics, students are taught particular new representations that help in solving problems in those domains. In addition, there are a number of more general representations that can be used across a wide variety of domains and which many people appear to know and use (see Novick et al., 1999, for more background). We mention two general representations: matrices and hierarchies.

Suppose you were faced with a problem that was very important to you—trying to figure out your class schedule for next semester. A common representation to help in solving such problems is to draw a *matrix*, a diagram that makes explicit the different combinations of the problem aspects (see Panel A of Figure 12.7). For example, when trying to schedule classes, many people construct a matrix with days of the week across five columns on the top and hours of the day for each row (beginning with 8 a.m. or 9 a.m. or whenever you are willing to have your first class). You

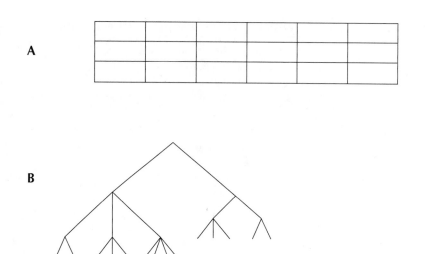

Figure 12.7   Two general representations: (A) matrix; (B) hierarchy.

can then fill in the times for each class, quickly see conflicts, and then try out different schedules until you get one that seems best for you. Notice that different people have different evaluation functions, ways of determining what is close to the goal, with some people giving more weight to late starts and others to having a day without classes. Matrix representations can be used for a variety of other problems as well. For example, in many bookstores, you can find books of logic problems that are best solved using a matrix representation. You might be told there are five people (Arthur, Brian, Carl, Douglas, and Edward) who have different last names (Fine, Goode, Hebb, Irwin, and Jacobs) and your task is to match the first and last names by combining information across a number of facts you are given (e.g., the person with the last name Fine does not play an instrument; Brian and Douglas play the harpsichord). You could then put an X at the combinations of Brian-Fine and Douglas-Fine, and with enough of these eliminations, you can match up the names correctly.

Another representation, hierarchies (see Panel B of Figure 12.7), can be illustrated with a common example—a family tree. If you have ever seen a family tree, it begins with a particular couple (for example, your great-great maternal grandparents) and then represents their offspring, the spouses of those offspring, the children of those couples, *their* spouses, etc., down to your generation (or further if there are children of people in your generation). This hierarchy allows you to quickly see a number of family facts, such as how many generations separate you and various relatives, and how various relatives are related to you and to each other. Also, by adding in further distinctions (such as different coloring or shapes for males and females), you can quickly see many other kinds of information. The hierarchies are commonly used in representing a number of other situations, such as company organization charts and athletic tournaments.

These kinds of representations are useful for solving problems, because the structure of the representation matches important aspects of the problem in some way. In a matrix, the key is to detect conflicts among situations. For example, you do not want to schedule two classes at the same time. Because each item in the problem has to be entered into a particular location in the matrix, it is easy to find cases where there are conflicts. Hierarchies have a different structure. They focus primarily on relationships between pairs of items that can be connected by a link. Thus, hierarchies are particularly good for understanding chains of relationships like family relationships or the teams someone beat in a tournament. More generally, if you are considering a particular representation to solve a problem, you should ensure that the representation has the same structure as the problem you are trying to solve (see the chapters in van Someren, Reimann, Boshuizen, & deJong, 1998, for discussions of this issue).

Summary of Problem Solving as Representation

In this section, we examined the representation of a problem. Because the problem representation determines what the problem space states and operators can be, it is crucial for problem solving. A number of different types of representations have been discussed, along with reasons for why some representations make problem solving easier or more difficult. The main point, repeated here, is that *the problem representation is crucial.* Although there is much we do not know about how people go from the problem to its representation, there is general agreement that this is one of the most important questions facing researchers in this area.

Summary of Problem Solving as Representation and Search

In this section, we have considered the dominant view of problem solving in psychology and AI over the last 35 (or more) years, the Newell and Simon view of problem solving as representation and search. A problem is represented as a problem space, consisting of states and operators. The problem is solved when the person (or program) has found a path from the initial state to the goal state. A primary focus of much of the work has been on understanding different search strategies that might be used, distinguishing between algorithms and heuristics. Heuristics are problem-solving methods that guide search, but do so at the expense of not guaranteeing a solution. We reviewed a number of heuristics, such as hill climbing, means-ends analysis, and working backward.

More recently, problem representation has become an area of much research interest. As we learned more about search, it became clear that *what* was being searched was at least as important has how it was searched. The representation is often crucial in determining whether a problem is solved. With this background on problem solving, we end the chapter by considering one of the most common means by which problems are solved—by analogy to other problems.

RELIANCE ON SPECIFIC RELEVANT KNOWLEDGE _____

Introduction

Experience plays a central role in problem solving. Many of the cases we have looked at so far required the problem solver to use knowledge that was very general. That is, besides the information presented with the problem, the problem solutions mainly called on general problem-solving methods. Often we have more specific relevant knowledge that we can use to improve our problem solving. In this section we consider a very important and often-used type of relevant knowledge, the solution of earlier problems.

Suppose you are trying to solve a homework problem for a math (or statistics) class. A very common strategy is to look through the chapter and see if you can find a problem that looks similar to your homework problem. If you can, you might use that problem to help guide you through solving the current one.

This issue of how problem solving transfers to similar problems is a crucial one. Much of education is spent having students solve problems. The goal of this problem solving is not to have the student learn to solve the specific problems given but rather to have students learn to solve related problems. This section addresses the issue of how knowledge of the solution of one problem can affect the solution of a later related problem.

The Influence of Related Problems

To benefit from earlier experience with a related problem, the problem solver must first *access* some knowledge about the earlier problem and then *apply* that knowledge to the current problem. The application or analogical mapping between an earlier situation and a current situation was discussed in the last chapter. Now we consider access: the process by which a problem solver may notice that the current problem is similar to one that had been solved earlier.

The Difficulty of Accessing Relevant Knowledge

Consider the following problem, which was introduced by Duncker (1945) and used in an important set of studies by Gick and Holyoak (1980, 1983). Try to come up with solutions to the problem.

> Suppose you are a doctor faced with a patient who has a malignant tumor in his stomach. It is impossible to operate on the patient, but unless the tumor is destroyed the patient will die. There is a kind of ray that can be used to destroy the tumor. If the rays reach the tumor all at once at a sufficiently high intensity, the tumor will be destroyed. Unfortunately, at this intensity the healthy tissue that the rays pass through on the way to the tumor will also be destroyed. At lower intensities the rays are harmless to healthy tissue, but they will not

affect the tumor either. What type of procedure might be used to destroy the tumor with the rays, and at the same time avoid destroying the healthy tissue?

There are several possible solutions to this problem, but the one that we will be interested in is what Gick and Holyoak call the convergence solution. In this solution, several machines use the low radiation, but they are placed around the patient and converge simultaneously at the tumor. Thus, the healthy tissue receives only low doses while the tumor receives the sum of several low doses (enough to destroy the tumor). If people are simply given the problem and asked to solve it, about 10% of them offer such a solution.

Gick and Holyoak were interested in how a similar solution in an earlier story might affect the proportion of convergence solutions. They had one group of subjects read the following story, which they called the General story.

> A small country was ruled from a strong fortress by a dictator. The fortress was situated in the middle of the country, surrounded by farms and villages. Many roads led to the fortress through the countryside. A rebel general vowed to capture the fortress. The general knew that an attack by his entire army would capture the fortress. He gathered his army at the head of one of the roads, ready to launch a full-scale direct attack. However, the general then learned that the dictator had planted mines on each of the roads. The mines were set so that small bodies of men could pass over them safely, since the dictator needed to move his troops and workers to and from the fortress. However, any large force would detonate the mines. Not only would this blow up the road, but it would also destroy many neighboring villages. It therefore seemed impossible to capture the fortress.
>
> However, the general devised a simple plan. He divided his army into small groups and dispatched each group to the head of a different road. When all was ready he gave the signal and each group marched down a different road. Each group continued down its road to the fortress so that the entire army arrived together at the fortress at the same time. In this way, the general captured the fortress and overthrew the dictator.

As you can see, this story uses a solution very much like the convergence solution for the tumor problem. After subjects read and summarized this story, they were asked to solve the tumor problem under the guise of a separate experiment. Given the clear analogy, you might think that performance would be near ceiling. Surprisingly, only 30% of the subjects offered a convergence solution. Moreover, when these same subjects were given the suggestion that they should use the General story, 80% provided a convergence solution. This finding demonstrates that half the subjects could apply the General story to the tumor problem when they were instructed to but did not do so on their own. Many subjects do not spontaneously notice that the General story is similar to the tumor problem. See the box, An Enigma, for some further examples.

AN ENIGMA
Accessing Earlier Problems Is Harder Than It Looks

The difficulty of accessing earlier problems often puzzles students (and even researchers). One reaction has been to try many different ways of presenting the problems to see whether the lack of access found in the earlier studies might be due to some procedural oddities. Although there are ways to overcome access difficulties (discussed in the next section), most of the results have confirmed how difficult it is for problem solvers to access similar earlier problems that are superficially very different. We mention two further findings to help make the problem more concrete to the reader.

First, perhaps the difficulty is that the participants in these studies did not really understand what principle was being illustrated in the story about the General. To check this possibility, Gick and Holyoak (1983, Experiment 2) ended the story with a clear statement of the principle. "The general attributed his success to an important principle: If you need a large force to accomplish some purpose, but are prevented from applying such a force directly, many smaller forces applied simultaneously from different directions may work just as well." Adding this principle to the story had no effect on performance on the tumor problem (32% before the hint and 80% after the hint).

Second, perhaps the difficulty is that people need to think about the problem and solution in a different way, maybe in more of a picture. To examine this possibility, Gick (1985) presented the General story along

(Continued)

Why is this analogy so difficult for problem solvers to notice? Remember, the problem is solved very shortly after the story is read, and the story and problem do seem rather closely analogous. Given the difficulty in spontaneously noticing the analogy, what do these results mean for more natural problem-solving situations?

These questions are currently the focus of much research, but we may offer some tentative answers. First consider the experiment from the subject's point of view. The subject reads a story about a general who overcomes a dictator through a tricky solution. Then the subject is asked to solve a problem in which a person has a tumor but the radiation machines are too strong or too weak. Given these characterizations of the story and problem, why would one think of the General story as being relevant? In addition, most subjects have knowledge about medical procedures and X rays that they might believe is more relevant to the solution of the tumor problem than is a story about a general.

AN ENIGMA
Accessing Earlier Problems Is Harder Than It Looks *(Continued)*

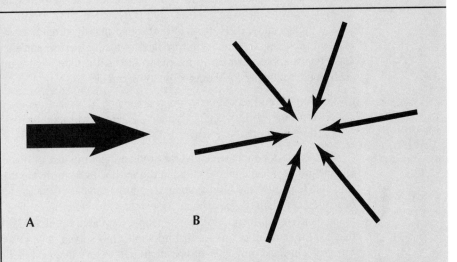

A   B

with the diagrams shown in the figure above. Diagram A was referred to in the story as an illustration of the General's first plan to stage a full assault, and Diagram B was referred to as an illustration of the solution. Participants were told to study the story and diagrams and then to write a summary that included the diagrams. When later asked to solve the tumor problem, performance did not improve. It has been a surprise to many researchers how difficult it is to overcome these access difficulties and has led to a rethinking about how people think back to earlier problems.

More succinctly, a major part of the difficulty with noticing the analogy may be that the story and problem are stored in memory in a content-dependent way. That is, the General story is not stored as a convergence solution that happened to have a military setting but rather as a military story. The convergence solution is embedded within this story, not abstracted out in a way that might make it more available for later noticing. When the subject is trying to solve the tumor problem, which has a medical cover story, the underlying similarity to the General story is masked by the great amount of dissimilarity in the contents. In determining what knowledge might be relevant to the current problem, the memory processes will tend to suggest medical-related knowledge (e.g., see the discussion of spreading activation in memory in Chapter 6).

One possibility is that this finding reflects the difficulty of using knowledge from one domain to solve problems in another. On this view, there should be less content dependence within a single domain. However, even when all the knowledge is in a single domain, people often learn in a much more restricted way than intended. For example, consider a common textbook in a mathematical or scientific field. The chapter may start with some principles and formulas and then provide an illustration of each principle. Although these illustrative examples are intended to help learners understand the principle, it appears that the principle is often understood in terms of the example (see, e.g., B. H. Ross, 1987, 1989).

In one study, B. H. Ross (1984) found that by simply varying the story line of word problems in elementary probability theory, performance changed dramatically. For example, each new principle would be illustrated with a different problem, such as the following for the principle of permutations:

> Sixteen golfers compete in a tournament. There are money prizes for the top nine golfers. In how many different ways might the prizes (first through ninth) be given?

As a test, people were given a problem requiring use of one of the principles, and the problem had either (1) the same story line as the problem that illustrated that principle (e.g., it would also be about a golf tournament), (2) a story line that had not been used before in the experiment, or (3) the same story line as a problem that illustrated a different principle. Although people were able to solve 77% of the problems that had the same story line for that principle, they solved only 43% of the new story line problems, and only 23% of ones that used a story line from a different principle (because they often tried to apply the inappropriate principle). Clearly, these problem solvers were using the superficial story line content to think back to and make use of earlier problems. In another study, Ross found that people learning to edit text on a computer were often reminded by superficial similarities of earlier text editings from the experiment and used those to figure out what to do. For example, people learned two different methods for inserting a word into text: one method illustrated on a shopping list and one on a review of a restaurant. Later, they were asked to insert a word in either another shopping list or another restaurant review. People were more likely to use the method that they had learned with the similar text (i.e., if they were given a shopping list, they tended to insert a word using the method illustrated with a shopping list). Thus, even though people know that the exact text being edited is not a relevant part of the methods for editing text, the similarity affects performance.

Nevertheless, this content dependence has certain advantages. If the current problem has contents similar to a relevant earlier problem, spontaneous noticing is much more likely (see, e.g., Gentner, Rattermann, & Forbus, 1993; Holyoak & Koh, 1987; Novick, 1988; Reeves & Weisberg, 1994; B. H. Ross, 1984). In this case, rather than acting to make the two problems seem dissimilar, the superficial similarity acts to make the two problems seem more similar. Thus, even if the deep underlying similarity between two problems is not sufficient to make a person notice the analogy, having similar contents may increase the similarity enough such that the earlier problem is accessed. So content dependence can hurt the access of superficially dissimilar problems but help the access of superficially similar problems. The overall utility depends on how often one needs to apply problems with very different contents versus problems with similar contents. Although analogies to very different contents occur (e.g., H. M. Johnson & Seifert, 1992; Wharton et al., 1994), for most relevant earlier problems, the content of that problem is not unrelated to the current problem contents. When one is trying to formulate a military strategy, earlier successful military strategies are usually most relevant. Such use of earlier problems in problem solving persists far beyond early learning and may often be a common technique of experts.

Overcoming Access Difficulties

There are at least two reasons why access is so difficult. First, as we have seen, much of the knowledge is stored in a content-dependent way, not abstracted away from many of the formally irrelevant details. Second, part of the difficulty may be that we have the knowledge, but we have not represented when such knowledge might be relevant. Simon (1980) observes that just to know facts is not enough—one needs to access the facts at the relevant point during problem solving. For example, in mathematics and certain sciences, textbooks commonly provide a great deal of information on how to perform some calculation or how to apply some principle, but they do not provide any information on when such a calculation should be performed or when such a principle should be applied. That is, the problem solver does not understand exactly what it is about the problem that requires an application of the principle.

What might help to make the earlier problem accessible from our representation of the current problem? First, we know that increased similarity between the problems will increase the likelihood of thinking back to the earlier problem.

Second, to the extent that the current problem is represented and processed in a similar way to the past problem, access will be increased (e.g., Lockhart, Lamon, & Gick, 1988; Needham & Begg, 1991; Seifert & Gray, 1990). That is, the representations of the problems may be more similar because they have been processed in similar ways. For example, suppose you were trying to repair some equipment, such as a bicycle, and found that you had made an error in your repair work that needed to be fixed (another problem to solve). You are probably more likely to think of an earlier situation in which this problem was caused by mistaken repair work than a situation in which it arose for some other reason (see Gick & McGarry, 1992; Johnson & Seifert, 1992, for experimental evidence). (Some readers may also notice the relation to the encoding specificity idea discussed in Chapter 5 and, especially, the transfer-appropriate processing idea examined in Chapter 6.)

A third means of overcoming the difficulties of access may be of particular theoretical importance and practical use. If the problem of access is largely due to content dependence and lack of understanding of the relevant problem conditions, then abstracting the content and improving this understanding should increase accessibility.

Let us consider two ways in which such content-dependence and understanding may be improved. First, if a problem solver is forced to compare several instances that all have the same underlying abstract structure, the representation may be abstract enough to be accessible by later superficially dissimilar instances (e.g., B. H. Ross & Kennedy, 1990). For example, the solution rate (without hints) to the tumor problem increases if subjects are forced to compare multiple instances (see,

AN APPLICATION
Case-Based Reasoning: An AI Approach

Much of the work on problem solving in AI (descended from the Newell and Simon approach discussed earlier) has focused on the idea of solving problems through the application of general principles or heuristics coupled with domain knowledge. Recently, however, similar to the work in psychology on analogical problem solving, **case-based reasoning** has examined the possibility that much of problem solving can be accomplished by using memory of earlier cases (instances) and adapting them to the current case.

Knowledge of how a similar problem was solved may be the most relevant knowledge that can be brought to bear during problem solving. Such a procedure may be especially useful when the chain of reasoning is very long or when one's understanding of the domain is incomplete or incorrect (Schank, 1982). Common examples of such case-based reasoning abound, such as the use of precedents in legal arguments and the pricing of houses by using the price of a recently sold house.

This idea has been incorporated into a large number of different computer simulations (see Kolodner, 1993, 1997, and Schank, Kass, & Riesbeck, 1994, for reviews; Seifert et al., 1994, provide an interesting case of combining AI and psychological experimentation). As a very simplified description, the case-based reasoning paradigm has the following parts:

1. A case is *selected* from memory. The current situation is characterized in some way, and this characterization is used to retrieve one or more cases with similar characterizations.

(Continued)

e.g., Catrambone & Holyoak, 1989; Gick & Holyoak, 1983). The comparison of instances can also help to point out important contrasts between two principles that seem very similar (e.g., Bransford, Franks, Vye, & Sherwood, 1989; VanderStoep & Seifert, 1993/1994). A second way to increase the access of just a single instance (as opposed to the generalization over several instances) is to help increase the understanding of the problem. Some findings suggest that if the problem solver has a clear understanding of the goal structure in the problem and an explanation of why each action was taken, then such knowledge may be more accessible for solving a later problem (see, e.g., A. L. Brown & Kane, 1988; B. H. Ross & Kilbane, 1997). The idea is that if a problem solver tries to explain each step in a problem solution in terms of what the goal is and how this step helps to accomplish the goal, this explanation provides an understanding that is abstracted (at least somewhat) away

AN APPLICATION

Case-Based Reasoning: An AI Approach *(Continued)*

2. The selected case is *adapted* to the present case. Usually the selected case is similar to the present case but not equivalent with respect to all important features. Thus, the system needs to take the solution of the selected case and modify it to be applicable to the current case.

3. The adapted solution is *evaluated*. Because the system relies on earlier instances, it requires good feedback about the usefulness of the solutions.

4. Memory is *updated*. The new case is stored in memory, along with the results of the evaluation. Learning is principally the storing of new cases.

The case-based approach has been applied to a large number of very different domains, ranging from dispute negotiations (Kolodner & Simpson, 1989) to recipe generation for Szechwan cooking (Hammond, 1989). For illustrative purposes, let us go over a possible situation in which a person may follow this general series of steps.

Suppose a real estate agent is asked to set a market price for a house that has just come on the market. Several means can be used for price setting, but one common means is to base it on an earlier house sale. Thus, the agent would characterize the new house using a set of features (age, square feet) and relations (layout, location in town). First, this description would remind the agent of some other house (or the agent might have a filing system in which the characteristics thought most

(Continued)

from the content of the problem. It may also allow the problem solver to adapt the solution for closely related problems, a task that is often difficult for learners (Catrambone, 1994; Novick & Holyoak, 1991; Reed, Dempster, & Ettinger, 1985).

Such explanations may seem to be a great amount of work, but the research suggests they may be quite helpful. Good problem solvers tend to explain the steps in examples to themselves and keep close tabs on what they do and do not understand in these explanations (Chi, Bassok, Lewis, Reimann, & Glaser, 1989; see also Pirolli & Recker, 1994; van Lehn, 1998), and asking people to give such explanations improves understanding and performance (Chi, de Leeuw, Chiu, & LaVancher, 1994). For example, suppose you were following a set of instructions on how to repair a malfunction with your bicycle. You may be able to make this repair (if the instructions are complete) even if you do not understand why any particular action

AN APPLICATION

Case-Based Reasoning: An AI Approach *(Continued)*

important would be used as indexes). Second, the agent would adjust the price of the new house by its differences with the old house (e.g., extra bathroom, more square feet, worse location). Third, when a price is set, the agent gets feedback. In this situation, feedback might be a house that sells too quickly (the price was too low) or too slowly (the price was too high), or perhaps the ridicule of other real estate agents. Fourth, the agent's memory (or filing system) for houses that have been priced would be updated to include this new house. In addition to the characteristics of the house, this case might be indexed by other useful information learned in the course of this pricing, such as what to do about a half-finished basement (in fact this technique for valuing houses is used by real estate appraisers).

Although the idea behind case-based systems may sound much simpler than the more search-oriented AI systems, earlier cases or problems implicitly contain a great deal of information that can be mined to solve later problems. Case-based reasoning takes advantage of this information to guide its problem solving without having to repeat much of what was done in solving earlier problems. Rather than emphasizing representation and search, this more memory-intensive type of problem solving emphasizes access and adaptation. As we will see in the next chapter on expertise, much of the power in problem solving comes from accessing relevant knowledge as opposed to general reasoning skills. Current work is also trying to understand how best to integrate this approach with more traditional AI problem-solving approaches so that a system can have the advantages of each approach.

is being done. But if you were able to explain why each step was done and what its role was in the repair, you would be more likely to be able to fix some slightly different problem in the future.

More generally, to increase the likelihood of accessing a relevant problem, try to store the earlier problem on the basis of the underlying abstract structure. When solving a problem, try to understand why each action is being taken. This explanation will help to access earlier problems with similar explanations and provide a useful basis for solving later problems of this type.

Summary

In this section, we have examined how specific earlier problems might be accessed and applied. The most surprising result from this research has been how difficult it is to access the appropriate earlier problem. We interpret this difficulty as a consequence of storing the knowledge in a content-dependent way. Some suggestions for overcoming this access are suggested, including comparing problems and explaining the goal structure of earlier examples.

Summary

In this chapter, we presented some fundamental components of problem solving. The problem space view of problem solving as representation and search, introduced by Newell and Simon, has been the prime organizing framework within problem solving in both psychology and artificial intelligence. The search of problem spaces can be distinguished by whether it involves algorithms (that are guaranteed to lead to a solution) or heuristics (means of guiding search, but with no guarantee). We examined a number of different heuristics, from simple hill climbing to planning beyond the next step, such as means-ends analysis. Researchers now also appreciate the huge influence that representation differences can have on problem solving. We illustrated a variety of cases in which the representation can affect problem solving and discussed why representation might matter in terms of its effect on the problem space. Although there are still many unanswered questions, the effects of representation is an area of much current work.

Even with a good representation, however, the vast number of possibilities can make exhaustive search impossible. Much of this chapter can be viewed as different ideas on how to reduce search. Clearly, heuristics are aimed exactly at ways of guiding search so that the more likely possibilities will be considered. Less obviously, perhaps, the work on the use of examples and case-based reasoning provides another way of guiding search. Rather than using general principles and heuristics to help choose the operators, one relies on earlier problem-solving episodes in which a similar problem was solved. Such an episode greatly reduces the search problem by focusing on a solution procedure that has already worked in a related situation. That is, these methods take advantage of a great deal of knowledge about the specific domain to reduce the need to search all possibilities. As we shall see in the next chapter, the use of domain knowledge is crucial in overcoming many problem-solving limitations.

Key Terms

algorithm

case-based reasoning

functional fixedness

heuristic

hill climbing

ill-defined problem

means-ends analysis

problem

problem operators

problem space

problem state

verbal protocol

well-defined problem

working backward

Recommended Readings _____

The classic account of human problem solving may be found in Newell and Simon (1972). The book is quite intimidating in its scope (and weight), but provides full treatments of problem spaces and their uses. A more general presentation is given in H. A. Simon (1978), and Wickelgren (1974) provides an excellent brief account of problems and search, with particular emphasis on mathematics. Hayes (1989) has a more thorough introductory treatment of problem solving. A clear theoretical discussion of verbal protocols and their uses can be found in a book by Ericsson and Simon (1993; see also Chi, 1997). Duncker (1945) presents a number of interesting demonstrations and thoughts on representation effects, and Kotovsky and Fallside (1989) provide a more recent case. Van Lehn (1989) offers an interesting perspective on these and other problem-solving ideas.

The Gick and Holyoak (1980, 1983) papers on the use of earlier related problems have been very influential. Other important work on this topic is presented in Holyoak and Thagard (1995), Reeves and Weisberg (1994), and Vosniadou and Ortony (1989). An extensive discussion of the background and mechanics of case-based reasoning can be found in Kolodner (1993). A very readable discussion of analogy and case-based reasoning that was written for a general audience is in the January 1997 issue of the *American Psychologist*.

Chapter 13

Expertise and Creativity

Introduction

Expertise
Introduction
Comparing Experts and Novices
Developing Expertise
Expert Systems
Adaptive Expertise
Summary

Creativity
Introduction
The Traditional View
Some Recent Views of Creativity
Summary

Summary

Key Terms

Recommended Readings

The first rule of discovery is to have brains and good luck. The second rule of discovery is to sit tight and wait until you get a bright idea.
—G. Polya, How to Solve It

INTRODUCTION

Expertise and creativity are fascinating topics because problem-solving ability is pushed beyond its everyday limits. These situations are excellent examples of our themes of constraints and relevance: The problem solver is given incomplete information and must augment it with knowledge, but the scope of the potentially relevant knowledge is vast. How can these problem solvers tap into the right knowledge and solve problems that most of the rest of us cannot? As we shall see, the quotation at the beginning of this chapter is not quite right—there *are* ways to increase all kinds of problem-solving performance, including the discovery of new ideas.

In this chapter, we take the ideas from the previous chapter on problem solving and apply them to cases of expert and creative problem solving. We begin by examining a variety of research results in expertise and current views of what it means to be an expert, and then we turn to creativity.

EXPERTISE

Introduction

We have all heard about extraordinary feats of expertise: a chess grandmaster playing blindfolded against a large number of opponents or a human calculator who can quickly do incredible arithmetic calculations without writing anything down. More mundane examples might include an expert in physics who can easily solve problems that others cannot or an expert diagnostician who can quickly and accurately assess medical problems. How do experts do what they do?

A common view is that experts are expert reasoners with exceptionally good memories. Although it is true, almost by definition, that experts are able to reason well within their domain, the view that they have some general expert reasoning abilities and good memories has been cast into doubt by recent research on expertise. Rather than reflecting some general abilities, expertise appears to be heavily domain-specific. In addition, the emphasis on reasoning has given way to an appreciation of the extraordinary domain knowledge that experts have. We first examine differences between novices and experts in a number of domains in order to clarify the notion of expertise.

Comparing Experts and Novices

The performance of experts and novices has been examined in a wide variety of domains, often using the methods of protocols and simulations. For purposes of exposition, we will focus on three areas: (1) chess and mental calculation, (2) rich formal domains (such as physics), and (3) the more perceptually oriented domain of radiology. Chess and mental calculation are interesting to explore, because they involve expertise in domains in which the problems are well defined. In contrast, expertise in physics requires developing methods for defining the problems. Finally, radiology has many of the characteristics of physics, but also involves perceptual expertise, where the expert must actually learn to see the world differently than the novice.

Chess and Mental Calculation

We start with a famous mental calculator, the mathematician A. C. Aitkin (Hunter, 1966/1977). As one example of his expertise, consider what happened when Aitkin was asked the square root of 851. (This is one problem we will not ask you to keep trying until you can get an answer.) After a short interval, he replied, "29.17." Following this, but within 15 seconds, he answered, "29.17190429." How was he able to do this?

Clearly Professor Aitkin had a remarkable ability, but let us analyze why it is so remarkable. First, most of us face severe memory limitations in performing arithmetic calculations, which is why we insist on using calculators or at least pencil and paper. Second, the task itself is difficult and involves a very long sequence of operations that most of us do not know and, even if we did, could not keep track of in our heads.

Aitkin was able to exploit his great experience with and understanding of numbers. He knew a tremendous amount about numbers and could perceive patterns where most of us could not. For instance, we all know factors for simple numbers (numbers which, when multiplied together, yield the number in question; the factors for 15 are 3 and 5). However, Aitkin knew the factors of every number up to 1,500. When asked to solve a problem with 851, he immediately noted that it is the product of 23 and 37. Aitkin also knew many different ways of calculating and knew which methods were most likely to be useful for specific calculations. The application of his chosen plan was greatly simplified by his ability to work in large steps. Because his plan freed him from deciding what to do at each step, he was able to concentrate on what he was doing. Some of the complexities of mental computation were avoided by his ability to remember many of the intermediate answers, rather than computing them.

Now let's shift to another domain. Why is chess such a hard game for novices? First, the representation of the board information is very complex. For most novices, the representation would need to include each individual piece separately, far beyond what can be kept immediately available. Second, the search space of possible move sequences is very large, and most novices do not have any good way to guide this search. A chess expert needs to overcome both of these difficulties. How do experts represent the board to avoid such memory limitations?

Short-term memory is limited in terms of the number of meaningful units or chunks that it can hold at any one time (see Chapter 5). Experts do not have a superior short-term memory capacity. Rather, experts represent the board positions as groups of chunks that include many more pieces than the chunks that novices use. For example, in one study (Chase & Simon, 1973) a master, an intermediate player (called Class A), and a novice were shown board positions with 24 to 26 pieces from the middle of a chess game for 5 seconds, an example of which is given in the top part of Figure 13.1. The board was then covered, and the subjects were asked to reconstruct the board position on another board. The results are shown in Figure 13.2. The master chess player was able to place considerably more pieces than the novice (16 vs. 4), with the performance of the Class A player falling in between. However, if the board position shown was randomly constructed so that any meaningful chess configurations

MIDDLE GAME
Black

White

RANDOM MIDDLE GAME

Figure 13.1   **Example of Chess Board Position Used in Memory Experiments**   Subjects are shown a 5-second glance and then have to reconstruct as much of it as they can.

Source: Chase & Simon, 1973.

---

were unlikely (as in the bottom part of Figure 13.2), there were no differences among the reconstructions (with all players placing 2 to 3 pieces). This result has been replicated in a variety of other domains, such as the game Go (Reitman, 1976) and electronics (Egan & Schwartz, 1979). Experts appear to chunk the information into larger units and perceive these units very quickly. These chunks are often hierarchically organized so that a master may recognize a whole board configuration.

It is important to bear this in mind: Which aspects of the environment are chunked together depends not only on the knowledge of the person, but also on the

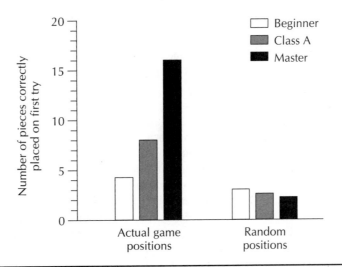

Figure 13.2   Results of chess board reconstruction experiment of Chase and Simon (1973)

Source: Data from Chase & Simon, 1973.

domain. For example, Allard and Starkes (1991) reviewed studies demonstrating that experts in some sports (like field hockey) were particularly good at remembering the configuration of players in a scene from a game. In contrast, experts in volleyball were not at all good at remembering the locations of players. While this result might seem surprising initially, volleyball experts pointed out that the locations of players on the court is often deceptive, and so focusing on the locations of the players can lead to poor performance. Instead, experts in volleyball are skilled at finding the ball given a scene from a game.

In Chapter 12, we described problem solving as a search through a space of possibilities. In domains like chess, where the pieces and moves are known, this idea of search is particularly useful. Studies of chess masters suggest that they are not searching more possibilities than novices, but rather that they are guiding their search much better. That is, they do not consider more moves than chess novices, but the moves they do consider are generally good ones. Experts use their perceptions of relevant chunks and their understanding of general principles of chess play to focus on what are likely to be the best possibilities. Another piece of evidence for the importance of fast chunk perception in chess play is that one grandmaster was found to play just as well against six grandmasters simultaneously as he was in tournament play when he had much more time per move (Gobet & Simon, 1996). Ericsson and Kintsch (1995) present ideas on how such expertise may also involve a combination of short-term memory and long-term memory access, as discussed in Chapter 5 (see also the examination of mnemonists in Chapter 7).

Thus the chess and mental calculation experts do not have unusual memories but rather have learned, for a very specific type of material, how to overcome difficulties imposed by memory limitations and the computational complexity of search.

Experts and Novices in More Formal Domains

In a formal domain like physics, the problems are less well defined than they are in chess. Even before a physics expert can search through a space of possible solution procedures, he or she must identify the type of problem being solved. Let's consider how a typical novice and a typical expert might try to solve a physics word problem (adapted from the findings of a number of papers, including Bedard & Chi, 1992; Chi, Feltovich, & Glaser, 1981; Larkin, McDermott, Simon, & Simon, 1980; D. P. Simon & Simon, 1978). The novice reads the problem carefully, underlining words she believes are important. Novice representations of problems rely heavily on the verbal statement of the problem and the concrete objects presented. Again, the problem solver is faced with too little information and needs to augment it with her knowledge. Unfortunately, her organization in memory of the relevant principles is very slight and does not allow her to understand how the problem might fit into these principles. To solve the problem, then, she must focus only on the information provided and hope for a connection. She first identifies the givens and the unknown. Then she works backward, searching for equations that contain the unknown. These equations often produce other unknowns, and she tries to find equations that contain these new unknowns until she gets one that contains only one unknown. These equations appear to be generated in a somewhat random way except for this constraint of containing the unknown.

The expert is also faced with the difficulty of too little information presented, but her expertise allows her performance to differ from the novice's. First, the expert often pauses before writing and then draws a simple qualitative diagram. (Larkin & Simon, 1987, provide some ideas about the general advantages of diagrams.) This representation may be added to as the expert elaborates the problem features until a promising avenue of solution is seen. The knowledge organization of the expert differs dramatically from the novice. The principles are richly organized with explanations and associations between principles. The solution strategy takes advantage of the plan developed from the representation and the organization of knowledge. The plan is successively refined until particular principles can be applied. Equations are then written down, but only in the service of this plan. Thus, there is a pattern of equations, pause, equations, and so on. Rather than working backward from the goal (the unknown), the expert is proceeding forward from the problem representation.

What are the differences in knowledge that lead to such differences in problem solving? A major difference is in the nature of the knowledge novices and experts have about problem types often called **problem schemas** or problem categories. These are general knowledge structures for understanding—in this case, understanding what type of problem is involved and how to solve it. (Thus, problem schemas are similar in structure to the schemas described in Chapter 7.) Suppose problem solvers are given a set of physics problems and asked to categorize them by solution procedure (Chi et al., 1981). Novices group together those problems that contain similar physical objects, such as inclined planes or springs (see the top part of Figure 13.3). Experts, however, categorize the problems by the laws of physics, such as conservation of momentum or Newton's Third Law (see the bottom part of Figure 13.3). Experts can use these categorizations to quickly access the relevant equations for solution. They use their extensive knowledge to augment the incomplete information in appropriate ways.

Novices:

<table>
<tr><th>Grouping</th><th>Explanation</th></tr>
</table>

Problem 23

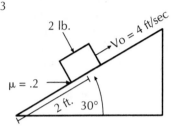

2 lb.

Vo = 4 ft/sec

μ = .2

2 ft. 30°

Novice 1: "These deal with blocks on an *incline plane*"

Novice 5: "*Inclined plane* problems, coefficient of *friction*"

Novice 6: "Blocks on *inclined planes* with angles"

Problem 35

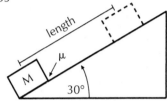

length

μ

M

30°

Experts:

<table>
<tr><th>Grouping</th><th>Explanation</th></tr>
</table>

Problem 21

K = 200 nt/m

ᴑᴑᴑᴑᴑᴑᴑᴑᴑᴑᴑ

.6 m

.15 m

equilibrium

Expert 2: "*Conservation of Energy*"

Expert 3: "*Work-Energy Theorem.* They are all straight-forward problems."

Expert 4: "These can be done from energy considerations. Either you should know the *Principle of Conversation of Energy,* or work is lost somewhere."

Problem 35

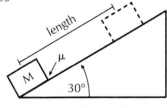

length

μ

M

30°

Figure 13.3   **An Example of Sortings of Physics Problems Made by Novices and Experts**   The sortings of the novices (top two problems) rely largely upon surface features, such as whether the problems include an inclined plane. The sortings of the experts, however, focus on the underlying principles, such as conservation of energy, for the bottom two problems.

Source: Chi, Feltovich, & Glaser, 1981.

Once the experts have the correct equations, they can substitute in the quantities given in the problem and rely upon their well-learned algorithms for solving the equations. In addition, they do not need to try all the many possible paths from their problem representations. As in chess and mental calculation, having a lot of experience with problems within their area of expertise has allowed experts to learn configurations and associated problem-solving procedures. Thus, experts are working forward, using their schemas to direct their search, while novices tend to work backward. We now look at expert-novice differences in a very different type of domain, radiology.

Radiological Expertise

Think about the first time you ever saw an X ray. Perhaps you were in the emergency room after a fall, and the doctor came into the room, put the film on a lighted screen and examined it. The doctor may have pointed to some part of the film and declared that you had a broken leg. Chances are you just took the doctor's word for it, because the X ray picture actually looked like a mass of light and dark splotches. Radiologists, who are experts in the interpretation of X ray films have learned to see the world in a different way from novices (like most of us) or even from medical residents who are developing expertise. How do their medical knowledge and perceptual ability interact?

This question has been studied by Alan Lesgold and his colleagues (Lesgold, Feltovich, Glaser, & Wang, 1981; Lesgold et al., 1988), who have examined differences between expert radiologists and radiology residents in their diagnosis of X rays. Although we might first guess that these diagnoses are largely dependent on just being able to detect information in the pictures, Lesgold and his fellow investigators provide strong evidence that detection is a minor part of the task, which is more properly viewed as problem solving. Indeed, the description of expert performance in this task closely parallels the descriptions of experts that we have already discussed.

In one set of studies (Lesgold et al., 1981), the task was similar to the one used by researchers investigating chess expertise. The experts and residents were presented with an X ray for 2 seconds and then asked to report any abnormalities they noticed. They were then shown the film for an unlimited amount of time and asked to think aloud while analyzing it and to dictate a formal report. Experts were more able to quickly detect the patterns in the film and ignore the irrelevant information. These differences in pattern detection were possible because the experts were using a very rich mental representation of the anatomy to allow them to "see" the third dimension. Again, experts were able to augment the incomplete information with their extensive domain knowledge. For example, Lesgold et al. (1988) mention one case in which the residents often discussed an enlarged heart, while the experts correctly attributed the increased heart shadow to irrelevant factors such as poor patient posture and breathing during the X ray. Experts used these augmented representations to keep track of various constraints, but they were deferring any decision making until the maximal data were available.

Experts are also able to focus on important perceptual aspects of a scene. For example, a medical resident asked to circle important parts of an X ray might point

AN ENIGMA
When Experience Hurts

The more we know about an area, the better we do, right? Usually, but not always. Consider the radiological expertise discussed in this section. As medical residents learn more, they begin to develop schemas (just as the experts do). For a while, these schemas are not totally correct, and experience is needed to help the residents to refine the schemas. Interestingly, this learning sometimes leads to a temporary decrease in performance while incorrect schemas are being refined (Lesgold et al., 1988, though there is some controversy about the prevalence of the effect and its interpretation; see, for example, Raufaste, Eyrolle, & Mariné, 1998).

Although such decrements with practice seem strange, many of us have experienced similar effects when developing a skill. Let's consider a physical skill for ease of exposition, such as hitting a tennis ball or shooting a basketball. As the learner practices, performance improves. After much initial improvement, the progress slows or may even plateau. A helpful coach or observer might make a suggestion about how to better hit the tennis ball or hold the basketball when shooting. As the learner practices this new technique, there is often an initial period in which performance is actually worse than it was before. Assuming the coach gave good advice, and the learner practices it properly, performance will later be even better than it was initially.

to large areas of the X ray as evidence for an abnormality. In contrast, experts tend to focus on specific small aspects of a film. Thus, like the chess experts, radiologists develop an ability to detect perceptual patterns that can be recognized quickly and provide associated hypotheses (see also Schyns, Goldstone, & Thibaut, 1998, for a discussion of perceptual feature learning).

Radiological expertise consists in part of developing these rich sets of configurations or schemas to use in reasoning forward from a recognized pattern. For example, examining a film of a patient with multiple chest tumors, the experts noticed the subtle differences in the haziness between the lungs and used this to diagnose the tumors. Less experienced radiology residents reason backward from possible hypotheses. For instance, an initial hypothesis of congestive heart failure might cause a resident to miss the differences between the two lungs. As residents gain more experience, they begin to form and use these schemas. The box, An Enigma, discusses how sometimes this learning can lead to worse performance for a short time. Overall, however, experience in such domains allows faster and more accurate analyses.

A DEBATE
Is Talent Important?

Many people believe that people who are able to perform exceptionally or expertly in some area have some innate talent in that area. That is, they have some predisposition for that general domain, such as music or athletics. This view is held by many researchers as well. For example, Gardner (1983) argues that we inherit not only physical and intellectual characteristics (such as IQ), but various other "intelligences" that constrain how well we can do in a variety of possible careers. No one denies the importance of hard work, but proponents of the talent view would argue that there also has to be an innate predisposition if the person is ever going to be an exceptional performer in that work.

The focus on knowledge as crucial in expertise suggests that determination may be more important than talent in becoming an expert. If the person can learn the necessary knowledge and skills, then expert performance may occur. Thus, this view is consistent with what is, for many of us, a very counterintuitive idea. In a series of fascinating papers, Anders Ericsson and his colleagues have provided surprisingly strong support for this claim that expertise is solely a matter of learning (Ericsson & Charness, 1994; Ericsson, Krame, & Tesch-Römer, 1993; Ericsson & Lehmann, 1996). These papers include careful reviews of studies (and some new studies) of elite performers, people who are at the top of their field: not just performers in intellectual fields, such as chess masters, but also exceptional musical performers and athletes. Their work involves a careful study of the practice of these performers compared to the practice of other performers who do not achieve the same level of expertise.

Their claim is a simple one, though very controversial: Performance is a direct function of the total (lifetime) amount of the performer's deliberate practice. The more practice, the higher the level of performance, and performance can be well predicted by knowing the amount of practice. What

(Continued)

Summary of Expert-Novice Differences

Novices have two major difficulties when trying to solve a problem. First, the problem information is incomplete and must be augmented with relevant knowledge from memory, but how do novices tell which knowledge is relevant? There are so many possibilities and often they just do not understand enough to know which of the possibilities is correct. Second, even if they are able to retrieve relevant knowledge, it

A DEBATE

Is Talent Important? *(Continued)*

does deliberate practice mean? **Deliberate practice** is not simply engaging in the activity but rather practicing in an effortful, intensive, self-monitored mode that is meant to improve specific aspects of performance through repetition and successive refinement. Deliberate practice in violin is not simply playing some violin music but, rather, playing a few notes over and over again until the tone, fingering, and the like are just right. Deliberate practice in basketball is not playing a game, but rather practicing the same move and shot 200 times with close attention paid to the various details of the movement. The legendary football coach, Vince Lombardi, is quoted as having said, "Practice does not make perfect. Perfect practice makes perfect."

For example, Ericsson et al. (1993) report a study of violinists from a music academy in Germany. Some students were said by the professors to have the potential to be international soloists (best), while others were said to be good, but not at as high a level of performance (good). The groups were matched for age and sex. Many details of their practice are included in the paper, but the one of interest here is the total amount of practice, based on a variety of diaries and self-estimates. The simple result is that the best violinists had averaged a total of 7,410 hours of practice (by age 18); the good students had an average of 5,301. This large difference occurs even though all the students are in a music academy.

Ericsson and his colleagues cannot disprove the idea that talent is innate, but they argue that there is no evidence for such talent and that the empirical findings can be understood in terms of the amount of deliberate practice. This view suggests that anyone can become an expert if they put in the needed amount of deliberate practice. Ericsson does acknowledge, however, that there may be individual differences in who is motivated enough to put in this amount of hard work.

may be very difficult to keep track of all the information because of short-term memory limitations. Novices often rely upon surface features of the problems to cue relevant knowledge and then work backward from the goal. This approach does have some advantages: In many domains, surface similarities predict deeper similarities (e.g., Blessing & Ross, 1996), and the goal is necessarily on the solution path (whereas not all the givens are). However, this problem-solving approach may often lead to the use of inappropriate knowledge and run into problems with the computational complexity of the search.

Experts can overcome these problems of accessing relevant knowledge, short-term memory limitations, and the complexity of the search by relying on knowledge built up from experience within the domain. They have stored a large number of rich perceptual units with associated procedures. In many situations, experts can use these units to recognize patterns. In more complex cases, experts use their extensive domain knowledge to elaborate the problem. They are likely to spend considerable time trying to represent the problem qualitatively, often using abstract diagrams to go beyond the simple objects and entities presented in the problem to a deeper representation. The deeper representation often allows the experts to categorize the problem as a particular type. In some cases, a problem category (a type of schema) has a standard procedure for solving instances of that type. In other cases, the experts can use the deeper representation and their organization of the domain knowledge to help determine what relevant knowledge to apply. This use often involves considerable working forward. Although the goal may not be explicitly taken into account, the expert has learned what types of information can be derived from the data and thus are likely to be useful for solving the problem. Another way of thinking about this working forward is that it is largely schema driven, as the knowledge of the problem category helps guide the experts in their use of the problem representation.

Overall, then, experts are using their extensive domain knowledge to help overcome the difficulties of too little information and too many possibilities. Expertise requires a great deal of knowledge to help represent problems, recognize large meaningful patterns, develop categories or problem schemas, and learn associated procedures for solving these problem types.

Developing Expertise

Assuming experts were not born as experts, how do they acquire their expertise? This question is central in current research on problem solving and learning. In this section, we discuss how people might learn to solve problems better, examine a theory of such learning, and consider computer systems that help people to become better solvers. The box, A Debate, examines the question of whether innate talent predisposes people to be exceptional in some domains, such as intellectual skills, music, or athletics.

Learning to Solve Problems

The box, A Debate, reminds us of an old joke: A violinist in New York for a concert gets lost and stops a pedestrian. "Excuse me, sir. How do I get to Carnegie Hall?" the violinist asks. The pedestrian looks down at the violin, then looks at the violinist, and replies, "Practice." Practice is necessary for gaining expertise. Simon (1980) estimates that a chess master knows well over 50,000 patterns and that it takes at least 10 years to become an expert in any complex domain. Practice helps in part by allowing the problem solver to learn the important conditions and actions of the domain and to make many of these actions "automatic."

In the last chapter, we spent considerable time explaining how people might use earlier examples in problem solving. One reason for that discussion is that people are generally not very good at learning from the abstract descriptions of principles that are presented along with the illustrating problems. Learning to solve problems appears to require the solution of many problems. How is this problem solving useful for learning? First, solving a variety of problems helps to "wean" the learner away from dependence on details of the content. One method for overcoming such content dependence (to some extent a necessary part of expertise) is to solve problems that vary these contents (see, e.g., Bassok, 1990).

Second, not all types of problem solving are equally effective for promoting learning. For example, means-ends analysis, in which the difference between the current state and the goal is used to guide search (see Chapter 12), is a very effective problem-solving technique. However, John Sweller and his colleagues (e.g., Owen & Sweller, 1985; Sweller, 1988; Sweller & Chandler, 1994) have convincingly demonstrated that the use of means-ends analysis to solve problems can interfere with learning. The argument is worth considering in detail because it helps to bring together a number of points from this chapter and the last chapter. As we have just discussed, expertise is characterized by the use of problem schemas to allow working forward from the givens. That is, experts often recognize a particular situation as an instance of something they have seen before, and then they apply the solution procedure used in the past to the new case.

Means-ends analysis, in contrast, involves focusing on both the current state, and also the goal. Keeping in mind (1) the beginning state, (2) the desired end state, (3) the differences between them, and (4) any operators that can be applied to reduce the differences between the beginning and end state is very taxing on working memory. Furthermore, the process of reducing the differences between the beginning state and end state is very different from the process of working forward using a previous example or learned schema. If we ultimately want people to be able to solve problems using a schema-driven approach, then early problem solving should focus on experiences with schema-driven problem solving rather than means-end analysis.

Sweller argues that many problem situations given to novices promote problem solving by means-end analysis. In contrast, he suggests that less directed problem-solving methods may be more effective in helping problem solvers acquire the appropriate schemas. For example, Owen and Sweller (1985) show that the learning of trigonometry problem solving may be enhanced if learners are simply told to calculate as many angles and sides as they can, rather than directed toward calculating a particular quantity. This nondirection allows them to learn the association between particular quantities (e.g., the givens) and the quantities that can be derived from them. (See Vollmeyer, Burns, & Holyoak, 1996, for similar results in a much more complex and dynamic domain.)

A third point about the effectiveness of practice is that the learner is aided by understanding the goal structure of the problem. The idea that an understanding of the problem promotes transfer is not new (see Katona, 1940), although the arguments supporting this idea were often very vague. The current view is that experts have well-refined problem schemas that allow them to identify the type of problem, provide an explanation of how the parts of the problem are related, and include associated procedures for solving problems. From this view, when learners understand a problem, they may be learning various parts of this schema: which features indicate the problem type, which features are irrelevant, how the relevant pieces fit together, and how they relate to the solution. We turn now to a theory that combines some of the ideas from expertise with the work on problem solving from Chapter 12 to address how people might learn a new problem-solving skill.

One Theory of Skill Acquisition

The last 15 years have seen a resurgence of theories of skill acquisition (e.g., Anderson, 1987, 1993a; Newell, 1990; Polson & Keiras, 1985; Rosenbloom & Newell, 1987). We consider here one theory that has been particularly influential in psychology, the theory of learning proposed by John Anderson within his ACT-R framework (the declarative part of which was discussed in Chapter 6). In this view, problem-solving skills progress through three "stages," which are summarized in Table 13.1. First, the situation and method for solving problems are encoded as *declarative* knowledge, usually from instructions and perhaps a worked-out example. (As discussed in Chapter 6, one may distinguish between declarative knowledge, knowledge about a topic, and procedural knowledge, knowledge of how to do some task.) In this stage, the problem solver can solve problems by carefully going over the declarative knowledge and figuring out how to apply it to a new problem. That is, the problem solver may have learned the relevant information, but it may not yet be in a form to allow quick, reliable access and application.

In the second stage, as a result of applying this knowledge, knowledge is transferred into a more efficient *procedural* representation. Anderson uses **productions** to capture this idea of procedural knowledge and has embodied his theory in a computer simulation. Productions are simple rules of the general form "IF certain conditions are true THEN perform some mental or physical action." Each production is constantly checking to see if its particular conditions are met, and when they are, its particular actions are performed. Thus, these productions can encode common situation-action pairings, so that they do not need to be recomputed from the declarative representation each time they are needed (reducing the difficulty of the computation). The point of this change from declarative to procedural knowledge is to encode the knowledge so that it is accessed at the relevant time during problem solving. (See Anderson & Lebiere, 1998, for arguments about the importance of productions in modeling human skill learning.)

Third, through further practice, this procedural knowledge is *refined and enlarged* so that bigger steps may be taken with each application. As we saw in the discussion of expertise, experts can recognize large patterns and have associated procedures for dealing with the situation signaled by these patterns. In addition, experts can combine multiple steps. Anderson captures this expertise by putting together productions so that the conditions can be quite complex (which is equiva-

Table 13.1   **Three Stages of Developing Expertise (Anderson, 1987)**

1. Use *declarative* knowledge
2. Develop *procedural* knowledge from the use of declarative knowledge
3. *Refine and enlarge* procedural knowledge

lent to recognizing a complex pattern) or so that successive steps can be accomplished more quickly.

A simplified example may help to illustrate these three stages. Suppose you are learning to use a word processor and you read the following:

> When you have finished making changes to the file, you will probably want to save it for later editing. To do this, you need to let the word processing program know that you wish to save it in place of the old file (before the changes were made). To do this, first press the F7 key, labeled SAVE, to let the program know that the file is to be saved. You will then be asked whether you wish to replace the old file. To do so, type Y (for "yes") and press the key labeled ENTER.

After reading these sentences, you could go through the steps for saving a file, though you would probably do so slowly, interpreting each sentence. This slow use of the information would be an instance of applying declarative knowledge (Stage 1). Once you have performed this procedure several times, you may have the information stored in a more efficient procedural way (Stage 2). For instance, you might have something like the following two productions:

> P1: If you are working on the word processor
> and the goal is to replace the file with a new version
> THEN press F7.

> P2: If you are working on the word processor and
> the goal is to replace the file with a new version and
> you have already pressed F7
> THEN press Y and press ENTER.

With further practice these two productions might be combined into a bigger production (Stage 3) that would enable you to replace a file:

> P3: If you are working on the word processor and
> the goal is to replace the file with a new version
> THEN press F7, Y, and ENTER.

This theory provides one set of ideas on how learners may gain knowledge about patterns and their associated actions. It has been used to predict in detail how performance speeds up with practice, as well as the degree of transfer between different tasks (see, e.g., Anderson, 1993a; Anderson & Labiere, 1998; Singley & Anderson, 1989). Although aspects of the theory have been questioned (see Carlson,

AN APPLICATION
Computer-Based Tutoring Systems

Computer systems that help people learn have been in schools since the 1960s. However, they have often consisted of inflexible programmed learning methods, and they have not been very widely available. Two major changes have occurred recently that promise systems that may be substantially more useful. First, our understanding of expertise and its development has increased greatly, providing some ideas about what the target skill should be and how people might best learn it. Second, computer capabilities have grown incredibly and become very widely available, so that even complex tutoring systems requiring sophisticated computers are not out of the range of many schools.

Tutoring systems currently being developed cover a variety of topics such as geometry and programming. To distinguish them from earlier types of systems and to highlight their use of cognitive analyses, these systems are usually called **intelligent tutoring systems** or intelligent computer-assisted instruction.

Although the various systems differ greatly, most of them consist of four general components. First, they include a representation of *expert knowledge.* This component captures the target knowledge, that is, what the tutoring system would like the learner to learn. Second, the systems keep a record of the **learner's model,** what knowledge the learner is assumed to have available. This record is kept for each user of the tutoring system and is updated during the learning sessions. The learner's model provides an analysis of what the learner knows, and the expert

(Continued)

Sullivan, & Schneider, 1989; Pennington, Nicolich, & Rahm, 1995), it has been influential in emphasizing certain issues about learning and, as presented in the box, An Application, in providing a theoretical base for instruction.

Teaching Heuristics

Most current theories of learning focus on how problem solving within a restricted domain improves with practice in the domain. But what about more general procedures, or heuristics, that can be applied across a wide variety of problems? Can they be taught?

George Polya, a mathematician, pioneered the study of problem-solving heuristics. His book *How to Solve It* outlines various heuristic procedures that may

AN APPLICATION
Computer-Based Tutoring Systems *(Continued)*

knowledge represents what the learner should eventually know, so the knowledge in the expert component that is not in the learner's model is the knowledge still needed to be learned. (The learner's model may also contain some misconceptions that need to be corrected.) Third, the system needs an *instructional component,* which determines what tutorial strategies will be applied to get the learner's knowledge closer to the expert's. This component must take into account what the learner knows and what the system is trying to teach (i.e., what difference between expert and learner is being worked on). Finally, because the computer needs to interact with the learner, the system needs some type of *interface* or means of communication. Some systems rely on simple displays and typed input; others use fancy color graphics and input by various pointing devices.

This discussion is rather abstract, so consider a particular tutoring system that relates to our study of developing expertise. John Anderson has applied his ACT-R theory of learning (discussed earlier) by building tutors that incorporate the ideas he thinks are important in learning. Anderson has developed a number of tutors, including ones to teach high school geometry and the programming language LISP (which is the most widely used language for programming in artificial intelligence). These tutors have been used in classrooms since 1984 and have been described and evaluated in a number of publications (e.g., J. R. Anderson, 1993a; Anderson, Conrad, & Corbett, 1990; Anderson, Corbett, Koedinger, &

(Continued)

be employed to help solve difficult problems. Given the importance of heuristics for expert problem solving, it was hoped that teaching them to nonexpert problem solvers may substantially aid their performance. A number of studies have been conducted examining the effects of teaching heuristics on problem-solving performance in a variety of settings (Schoenfeld, 1985, Chapter 6, provides a good review). Surprisingly, teaching heuristics appears to have very little effect on problem-solving performance. That is, these studies generally show little or no effect of such instruction.

Why? Schoenfeld (1985) argues that heuristics may be good descriptions of what experts are doing, but they are not specific enough to tell a novice how to perform this action. Let's consider a simple case, and then apply it to more complex forms of expertise. A parent may tell a young child learning to sit at the dinner table

AN APPLICATION

Computer-Based Tutoring Systems *(Continued)*

Pelletier, 1995). For the level of LISP knowledge being taught, Anderson claims that 500 productions (i.e., condition-action pairs) are needed. These productions represent the expert knowledge of the domain and have been derived through an extensive series of investigations. The students' problem-solving performances are used to infer which productions they are likely to have mastered and which ones need to be worked on. The LISP tutor then provides examples that require the use of one of these still-to-be-learned productions. As in his learning theory, Anderson assumes that productions can be learned from declarative knowledge encoded by the learner or by refining earlier productions. The tutor depends entirely on Anderson's expert model and theory of learning for deciding what knowledge is known and what knowledge needs to be taught.

Among the instructional principles used are (1) almost all instruction occurs by having learners solve problems, an idea discussed as a means of overcoming access difficulties; (2) feedback needs to be immediate; and (3) the load on working memory should be minimized, following the research of Sweller discussed earlier in this chapter. Although many of Anderson's instructional ideas seem quite reasonable, they are not based simply on intuition but derive from theoretical and empirical motivations. In addition, his approach combines a learning theory with this set of instructional strategies to provide a strong hypothesis about how people can best be taught to learn problem solving within a domain. Although the evaluation of the tutor is still in progress, the results are encouraging (Anderson et al., 1995).

not to break anything fragile. Unfortunately, the young child might not know which actions will cause things to break. Only after hitting a plate too hard with a fork, or knocking a glass onto the floor, does the child learn how to apply this heuristic. Similarly, an expert in physics problem solving might tell a novice to look beyond the surface form of a problem to determine what physical principle is being tested by the problem. If the novice has not yet learned to recognize the relationship between particular principles and the way they are incorporated into word problems, then this advice, while useful to the expert, is not helpful to the novice.

Does this mean that the teaching of heuristics is a bad idea? No, it only means that the teaching of heuristics described at a general level may be a bad idea. Rather, nonexperts need to be taught how to implement these heuristics so that they can learn the various substrategies and when they are applicable. Schoenfeld has developed instructional methods to teach problem solvers how to understand and analyze problems, and these instructional methods appear to show positive effects on later problem solving. For instance, Schoenfeld and Herrmann (1982) provided a one-month course in mathematical problem solving. The students were asked to sort a set of 32 problems before they took the course and after they took the course. These sortings were compared to expert sortings and the sortings of a control group consisting of students who took a course in another form of problem solving (structured programming). Recall that problem categorization by experts is usually done on the basis of the underlying principles, while novices tend to use the surface objects to categorize problems. Schoenfeld and Herrmann found that the two nonexpert groups sorted similarly before their courses (and very differently from the experts). However, in the second sorting, the students who had taken the course on problem solving were sorting much more like the experts, whereas the students who took the structured programming course were still relying on surface objects. Therefore, a course that focuses on understanding and analysis of mathematical problems can have an impact on the categorization of such problems.

Schoenfeld's work and the recent related work of some other investigators provide some optimism on the teaching of general heuristics. Nonetheless, two cautionary notes are in order. First, although the course covered a variety of mathematical problem types, the generality of the heuristics learned is not clear. Would they be successfully applied to very different types of math problems or to non-math problems? Second, often the ability to apply a heuristic depends on domain knowledge. Although it may be possible to learn some general heuristics, their successful application will usually require considerable specific knowledge about the domain. For example, the recognition of relevant domain patterns is crucial for expertise and cannot be gotten around by the use of general heuristics. Nonetheless, the careful explicit teaching of heuristics in several domains may make their transfer across domains much easier. Although there may be no substitute for domain experience, the effectiveness of the experience may be increased by such teaching of heuristics.

Summary of Developing Expertise

In this section, we have discussed a number of ideas about how people may develop their expertise within a domain. All of these ideas have focused on how practice within a domain may allow people to better learn to perform within the domain. As presented in the box A Debate, Ericsson and his colleagues take a strong stand that deliberate practice predicts performance. The rest of this section addressed particular aspects of performance that might be learned with practice. We examined the ACT-R theory of skill acquisition, in which declarative knowledge is turned into highly specific productions, as one account of what happens during the development of expertise. Finally, we discussed Schoenfeld's work, which provides some ideas on how people might also learn more general heuristics. The research on developing expertise is of great interest these days, and there may soon be further developments that can improve instruction for problem-solving skills (as briefly outlined in the box, An Application).

Expert Systems

Introduction

Throughout the book, we have described different computer programs that have been used to understand aspects of psychological processing. An important type of program that has been based on studies of expert performance is the **expert system,** which is a computer system that attempt to simulate the reasoning of experts. The idea underlying the expert system is that experts are reasoning on the basis of domain-specific rules, and so making a computer program that reasons as well as an expert does requires capturing this domain-specific knowledge within the program.

One of the pioneers in the development of expert systems, Edward Feigenbaum, describes the enterprise as follows: "The goal of an expert system project is to write a program that achieves a high level of performance on problems that are difficult enough to require significant human expertise for their solution" (1983, p. 38). For our purposes, work on expert systems has been valuable for increasing our understanding of expertise.

The research on expert systems began as a scientific study of expertise. Following the protocol-simulation methodology of Newell and Simon, early investigators reasoned that if they could program a computer to provide the same solutions as experts, they had at least a sufficient set of processes for expertise. As the performance of these expert systems improved, however, the commercial potential became clear. Many hundreds of expert systems have been or are being developed for all types of expertise, such as geological decisions, accounting, computer system design, and medical diagnosis, and many have been incorporated into commercial enterprises. The work of Feigenbaum and his students has influenced business enough that *Forbes* magazine did a profile on him and expert systems (November 30, 1998).

Building an Expert System

The basic idea behind an expert system is to try to simulate the thinking of a particular expert. The developers of the expert system obtain the cooperation of an expert. A long procedure then begins, illustrated in Figure 13.4. The expert is asked for various facts and heuristics used in the area (Step 1). For example, for an expert system of some specialty of medical diagnosis, the physician diagnostician would explain what symptoms would be evidence for which diseases. This knowledge is then incorporated into a computer program, often using productions (Step 2). After quite a bit of this knowledge has been incorporated, the system is evaluated on a series of problems (Step 3). Invariably the program performs poorly, even on some cases that the expert used to generate the rules. When the expert is confronted with the poor performance of the system, the usual response is something like, "Well, no wonder. Of course, you also need to take into account. . . ." The expert has not been negligent. As we have discussed, expertise consists of a large number of perceptual patterns and memory-intensive procedures, many of which are not carried out at a conscious level. Nonetheless, experts can sometimes figure out how they solved a

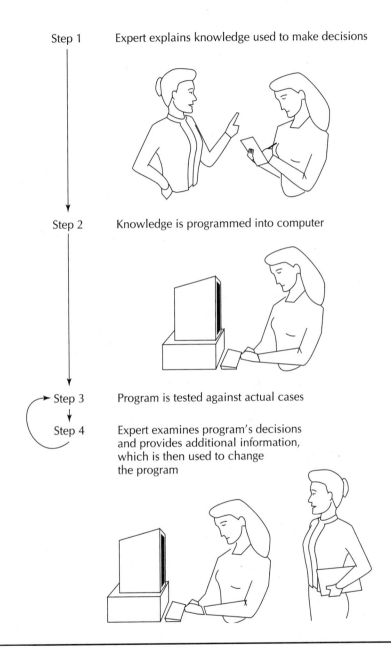

Step 1   Expert explains knowledge used to make decisions

Step 2   Knowledge is programmed into computer

Step 3   Program is tested against actual cases

Step 4   Expert examines program's decisions
and provides additional information,
which is then used to change
the program

Figure 13.4   **The Steps in Building an Expert System**   The expert is queried for information (Step 1), and that knowledge is programmed (Step 2). The program is tested against actual cases (Step 3), and changes are made after the expert examines the program's correct and incorrect decisions (Step 4). Steps 3 and 4 are repeated until performance is satisfactory.

problem by seeing how the stated rules fail to make the same decision the expert might. For instance, continuing with the medical diagnosis example, the expert might be shown a set of symptoms and told that the rules diagnosed it as one disease when, in fact, it was another. The expert might reply that each of two symptoms is only weak evidence for a particular disease, but when both the symptoms occur together, then it is much stronger evidence for that disease. The new rules and amendments are then added to the system (Step 4), and then the new system is tested again and modified again (Steps 3 and 4 again). Frequently, building an expert system requires many repeated queries of the expert to clarify and refine these rules as well as to elicit other rules. At the present time, the primary limitation of the work on expert systems is this "knowledge bottleneck"; that is, it is difficult to get knowledge out of an expert and into a system. Current systems usually have knowledge directly programmed into them and do not learn from experience, although doing so is likely to be a goal of future systems.

The end result of this iterative process is an expert system. The typical expert system consists of two main parts: First, there is the *knowledge base,* the set of rules that have been taken from the expert's suggestions and elicited in the course of the expert's problem-solving performance. Second, there is the *inference method* (often called the *inference engine*), which decides how to use the knowledge (e.g., whether to reason backward or forward). Most expert systems cover a very specific (and small) domain, but, as we saw, so do human experts. In addition, many expert systems are able to request information to help them make their decisions, such as the results of a lab test or the personal history of a patient.

What Can These Systems Do?

Although it may be a long time before expert systems are able to meet the expectations of those of us who enjoy science fiction books, there have been a number of successes. For example, one system, Meta-Dendral, helped in designing chemistry experiments that led to a publication in the *Journal of the American Chemical Society* (see Feigenbaum, 1983, for a description).

A major area of application of expert systems has been in medicine (see Feigenbaum, 1983; Lundsgaarde, 1987; Shortliffe, Buchanan, & Feigenbaum, 1979, for general reviews). One of the earliest systems, MYCIN (Shortliffe, 1976), helps select antibiotics for bacterial infections through the use of extensive backward reasoning from hypotheses through its approximately 500 rules. Although MYCIN is an older program, later versions have built on it. For example, NEOMYCIN (Clancey & Letsinger, 1984; also see Clancey, 1988) is able to give explanations of why it requested some type of information or how it arrived at a particular conclusion. This explanation capability is crucial for two reasons. First, in many situations people are willing to use an expert system as a consultation program (as one physician might ask the opinion of another) but may be unwilling to simply let it make the decisions. The consulting aspect requires the expert system not only to be able to arrive at a correct conclusion but also to be able to explain how it did so in a way that the user can understand. Second, if the explanation can be made explicit, it may be used to help teach nonexperts in the domain. For example, Clancey (1987) has built a tutoring system to teach some of the expert knowledge contained in NEOMYCIN.

What have we learned from these expert systems? We mention here four general principles that are relevant for our understanding of expertise (from Aikins, 1993; Feigenbaum, 1983, 1989). First, "knowledge is power." As we saw in the work on expertise, domain-specific knowledge is the key. The work on expert systems provides an interesting test of this idea, because the results in developing these systems have generally been that the exact inference method used is not very important. The general reasoning strategy used does not appear to be crucial. The extent and correctness of the knowledge base is what determines the performance of the expert system. In fact, this idea is so crucial, that many current expert systems are called *knowledge systems*. Second, much of the knowledge that is important is not simple facts but rather heuristics—what Feigenbaum calls "judgmental, experiential, uncertain." This knowledge reflects the experts' ability to see complex patterns and to know how these patterns are related to each other and to outcomes. Third, the system developers have found that the particular representation used for encoding the knowledge greatly influences how well the system works. Rather than trying to use a single uniform representation for encoding knowledge from all the expert systems, the programmers try to choose a way of representing the knowledge that will be most appropriate for the particular application. We saw in Chapter 12 how different representations, even if they are formally equivalent, can lead to large differences in ease of use. Fourth, expert system reasoning is *brittle*. That is, an expert system reasons exceptionally well within its domain of expertise, but quite poorly (or not at all) outside of that domain of expertise. Indeed, one movement in computer science is to embed expert systems within a larger system that has commonsense knowledge in order to permit expert systems to reason more broadly (see Lenat & Guha, 1994, for a discussion of this issue).

Although expert systems have been developed in many areas, it is important to keep in mind their limitations for our understanding of expertise. Their goal is to perform well in one difficult area, not to exhibit generally intelligent behavior. Their lack of knowledge that is not directly in their area of expertise means that they will have difficulty, without new programming, in adapting to changes in goals, unexpected changes in the environment, or even to changes in domain understandings.

Adaptive Expertise

Before ending this section on expertise, let's consider whether any important aspects of expertise have been missed. Everyone would agree that experts know more than nonexperts. The greater knowledge and the richer organization of that knowledge allows experts to solve with relative ease the usual problems they face. But what happens when they are faced with a new problem for which they do not have schemas or sufficient relevant knowledge to quickly piece together an appropriate solution?

Holyoak (1991) claims that most of the current research focuses on experts solving routine tasks but does not examine this crucial aspect of expertise—the ability to adapt to new situations and invent procedures for solving new types of problems. The production-based systems do a good job of building up large sets of rules and heuristics that allow the solution of routine problems. However, the nonroutine problems often require solvers to adapt their solutions in new ways. The difficulty is this: The experts need to use the great deal of expert knowledge they possess, but they should be able to adapt it flexibly so that changes in the situation can be dealt with. Indeed, one mark of experts is that they are able to solve both routine problems as well as novel problems within their domain of expertise. How can this be done?

The short answer is that we do not yet know. Holyoak suggests that we may need hybrid systems that combine the important representational power of symbolic systems (such as their ability to represent relational information, as discussed in the propositional model of Chapter 6) with the flexible processing of PDP or connectionist systems. In Chapter 6, we went over a simple type of PDP system, in which the many simple units would each activate other units and the resulting pattern of activation would be the "response." Holyoak is arguing that this interactive passing of activation allows great flexibility because small changes in the situation can lead to changes in the activation that get propagated and may lead to major changes in the overall pattern. Such hybrid systems are still new, though they have been used in text understanding (Kintsch, 1988) and have been applied in some work on expertise (Doane et al., 1992). Although we cannot be sure that this hybrid approach will solve the difficulties, the examination of adaptive expertise is becoming an important area of research. With the rapid changes in our information-based businesses, there is much interest in developing expertise that will adapt to changes in the workplace (e.g., E. M. Smith, Ford, & Kozlowski, 1997).

Summary

In this section, we examined expertise and its development. A common theme is the importance of domain knowledge. Experts augment the incomplete information presented in order to get a rich and deep representation of the problem. They also reduce the great computational complexity of some problems by substituting memorized procedures. Novices do not have the extensive knowledge of the domain or an understanding of various underlying principles and relations, so their augmentation is much less useful. For example, in formal domains, they rely more on the surface elements mentioned in the problem and in working backward from the goal.

We then examined how such expertise might be learned. Anderson's ACT-R theory illustrated one set of ideas on how expertise develops and how these ideas might be incorporated into a tutoring system. We also considered work showing that if the goal is to develop working forward or schema-driven problem solving, then some common heuristics, such as means-ends analysis, may not be helpful.

The work on expert systems illustrates the importance of knowledge for expert performance, and allows a clear way of examining the extent to which the knowledge is crucial (as opposed to the reasoning methods). We ended this section by pointing out that much of the expertise research has focused on routine expertise, as opposed to adaptive expertise. Given the rate of change in many domains, being able to adapt one's expertise may turn out to be one of the most important skills for an expert.

Throughout this chapter and the previous chapter, we have often been focusing on problem solving and expertise in situations in which there is some "correct" (or best) answer. A common question that nonpsychologists have when they hear about problem solving is how it relates to creativity. In addition, the previous section has just argued that we need to consider how experts might creatively adapt to new situations in their area of expertise. We examine creativity in the next section.

CREATIVITY

Introduction

Almost everyone finds creativity to be an interesting topic. We all have heard wonderful stories about tortured artists whose creative genius drives them mad or inspired scientists who solve, with a single flash of insight, questions that have plagued humankind for many years. On a less grand scale, we are often faced with problems for which we need to generate a novel solution. What can we say about the cognitive processes of creativity?

As you might guess, creativity is a difficult topic to research. Reasons for this difficulty include disagreements about how to tell whether something is creative and the inability to easily foster creative solutions in a controlled laboratory setting. To discuss this topic, we first look at a case that we would all view as *not* being creative.

Rigidity in Problem Solving

Consider the following experiment by Luchins (1942; or see Luchins & Luchins, 1950, for some interesting follow-up studies). A subject is told that there are three containers of different sizes that can hold some fluid. There is an unlimited supply of fluid, and the subject's job is to pour the fluids between the supply and the containers so as to end up with a specified amount of fluid. For example, as in the second line of Table 13.2 (the first task was used to illustrate the idea to subjects), the containers are of capacity (a) 21 quarts, (b) 127 quarts, and (c) 3 quarts. The goal is to end up with 100 quarts (clearly in container b). How would this be done? An alert participant might notice that $127 - 100$ is 27, which can be gotten by pouring off fluid to fill container a, then pouring it twice to fill container c. That is, the answer can be thought of as $b - a - 2c$. In fact, problems 2 through 6 can be solved by this same formula. The next two problems, 7 and 8, can be solved by this formula but can also be solved by a simple formula ($a - c$ for 7 and $a + c$ for 8). Problem 9 cannot be solved by $b - a - 2c$, but only by $a - c$. Finally, problems 10 and 11 can be solved by the formula $b - a - 2c$ or by $a + c$ and $a - c$, respectively.

What is the point of this experiment? Luchins was interested in the "mechanization" of problem-solving procedures. Problems 2 through 6 were used to induce

Table 13.2   **Water Jug Problems Used in Luchins and Luchins (1950)**

	The Tasks			
	Containers given (capacity in quarts)			
Problem	a	b	c	To get
1	29	3		20 quarts
2	21	127	3	100 "
3	14	163	25	99 "
4	18	43	10	5 "
5	9	42	6	21 "
6	20	59	4	31 "
7	23	49	3	20 "
8	15	39	3	18 "
9	28	76	3	25 "
10	18	48	4	22 "
11	14	36	8	6 "

Source: Luchins & Luchins, 1950.

the subject to mechanize the solution procedure. The results (which Luchins collected over the years from many thousands of subjects) are quite striking. Almost three quarters of the subjects solve problems 7, 8, 10, and 11 by the mechanized procedure (i.e., $b - a - 2c$) rather than the much more direct solution of $a + c$ or $a - c$. (Note that other subjects who did not get problems 2 through 6 first almost always used the direct solutions for problems 7, 8, 10, and 11, indicating that the first problems were leading to the application of these more complex procedures.) Even after problem 9, which could not be solved by the $b - a - 2c$ procedure, not many subjects applied the direct solutions.

This phenomenon, called **Einstellung** (German for "attitude"), was used to demonstrate that people often apply their past experiences directly, to the detriment of simple or more elegant solutions. Clearly, the ability to make use of past experience is necessary to our survival. The point of this demonstration is that we may perseverate in applying this past experience in routinized situations, even when it is not appropriate.

From this work (and many anecdotes we can all generate), it does appear that sometimes it is useful to approach a problem differently and try to come up with an alternative type of solution. The ability to know when such a change might be profitable and how to accomplish it are important aspects of what most of us think of as creativity.

What Is Creativity?

What does it take to be creative or have a creative solution? Sometimes it seems as if the definition is somewhat circular: Creative solutions are those solutions produced by creative people, and creative people are those people who come up with creative solutions. In fact, we can do a little better than that. For a solution to be creative, it must be both *original* and *relevant*. That is, the solution must be new and it must be a solution, not just some original, irrelevant proposal. For example, a novel solution to world hunger might be to jump in the air 20 times, but we would not consider it a creative solution because it will not cure world hunger (or even have the possibility of doing so).

Boden (1994) distinguishes between historical creativity and personal creativity. Historical creativity is the first proposal of a given solution to a difficult problem. For example, Newton's description of the solar system as a central force system (with the sun pulling the planets toward it to keep them in orbit) was historically creative. Personal creativity is the generation of a novel idea for an individual (even if that idea has been had elsewhere by someone else). From the standpoint of psychology, personal creativity is important, because it reflects the operation of processes that lead to new ideas. Discussions of historically creative ideas may illuminate psychological processes, but it is unlikely that participants in psychological experiments will uncover historically creative ideas in the course of a study.

Creative thinking is often thought to involve *divergent thinking* (Guilford, 1959); that is being able to consider a solution in lots of different ways rather than converging on a single answer. Some creativity tests (e.g., Torrance, 1966) include tests of divergent thinking, such as to think of as many uses as you can for a common object, such as a paperclip. These answers are scored in terms of *fluency,* how many different ideas were generated (related to the divergent thinking aspect), and *flexibility,* how many different types of uses were generated, as well as in terms of *originality,* how different it was from the answers of other people.

It is important to note that we have defined **creativity** with respect to a *product* or solution being original and relevant, not with respect to the processes that led to the solution. This might seem a little strange, because in a book on cognition we are really interested in the cognitive processes people go through. The question, then, is whether there is something special about the cognitive processes that lead to creative products (as opposed to noncreative products).

The Traditional View

The Idea of Creativity

Although psychologists might argue about what it means to be creative, many nonpsychologists feel quite confident about which of their acquaintances are creative and which ones are not. On a grander scale, most people have strong views that creativity is closely related to imagination, especially involving flashes of insight.

Weisberg (1986, 1993) provides details on many illustrations of creativity taken from personal diaries or journals that were kept by creative people. For instance, an important mathematician, Poincaré, described how he had spent weeks working without success on a problem, only to have the answer occur to him in a flash while he vacationed. Another famous example is the story of how the poet Coleridge wrote the poem *Kubla Khan* from scratch after having it appear to him during (drug-induced) sleep.

Gestalt psychologists such as Kohler and Wertheimer distinguished "productive" thought, in which novel ideas are generated, from "reproductive" thought, in which the earlier responses are simply applied mechanically, as in the Luchins water jug problem. The Gestalt view of problem solving (and perception) emphasized the importance of the relations among the parts (as discussed in Chapter 3). By this view, understanding the problem, a crucial step toward solving it, requires one to "see" how all the parts fit together to form the whole. Sometimes when one approaches a problem, the structuring one gets of the parts is not adequate to solve the problem (perhaps due to the inappropriate influence of past experience). However, an appropriate understanding sometimes comes about through a *spontaneous restructuring* of the problem in which the parts are seen as fitting together in a different way, leading to a new understanding. Although the view is sometimes faulted for vagueness, the central point for our current purpose is that the parts are seen as going together differently, often leading to a feeling of "Eureka!" or "Aha!" Common to many ideas on creativity is this phenomenology of sudden insight.

Although most researchers agree that the solving of insight and noninsight problems share many of the same processes, there is disagreement over whether there are unique processes used in solving insight problems. As one example of a difference between such problems, Schooler and Melcher (1995) report studies in which people have to give verbal protocols of their solutions—talking aloud about how they are solving the problem (see Chapter 12). They found that these protocols interfere with insight problem solutions but not noninsight problem solutions.

Stages of Creativity

Several suggestions for the stages one goes through in creativity have been based on introspections or on accounts of how creative people came up with their creative ideas. For example, Wallas (1926) proposed four stages of creative thought. First, there is *preparation*. The problem solver (e.g., scientist, artist) gains knowledge about the area, starts to work on a task, and runs into difficulty. Second, during a period of **incubation,** the problem solver puts the problem aside and does something else, such as Poincaré going on vacation. Third, the solution (or a crucial part of it) occurs in a sudden insight labeled *illumination* (such as the cartoon idea of a light-bulb turning on over a character's head). Finally, there is a stage of *verification,* in which the insight is checked, because not all insights turn out to be correct. Common to many reports of creativity, as in many people's view, is the idea of a prolonged mental block or obstacle followed by sudden insight.

Despite the plausibility of such a view, a number of points argue against accepting creativity as a fixed set of stages by which novel solutions are produced. First, not all accounts include all the stages and many accounts seem to have some of the stages interleaved. Second, as in memory for anything, these accounts by creative people may contain some distortions. Weisberg (1986) takes several well-known cases and provides strong evidence for alternative accounts that do not support the stage view. As an extreme example, it was later found that Coleridge had a number of earlier drafts of part of *Kubla Khan* written before his alleged insight.

In addition, although it is not documented, it seems likely that many creative solutions simply come to the person during problem solving, but their arrival is not considered unusual enough to record for posterity. Third, and perhaps most important, the stage idea is really at best a description of the *phenomenology* of creative thinking. It is not an explanation of what cognitive processes occur. That is, these stages propose what it "feels like" to go through creative thought, rather than what one is actually doing. This criticism is especially true of the crucial stage of illumination. Thus, Metcalfe and Wiebe (1987) have shown that when people solve insight problems, they often do not feel that they are getting closer to the answer even right before they solve it, while in more usual problems they do feel that they are getting closer (though the absence of a feeling that one is progressing toward a solution does not mean that associative cues that will lead to insight are not being accumulated; see Bowers, Farvolden, & Mermigis, 1995). Of course, the feeling that one is approaching a solution is an indication of a possible difference, but not an explanation of it. Even if one assumes the validity of this stage approach, the real question is what leads to illumination. We now examine some recent views that have addressed this question or provided alternative accounts of creativity.

Some Recent Views of Creativity

What would it mean to argue that creativity is not anything special, that is, not any different from noncreative problem solving? Clearly, creative products are different from noncreative products (by definition), but the question is: Are creative products produced by cognitive processes that are fundamentally different than the cognitive processes producing noncreative products?

In the last section, we suggested some problems with the traditional analysis of creativity. What might be a more useful approach? We discuss how creativity might be considered within a general cognitive framework. Creativity is attracting an increasingly large amount of research. Because it is not possible in a book like this one to discuss all of this work, we have chosen some different cognitive approaches. The interested reader might want to consider other theories that examine creativity from other perspectives (e.g., Amabile, 1996; Csikszentmihalyi, 1996). The focus in this section will be on (1) cognitive analyses of the traditional view, (2) creativity as incremental problem solving, (3) creativity as problem finding, and (4) the creative cognition approach.

Cognitive Analyses of the Traditional View

Although we have argued that there are problems with the traditional view of creativity as a series of stages—preparation, incubation, illumination, and verification—that does not mean that it cannot be useful in helping us understand creativity. Many researchers have tried to analyze these stages with cognitive concepts.

For example, Smith and Blankenship (1991) examined incubation. Most researchers would agree that some time spent away from the problem can sometimes help, but the question is why. Although the traditional view that unconscious problem solving may occur while the mind is occupied with other things is possible, there is little support for this idea (despite many attempts to gather such support). Smith and Blankenship address the possibility that what may be happening is that the solver gets fixated on an inappropriate approach to the problem (i.e., inappropriate knowledge is highly activated) and gets nowhere. This proposal is like the idea of finding a local maximum that we discussed when talking about hill-climbing search in Chapter 12. The solution that the solver fixates on is not the best one, but without finding a way to get away from that local maximum, the problem solver may have difficulty finding an even better solution.

The focus on this inappropriate approach blocks the retrieval of useful information. Such retrieval blocks have been shown in a variety of memory results (see the discussion of interference in Chapter 5 or Roediger & Neely, 1982, for more information), so Smith and Blankenship are arguing that these same types of blocks are happening here. Further attempts at solving will not help because the appropriate knowledge is blocked (i.e., they keep returning to the local maximum). If, however, there is a period during which other things are worked on, the highly activated inappropriate knowledge will become less activated and less effective at blocking the appropriate knowledge. Thus, a period of doing something else might help for reasons other than unconscious problem solving.

Smith and Blankenship tested this idea by examining what happens in a common creativity test when the person is given misleading information. They used the Remote Associates Test (RAT) in which three words are presented (e.g., *arm, coal, peach*) and the solution is a single word that combines with each of the three words to form a common word or phrase. Try to solve this one for a minute before looking at the answer in parentheses (in this example, the answer is pit: *armpit, coal pit, peach pit*). As you can see, the target word may have different meanings or senses, so the solutions are thought to require considerable fluency and flexibility of thought, related to the idea of divergent thinking mentioned earlier. Along with each set of words, Smith and Blankenship sometimes included italicized words that they said were associated to the target word (for example, *leg* for the target word *arm*). In fact, however, the italicized words were not associated to the target (*pit*) but meant to mislead people to think about inappropriate responses. Clearly, such misleading information will hurt performance, relative to a condition in which people did not get such misleading information, but the question of interest is what happens with a period of incubation. The design and results of one experiment are presented in Table 13.3. Half the subjects immediately took the same RAT again (without any misleading information), while half read a science fiction story and then retook the RAT. If the misleading associates led solvers to fixate on inappropriate possible solutions, interfering with the retrieval of appropriate responses, then reading the story would allow this fixation to go away and make the appropriate responses more available. Thus, the improvement of this intervening story should be greater for the misled word sets than the ones without misleading information. Although such improvement during another activity would usually be attributed to incubation, here the appropriate interpretation seems to be less blocking of retrieval. The results were consistent with this prediction. For example, in Experiment 1, the improvement

Table 13.3   **Design and Results of Smith & Blankenship (1991, Experiment 1)**
Performance on second time with the same Remote Associate Test

	First Remote Associate Test	
	Misleading Information	**No Misleading Information**
Incubation	.41	.32
No Incubation	.19	.22
Incubation Effect	.22	.10

in performance with incubation was more than twice as large for the misleading word sets than for the other word sets (22% vs. 10%). The point of this work is that incubationlike effects may at least sometimes be due to factors other than unconscious problem solving.

Creativity as Incremental Problem Solving

Weisberg (1986) presents a convincing case that creativity occurs through a series of small steps in which earlier ideas are modified and elaborated (e.g., the *Kubla Khan* example mentioned earlier). The incremental nature of creativity occurs as the problem solver runs into obstacles, proposes solutions, runs into further obstacles, and so on, refining and elaborating the earlier solutions. Rather than viewing creative ideas as springing without warning, we should be trying to understand the details of how they develop.

Weber and Dixon (1989) apply the same point about the incremental nature of creativity to the historical analysis of inventions. They argue that inventions often evolve over long periods of time by the gradual accumulation of the best ideas. To illustrate this point, they describe the historical evolution of a simple hand tool, the sewing needle, some early versions of which are estimated to be 25,000 years old. Although it may seem a quite simple invention, it is an elegant solution to the problem of having a device that (1) penetrates the material, (2) conveys the thread, and (3) allows the user to pull and push it. Figure 13.5 presents a set of possible precursors to the current butt-eye needle (the eye is in the butt of the needle). The awl was used to penetrate the material, but a separate tool, a fork, then had to be used to push the thread through. These tools were then combined into one in the joined awl and fork. The middle-eye needle improves upon this by allowing the penetration and conveying of the thread to be done together, though it causes some binding of the thread and may break more easily (the maximum stress is at the middle, but that is already weakened by having the eye there). Thus, the final "invention" did not just spontaneously emerge but slowly evolved (see also Ward, 1995).

Artistic creations and scientific discoveries are no less important or impressive because they did not occur by sudden insight. Although some readers may feel that this approach misses some of the essence of the creative process, it allows us to consider the importance of other factors in trying to explain how creativity develops, such as, "What is the role of knowledge?"

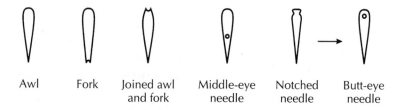

| Awl | Fork | Joined awl and fork | Middle-eye needle | Notched needle | Butt-eye needle |

Figure 13.5   **Possible Precursors to the Modern Butt-Eye Sewing Needle**   The figure shows how the precursors might have evolved (from left to right) to the needle we are familiar with.

Source: Weber & Dixon, 1989.

Creativity requires knowledge. Even the traditional view includes in the stage of preparation all the background knowledge that creative people have as necessary for their creative insights. Although one hears stories about people coming to a new problem area and solving problems that have long been agonized over, such occurrences are rare, and the few that occur may be due to an analogy to an area in which the person is expert. In terms of the incremental view, knowledge is also crucial. As in our discussion of expertise, domain knowledge guides search and allows the recognition of patterns that may suggest useful avenues to try.

Creativity as Problem Finding

Another possibility in the general problem-solving framework is that creative problem solving often involves viewing the problem in a new way. When the problem has been "appropriately" represented, the solution is often clear. Thus, suggestions that creative thinking involves sudden insights (e.g., Wallas, 1926) often bring in the idea that the problem has been re-represented. Creativity training techniques (see, e.g., Gordon, 1961) often try to get the problem solvers to think about the problem in new ways until a solution comes to them. The use of analogy is a common tool in creativity training and creative problem solving (Holyoak & Thagard, 1995).

One suggestion that is generally consistent with these ideas is that real creativity involves not just representing a given problem but "finding" the real problem and representing that. Creative people may not be creative in their solutions but rather creative in their choice of problems. For example, Getzels and Csikszentmihalyi (1976) analyzed how artists painted, starting with the composition. The artists were provided with a table of objects and asked to choose some of the objects, compose a still life, and paint it. The pertinent result is that artists whose paintings were judged to be more original tended to spend more effort choosing objects, sometimes biting into the objects to help make the decision. Perkins (1988) suggests that a hallmark of such problem finding is the extensive exploration of possibilities before committing to an approach.

In fact, a process similar to problem finding was proposed within the general problem-solving framework many years ago (e.g., Newell, Shaw, & Simon, 1962). More recently, Simon (1989) further explains the importance of this problem finding with the term **problem formulation.** The reason for this term is to make clear that such an activity can be viewed as another type of problem solving in which the problem is to decide how best to formulate the problem. Often in trying to solve one problem we need to pose and solve some other problem. For example, Weisberg (1993) argues that the inventor Watt was greatly bothered by what he saw as the inefficiencies of the current engines, so he set as his problem not to invent a new engine but to improve the efficiency. Many political issues illustrate this idea of problem finding, in which there may be some agreed-on situation but multiple formulations of the problem. For example, almost everyone would agree that the degree of homelessness in the United States is shameful, but there would be great disagreement as to what the problem is. How the problem is formulated (is it the lack of adequate welfare, lack of adequate economic incentives, or what?) will have great effects on the type of solutions proposed.

Finally, the incremental and problem-finding views are not mutually exclusive, but rather different in emphasis. Combining these ideas, we might best think about creativity as arising from a great deal of refining, elaborating, and reformulating of the problem and its possible solutions. Much problem solving involves reformulating the problem by using information gained from failed solution attempts. Dunbar (1995) provides a fascinating description of this cycle in his examination of scientific reasoning taking place over a one-year period in four major molecular biology laboratories. For example, he points out how the problem reformulation often takes place at lab meetings, prompted by tough questions from others in the lab. Thus, creative products may emerge from failures, through incremental problem reformulation. The final work we examine tries to incorporate many of the earlier ideas in a single framework.

The Creative Cognition Approach

The goal of the creative cognition approach is to provide a thorough analysis of creativity by using the experimental methods of cognitive science, including the development of a variety of experimental paradigms that can be used to study creative behavior in the laboratory approach (Finke, Ward, & Smith, 1992; Smith, Ward, & Finke, 1995; Ward, Smith, & Finke, 1999). First, these researchers argue, consistent with some of the work just described, that there is no single creative process; rather, creativity is the result of many types of mental processes working together. Second, they claim (and test the idea) that the processes used to produce creative thoughts are exactly the same as those used in producing noncreative thoughts, so much of their work draws on relevant work in cognitive psychology. Third, they believe that rather than focus on only a single type of creativity, it is important to construct global information-processing models that can capture a variety of creative thought. They offer one such model, which they call GENEPLORE, which distinguishes between processes that *generate* various mental structures and processes that *explore* the creative implications of these structures.

Let us try to explain this view by examining some work on a topic that seems very creative: imagination. Imagine that you went to a planet that was very different from earth and found an animal there. What might it be like? Ward (1994) asked people to imagine exactly that and then to draw and describe this creature. Figure 13.6 provides some examples of the drawings that subjects made in this study. Interestingly, Ward found that while some of the creatures looked little like any earth creature, a number of basic characteristics of earth animals were observed in a large majority of the imagined animals. For example, 89% of the imagined animals were symmetric (i.e., had two halves that were the same but mirror images, such as people and most earth animals have), and 92% had a visible sensory organ (nose, ear, or eye). Ward discusses much evidence that argues for the idea that the construction of these imaginary creatures is structured by the properties that are usually found in earth animals (see also Karmiloff-Smith, 1992, for evidence of this process in children). That is, although people are imagining creatures, they use the knowledge they have of earth animals to help them develop the new creatures. Because earth animals are symmetric and have sense organs, many of the imaginary animals do as well. However, once they decide that the animal will have an eye, they may think of very different types of eyes than are found on earth animals. In terms of the GENE-PLORE model, the generation occurs by the usual category-related processes, leading to structures from earth animals. The creativity occurs with the exploration of these structures, including deletions of some features or very different instantiations. Thus, the knowledge of animal categories is not determining their imaginary animals, but it is providing a strong structure in which they can make new particulars, such as the exact type of eyes. The claim of the creative cognition approach is that all creative products greatly rely upon our knowledge and usual, noncreative processes (see also Marsh, Landau, & Hicks, 1996).

Summary

In this section, we have examined creativity, which was contrasted with reproductive or mechanized thinking. A central issue in the research has been how to best define creativity. Although no current proposal satisfies all researchers, important ingredients include originality and relevance. How has creativity been examined?

The traditional view has been to consider creativity as a process very different from other cognitive processes. One characterization has been in terms of the stages of preparation, incubation, illumination, and verification. The importance of incubation and the suddenness of illumination have been the focus of much work. Our evaluation is that although this traditional view has been very influential, it ultimately fails to provide a satisfactory cognitive explanation of creativity.

The bulk of this section has considered how creativity might be conceptualized within a general cognitive framework. First we examined whether the incubation effects might be akin to a well-known cognitive phenomenon, retrieval blocking. Although we do not think there is a definitive answer, it does seem that some results that are attributed to incubation effects might instead be due to retrieval blocks. Second, we discussed the idea that creative ideas often do not appear whole cloth, but rather develop incrementally. Third, we investigated the idea that a main

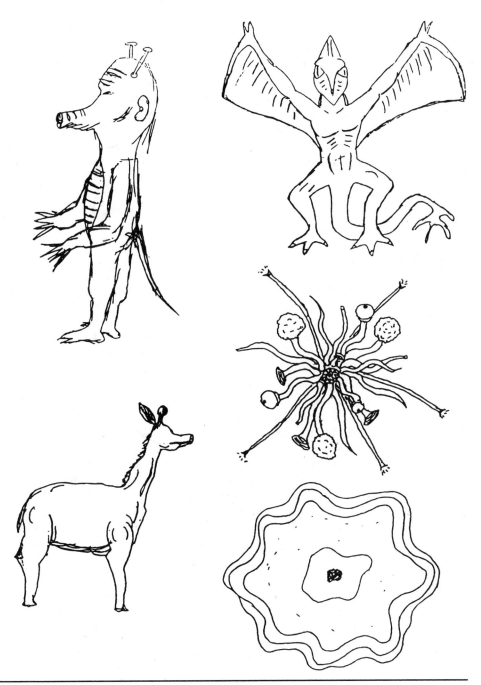

Figure 13.6   Some creatures drawn by subjects asked to imagine animals on a planet very different from earth.

Source: Ward, T. B., 1994.

part of creativity might not be in problem solving, but rather in problem finding. This view stresses the importance of how problems are represented, much as in Chapter 12. Finally, the creative cognition approach was described, in which a proposal is made for how creative products emerge from usual cognitive processes.

We end this discussion of creativity with a final point that has not come up yet—passion. Across many reports of creative people is a common incredibly strong commitment to their activity. Although one can view this in terms of personality traits, it also has important consequences for some cognitive aspects that we have discussed. This passion allows them to work hard (or practice) to gain the great deal of domain knowledge they need, to try many ways of thinking about the problem, and to persevere in the face of repeated failures. By all of the views we have considered, a strong commitment to the activity is essential.

Summary

In this chapter we expanded on two important topics in problem solving. First, we discussed expertise. Experts and novices differ in many ways. Experts use high-level principles to represent and categorize problems and have highly organized knowledge about the relations among the various problem types and principles. They tend to solve problems by working forward from the givens, whereas novices tend to work backward from the goal. These differences all depend on the experts' greater domain knowledge. Although we may learn how to better instruct people on general problem-solving strategies, acquiring extensive domain knowledge will still be crucial for becoming an expert. We ended the section by discussing two current controversies: talent vs. learning views of exceptional performance and adaptive vs. routine expertise.

Second, we examined creativity. We argued that a traditional view of creativity is inadequate. We then considered cognitive analyses of this traditional view, as well as ideas of creativity as incremental problem solving and problem finding. Finally, the creative cognition approach was discussed. Although we are clearly far from a full understanding of creativity, our evaluation is that these ideas indicate that much can be learned by considering creativity in the usual cognitive framework.

Key Terms

creativity

deliberate practice

Einstellung

expert system

incubation

intelligent tutoring systems

learner's model

problem formulation

problem schemas

productions

Recommended Readings _____

Expertise is currently being studied intensively. In addition to the experiments presented here, some useful reviews can be found in Gick (1986), Reimann and Chi (1989), and Ericsson and Lehmann (1996). An edited volume on expertise by Chi, Glaser, and Farr (1988) contains many interesting chapters. These readings include some ideas on the development of expertise as well, but other useful sources are Anderson (1987, 1993a). Zsambok and Klein (1997) provide an up-to-date treatment of expertise in naturalistic situations. Readers interested in heuristics should look at Polya (1945, 1957), Wickelgren (1974), and Schoenfeld (1985). A number of books have been published on intelligent tutoring systems, such as the one by Mandl and Lesgold (1988), and Anderson et al. (1995) provide an overview and evaluation of tutors built in the ACT* framework. Ericsson and Charness (1994) give a very readable presentation of the work on exceptional performers and deliberate practice.

Discussions of creative thinking were emphasized by Gestalt psychologists, including Wertheimer's (1945/1982) very readable and enjoyable book. Seifert, Meyer, Davidson, Patalano, and Yaniv (1994) provide an outline of a thorough cognitive analysis of the stage approach, with specific hypotheses about the different parts and functions of these stages. Weisberg (1986, 1993) has written clear and interesting short books (with several detailed case studies) that argue against creativity as a special mental activity. Simon (1989) makes a similar argument examining how creativity can be viewed from the traditional human problem-solving framework that he helped to develop. The creative cognition project is outlined in Finke et al. (1992), and some more recent work can be found in Smith et al. (1995) and Ward et al. (1999). Very different cognitive views of creativity may be found in other work, such as Sternberg and Lubart (1999). In addition, Amabile (1996) provides an examination of creativity from a social psychological perspective (with a focus on the idea of intrinsic motivation), and Csikszentmihalyi (1996) proposes a view based on extensive interviews with 91 eminent creative artists, scientists, and writers. Simonton (1997) provides an intriguing view of creativity over the lifespan. Finally, current studies of the relationship between expertise, creativity, and emotion can be found in the journal *Cognition and Emotion*.

Chapter 14

Judgment and Decision Making

Introduction

Rational and Normative Models
Expected Value Theory
Expected Utility Theory

Limitations of Expected Utility and Alternatives to It
Violations of Expected Utility
Prospect Theory
Regret Theory
Decision Making Over Time
Summary

Dealing With Complexity
Strategies for Dealing With Complexity
Adaptive Decision Making

Further Heuristics and Biases
Availability Heuristic
Representativeness Heuristic
Anchoring and Adjustment
Causal Schemas
Hindsight Bias
Overconfidence
Relativity of Judgment and Use of Norms
Summary

Are There Kinds of Decisions?
Mental Accounting

Summary

Key Terms

Recommended Readings

*There is no more miserable human being than in
whom nothing is habitual but indecision.*
—William James

INTRODUCTION _____

One of the hardest things about decision making is to define it, for it is so pervasive that we could equate it with virtually all voluntary human behavior. If a behavior is voluntary, then it might have been different, and the processes that led to that behavior rather than another can be thought of as involving decision making. Then again, brushing one's teeth in the morning seems to be more a matter of habit than a conscious selection from a set of potential behaviors. And just what constitutes this set? Certainly the fact that you did not pour oatmeal into your coffee, stir it with scissors, and then attempt to use the mixture as shaving cream does not mean that you explicitly decided not to do so. So it seems that we would want to restrict decision making to choosing among alternatives that are in some sense explicitly available.

But equating decision making with selecting among explicit choices may be too narrow. Part of good decision making may involve generating new options. A commuter faced with traffic jams or crowded public transportation may learn that there is another route or consider working at home. Gettys, Manning, Mehle, and Fisher (1980) noted that even experts were not very good at generating a full set of hypotheses about the cause of a problem, such as a car failing to start. Furthermore, field studies indicate that people in flood plain areas do not know much about the range of options for reducing the risk of flood damage or insuring against it (Kunreuther et al., 1978).

A key aspect of decision making is that it involves risk in one form or another. A person offered a choice between buying a car for $15 versus $15,000 finds the task so obvious that the first reaction would surely be "What's the catch?" or "What else haven't you told me?" To make effective decisions, we must assess risks. We criticize someone who ignores the warning signal at a railroad crossing for not weighing the risks properly. Overall, then, decision making can be roughly defined as generating, evaluating, and selecting among a set of relevant choices. Another important element of many decisions is that they involve some element of uncertainty or risk.

A moment's thought will tell you that decision making is rife with issues of computational complexity. How do people select from a potentially infinite set of choices only those that are relevant in a particular situation? And for each alternative there may be a vast if not unlimited amount of information that could be collected and evaluated prior to reaching a decision. To make the objectively optimal choice in these circumstances, a person would need an infinite amount of time to decide. To cope with these complexity problems, people seem to adopt strategies or heuristics that are efficient (in that they reduce the complexity) and effective (in that many undesirable alternatives are eliminated and the alternative selected satisfies the goal, even if it is not optimal).

If you find these arguments plausible, then you might be surprised to find that much of the history of research on decision making has been organized around the question of whether human decision making is perfectly optimal. The study of decision making owes much of its origins to philosophy and economics. Traditionally, theories of economic behavior have assumed that people's purchasing decisions follow a **rational model.** A rational model is one that assumes people always select the *best* option from a set (we will have more to say about what constitutes the "best" decision later). From the perspective of these theories, the question was not *whether* people optimized but *what* they optimized. Therefore, studies were aimed at different ways of measuring what people value because, knowing that, we ought to be able to predict what choices people will make.

A major contribution of psychological research on decision making has been to undermine the view that computational complexity and the associated demands on resources in decision making can be ignored. Decision making has its costs, and they must be given important consideration in theories of human choice behavior. Some people continue to have the bedrock faith that human decision making is always optimal or at least rational (in a bit we'll define what we mean by *rational*), and they attribute any nonoptimality or irrationality to the researcher's failure to analyze the task properly (see L. J. Cohen, 1981, for a modest version of this view and Camerer, 1995; Cosmides & Tooby, 1994; Gigerenzer & Hoffrage, 1995; and Kahneman & Tversky, 1996, for further discussion and debate). The body of research on choice behavior, however, motivates the consensus view that human decision making often shows clear departures from optimality.

Just as researchers in the area of perception may study visual illusions to get an idea of how the visual system works, decision researchers often focus on situations in which strategies and heuristics may fail or be misleading. These failures are illuminating, but they should not be read as indicating that, in general, human decision making is ineffective, any more than visual illusions prove that our perceptual system is ineffective. Nevertheless, human shortcomings in decision making can be quite serious. Furthermore, decision making can be improved, so it behooves us to understand it better. At the same time, we would argue that decision making must be understood in the context of computational complexity and that, for the most part, the procedures used in decision making serve people well. Herbert Simon has suggested that decision making might show **bounded rationality.** By that he means that, instead of making perfect or optimal decisions all of the time, people may make pretty good decisions most of the time.

This chapter first focuses on reasoning involving uncertainty and describes cases in which people's decisions depart from what is normatively correct in the sense of being optimal. As we extend our analysis, it will become clear that psychological models of decision making cannot be built on the idea that people invariably optimize (as models in economics often assume). Then we step back from a normative analysis to ask what psychological processes and strategies underlie decision making. Finally, we provide an overview on judgment tasks.

RATIONAL AND NORMATIVE MODELS

First, let's define what we mean by *rational*. Following the lead of Dawes (1988), we can define irrational by the **law of contradiction:** Reasoning processes based on the same evidence that reach contradictory conclusions are irrational. That is, a person who believes that overall choice A is better than B, and that overall choice B is better than A, is being irrational. This definition focuses on consistency, and we shall see that people systematically violate consistency. By this same criterion, a person who prefers A to B and B to C, ought to prefer A to C. That is, choices should show **transitivity.** Rationality is not based on what most people value. If John would rather have a paper clip than a CD player and would rather have a CD player than a free trip around the world, then John meets the consistency criterion for rationality as long as he prefers a paper clip to a free trip around the world (regardless of how silly his choice may seem to us).

Models that provide an ideal standard or norm hold people to a stricter criterion. Given certain assumptions about a person's goals and values and a description of some task, normative models prescribe what choice should be made. That is, normative models are prescriptive, and they set norms by which human decision making can be evaluated. Sometimes normative models are treated as candidates for psychological models, but people's performance departs sufficiently from optimality to undermine this practice. In fact, we will see that people's choices often violate rationality assumptions. In this section we consider both rational and normative models but note that if choices do not conform to a rationality criterion they will also violate normative standards.

Expected Value Theory

How should options be evaluated when making a choice? An early normative model in economics was **expected value theory,** which assumed that people calculate the monetary value of a set of choices, and then select the option with the highest value. To determine the value of an option, the decision maker must determine all of the possible outcomes if that option is selected, and the probability that each of those outcomes will occur. Each outcome then needs to be given a monetary value. The expected value of the option can then be calculated by multiplying the probability of each outcome by the value of that outcome, and adding together these values. The expected value is the amount of value you would expect to have in the long run if a particular option was selected.

For example, if the options were gambles, the expected value is just the average amount you would win on each gamble if you played it many times. Consider the following two options:

1. Winning $40 with probability .20, otherwise winning nothing

2. Winning $30 with probability .25 otherwise winning nothing

The expected value of the first option is just the sum of each possible outcome multiplied by the probability of that outcome. That is ($40 × .20) + ($0 × .80) = $8.00. The expected value of the second outcome involves a similar calculation ($30 × .25) + ($0 × .75) = $7.50. Thus, if people are using an expected value model for making choices, they should select option 1 rather than option 2.

As it turns out, people's behavior often violates expected value. People gamble in casinos and buy lottery tickets, even though the expected value for playing these games is less than the expected value for not playing. More generally, expected value theory fails as a description of human decision making because it does not take into account the *utility* of different choices to people. That is, people select options because of what the possible outcomes can do for them rather than because of some arbitrary value that can be given to them. Psychological utility is not necessarily the same as objective value. For example, psychologically speaking, the difference between 0 and $10,000 is much larger than the difference between $1,000,000 and $1,010,000.

Expected Utility Theory

In response to the idea that the personal value of an outcome is different from its objective monetary value, economic theories moved from expected value to **expected utility** (von Neumann & Morgenstern, 1944). The expected utility theory is very similar in spirit to the expected value theory, except that it explicitly acknowledges that the value of an outcome will depend on goals of a particular individual. In this case, evaluating an option requires determining the *utility* of each possible outcome, and then multiplying this utility by the probability that the outcome will occur.

It is easy to imagine situations in which expected utility and expected value disagree. Consider a college student with no money who needs $25 for bus fare to return home. Both choices described earlier provide at least that much money and the extra $10 associated with the first choice may have little additional utility. In that case, the extra probability associated with the second choice could make it the preferred decision. The college student would have violated expected value, but the choice would be perfectly consistent with expected utility.

Evaluating expected utility theory in experiments is somewhat more difficult than evaluating expected value, because we cannot make a prediction about which option a person will select without knowing his or her utilities for each of the outcomes. In the gambles above, for example, we cannot say whether option 1 or option 2 should be chosen. On this basis, one might think that expected utility theory would prove impossible to test or falsify. But the theory is quite testable, mainly because it implies that people will be consistent across a set of choices. For example, consider the following two alternatives:

3. Winning $40 with probability .40

4. Winning $30 with probability .50

Obviously, choices 3 and 4 are just like choices 1 and 2, except that the probabilities have been doubled. Expected utility theory assumes that utilities and probabilities are independent, so that the utility of $40 would be identical for the first and third choices as would the utility of $30 for the second and fourth choices. Therefore, expected utility theory imposes a consistency constraint: if you prefer choice 1 over choice 2, then you should also prefer choice 3 over choice 4; if you prefer choice 2 to choice 1 then you ought to prefer choice 4 to choice 3. In fact, for the four choices outlined here, people generally *are* consistent, just as expected utility theory predicts.

But now consider two more choices:

5. Winning $40 with probability .80

6. Winning $30 with probability 1.00

Again we have left the amount unchanged but doubled the probabilities once more. In this circumstance, many people who prefer choices 1 and 3 to choices 2 and 4 nonetheless generally prefer choice 6 to choice 5. This observation is inconsistent with expected utility theory, so the theory is not only testable but also incorrect. As we shall see, people show a tendency to prefer certain sure gains (and to avoid certain losses), and a preference for choice 6 over choice 5 is consistent with this observation. This tendency is known as the **certainty effect.** Let's take a closer look at violations of expected utility. They are important because they provide useful information about what factors guide human decision making.

LIMITATIONS OF EXPECTED UTILITY AND ALTERNATIVES TO IT

A number of observations suggest that models based on expected utility do not fully describe human decision making. We begin with a more detailed discussion of the certainty effect. As we shall see, there are clear cases where people's choices do not satisfy the normative criterion of consistency.

Violations of Expected Utility

The Allais Paradox

Allais (1953) proposed the following hypothetical pair of decision problems:

Pair 1:

Choice 7 $1,000 with probability 1.00 vs.

Choice 8 $1,000 with probability .89,

$5,000 with probability .10,

and $0 with probability .01.

Pair 2:

Choice 9 $1,000 with probability .11

and $0 with probability .89 vs.

Choice 10 $5,000 with probability .10

and $0 with probability .90.

What is the relation of the two pairs? Choices 9 and 10 are created by subtracting exactly the same probability and amount from Choices 7 and 8—$1000 with probability .89. (This is obvious in comparing Choices 8 and 10 and you can see it by simple subtraction for Choices 7 and 9.) The fact that the same probability and amount was subtracted to create Choices 9 and 10 forces utility theory to predict that people who prefer Choice 7 to Choice 8 will also prefer Choice 9 to Choice 10. In contrast, most people pick choice 7 over choice 8 but select choice 10 over choice 9. In pair 1, people are not willing to give up the certainty of the $1,000 payoff to take a chance on winning $5,000. (If you would be inclined to pick choice 8, then reduce the $5,000 in choices 8 and 10 to $2,000 or $1,500 and you will likely find yourself preferring choices 7 and 10 to 8 and 9, respectively.) This example illustrates what is known as the **Allais paradox.**

A similar example comes from work by Tversky and Kahneman (1981). They found that in questions dealing with the effects of a hypothetical epidemic, most people preferred an 80% probability of losing 100 lives to a sure loss of 75 lives (that is, they preferred to avoid a certain loss). The subjects also preferred a 10% chance to lose 75 lives to an 8% chance of losing 100 lives. Note that the second situation is just the first one with each probability reduced by a factor of 10. The key difference (psychologically) is that the first situation involves certainty and the second does not. The certainty effect shows that outcomes perceived with certainty loom larger and are overweighted relative to uncertain outcomes. Expected utility has no way of capturing this overweighting.

Preference Reversals

Many theories of decision making, including expected utility theory, require that different measures of preferences yield consistent outcomes. For example, if you value A more than B, then you should choose A when selecting between A and B. This seems pretty straightforward, but psychologists have identified numerous exceptions to this principle (e.g., Slovic & Lichtenstein, 1968; A. Tversky, Sattath, & Slovic, 1988). Consider the following pair of gambles:

> Bet A: 11/12 chance to win 12 chips
>
> 1/12 chance to lose 24 chips
>
> Bet B: 2/12 chance to win 79 chips
>
> 10/12 chance to lose 5 chips

Lichtenstein and Slovic (1973) asked people to choose a bet and to give a minimum price they would sell each bet for. Expected utility theory requires that both measures be equivalent and agree with each other. For example, if a person chooses A over B, it must be because its expected utility is higher. It follows that, in selling, such a person should ask more money for A than for B. Overall, bets A and B were selected equally often, but bet B received a higher selling price 88% of the time. Even the people who selected bet A gave a higher selling price to bet B 87% of the time. (By the way, this study was conducted on the floor of a casino in Las Vegas, so it cannot be argued that the participants were unfamiliar with gambling.)

As an interesting sidelight, two economists were skeptical about these **preference reversals** and ran a series of studies (Grether & Plott, 1979) with the explicit goal "to discredit the psychologists' works as applied to economics" (p. 623). They developed a number of criticisms of earlier work and ran a number of "improved" studies. Despite their considerable efforts and much to their surprise, they also observed preference reversals.

Preference reversals are even seen for seemingly equivalent choice measures. Consider the following example from Shafir (1993). People were asked to consider two alternative vacations (Spot A and Spot B, described next). Half the participants were asked which option they would prefer, whereas the other half were asked to choose by canceling the less desirable option. The wording of instructions and selection percentages were as follows:

Prefer:
Imagine that you are planning a week vacation in a warm spot over spring break. You currently have two options that are reasonably priced. The travel brochure gives only a limited amount of information about the two options. Given the information available, which vacation spot would you prefer?

Cancel:
Imagine that you are planning a week vacation in a warm spot over spring break. You currently have two options that are reasonably priced, but you can no longer retain your reservation in both. The travel brochure gives only a limited amount of information about the two options. Given the information available, which reservation do you decide to cancel?

		Prefer	*Cancel*
Spot A:	average weather average beaches medium-quality hotel medium-temperature water average nightlife	33%	52%
Spot B:	lots of sunshine gorgeous beaches and coral reefs ultramodern hotel very cold water very strong winds no nightlife	67%	48%

If the two ways of responding were equivalent, we would expect that if a choice was preferred two thirds of the time it should be rejected a third of the time. Instead, Spot B was strongly preferred but was as likely to be rejected as Spot A. Shafir (see also Shafir, Simonson, & Tversky, 1993) argues that people like to have reasons to justify their decisions. Spot A is fairly bland, whereas Spot B has clear positive and clear negative aspects. Furthermore, the preference framing may direct people toward positive reasons, whereas the "cancel frame" may bias people toward negative properties. In short, there are more reasons to go to Spot B and more reasons not to go to Spot B, such that the total selections sum to 115% (67% plus 48%). It appears that the compatibility or match between the form of questions and the properties or components of choices affects selective attention to choice components (Tversky, Sattath, & Slovic, 1988, see also Chapman & Johnson, 1995).

Hsee, Loewenstein, Blount, and Bazerman (1999) review a number of other cases of preference reversals. They suggest that when options are evaluated individually (particularly when a person sees only one of the options) some attributes may be difficult to evaluate, and so people may not use them in an evaluation. For example, when evaluating a CD player, it may be obvious to people that being able to hold 20 discs at once is good, but it may not be clear whether a noise reduction value of .02% is good or bad. Thus, people in this case might focus primarily on the number of discs the player holds. In contrast, when two or more options are compared, people need to attend only to the relative goodness of values, and so it can be easier to evaluate all of the attributes. For example, while the absolute goodness of a noise reduction value of .02% is not known, it may be judged as better than a noise reduction value of .01% possessed by another model to which it is compared. As these examples demonstrate, reasoning processes and selective attention affect decisions. Again, expected utility theory comes up short.

Context Effects

One thing to notice about the expected utility model is that it assumes each option is evaluated individually without regard to the other options in the set. Despite this prediction, there are demonstrations that people's evaluation of one option is influenced by the presence of other options in the set. This phenomenon is called a context effect, because the context (i.e., the other options in the set) are affecting how a particular option is evaluated. One particularly striking context effect is called the **attraction effect** for reasons that will become clear (Huber, Payne, & Puto, 1982; Simonson & Tversky, 1992).

The attraction effect occurs in situations like the one illustrated in Figure 14.1, which shows two dimensions that might describe a set of options. For example, if the options were brands of cars, the dimensions might be price and quality. Options A and B are set up in this example so that A is better than B along one dimension (in this case dimension 1) and B is better than A along the other dimension. In the set of options in the left panel, a third option (C) is added that is also better than option B along one dimension and worse along the other. Notice, however, that C is worse than A along both dimensions so that A *dominates* C. Given this choice set, people tend to select option A. Now, it could be that people just prefer option A in general. However, if the choice set in the right panel of Figure 14.1 is given to people, then people tend to select option B. Notice that this choice set consists of A, B, and D, where D is dominated by option B. Thus, the presence of a dominated option in a choice set tends to *attract* choices to the option that dominates it (hence the term *attraction effect*).

It should be obvious that context effects are a problem for expected utility theory: Preference between A and B should depend on their intrinsic properties, not

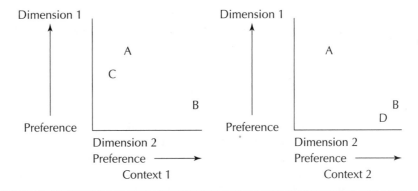

Figure 14.1   **Paradigm for evaluating context effects on choice**   A and B are available in both contexts and in Context 1 a third choice, C, is available, whereas in Context 2, the third choice is D. The direction of the arrow indicates increasing preference.

on which inferior alternative (e.g., C, D) happen to be present. One possibility is that the attraction effect occurs, because the presence of the dominated option provides a reason for selecting the dominating option.

Framing

Another direct way to demonstrate an inconsistent (and in that sense, irrational) component to human decision making is to show that the same information presented in different forms can lead to different decisions. Again, utility theory does not address these effects. Changes in decisions made as a function of different presentation forms are known as **framing effects.** Consider the following problem originated by Kahneman and Tversky (see Tversky & Kahneman, 1974; Kahneman, Slovic, & Tversky, 1982).

1. Imagine that the United States is preparing for the outbreak of an unusual disease, which is expected to kill 600 people. Two alternative programs have been proposed. Assume that the exact scientific estimate of the consequences of the programs is as follows:

    If Program A is adopted, 200 people will be saved.

    If Program B is adopted, there is a one-third probability that 600 people will be saved and a two-thirds probability that no people will be saved.

    Which of the two programs would you favor?

2. Imagine the identical situation with the following choices:

    If Program C is adopted, 400 people will die.

    If Program D is adopted, there is a one-third probability that nobody will die, and a two-thirds probability that 600 people will die.

    Which of the two programs would you favor?

In reading over the problem, you probably realized that program A and program C are identical, as are program B and program D. On logical grounds, then, and according to expected utility theory, people who prefer program A to program B ought to prefer program C to program D. Usually this problem is presented to two groups of subjects, one of which is shown the first phrasing, and the other of which is shown the second phrasing. The typical result is that people prefer program A over B, and program D over C. Deaths seem to loom larger in program C than in program A. We have presented this problem to different groups of medical school students, and they show this same pattern of results, but they show a higher overall willingness to gamble (select programs B and D). It is not clear how to interpret this willingness to take a risk, but we prefer to think of it as a sign that idealism is not dead and that these students want to save everyone.

Framing effects can be important. McNeil, Pauker, Cox, and Tversky (1982) found that both physicians and patients varied their ratings of how preferable different treatments were as a function of whether they were described in terms of probability of living versus probability of dying. Obviously, this factor is a problem if we want decisions to be based on objective properties of choices rather than on how we talk about them. In facing situations in which framing effects are likely to be present, a good strategy may be to try to develop multiple frames. If these frames suggest different choices, then at least one is aware of the fact that framing effects are operating.

Another version of the framing effect can be seen in the way people treat **sunk costs.** A sunk cost is some resource (e.g., money or time) that has already been spent pursuing a goal. Imagine you are watching a play. The money you spent for the ticket is a sunk cost, because it has already been spent and cannot be retrieved. For example, if you paid $10, that $10 is gone. If you paid $50, that $50 is gone. Now suppose that the play is lousy. Does whether you walk out of the play at intermission and skip the second act depend on whether you paid $10 or $50 for the play? Logically, it should not. After all, the money has already been spent, and cannot be gotten back. The only thing that should matter in your decision is how you would like to spend the next hour of your life.

Despite the fact that the sunk costs should not matter in decisions, they often do. If you paid $50 for a ticket rather than $10, you are probably more likely to stay. As another example, imagine the following situation (taken from Thaler, 1980): "A man joins a tennis club and pays a $300 yearly membership fee. After two weeks of playing he develops tennis elbow. He continues to play (in pain) saying 'I don't want to waste the $300.'" Note that the man probably would not have played if given a free membership. The point is that our ideas about sinking resources into choices seem to influence our future choices in ways that, objectively speaking, do not appear to be very logical. Sunk costs should not influence decisions about the future. If the man would rather not be playing tennis in pain, he should stop.

If people ignore sunk costs, are they really making better decisions? To test this possibility, Larrick, Nisbett, and Morgan (1993) surveyed college faculty in economics, biology, and the humanities, and asked them questions about the degree to which their own decisions would be affected by sunk costs. For example, they were asked whether they often abandon projects that do not seem to be working out but they have spent a lot of time on. They found that the degree to which people were able to ignore sunk costs was positively correlated with their salary, which is one objective indicator of their professional success. Thus, it seems that people should ignore sunk costs, although they often do not.

While it is often important to ignore sunk costs, there may be many cases in which persistence in a task is adaptive. For example, it is important to keep working at tasks that involve initial modest negative outcomes followed by strongly positive outcomes (e.g., starting out completely incompetent at tennis and then developing skill). Indeed, Heath (1995) has identified situations in which people show the opposite of sunk costs and abandon options prematurely. As he demonstrates, it is often difficult to gain access to information that would dictate the right decision (will I get better at tennis or won't I?). In addition, Tan and Yates (1995) describe some business situations in which persisting in a project can help recoup some of the previous investment.

Finally, evidence suggests that lower animals (like fish and birds) and human children do not attend to sunk costs when making decisions. Arkes and Ayton (1999) review animal studies demonstrating that the strength of a response by an animal is typically proportional to the future value of the investment they are protecting rather than to the effort already expended. Thus, it seems that evolution led lower animals to act more normatively than adult humans. Arkes and Ayton suggest that people's tendency to use rules such as "waste not want not" may lead them to attend to sunk costs too heavily. In support of this explanation, Arkes and Ayton describe studies showing that young children (who are probably less likely than adults to know rules like "waste not want not") are unlikely to attend to sunk costs when making decisions.

Summary

The various phenomena examined in this section show that people's choices are often inconsistent in a way that cannot be handled by expected utility theory. Perhaps the key problem for utility theory is that it assumes that people have subjective values or utilities for options that do not vary across contexts. The theory is silent about the psychological processes that go into creating these values or utilities. We turn now to a pair of theories that are more psychologically motivated. These theories attempt to address the phenomena we have just been considering.

Prospect Theory

The appeal of expected utility theory is that it provides a fairly simple account of how people evaluate options and make choices. Thus, rather than dispensing with expected utility theory altogether, it would be nice to be able to modify it in a way that makes it more compatible with psychological data. Kahneman and Tversky (1979) took just this approach in developing a descriptive theory of human decision called **prospect theory.** Prospect theory aims to account for the nonnormative aspects of decision making that caused problems for expected utility theory, while still maintaining the basic framework of expected utility theory.

Recall that expected utility theory evaluates options by finding the utility of each possible outcome from an option, and then multiplies this utility by the probability that the outcome will occur. The evaluation of an option is just the sum of these weighted outcome utilities. Prospect theory makes two key adjustments to this theory. First, the utility of each outcome is evaluated relative to a reference point rather than with respect to its absolute utility. This assumption is made to help account for framing effects. Framing effects can be interpreted as affecting the reference point. Consider again the example of the disease expected to kill 600 people. Programs A and B take the anticipated loss of 600 people as the reference point. Subjects are reluctant to give up saving 200 lives for sure to gamble for the chance to save 600 lives. For programs C and D, the current situation is provided as the reference point. Subjects apparently see the loss of 400 lives as not too different from the loss of 600 lives and so appear willing to gamble on the chance that no one will die.

The second major change is that utilities are not multiplied by objective probabilities (as assumed by expected utility theory) but rather by a distorted "psychological probability" that Kahneman and Tversky call the π (pi) function. Figure 14.2 illustrates this function (p refers to objective probability, and π refers to the weight associated with a given probability). According to this function, very low and very high probabilities are overweighted relative to intermediate probabilities. To see this, note that the middle part of the function is bowed so that the π value associated with a probability of .80 is more than twice as large as the π value associated with a probability of .40. The π function can account for the Allais paradox discussed earlier, because objective probabilities cannot simply be broken down into additive constituents. That is, the π value associated with a probability of 1.0 is greater than the sum of the π value for probability .11 plus the π value for probability .89. In brief, prospect theory handles certainty effects by assuming a π function that departs from

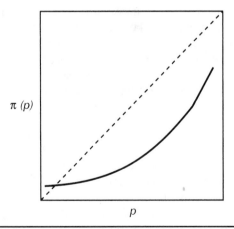

| **Figure 14.2** | π, the weight applied to the utility of each outcome, as a function of p, the probability of the outcome, according to Prospect theory. |

Source: Kahneman & Tversky, 1979.

objective probabilities and it addresses at least some framing effects by the idea that reference points can be altered by how a problem is described.

Regret Theory

Another way to address certainty effects is to describe decision situations in terms of anticipated reactions to various outcomes. For example, a reason for preferring choice 7 to choice 8 in the Allais paradox is that one may focus on the 1% chance of obtaining nothing for choice 8 and imagine how miserable one might feel about not getting $1,000 that one could have had for sure. **Regret theory** suggests that we overweight anticipated feelings of regret when the difference between outcomes is large (Bell, 1982; Loomes & Sugden, 1982).

A clever observation in support of regret theory comes from an experiment by Loomes (1987). Subjects were given choices like those in Table 14.1. Participants were told that a ticket had been randomly selected from a set of tickets numbered from 1 to 24. They were given a choice between options A and B and between options C and D. The amount won would depend on the ticket selected. Options A and C are identical, and options B and D both offer a 50% chance to win $16.

Despite the parallels between the two sets of options, people choose A slightly more often than B, and D more often than C. According to regret theory, option A might be preferred because the regret associated with drawing a ticket number between 1 and 9 approximately offsets the regret associated with a ticket number between 10 and 21. But for options C and D, the major regret factor involves the possible drawing of ticket numbers 10 through 12, which would favor option D (the difference between $24 and $16 for ticket numbers 1 through 9 would produce only modest regret). This observation is exactly as predicted by regret theory.

Table 14.1   **Two Sets of Options With Identical Probabilities and Outcomes but With Different Possibilities for Regret***

	Ticket Number		
Option	**1–9**	**10–21**	**22–24**
A	$24	$ 0	$ 0
B	$ 0	$16	$ 0

	Ticket Number		
Option	**1–9**	**10–12**	**13–24**
C	$24	$ 0	$ 0
D	$16	$16	$ 0

*For simplicity, we have changed the monetary units from pounds to dollars.

Source: Loomes, 1987.

AN APPLICATION
When More Is Less

It seems obvious that people prefer to minimize negative or undesirable experiences or outcomes. Indeed, it may seem that this has to be true by the very definition of *undesirable*. Surprisingly, however, there is an exception to this rule involving unpleasant events that unfold over time. In one study by Kahneman, Fredrickson, Schreiber, and Redelmeier (1993), participants were first exposed to two aversive experiences: (1) immersing one hand in 14°C water for 60 seconds and (2) immersing the other hand in 14°C water for 60 seconds followed by 30 seconds more while the temperature was gradually raised to 15°C (still painful but distinctly less so for most participants). When given a choice of which event to repeat, 69% chose the second, longer trial. In a sense, more pain was preferred to less. Apparently the improvement in temperature in the final 30 seconds made the over-all evaluation of the second experience more positive. This demonstrates that subjective experience cannot be simply described in terms of adding up the pleasantness of each of the components of that

(Continued)

Summary

Prospect theory and regret theory represent two interesting attempts to capture the irrationality of human decision making. In fact, one might argue that anticipated feelings (e.g., regret) are an important ingredient in a decision-making situation and that these reactions must be included in the evaluation of utilities and probabilities. (For interesting discussions of this issue, see Gilovich and Medvec, 1995, and Chapters 16 and 17 of Baron, 1988.) We now turn to another important aspect of decision making: how decisions are affected by the context of events in time.

Decision Making Over Time

Many decisions people face have a temporal component to them. For example, a person may choose between taking a job with a certain salary now or going back to school in hopes of getting a higher-paying job two years from now. Research on time and decision making shows many of the same sorts of anomalies that we saw earlier with choices involving probabilities (Prelec & Loewenstein, 1991). For example, people who prefer receiving $20 immediately to receiving $30 a month from now are likely to prefer $30 in 13 months to $20 in 12 months (we just added

AN APPLICATION
When More Is Less *(Continued)*

experience. Kahneman et al. argue that memory for unpleasant experiences is determined primarily by the peak unpleasantness and the final moments of the experience.

These observations are also of practical significance. Memory of a painful medical treatment is likely to be less negative if relief from the pain is gradual than if relief is abrupt. Redelmeier and Kahneman (1996) performed a study with patients who underwent an unpleasant rectal colonoscopy examination that was either terminated normally and abruptly (this was the Control group) or terminated by a more gradual withdrawal of the probe (the Experimental group). Patients rated their experienced pain both during the procedure and retrospectively. The Experimental group judged the procedure as less unpleasant than the Control group. These results may have important practical applications. Memory for a medical treatment can affect patient morale and likelihood of following treatment recommendations.

a year to each choice). Note that after those 12 months have passed, they will be back in the first situation, but committed to waiting a month for $30 rather than getting $20 immediately.

Loewenstein and Prelec (1993) have also shown distinctive framing effects involving options unfolding over time. Normally, people prefer valuable outcomes sooner rather than later, but they also prefer outcomes to improve over time. This leads to some striking context effects. For example, Loewenstein and Prelec found that people showed the following pattern of preferences:

1. They strongly prefer a free dinner at a fancy French restaurant to a free dinner at a fancy Greek restaurant.

2. They strongly prefer dinner at the French restaurant in one month rather than in two months.

Now imagine the following pair of options:

3. Free dinner at a French restaurant in one month and at a Greek restaurant in two months.

4. Free dinner at a Greek restaurant in one month and at a French restaurant in two months.

From the first two preferences, we should predict that people would prefer option 3 to option 4. The only way to avoid this prediction is to argue that the preference for a Greek restaurant in one month versus two months is greater than the known, strong preference for a French restaurant in one month rather than two. Instead, people generally choose to eat at the Greek restaurant first (preferring outcomes that improve over time).

Summary

We have covered a number of observations and phenomena, so let's take a minute to see where we are. The idea that people's decision making always optimizes either objective or subjective utility is simply incorrect. In fact, people's decision making cannot even be said to be rational, if we use criteria such as consistency. However, to conclude from these observations that people are simply bad decision makers would be to miss the point, in our opinion. As we stressed earlier, the computational costs of picking the very best alternative are prohibitive, and there is every reason to expect that human decision making is guided by heuristics and strategies that are generally effective but not infallible. These strategies may be embedded in contexts (e.g., I don't know exactly how much I like A, but it's certainly better than B) and, therefore, the inconsistencies associated with context effects should not come as a surprise. Even if our single-minded goal is to improve decision making, we need to analyze how people do it rather than simply pointing to human shortcomings. Prospect theory and regret theory are important steps in the right direction. In the remainder of this chapter, we review research aimed at understanding the psychological dimensions associated with decision making. We begin by a further look at strategies people use to cope with complex decision-making tasks.

DEALING WITH COMPLEXITY

Imagine that Leigh has just received her PhD in clinical psychology and must decide where to set up her practice. Obviously she has many, many choices available, and for each choice there is a wealth of potentially important information she might gather (e.g., cost of living, quality of schools, number of other clinicians practicing, cultural events available, malpractice insurance costs, types of restaurants, access to recreation, and so on). She would need several lifetimes to completely evaluate all the choices, so some shortcuts or strategies must be employed to make the decision manageable. There are two aspects to this problem. Leigh must decide how much information to gather and then how to combine this information to make a choice. Several strategies have been identified for dealing with this sort of information-rich situation.

Strategies for Dealing With Complexity

Satisficing

Herbert Simon (1957) has argued that people and organizations often abandon the goal of making the optimal choice in favor of one that is satisfactory. The idea is to search through a set of alternatives until a satisfactory one is found. A related idea is to sample a set of n alternatives and pick the best one, provided that at least one is satisfactory. For example, a company hiring a secretary would not examine the complete pool of potential employees but might set up interviews for eight candidates and pick the best of these. This **satisficing** strategy implies a very strong sensitivity to the exact sampling procedure, such as which factors are used to reduce the pool. Getting into the pool of n alternatives is critically important and for satisficing, the exact order of considering choices is crucial.

Elimination by Aspects

The **elimination by aspects** procedure focuses not on the overall desirability of choices but rather on the individual aspects or components (A. Tversky, 1972). The idea is that some aspect is selected and all alternatives that fail to meet some criterion with respect to this aspect are eliminated. Then a new aspect is picked, and further unsatisfactory alternatives are eliminated until one is left with a single choice. For example, Leigh might decide first to live in the Midwest and eliminate from consideration all alternatives that are not in the Midwest. Next she might choose to locate within 100 miles of a university, and then to require a city with a population of between 100,000 and 300,000 and so on, until either just one alternative remains or until the choice set is small enough to be examined in detail. Elimination by aspects is also nonoptimal in that it depends on the order in which various aspects are considered. An optimal decision rule would pick the "best" choice regardless of order. (Of course, much more processing effort would be needed to determine the best choice.)

Elimination by aspects and satisficing are two useful strategies for reducing a wealth of information. Just how useful are they? The perspective in the next section suggests that they can be very effective.

Adaptive Decision Making

There may be situations in which the choice set is small and the amount of relevant information concerning each alternative is modest. In this case it would be sensible for people to examine each alternative fully and weight each aspect by its (psychological) importance, as expected utility theory would prescribe.

There is evidence that people adjust their decision-making strategies in an adaptive manner. Payne, Bettman, and Johnson (1988, 1993) combined computer simulation with experimental investigations to demonstrate this point. They first ran simulations of different decision procedures under various time constraints. That is, they assumed that each step in a decision procedure would take one unit of time and then cut off the decision-making process after various time periods had passed. For example, when satisficing was simulated, if no satisfactory choice had been identified by the cutoff time, the program randomly selected from the remaining alternatives. In addition to heuristics such as elimination by aspects and satisficing, the Payne et al. simulations included normative decision procedures (e.g., examining all aspects of all alternatives and picking the one with the best overall weighted average). They found that under time pressure some of the nonnormative heuristics such as elimination by aspects actually performed much better than the normative procedure. The reason is that the normative procedure may take too long, and it does not take into account processing effort. Therefore, the simulation often had to pick at random when time ran out.

These simulations demonstrate that heuristics that are nonoptimal may be better than normative procedures when time limitations are significant. That is to say, normative models do not take into account the costs associated with gathering and evaluating information. Where time costs are critical, normative models may be inappropriate.

Payne et al. (1988) went on to conduct experiments with human subjects in which they varied the complexity of the choice task and time pressure. They found that people adjusted their decision procedures in an adaptive manner. When there was little time pressure and the decision task was not overly complex, strategies shifted in the direction of normative procedures. Under time pressure in complex environments, strategies shifted toward simplifying heuristics (see also Payne, 1976, 1982; Payne, Bettman, & Johnson, 1992). These observations provide an appreciation of some of the positive aspects of heuristics.

In the next section, we take a more extensive look at the use of heuristics in judgment and decision making. Although the examples reveal systematic biases and misperceptions, bear in mind that, for the most part, they represent adaptive responses to computational complexity.

FURTHER HEURISTICS AND BIASES

Judgment heuristics are easy or natural ways of thinking that are very often useful and powerful. Because they are shortcuts, however, they represent oversimplifications and, consequently, may lead to systematic biases or misperceptions. In the last section, we described strategies for dealing with complex information that constituted effective heuristics. In this section we describe strategies for generating and evaluating information used in judgments as well as heuristics for monitoring the decision-making process itself.

An important aspect of **cognitive heuristics** or biases is that they are very strong in two senses: (1) They are used by experts in technical areas such as medicine, as well as by novices, and (2) they are difficult to overcome. Cognitive heuristics are two-sided. They can be both very effective in some cases and very misleading in others. We shall focus on the biases associated with cognitive heuristics, as most heuristics do not come equipped with warning labels. Bear in mind, however, that in general these strategies are efficient and effective, especially in relation to the complexity of judgment and decision-making tasks. Still, the consequences in terms of systematic biases must be taken seriously.

Research over the last two decades has led to a major shift in our thinking about human bias. The earlier view was that human thought could be neatly partitioned into a logical, rational component and an irrational, blind, emotion-laden component, the latter giving rise to certain human shortcomings such as racial prejudice. Although we still do not understand the role of emotion in cognition, it has become increasingly clear that normal cognitive processes frequently give rise to nonrational by-products that are associated with systematic misperceptions of other individuals and groups. In some respects, this newer view is more sobering than the earlier one because it suggests that human rationality is not segregated from processes that lead to cognitive biases.

Many of the examples that follow are based on the pioneering work of Kahneman and Tversky (e.g., A. Tversky & Kahneman, 1974; Kahneman, Slovic, & Tversky, 1982). As we noted earlier, initial work on decision making or judgment in uncertain situations was based on determining what the optimal decision-making procedure would be in a given situation, but it soon became clear that people typically do not perform optimally (Edwards, Lindman, & Savage, 1963; see Fischhoff, 1988; Hogarth, 1990, for more recent reviews). Kahneman and Tversky demonstrated that many violations of what would be rationally or optimally correct can be traced to the use of cognitive heuristics.

Availability Heuristic

The **availability heuristic** refers to a tendency to form a judgment on the basis of what is readily brought to mind. For example, a person who is asked whether there are more English words that begin with the letter *t* or the letter *k* might try to think of words that begin with each of these letters. Since a person probably can think of more words beginning with *t*, he or she would (correctly) conclude that *t* is more frequent than *k* as the first letter of English words. So far, so good.

As long as the retrieval process is unbiased, the availability heuristic works quite well. Of course, anything that biases the retrieval process may lead to incorrect judgments. Consider the following experiment: We ask different groups of subjects to judge how many English words end with either this pattern: _n_, or this pattern: *ing*. Objectively, the answer has to be greater in the first case because the first pattern includes the second pattern as a special case. Then again, the group shown the first pattern may not think of the *ing* ending, which the other group is given. In fact, groups of subjects give higher estimates for the second pattern than the first. One recent demonstration produced a median estimate of 125 words fitting the first pattern and a median estimate of 880 words for the second pattern.

AN ENIGMA
The Role of Emotions in Decision Making

When it comes to decision making do emotions just get in the way? Or are emotions indispensable to good decision making? To address these sorts of questions, we need to know much more about the role of emotions in decision making. From one perspective, emotional reactions lead to impulsiveness and get in the way of good decisions. This issue is often addressed in the context of individuals who can satisfy an immediate goal (e.g., going out to have fun with friends) only at the cost of a long-term goal (e.g., getting an A in a course where there is a major exam the next day). On this view emotions create desires that may lead us to yield to temptation. There has been a considerable amount of research studying variables that determine how well people can delay immediate gratification in favor of larger long-time goals (e.g., see Metcalfe & Mischel, 1999, for a recent review and analysis). Related research draws on a distinction between a *want self* and a *should self* and studies their interplay in decision making (Bazerman, Tenbrunsel, & Wade-Benzoni, 1998; Crowe & Higgins, 1997; see also Loewenstein, 1996).

But there are other perspectives on emotions. In a provocative book Frank (1988) argues that "passions" serve an important function in decision making contexts, precisely because emotions do not constitute a *rational* calculation of self-interest. He gives the example of a person who is upset that the person next door lets his dogs wander into neighboring yards and doesn't clean up the "messes" his dog leaves. The angry person threatens

(Continued)

Many factors can influence the accessibility of information and consequently influence judgments. Let's look at one of them in detail.

"Solo" or Token Members

One robust finding from memory research is that if one word in a list of words to be remembered is different from the others in some way (e.g., an animal name in a list of plant names), that word is much more likely to be remembered than any other word. This is known as the *Von Restorff effect* (after its original investigator).

Consider the situation of a black person in an otherwise all-white group or a female in an otherwise all-male group. They will be distinctive in that group context. Taylor, Fiske, Etcoff, and Ruderman (1978) showed that the perception of a group member is strongly influenced by the member's status as a solo. The subjects in their experiments listened to a tape recording of a group discussion. As the tape was played,

AN ENIGMA
The Role of Emotions in Decision Making *(Continued)*

to take the neighbor to court unless he controls his dog. The offending neighbor could reasonably assume that a rational person would analyze the costs and benefits of going though a court action and quickly realize that it would involve too much time and trouble to pursue a legal remedy. Therefore, he could assume that he could continue to let his dog wander without needing to clean up after it. But, Frank reminds us, the person is very angry, so angry that he might ignore personal costs in order to punish the offender. Therefore, the neighbor might well decide that he had better keep his dog under control. In this instance, the person's passionate reaction produces a better outcome than would have been expected from cold calculations.

Currently, there is a great deal of interest in specifying the various roles or functions of emotions in decision making (e.g., Busemeyer & Townsend, 1993; Isen, 1993; Peters & Slovic, 1996; Finucane, Alhakami, & Slovic, in press; Loewenstein & Mather, 1990; Luce, Bettman, & Payne, 1997). It seems likely that emotions will turn out to have both positive and negative properties just as cognitive heuristics have their pluses and minuses. We sum up our puzzle with a striking observation from studies of brain damage and decision making. Damasio (1994) reports that people with frontal lobe damage show seriously impaired decision making skills despite having normal IQ. Frontal lobe damage is associated with diminished emotional reactions and it appears that this leads to an inability to anticipate the negative aspects of risky decisions. This syndrome is as fascinating as it is tragic.

subjects were shown slides of the participant who presumably was speaking at the time. By using the same tape but varying the slides shown, Taylor et al. were able to change the assumed group composition while keeping the content of the discussion constant. For example, in one condition, the slides indicated that the discussion involved five whites and one black, and in another that the discussion involved three whites and three blacks. The observers then rated the group members on a number of scales.

These ratings showed that solo members were perceived as having been more active and influential during the discussion than the same stimulus person in the fully integrated group. Subjects also remembered more of what the solo person said. Ratings on evaluative dimensions were also more extreme for solo members, perhaps because distinctiveness in memory amplified any differences. If the rating was slightly negative in the fully integrated group, it became far more negative for the same stimulus person in the solo context. These results were as predicted. Based on the Von Restorff effect, we would expect better memory for what a person said when he or she was a solo, distinctive member of a group. The greater availability of any distinctive information about her or him should lead to more extreme ratings. These findings and others (see, e.g., Hamilton, 1976) suggest that people tend to systematically misperceive minorities, simply on the basis of the Von Restorff effect and the availability heuristic.

Representativeness Heuristic

The **representativeness heuristic** refers to a tendency to judge an event as likely if it "represents" the typical features of (or is similar in its essential properties to) its category. As a consequence, people may use similarity as a guideline in situations where, objectively, they should focus on probability.

Conjunction Fallacy

Using the representativeness heuristic can lead to systematic errors in judgment, as seen in what is known as the **conjunction fallacy.** Consider the following example:
Which of the following events is the most likely?

1. that a man is under 55 and has a heart attack

2. that a man has a heart attack

3. that a man smokes and has a heart attack

4. that a man is over 55 and has a heart attack

Many people might select the third or fourth choice as most likely because these alternatives seem to conform most closely to their ideas about typical heart attack victims. The correct answer is the second choice, as a moment's reflection will reveal. The reason is that the second alternative encompasses all the others; it includes heart attack victims both under and over 55, regardless of whether or not they smoke. More formally, the conjunction of probabilistic events (such as smoking, being over 55, or having a heart attack) cannot be more probable than any individual events. In short, people seem to use similarity to some prototypical example rather than probability as the basis for judgment (see Fiedler, 1988; Massaro, 1994; A. Tversky & Kahneman, 1983, for alternative perspectives on this phenomenon). This tendency is known as the conjunction fallacy, and Kahneman and Tversky argued that it is caused by people's tendency to use the representativeness heuristic.

Misconceptions of Chance

A key problem with the use of the representativeness heuristic is that random patterns will appear nonrandom and people may inappropriately attribute the apparent pattern to a cause. For example, people tend to think extremes are less likely to occur than they actually are. If a baseball player fails to get a hit 12 times in a row, people assume that he is in a "batting slump," even though it might be that the streak is simply due to chance factors. At the other extreme is the notion that a batter who has not had a hit in several at bats is somehow "due to get a hit," such that the probability of his getting a hit is much greater than normal. Although a string of failures at bat may demoralize a player or perhaps lead her or him to try harder, many probabilistic events, like the roll of dice, are not affected by previous success and failure. This idea that prior outcomes can influence the outcome of probabilistic events (like a coin toss or the roll of dice) is known as the **gambler's fallacy.** Because of this belief, a person who believes that the airline with the best safety record is "due for a crash" might make an unwise choice in picking an airline for a trip.

Anchoring and Adjustment

A common strategy in making estimates is to start with some initial estimate or anchor and then adjust it in light of new information to come up with an answer or final estimate. Again, this strategy is useful, but frequently people fail to make sufficiently large adjustments to appropriately overcome the influence of the initial anchoring. For example, in one study of **anchoring and adjustment** by Tversky and Kahneman (1974), two groups of high school students were asked to estimate within a few seconds the value of a numerical expression written on the board. One group estimated the product

$$1 \times 2 \times 3 \times 4 \times 5 \times 6 \times 7 \times 8$$

whereas the other group estimated the product

$$8 \times 7 \times 6 \times 5 \times 4 \times 3 \times 2 \times 1.$$

The initial numbers ought to act as an anchor and, therefore, Tversky and Kahneman predicted, the second group would come up with higher estimates. The median estimate for the first sequence was 512, whereas the corresponding estimate for the second group was 2,250. (The correct answer is 40,320.)

An important aspect of anchoring is that we may be influenced by initial anchors even when these anchors are generated by an arbitrary or biased source. This tendency is exploited by salespeople and auctioneers to influence people's willingness to pay higher prices for goods. An auctioneer who starts the bidding for a lamp by saying, "Who will give me $300?" may have no expectation of selling the lamp for $300 but may succeed in inserting a high anchor that will not be adjusted downward appropriately as the bidding proceeds.

Causal Schemas

Causal schema is a term used to refer to a tendency to expect predictions to be more accurate when they are presented in a way that is consistent with one's expectations about causes or notions about underlying stability. Consider the following two questions. Which would be more accurate:

1. Predicting a daughter's eye color from her mother's eye color or predicting a mother's eye color from her daughter's eye color?

2. Predicting scores on a short quiz from performance on a 10-hour exam or predicting scores on a 10-hour exam from scores on a short quiz?

People are very likely to indicate that the first prediction would be more accurate on each of the two questions. In fact, since both directions of prediction involve just a correlation, there is no basis for expecting any differences in predictability. Apparently this bias arises because, based on our understanding of genetics, we think of a mother as causing or directly influencing her daughter's eye color and, based on notions of stability, we think that a 10-hour exam would better predict quiz performance than vice versa. This bias may lead people to interpret correlations in ways consistent with prior expectations and fail to consider alternative possibilities, such as the idea that smoking does not cause cancer but rather that cancer causes the urge to smoke; of course, proper experiments can disentangle such correlations. A key aspect of causal schemas is that they can lead people to ignore other potentially relevant information (as we shall see later in this chapter).

Hindsight Bias

Hindsight bias refers to the tendency for people to think after the fact that they would have known something before the fact when, in actuality, they would not have. This problem seems intuitively plausible but one might wonder how it could be established experimentally. Again we will take an example from medicine, but the phenomenon appears to be quite general (see Fischhoff, 1982). Arkes, Wortmann, Saville, and Harkness (1981) gave the same medical history to five different groups of clinicians. The foresight group was asked to assign a probability estimate to each of four possible diagnoses. The four hindsight groups were asked to do the same thing but were told the diagnosis (each group was told that a different diagnosis was correct). Specifically, they were asked to disregard their knowledge of the correct diagnosis and give estimates only on the basis of other information presented. The hindsight groups that were told that the least likely diagnoses were correct (likelihood was determined by the judgments of the foresight group) then assigned probability estimates for these "correct" diagnoses that were 2 or 3 times higher than the probabilities given by the foresight group. That is, the hindsight groups were unable to disregard information about the correct diagnosis. This hindsight bias may lead to an inadequate appreciation of the original difficulty of a diagnosis.

Overconfidence

For reasons that are not entirely clear, both novices and experts appear to be more confident in their judgments than is objectively justifiable (see Lichtenstein, Fischhoff, & Phillips, 1982, for a review). Part of the problem may be hindsight bias, and part of the problem is that experts often do not receive feedback on their

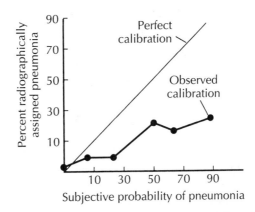

Figure 14.3   Relationship between physicians' subjective probability of pheumonia and the actual probability of pheumonia.

Source: Christensen-Szalanski & Bushyhead, 1981.

judgments (see, e.g., Einhorn & Hogarth, 1978) and therefore do not know when they are in error. Figure 14.3 is taken from a study by Christensen-Szalanski and Bushyhead (1981) that involved diagnosis of possible pneumonia at an outpatient clinic. In the study, physicians interviewed the patients and then estimated the probability that the patients had pneumonia. In all cases, regardless of the probability estimates, X-rays were given to determine radiographically whether a patient did have pneumonia.

As Figure 14.3 indicates, as the probability estimates increased, so also did the objective likelihood that the patients had pneumonia, indicating that the physicians were sensitive to the predictive value of different symptoms. However, subjective probabilities were far higher than objective probabilities. For example, when the physicians were 90% sure that pneumonia was present, there was less than a 30% chance that the diagnosis would be confirmed by the X rays. There has been, for obvious reasons, a fair amount of effort to figure out how to make expert judgments more accurate. Interestingly, among populations of experts, meteorologists' predictions of precipitation appear to be least susceptible to overconfidence effects (Murphy & Winkler, 1977). Meteorologists are directly trained to reason with probabilities, and they receive accurate feedback about their judgments (and they also have computer models to help them). As another way of adjusting for biased estimates, in the United Kingdom, the Electricity Board has a policy of doubling engineers' chronic underestimates of the time needed for production (Kidd, 1970).

Relativity of Judgment and Use of Norms

Kahneman and Miller (1986) have argued that judgments are often based on norms or standards that are recruited or retrieved by the events themselves. Consider the following scenario:

Two businesspeople, John and Jill, are sharing a cab to the airport, where they intend to take separate flights, each of which is scheduled to leave at 11:00 a.m. Traffic proves to be very heavy, and the cab arrives at 11:30 a.m. Both miss their flight, but Jill finds out that her flight left on time and John finds out that his flight left at 11:25 a.m. Which traveler will experience greater regret?

Most people judge that John, who missed his flight by 5 minutes, will be more upset. Given that the flights were scheduled to leave at the same time, that they shared the cab, and that they both missed their flight, clearly this judgment is based on more than outcomes alone. According to Kahneman and Miller, John is more upset than Jill because he can imagine more similar possible worlds (e.g., less traffic) in which he would have made the flight than can Jill.

The general idea is that people form judgments based on comparisons of alternative possible worlds where the possible worlds are based on imagined changes from the present world. Certain changes are easier to imagine than others, and judgments should tend to reflect influences of changeability or what Kahneman and Miller (1986) refer to as mutability.

What determines mutability? One factor is that information that is part of the background of a scenario may be less mutable than the aspects that are the focus of attention. This can lead to systematic biases. As Kahneman and Miller note, the idea that the actions of an individual who is in focus are mutable may help explain the well-established tendency for victims of violence to be assigned an unreasonable degree of responsibility for their fate (Lerner & Miller, 1978). Imagine that a victim took an unusual rather than a typical route on just the evening that he was robbed on the way home. The ready availability of an alternative scenario can lead to the victim's receiving a disproportionate responsibility for being robbed.

Summary

We have deliberately presented the strongest case for paying attention to heuristics and biases, because they are important and appear in many judgmental contexts. Heuristics are generally effective rules of thumb but sometimes they are applied where they should not be. Furthermore, being aware of these strategies provides the opportunity for improving decision making.

We end this section on a note of optimism. Hogarth (1981) points out that most judgment research has focused on discrete situations. He argues that many decision tasks are continuous and interactive, in which a person's initial decisions can be modified and refined on the basis of feedback. Therefore, it may often suffice to get the decision process headed roughly in the right direction rather than exactly on target. Although it is very important to keep in mind the limitations of various cognitive heuristics, there may be compensatory factors associated with the decision context that keep us from being led too far astray.

ARE THERE KINDS OF DECISIONS? _____

Much of the discussion so far has assumed that the various components of a decision are readily combined into an overall value or subjective utility. This seems almost logically necessary. Nonetheless, from another perspective there may be distinct *kinds* of decisions that would be difficult to understand in terms of utility theory. For example, Tenbrunsel and Messick (in press) presented research participants with a role-playing game involving businesses that could cooperate to control pollution, but where such controls would reduce profits. Surprisingly, they found that introducing small penalties for polluting actually produced *less* cooperation than a control condition that had no penalties. Tenbrunsel and Messick also asked participants how they interpreted the task. Without penalties, most people thought of the game as requiring a personal or ethical decision; with penalties, most people saw the game as involving a business decision. In short, decision making was more a function of how the game was interpreted than objective costs and benefits (see Larrick & Blount, 1997, for related evidence).

Fiske and Tetlock (1997) proposed that rules governing decisions and exchanges are a function of the kinds of social relationship involved. For example, parents who help their daughter move into a new apartment would not expect to be compensated (monetarily or otherwise). Violations of these rules of exchange are met with confusion or anger. It will not do to respond to a nice dinner in a restaurant by saying "Thank you, you must come to our house for dinner soon" or to respond to an equally nice dinner at a friend's house by saying, "Do you take credit cards?" Nor is the problem in the latter case simply one of introducing money—it would be equally bad to offer to mow your friend's lawn as a form of immediate reciprocation. The straightforward exchange of money for goods and services is appropriate mainly for business or market transactions where the relationship between buyer and seller does not go much beyond that role. The general point is that market pricing applies to markets but not everything is a simple market—in our culture it is perfectly acceptable to decide to sell cars and houses but we do not sell children or human body parts. In the next section we will examine evidence that even money is not treated as a homogenous thing.

Mental Accounting

Consider the following scenario taken from Thaler and Johnson (1990, p. 643):

> Imagine that you are attending a vacation in Las Vegas, and you walk into a casino. While passing the slot machines, you put a quarter into a slot machine and, surprisingly, you win $100. Now what? Will your gambling behavior for the rest of the evening be altered? Might you make a few more wagers, even if you usually abstain? Suppose you had $100 stolen from your wallet while taking a swim at the pool? How will that alter your behavior? Are either of these events equivalent to discovering, just before

A DEBATE
Is Rational Choice Theory the Correct Standard?

Psychological research on decision making has benefited greatly from utility theory, if only in showing that people consistently depart from optimality. This theory, with its idea that people act to maximize utility, provides a normative standard or benchmark that is often useful in analyzing human choice behavior. Nonetheless, rational choice theory is being increasingly criticized as inadequate.

The criticisms take several forms. One is that it is not a good description of what people actually do. Another is that it may not be a good description of what people are even trying to do (e.g., Fiske & Tetlock, 1997; Messick, 1999). Consider, for example, studies on what is known as the ultimatum game (e.g., Roth, 1991). Participants are paired off and one player is allowed to propose the allocation of some resource (e.g., $10) and the other player must accept or reject it. If the proposal is accepted, then both players get the proposed split; if the proposal is rejected, neither player gets anything. Rational choice theory would suggest that the second player faces an easy choice—he or she should accept any nonnegative offers because it is better than nothing. To the contrary, players tend to reject proposals involving unequal distributions on the grounds that the proposed split is not fair. And the most common proposal is for an equal split, even though the participants do not know each other and are unlikely

(Continued)

you entered the casino, that a stock in which you own 100 shares has gone up (or down) one dollar a share that day?

The answer suggested by research (e.g., Thaler, 1985; Thaler & Johnson, 1990; Hirst, Joyce, & Schadewald, 1994) is that your behavior would vary as a function of the above events, even though each of them decreased or increased your wealth by an identical amount. For example, the fact that your stock is worth $100 more will be unlikely to affect your gambling, but winning $100 with your first quarter in the slot machine might lead you to bet more (because you are "playing with the house money"). In a similar way people typically do not spend money they receive as a gift in the same way that they spend money they have earned. **Mental accounting** refers to the fact that people tend to treat financial resources as falling into distinct accounts or categories that are not completely interchangeable. Thaler (1985) suggests that people form these accounts as a means of self-control. For

A DEBATE

Is Rational Choice Theory the Correct Standard? *(Continued)*

to interact again in the future. Instead of focusing on maximizing utility, participants appear to be motivated by considerations of fairness.

Yet another reason to question rational choice theory is that people may behave "better than rational." Consider resource dilemmas that have been said to lead to the "tragedy of the commons" (Hardin, 1968). Imagine a community of sheep herders whose sheep graze on a common ground. If each herder restrains the number of sheep feeding on the commons, then the commons will not become exhausted from overgrazing. Note, however, that no individual herder can protect the commons from overgrazing because any individual restraint can be outweighed by greediness on the part of other herders. Furthermore, each sheep only does a small part of the damage, and a herder who adds one more sheep gains more than he loses. In this situation rational choice theory predicts that each herder should act in his own interest with the consequence being a race to exhaust the resource. Nonetheless, both laboratory studies and field studies conducted around the world show that often what emerges is cooperation that conserves the resource (e.g., Ostrom, 1998). In short, the outcome is "better than rational." Findings such as these suggest that a different framework may be needed, especially in the case of collective action. Of course, theories rarely die out of their own accord—they hang on until they are replaced by better theories.

example, a couple might borrow money at a high interest rate to buy a car, even when they have a savings account that they could use to pay cash for it, because they know they have to make the loan payments and they are not so sure they would have the self-discipline to "repay" their savings account with the same regularity. Mental accounting violates standard economic theory, which treats money just as money.

Mental accounting is also evident in examinations of how people use money outside the lab (Zelizer, 1994). Money is a method that governments use to establish a common system of value across situations. Yet people go to great lengths to distinguish forms of money (often physically) in order to differentiate functions of money. For example, when money is given as a gift, it is often given in a greeting card, or with a new bill. That helps distinguish a gift from charity or from wages. Furthermore, people treat gift money differently from wages, and often spend it on luxuries rather than on necessities (Henderson & Peterson, 1992).

Summary

The research reviewed in this section suggests that there may be distinct kinds of decisions. People may treat things as falling into distinct categories rather than lumping all valued things into a single mental account. As we have seen, these categorization or mental accounting principles affect decision making and therefore it is important to understand them.

Summary

In this chapter, we started by pointing out that psychological research on decision making has its roots in economic models. Whereas economic models predict that humans are rational decision makers, the evidence suggests that people's choices depart systematically from optimal choices because they use heuristics and strategies that make good choices most of the time. People's judgments are also susceptible to framing and other sorts of context effects that demonstrate that human decision making is far from optimal.

As we suggested at the beginning of this chapter, the shortcomings of human decision making have come as big news and have had a major impact in economics and in a variety of applied areas ranging from stock market forecasting to medical decision making. Cognitive biases can produce serious errors. Normative models of decision making are not, in general, very accurate models of human choice behavior. The current challenge is to formulate models of decision making that are more realistic and describe decision making processes as they occur, including the influence of goals, emotions, mental accounts, and the like.

Optimality is a very tough standard, given the complexities of decision making. Although we may be accused of taking too charitable a view, how effective and efficient human decision-making strategies often prove to be is surprising to us. If we consider computational costs and time limitations, as we have seen, heuristics may outperform normative strategies because the "correct" or optimal strategies take too long to compute. In short, human decision processes can be seen as adaptive, even if they are not flawless.

Key Terms

Allais paradox

anchoring and adjustment

attraction effect

availability heuristic

bounded rationality

certainty effect

cognitive heuristics

conjunction fallacy

elimination by aspects

expected utility

expected value

framing effects

gambler's fallacy

hindsight bias

mental accounting	regret theory
law of contradiction	representativeness heuristic
preference reversals	satisficing
prospect theory	sunk costs
rational model	transitivity

Recommended Readings _____

Decision making is an important and intriguing subject. Even though one may understand framing effects, they may remain compelling. For a review and survey of work on judgment heuristics, see the edited volume by Kahneman et al. (1982), Fischhoff's (1988) article, and the textbooks by Dawes (1988), Baron (1988), and Bazerman (1998). Payne, Bettman, and Johnson (1993) review a substantial body of work on the adaptive-decision-maker view of choice. For work on the interesting question of cross-cultural differences in decision making see Weber and Hsee (1999) and Yates, Lee and Shinotsuka (1996).

A more salient reason to be intrigued by decision-making research is that it raises questions about human rationality. To get a flavor for the different perspectives on this issue, see Simon (1957), Hogarth (1981), L. J. Cohen's (1981) article and the associated commentaries, Cosmides and Tooby (1994), Gigerenzer and Hoffrage (1995), and Kahneman and Tversky (1996). Readers interested in clinical judgment should look at Meehl (1954), Dawes and Corrigan (1974), and Dawes (1988). An interesting sidelight on the role of reasons in choice is some evidence by Tim Wilson and his associates suggesting that providing justifications can interfere with people's ability to know what their preferences are (e.g., Wilson, Dunn, Kraft, & Lisle, 1989; Wilson & Schooler, 1991).

Pennington and Hastie (1988) have argued that complex decision making often involves the construction of explanations. They have gathered clear empirical support that these explanations play a direct or causal role in decision making. Finally, W. M. Goldstein and Weber (1995) offer a provocative critique of decision-making studies involving just probabilities and amounts of money, and they argue that decision processes may be content- and domain-specific. Their paper appears in an edited book that attempts to integrate decision-making research with other sub-areas of cognition (Busemeyer, Hastie, & Medin, 1995; see also Baron & Spranca, 1997, and Fiske & Tetlock, 1997). For a review paper that develops these and related arguments see Medin and Bazerman (1999).

GLOSSARY

ad hoc categories   categories that are spontaneously created, typically in the service of some goal (e.g., things to take on a camping trip).

affirming the consequent   logical error in reasoning; assuming that if the consequent is true, then the premise must be true (that "P implies Q" and "Q" leading to the conclusion "P").

algorithm   a systematic procedure that is guaranteed to lead to a correct solution to a problem.

algorithmic level   level of analysis that describes in a general way what computational steps are needed and what representations are used.

Allais paradox   an example of the certainty effect in which adding the same amount to two choices reverses the preference.

analog representation   a representation that mimics or simulates the structure of its referent in a more or less direct manner. In the case of spatial representations, continuous spatial information and spatial relationships might be the relevant structure.

analogical reasoning   reasoning by finding corresponding aspects (often relations) of two domains.

anchoring and adjustment   judgment strategy of starting with some initial estimate or anchor and then adjusting the estimate in light of new information.

anterograde amnesia   an inability to learn new information after some trauma.

artificial intelligence   the science of writing computer programs to do intelligent things.

attentional blink   a phenomenon in which people are not aware of stimuli presented for a brief period after making a response.

attraction effect   a context effect in decision making in which adding an inferior alternative to a choice set increases choices to the most similar alternative.

auditory theory   theory that speech perception follows general principles of auditory perception (speech is not special).

automaticity   the development of processes that can be run off without the use of attentional resources.

autoshaping   a procedure in an operant learning situation in which a signal (a key lighting) is paired with the presentation of reward (as in a classical conditioning situation) and the organism "learns" a response (e.g., key pecking, in the case of pigeons) even though none is required.

availability heuristic   a judgment strategy in which probability judgments are based on the readiness with which examples are brought to mind.

base rate   the relative frequency of some event or outcome in some general population of events.

basic level   intermediate level of categorization that appears to be psychologically privileged in that it is the first one learned, shows cross-cultural consistency, and is the natural level at which objects are named.

behaviorism   approach to research that focuses on behavior as the subject matter of psychology.

blocking   failure to learn about the association between a stimulus and some outcome because of the presence of some other stimulus that already predicts or has been associated with that outcome.

bottleneck model   theory of attention in which the perceptual system selects one signal (or a small number) from many sources for further perceptual processing.

bottom-up processing   information processing that starts with low-level information (like the features of letters) and constructs higher-level units (like letters) from this low-level information.

bounded rationality   the idea of taking computational costs and limitations into account to determine what is rational.

Broca's aphasia   a disorder associated with cortical damage (to Broca's area) leading to impairments in speech production.

case-based reasoning   an artificial intelligence approach in which earlier cases (or instances) are retrieved and adapted to help solve the current problem.

categorical perception   the observation that continuous variations on a dimension relevant to a phonemic contrast are often perceived in a discrete (all-or-none) rather than a graded manner.

category   the set of entities or examples "picked out" by a concept.

category-specific deficits   refers to a brain damage where patients lose their ability to recognize and name examples of some kinds of categories (e.g., living kinds) but not others.

certainty effect   tendency for people to violate expected utility in the direction approaching sure gains and avoiding sure losses.

change blindness   A phenomenon in which people fail to notice large perceptual changes that occur in peripheral vision or that occur in successive views of a pair of pictures.

chunking   combining several pieces of information into a single unit or code.

chunks   units of organized information.

classical conditioning   a form of learning in which a hitherto neutral stimulus, the conditioned stimulus (CS), is paired with an unconditioned stimulus (US), regardless of what the animal does.

classical view   theory of conceptual structure that argues that concepts are based on defining features.

coarticulation   in speech production, the form in which a phoneme is produced varies as a function of the surrounding context of other phonemes being produced.

cognitive heuristics   reasoning strategies that are easy or natural shortcuts that often work well but sometimes introduce biases and misconceptions.

cognitive psychology   the research approach that views intelligent behavior within an information-processing framework and is characterized by a willingness to develop and evaluate ideas about internal mechanisms and procedures that mediate behavior.

cognitive science   the interdisciplinary approach to the study of the mind that includes artificial intelligence, cognitive psychology, linguistics, anthropology, and philosophy.

compensatory response model   theory of classical conditioning that argues that conditioned responses are adaptive and that the conditioned response will either be similar in form or opposite in form to the unconditioned response, depending on what is adaptive.

computational complexity   the observation that many cognitive procedures are impractical because of the time and effort needed to evaluate the very large number of alternative possibilities.

computational level   abstract level of analysis that tells what is being computed and why. In a sense it is a theory of competence.

concept   a mental representation of a category.

conceptual combination   the problem of understanding the meaning of novel concepts derived from combinations of simple concepts (e.g., paper bee).

conditioned response   the learned or acquired response to a conditioned stimulus.

conditioned stimulus   a previously neutral stimulus that comes to elicit a conditioned response through association within an unconditioned stimulus.

confirmation bias   tendency to seek out evidence that would support a hypothesis rather than evidence that might disconfirm it.

confounding factor   a factor that varies simultaneously with an independent variable. For example, when a new educational technique is introduced, improvements in learning may arise either because the technique is indeed more effective or because the new technique is novel and different from the usual routine. In this event, novelty would be a confounding factor.

conjunction fallacy   tendency to think the conjunction of two events is more likely than one or more of the individual events. It may arise when people use similarity to some prototypic situation rather than probability as the basis of judgment.

connection weights   in PDP models, the weights determining how much the activation of one unit affects the activation of another unit. These weights serve to encode long-term memories.

connectionist models   approach to cognitive modeling that typically views information as a pattern of activation over a network of interconnected cells.

consistent mapping procedure where the response associated with a stimulus is consistent across trials. This procedure leads to automaticity.

constraints natural assumptions or biases that favor some possibilities over others. For example, rats tend to associate illness with odors and tastes rather than with visual cues.

context effects the improvement (or decrement) in memory of having information occur with the same (or different) context.

conversational maxims principles or guidelines for cooperative communication.

correlation a measure of the extent to which two variables are related. The relation is not necessarily causal. Correlation coefficients can vary from 21.00 to 1.00 (.00 means the variables are unrelated), and the bigger the absolute correlation (the more it departs from zero, either positively or negatively), the stronger the relation.

creativity the cognitive activity leading to original and relevant solutions to a problem.

credit assignment the problem of identifying why some action succeeded or failed so that the learner can perform more successfully in the future.

critical period period in the development of an organism when it is particularly sensitive to environmental influences. Outside this critical period, learning may not take place at all.

declarative memory knowledge of factual information, including both episodic and semantic information, "knowing that."

deductive reasoning concerned with which beliefs are licensed or entailed by other beliefs by necessity or logic.

deep structure grouping of words that represents the basic meaning of a sentence.

deliberate practice intensive, effortful training activities designed to improve particular aspects of performance by repetition and successive refinement.

denying the antecedent reasoning error in which people incorrectly interpret "P implies Q" and "not P" as leading to the conclusion "not Q."

dependent variable the variable measured and recorded by the experimenter.

dichotic listening experiment listening to two unrelated messages played over headphones. This technique is often used in studies of selective attention.

dual-coding hypothesis the idea that pictures are remembered better than words because pictures are encoded both verbally and as images.

early selection theory of attention in which a signal is selected early in processing and unattended signals are lost and unavailable to the perceiver.

echoic memory auditory sensory storage buffer.

ecological validity approach with the ideal of developing theories that operate in realistic everyday situations. Some advocates of this approach would argue that artificial laboratory experiments are sometimes "ecologically invalid" because they fail to capture critical aspects of real-world situations.

Einstellung the rigid or mechanical application of a solution procedure to a problem.

elimination by aspects theory of choice behavior that suggests that successive criteria or aspects are considered and any choices not meeting a criterion are eliminated. This process continues until only one choice remains.

empiricism the idea that knowledge derives from experience.

encoding the initial processing of a stimulus that leads to a mental representation in memory.

encoding specificity effect retrieval depends on the extent to which the retrieval cue matches the information available at encoding.

episodic memory memory for autobiographical events, including the context (time, place, setting) in which they occurred.

exemplar models categorization models that assume that classification decisions for new examples are based on their similarity to specific, stored examples rather than similarity to a summary prototype.

expected utility idea that people maximize their subjective value or utility, which is equal to the subjective value of outcomes multiplied by their probability.

expected value   idea that says people maximize objective value which is equal to the value of outcomes multiplied by their probability of occurrence.

expert system   a computer system that is designed to simulate the reasoning of a particular expert. It consists of a knowledge base (including facts and heuristics) and an inference method for applying this knowledge.

explicit memory   uses of memory requiring the conscious recollection of an experience.

extinction   the weakening of response tendencies when reinforcement is withdrawn.

family resemblance   principle of category organization by which members of the category tend to share properties but there is no property or feature that every member has to have. Family resemblance categories are consistent with the probabilistic view.

feature integration theory   theory of attention that suggests that conjunctions or combinations of features can only be encoded in a serial manner, which requires attention.

features   separable, distinct components that are combined in various ways to create complex entities.

figure-ground relations   determining which parts of a scene form connected and cohesive objects and which parts are background.

fixed-action patterns   stereotyped, species-specific behaviors triggered by genetically preprogrammed releasing stimuli.

flashbulb memory   highly vivid, almost photograph-like, memory for the details of an event and the setting.

frame   structural component of a schema that provides relevant dimensions of information. See also schema.

framing effects   phenomenon in decision making, in which the same information presented in different forms can lead to different decisions.

free recall   a test of memory in which the subjects are asked to reproduce from memory as much of the presented material as possible.

functional fixedness   the tendency to see only the typical use of an object, rather than some new use that might help in solving a problem (i.e., being fixed on its usual function).

gambler's fallacy   tendency to think that prior events can influence the outcome of an independent probabilistic event (as when something is "due" to happen).

garden path sentence   sentence like "The horse raced past the barn fell" where we suddenly realize that we have been constructing the wrong interpretation of the sentence. These sentences make the point that comprehension proceeds "on line" rather than by taking in entire sentences before interpreting them.

geons   features in the form of three-dimensional shapes such as cylinders, cones, and wedges, which are assumed to be the constituents of objects in Biederman's theory of object recognition.

given-new strategy   principle of communication in which new information is presented only after a relevant context of old information is provided.

good continuation   the Gestalt principle that contours that vary smoothly along their course tend to be part of the same object.

government and binding theory   Chomsky's grammatical theory that aims to reduce differences between languages to variations in a small number of parameters. In this theory there is only one transformation, "move x," where x is a parameter that can vary across languages.

Gricean maxims   conversational maxims such as tell the truth, be informative, be relevant, and be clear.

habituation   a form of learning manifested in reduced response to repeated stimulation.

heuristic   a rule of thumb for problem solving or reasoning, which may lead to a correct answer but is not guaranteed to do so.

hierarchical model   a model of semantic knowledge in which knowledge about objects is stored in a hierarchy or ranking, with instances connected to their superordinates by is-a links.

hill climbing   a problem-solving heuristic in which one chooses whichever next step brings one closer to the goal.

hindsight bias   inflated estimate after the fact for how likely one would have been to know or predict something before the fact.

homeopathy   belief that causes and effects tend to be similar.

iconic memory   visual sensory storage buffer with large information capacity and brief duration.

ill-defined problem   a problem in which the givens, goals, or means of transforming the conditions are not clearly specified.

illusory correlation   a tendency to see relationships between two variables that are not objectively present in the data.

implementation level   level of analysis where the physical realization of an algorithm or procedure is instantiated.

implicit learning   learning complex information without expressible knowledge of what is learned.

implicit memory   uses of memory in which some previous experience can affect performance without any conscious recollection of the experience.

imprinting   a learned attachment that is formed at a particular period in life (the critical or sensitive period) and is difficult to reverse.

incidental learning   learning that takes place without any intent to learn. In memory research, it usually involves a test of memory in which subjects are not aware during study that they will be tested for their memory of the material.

incubation   in the traditional view of creativity, the time in which a problem is put aside and the solution is worked upon at an unconscious level.

independent variable   the factor that is varied by the experimenter.

induction   the use of inductive inferences or the process of reasoning from partial knowledge to more general situations. Inductive inferences are not logical truths, but they may often be true in experience.

inductive reasoning   concerned with which beliefs support or are supported by other beliefs.

information processing   approach to research that views cognition as involving the encoding, storage, and retrieval of information.

instrumental learning   a form of learning in which a reward is given only if the organism performs the instrumental response (e.g., key peck). What is learned is the relationship between the response and the reinforcer.

intelligent tutoring systems   computer systems that guide a student through the learning of some new information. The tutor keeps track of what the student knows and tries to increase this knowledge until it matches the expert knowledge of the material.

intentional forgetting   an experimental procedure in which subjects are sometimes signaled that they can forget the items presented so far on the list.

interactive activation   assumption typically associated with connectionist models that processing (e.g., in perception) depends on interactive influences at multiple levels of abstraction (e.g., feature, letter, word).

introspectionism   approach to cognition that focuses on the contents of consciousness as the subject matter of psychology.

intuitive physics   naive or intuitive theories about how the world works.

invariants   properties of the proximal (retinal) stimulus pattern that remain unchanged despite various transformations of the distal stimulus or object.

joint action   Any action, like communication or dancing a tango, that requires the coordinated effort of two or more people to be carried out.

late selection   a theory of attention that suggests that processing limitations arise primarily at late stages of processing when information is being integrated and decisions made.

law of contradiction   one criterion of rationality that states that reasoning processes that operate on the same evidence should not reach contradictory conclusions.

learner's model   in intelligent tutoring systems, the representation of what the learner is assumed to know at a given time. It is updated throughout the tutoring sessions.

learning   a relatively permanent change in behavior or knowledge as a result of experience.

learning-performance distinction   what is learned is not necessarily directly manifested in performance (contrary to some early theories of learning that equate the two).

levels of processing   the proposal that different encodings vary in how deeply the material is processed and that deeper processings lead to the material being better remembered. The memory is established as a by-product of the processing.

lexical decision task   An experimental technique in which a string of letters is presented (e.g., NURSE) and the participant must say whether the string forms a word.

linear separability   categories are linearly separable if some weighted additive combination of properties can be used to correctly classify examples.

links   in network models, the pointers designating the relation between two nodes, representing which ideas can access which other ideas.

Logic   a system of operators, facts, and schemas that allow conclusions to be drawn from a set of premises.

long-term memory   the term referring to the retention of information over long (i.e., more than 30 seconds) periods of time, with a large (unlimited?) capacity. Forgetting from long-term memory is usually thought to be due to retrieval failures caused by interference from other knowledge.

maintenance rehearsal   repeating by rote some information without any effort to develop meaningful associations to it. This is an effective way of holding information in short-term memory but is not very effective for later remembering.

mathematical models   models of cognition that can be cast into mathematical form and that often yield quantitative predictions about behavior.

McGurk effect   the phenomenon when visual information from articulatory movements and the acoustic speech signal are integrated to yield a unitary percept. For example, the articulation of /pa-pa/ coupled with the speech sound /na-na/ produces the percept /ma-ma/.

means-ends analysis   a problem-solving search heuristic in which one compares the current state to the goal state and then chooses the problem operator that will most reduce the difference.

memory decay hypothesis   an idea about the cause of forgetting, in which items that are not recalled or studied for a period of time tend simply to lose strength in memory as a result of an automatic process of decay.

memory span   the number of items (usually digits or words) that a person can immediately repeat back accurately. In adults, a typical memory span would be about seven items.

mental accounting   refers to people's tendency to assign financial resources to separate categories or budgets and to impose rules on exchanges between accounts. One idea is that these rules are in response to problems of self-control (spending money intended for other uses).

mental models   knowledge structures that are constructed in the service of understanding and explaining experience. Mental models are constrained by theories about the world rather than empirically derived generalizations.

mental rotation   subjects are asked to determine if two objects differ only in rotation. Results from these studies have been used to argue for the existence of analog representations.

metamemory   knowledge about one's own memory and memory abilities, as well as about different memory strategies and their effectiveness for different situations.

method of loci   mnemonic technique for remembering a set of items in order by mentally moving along a familiar path and "dropping off" a to-be-remembered item at each landmark.

minimal attachment   comprehension strategy that favors attaching a new phrase to an old node rather than building up a new phrasal node.

misinformation effect   when misinformation provided after the event leads people to be less likely to choose the correct alternative on a later test.

mnemonics strategies or procedures for remembering material, many of which rely on visual imagery.

modus ponens the valid argument structure that says that if P implies Q is true and P is true, then Q must be true.

modus tollens the valid argument structure that says that if P implies Q is true and Q is false, then P must be false.

morpheme the smallest significant unit of meaning in language.

motion parallax a perceptual cue to depth in which, as one moves back and forth, the images of nearby objects move across the field of vision faster than more distant objects.

naïve realism the assumption that perception involves directly seeing the world as it truly is

nodes in network models, a unit that represents a particular concept or idea.

object centered representation a method for representing visual objects in which the description relates the parts of the objects and their orientations relative to each other.

operant behaviors responses resulting in or followed by a particular effect on the environment.

parallel distributed processing (PDP) also referred to as connectionist models. The models consist of a large number of interconnected units. Concepts are represented as patterns of activations over these units, and learning proceeds by changes in the weights of the connections between the units.

partial report technique procedure for separating memory loss from limited attention by providing a postdisplay signal indicating which part of the display is to be reported.

PDP models also referred to as parallel distributed processing or connectionist models. The models consist of a large number of interconnected units. Concepts are represented as patterns of activations over these units, and learning proceeds by changes in the weights of the connections between the units.

phoneme the smallest significant unit of sound in language.

phonological loop a subsystem of working memory that accounts for much of the auditory temporary storage capabilities. It consists of a phonological store to hold acoustic or speech-based information for about 2 seconds and an articulatory control process, which produces inner speech.

phonology the rules governing the sequence in which phonemes can be arranged.

phrase structure building blocks or organizational units of sentences that are themselves comprised of words. For example, sentences are naturally broken into a noun phrase and a verb phrase.

picture-superiority effect empirical generalization that pictures are remembered better than words.

positive test strategy tendency to test an implication that will be true if a hypothesis is true.

pragmatic reasoning schemas reasoning strategies associated with social contracts such as permission and obligation that may or may not be activated in conditional reasoning tasks.

pragmatics aspects of language that refer to the practical knowledge a language user needs to have in order to communicate effectively.

preference reversals refers to the inconsistencies between people's choices and the prices or values they place on alternatives.

primacy effect the superiority in memory for items in the first part of the list compared to items in the middle part of the list.

proactive interference memory loss for recently acquired information that is caused by interference from memories acquired earlier.

probabilistic view theory of conceptual structure that argues that concepts are based on characteristic or typical features rather than strict definitions.

problem a person who has some goal for which no simple direct means are known is said to face a problem. A problem consists of a goal, givens, means of transforming conditions, and obstacles.

problem formulation taking an ill-defined problem and determining how to represent the problem. In many situations, the determination of what problem really should be solved is thought to be where much of the creative activity lies.

problem operators   in a problem space, the processes that "move" the solver from one state to another state.

problem schemas   structured knowledge about a type of problem that allows the problem solver to identify problems of that type, as well as the associated procedures for solving those problems.

problem space   the internal representation of the problem, consisting of states and operators.

problem state   in a problem space, a state represents the information available to the problem solver in that situation, a "state" of knowledge. The problem solver moves among the states by applying problem operators.

procedural memory   memory about how to do something, "knowing how." Usually thought to be gradually acquired through practice and not easily communicated verbally to others.

productions   a simple means of representing knowledge in terms of condition-action pairs: if some conditions are met, then some action is taken. Often used for representing procedural knowledge.

propositional representation   representation that takes the form of abstract languagelike propositions that are not tied to any particular sensory modality.

propositions   smallest units of meaning about which one can reasonably assert truth or falsity.

prosopagnosia   the inability to recognize familiar faces.

prospect theory   theory of decision making that attempts to account for violations of expected utility by assuming that utilities are evaluated relative to a reference point and that subjective probability (which does not correspond in a simple way to objective probability) is integrated with utility to determine choices.

prototype   a mental representation of a category that reflects the central tendency or what is, on the average, true of a category.

proximity principle   Gestalt principle that suggests that the closer two figures are, the more likely they are to be grouped perceptually.

psychological essentialism   belief that things have underlying natures that make them the thing that they are.

rapid serial visual presentation   An experimental technique in which a series of items is flashed quickly one after another.

rational model   normative model of decision making based on maximizing utility.

reasoning schema   A template or rule for doing logical reasoning.

recency effect   the superiority in memory (usually in free recall tests) for the items at the end of the list relative to items in the middle of the list.

reconstructive memory   remembering by integrating partial information from the event with other information, such as schemas or beliefs.

recursive decomposition   idea that an event at one level of description can be specified more fully at a lower level of description by analyzing the event into components and processes that operate on these components.

reductionism   idea that the best or correct level of description is the most specific one.

regret theory   theory of decision making that assumes that choices are determined in part by considering how one will feel if different outcomes occur.

reinforcement   an event that can serve to change the likelihood of the behavior that precedes it.

release from PI   an experimental procedure for studying what type of information about the stimulus is being encoded by examining the extent of proactive interference when different types of information are changed.

releasers   particular stimulus patterns that lead to or elicit species-specific behaviors such as fixed action patterns.

repetition blindness   A phenomenon in which people are unable to detect the repetition of an item from a rapidly presented sequence.

repetition priming   the finding that a recent exposure to a stimulus affects its subsequent processing.

representation internal model linked to external (real-world) objects and events so as to preserve functionally relevant information.

representativeness heuristic heuristic whereby people judge probabilities in terms of resemblance or similarity rather than probability.

respondent behaviors responses that are directly elicited by the environment, as in classical conditioning.

retinal disparity source of depth information associated with stereopsis.

retrieval plan an organized set of cues to be used in helping to retrieve information.

retroactive interference memory loss for previously learned information that is caused by interference from recently acquired information.

retrograde amnesia a loss of memory for events that occurred prior to some trauma.

route knowledge spatial knowledge in the form of the appropriate procedure for navigating from one point to another.

SAM search of associative memory theory, in which long-term memory consists of a set of interconnected concepts and retrieval is cue-dependent. This theory provides quantitative fits of many data and relates different memory tests.

satisficing using the criteria of whether an alternative is satisfactory (as opposed to optimal)

savings in relearning improvement in learning performance for material learned earlier.

schema a generalized knowledge structure used in understanding. A schema tells what to expect and what unstated information may nonetheless be inferred as present.

script a knowledge structure containing information about the sequence of events in routine or stereotypical situations, such as going to a restaurant.

self-fulfilling prophecy the tendency of people to act in such a way as to make what they predicted would happen actually happen. For example, if one expects a person to be hostile, one might behave in a way that brings out unfriendliness.

semantic memory memory for general knowledge of the world and language; the type of knowledge often found in encyclopedias and dictionaries but not knowledge about particular events.

semantics the aspect of language dealing with meaning.

serial position effect recall of an item in a list depends on where in the list it was presented, with middle items recalled worse than items at the beginning or end.

short-term memory the term referring to a limited amount of information being retained over a brief period of time; sometimes thought of as a separate memory store for information before it is transferred to long-term memory or as the activated portion of long-term memory.

size constancy the tendency for people to see a given object as being the same size, regardless of the size of the retinal image.

slot component of a frame that is filled in by particular information. In the absence of specific information, a slot may have a default value.

spacing effect the result that repeated items are better remembered if their repetitions occur apart from each other, rather than being massed or successive.

span of apprehension the number of items one can identify in a single glance.

span of attention the number of distinct items a person is aware of from a brief presentation of an array of items.

spatial neglect deficit associated with brain injury in which the person acts unaware of objects and events on the neglected side of space and may include neglect of the limbs and body surface.

spotlight metaphor theory of attention that suggests that attention is like a spotlight in the sense that it is continuous, can be narrowly or broadly focused, and moves continuously from location to location.

spreading activation a process in network models in which nodes are activated (made available for processing) by their links to other nodes, as if the activation were spreading from node to node through the links.

state-dependent recall   the improvement (or decrement) in recall of information learned when the person's internal state is similar to (or different from) the current state.

stereopsis   cues to depth perception deriving from the fact that each of a person's eyes has a slightly different view of a scene.

structural descriptions   theory of object perception based on the idea that recognition is based on comparing images with descriptions that include parts and their spatial relationships to each other.

sunk costs   framing effect in which people continue to engage in unrewarding behavior because of prior investment of resources. Sitting through a terrible movie just because you have paid to get in is an example of sunk costs.

surface structure   the organization of sentences as they are spoken or written.

survey knowledge   spatial knowledge that preserves relevant information about spatial relationships, as in a map.

syntax   aspect of language concerned with the way that words combine to form sentences.

systematicity   principle for interpreting analogies by which one gives more weight to properties and relations that have corresponding higher-order relations.

template matching   theory of perception that assumes that object recognition is based on comparing images of objects with stored patterns or templates.

texture gradients   the elements of a textured surface appear to be packed closer and closer together as the surface recedes and therefore texture gradients provide depth information.

top-down processing   information processing that starts with high-level information (like a word) and guides the search for lower-level information (like letters from that word).

transfer-appropriate processing   a framework with the main assumption that memory performance is greater, the more the cognitive processes required at test overlap with the cognitive processes required at learning.

transformational grammar   theory of grammar that suggests many forms (surface structures) result from applying a transformation to a base or underlying structure.

transitivity   a criterion of rationality that says if you prefer A to B and B to C then you should prefer A to C. That is, preferences should be transitive.

Turing machine   a simple machine consisting of a tape, a reading device, and a table of actions for each state of the machine. Turing proved that such a machine could do any computation that could be performed on a digital computer.

Turing test   a test in which a person is communicating over a keyboard with either another person or with a computer. If people are unable to tell which is which, then we should agree that computers are intelligent and can think, Turing argued.

type-token distinction   a representation distinction in network models in which the nodes representing general concepts (types) are connected to but distinct from the nodes representing particular instances of that concept (tokens).

typicality   the observation that some examples of a category may be "better" examples or more typical than others. Typical category members have more characteristic features of the category than atypical category members.

typicality effect   in category verification tasks, the finding that typical instances of a category (e.g., robin-bird) are verified more quickly than less typical instances (e.g., penguin-bird).

unconditioned response   in classical conditioning, the response that is elicited by the unconditioned stimulus without prior training (e.g., air puff to the eye elicits an eyeblink).

unconditioned stimulus   in classical conditioning, the stimulus that elicits the UR and the presentation of which acts as reinforcement.

unusualness heuristic   a general bias or strategy for linking surprising events to unusual preceding stimuli or events.

valid argument   an argument is deductively valid if its conclusion necessarily follows from the premise. The conclusion need not be true in the sense of corresponding to some state of affairs in the world.

varied mapping   procedure in search task in which items that are targets on some trials may be distractors on other trials.

verbal protocol   the data of a person talking during some task. Often these protocols are taken during problem solving, with the person asked to think aloud while solving the problem.

viewer centered representation   A method for representing visual objects in which the description relates the parts of the objects and their orientations relative to the viewer.

visuospatial sketchpad   a subsystem of working memory that allows us to maintain and manipulate visual and spatial images.

voice onset time   in speech production, the time between the release of air and the beginning of vocal cord vibration. For example, [b] has a shorter voice onset time than [p].

well-defined problem   a problem in which the goal, givens, and means of transforming the conditions are completely specified.

Wernicke's aphasia   disorder associated with damage (to Wernicke's area) leading to impairments in language perception.

what system   distinct neuroanatomical system associated with identifying what something is.

where system   distinct neuroanatomical system associated with determining where something is.

Williams syndrome   A disorder marked by profound intellectual deficits combined with preserved language ability.

working backward   a problem-solving heuristic that initially focuses on the goal. The solver applies operators to the goal state until it is transformed into one or more of the givens. The solution is then the inverse of each of these operators in the opposite order (i.e., from givens to goal).

working memory   a cognitive system that provides temporary storage and manipulation of information that is necessary for a wide variety of complex cognitive tasks. Consists of a central executive control process and two subsystems: phonological loop and visuospatial sketchpad.

REFERENCES

Ader, R. (1982). Conditioned suppression of humoral immunity in the rat. *Journal of Comparative and Physiological Psychology, 96,* 517–521.

Ader, R., & Cohen, N. (1985). CNS-immune system interaction: Conditioning phenomena. *The Behavioral and Brain Sciences, 8,* 379–394.

Aikins, J. S. (1993). Prototypical knowledge for expert systems: A retrospective analysis. *Artificial Intelligence, 59,* 207–211.

Alcock, J. (1989). *Animal behavior (4th edition).* Sunderland, MA: Sinauer Associates.

Allais, M. (1953). Le comportement de phonomme rationnel devant le risque: Critique des postulates et axioms de l'ecole americaine. *Econometrica, 21,* 503–546.

Allard, F., & Starkes, J. L. (1991). Motor-skill experts in sports, dance, and other domains. In K. A. Ericsson & J. Smith (Eds.) *Toward a general theory of expertise.* (pp. 126–152). New York: Cambridge University Press.

Allport, A. (1989). Visual attention. In M. I. Posner (Ed.), *Foundation of cognitive science.* Cambridge, MA: MIT Press.

Amabile, T. M. (1996). *Creativity in context.* Boulder, CO: Westview Press.

Anderson, J. A. (1995). *An Introduction to Neural Networks.* Cambridge, MA: The MIT Press.

Anderson, J. R. (1976). Language, memory, and thought. Hillsdale, NJ: Erlbaum.

Anderson, J. R. (1978). Arguments concerning representations for mental imagery. Psychological Review, 85, 249–277.

Anderson, J. R. (1983). The architecture of cognition. Cambridge, MA: Harvard University Press.

Anderson, J. R. (1987). Skill acquisition: Compilation of weak-method problem solutions. Psychological Review, 94, 192–210.

Anderson, J. R. (1990a). *The adaptive character of thought.* Hillsdale, NJ: Erlbaum.

Anderson, J. R. (1990b). The adaptive nature of human categorization. *Psychological Review, 98,* 409–429.

Anderson, J. R. (1993). *Rules of the mind.* Hillsdale, NJ: Erlbaum.

Anderson, J. R., & Bower, G. H. (1973). *Human associative memory.* Hillsdale, NJ: Erlbaum.

Anderson, J. R., & Lebiere, C. (1998). *The atomic components of thought.* Mahwah, NJ: Erlbaum.

Anderson, J. R., & Lebiere, C. (1998). *The atomic components of thought.* Mahwah, NJ: Erlbaum..

Anderson, J. R., & Ross, B. H. (1980). Evidence against a semantic-episodic distinction. *Journal of Experimental Psychology: Human Learning & Memory, 6*(5), 441–466.

Anderson, J. R., Conrad, F. G., & Corbett, A. T. (1990). Skill acquisition and the LISP tutor. *Cognitive Science, 13,* 467–505.

Anderson, J. R., Corbett, A. T., Koedinger, K. R., & Pelletier, R. (1995). Cognitive tutors: Lessons learned. *The Journal of the Learning Sciences, 4,* 167–207.

Anderson, J. R., Reder, L. M., & Lebiere, C. (1996). Working memory: Activation limitations on retrieval. *Cognitive Psychology, 30*(3), 221–256.

Anderson, R. C., & Pichert, J. W. (1978). Recall of previously unrecallable information following a shift in perspective. *Journal of Verbal Learning and Verbal Behavior, 17,* 1–12.

Anderson, R. C., Reynolds, R. C., Schallert, D. L., & Goetz, E. T. (1977). Frameworks for comprehending discourse. *American Education Research Journal, 14,* 367–381.

Arbib, M. A. (1995). *The handbook of brain theory and neural networks.* Cambridge, MA: MIT Press.

Arkes, H. R., & Ayton, P. (1999). The sunk cost and Concorde effects: Are humans less rational than lower animals? *Psychological Bulletin, 125*(5), 591–600.

Arkes, H. R., & Harkness, A. R. (1983). Estimates of contingency between two dichotomous variables. *Journal of Experimental Psychology: General, 112,* 117–135.

Arkes, H. R., Wortmann, R. L., Saville, P. D., & Harkness, A. R. (1981). Hindsight bias among physicians weighing the likelihood of diagnosis. *Journal of Applied Psychology, 66,* 252–254.

Ashby, F. G., Alfonso-Reese, L. A., Turken, A. U., & Waldron, E. M. (1998). A neuropsychological theory of multiple systems in category learning. *Psychological Review, 105,* 442–481.

Atkinson, R. C. (1975). Mnemotechnics in second-language learning. *American Psychologist, 30,* 821–828.

Atkinson, R. C., & Shiffrin, R. (1968). Human memory: A proposed system and its control processes. In K. Spence & J. Spence (Eds.), *The psychology of learning and motivation, vol. 2.* New York: Academic Press.

Atran, S. (1990). *Cognitive foundations of natural history: Towards an anthropology of science.* Cambridge: Cambridge University Press.

Atran, S. (1998). Folk biology and the anthropology of science: Cognitive universals and cultural particulars. *Behavioral and Brain Sciences, 21,* 547–611.

Atran, S., Estin, P., Coley, J. D., & Medin, D. L. (1997). Generic Species and Basic Levels: Essence and Appearance in Folk Biology. *Journal of Ethnobiology, 17,* 22–45.

Au, T. K. (1994). Developing an intuitive understanding of substance kinds. *Cognitive Psychology, 27*(1), 71–111.

Au, T. K., & Romo, L. F. (1996). Building a coherent conception of HIV transmission: A new approach to AIDS education. In D. L. Medin, (Ed)., *The Psychology of Learning and Motivation, vol. 35* (pp. 193–241). San Diego: Academic Press.

Au, T. K., & Romo, L. F. (1999). Mechanical causality in children's "Folkbiology." In D. L. Medin & S. Atran (Eds.), *Folkbiology* (pp. 355–402). Cambridge, MA: Bradford.

Ayers, M. S., & Reder, L. M. (1998). A theoretical review of the misinformation effect: Predictions from an activation-based memory model. *Psychonomic Bulletin & Review, 5,* 1–21.

Baddeley, A. D. (1978). The trouble with levels: A reexamination of Craik & Lockhart's framework for memory research. *Psychological Review, 85,* 139–152.

Baddeley, A. D. (1986). *Working memory.* Oxford: Oxford University Press.

Baddeley, A. D. (1990). *Human memory: Theory and practice.* Needham Heights, MA: Allyn & Bacon.

Baddeley, A. D. (1996). Exploring the central executive. *Quarterly Journal of Experimental Psychology. A, Human Experimental Psychology, 49A(1),* 5–28.

Baddeley, A. D., & Hitch, G. J. (1974). Working memory. In G. H. Bower (Ed.), *The psychology of learning and motivation, vol. 8.* New York: Academic Press.

Baddeley, A. D., Gathercole, S., & Papagno, C. (1998). The phonological loop as a language learning device. *Psychological Review, 105,* 158–173.

Baddeley, A. D., Thomson, N., & Buchanan, M. (1975). Word length and the structure of short-term memory. *Journal of Verbal Learning & Verbal Behavior, 14*(6), 575–589.

Bahrick, H. P., Bahrick, L. E., Bahrick, A. S., & Bahrick, P. E. (1993). Maintenance of foreign language vocabulary and the spacing effect. *Psychological Science, 4,* 316–321.

Bahrick, H. P., Bahrick, P. O., & Wittlinger, R. P. (1975). Fifty years of memory for names and faces: A cross-sectional approach. *Journal of Experimental Psychology: General, 104*(1), 54–75.

Baker, D. P., Chabris, C. F., & Kosslyn, S. M. (1999). Encoding categorical and coordinate spatial relations without input-output correlations: New simulation models. *Cognitive Science, 23,* 33–51.

Balch, W. R., Myers, D. M., & Papotto, C. (1999). Dimensions of mood in mood-dependent memory. *Journal of Experimental Psychology: Learning, Memory, & Cognition, 25*(1), 70–83.

Baldwin, D. A. (1993). Early referential understanding: Infants' ability to recognize referential acts for what they are. *Developmental Psychology, 29,* 832–843.

Ball, G. F. & Hulse, S. H. (1998). Birdsong. *American Psychologist, 53,* 37–58.

Bandura, A. (1982). The psychology of chance encounters and life paths. *American Psychologist, 37,* 747–761.

Bargh, J. A. (1994). The four horsemen of automaticity: Awareness, intention, efficiency, and control in social cognition. In R. S. Wyer, Jr., T. K. Srull (Eds.), *Handbook of social cognition, Vol. 1: Basic processes* (pp. 1–40). Hillsdale, NJ: Erlbaum.

Bar-Hillel, M., & Fischhoff, B. (1981). When do base rates affect predictions? *Journal of Personality and Social Psychology, 41,* 671–680.

Barkley, R. A. (1997a). Behavioral inhibition, sustained attention, and executive functions: Constructing a unifying theory of ADHD. *Psychological Bulletin, 121,* 65–94.

Barkley, R. A. (1997b). *ADHD and the nature of self control.* New York: Guilford Press.

Baron, J. (1988). *Thinking and deciding.* Cambridge: Cambridge University Press.

Baron, J., & Spranca, M. (1997). Protected values. *Organizational Behavior and Human Decision Processes, 70,* 1–16.

Barsalou, L. W. (1983). Ad hoc categories. *Memory & Cognition, 11,* 211–217.

Barsalou, L. W. (1985). Ideals, central tendency, and frequency of instantiation as determinants of graded structure in categories. *Journal of Experimental Psychology: Learning, Memory, and Cognition, 11,* 629–654.

Barsalou, L. W. (1987). The instability of graded structure: Implications for the nature of concepts. In U. Neisser (Ed.), *Concepts and conceptual development: Ecological and intellectual factors in categorization* (pp. 101–140). New York: Cambridge University Press.

Barsalou, L. W. (1989). Intraconcept similarity and its implications for interconcept similarity. In S. Vosniadon & A. Ortony (Eds.), *Similarity and analogical reasoning* (pp. 76–121). New York: Cambridge University Press.

Barsalou, L. W. (1994). Flexibility, structure, and linguistic vagary in concepts: Manifestations of a compositional system of perceptual symbols. In A. F. Collins, S. E. Gathercole, M. A. Conway, & P. E. Morris (Eds.), Theories of memory, Hillsdale, NJ: Erlbaum.

Barsalou, L. W. (1999). Perceptual symbol systems. *Behavioral and Brain Sciences, 22,* 577–609.

Barsalou, L. W., & Medin, D. L. (1986). Concepts: Fixed definitions or dynamic context-dependent representations? *Cahiers de Psychologie Cognitive, 6,* 187–202.

Barsalou, L. W., Huttenlocher, J., & Lamberts, K. (1998). Basing categorization on individuals and events. *Cognitive Psychology, 36,* 203–272.

Barsalou, L. W., Solomon, K. O., & Wu, L. L. (1999). Perceptual simulation in conceptual tasks. In M. K. Hiraga, C. Sinha, & S. Wilcox (Eds.), *Cultural, typological, and psychological perspectives in cognitive linguistics: The proceedings of the 4th conference of the International Cognitive Linguistics Association, Vol. 3.* Amsterdam: John Benjamins.

Bartlett, F. C. (1932). *Remembering.* Cambridge: Cambridge University Press.

Bassok, M. (1990). Transfer of domain-specific problem-solving procedures. *Journal of Experimental Psychology: Learning, Memory, and Cognition, 16,* 522–533.

Bassok, M., Wu, L., & Olseth, K. L. (1995). Judging a book by its cover: Interpretative effects of content on problem solving transfer. *Memory & Cognition, 23,* 354–367.

Batsell, W. R., Jr., & Brown, A. S. (1998). Human flavor-aversion learning: A comparison of traditional aversions and cognitive aversions. *Learning & Motivation, 29*(4), 383–396.

Bazerman, M. H. (1998). *Judgment in managerial decision making* (4th ed.). New York: John Wiley & Sons.

Bazerman, M. H., Tenbrunsel, A. E. & Wade-Benzoni, K. A. (1998). Negotiating with Yourself and Losing: Understanding and Managing Conflicting Internal Preferences. *Academy of Management Review, 23,* 225–241.

Bedard, J., & Chi, M. T. H. (1992). Expertise. *Current Directions in Psychological Science, 1,* 135–139.

Bell, D. E. (1982). Regret in decision making under uncertainty. *Operations Research, 30,* 961–981.

Bellezza, F. S. (1982). *Improve your memory skills.* Englewood Cliffs, NJ: Prentice-Hall.

Bellezza, F. S. (1984). Reliability of retrieval from semantic memory: Noun meanings. *Bulletin of the Psychonomic Society, 22,* 377–380.

Bellezza, F. S. (1996). Mnemonic methods to enhance storage and retrieval. In E. L. Bjork, & R. A. Bjork (Eds.), *Memory. Handbook of perception and cognition* (2nd ed., pp. 345–380). San Diego, CA: Academic Press.

Bellezza, F. S., & Young, D. R. (1989). Chunking repeated events in memory. *Journal of Experimental Psychology: Learning, Memory, and Cognition, 15,* 990–997.

Bellezza, F. S., Winkler, H. B., & Andrasik, F. (1975). Encoding processes and the spacing effect. *Memory & Cognition, 3,* 451–457.

Belli, R. F., Lindsay, D. S., Gales, M. S., & McCarthy, T. T. (1994). Memory impairment and source misattribution in postevent misinformation experiments with short retention intervals. *Memory & Cognition, 22,* 40–54.

Bellugi, U., Bihrle, A., Jernigan, T., Trauner, D., & Doherty, S. (1990). Neuro-psychological, neurological, and neuroanatomical profile of Williams syndrome. *American Journal of Medical Genetics Supplement, 6,* 115–125.

Benson, D. F., & Ardila, A. (1996). *Aphasia: A clinical perspective.* New York: Oxford University Press.

Berkeley, G. (1975). *Philosophical Works, Including the Works on Vision.* Totowa, NJ: Rowman and Littlefield.

Berlin, B. (1992). *Ethnobiological classification: Principles of categorization of plants and animals in traditional societies.* Princeton, NJ: Princeton University Press.

Berlin, B., Breedlove, D., & Raven, P. (1973). General principles of classification and naming in folkbiology. *American Anthropologist, 74,* 214–242.

Bernstein, I. L. (1978). Learned taste aversions in children receiving chemotherapy. *Science, 200,* 1302–1303.

Bernstein, I. L., & Borson, S. (1986). Learned food aversion: A component of anorexia syndromes. *Psychological Review, 93,* 462–472.

Bernstein, I. L., Webster, M. M., & Berstein, I. D. (1982). Food aversions in children receiving chemotherapy for cancer. *Cancer, 50,* 2961–2963.

Bever, T. G. (1970). The cognitive basis for linguistic structures. In J. P. Hayes (Ed.), *Cognition and development of language.* New York: Wiley.

Biederman, I. & Ju, G. (1988). Surface and edge-based determinants of visual recognition. *Cognitive Psychology, 20,* 38–64.

Biederman, I. (1987). Recognition by components: A theory of human image understanding. *Psychological Review, 94,* 115–147.

Biederman, I. (1990). Higher-level vision. In D. N. Osherson, S. M. Kosslyn, and J. M. Hollerback (Eds.), *Visual cognition and action: An invitation to cognitive science.* Cambridge, MA: MIT Press.

Bisiach, E. (1996). Unilateral neglect and the structure of space representation. *Current Directions in Psychological Science, 5,* 62–65.

Bisiach, E., Perani, D., Vallar, G., & Berti, A. (1986). Unilateral neglect: Personal and extra-personal. *Neuropsychological, 24,* 759–767.

Bjork, R. A. (1972). Theoretical implications of directed forgetting. In A. W. Melton & E. Martin (Eds.), *Coding processes in human memory.* Washington, D. C.: V. H. Winston & Sons.

Blumstein, S. E. (1997). A perspective on the neurobiology of language. *Brain and Language, 60,* 335–346.

Boden, M. A. (Ed.). (1994). *Dimensions of creativity.* Cambridge, MA: Mit Press.

Bolles, R. C. (1970). Species-specific defense reactions and avoidance learning. *Psychological Review, 77,* 32–48.

Boring, E. G. (1950). *A history of experimental psychology.* New York: Appleton-Century-Crofts.

Bower, G. H. (1961). Application of a model to paired-associate learning. *Psychometrika, 26,* 255–280.

Bower, G. H. (1981). Mood and memory. American Psychologist, 36, 129–148.

Bower, G. H. (1997). An associative theory of implicit and explicit memory. In M. A. Conway, C. Cornold, &S. E. Gathercole (Eds.), *Theories of memory II.* Hove, Sussex: Psychological Press.

Bower, G. H., & Springston, F. (1970). Pauses as recoding points in letter series. *Journal of Experimental Psychology, 83,* 421–430.

Bower, G. H., Black, J. B., & Turner, T. F. (1979). Scripts in memory for text. *Cognitive Psychology, 11,* 177–220.

Bower, G. H., Clark, M. C., Lesgold, A. M., & Winzenz, D. (1969). Hierarchical retrieval schemes in recall of categorized word lists. *Journal of Verbal Learning and Verbal Behavior, 8,* 323–343.

Bowerman, M. (1996). Learning how to structure space for language: A crosslinguistic perspective. In P. Bloom, M. A. Peterson (Eds.), *Language and space. Language, speech, and communication* (pp. 385–436). Cambridge, MA: MIT Press.

Bowers, K. S., Farvolden, P., & Mermigis, L. (1995). Intuitive antecedents of insight. In S. M. Smith, T. B. Ward, & R. A. Finke (Eds.), *The creative cognition approach.* Cambridge, MA: MIT Press.

Bowlby, J. (1969). *Attachment (Vol. 1).* New York: Basic Books.

Braine, M. D. S., Reiser, B. J., & Rumain, B. (1984). Some empirical justification for a theory of natural propositional logic. In G. Bower (Ed.), *The psychology of learning and motivation, vol. 18.* Orlando, FL: Academic Press.

Braitenberg, V. (1984). *Vehicles: Experiments on synthetic psychology.* Cambridge, MA

Bransford, J. D., & Johnson, M. K. (1972). Contextual prerequisites for understanding: Some investigations of comprehension and recall. *Journal of Verbal Learning and Verbal Behavior, 11,* 717–726.

Bransford, J. D., Barclay, J. R., & Franks, J. J. (1972). Sentence memory: A constructive versus interpretive approach. *Cognitive Psychology, 3,* 193–200.

Bransford, J. D., Franks, J. J., Vye, N. J., & Sherwood, R. D. (1989). New approaches to instruction: Because wisdom can't be told. In S. Vosniadou & A. Ortony (Eds.), *Similarity and analogical reasoning.* Cambridge: Cambridge University Press.

Brennan, S. E., & Clark, H. H. (1996). Conceptual pacts and lexical choice in conversation. *Journal of Experimental Psychology: Learning, Memory, and Cognition, 22*(6), 1482–1493.

Bresnan, J. (1978). A realistic transformational grammar. In M. Hall, J. Bresnan, & G. Miller (Eds.), *Linguistic theory and psychological reality.* Cambridge, MA: MIT Press.

Brewer, W. F. (1977). Memory for the pragmatic implications of sentences. *Memory & Cognition, 5,* 673–678.

Brewer, W. F. (1988). Memory for randomly sampled autobiographical events. In U. Neisser & E. Winograd (Eds.), *Remembering reconsidered: Ecological and traditional approaches to the study of memory.* Cambridge: Cambridge University Press.

Brewer, W. F. (1992). An analysis of the theoretical and empirical status of the flashbulb memory hypothesis. In E. Winograd & U. Neisser (Eds.), *Affect and accuracy in recall: Studies of "flashbulb memories".* Cambridge: Cambridge University Press.

Brewer, W. F., & Treyens, J. C. (1981). Role of schemata in memory for places. *Cognitive Psychology, 13,* 207–230.

Broadbent, D. E. (1958). *Perception and communication.* London: Pergamon Press.

Broadbent, D. E., & Broadbent, M. H. P. (1987). From detection to identification: Response to multiple targets in rapid serial visual presentation. *Perception and Psychophysics, 42*(2), 105–113.

Brooks, L. R. (1968). Spatial and verbal components of the act of recall. *Canadian Journal of Psychology, 22,* 349–368.

Brooks, L. R. (1978). Nonanalytic concept formation and memory for instances. In E. Rosch & B. B. Lloyd (Eds.), *Cognition and categorization.* New York: Wiley.

Brooks, L. R., Norman, G. R., & Allen, S. W. (1991). Role of specific similarity in a medical diagnostic task. *Journal of Experimental Psychology: General, 120,* 278–287.

Brown, A. L., & Kane, M. J. (1988). Preschool children can learn to transfer: Learning to learn and learning from example. *Cognitive Psychology, 20,* 493–523.

Brown, J. (1958). Some tests of the decay theory of immediate memory. *Quarterly Journal of Experimental Psychology, 10,* 12–21.

Brown, P. L., & Jenkins, H. M. (1968). Autoshaping the pigeon's key peck. *Journal of the Experimental Analysis of Behavior, 11,* 1–8.

Brown, R., & Kulik, J. (1977). Flashbulb memories. *Cognition, 5,* 73–99.

Bryant, D. J., & Tversky, B. (1999). Mental representations of perspective spatial relations from diagrams and models. *Journal of Experimental Psychology: Learning, Memory, and Cognition, 25,* 137–156.

Budescu, D. V., & Wallsten, T. S. (1995). Processing linguistic probabilities: General principles and empirical evidence. In J. Busemeyer, R. Hastie, & D. L. Medin (Eds.), *The Psychology of Learning and Motivation* (pp. 275–318). New York: Academic Press.

Burtt, H. E. (1941). An experimental study of early childhood memory: Final report. *The Journal of Genetic Psychology, 58,* 435–439.

Busemeyer, J. R., & Townsend, J. T. (1993). Decision field theory: A dynamic-cognitive approach to decision making in an uncertain environment. *Psychological Review, 100*(3), 432–459.

Busemeyer, J. R., Hastie, R., & Medin, D. L. (Eds.) (1995). *The psychology of learning and motivation, vol. 32.* New York: Academic Press.

Buss, D. M., Haselton, M. G., Shackelford, T. K., Bleske, A. L., & Wakefield, J. C. (1998). Adaptations, exaptations, and spandrels. *American Psychologist, 53,* 533–548.

Butters, N. (1984). Alcoholic Korsakoff's syndrome: An update. *Seminars in Neurology, 4,* 226–244.

Butters, N., & Cermak, L. S. (1986). A case study of the forgetting of autobiographical knowledge: Implications for the study of retrograde amnesia. In D. C. Rubin (Ed.), *Autobiographical memory.* Cambridge: Cambridge University Press.

Byrne, R. W. (1982). Geographical knowledge and orientation. In A. W. Ellis (Ed.), *Normality and pathology in cognitive functions.* New York: Academic Press.

Camerer, C. F. (1995). Individual Decision making. In J. H. Kagel & A. E. Roth (Eds.), *The Handbook of Experimental Economics* (pp. 587–703). Princeton: Princeton University Press.

Caplan, D. (1972). Clause boundaries and recognition latencies for words in sentences. *Perception & Psychophysics, 12,* 73–76.

Caramazza, A., & Shelton, J. R. (1998). Domain-specific knowledge systems in the brain: The animate-inanimate distinction. *Journal of Cognitive Neuroscience, 10*(1), 1–34.

Carey, S. (1982). Semantic development, state of the art. In E. Wanner & L. R. Gleitman (Eds.), *Language acquisition: The state of the art* (pp. 347–389). Cambridge: Cambridge University Press.

Carey, S. (1985). *Conceptual change in childhood.* Cambridge, MA: MIT Press.

Carey, S. (1995). On the origins of causal understanding. In A. Premack (Ed.), *Casual understanding in cognition and culture* (pp. 268–308). New York: Oxford University Press.

Carlson, R. A., Sullivan, M. A., & Schneider, W. (1989). Practice and working memory effects in building procedural skill. *Journal of Experimental Psychology: Learning, Memory, and Cognition, 15,* 517–526.

Catrambone, R. (1994). Improving examples to improve transfer to novel problems. *Memory & Cognition, 22,* 606–615.

Catrambone, R., & Holyoak, K. J. (1989). Overcoming contextual limitations on problem-solving transfer. *Journal of Experimental Psychology: Learning, Memory, and Cognition, 15,* 1147–1156.

Cattell, J. M. (1886). The time taken up by the cerebral operations. *Mind, 11,* 220–242, 377–392, 524–538.

Cavanagh, P., & Leclerc, Y. G. (1989). Shape from shadows. *Journal of Experimental Psychol-*

ogy: Human Perception and Performance, 15, 3–27.

Cave, K. R., & Wolfe, J. M. (1990). Modeling the role of parallel processing in visual search. *Cognitive Psychology, 22*, 225–271.

Ceci, S. J., & Bruck, M. (1993) Suggestibility of the child witness: A historical review and synthesis. *Psychological Bulletin, 113*, 403–439.

Ceci, S. J., & Tishman, J. (1984). Hyperactivity and incidental memory: Evidence for attentional diffusion. *Child Development, 55*, 2192–2203.

Chalmers, D. J. (1996). *The conscious mind: In search of a fundamental theory.* New York: Oxford University Press.

Chambers, D., & Reisberg, D. (1985). Can mental images be ambiguous? Journal of Experimental Psychology: *Human Perception and Performance, 11*, 317–328.

Chapman, G. B., & Johnson, E. J. (1995). Preference reversals in monetary and life expectancy evaluations. *Organizational Behavior & Human Decision Processes, 62*(3), 300–317.

Chapman, L. J., & Chapman, J. P. (1969). Illusory correlation as an obstacle to the use of valid diagnostic signs. *Journal of Abnormal Psychology, 74*, 271–280.

Charniak, E. (1973). Jack and Janet in search of a theory of knowledge. *IJCAI Proceedings,* 337–343.

Chase, W. G., & Ericsson, K. A. (1981). Skilled memory. In J. R. Anderson (Ed.), *Cognitive skills and their acquisition.* Hillsdale, NJ: Erlbaum.

Chase, W. G., & Simon, H. A. (1973). The mind's eye in chess. In W. G. Chase (Ed.), *Visual information processing.* New York: Academic Press.

Chatterjee, S. H., Freyd, J. J., & Shiffrar, M. (1996). Configural processing in the perception of apparent biological motion. *Journal of Experimental Psychology: Human Perception and Performance, 22*, 916–929.

Chedru, F. (1976). Space representation in unilateral spatial neglect. *Journal of Neurology, Neurosurgery and Psychiatry, 39*, 1057–1061.

Cheney, D. L., & Seyfarth, R. M. (1990). *How monkeys see the world.* Chicago: University of Chicago Press.

Cheng, P. W. (1985). Restructuring versus automaticity: Alternative accounts of skill acquisition. *Psychological Review, 92*, 414–423.

Cheng, P. W. (1997). From covariation to causation: A causal power theory. *Psychological Review, 104*, 367–405.

Cheng, P. W., & Holyoak, K. J. (1985). Pragmatic reasoning schemas. *Cognitive Psychology, 17*, 391–416.

Cheng, P. W., & Holyoak, K. J. (1989). On the natural selection of reasoning theories. *Cognition, 33*, 285–313.

Cheng, P. W., Holyoak, K. J., Nisbett, R. E., & Oliver, L. M. (1986). Pragmatic versus syntactic approaches to training deductive reasoning. Cognitive Psychology, 18, 293–328.

Cheng, P. W., & Novick, L. R. (1992). Covariation in natural causal induction. *Psychology Review, 99*, 365–382.

Cherniak, C. (1986). *Minimal rationality.* Cambridge, MA: MIT Press.

Cherry, E. C. (1953). Some experiments on the recognition of speech with one and with two ears. *Journal of the Acoustical Society of America, 25*, 975–979.

Cherry, K. E., Park, D. C., Frieske, D. A., & Rowley, R. L. (1993). The effect of verbal elaborations on memory in young and older adults. *Memory & Cognition, 21*, 725–738.

Chi, M. T. H. (1997). Quantifying qualitative analyses of verbal data: A practical guide. *The Journal of the Learning Sciences, 6*, 271–315.

Chi, M. T. H., Bassok, M., Lewis, M. W., Reimann, P., & Glaser, R. (1989). Self-explanations: How students study and use examples in learning to solve problems. *Cognitive Science, 13*, 145–182.

Chi, M. T. H., de Leeuw, N., Chiu, M., & LaVancher, C. (1994). Eliciting self-explanations improves understanding. *Cognitive Science, 18*, 439–477.

Chi, M. T. H., Feltovich, P. J., & Glaser, R. (1981). Categorization and representation of physics problems by experts and novices. *Cognitive Science, 5,* 121–152.

Chi, M. T. H., Glaser, R., & Farr, M. J. (Eds.). (1988). *The nature of expertise.* Hillsdale, NJ: Erlbaum.

Chiu, C. Y., Krauss, R. M., & Lau, I. Y. M. (1998). Some cognitive consequences of communication. In S. R. Fussell & R. J. Kreuz (Eds.), *Social and cognitive approaches to interpersonal communication* (pp. 259–278). Mahwah, NJ: Erlbaum.

Choi, I., Nisbett, R. E., & Smith, E. E. (1997). Culture, category salience, and inductive reasoning. *Cognition, 65,* 15–32.

Choi, S., & Bowerman, M. (1991). Learning to express motion events in English and Korean: The influence of language-specific lexicalization patterns. *Cognition, 41,* 83–121.

Chomsky, N. (1957). *Syntactic structures.* The Hague, Netherlands: Mouton.

Chomsky, N. (1959). Review of Skinner's Verbal behavior. *Language, 35,* 26–58.

Chomsky, N. (1981). *Lectures on government and binding.* Dordrecht, Netherlands: Foris.

Chomsky, N. (1988). *Language and problems of knowledge: The Managua Lectures.* Cambridge, MA: MIT Press.

Chomsky, N., & Halle, M. (1968). *The sound pattern of English.* New York: Harper & Row.

Christensen-Szalanski, J. J. J., & Bushyhead, J. B. (1981). Physicians' use of probabilistic information in a real clinical setting. *Journal of Experimental Psychology: Human Perception and Performance, 7,* 928–935.

Chun, M. M. (1997). Types and tokens in visual processing: A double dissociation between the attentional blink and repetition blindness. *Journal of Experimental Psychology: Human Perception and Performance, 23*(3), 738–755.

Clancey, W. J. (1987). *Knowledge-based tutoring: The GUIDON program.* Cambridge, MA: MIT Press.

Clancey, W. J. (1988). Acquiring, representing, and evaluating a competence model of diagnostic strategy. In M. T. H. Chi, R. Glaser, & M. J. Farr (Eds.), *The nature of expertise.* Hillsdale, NJ: Erlbaum.

Clancey, W. J., & Letsinger, R. (1984). NEOMYCIN: Reconfiguring a rule-based expert system for application to teaching. In W. J. Clancey & E. H. Shortliffe (Eds.), *Readings in medical artificial intelligence: The first decade.* Reading, MA: Addison-Wesley.

Clark, H. H. (1996). *Using Language.* New York: Cambridge University Press.

Clark, H. H., & Schaefer, E. F. (1987a). Collaborating on contributions to conversation. *Language and Cognitive Processes, 2,* 19–41.

Clark, H. H., & Schaefer, E. F. (1987b). Concealing one's meaning from overhearers. *Journal of Memory and Language, 26,* 209–225.

Clement, C. A., & Gentner, D. (1991). Systematicity as a selectional constraint in analogical mapping. *Cognitive Science, 15,* 89–132.

Cochran, B. P., McDonald, J. L., & Parault, S. J. (1999). Too smart for their own good: The disadvantage of a superior processing capacity for adult language learners. *Journal of Memory & Language, 41*(1), 30–58.

Cohen, J. D., & Servan-Schreiber, D. (1992). Context, cortex, and dopamine: A connectionist approach to behavior and biology in schizophrenia. *Psychological Review, 99,* 45–77.

Cohen, J. D., Dunbar, K., & McClelland, J. L. (1990). On the control of automatic processes: A parallel distributed processing account of the stroop effect. *Psychological Review, 97,* 332–361.

Cohen, L. J. (1981). Can human irrationality be experimentally demonstrated? *Behavioral and Brain Sciences, 4,* 317–370.

Cohen, N. J. (1984). Preserved learning capacity in amnesia: Evidence for multiple memory systems. In L. Squire & N. Butters (Eds.), *Neuropsychology of memory.* New York: Guilford Press.

Cohen, N. J., & Eichenbaum, H. (1993). *Memory, amnesia, and the hippocampal system.* Cambridge, MA: MIT Press.

Cohen, N. J., & Squire, L. R. (1980). Preserved learning and retention of pattern-analyzing skill in amnesia: Dissociation of knowing how and knowing that. *Science, 210,* 207–210.

Cohen, N. J., & Squire, L. R. (1981). Retrograde amnesia and remote memory impairment. *Neuropsychologia, 19,* 337–356.

Coley, J. D. (1995). Emerging differentiation of folkbiology and folkpsychology: Attributions of biological and psychological properties to living things. *Child Development, 66,* 1856–1874.

Coley, J. D., Medin, D. L., & Atran, S. (1997). Does rank have its privilege? Inductive inferences within folkbiological taxonomies. *Cognition, 64,* 73–112.

Coley, J. D., Medin, D. L., Proffitt, J. B., Lynch, E., & Atran, S. (1999). Inductive reasoning in folkbiological thought. In D. L. Medin & S. Atran (Eds.), *Folkbiology* (pp. 205–232). Cambridge, MA: Bradford.

Collins, A. M., & Loftus, E. F. (1975). A spreading-activation theory of semantic processing. *Psychological Review, 82,* 407–428.

Collins, A. M., & Quillian, M. R. (1969). Retrieval time from semantic memory. *Journal of Verbal Learning and Verbal Behavior, 8,* 240–247.

Collins, A. M., & Quillian, M. R. (1972). Experiments on semantic memory and language comprehension. In L. W. Gregg (Ed.), *Cognition in learning and memory.* New York: Wiley.

Conrad, R. (1964). Acoustic confusion in immediate memory. *British Journal of Psychology, 55,* 75–84.

Conway, M. A. (1995). *Flashbulb memories.* Hove, England UK: Erlbaum.

Conway, M. A. (Ed.). (1997). *Recovered memories and false memories. Debates in Psychology.* Oxford, England UK: Oxford University Press.

Conway, M. A., Anderson, S. J., Larsen, S. F., Donnelly, C. M., McDaniel, M. A., McClelland, A. G. R., Rawles, R. E., & Logie, R. H. (1994). The formation of flashbulb memories. *Memory & Cognition, 22,* 326–343.

Cooke, N. J., & Breedin, S. D. (1994). Constructing naive theories of motion on the fly. *Memory & Cognition, 22,* 474–493.

Cooper, L. A. (1975). Mental rotation of random two-dimensional shapes. *Cognitive Psychology, 7,* 120–143.

Cooper, L. A. (1976). Demonstration of a mental analog of an external rotation. *Perception & Psychophysics, 19,* 296–302.

Cooper, L. A., & Shepard, R. N. (1973). The time required to prepare for a rotated stimulus. *Memory & Cognition, 1,* 246–250.

Cooper, L. A., & Shepard, R. N. (1978). Transformations on representations of objects in space. In E. C. Carterette & M. P. Friedman (Eds.), *Handbook of perception* (Vol. 8). New York: Academic Press.

Corkin, S., Sullivan, E. V., Twitchell, T. E., & Grove, E. (1981). The amnesic patient H. M.: Clinical observations and test performance 28 years after operation. *Society for Neuroscience Abstracts, 7,* 235.

Cosmides, L. (1989). The logic of social exchange: Has natural selection shaped how humans reason? Studies with the Wason selection task. *Cognition, 31,* 187–276.

Cosmides, L., & Tooby, J. (1994). Origins of domain specificity: The evolution of functional organization. In L. A. Hirschfeld & S. A. Gelman (Eds.), *Mapping the mind: Domain specificity in cognition and culture* (pp. 85–116). New York, NY: Cambridge University Press.

Cover, T. M., & Hart, P. E. (1967). Nearest neighbor pattern classification. *IEEE Trans Inform Theory, Vol. IT-B,* 21–27.

Cowan, N. (1994). Mechanisms of verbal short-term memory. *Current Directions in Psychological Science, 3,* 185–189.

Craik, F. I. M., & Lockhart, R. S. (1972). Levels of processing: A framework for memory research. *Journal of Verbal Learning and Verbal Behavior, 11,* 671–684.

Craik, F. I. M., & Tulving, E. (1975). Depth of processing and the retention of words in episodic memory. *Journal of Experimental Psychology: General, 104,* 268–294.

Crick, F. & Koch, C. (1990). Towards a neurobiological theory of consciousness. *Seminars in the Neurosciences, 2,* 263–275.

Crowder, R. G. (1982). Decay of auditory memory in vowel discrimination. *Journal of Experimental Psychology: Learning, Memory, and Cognition, 8,* 153–162.

Crowder, R. G. (1993). Short-term memory: Where do we stand? *Memory & Cognition, 21,* 142–145.

Crowder, R. G., & Morton, J. (1969). Precategorical acoustic storage (PAS). *Perception & Psychophysics, 5,* 365–373.

Crowe, E., & Higgins, E. T. (1997). Regulatory focus and strategic inclinations: Promotion and prevention in decision-making. *Organizational Behavior & Human Decision Processes, 69*(2), 117–132.

Crowell, C. R., Hinson, R. E., & Siegel, S. (1981). The role of conditional drug responses in tolerance to the hypothermic effects of ethanol. *Psychopharmacology, 73,* 51–54.

Csikszentmihalyi, M. (1996). *Creativity.* New York, NY: HarperCollins Publishers.

Curiel, J. M., & Radvansky, G. A. (1998). Mental organization of maps. *Journal of Experimental Psychology: Learning, Memory, & Cognition, 24*(1), 202–214.

D'Esposito, M., Zarahn, E., & Aguirre, G. K. (1999). Event-related functional MRI:Implications for cognitive psychology. *Psychological Bulletin, 125,* 155–164.

Dadds, M. R., Bovbjerg, D. H., Redd, W. H., & Cutmore, T. R. H. (1997). Imagery in human classical conditioning. *Psychological Bulletin, 122*(1), 89–103.

Dafters, R., Hetherington, M., & McCartney, H. (1983). Blocking and sensory preconditioning effects in morphine analgesic tolerance: Support for a Pavlovian conditioning model of drug tolerance. *Quarterly Journal of Experimental Psychology, 35B,* 1–11.

Dagenback, D., & Carr, T. H. (Eds). (1994). *Inhibitory processes in attention, memory, and language.* San Diego: Academic Press.

Damasio, A. R. (1994). The brain binds entities and events by multiregional activation from convergence zones. In H. T. G. Gutfreund (Ed.), *Biology and computation: A physicist's choice. Advanced series in neuroscience* (Vol. 3, pp. 749–758). , Singapore: World Scientific Publishing Co.

Damasio, H., Grabowski, T. J., Tranel, D., & Hichwa, R. D. (1996). A neural basis for lexical retrieval. *Nature, 380*(6574), 499–505.

Dawes, R. M. (1988). *Rational choice in an uncertain world.* San Diego: Harcourt Brace Jovanovich.

Dawes, R. M., & Corrigan, B. (1974). Linear models in decision making. *Psychological Bulletin, 81,* 95–106.

De Groot, A. D. (1965) *Thought and choice in chess.* The Hague, Netherlands: Mouton.

Deci, E. L. (1971). Effects of externally mediated rewards on intrinsic motivation. *Journal of Personality and Social Psychology, 18,* 105–115.

DeLoache, J. S. (1995). Early symbol understanding and use. In D. L. Medin (Ed.), *The psychology of learning and motivation, vol. 33.* New York: Academic Press.

DeLoache, J. S., Miller, K. F., & Rosengren, K. S. (1997). The credible shrinking room: Very young children's performance with symbolic and nonsymbolic relations. *Psychological Science, 8*(4), 308–313.

Dennett, D. C. (1991). *Consciousness explained.* Boston: Little, Brown, and Company.

Dennett, D. C., & Kinsbourne, M. (1992). Time and the observer: The where and when of consciousness in the brain. *Behavioral & Brain Sciences, 15*(2), 183–247.

Denniston, J. C., Miller, R. R., & Matute, H. (1996). Biological significance as a determinant of cue competition. *Psychological Science, 7,* 325–331.

Desimone, R., & Duncan, J. (1995). Neural mechanisms of selective visual attention. *Annual Review of Neuroscience, 18,* 193–222.

Deutsch, J. A., & Deutsch, D. (1963). Attention: Some theoretical considerations. *Psychological Review, 70,* 80–90.

Devine, P. G. (1989). Stereotypes and prejudice: Their automatic and controlled components. *Journal of Personality and Social Psychology, 56,* 5–18.

Di Sessa, A. A. (1982). Unlearning Aristotelian physics: A case study of knowledge-based learning. *Cognitive Science, 6,* 37–75.

Dickinson, A., Shanks, D., & Evenden, J. (1984). Judgment of act-outcome contingency: The role of selective attribution. *Quarterly Journal of Experimental Psychology, 36A,* 29–50.

Diehl, R. L., & Kluender, K. R. (1987). On the categorization of speech sounds. In S. Harnad (Ed.), *Categorical perception.* Cambridge: Cambridge University Press.

Diwadkar, V. A., & McNamara, T. P. (1997). Viewpoint dependence in scene recognition. *Psychological Science, 8*(4), 302–307.

Doane, S. M., McNamara, D. S., Kinstch, W., Polson, P. G., Clawson, D. M., & Dungca, R. G. (1992). Prompt comprehension of UNIX command production. *Memory & Cognition, 20,* 327–343.

Domjan, M., & Burkhard, B. (1986). *The principles of learning and behavior.* Monterey, CA: Brooks/Cole.

Downing, C. & Pinker, S. (1985). The spatial structure of visual attention. In M. Posner and O. Marin (Eds.) *Attention and Performance XI* (pp. 171–187). Hillsdale, NJ: Erlbaum.

Driskell, J. E., Copper, C., & Moran, A. (1994). Does mental practice enhance performance? *Journal of Applied Psychology, 79,* 481–492.

Driver, J., & Baylis, G. C. (1998). Attention and visual object segmentation. In R. Parasuraman (Ed.) *The attentive brain* (pp. 299–325). Cambridge, MA: The MIT Press.

Dunbar, K. (1995). How scientists really reason: Scientific reasoning in real-world laboratories. In R. J. Sternberg & J. E. Davidson (Eds.), *The Nature of Insight* (pp. 365–396). Cambridge, MA: The MIT Press.

Dunbar, K. (1997). How scientists think: On-line creativity and conceptual change in science. In T. B. Ward, S. M. Smith, & J. Vaid (Eds.), *Creative Thought: An investigation of conceptual structures and processes* (pp. 461–493). Washington, DC: American Psychological Association.

Dunbar, K., & MacLeod, C. M. (1984). A horse race of a different color: Stroop interference patterns with transformed words. *Journal of Experimental Psychology: Human Perception and Performance, 10,* 622–639.

Duncan, J., & Humphreys, G. W. (1989). Visual search and stimulus similarity. *Psychological Review, 96,* 433–458.

Duncker, K. (1945). On problem solving. *Psychological Monographs, 58:5,* Whole No. 270.

Ebbinghaus, H. (1885). *Uber das gedachtnis.* Leipzig: Duncker and Humbolt.

Eddy, D. M. (1982). Probabilistic reasoning in clinical medicine: Problems and opportunities. In D. Kahneman, P. Slovic, & A. Tversky (Eds.), *Judgment under uncertainty: Heuristics and biases.* Cambridge: Cambridge University Press.

Edwards, W., Lindman, H., & Savage, L. J. (1963). Bayesian statistical inferences for psychological research. *Psychological Review, 70,* 193–242.

Egan, D., & Schwartz, B. (1979). Chunking in recall of symbolic drawings. *Memory & Cognition, 7,* 149–158.

Egeth, H. E., & Yantis, S. (1997). Visual attention: Control, representation, and time course. In J. T. Spence, J. M. Darley, & D. J. Foss (Eds.), *Annual Review of Psychology, Vol. 48* (pp. 269–297). Palo Alto, CA: Annual Reviews Inc.

Egly, R., Driver, J., & Rafal, R. D. (1994). Shifting visual attention between objects and locations: Evidence from normal and parietal lesion patients. *Journal of Experimental Psychology: General, 123,* 161–177.

Eich, E. (1995). Searching for mood dependent memory. *Psychological Science, 6,* 67–75.

Einhorn, H. J., & Hogarth, R. M. (1978). Confidence in judgment: Persistence of the illusion of validity. *Psychological Review, 85,* 395–416.

Einhorn, H. J., & Hogarth, R. M. (1986). Judging probable cause. *Psychological Bulletin, 99,* 3–19.

Einstein, G. O., & McDaniel, M. A. (1987). Distinctiveness and the mnemonic benefits of bizarre imagery. In M. A. McDaniel & M. Pressley (Eds.), *Imagery and related mnemonic processes: Theories, individual differences and applications.* New York: Springer-Verlag.

Eisenberger, R. & Cameron, J. (1996). Detrimental effects of reward: Reality or myth? *American Psychologist, 11,* 1153–1166.

Ellis, A. W., & Young, A. M. (1988). *Human cognitive neuropsychology.* Hillsdale, NJ: Erlbaum.

Ellman, T. (1989). Explanation-based learning: A survey of programs and perspectives. *Computing Surveys, 21,* 163–221.

Elman, J. L., Bates, E. A., Johnson, M. H., Karmiloff-Smith, A., Parisi, D., & Plunkett, K. (1996). *Rethinking innateness.* Cambridge, MA: The MIT Press.

Erdfelder, E., & Bredenkamp, J. (1998). Recognition of script-typical versus script-atypical information: Effects of cognitive elaboration. *Memory & Cognition, 26,* 922–938.

Erickson, M. A., & Kruschke, J. K. (1998). Rules and exemplars in category learning. *Journal of Experimental Psychology: General, 127,* 107–140.

Ericsson, K. A., & Charness, N. (1994). Expert performance: Its structure and acquisition. *American Psychologist, 49,* 725–747.

Ericsson, K. A., & Kintsch, W. (1995) Long-term working memory. *Psychological Review, 102,* 211–245.

Ericsson, K. A., Krampe, R. T., & Tesch-Römer, C. (1993). The role of deliberate practice in the acquisition of expert performance. *Psychological Review, 100,* 363–406.

Ericsson, K. A., & Lehmann, A. C. (1996). Expert and exceptional performance: Evidence of maximal adaptation to task constraints. *Annual Review of Psychology, 47,* 273–305.

Ericsson, K. A., & Simon, H. A. (1993). *Protocol analysis: verbal reports as data.* Cambridge, MA: MIT Press.

Estes, W. K. (1969). Reinforcement in human learning. In J. Tapp (Ed.), *Reinforcement and behavior.* New York: Academic Press.

Estes, W. K. (1976). Structural aspects of associative models for memory. In C. F. Cofer (Ed.), *The structure of human memory.* San Francisco: W. H. Freeman.

Estes, W. K. (1994). *Classification and cognition.* Oxford: Oxford University Press.

Estes, W. K., (1986). Array models for category learning. *Cognitive Psychology, 18,* 500–549.

Evans, J. St. B. T. (1977). Linguistic factors in reasoning. *Quarterly Journal of Experimental Psychology, 29,* 297–306.

Evans, J. St. B. T. (1982). *The psychology of deductive reasoning.* London: Routledge and Kegan Paul.

Evans, J. St. B. T. (1983). Selective processes in reasoning. In J. St. B. T. Evans (Ed.), *Thinking and reasoning.* London: Routledge and Kegan Paul.

Evans, J. St. B. T., & Lynch, J. S. (1973). Matching bias in the selection task. *British Journal of Psychology, 64,* 391–397.

Falkenhainer, B., Forbus, K. D., & Gentner, D. (1990). The structure-mapping engine. *Artificial Intelligence, 41,* 1–63.

Farah, M. J. (1988). Is visual imagery really visual? Overlooked evidence from neuropsychology. *Psychological Review, 95,* 307–317.

Farah, M. J. (1990). *Visual agnosia: Disorders of object recognition and what they tell us about normal vision.* Cambridge, MA: MIT Press.

Farah, M. J. (1992). Is an object an object and object? Cognitive and neuropsychological investigations of domain specificity in visual object recognition. *Current Directions in Psychological Science, 2,* 55–82.

Farah, M. J., Hammond, K. M., Levine, D. N., & Calvanio, R. (1988). Visual and spatial mental imagery: Dissociable systems of representation. *Cognitive Psychology, 20,* 439–462.

Farah, M. J., Peronnet, F., Gonon, M. A., & Giard, M. G. (1988). Electrophysiological evidence for a shared representational medium for visual images and visual percepts. *Journal of Experimental Psychology: General, 117,* 248–257.

Farah, M. J., Wilson, K. D., Drain, M., & Tanaka, J. N. (1998). What is "special" about face perception. *Psychological Review, 105*(3), 482–498.

Feigenbaum, E. A. (1983). Knowledge engineering: The applied side. In J. E. Hayes & D. Michie (Eds.), *Intelligent systems.* West Sussex: Ellis Horwood.

Feigenbaum, E. A. (1989). What hath Simon wrought? In D. Klahr & K. Kotovsky

(Eds.), *Complex information processing: The impact of Herbert A. Simon.* Hillsdale, NJ: Erlbaum.

Ferguson, E. L., & Hegarty, M. (1994). Properties of cognitive maps constructed from texts. *Memory and Cognition, 22,* 455–473.

Fernandez-Duque, D. & Johnson, M. L. (1999). Attention metaphors: How metaphors guide the cognitive psychology of attention. *Cognitive Science, 23,* 83–116.

Ferster, C. S., & Skinner, B. F. (1957). *Schedules of reinforcement.* New York: Appleton-Century-Crofts.

Fiedler, K. (1988). The dependence of the conjunction fallacy on subtle linguistic factors. *Psychological Research, 50,* 123–129.

Fiez, J. A., & Peterson, S. E. (1993). PET as part of an interdisciplinary approach to understanding processes involved in reading. *Psychological Science, 4,* 287–293.

Finke, R. A. (1985). Theories relating mental imagery to perception. *Psychological Bulletin, 98,* 236–259.

Finke, R. A., Pinker, S., & Farah, M. J. (1989). Reinterpreting visual patterns in mental imagery. *Cognitive Science, 13,* 51–78.

Finke, R. A., Ward, T. B., & Smith, S. M. (1992). *Creative cognition: Theory, research, and applications.* Cambridge, MA: MIT Press.

Finkenauer, C., Luminet, O., Gisle, L., El-Ahmadi, A., van der Linden, M., & Philippot, P. (1998). Flashbulb memories and the underlying mechanisms of their formation: Toward an emotional-integrative model. *Memory & Cognition, 26,* 516–531.

Finucane, M. L., Alhakami, A., & Slovic, P. (in press). The heuristic affect in jedgmenets of risks and benefits. *Journal of Behavioral Decision Making.*

Fischhoff, B. (1982). For those condemned to study the past: Heuristics and biases in hindsight. In D. Kahneman, P. Slovic, & A. Tversky (Eds.), *Judgment under uncertainty: Heuristics and biases.* Cambridge: Cambridge University Press.

Fischhoff, B. (1988). Judgement and decision making. In R. J. Sternberg & E. E. Smith (Eds.), *The psychology of human thought.* Cambridge: Cambridge University Press.

Fisher, R. P., & Craik, F. I. M. (1977). Interaction between encoding and retrieval operations in cued recall. *Journal of Experimental Psychology: Human Learning and Memory, 3,* 701–711.

Fiske, A. P., & Tetlock, P. E. (1997). Taboo trade-offs: Reactions to transactions that transgress the spheres of justice. *Political Psychology, 18*(2), 255–297.

Fiske, S. T., Lin, M., Neuberg, S. L. (1999). The continuum model: Ten years later. In S. Chaiken, Y. Trope (Eds.), *Dual process theories in social psychology.* New York: Guildford.

Fiske, S. T., Neuberg, S. L., Beattie, A. E., & Milberg, S. J. (1987). Category-based and attribute-based reactions to others: Some informational conditions of stereotyping and individuating processes. *Journal of Experimental Social Psychology, 23*(5), 399–427.

Flaherty, C. F., & Becker, H. C. (1984). Influence of conditioned stimulus context on hyperglycemic conditioned responses. *Physiology & Behavior, 33,* 587–593.

Flann, N. S., & Dietterich, T. G. (1989). A study of explanation-based methods for inductive learning. *Machine Learning, 4,* 187–226.

Flannagan, M. J., Fried, L. S., & Holyoak, K. J. (1986). Distributional expectations and the induction of category structure. *Journal of Experimental Psychology: Learning, Memory, and Cognition, 12,* 241–256.

Flannagan, O. (1998). Consciousness. In W. Bechtel & G. Graham, (Eds.), *A Companion to Cognitive Science* (pp. 176–185). Malden, Mass.: Blackwell Publishers.

Fodor, J. A. (1981). *Representations.* Cambridge, MA: MIT Press.

Fodor, J. A., Bever, T. G., & Garrett, M. F. (1974). *The psychology of language.* New York: McGraw-Hill.

Fodor, J., & Lepore, E. (1996). The red herring and the pet fish: Why concepts still can't be prototypes. *Cognition, 58,* 253–270.

Fodor, J. A., & Pylyshyn, Z. W. (1981). How direct is visual perception? Some reflections on Gibson's "ecological approach." *Cognition, 9,* 139–196.

Forde, E. M. E., & Humphreys, G. W. (1999). Category-specific recognition impairments: A review of important case studies and influential theories. *Aphasiology, 13*(3), 169–193.

Frank, R. H. (1988). *Passions within reason: The strategic role of the emotions.* New York, NY: W.

Frazer, J. G. (1959). *The new golden bough.* New York: Criterion Books.

French, R. M. (1999). Catastrophic forgetting in connectionist network. *Trends in Cognitive Sciences, 3*(4), 128–135.

Fried, L. S., & Holyoak, K. J. (1984). Induction of category distributions: A framework for classification learning. *Journal of Experimental Psychology: Learning, Memory, and Cognition, 10,* 234–257.

Fujisaki, H., & Kawashima, T. (1970). Some experiments on speech perception and a model for the perceptual mechanism. *Annual Report of the Engineering Institute (University of Tokyo), 29,* 207–219.

Fussell, S. R., & Kreuz, R. J. (Eds.) (1998). *Social and cognitive approaches to interpersonal communication.* Mahwah, NJ: Erlbaum..

Gabrieli, J. D. E. (1998). Cognitive neuroscience of human memory. *Annual Review of Psychology, 49,* 87–115.

Gabrieli, J. D. E., Cohen, N. J., & Corkin, S. (1988). The impaired learning of semantic knowledge following bilateral medial temporal-lobe resection. *Brain and Cognition, 7,* 157–177.

Gadzar, G., Klein, E., Pullum, G., & Sag, I. (1985). *Generalized phrase structure grammar.* Cambridge, MA: Harvard University Press.

Gagne, C. L., & Shoben, E. J. (1997). Influence of thematic relations on the comprehension of modifier-noun combinations. *Journal of Experimental Psychology: Learning, Memory, & Cognition, 23*(1), 71–87.

Gallistel, C. R. (1990). *The organization of learning.* Cambridge, MA: MIT Press.

Garcia, J., Hawkins, W. G., & Rusiniak, K. W. (1974). Behavioral regulation of the milieu interne in man and rat. *Science, 85,* 824–831.

Gardner, H. (1974). *The shattered mind.* New York: Vintage.

Gardner, H. (1983). *Frames of mind: The theory of multiple intelligences.* New York: Basic Books.

Garnsey, S. M., Pearlmutter, N. J., Myers, E., & Lotocky, M. A. (1997). The contributions of verb bias and plausibility to the comprehension of temporarily ambiguous sentences. *Journal of Memory and Language, 37*(1), 58–93.

Garry, M., Manning, C. G., Loftus, E. F., & Sherman, S. J. (1996). Imagination inflation: Imagining a childhood event inflates confidence that it occurred. *Psychonomic Bulletin and Review, 3*(2), 208–214.

Gati, I., & Tversky, A. (1984). Weighting common and distinctive features in perceptual and conceptual judgments. *Cognitive Psychology, 16,* 341–370.

Gauthier, I., & Tarr, M. J. (1997). Becoming a "greeble" expert: Exploring mechanisms for face recognition. *Vision Research, 37,* 1673–1682.

Gelman, S. A. (1996). Concepts and theories. In R. Gelman & T. Au (Eds.), *Handbook of perception and cognition (Volume 13): Perceptual and cognitive development* (pp. 117–150). New York: Academic Press.

Gelman, S. A. (1998). Categories in young children's thinking. *Young Children, 53,* 20–26.

Gelman, S. A., Coley, J. D., & Gottfried, G. M. (1994). Essentialist beliefs in children: The acquisition of concepts and theories. In L. A. Hirschfeld & S. A. Gelman (Eds.), *Mapping the mind: Domain specificity in cognition and culture* (pp. 341–366). New York: Cambridge University Press.

Gelman, S. A., & Hirschfeld, L. A. (1999). How biological is essentialism? In D. L. Medin & S. Atran (Eds.), *Folkbiology* (pp. 403–446). Cambridge, MA: Bradford.

Gelman, S. A., & Markman, E. M. (1986). Categories and induction in young children. *Cognition, 23,* 183–209.

Gelman, S. A., & Wellman, H. M. (1991). Insides and essence: Early understandings of the non-obvious. *Cognition, 38,* 213–244.

Gentner, D. (1981). Some interesting differences between nouns and verbs. *Cognition and Brain Theory, 4,* 161–178.

Gentner, D. (1983). Structure-mapping: A theoretical framework for analogy. *Cognitive Science, 1,* 155–170.

Gentner, D. (1989). The mechanisms of analogical reasoning. In S. Vosniadou & A. Ortony (Eds.), *Similarity and analogical reasoning.* Cambridge: Cambridge University Press.

Gentner, D., & Markman, A. B. (1994). Structural alignment in comparison: No difference without similarity. *Psychological Science, 5*(3), 152–158.

Gentner, D., & Markman, A. B. (1997). Structural alignment in analogy and similarity. *American Psychologist, 52*(1), 45–56.

Gentner, D., Rattermann, M. J., & Forbus, K. D. (1993). The roles of similarity in transfer: Separating retrievability from inferential soundness. *Cognitive Psychology, 25,* 524–575.

Gentner, D., & Stevens, A. L. (Eds.). (1983). *Mental models.* Hillsdale, NJ: Erlbaum.

Gerrig, R. J., & Murphy, G. L. (1992). Contextual influences on the comprehension of complex concepts. *Language & Cognitive Processes, 7,* 205–230.

Gettys, C. F., Manning, C., Mehle, T., & Fisher, S. (1980). *Hypothesis generation: A final report of three years of research (Report No. TR-15-10–80).* Decision Processes Laboratory, Dept. of Psychology, University of Oklahoma, Norman, OK.

Getzels, J., & Czikszentmihalyi, M. (1976). *The creative vision: A longitudinal study of problem finding in art.* New York: John Wiley.

Gibbon, J., & Balsam, P. (1981). Spreading association in time. In C. M. Locurto, H. S. Terrace, & J. Gibbon (Eds.), *Autoshaping and conditioning theory.* New York: Academic Press.

Gibson, J. J. (1950). *The perception of the visual world.* Boston: Houghton Mifflin.

Gibson, J. J. (1979). *The ecological approach to visual perception.* Boston: Houghton Mifflin.

Gibson, J. J. (1986). The ecological approach to visual perception. Hillsdale, NJ: Lawrence Erlbaum Associates.

Gick, M. L. (1985). The effect of a diagram retrieval cue on spontaneous analogical transfer. *Canadian Journal of Psychology, 39,* 460–466.

Gick, M. L. (1986). Problem-solving strategies. *Educational Psychologist, 21,* 99–120.

Gick, M. L., & Holyoak, K. J. (1980). Analogical problem solving. *Cognitive Psychology, 12,* 306–355.

Gick, M. L., & Holyoak, K. J. (1983). Schema induction and analogical transfer. *Cognitive Psychology, 15,* 1–38.

Gick, M. L., & McGarry, S. J. (1992). Learning from mistakes: Inducing analogous solution failures to a source problem produces later successes in analogical transfer. *Journal of Experimental Psychology: Learning, Memory, and Cognition, 18,* 623–639.

Gigerenzer, G. (1994). Why the distinction between single-event probabilities and frequencies is important for psychology (and vice versa). In G. Wright & P. Ayton (Eds.), *Subjective probability* (pp. 129–161). New York: John Wiley and Sons.

Gigerenzer, G. (1996). On narrow norms and vague heuristics: A reply to Kahneman and Tversky (1996). *Psychological Review, 103*(3), 592–596.

Gigerenzer, G., Hell, W., & Blank, H. (1988). Presentation and content: The use of base rates as a continuous variable. *Journal of Experimental Psychology: General, 14,* 513–525.

Gigerenzer, G., & Hoffrage, U. (1995). How to improve Bayesian reasoning without instruction: Frequency formats. *Psychological Review, 102*(4), 684–704.

Gigerenzer, G. & Hug, K. (1992). Domain specific reasoning: Social contracts, cheating, and perspective change. *Cognition, 43,* 127–171.

Gilovich, T., & Medvec, V. H. (1995). The experience of regret: What, when, and why. *Psychological Review, 102,* 379–395.

Glenberg, A. M. (1976). Monotonic and nonmonotonic lag effects in paired-associate and recognition memory. *Journal of Verbal Learning and Verbal Behavior, 15,* 1–16.

Glenberg, A. M. (1979). Component-levels theory of the effect of spacing of repetitions on recall and recognition. *Memory & Cognition, 7,* 95–112.

Glenberg, A. M., Kruley, P., & Langston, W. E. (1994). Analogical processes in comprehension: Simulation of a mental model. In M. A. Gernsbacher (Ed.), *Handbook of Psycholinguistics* . New York: Academic Press.

Glisky, E. L., Schacter, D. L., & Tulving, E. (1986). Learning and retention of computer-related vocabulary in amnesic patients: Method of vanishing cues. *Journal of Clinical and Experimental Neuropsychology, 8,* 292–312.

Glucksberg, S., & Danks, J. (1968). Effects of discriminative labels and of nonsense labels upon availability of novel function. *Journal of Verbal Learning and Verbal Behavior, 7,* 72–76.

Glushko, R. J. (1979). The organization and activation of orthographic knowledge in reading aloud. *Journal of Experimental Psychology: Human Perception and Performance, 5,* 674–691.

Gobet, F., & Simon, H. A. (1996). The roles of recognition processes and look-ahead search in time-constrained expert problem-solving: Evidence from grand-master-level chess. *Psychological Science, 7,* 52–55.

Godden, D. R., & Baddeley, A. D. (1975). Context-dependent memory in two natural environments: On land and underwater. *British Journal of Psychology, 66,* 325–331.

Golding, E. (1981). The effect of past experience on problem solving. Paper presented at the *Annual Conference of the British Psychological Society,* Surrey University.

Goldmeier, E. (1972). Similarity in visually perceived forms. *Psychological Issues Monograph, 8*(1), 135.

Goldowsky, B. N., & Newport, E. L. (1993). Modeling the effects of processing limitations on the acquisition of morphology: The less is more hypothesis. In J. Mead (Ed.), *Proceedings of the 11th West Coast Conference on Formal Linguistics* (pp. 124–138). Stanford, CA: Center for the Study of Language and Information.

Goldstein, W. M., & Weber, E. U. (1995). Content and discontent: Indications and implications of domain specificity in preferential decision making. In J. Busemayer, R. Hastie, & D. L. Medin (Eds.), *The psychology of learning and motivation, vol. 32.* San Diego: Academic Press.

Goldstone, R. L. (1994a). The role of similarity in categorization: Providing a groundwork. *Cognition, 52,* 125–157.

Goldstone, R. L. (1994b). Influences of categorization on perceptual discrimination. *Journal of Experimental Psychology: General, 123,* 178–200.

Goldstone, R. L. (1998). Perceptual Learning. *Annual Review of Psychology, 49,* 585–612.

Goldstone, R. L., & Medin, D. L. (1994). Time course of comparison. *Journal of Experimental Psychology: Learning, Memory, and Cognition, 20,* 29–50.

Goodglass, H., & Geschwind, N. (1976). Language disorders (APHASIA). *Handbook of Perception, 7,* 389–428.

Goodman, N. (1955). *Fact, fiction, and forecast.* Cambridge: Harvard University Press.

Goodman, N. (1972). Seven strictures on similarity. In N. Goodman (Ed.), *Problems and projects.* New York: Bobbs-Merrill.

Gopnik, A., & Meltzoff, A. N. (1997). *Words, thoughts, and theories.* Cambridge, MA: MIT Press.

Gopnik, A., & Wellman, H. M. (1994). The theory theory. In L. A. Hirschfeld & S. A. Gelman (Eds.), *Mapping the mind: Domain specificity in cognition and culture* (pp. 257–293). New York: Cambridge University Press.

Gordon, W. J. J. (1961). *Synectics.* New York: Harper & Row.

Gotlib, I. H., & McCann, C. D. (1984). Construct accessibility and depression: An examination of cognitive and affective factors. *Journal of Personality and Social Psychology, 47,* 427–439.

Grabowecky, M., Robertson, L. C., & Treisman, A. (1993). Preattentive processes guide visual search: Evidence from patients with unilateral neglect. *Journal of Cognitive Neuroscience, 5,* 288–302.

Graesser, A. C., Millis, K. K., & Zwaan, R. A. (1997). Discourse comprehension. *Annual Review of Psychology, 48*, 163–189.

Graesser, A. C., Singer, M., & Trabasso, T. (1994). Constructing inferences during narrative text comprehension. *Psychological Review, 101*, 371–395.

Graf, P., Squire, L. R., & Mandler, G. (1984). The information that amnesic patients do not forget. *Journal of Experimental Psychology: Learning, Memory, and Cognition, 10*, 164–178.

Graham, N. (1992). Breaking the visual stimulus into parts. *Current Directions in Psychological Science, 1*(2), 55–61.

Greene, R. L. (1989). Spacing effects in memory: Evidence for a two-process account. *Journal of Experimental Psychology: Learning, Memory, and Cognition, 15*, 371–377.

Greenwald, A. G., & Banaji, M. R. (1995). Implicit social cognition: Attitudes, self-esteem, and stereotypes. *Psychological Review, 102*(1), 4–27.

Grether, D. M., & Plott, C. R. (1979). Economic theory of choice and the preference reversal phenomenon. *American Economic Review, 69*, 623–638.

Grice, H. P. (1975). Logic and conversation. In P. Cole and J. L. Morgan (Eds.), *Syntax and semantics III: Speech acts.* New York: Seminar Press.

Griggs, R. A. (1983). The role of problem content in the selection task and in the THOG problem. In J. St. B. T. Evans (Ed.), *Thinking and reasoning: Psychological approaches.* London: Routledge.

Griggs, R. A., & Cox, J. R. (1982). The elusive thematic materials effect in Wason's selection task. *British Journal of Psychology, 73*, 407–420.

Grimes, J. (1996). On the failure to detect changes in scenes across saccades. In K. Akins (Ed.), *Perception* (pp. 89–110). New York: Oxford University Press.

Guilford, J. P. (1959). The three faces of intellect. *American Psychologist, 14*, 469–479.

Gutheil, G., & Gelman, S. A. (1997). Children's use of sample size and diversity information within basic-level categories. *Journal of Experimental Child Psychology, 64*, 159–174.

Halpern, A. R. (1986). Memory for tune titles after organized or unorganized presentation. *American Journal of Psychology, 99*, 57–70.

Hamilton, D. L. (1976). Cognitive biases in the perception of social groups. In J. S. Carroll & J. W. Payne (Eds.), *Cognition and social behavior.* Hillsdale, NJ: Erlbaum.

Hamilton, W. J., & Orians, G. H. (1965). Evolution of brood parasitism in altricial birds. *Condor, 67*, 361–382.

Hammond, K. J. (1989). *Case-based planning: Viewing planning as a memory task.* San Diego: Academic Press.

Hampton, J. A. (1987). Inheritance of attributes in natural concept conjunctions. *Memory & Cognition, 15*, 55–71.

Hampton, J. A. (1993). Prototype models of concept representation. In I. van Mechelen, J. A. Hampton, R. S. Michalski & P. Theuns (Eds.), *Categories and concepts: Theoretical views and inductive data analysis* (pp. 67–95). London: Academic.

Hampton, J. A. (1996). Conjunctions of visually based categories: Overextension and compensation. *Journal of Experimental Psychology: Learning, Memory & Cognition, 22*, 378–396.

Hardin, G. (1968). The tragedy of the commons. *Science, 162*, 1243–1248.

Hastorf, A. & Cantril, H. (1954). They saw a game: A case study. *Journal of Abnormal and Social Psychology, 49*, 129–134.

Hatano, G. & Inagaki, K. (1994). Young children's naive theory of biology. *Cognition, 50*, 171–188.

Hauser, M. D. (1996). *The evolution of communication.* Cambridge, MA: The MIT Press.

Haviland, S. E., & Clark, H. H. (1974). What's new? Acquiring new information as a process in comprehension. *Journal of Verbal Learning and Verbal Behavior, 13*, 512–521.

Hawkins, R. D., & Bower, G. H. (Eds.). (1989). Computational models of learning in simple neural systems. *The psychology of learning and motivation, vol. 23.* San Diego: Academic Press.

Hayes, J. R. (1989). *The complete problem solver (2nd ed.).* Hillsdale, NJ: Erlbaum.

Heath, C. (1995). Escalation and de-escalation of commitment in response to sunk costs: The role of budgeting in mental accounting. *Organizational Behavior and Human Decision Processes, 62,* 38–54.

Heit, E. (1994). Models of the effects of prior knowledge on categorization. *Journal of Experimental Psychology: Learning, Memory, and Cognition, 20,* 11–19.

Hellige, J. B., & Michimata, C. (1989). Categorization versus distance: Hemispheric differences for processing spatial information. *Memory & Cognition, 17,* 770–776.

Henderson, P. W., & Peterson, R. A. (1992). Mental accounting and categorization. *Organizational Behavior and Human Decision Processes, 51,* 92–117.

Henle, M. (1962). On the relation between logic and thinking. *Psychological Review, 69,* 366–378.

Herz, R. S. (1998). Emotion experienced during encoding enhances odor retrieval cue effectiveness. *American Journal of Psychology, 110,* 489–505.

Hesse, M. B. (1966). *Models and Analogies in Science.* Notre Dame, IN: University of Notre Dame Press.

Hildreth, E. C., & Ullman, S. (1989). The computational study of vision. In M. I. Posner (Ed.), *Foundations of cognitive science.* Cambridge, MA: MIT Press.

Hilton, D. J., & Slugoski, B. R. (1986). Knowledge-based causal attribution: The abnormal conditions focus model. *Psychological Review, 93,* 75–88.

Hinton, G. E. (1979). Some demonstrations of the effects of structural descriptions in mental imagery. *Cognitive Science, 3,* 231–250.

Hintzman, D. L. (1976). Repetition and memory. In G. H. Bower (Ed.), *The psychology of learning and motivation, vol. 11.* New York: Academic Press.

Hintzman, D. L. (1984). Episodic versus semantic memory: A distinction whose time has come" and gone? *Behavioral and Brain Sciences, 7,* 240–241.

Hintzman, D. L. (1986). "Schema abstraction" in a multiple-trace memory model. *Psychological Review, 93,* 411–428.

Hintzman, D. L. (1988). Judgments of frequency and recognition memory in a multiple-trace memory model. Psychological Review, 95, 528–551.

Hirschfeld, L. A. (1994). The child's representation of human groups. In D. L. Medin (Ed.), *The psychology of learning and motivation, vol. 31* (pp. 131–185). New York: Academic Press.

Hirschfeld, L. A. (1996). *Race in the making: Cognition, culture, and the child's construction of human kinds.* Cambridge, MA: MIT Press.

Hirschfeld, L. A., & Gelman, S. A. (Eds.). (1994). *Mapping the mind: Domain specificity in cognition and culture.* New York: Cambridge University Press.

Hirsh, K. W., & Ellis, A. W. (1994). Age of acquisition and aphasia: A case study. *Cognitive Neuropsychology, 11,* 435–458.

Hirst, D. E., Joyce, E. J., & Schadewald, M. S. (1994). Mental accounting and outcome contiguity in consumer-borrowing decisions. *Organizational Behavior & Human Decision Processes, 58*(1), 136–152.

Hirst, W., Spelke, E. S., Reaves, C. C., Caharack, G., & Neisser, U. (1980). Dividing attention without alternation or automaticity. *Journal of Experimental Psychology: General, 109,* 98–117.

Hirtle, S. C., & Jonides, J. (1985). Evidence of hierarchies in cognitive maps. *Memory & Cognition, 13,* 208–217.

Hochberg, J. E. (1964). *Perception.* Englewood Cliffs, NJ: Prentice-Hall.

Hodgson, C., & Ellis, A. W. (1998). Last in, first to go: Age of acquisition and naming in the elderly. *Brain and Language, 64,* 146–163.

Hoffman, H. W., & Ratner, A. M. (1983). A reinforcement model of imprinting: Implications for socialization in monkeys and men. *Psychological Review, 80,* 527–544.

Hogarth, R. M. (1981). Beyond discrete biases: Functional and dysfunctional aspects of judgmental heuristics. *Psychological Bulletin, 90,* 197–217.

Hogarth, R. (Ed.). (1990). *Insights in decision making.* Chicago: University of Chicago Press.

Holding, D. H. (1985). *The psychology of chess skill.* Hillsdale, NJ: Erlbaum.

Holland, J. H., Holyoak, K. J., Nisbett, R. E., & Thagard, P. R. (1986). *Induction.* Cambridge, MA: MIT Press.

Holland, P. C. (1984). Origins of behavior in Pavlovian conditioning. In G. H. Bower (Ed.), *The psychology of learning and motivation, vol. 18.* Orlando, FL: Academic Press.

Hollis, K. L. (1997). Contemporary research on Pavlovian conditioning: A "new" functional analysis. *American Psychologist, 52,* 956–965.

Holyoak, K. J. (1991). Symbolic connectionism: Toward third-generation theories of expertise. In K. A. Ericsson & J. Smith (Eds.), Toward a general theory of expertise: Prospects and limits. Cambridge: Cambridge University Press.

Holyoak, K. J., & Koh, K. (1987). Surface and structural similarity in analogical transfer. Memory & Cognition, 15, 332–340.

Holyoak, K. J., & Thagard, P. (1989). Analogical mapping by constraint satisfaction. *Cognitive Science, 13,* 295–355.

Holyoak, K. J., & Thagard, P. (1995). *Mental leaps.* Cambridge, MA: MIT Press.

Holyoak, K. J., Koh, K., & Nisbett, R. E. (1989). A theory of conditioning: Inductive learning with rule-based default hierarchies. *Psychological Review, 96,* 315–340.

Homa, D. (1984). On the nature of categories. In G. H. Bower (Ed.), *The psychology of learning and motivation, vol. 18.* Orlando, FL: Academic Press.

Homa, D., & Vosburgh, R. (1976). Category breadth and the abstraction of prototypical information. *Journal of Experimental Psychology: Human Learning and Memory, 2,* 322–330.

Howard, J., & Rothbart, M. (1980). Social categorization and memory for ingroup and outgroup behavior. *Journal of Personality and Social Psychology, 38,* 301–310.

Hsee, C. K., Blount, S., Loewenstein, G. F., & Bazerman, M. H. (1999). Preference reversals between joint and separate evaluations of options: A review and theoretical analysis. *Psychological Bulletin, 125*(5), 576–590.

Huber, J., Payne, J. W., & Puto, C. (1982). Adding asymmetrically dominated alternatives: Violations of regularity and the similarity hypothesis. *Journal of Consumer Research, 9,* 90–98.

Hummel, J. E., & Biederman, I. (1992). Dynamic binding in a neural network for shape recognition. *Psychological Review, 99,* 480–517.

Hummel, J. E., & Holyoak, K. J. (1997). Distributed representations of structure: A theory of analogical access and mapping. *Psychological Review, 104*(3), 427–466.

Humphreys, G. W., & Muller, H. J. (1993). Search via recursive rejection (SERR): A connectionist model of visual search. Cognitive Psychology, 25, 43–110.

Hunter, I. M. L. (1966/1977). Mental calculation. In P. N. Johnson-Laird & P. C. Wason (Eds.), *Thinking: Readings in cognitive science.* Cambridge: Cambridge University Press.

Hyde, T. S., & Jenkins, J. J. (1969). The differential effects of incidental tasks on the organization of recall of a list of highly associated words. *Journal of Experimental Psychology, 82,* 472–481.

Inagaki, K. (1997). Emerging distinctions between naive biology and naive psychology. In H. M. Wellman & K. Inagaki (Eds.), *The emergence of core domains of thought: Children's reasoning about physical, psychological, and biological phenomena. New directions for child development, No. 75* (pp. 27–44). San Francisco, CA: Jossey-Bass.

Intons-Peterson, M. J. (1983). Imagery paradigms: How vulnerable are they to experimenters' expectancies? *Journal of Experimental Psychology: Human Perception and Performance, 9,* 394–412.

Intons-Peterson, M. J., & White, A. R. (1981). Experimenter naivete and imagined judgments. *Journal of Experimental Psychology: Human Perception and Performance, 11,* 317–328.

Irwin, D. (1996). Integrating information across saccadic eye movements. *Current Directions in Psychological Science, 5,* 94–100.

Irwin, D. E. (1991). Information integration across saccadic eye movements. *Cognitive Psychology, 23,* 420–456.

Isen, A. M. (1993). Positive affect and decision making. In M. H. J. M. Lewis (Ed.), *Handbook of emotions* (pp. 261–277). New York, NY: Guilford Press.

Ivry, R. B., & Robertson, L. C. (1998). *The two sides of perception.* Cambridge, MA: The MIT Press.

Jackendoff, R. (1994). *Patterns in the mind.* New York: Basic Books.

Jacoby, L. L. (1983). Remembering the data: Analyzing interactive processes in reading. *Journal of Verbal Learning and Verbal Behavior, 22,* 485–508.

Jacoby, L. L., & Dallas, M. (1981). On the relationship between autobiographical memory and perceptual learning. *Journal of Experimental Psychology: General, 110,* 306–340.

Jacoby, L. L., Kelley, C., Brown, J., & Jasechko, J. (1989a). Becoming famous overnight: Limits on the ability to avoid unconscious influences of the past. *Journal of Personality and Social Psychology, 56*(3), 326–338.

Jacoby, L. L., Woloshyn, V., & Kelley, C. M. (1989). Becoming famous without being recognized: Unconscious influences of memory produced by dividing attention. Journal of Experimental Psychology: General, 118, 115–125.

James, W. (1890). *Principles of psychology (Vol. 1).* New York: Holt.

Jenkins, J. G., & Dallenbach, K. M. (1924). Obliviscence during sleep and waking. *American Journal of Psychology, 35,* 605–612.

Johnson, H. M. (1994) Processes of successful intentional forgetting. *Psychological Bulletin, 116,* 274–292.

Johnson, H. M., & Seifert, C. M. (1992). The role of predictive features in retrieving analogical cases. *Journal of Memory and Language, 31,* 648–667.

Johnson, H. M., & Seifert, C. M. (1994). Sources of the continued influence effect: When discredited information in memory affects later inferences. *Journal of Experimental Psychology: Learning, Memory, and Cognition, 20,* 1420–1436

Johnson, J. S., & Newport, E. L. (1989). Critical period effect in second language learning: The influence of maturational state on the acquisition of English as a second language. *Cognitive Psychology, 21,* 60–99.

Johnson, K. E., & Mervis, C. B. (1997). Effects of varying levels of expertise on the basic level of categorization. *Journal of Experimental Psychology: General, 126,* 248–277.

Johnson, K. E., & Mervis, C. B. (1998). Impact of intuitive theories on feature recruitment throughout the continuum of expertise. *Memory and Cognition, 26,* 382–401.

Johnson, M. K., Hashtroudi, S., & Lindsay, D. S. (1993). Source monitoring. *Psychological Bulletin, 114*(1), 3–28.

Johnson, M. K., & Raye, C. L. (1981). Reality monitoring. *Psychological Review, 88,* 67–85.

Johnson-Laird, P. N. (1983). *Mental models: Towards a cognitive science of language, inference, and consciousness.* Cambridge, MA: Harvard University Press.

Johnson-Laird, P. N. (1988). *The computer and the mind.* Cambridge, MA: Harvard University Press.

Johnson-Laird, P. N., & Byrne, R. M. (1989). Only reasoning. *Journal of Memory & Language, 28*(3), 313–330.

Johnson-Laird, P. N., & Byrne, R. M. J. (1991). *Deduction.* Hove, Sussex: Erlbaum.

Johnson-Laird, P. N., Legrenzi, P., & Legrenzi, M. (1972). Reasoning and a sense of reality. *British Journal of Psychology, 63,* 395–400.

Johnston, W. A., & Dark, V. A. (1986). Selective attention. *Annual Review of Psychology, 37,* 43–75.

Jones, G. V. (1990). Misremembering a common object: When left is not right. *Memory & Cognition, 18,* 174–182.

Jonides, J., Reuter-Lorenz, P. A., Smith, E. E., Awh, E., Barnes, L. L., Drain, M., Glass, J., Lauber, E. J., Patalano, A., & Schumacher, E. (1996). Verbal and spatial working memory in humans. In D. L. Medin (Ed.)

The psychology of learning and motivation, vol. 35. San Diego: Academic Press.

Just, M. A., & Carpenter, P. A. (1976). Eye fixations and cognitive processes. *Cognitive Psychology, 8,* 441–480.

Kahneman, D. (1973). *Attention and effort.* Englewood Cliffs, NJ: Prentice-Hall.

Kahneman, D., Fredrickson, B. L., Schreiber, C. A., & Redelmeier, D. A. (1993). When more pain is preferred to less: Adding a better end. *Psychological Science, 4,* 401–405.

Kahneman, D., & Miller, D. T. (1986). Norm theory: Comparing reality to its alternatives. *Psychological Review, 93,* 136–153.

Kahneman, D., Slovic, P., & Tversky, A. (1982). *Judgment under uncertainty: Heuristics and biases.* Cambridge: Cambridge University Press.

Kahneman, D., & Treisman, A. M. (1984). Changing views of attention and automaticity. In R. Parasuraman & D. R. Davies (Eds.), *Varieties of attention.* New York: Academic Press.

Kahneman, D., Treisman, A., & Gibbs, B. J. (1992). The reviewing of object files: Object specific integration of information. *Cognitive Psychology, 24*(2), 175–219.

Kahneman, D., & Tversky, A. (1979). Prospect theory: An analysis of decisions under risk. *Econometrica, 97,* 263–291.

Kahneman, D., & Tversky, A. (1996). On the reality of cognitive illusions. *Psychological Review, 103*(3), 582–591.

Kaiser, M. K., McCloskey, M., & Proffitt, D. R. (1986). Development of intuitive theories of motion: Curvilinear motion in the absence of external forces. *Developmental Psychology, 22,* 1–5.

Kamin, L. J. (1969). Predictability, surprise, attention and conditioning. In B. A. Campbell & P. M. Church (Eds.), *Punishment and aversive behavior.* New York: Appleton-Century-Crofts.

Kamp, H., & Partee, B. (1995). Prototype theory and compositionality. *Cognition, 57,* 129–191.

Kandel, E. R. (1976). *Cellular basis of behavior: An introduction to behavioral neurobiology.* San Francisco: W. H. Freeman.

Kandel, E. R., & Schwartz, J. H. (1982). Molecular biology of learning: Modulation of transmitter release. *Science, 218,* 433–443.

Kanwisher, N. G. (1987). Repetition blindness: Type recognition without token individuation. *Cognition, 27,* 117–143.

Karmiloff-Smith, A. (1992). *Beyond modularity: A developmental perspective on cognitive science.* Cambridge, MA: MIT Press.

Katona, G. (1940). *Organizing and memorizing.* New York: Columbia University Press.

Keane, M. T., Ledgeway, T., & Duff, S. (1994). Constraints on analogical mapping: A comparison of three models. *Cognitive Science, 18,* 387–438.

Keil, F. C. (1979). *Semantic and conceptual development: An ontological perspective.* Cambridge, MA: Harvard University Press.

Keil, F. C. (1981). Constraints on knowledge and cognitive development. *Psychological Review, 88,* 199–227.

Keil, F. C. (1986). The acquisition of natural kind and artifact terms. In W. Demopoulos & A. Marras (Eds.), *Language learning and concept acquisition.* Norwood, NJ: Ablex.

Keil, F. C. (1989). *Concepts, kinds, and cognitive development.* Cambridge, MA: MIT Press.

Keil, F. C. (1995). The growth of causal understandings of natural kinds. In D. Sperber & D. Premack (Eds.), *Causal cognition: A multidisciplinary debate. Symposia of the Fyssen Foundation* (pp. 234–267). New York: Clarendon Press/Oxford University Press.

Kelly, H. H., and Michela, J. (1980). Attribution theory and research. *Annual Review of Psychology, 31,* 457–501.

Kemler-Nelson, D. G. (1984). The effect of intention on what concepts are acquired. *Journal of Verbal Learning and Verbal Behavior, 23,* 734–759.

Kempton, W. (1986). Two theories of home heat control. *Cognitive Science, 10*(1), 75–90.

Kendall, R. E. (1975). *The role of diagnosis in psychiatry.* Oxford: Blackwell Scientific.

Kennell, J. H., & Klaus, M. H. (1984). Mother-infant bonding: Weighing the evidence. *Developmental Review, 4*(3), 275–282.

Kersten, A. W. (1998a). A division of labor between nouns and verbs in the representation of motion. *Journal of Experimental Psychology: General, 127*(1), 34–54.

Kersten, A. W. (1998b). An examination of the distinction between nouns and verbs: Associations with two different kinds of motion. *Memory and Cognition, 26,* 1214–1232.

Keysar, B. (1994). The illusory transparency of intention: Linguistic perspective taking in text. *Cognitive Psychology, 26,* 165–208.

Keysar, B., & Bly, B. (1995). Intuitions of the transparency of idioms: Can one keep a secret by spilling the beans? *Journal of Memory and Language, 34*(1), 89–109.

Kibler, D., & Aha, D. W. (1987). Learning representative exemplars of concepts: An initial case study. In *Proceedings of the Fourth International Workshop on Machine Learning.* Irvine, CA: Morgan Kaufmann.

Kidd, J. B. (1970). The utilization of subjective probabilities in production planning. Acta *Psychologica, 34,* 338–347.

Kiecolt-Glaser, J. K., Page, G. G., Marucha, P. T., MacCallum, R. C., & Glaser, R. (1998). Psychological influences on surgical recovery: Perspectives from psychneuroimmunology. *American Psychologist, 53,* 1209–1218.

Kim, J. J., Pinker, S., Prince, A., & Prasada, S. (1991). Why no mere mortal has ever flown out to center field. *Cognitive Science, 15*(2), 173–218.

Kimberg, D. Y., D'Esposito, M. ,& Farah, M. J. (1997). Cognitive functions in the prefrontal cortex—working memory and executive control. *Current Directions in Psychological Science, 6,* 185–192.

Kinchla, R. A., & Wolf, J. M. (1979). The order of visual processing: "Topdown," "bottomup," or "middle-out." *Perception and Psychophysics, 25,* 225–231.

Kintsch, W. (1988). The use of knowledge in discourse processing. *Psychological Review, 95,* 163–182.

Kintsch, W. (1994). Text comprehension, memory, and learning. *American Psychologist, 49,* 294–303.

Kintsch, W., & van Dijk, T. A. (1978). Toward a model of text comprehension and production. *Psychological Review, 85,* 363–394.

Klaczynski, P. A., Gelfund, H., & Reese, H. W. (1989). Transfer of conditional reasoning: Effects of explanations and initial problem types. *Memory & Cognition, 17,* 208–220.

Klaus, M. H., & Kennell, J. H. (1976). *Mother-infant bonding.* St. Louis: Mosby.

Klayman, J. (1988). Cue discovery in probabilistic environments. *Journal of Experimental Psychology: Learning, Memory, and Cognition, 14,* 317–330.

Klayman, J., & Ha, Y-W. (1987). Confirmation, disconfirmation, and information in hypothesis testing. *Psychological Review, 94,* 211–228.

Kleffner, D. A., & Ramachandran, V. S. (1992). On the perception of shape from shading. *Perception and Psychophysics, 52,* 18–36.

Knowlton, B. J., Squire, L. R., & Gluck, M. A. (1994). Probabilistic classification learning in amnesia. *Learning and Memory, 1,* 106–120.

Koehler, J. J. (1993). The influence of prior beliefs on scientific judgments of evidence quality. *Organizational Behavior and Human Decision Processes, 56,* 28–55.

Koehler, J. J. (1996). The base rate fallacy reconsidered: Descriptive, normative, and methodological challenges. *Behavioral and Brain Sciences, 19*(1), 1–53.

Kolers, P. A. (1975). Specificity of operations in sentence recognition. *Cognitive Psychology, 7,* 289–306.

Kolodner, J. L. (1993). *Case-based reasoning.* San Mateo, CA: Morgan Kaufmann.

Kolodner, J. L. (1997). Educational implications of analogy: A view from case-based reasoning. *American Psychologist, 52,* 57–66.

Kolodner, J. L., & Simpson, R. L. (1989). The MEDIATOR: Analysis of an early case-based problem solver. *Cognitive Science, 13,* 507–549.

Komatsu, L. K. (1992). Recent views of conceptual structure. *Psychological Bulletin, 112,* 500–526.

Kosslyn, S. M. (1973). Scanning visual images: Some structural implications. *Perception & Psychophysics, 14,* 90–94.

Kosslyn, S. M. (1975). Information representation in visual images. *Cognitive Psychology, 7,* 341–370.

Kosslyn, S. M. (1976). Can imagery be distinguished from other forms of internal representation? Evidence from studies of information retrieval times. *Memory & Cognition, 4,* 291–297.

Kosslyn, S. M. (1983). *Ghosts in the mind's machine: Creating and using images in the brain.* New York: Horizon.

Kosslyn, S. M. (1987). Seeing and imagining in the cerebral hemispheres: A computational approach. *Psychological Review, 94,* 148–175.

Kosslyn, S. M. (1994). *Image and brain: The resolution of the imagery debate.* Cambridge, MA: MIT press.

Kosslyn, S. M., Ball, T. M., & Reiser, B. J. (1978). Visual images preserve metric spatial information: Evidence from studies of image scanning. *Journal of Experimental Psychology: Human Perception and Performance, 4,* 47–60.

Kosslyn, S. M., & Koenig, G. (1992). *Wet mind: The new cognitive neuroscience.* New York: Free Press.

Kosslyn, S. M., & Pomerantz, J. R. (1977). Imagery, propositions, and the form of internal representations. *Cognitive Psychology, 9,* 52–76.

Kosslyn, S. M., & Shwartz, S. P. (1977). A simulation of visual imagery. *Cognitive Science, 1,* 265–295.

Kotovsky, K., & Fallside, D. (1989). Representation and transfer in problem solving. In D. Klahr & K. Kotovsky (Eds.), *Complex information processing: The contributions of Herbert A. Simon.* Hillsdale, NJ: Erlbaum.

Kotovsky, K., Hayes, J. R., & Simon, H. A. (1985). Why are some problems hard? Evidence from Tower of Hanoi. *Cognitive Psychology, 17,* 248–294.

Koutstaal, W., & Schacter, D. L. (1997). Gist-based false recognition of pictures in older and younger adults. *Journal of Memory and Language, 37,* 555–583.

Kramer, A. F., Weber, T. A., & Watson, S. E. (1997). Object-based attentional selection—Grouped arrays or spatially invariant representations? Comment on Vecera and Farah (1994). *Journal of Experimental Psychology: General, 126,* 3–13.

Krasner, L., & Ullman, L. P. (Eds.). (1965). *Research in behavior modification: New developments and implications.* New York: Holt.

Kristofferson, M. (1972). When item recognition and visual search functions are similar. *Perception & Psychophysics, 12,* 379–384.

Krumhansl, C. L. (1992). Internal representations for music perception and performance. In M. R. Jones & S. Holleran (Eds.), *Cognitive bases of musical communication* (pp. 197–211). Washington, DC: American Psychological Association.

Kruschke, J. K. (1992) ALCOVE: An exemplar-based connectionist model of category learning. *Psychological Review, 99,* 22–44.

Kuhl, P. K., & Meltzoff, A. N. (1982). The bimodal perception of speech in infancy. *Science, 218,* 1138–1141.

Kuhl, P. K., & Miller, J. D. (1978). Speech perception by the chinchilla: Identification functions for syntactic VOT stimuli. *Journal of the Acoustical Society of America, 63,* 905–917.

Kuhn, D. (1997). Is good thinking scientific thinking? In D. R. Olson & N. Torrance (Eds.), *Modes of thought: Explorations in culture and cognition* (pp. 261–281). New York: Cambridge University Press.

Kunreuther, H., Ginsberg, R., Miller, L., Sagi, P., Slovic, P., Borkan, B., & Katz, N. (1978). *Disaster insurance protection: Public policy lessons.* New York: Wiley.

Kurbat, M. A. (1994). Structural description theories: Is RBC/JIM a general purpose theory of human entry-level object recognition? *Perception, 23,* 1339–1368.

Kutas, M., & Hillyard, S. A. (1984). Brain potentials during reading reflect word expectancy and semantic association. *Nature, 307,* 161–163.

Lakoff, G., & Johnson, M. (1980). *Metaphors we live by.* Chicago: University of Chicago Press.

Lamberts, K. (1995). Categorization under time pressure. *Journal of Experimental Psychology: General, 124,* 161–180.

Lamberts, K., & Shanks, D. R. (Eds.) (1997). *Knowledge, concepts and categories.* Cambridge, MA: MIT Press.

Landauer, T. K., & Bjork, R. A. (1978). Optimum rehearsal patterns and name learning. In M. M. Gruneberg, P. E. Morris, & R. N. Sykes (Eds.), *Practical Aspects of Memory.* New York: Academic Press.

Landauer, T. K., & Freedman, J. L. (1968). Information retrieval from long-term memory: Category size and recognition time. *Journal of Verbal Learning and Verbal Behavior, 7,* 291–295.

Larkin, J. H., McDermott, J., Simon, D. P., & Simon, H. A. (1980). Models of competence in solving physics problems. *Cognitive Science, 4,* 317–345.

Larkin, J. H., & Simon, H. A. (1987). Why a diagram is (sometimes) worth 10,000 words. *Cognitive Science, 11,* 65–100.

Larkin, M. J. W., Aitken, M. R. F., & Dickinson, A. (1998). Retrospective reevaluation of causal judgments under positive and negative contingencies. *Journal of Experimental Psychology: Learning, Memory, and Cognition, 24,* 1331–1352.

Larrick, R. P., & Blount, S. (1997). The claiming effect: Why players are more generous in social dilemmas than in ultimatum games. *Journal of Personality & Social Psychology, 72*(4), 810–825.

Larrick, R. P., Nisbett, R. E., & Morgan, J. N. (1993). Who uses the cost-benefit rules of choice? Implications for the normative status of microeconomic theory. *Organizational Behavior & Human Decision Processes, 56*(3), 331–347.

Lassaline, M. E. (1996). Structural alignment in induction and similarity. *Journal of Experimental Psychology: Learning, Memory, and Cognition, 22*(3), 754–770.

Lassaline, M. L., & Logan, G. D. (1993). Memory-based automaticity in the discrimination of visual numerosity. *Journal of Experimental Psychology: Human Learning and Cognition, 19,* 561–581.

Lenat, D., & Guha, R. V. (1990). *Building large knowledge-based systems.* San Francisco: Addison Wesley.

Lenat, D. B. & Guha, R. V. (1994). Enabling agents to work together. *Communications of the ACM, 37,* 203–215.

Lepper, M. R., Greene, D., & Nisbett, R. E. (1975). Undermining children's intrinsic interest with extrinsic reward: A test of the "overjustification" hypothesis. *Journal of Personality and Social Psychology, 28,* 129–137.

Lerner, M. J., & Miller, D. T. (1978). Just world research and the attribution process: Looking back and ahead. *Psychological Bulletin, 85,* 1030–1051.

Lesgold, A. M., Feltovich, P. J., Glaser, R., & Wang, Y. (1981). *The acquisition of perceptual diagnostic skill in radiology. (Tech. Rep. No. PDS-1).* Pittsburgh: University of Pittsburgh, LRDC.

Lesgold, A. M., Rubinson, H., Feltovich, P., Glaser, R., Klopfer, D., & Wang, Y. (1988). Expertise in a complex skill: Diagnosing X-ray pictures. In M. Chi, R. Glaser, & M. Farr (Eds.), *The nature of expertise.* Hillsdale, NJ: Erlbaum.

Leslie, A. M. (1988). Some implications of pretense for mechanisms underlying the child's theory of mind. In J. W.. Astington & P. L. Harris (Eds.), *Developing theories of mind* (pp. 19–46). Cambridge, England: Cambridge University Press.

Lettvin, J. Y., Maturana, H. R., McCulloch, W. S., & Pitts, W. H. (1959). What the frog's eye tells the frog's brain. *Proceedings of the IRE, 47,* 1940–1951.

Levelt, W. J. M. (1989). *Speaking: From intention to articulation.* Cambridge, MA: The MIT Press.

Leventhal, H., Meyer, D., and Nerenz, D. (1980). The common sense representation of illness danger. In S. Rachman (Ed.), *Medical psychology (Vol. 2).* New York: Pergamon Press.

Levine, M. (1971). Hypothesis theory and nonlearning despite ideal S-R reinforcement contingencies. *Psychological Review, 78,* 130–140.

Levinson, S. C. (1994). Vision, shape, and linguistic description: Tzeltal body-part terminology and object description. *Linguistics, 33*(4–5), 791–855.

Lewis, C. H., & Anderson, J. R. (1976). Interference with real world knowledge. *Cognitive Psychology, 8,* 311–335.

Lewis, D. K. (1973). *Counterfactuals.* Cambridge, MA: Harvard University Press.

Liberman, A. M., & Mattingly, I. G. (1985). The motor theory of speech perception revised. *Cognition, 21,* 1–36.

Lichtenstein, S., Fischhoff, B., & Phillips, B. (1982). Calibration of probabilities: The state of the art to 1980. In D. Kahneman, P. Slovic, & A. Tversky (Eds.), *Judgment under uncertainty: Heuristics and biases.* Cambridge: Cambridge University Press.

Lichtenstein, S., & Slovic, P. (1973). Response-induced reversals of preference in gambling: An extended replication in Las Vegas. *Journal of Experimental Psychology, 101,* 16–20.

Light, L. L., & Carter-Sobell, L. (1970). Effects of changed semantic context on recognition memory. *Journal of Verbal Learning and Verbal Behavior, 9,* 1–11.

Lillard, A. (1998). Ethnopsychologies: Culture variations in theories of mind. *Psychological Bulletin, 123,* 3–32.

Lindsay, D. S. (1990). Misleading suggestions can impair eyewitnesses' ability to remember event details. *Journal of Experimental Psychology: Learning, Memory, and Cognition, 16,* 1077–1083.

Lindsay, D. S. (1993). Eyewitness suggestibility. *Current Directions in Psychological Science, 2,* 86–89.

Lindsay, D. S., & Johnson, M. K. (1989). The eyewitnesses suggestibility effect and memory for source. *Memory & Cognition, 17,* 349–358.

Lisker, L., & Abramson, A. S. (1970). The voicing dimension: some experiments in comparative phonetics. In H. Bohuslav, R. Milan, & J. Permysl (Eds.), *Proceedings of the Sixth International Congress of Phonetic Sciences (Prague 1967)* (pp. 563–567). Prague: Academic Publishing House of the Czechoslovakian Academy of Sciences.

Lively, S. E., Logan, J. S., & Pisoni, D. B. (1993). Training Japanese listeners to identify English /r/ and /l/. II: The role of phonetic environment and talker variability in learning new perceptual categories. *Journal of the Acoustical Society of America, 94*(3), 1242–1255.

Lively, S. E., Pisoni, D. B., Yamada, R. A., Tohkura, Y., & Yamada, T. (1994). Training Japanese listeners to identify English /r/ and /l/. III. Long-term retention of new phonetic categories. *Journal of the Acoustical Society of America, 96*(4), 2076–2087.

Livingstone, M., & Hubel, D. (1988). Segregation of form, color, movement, and depth: Anatomy, physiology, and perception. *Science, 240,* 740–750.

Lockhart, R. S., Lamon, M., & Gick, M. L. (1988). Conceptual transfer in simple insight problems. *Memory & Cognition, 16,* 36–44.

Locksley, A., Borgida, E., Brekke, N., & Hepburn, C. (1980). Sex stereotypes and social judgment. *Journal of Personality and Social Psychology, 39,* 821–831.

Loewenstein, G. (1996). Out of control: Visceral influences on behavior. *Organizational Behavior & Human Decision Processes, 65*(3), 272–292.

Loewenstein, G. L., & Mather, J. (1990). Dynamic processes in risk perception. *Journal of Risk and Uncertainty, 3,* 155–170.

Loewenstein, G. L., & Prelec, D. (1993). Preferences for sequences of outcomes. *Psychological Review, 100,* 91–108.

Loftus, E. F. (1993) The reality of repressed memories. *American Psychologist, 48,* 518–537.

Loftus, E. F. (1994). The repressed memory controversy. *American Psychologist, 49,* 443–445.

Loftus, E. F. (1997). Memory for a past that never was. *Current Directions in Psychological Science, 6,* 60–65.

Loftus, E. F., Burns, H. J. & Miller, D. G., (1978). Semantic integration of verbal information into a visual memory. *Journal of Experimental Psychology: Human Learning and Memory, 4,* 19–31.

Loftus, E. F., & Ketcham, K. (1994). *The myth of repressed memory.* New York: St. Martin's Press.

Loftus, E. F., & Palmer, J. C. (1974). Reconstruction of automobile destruction: An example of the interaction between language and memory. *Journal of Verbal Learning and Verbal Behavior, 13,* 585–589.

Logan, G. D. (1988). Toward an instance theory of automatization. *Psychological Review, 95,* 492–527.

Logan, J. S., Lively, S. E., & Pisoni, D. B. (1991). Training Japanese listeners to identify English /r/ and /l/: A first report. *Journal of the Acoustical Society of America, 89*(2), 874–886.

Logie, R. H., Zucco, G. M., & Baddelely, A. D. (1990). Interference with visual short-term-memory. *Acta Psychologica, 75,* 55–74.

LoLordo, V. M., Jacobs, W. J., & Foree, D. D. (1982). Failure to block control by a relevant stimulus. *Animal Learning & Behavior, 10,* 183–193.

Loomes, G. (1987). Testing for regret and disappointment in choice under uncertainty. *Economic Journal, 97,* 118–129.

Loomes, G., & Sugden, R. (1982). Regret theory: An alternative theory of rational choice under uncertainty. *Economic Journal, 92,* 805–824.

Lopez, A., Atran, S., Coley, J. D., Medin, D. L., & Smith, E. E. (1997). The tree of life: Universal and cultural features of folkbiological taxonomies and inductions. *Cognitive Psychology, 32,* 251–295.

Lopez, A., Gelman, S. A., Gutheil, G., & Smith, E. E. (1992). The development of category-based induction. *Child Development, 63,* 1070–1090.

Lopez, F. J., Shanks, D. R., Almaraz, J. & Fernandez, P. (1998). Effects of trial order on contingency judgments: A comparison of associative and probabilistic contrast accounts. *Journal of Experimental Psychology: Learning, Memory, and Cognition, 24,* 672–694.

Lorayne, H., & Lucas, J. (1974). *The memory book.* New York: Ballantine Books.

Love, B. C., Rouder, J. N., & Wisniewski, E. J. (1999) A structural account of global and local processing. *Cognitive Psychology, 38,* 291–316.

Luce, M. F., Bettman, J. R., & Payne, J. W. (1997). Choice processing in emotionally difficult decisions. *Journal of Experimental Psychology: Learning, Memory, & Cognition, 23*(2), 384–405.

Luchins, A. S. (1942). Mechanization in problem solving. *Psychological Monographs, 54, No. 248.*

Luchins, A. S., & Luchins, E. H. (1950). New experimental attempts at preventing mechanization in problem solving. *Journal of General Psychology, 42,* 279–297.

Lundsgaarde, H. P. (1987). Evaluating medical expert systems. *Social Science and Medicine, 24,* 805–819.

Luria, A. R. (1968). *The mind of a mnemonist.* New York: Basic Books.

Lynch, E. B., Coley, J. D., & Medin, D. L. (in press). Tall is Typical: Central Tendency, Ideal Dimensions and Graded Category Structure Among Tree Experts. *Memory and Cognition.*

Lynn, S. J., Lock, T. G., Myers, B., & Payne, D. G. (1997). Recalling the unrecallable: Should hypnosis be used to recover memories in psychotherapy? *Current Directions in Psychological Science, 6*(3), 79–83.

Macnamara, J. (1972). Cognitive basis of language learning in infants. *Psychological Review, 79*(1), 1–13.

MacQueen, G. M., & Siegel, S. (1989). Conditional immunomodulation following training with cyclophosphamide. *Behavioral Neuroscience, 103,* 638–647.

MacQueen, G. M., Siegel, S., & Landry, J. O. (1990). Acquisition and extinction of conditional immunoenhancement following training with cyclophosphamide. *Psychobiology, 18,* 287–292.

Macrae, C. N., Milne, A. B., & Bodenhausen, G. V. (1994). Stereotypes as energy-saving devices: A peek inside the cognitive toolbox. *Journal of Personality and Social Psychology, 66,* 37–47.

Maddox, W. T., & Ashby, F. G. (1993). Comparing decision bound and exemplar models of categorization. *Perception & Psychophysics, 53,* 29–70.

Madigan, S. A. (1969). Intraserial repetition and coding processes in free recall. *Journal of Verbal Learning and Verbal Behavior, 8,* 828–835.

Maier, S. F., Watkins, L. R., & Fleshner, M. (1994). Psychoneuroimmunology: The interface between behavior, brain, and immunity. *American Psychologist, 49,* 1004–1017.

Malt, B. C. (1995). Category coherence in cross-cultural perspective. *Cognitive Psychology, 29,* 85–148.

Malt, B. C., Sloman, S. A., Gennari, S., Shi, M., & Wang, Y. (1999). Knowing versus naming: Similarity and the linguistic categorization of artifacts. *Journal of Memory and Cognition, 40,* 230–262.

Malt, B. C., & Smith, E. E. (1983). Correlated properties in natural categories. *Journal of Verbal Learning and Verbal Behavior, 23,* 250–269.

Mandl, H., & Lesgold, A. M. (1988). *Learning issues for intelligent tutoring systems.* New York: Springer-Verlag.

Mandler, G. (1982). The structure of value: Accounting for taste. In M. S. Clark, & S. T. Fiske (Eds.) *Affect and cognition: The seventeenth annual Carnegie Symposium on Cognition* (pp. 3–36). Hillsdale, NJ: Erlbaum.

Manis, M., Dovalina, I., Avis, N. E., & Cardoze, S. (1980). Base rates can affect individual predictions. *Journal of Personality and Social Psychology, 38,* 287–298.

Manktelow, K. I., & Evans, J. St. B. T. (1979). Facilitation of reasoning by realism: Effect or non-effect? *British Journal of Psychology, 73,* 407–420.

Manktelow, K. I., & Over, D. E. (1991). Social roles and utilities in reasoning with deontic conditionals. *Cognition, 39,* 85–105.

Marcus, S. L., & Rips, L. J. (1979). Conditional reasoning. *Journal of Verbal Learning and Verbal Behavior, 18,* 199–224.

Markman, A. B. (1997). Constraints on analogical inference. *Cognitive Science, 21*(4), 373–418.

Markman, A. B. (1999). *Knowledge representation.* Mahwah, NJ: Erlbaum..

Markman, A. B., & Gentner, D. (1993). Splitting the differences: A structural alignment view of similarity. *Journal of Memory and Language, 32*(4), 517–535.

Markman, A. B., & Gentner, D. (1997). The effects of alignability on memory. *Psychological Science, 8*(5), 363–367.

Markman, A. B., & Makin, V. S. (1998). Referential communication and category acquisition. *Journal of Experimental Psychology: General, 127,* 331–354.

Markman, A. B., Yamauchi, T., & Makin, V. S. (1997). The creation of new concepts: A multifaceted approach to category learning. In T. B. S. S. M. Ward (Ed.), *Creative thought: An investigation of conceptual structures and processes* (pp. 179–208). Washington, DC: American Psychological Association.

Markman, A.B, & Wisniewski, E. J. (1997). Similar and different: The differentiation of basic level categories. *Journal of Experimental Psychology: Learning, Memory, and Cognition, 23,* 54–70.

Markman, E. M. (1989). *Categorization and naming in children: Problems of induction.* Cambridge, MA: MIT Press.

Marler, P. (1970). A comparative approach to vocal learning: Song development in white-crowned sparrows. *Journal of Comparative & Physiological Psychology, 71*(2, Pt.2), 1–25.

Marler, P., & Peters, S. (1977). Selective learning in a sparrow. *Science, 198,* 519–521.

Marler, P., & Peters, S. (1988). The role of song phonology and syntax in vocal learning preferences in the song sparrow, Melospiza melodia. *Ethology, 77,* 125–149.

Marler, P., & Sherman, V. (1983). Song structure without auditory feedback: Emendations of the auditory template hypothesis. *Journal of Neuroscience, 3,* 517–531.

Marr, D. (1982). *Vision.* San Francisco: W. H. Freeman.

Marr, D., & Poggio, T. (1976). Cooperative computation of stereo disparity. *Science, 194*, 283–287.

Marsh, R. L., Landau, J. D., & Hicks, J. L. (1996). How examples may (and may not) constrain creativity. *Memory & Cognition, 24*, 669–680.

Martin, R. C. (1993). Short-term memory and sentence processing: Evidence from neuropsychology. *Memory & Cognition, 21*, 176–183.

Massaro, D. W. (1987). *Speech perception by ear and eye: A paradigm for psychological inquiry.* Hillsdale, NJ: Erlbaum.

Massaro, D. W. (1994). A pattern recognition account of decision making. *Memory and Cognition, 22*, 616–627.

Massaro, D. W., & Cohen, M. M. (1983). Evaluation and integration of visual and auditory information in speech perception. *Journal of Experimental Psychology: Human Perception and Performance, 9*, 753–771.

Massaro, D. W., & Friedman, D. (1990). Models of integration given multiple sources of information. *Psychological Review, 97*, 225–252.

McClelland, J. L., McNaughton, B. L., & O'Reilly, R. C. (1995). Why there are complementary learning systems in the hippocampus and neocortex: Insights from the successes and failures of connectionist models of learning and memory. *Psychological Review, 102*, 419–457.

McClelland, J. L., & Rumelhart, D. E. (1981). An interactive activation model of context effects in letter perception, Part 1. An account of basic findings. *Psychological Review, 88*, 375–407.

McClelland, J. L., & Rumelhart, D. E. (1986a). A distributed model of human learning and memory. In J. L. McClelland & D. E. Rumelhart (Eds.), *Parallel distributed processing: Explorations in the microstructure of cognition: Vol. 2. Psychological and biological models.* Cambridge, MA: MIT Press.

McClelland, J. L., & Rumelhart, D. E. (1986b). Amnesia and distributed memory. In J. L. McClelland & D. E. Rumelhart (Eds.), *Parallel distributed processing: Explorations in the microstructure of cognition. Vol. 2. Psychological and biological models.* Cambridge, MA: MIT Press.

McClelland, J. L., & Rumelhart, D. E. (Eds.). (1986c). *Parallel distributed processing: Explorations in the microstructure of cognition. Vol. 2. Psychological and biological models.* Cambridge, MA: MIT Press.

McClelland, J. L., Rumelhart, D. E., & Hinton, G. E. (1986). The appeal of parallel distributed processing. In D. E. Rumelhart & J. L. McClelland (Eds.), *Parallel distributed processing: Explorations in the microstructure of cognition. Vol. 1. Foundations.* Cambridge, MA: MIT Press.

McCloskey, M. (1983). Intuitive physics. *Scientific American, 248*, 122–130.

McCloskey, M. (1991). Networks and theories: The place of connectionism in cognitive science. *Psychological Science, 2*, 387–395.

McCloskey, M. (1992). Special versus ordinary memory mechanisms in the genesis of flashbulb memories. In E. Winograd & U. Neisser (Eds.) *Affect and accuracy in recall: Studies of "flashbulb memories".* Cambridge: Cambridge University Press.

McCloskey, M., & Cohen, N. J. (1989). Catastrophic interference in connectionist networks: The sequential learning problem. In G. H. Bower (Ed.), *The psychology of learning and motivation: Advances in research and theory, vol. 24.* New York: Academic Press.

McCloskey, M., & Glucksberg, S. (1978). Natural categories: Well-defined or fuzzy sets? *Memory & Cognition, 6*, 462–472.

McCloskey, M., Wible, C. G., & Cohen, N. J. (1988). Is there a special flashbulb-memory mechanism? *Journal of Experimental Psychology: General, 117*, 171–181.

McCloskey, M., & Zaragoza, M. (1985). Misleading postevent information and memory for events: Arguments and evidence against memory impairment hypotheses. *Journal of Experimental Psychology: General, 114*, 1–16.

McGurk, H., & MacDonald, J. (1976). Hearing lips and seeing voices. *Nature, 264*, 746–748.

McKenzie, B. E., Tootell, H. S., & Day, R. H. (1980). Development of size constancy during the 1st year of human infancy. *Developmental Psychology, 16,* 163–174.

McKoon, G., & Ratcliff, R. (1986). Inferences about predictable events. *Journal of Experimental Psychology: Learning, Memory, and Cognition, 12,* 82–91.

McKoon, G., & Ratcliff, R. (1992). Inference during reading. *Psychological Review, 99,* 440–466.

McKoon, G., Ratcliff, R., & Dell, G. S. (1986). A critical evaluation of the semantic/episodic distinction. *Journal of Experimental Psychology: Learning, Memory, and Cognition, 12,* 295–306.

McNamara, T. P. (1986). Mental representations of spatial relations. *Cognitive Psychology, 18,* 87–121.

McNamara, T. P. (1992). Priming and constraints in places on theories of memory and retrieval. *Psychological Review, 99,* 650–662.

McNamara, T. P. (1994). Priming and theories of memory: A reply to Ratcliff and McKoon. *Psychological Review, 101,* 185–187.

McNamara, T. P., Halpin, J. A., & Hardy, J. K. (1992). Spatial and temporal contributions to the structure of spatial memory. *Journal of Experimental Psychology: Learning, Memory, and Cognition, 18,* 554–564.

McNeil, B. J., Pauker, S. G., Cox, H. C., Jr., & Tversky, A. (1982). On the elicitation of preferences for alternative therapies. *New England Journal of Medicine, 306,* 1259–1262.

Medin, D. L., Altom, M. W., Edelson, S. M., & Freko, D. (1982). Correlated symptoms and simulated medical classification. *Journal of Experimental Psychology: Learning, Memory, and Cognition, 8,* 37–50.

Medin, D. L., & Atran, S. (Eds.) (1999). *Folkbiology.* Cambridge, MA: Bradford.

Medin, D. L., & Bazerman, M. H. (in press). Broadening Behavioral Decision Research: Multiple Levels of Cognitive Processing. *Psychonomic Bulletin and Review.*

Medin, D. L., & Coley, J. D. (1998). Concepts and categorization. In J. Hochberg & J. E. Cutting (Eds.), *Handbook of perception and Cognition. Perception and cognition at century's end: History, philosophy, theory* (pp. 403–439). San Diego: Academic Press.

Medin, D. L., & Edelson, S. E. (1988). Problem structure and the use of base-rate information from experience. *Journal of Experimental Psychology: General, 117,* 68–85.

Medin, D. L., Goldstone, R. L., & Gentner, D. (1993). Respects for similarity. *Psychological Review, 100,* 254–278.

Medin, D. L., & Heit, E. J. (1999). Categorization. In D. Rumelhart & B. Martin (Eds.), *Handbook of cognition and perception* (pp. 99–143). San Diego: Academic Press.

Medin, D. L., Lynch, E. B., Coley, J. D., & Atran, S. (1997). Categorization and reasoning among tree experts: Do all roads lead to Rome? *Cognitive Psychology, 32*(1), 49–96.

Medin, D. L., Lynch, E. B., & Solomon, K. O. (in press). Are there kinds of concepts? *Annual Review of Psychology.*

Medin, D. L., & Ortony, A. (1989). Psychological essentialism. In S. Vosniadou and A. Ortony (Eds.), *Similarity and analogical reasoning* (pp. 179–195). New York: Cambridge University Press.

Medin, D. L., & Ross, B. H. (1989). The specific character of abstract thought: Categorization, problem-solving, and induction. In R. J. Sternberg (Ed.), *Advances in the psychology of human intelligence, Vol. 5* (pp. 189–223). Hillsdale, NJ: Erlbaum.

Medin, D. L., & Schaffer, M. M. (1978). A context theory of classification learning. *Psychological Review, 85,* 207–238.

Medin, D. L., & Schwanenflugel, P. J. (1981). Linear separability in classification learning. *Journal of Experimental Psychology: Human Learning and Memory, 7,* 355–368.

Medin, D. L., & Shoben, E. J. (1988). Context and structure in conceptual combination. *Cognitive Psychology, 20,* 158–190.

Medin, D. L., & Wattenmaker, W. D. (1987). Category cohesiveness, theories and cognitive archeology. In U. Neisser (Ed.), *Concepts and conceptual development: Ecological and intellectual factors in categorization* (pp. 25–62). Cambridge: Cambridge University Press.

Meehl, P. E. (1954). *Clinical vs. statistical prediction: A theoretical analysis and review of the evidence.* Minneapolis: University of Minnesota Press.

Melton, A. W. (1970). The situation with respect to the spacing of repetitions and memory. *Journal of Verbal Learning and Verbal Behavior, 9,* 596–606.

Merton, R. K. (1948). The self-fulfilling prophecy. *Antioch Review, 8,* 193–210.

Messick, D. M. (1999). Models of decision making in social dilemmas. In M. S. M. Foddy (Ed.), *Resolving social dilemmas: Dynamic, structural, and intergroup aspects* (pp. 209–217). Philadelphia, PA: Psychology Press/Taylor & Francis.

Metcalfe, J., & Mischel, W. (1999). A hot/cool-system analysis of delay of gratification: Dynamics of willpower. *Psychological Review, 106*(1), 3–19.

Metcalfe, J., & Shiamura, A. P. (1994). *Metacognition: Knowing about knowing.* Cambridge, MA: MIT Press.

Metcalfe, J., & Wiebe, D. (1987). Intuition in insight and noninsight problem solving. *Memory & Cognition, 15,* 238–246.

Meyer, D., Leventhal, H., & Gutmann, M. (1985). Common-sense models of illness: The example of hypertension. *Health Psychology, 4,* 115–135.

Meyer, D. E., & Schvaneveldt, R. W. (1971). Facilitation in recognizing pairs of words: Evidence of a dependence between retrieval operations. *Journal of Experimental Psychology, 90,* 227–234.

Meyer, D. E., Osman, A. M., Irwin, D. E., & Yantis, S. (1988). Modern mental chronometry. *Biological Psychology, 26,* 3–67.

Michotte, A. (1963). *The perception of causality.* London: Methuen.

Milich, R., & Lorch, E. P. (1994). Television viewing methodology to understand cognitive processing of ADHD children. In T. H. Ollendick & R. J. Prinz (Eds.), *Advances in Clinical Child Psychology, Vol. 16* (pp. 177–201). New York: Plenum Press.

Miller, G. A. (1956). The magical number seven plus or minus two: Some limits on our capacity for processing information. *Psychological Review, 63,* 81–97.

Miller, G. A. (1962). Some psychological studies of grammar. *American Psychologist, 17,* 748–762.

Miller, J. L. (1990). Speech perception. In D. N. Osherson & H. Lasnik (Eds.), *Language: An invitation to cognitive science (Vol. 1).* Cambridge, MA: MIT Press.

Miller, J. L., & Jusczyk, P. W. (1989). Neurobiological bases of speech perception. *Cognition, 13,* 111–137.

Miller, N. E. (1995). Clinical-experimental interactions in the development of neuroscience. *American Psychologist, 50,* 901–911.

Miller, R. R. & Matute, H. (1996). Biological significance in forward and backward blocking: Resolution of a discrepancy between animal conditioning and human causal judgment. *Journal of Experimental Psychology: General., 125,* 370–386.

Milner, B. (1965). Visually guided maze learning in man: Effects of bilateral hippocampal, bilateral frontal, and unilateral cerebral lesions. *Neuropsychologia, 3,* 317–338.

Milner, B. (1966). Amnesia following operation on the temporal lobes. In C. W. M. Whitty & O. L. Zangwill (Eds.), *Amnesia.* London: Butterworths.

Mineka, S. (1992). Evolutionary memories, emotional processing, and the emotional disorders. In D. L. Medin (Ed.), *The Psychology of Learning and Motivation, vol. 28.* New York: Academic Press.

Minsky, M. L. (1975). A framework for representing knowledge. In P. H. Winston (Ed.), *The psychology of computer vision.* New York: McGraw-Hill.

Minsky, M. L., & Papert, S. A. (1988). *Perceptrons.* Cambridge, MA.: MIT Press.

Mitchell, D. B., & Richman, C. L. (1980). Confirmed reservations: Mental travel. *Journal of Experimental Psychology: Human Perception and Performance, 6,* 58–66.

Miyake, A., & Shah, P. (Eds.). (1999). *Models of working memory: Mechanisms of active maintenance and executive control.* New York: Cambridge University Press.

Moray, N. (1959). Attention in dichotic listening: Affective cues and the influence of instructions. *Quarterly Journal of Experimental Psychology, 11,* 56–60.

Morey, L. C., & McNamara, T. P. (1987). On definitions, diagnosis, and DSM-III. *Journal of Abnormal Psychology, 96,* 283–285.

Morris, C. D., Bransford, J. P., & Franks, J. J. (1977). Levels of processing versus transfer appropriate processing. *Journal of Verbal Learning and Verbal Behavior, 16,* 519–533.

Murnane, K., & Phelps, M. P. (1993). A global activation approach to the effect of changes in environmental context on recognition. *Journal of Experimental Psychology: Learning, Memory, and Cognition, 19,* 882–894.

Murphy, A. H., & Winkler, R. C. (1977). Can weather forecasters formulate reliable probability forecasts of weather and temperature? *National Weather Digest, 2,* 2–9.

Murphy, G. L. (1988). Comprehending complex concepts. *Cognitive Science, 12,* 529–562.

Murphy, G. L. (1993). A rational of concepts. In G. V. Nakamura & D. L. Medin (Eds.), *Categorization by humans and machines. The psychology of learning and motivation: Advances in research and theory, vol. 29* (pp. 327–359). San Diego: Academic Press.

Murphy, G. L., & Medin, D. L. (1985). The role of theories in conceptual coherence. *Psychological Review, 92,* 289–316.

Murphy, G. L., & Ross, B. H. (1994). Predictions from uncertain categorizations. *Cognitive Psychology, 27,* 148–193.

Murphy, G. L., & Smith, E. E. (1982). Basic-level superiority in picture categorization. *Journal of Verbal Learning and Verbal Behavior, 21,* 1–20.

Murphy, G. L., & Wisniewski, E. J. (1989). Categorizing objects in isolation and in scenes: What a superordinate is good for. *Journal of Experimental Psychology: Learning, Memory, and Cognition, 15,* 572–586.

Musen, G., & Squire, L. R. (1991). Normal acquisition of novel verbal information in amnesia. *Journal of Experimental Psychology:*

Learning, Memory, and Cognition, 17, 1095–1104.

Myers, B. P. (1987). Mother-infant bondings: A critical period. In M. H. Bornstein (Ed.), *Sensitive periods in development: Interdisciplinary perspective.* Hillsdale, NJ: Erlbaum.

Mynatt, C. R., Doherty, M. E., & Tweney, R. D. (1977). Confirmation bias in a simulated research environment: An experimental study of scientific inference. *Quarterly Journal of Experimental Psychology, 29,* 85–95.

Nadel, L., & Jacobs, W. J. (1998). Traumatic memory is special. *Current Directions in Psychological Science, 7,* 154–157.

Naigles, L. (1990). Children use syntax to learn verb meaning. *Journal of Child Language, 17*(2), 357–374.

Nakayama, K. (1985). Biological image motion processing: A review. *Vision Research, 25,* 625–660.

Navon, D. (1984). Resource—a theoretical stone soup? *Psychological Review, 91,* 216–234.

Needham, D. R., & Begg, I. M. (1991). Problem-oriented training promotes spontaneous analogical transfer: Memory-oriented training promotes memory for training. *Memory & Cognition, 19,* 543–557.

Neisser, U. (1967). *Cognitive psychology.* Englewood Cliffs, NJ: Prentice-Hall.

Neisser, U. (1981). John Dean's memory: A case study. *Cognition, 9,* 1–22.

Neisser, U., & Harsch, N. (1992). Phantom flashbulbs: False recollections of hearing the news about Challenger. In E. Winograd & U. Neisser (Eds.), *Affect and accuracy in recall: Studies of "flashbulb memories."* Cambridge: Cambridge University Press.

Nelson, J. M. (1946*). Agnosia, Apraxia, Aphasia: Their Value in Cerebral Localization (2nd edition).* New York: Hoeben.

Nelson, T. O., Dunlosky, J., Graf, A., & Narens, L. (1994). Utilization of metacognitive judgments in the allocation of study during multitrial learning. *Psychological Science, 5,* 207–213

Nelson, T. O., Fehling, M. R., & Moore-Glascock, J. (1979). The nature of semantic savings for items forgotten from long-term memory. *Journal of Experimental Psychology: General, 108*, 225–250.

Nelson, T. O., & Narens, L. (1990). Metamemory: A theoretical framework and some new findings. In G. H. Bower (Ed.), *The psychology of learning and motivation, vol. 26*. San Diego: Academic Press.

Newell, A. (1990). *Unified theories of cognition*. Cambridge, MA: Harvard University Press.

Newell, A., & Simon, H. A. (1972). *Human problem solving*. Englewood Cliffs, NJ: Prentice-Hall.

Newell, A., Shaw, J. C., & Simon, H. A. (1959). A report on a general problem-solving program. In *Proceedings of the International Conferences on Information Processing*. New York: UNESCO.

Newell, A., Shaw, J. C., & Simon, H. A. (1962). The process of creative thinking. In H. E. Gruber, G. Terrell, & M. Wertheimer (Eds.), *Contemporary approaches to creative thinking*. New York: Atherton Press.

Newport, E. L. (1984). Constraints on learning: Studies in the acquisition of American sign language. *Papers and Reports on Child Language Development, 23*, 1–22.

Newport, E. L. (1988). Constraints on learning and their role in language acquisition: Studies of the acquisition of American sign language. *Language Sciences, 10*, 147–172.

Newport, E. L. (1990). Maturational constraints on language learning. *Cognitive Science, 14*, 11–28.

Nickerson, R. S., & Adams, M. J. (1979). Long-term memory for a common object. *Cognitive Psychology, 11*, 287–307.

Nisbett, R. E., Krantz, D. H., Jepson, D., & Kunda, Z. (1983). The use of statistical heuristics in everyday inductive reasoning. *Psychological Review, 90*, 339–363.

Nolde, S. F., Johnson, M. K., & Raye, C. L. (1998). The role of prefrontal cortex during tests of episodic memory. *Trends in Cognitive Sciences, 2*, 399–406.

Norman, D. A. (1968). Toward a theory of memory and attention. *Psychological Review, 75*, 522–536.

Nosofsky, R. M. (1986). Attention, similarity, and the identification-categorization relationship. *Journal of Experimental Psychology: General, 115*, 39–57.

Nosofsky, R. M. (1988a). Exemplar-based accounts of relations between classification, recognition, and typicality. *Journal of Experimental Psychology: Learning, Memory, and Cognition, 14*, 700–708.

Nosofsky, R. M. (1988b). Similarity, frequency, and category representations. *Journal of Experimental Psychology: Learning, Memory, and Cognition, 14*, 54–65.

Nosofsky, R. M. (1991). Tests of an exemplar model for relating perceptual classification and recognition in memory. *Journal of Experimental Psychology: Human Perception and Performance, 17*, 3–27.

Nosofsky, R. M., & Palmeri, T. J. (1997). An exemplar-based random walk model of speeded classification. *Psychological Review, 104*, 266–300.

Nosofsky, R. M., Palmeri, T. J., & McKinley, S. C. (1994). Rule-plus-exception model of classification learning. *Psychological Review, 97*, 53–79.

Novick, L. R. (1988). Analogical transfer, problem similarity, and expertise. *Journal of Experimental Psychology: Learning, Memory, and Cognition, 14*, 510–520.

Novick, L. R., & Holyoak, K. J. (1991). Mathematical problem solving by analogy. *Journal of Experimental Psychology: Learning, Memory, and Cognition, 17*, 398–415.

Novick, L. R., Hurley, S. M., & Francis, M. (1999). Evidence for abstract, schematic knowledge of three spatial diagram representations. *Memory & Cognition, 27*, 288–308.

Nussbaum, J. (1979). Children's conceptions of the earth as a cosmic body: A cross-age study. *Science Education, 63*, 83–93.

Nyberg, L., Cabeza, R., & Tulving, E. (1996). PET studies of encoding and retrieval: The HERA model. *Psychonomic Bulletin & Review, 3*, 135–148.

Oaksford, M., & Chater, N. (1994). A rational analysis of the selection task as optimal data selection. *Psychological Review, 101*, 608–631.

Obal, F. (1966). The fundamentals of the central nervous system of vegetative homeostasis. *Acta Physiologica Academiae Scientiarum Hungaricae, 30,* 15–29.

Oliva, A., & Schyns, P. G. (1997). Coarse blobs or fine edges? Evidence that information diagnosticity changes the perception of complex visual stimuli. *Cognitive Psychology, 34,* 72–107.

Ortony, A., Vondruska, R. J., Foss, M. A., & Jones, L. E. (1985). Salience, similes, and the asymmetry of similarity. *Journal of Memory & Language, 24*(5), 569–594.

Osherson, D. N., & Lasnik, H. (Eds.). (1990). *Language: An introduction to cognitive science (Vol. 1).* Cambridge, MA: MIT Press.

Osherson, D., & Smith, E. E. (1982). Gradedness and conceptual combination. *Cognition, 12,* 299–318.

Osherson, D., & Smith, E. E. (1997). On typicality and vagueness. *Cognition, 64,* 189–206.

Osherson, D. N., Smith, E. E., & Shafir, E. B. (1986). Some origins of belief. *Cognition, 24,* 197–224.

Osherson, D. N., Smith, E. E., Wilkie, O., Lopez, A., & Shafir, E. (1990). Category-based induction. *Psychological Review, 97,* 185–200.

Osherson, D., Perani, D., Cappa, S., Schnur, T., Grassi, F., & Fazio, F. (1998). Distinct brain loci in deductive versus probabilistic reasoning. *Neuropsychologica, 36,* 369–376.

Osterhout, L., & Holcomb, P. J. (1992). Event-related potentials elicited by syntactic anomaly. *Journal of Memory and Language, 31,* 785–806.

Osterhout, L., & Swinney, D. (1989). On the role of the simplicity heuristic in language processing: Evidence from structural and inferential processing. *Journal of Psycholinguistic Research, 18,* 553–562.

Ostrum, E. (1998). A behavioral approach to the rational choice theory of collective action. *American Political Science Review, 92,* 1–22.

O'Sullivan, J. T., Howe, M. L., & Marche, T. A. (1996). Children's beliefs about long-term retention. *Child Development, 67,* 2989–3009.

Owen, E., & Sweller, J. (1985). What do students learn while solving mathematics problems? *Journal of Educational Psychology, 77,* 272–284.

Paivio, A. (1971). *Imagery and verbal processes.* New York: Holt, Rinehart and Winston.

Palmer, C. (1997). Music performance. *Annual Review of Psychology, 48,* 115–138.

Palmer, S. E. (1977). Hierarchical structure in perceptual recognition. *Cognitive Psychology, 9,* 441–474.

Palmer, S. E. (1978). Fundamental aspects of cognitive representation. In E. Rosch & B. Lloyd (Eds.), Cognition and categorization. Hillsdale, NJ: Erlbaum.

Palmer, S. E. (1992). Common region: A new principle of perceptual grouping. *Cognitive Psychology, 9*(3), 441–474.

Palmer, S. E., & Kimchi, R. (1986). The information processing approach to cognition. In T. J. Knapp & L. C. Robertson (Eds.), *Approaches to cognition: Contrasts and controversies* (pp. 37–77). Hillsdale, NJ: Erlbaum.

Palmeri, T. J. (1997). Exemplar similarity and the development of automaticity. *Journal of Experimental Psychology: Learning, Memory, and Cognition, 23*(2), 324–354.

Parasuraman, R. (1998). *The attentive brain.* Cambridge, MA: The MIT Press.

Parasuraman, R., & Greenwood, P. M. (1998). Selective attention in aging and dementia. In R. Parasuraman (Ed.) *The attentive brain* (pp. 461–488). Cambridge, MA: The MIT Press.

Pashler, H. (1989). Dissociations and dependencies between speed and accuracy: Evidence for a two-component theory of divided attention in simple tasks. *Cognitive Psychology, 21,* 469–514.

Pashler, H. (1991). Shifting visual attention and selecting motor response: Distinction attentional mechanisms. *Journal of Experimental Psychology: Human Perception and Performance, 17,* 1023–1040.

Pashler, H. (1994a). Graded capacity-sharing in dual task interference? *Journal of Experimental Psychology: Human Perception and Performance, 20,* 330–342.

Pashler, H. E. (1998). *The psychology of attention.* Cambridge, MA: The MIT Press.

Payne, J. W. (1976). Task complexity and contingent processing in decision making: An information search and protocol analysis. *Organizational Behavior and Human Performance, 16,* 366–387.

Payne, J. W., Bettman, J. R., & Johnson, E. J. (1988). Adaptive strategy selection in decision making. *Journal of Experimental Psychology: Learning, Memory, and Cognition, 14,* 534–552.

Payne, J. W., Bettman, J. R., & Johnson, E. J. (1992). Behavioral decision research: A constructive processing perspective. *Annual Review of Psychology, 43,* 87–131.

Payne, J. W., Bettman, J. R., & Johnson, E. J. (1993). *The adaptive decision maker.* New York, NY: Cambridge University Press.

Penfield, W. (1959). The interpretive cortex. *Science, 129,* 1719–1725.

Pennebaker, J. W., & Epstein, D. (1983). Implicit psychophysiology: Effects of common beliefs and idiosyncratic physiological responses on symptom reporting. *Journal of Personality, 51,* 468–496.

Pennington, N., & Hastie, R. (1988). Explanation-based decision making: Effects of memory structure on judgment. *Journal of Experimental Psychology: Learning, Memory, and Cognition, 14,* 521–533.

Pennington, N., Nicolich, R., & Rahm, J. (1995). Transfer of training between cognitive subskills: Is knowledge use specific? *Cognitive Psychology, 28,* 175–224.

Perkins, D. N. (1988). Creativity and the quest for mechanism. In R. J. Sternberg & E. E. Smith (Eds.), *The psychology of human thought* (pp. 309–336). New York, NY: Cambridge University Press.

Peters, E., & Slovic, P. (1996). The role of affect and worldviews as orienting dispositions in the perception and acceptance of nuclear power. *Journal of Applied Social Psychology, 26*(16), 1427–1453.

Peterson, L. R., & Peterson, M. J. (1959). Short-term retention of individual verbal items. *Journal of Experimental Psychology, 58,* 193–198.

Peterson, M. A., Kihlstrom, J. K., Rose, P., & Glisky, M. L. (1992). Mental images can be ambiguous: Reconstruals and reference-frame reversals. *Memory and Cognition, 20,* 107–123.

Peterson, M. J., Meagher, R. B., Jr., Chait, H., & Gillie, S. (1973). The abstraction and generalization of dot patterns. *Cognitive Psychology, 4,* 378–398.

Peterson, S. E., Fox, P. T., Snyder, A. Z., & Raichle, M. E. (1990). Activation of extrastriate and frontal cortical areas by visual words and word-like stimuli. *Science, 249,* 1041–1044.

Pezdek, K., Finger, K., & Hodge, D. (1997). Planting false childhood memories: The role of event plausibility. *Psychological Science, 8,* 437–441.

Pichert, J. W., & Anderson, R. C. (1977). Taking different perspectives on a story. *Journal of Educational Psychology, 69,* 309–315.

Pinker, S. (1994). *The language instinct.* New York: W. Morrow.

Pirolli, P. & Recker, M. (1994). Learning strategies and transfer in the domain of programming. *Cognition and Instruction, 12,* 235–275.

Pisoni, D. B. (1973). Auditory and phonetic memory codes in the discrimination of consonants and vowels. *Perception & Psychophysics, 13,* 253–260.

Poggio, T. (1984). Vision by man and machine. *Scientific American, 62–63,* 107–116.

Poggio, T., Torre, V., & Koch, C. (1985). Computational vision and regularization theory. *Nature, 317,* 314–319.

Pollack, I., & Pickett, J. M. (1964). Intelligibility of excerpts from fluent speech: Auditory vs. structural context. *Journal of Verbal Learning and Verbal Behavior, 3,* 79–84.

Polson, P. G., & Kieras, D. E. (1985). A quantitative model of the learning and performance of text-editing knowledge. *Proceedings of the CHI '85 Conference on Human Factors in Computing Systems.* New York: ACM.

Polya, G. (1945). *How to solve it.* Princeton, NJ: Princeton University Press.

Polya, G. (1957). *How to solve it: A new aspect of mathematical method (2nd ed.).* Princeton, NJ: Princeton University Press.

Posner, M. I. (1988). Structures and functions of selective attention. In T. Boll & B. K. Bryant (Eds.), *Clinical neuropsychology and brain function.* Washington, DC: American Psychological Association.

Posner, M. I., & Raichle, M. E. (1994). *Images of mind.* New York: Scientific American.

Postman, L., & Phillips, L. W. (1965). Short-term temporal changes in free recall. *Quarterly Journal of Experimental Psychology, 17,* 132–138.

Prelec, D., & Loewenstein, G. L. (1991). Decision making over time and under uncertainty: A common approach. *Management Science, 37,* 770–786.

Presson, C. C., DeLange, N., & Hazelrigg, M. D. (1989). Orientation specificity in spatial memory: What makes a path different from a map of the path? *Journal of Experimental Psychology: Learning, Memory, and Cognition, 15,* 887–897.

Provine, R. R. (1986). Yawning as a stereotyped action pattern and releasing stimulus. *Ethology, 72,* 109–122.

Putnam, H. (1960). Minds and machines. In S. Hook (Ed.), *Dimensions of mind.* New York: New York University Press.

Pylyshyn, Z. W. (1979). The rate of "mental rotation" of images: A test of the holistic analogue hypothesis. *Memory & Cognition, 7,* 19–28.

Pylyshyn, Z. W. (1981). The imagery debate: Analogue media versus tacit knowledge. *Psychological Review, 88,* 16–45.

Quillian, M. R. (1968). Semantic memory. In M. Minsky (Ed.), *Semantic information processing.* Cambridge, MA: MIT Press.

Raaijmakers, J. G., & Shiffrin, R. M. (1981). Search of associative memory. *Psychological Review, 88,* 93–134.

Rajamoney, S., & DeJong, G. (1987). The classification, detection, and handling of imperfect theory problems. In *Proceedings of the Tenth International Joint Conference on Artificial Intelligence.* Milan, Italy.

Rajaram, S., & Roediger, H. L. (1993). Direct comparison of four implicit memory tests. *Journal of Experimental Psychology: Learning, Memory, and Cognition, 19,* 765–776

Ranney, M. (1994). Relative consistency and subjects' "theories" in domains such as naive physics: Common research difficulties illustrated by Cooke and Breedin. *Memory & Cognition, 22,* 494–502.

Ratcliff, R. (1990). Connectionist models of recognition memory: Constraints imposed by learning and forgetting functions. *Psychological Review, 97,* 285–308.

Ratcliff, R., & McKoon, G. (1988). A retrieval theory of priming in memory. *Psychological Review, 95,* 385–408.

Ratcliff, R., & McKoon, G. (1989). Similarity information versus relational information: Differences in the time course of retrieval. *Cognitive Psychology, 21,* 139–155.

Ratcliff, R., & McKoon, G. (1994). Retrieving information from memory: Spreading-activation theories versus compound-cue theories. *Psychological Review, 101,* 177–184.

Ratcliff, R., & McKoon, G. (1995a). Bias in the priming of object decisions. *Journal of Experimental Psychology: Learning, Memory, and Cognition, 21*(3), 754–767.

Ratcliff, R., & McKoon, G. (1995b) Sequential effects in lexical decision: Tests of compound-cue retrieval theory. *Journal of Experimental Psychology: Learning, Memory, & Cognition, 21*(5), 1380–1388.

Ratcliff, R., & McKoon, G. (1997). A counter model for implicit priming in perceptual word identification. *Psychological Review, 104*(2), 319–343.

Raufaste, E., Eyrolle, H., & Marine, C. (1998). Pertinence generation in radiological diagnosis: Spreading activation and the nature of expertise. *Cognitive Science, 22,* 517–546.

Rayner, K., Carlson, M., & Frazier, L. (1983). The interaction of syntax and semantics during sentence processing: Eye movements in the analysis of semantically biased sentences. *Journal of Verbal Learning and Verbal Behavior, 22,* 358–374.

Redd, W. H., Jacobson, P. B., Die-Trill, M., & Dermatis, H. (1987). Cognitive/attention distraction in the control of conditioned nausea in pediatric cancer patients receiving chemotherapy. *Journal of Consulting and Clinical Psychology, 55,* 391–395.

Redelmeier, D., & Kahneman, D. (1996). Patients' memories of painful medical treatments: real-time and retrospective evaluations of two minimally invasive procedures. *Pain, 66,* 3–8.

Reder, L. M. (1979). The role of elaborations in memory for prose. *Cognitive Psychology, 11,* 221–234.

Reder, L. M. (1982). Plausibility judgments versus fact retrieval: Efficient strategies for question-answering. *Psychological Review, 89,* 250–280.

Reder, L. M. (1996). Different research programs on metacognition: Are the boundaries imaginary? *Learning & Individual Differences, 8,* 383–390.

Reder, L. M., & Ross, B. H. (1983). Integrated knowledge in different tasks: The role of retrieval strategy on fan effects. *Journal of Experimental Psychology: Learning, Memory, and Cognition, 9,* 55–72.

Reder, L. M., Charney, D. H., & Morgan, K. I. (1986). The role of elaborations in learning a skill from an instructional text. *Memory & Cognition, 14,* 64–78.

Reed, S. K. (1974). Structural descriptions and the limitations of visual images. *Memory & Cognition, 2,* 329–336.

Reed, S. K., Dempster, A., & Ettinger, M. (1985). Usefulness of analogous solutions for solving algebra word problems. *Journal of Experimental Psychology: Learning, Memory, and Cognition, 11,* 106–125.

Reeves, L. M., & Weisberg, R. W. (1994). The role of content and abstract information in analogical transfer. *Psychological Bulletin, 115,* 381–400.

Reicher, G. M. (1969). Perceptual recognition as a function of meaningfulness of stimulus material. *Journal of Experimental Psychology, 81,* 274–280.

Reimann, P., & Chi, M. T. H. (1989). Human expertise. In K. J. Gilhooly (Ed.), *Human and machine problem solving.* London: Plenum.

Reisberg, D. (1998). Constraints on image-based discovery: A comment on Rouw et al. (1997). *Cognition, 66,* 95–102.

Reitman, J. S. (1976). Skilled perception in Go: Deducing memory structures from inter-response times. *Cognitive Psychology, 8,* 336–356.

Reitman, W. (1965). *Cognition and thought.* New York: Wiley.

Rensink, R. A., O'Regan, J. K., & Clark, J. J. (1997). To see or not to see: The need for attention to perceive changes in scenes. *Psychological Science, 8*(5), 368–373.

Rescorla, R. A. (1967). Pavlovian conditioning and its proper control procedures. *Psychological Review, 74,* 71–80.

Rescorla, R. A. (1988). Pavlovian conditioning: It's not what you think it is. *American Psychologist, 45,* 151–160.

Rescorla, R. A., & Wagner, A. R. (1972). A theory of Pavlovian conditioning: Variations in the effectiveness of reinforcement and nonreinforcement. In A. H. Black & W. F. Prokasy (Eds.), *Classical conditioning II: Current theory and research.* New York: Appleton-Century-Crofts.

Richardson, J. T. E. (1980). *Mental imagery and human memory.* New York: St. Martin's.

Richardson, J. T. E. (1998). The availability and effectiveness of reported mediators in associative learning: A historical review and experimental investigation. *Psychonomic Bulletin & Review, 5,* 597–614.

Rickard, T. C. (1997). Bending the power law: A CMPL theory of strategy shifts and the automatization of cognitive skills. *Journal of Experimental Psychology: General, 126,* 288–311.

Rips, L. J. (1975). Inductive judgments about natural categories. *Journal of Verbal Learning and Verbal Behavior, 14,* 665–681.

Rips, L. J. (1986). Mental muddles. In M. Brand & R. M. Harnish (Eds.), *Representation of knowledge and belief.* Tucson: University of Arizona Press.

Rips, L. J. (1989). Similarity, typicality, and categorization. In S. Vosniadou & A. Ortony (Eds.), *Similarity and analogical reasoning* (pp. 21–59). New York: Cambridge University Press.

Rips, L. J. (1990). Reasoning. In M. R. Rosenzweig & L. W. Porter (Eds.), *Annual Review of Psychology, 41,* 321–353.

Rips, L. J. (1994). *The psychology of proof.* Cambridge, MA: MIT Press.

Rips, L. J., & Collins, A. (1993). Categories and resemblance. *Journal of Experimental Psychology: General, 122,* 468–486.

Roberts, W. A. (1972). Free recall of word lists varying in length and rate of presentation: A test of total-time hypotheses. *Journal of Experimental Psychology, 92,* 365–372.

Robins, A. (1995). Catastrophic forgetting, rehearsal, and pseudo-rehearsal. *Connection Science, 7,* 123–146.

Robins, R. W., Gosling, S. D., & Craik, K. H. (1999). An empirical analysis of trends in psychology. *American Psychologist, 54,* 117–128.

Roediger, H. L. (1990). Implicit memory: Retention without remembering. *American Psychologist, 45,* 1043–1056.

Roediger, H. L., & Blaxton, T. A. (1987). Effects of varying modality, surface features, and retention interval on priming in word-fragment completion. *Memory & Cognition, 15,* 379–388.

Roediger, H. L., & McDermott, K. B. (1993). Implicit memory in normal human subjects. In H. Spinnler & F. Boller (Eds.). *Handbook of neuropsychology.* Amsterdam: Elsevier.

Roediger, H. L., & McDermott, K. B. (1995). Creating false memories: Remembering words not presented in lists. *Journal of Experimental Psychology: Learning, Memory, and Cognition, 21*(4), 803–814.

Roediger, H. L., & Neely, J. H. (1982). Retrieval blocks in episodic and semantic memory. *Canadian Journal of Psychology, 36,* 213–242.

Roediger, H. L., Srinivas, K., & Weldon, M. S. (1989). Dissociations between implicit measures of retention. In S. Lewandowsky, J. C. Dunn, & K. Kirsner (Eds.), *Implicit memory: Theoretical issues.* Hillsdale, NJ: Erlbaum.

Roland, P. E., & Friberg, L. (1985). Localization of cortical areas activated by thinking. *Journal of Neurophysiology, 53,* 1219–1243.

Rosch, E., & Lloyd, B. B. (Eds.). (1978). *Cognition and categorization.* New York: Wiley.

Rosch, E., & Mervis, C. B. (1975). Family resemblances: Studies in the internal structure of categories. *Cognitive Psychology, 7,* 573–605.

Rosch, E., Mervis, C. G., Gray, W. D., Johnson, D. M., & Bayes Braem, P. (1976). Basic objects in natural categories. *Cognitive Psychology, 8,* 382–439.

Rosenbloom, P., & Newell, A. (1987). Learning by chunking: A production system model of practice. In D. Klahr, P. Langley, & R. Neches (Eds.), *Production system models of learning and development.* Cambridge, MA: MIT Press.

Rosenthal, R. (1967). Covert communication in the psychological experiment. *Psychological Bulletin, 67,* 356–367.

Ross, B. H. (1984). Remindings and their effects in learning a cognitive skill. *Cognitive Psychology, 16,* 371–416.

Ross, B. H. (1987). This is like that: The use of earlier problems and the separation of similarity effects. *Journal of Experimental Psychology: Learning, Memory, and Cognition, 13,* 629–639.

Ross, B. H. (1989). Distinguishing types of superficial similarities: Different effects on the access and use of earlier problems. *Journal of Experimental Psychology: Learning, Memory, and Cognition, 15,* 456–468.

Ross, B. H. (1997). The use of categories affects classification. *Journal of Memory and Language, 37,* 240–267.

Ross, B. H., & Kennedy, P. T. (1990). Generalizing from the use of earlier examples in problem solving. *Journal of Experimental Psychology: Learning, Memory, and Cognition, 16,* 42–55.

Ross, B. H., & Kilbane, M. C. (1997). Effects of principle explanation and superficial similarity on analogical mapping in problem solving. *Journal of Experimental*

Psychology: Learning, Memory, and Cognition, 23, 427–440.

Ross, L. (1977). The intuitive psychologist and his shortcomings: Distortions in the attribution process. In L. Berkowitz (Ed.), *Advances in experimental social psychology (Vol. 10).* New York: Academic Press.

Ross, L., Lepper, M. R., & Hubbard, M. (1975). Perseverance in self-perception and social perception: Biased attributional processes in the debriefing paradigm. *Journal of Personality and Social Psychology, 32,* 880–892.

Ross, L., & Nisbett, R. E. (1991). *The person and the situation: Perspectives of social psychology.* New York, NY: Mcgraw-Hill Book Company.

Roth, E. M., & Shoben, E. J. (1983). The effect of context on the structure of categories. *Cognitive Psychology, 15,* 346–378.

Rouw, R., Kosslyn, S. M., & Hamel, R. (1997). Detecting high-level and low-level properties in visual images and visual perepts. *Cognition, 63,* 209–226.

Rozin, P., Haidt, J., & McCauley, C. R. (1993). Disgust. In A. M. Brandt & P. Rozin (Eds.), *Morality and Health* (pp. 379–401). New York: Routledge.

Rozin, P., & Kalat, J. W. (1971). Specific hungers and poison avoidance as adaptive specializations of learning. *Psychological Review, 78,* 459–486.

Rozin, P., Millman, L., & Nemeroff, C. (1986). Operations of the laws of sympathetic magic in disgust and other domains. *Journal of Personality and Social Psychology, 50,* 703–712.

Rozin, P., Wrzesniewski, A., & Barnes, D. (1998). The elusiveness of evaluative conditioning. *Learning and Motivation, 29,* 397–415.

Ruddle, R. A., Payne, S. J., & Jones, D. M. (1999). The effects of maps on navigation and search strategies in very-large-scale virtual environments. *Journal of Experimental Psychology: Applied, 5,* 54–75.

Rumelhart, D. E., & McClelland, J. L. (1986a). On learning the past tenses of English verbs. In J. L. McClelland & D. E. Rumelhart (Eds.), *Parallel distributed processing. Explorations in the microstructure of cognition:*

Vol. 2. Psychological and biological models. Cambridge, MA: Bradford Books/MIT Press.

Rumelhart, D. E., & McClelland, J. L. (Eds.). (1986b). *Parallel distributed processing. Explorations in the microstructure of cognition. Vol. 1. Foundations.* Cambridge, MA: MIT Press.

Rumelhart, D. E., & Ortony, A. (1977). The representation of knowledge in memory. In R. C. Anderson, R. J. Spiro, & W. E. Montague (Eds.), *Schooling and the acquisition of knowledge.* Hillsdale, NJ: Erlbaum.

Rumelhart, D. E., Smolensky, P., McClelland, J. L., & Hinton, G. E. (1986). Schemata and sequential thought processes in PDP models. In J. L. McClelland & D. E. Rumelhart (Eds.), *Parallel distributed processing: Explorations in the microstructure of cognition (Vol. 2).* Cambridge, MA: MIT Press.

Russo, J. E., Johnson, E. J., & Stephens, D. L. (1989). The validity of verbal protocols. *Memory & Cognition, 17,* 759–769.

Sacks, H., Schegloff, E. A., & Jefferson, G. (1974). A simplest systematics for the organization of turn-taking for conversation. *Language, 50,* 696–735.

Samarapungavan, A., Vosniadou, S., & Brewer, W. F. (1996). Mental models of the earth, sun, and moon: Indian children's cosmologies. *Cognitive Development, 11,* 491–521.

Sanders, G. S., & Simmons, W. L. (1983). Use of hypnosis to enhance eyewitness accuracy: Does it work? *Journal of Applied Psychology, 68,* 70–77.

Sanocki, T. (1993). Time course of object identification: Evidence for a global-to-local contingency. *Journal of Experimental Psychology: Human Perception and Performance, 19,* 878–898.

Sartori, G., & Job, R. (1988). The oyster with four legs: A neuropsychological study on the interaction of visual and semantic information. *Cognitive Neuropsychology, 5*(1), 105–132.

Schacter, D. L. (1989). Memory. In M. Posner (Ed.), *Foundations of cognitive science.* Cambridge, MA: Bradford Books.

Schacter, D. L. (1992). Understanding implicit memory: A cognitive neuroscience approach. *American Psychologist, 47,* 559–569.

Schacter, D. L. (1996). *Searching for memory: The brain, the mind, and the past.* New York: BasicBooks.

Schacter, D. L. (1999). The seven sins of memory: Insights from psychology and cognitive neuroscience. *American Psychology, 54,* 182–203.

Schacter, D. L., Church, B., & Treadwell, J. (1994). Implicit memory in amnesic patients: Evidence for spared auditory priming. *Psychological Science, 5,* 20–25.

Schank, R. C. (1982). *Dynamic memory.* Cambridge: Cambridge University Press.

Schank, R. C., & Abelson, R. (1977). *Scripts, plans, goals and understanding.* Hillsdale, NJ: Erlbaum.

Schank, R. C., Collins, G. C., & Hunter, L. E. (1986). Transcending inductive category formation in learning. *Behavioral and Brain Sciences, 9,* 639–686.

Schank, R. C., Kass, A., & Riesbeck, C. K. (Eds.). (1994). *Inside case-based explanation.* Hillsdale, NJ, : Erlbaum.

Schneider, W., & Detweiler, M. (1987). A connectionist/control architecture for working memory. In G. H. Bower (Ed.), *The psychology of learning & motivation (Vol. 21).* New York: Academic Press.

Schneider, W., & Shiffrin, R. M. (1977). Controlled and automatic human information processing: 1. Detection, search, and attention. *Psychological Review, 84,* 1–66.

Schober, M. F., & Clark, H. H. (1989). Understanding by addressees and overhearers. *Cognitive Psychology, 21*(2), 211–232.

Schoenfeld, A. H. (1985). *Mathematical problem solving.* Orlando, FL: Academic Press.

Schoenfeld, A. H., & Herrmann, D. J. (1982). Problem perception and knowledge structure in expert and novice mathematical problem solvers. *Journal of Experimental Psychology: Learning, Memory, and Cognition, 8,* 484–494.

Schooler, J. W., Bendiksen, M., & Ambadar, Z. (1997). Taking the middle line: Can we accommodate both fabricated and recovered memories of sexual abuse? In M. A. Conway (Ed.), *Recovered memories and false memories. Debates in Psychology.* (pp. 251–292). Oxford, England UK: Oxford University Press.

Schooler, J. M., Ohlsson, S., & Brooks, K. (1993). Thoughts beyond words: When language overshadows insight. *Journal of Experimental Psychology: General, 122,* 166–184.

Schooler, J. W. & Melcher, J. (1995). The ineffability of insight. In S. M. Smith, T. B. Ward, & R. A. Finke (Eds.), *The creative cognition approach.* Cambridge, MA: MIT Press.

Schwartz, B. L., Benjamin, A. S., & Bjork, R. A. (1997). The inferential and experiential bases of metamemory. *Current Directions in Psychological Science, 6,* 132–138.

Schwartz, D. L., & Black, J. B. (1996). Shuttling between depictive models and abstract rules: Induction and fallback. *Cognitive Science, 20*(4), 457–498.

Schwartz, D. L., & Black, T. (1999). Inferences through imagined actions: Knowing by simulated doing. *Journal of Experimental Psychology: Learning, Memory, and Cognition, 25*(1), 116–136.

Schyns, P. G., Goldstone, R. L., & Thibaut, J. P. (1998). The development of features in object concepts. *Behavioral and Brain Sciences, 21*(1), 1–54.

Schyns, P. G., & Oliva, A. (1994). From blobs to boundary edges: Evidence for time- and spatial-scale-dependent scene recognition. *Psychology Science, 5,* 195–200.

Schyns, P. G., & Oliva, A. (1999). Dr. Angry and Mr. Smile: When categorization flexibly modifies the perception of faces in rapid visual presentations. *Cognition, 69,* 243–265.

Schyns, P. G., & Rodet, L. (1997). Categorization creates functional features. *Journal of Experimental Psychology: Learning, Memory, & Cognition, 23,* 681–696.

Segal, S. J., & Fusella, V. (1970). Influence of imaged pictures and sounds on detection of visual and auditory signals. *Journal of Experimental Psychology, 83,* 458–464.

Seidenberg, M. S. (1993). Connectionist models and cognitive theory. *Psychological Science, 4,* 228–235.

Seidenberg, M. S., & McClelland, J. L. (1989). A distributed, developmental model of word recognition and naming. *Psychological Review, 96,* 523–568.

Seifert, C. M., & Gray, K. C. (1990). Representational issues in analogical transfer. In *Proceedings of the twelfth annual conference of the Cognitive Science Society.* Hillsdale, NJ: Erlbaum.

Seifert, C. M., Hammond, K. J., Johnson, H. M., Converse, T. M., McDougal, T. F., & VanderStoep, S. W. (1994). Case-based learning: Predictive features in indexing. *Machine Learning, 16,* 37–56.

Seifert, C. M., Meyer, D. E., Davidson, N., Patalano, A. L., & Yaniv, I. (1994). Demystification of cognitive insight: Opportunistic assimilation and the prepared-mind perspective. In R. J. Sternberg & J. E. Davidson (Eds.), *The nature of insight.* Cambridge, MA: MIT Press.

Sekuler, R., & Blake, R. (1994). *Perception.* (3rd Edition ed.). New York: McGraw-Hill.

Seligman, M. E. P. (1970). On the generality of the laws of learning. *Psychological Review, 77,* 406–418.

Semin, G. R., & DePoot, C. (1997a). Bringing partiality to light: Question wording and choice as indicators of bias. *Social Cognition, 15*(2), 91–106.

Semin, G. R., & DePoot, C. J. (1997b). The question—answer paradigm: You might regret not noticing how a question is worded. *Journal of Personality and Social Psychology, 73*(3), 472–480.

Shafir, E. (1993). Choosing versus rejecting: Why some options are both better and worse than others. *Memory & Cognition, 21,* 546–556.

Shafir, E., Simonson, I., & Tversky, A. (1993). Reason-based choice. *Cognition, 49,* 11–36.

Shaklee, H., & Mims, M. (1982). Sources of error in judging event covariation: Effects of memory demands. *Journal of Experimental Psychology: Human Learning and Memory, 8,* 208–224.

Shaklee, H., & Tucker, D. (1980). A rule analysis of judgements of covariation between events. *Memory & Cognition, 8,* 459–467.

Shanks, D. R. (1985). Forward and backward blocking in human contingency judgment. *Quarterly Journal of Experimental Psychology, 37B,* 1–21.

Shanks, D. R. (1986). Selective attribution and the judgment of causality. *Learning & Motivation, 17,* 311–334.

Shanks, D. R. (1989). Selectional processes in causality judgments. *Memory & Cognition, 17,* 27–34.

Shanks, D. R., & Dickinson, A. (1988). The role of selective attribution in causality judgment. In D. J. Hilton (Ed.), *Contemporary science and natural explanation: Commonsense conceptions of causality* (pp. 94–126). New York, NY: New York University Press.

Shanks, D. R., Holyoak, K. J., & Medin, D. L. (Eds.). (1996). *The Psychology of Learning and Motivation: Causal Learning, vol. 34.* New York: Academic Press.

Shapiro, K. L. (1994). The attentional blink: The brain's "eyeblink". *Current Directions in Psychological Science, 3*(3), 86–89.

Shapiro, K. L., Jacobs, W. J., & LoLordo, V. M. (1980). Stimulus-reinforcer interactions in Pavlovian conditioning of pigeons: Implications for selective associations. *Animal Learning & Behavior, 8,* 586–594.

Shepard, R. N. (1967). Recognition memory for words, sentences, and pictures. *Journal of Verbal Learning and Verbal Behavior, 6,* 156–163.

Shepard, R. N. (1978). The mental image. *American Psychologist, 33*(2), 125–137.

Shepard, R. N. (1981). Psychophysical complementarity. In M. Kubovy & J. R. Pomerantz (Eds.), *Perceptual organization.* Hillsdale, NJ: Erlbaum.

Shepard, R. N. (1984). Ecological constraints on internal representation: Resonant kinematics of perceiving, imaging, thinking, and dreaming. *Psychological Review, 91,* 417–447.

Shepard, R. N. (1987). Toward a universal law of generalization for psychological science. *Science, 237,* 1317–1323.

Shepard, R. N., & Cooper, L. A. (1982). *Mental images and their transformations.* Cambridge, MA: MIT Press.

Shepard, R. N., & Metzler, J. (1971). Mental rotation of three-dimensional objects. *Science, 171,* 701–703.

Sherry, D. F., & Schacter, D. L. (1987). The evolution of multiple memory systems. *Psychological Review, 94,* 439–454.

Shiffrin, R. M. (1997). REM:A model for explicit, generic, and implicit memory. In M. A. Conway, C. Cornoldi, & S. E. Gathercole (Eds.), *Theories of memory II.* Hove, Sussex: Psychological Press.

Shiffrin, R. M., & Raaijmakers, J. (1992). The SAM retrieval model: A retrospective and prospective. In A. Healy, S. Kosslyn, & R. Shiffrin (Eds.), *From learning processes to cognitive processes: Essays in honor of William K. Estes, Vol. 2.* Hillsdale, NJ: Erlbaum.

Shiffrin, R. M., Ratcliff, R., & Clark, S. E. (1990). List-strength effect: II. Theoretical mechanims. *Journal of Experimental Psychology: Learning, Memory, and Cognition, 16,* 179–195.

Shiffrin, R. M., & Steyvers, M. (1997). A model for recognition memory: REM—retrieving effectively from memory. *Psychonomic Bulletin & Review, 4,* 145–166.

Shortliffe, E. H. (1976). *Computer-based medical consultations: MYCIN.* New York: Elsevier.

Shortliffe, E. H., Buchanan, B. G., & Feigenbaum, E. A. (1979). Knowledge engineering for medical decision-making: A review of computer-based clinical decision aids. *Proceedings of the IEEE, 67,* 1207–1244.

Shweder, R. A. (1977). Likeness and likelihood in everyday thought: Magical thinking in judgments about personality. *Current Anthropology, 18,* 637–638.

Siegel, S. (1977a). Morphine tolerance acquisition as an associative process. Journal of Experimental Psychology: *Animal Behavior Processes, 3,* 1–13.

Siegel, S. (1977b). A Pavlovian conditioning analysis of morphine tolerance (and opiate dependence). In N. A. Krasnegor (Ed.), *Behavioral tolerance: Research and treatment implications.* National Institute for Drug Abuse, Monograph No. 18.

Siegel, S. (1989). Pharmacological conditioning and drug effects. In M. W. Emmett-Oglesby & A. J. Goudie (Eds.), *Tolerance and sensitization to psychoactive drugs.* Clifton, NJ: Human Press.

Simon, D. P., & Simon, H. A. (1978). Individual differences in solving physics problems. In R. Siegler (Ed.), *Children's thinking: What develops?* Hillsdale, NJ: Erlbaum.

Simon, H. A. (1957). *Models of man: Social and rational.* New York: Wiley.

Simon, H. A. (1973). The structure of ill-structured problems. *Artificial Intelligence, 4,* 181–201.

Simon, H. A. (1978). Information processing theory of human problem solving. In W. K. Estes (Ed.), *Handbook of learning and cognitive processes (Vol. 5).* Hillsdale, NJ: Erlbaum.

Simon, H. A. (1980). Problem solving and education. In D. T. Tuma & F. Reif (Eds.), Problem solving and education: Issues in teaching and learning. Hillsdale, NJ: Erlbaum.

Simon, H. A. (1989). The scientist as problem solver. In D. Klahr & K. Kotovsky (Eds.), *Complex information processing: The impact of Herbert A. Simon.* Hillsdale, NJ: Erlbaum.

Simons, D. J., & Keil, F. C. (1995). An abstract to concrete shift in the development of biological thought: the insides story. *Cognition, 56,* 129–163.

Simons, D. J., & Levin, D. T. (1997). Change blindness. *Trends in Cognitive Sciences, 1,* 261–267.

Simons, D. J., & Levin, D. T. (1998). Failure to detect changes to people duing a real-world interaction. *Psychonomic Bulletin & Review, 5,* 644–649.

Simons, D. J., & Levin, D. T. (1998). Failure to detect changes to people during a real-world interaction. *Psychonomic Bulletin and Review, 5*(4), 644–649.

Simonson, I., & Tversky, A. (1992). Choice in context: Tradeoff contrast and extremeness aversion. *Journal of Marketing Research, 29,* 281–295.

Simonton, D. K. (1997). Creative productivity: A predictive and explanatory model of career trajectories and landmarks. *Psychological Review, 104,* 66–89.

Singley, M. K., & Anderson, J. R. (1989). *The transfer of cognitive skill.* Cambridge, MA: Harvard University Press.

Skinner, B. F. (1950). Are theories of learning necessary? *Psychological Review, 57,* 193–216.

Skinner, B. F. (1957). *Verbal behavior.* Englewood Cliffs, NJ: Prentice-Hall.

Slamecka, N. J., & Graf, P. (1978). The generation effect: Delineation of a phenomenon. *Journal of Experimental Psychology: Human Learning, and Memory, 4,* 592–604.

Slobin, D. (1966). Grammatical transformation and sentence comprehension in childhood and adulthood. *Journal of Verbal Learning and Verbal Behavior, 5,* 219–277.

Sloman, S. A. (1993). Feature-based induction. *Cognitive Psychology, 25,* 231–280.

Sloman, S. A. (1994). When explanations compete: The role explanatory coherence on judgments of likelihood. *Cognition, 52,* 1–21.

Sloman, S. A. (1998). Categorical inference is not a tree: The myth of inheritance hierarchies. *Cognitive Psychology, 35,* 1–33.

Sloman, S. A., & Rips, L. J. (Eds.) (1998). Rules and similarity in human thinking. *Cognition (special issue), 2–3.*

Sloman, S. A., & Rumelhart, D. E. (1992). Reducing interference in distributed memories through episodic gating. In A. Healy, S. Kosslyn, & R. Shiffrin (Eds.), *From learning theory to connectionist theory: Essays in honor of William K. Estes, Vol. 1.* Hillsdale, NJ: Erlbaum.

Slovic, P., & Lichtenstein, S. (1968). The relative importance of probabilities and payoffs in risk taking. *Journal of Experimental Psychology Monograph Supplement, 78 (3 pt 2).*

Smedslund, J. (1963). The concept of correlation in adults. *Scandinavian Journal of Psychology, 4,* 165–173.

Smith, E. E. (1978). Theories of semantic memory. In W. K. Estes (Ed.), *Handbook of learning and cognitive processes (Vol. 6).* Hillsdale, NJ: Erlbaum.

Smith, E. E., & Jonides, J. (1997). Working memory: A view from neuroimaging. *Cognitive Psychology, 33,* 5–42.

Smith, E. E., Langston, C., & Nisbett, R. E. (1992). The case for rules in reasoning. *Cognitive Science, 16,* 1–40.

Smith, E. E., & Medin, D. L. (1981). *Categories and concepts.* Cambridge, MA: Harvard University Press.

Smith, E. E., & Osherson, D. N. (1984). Conceptual combination with prototype concepts. *Cognitive Science, 8,* 337–361.

Smith, E. E., Osherson, D. N., Rips, L. J., & Keane, M. (1988). Combining prototypes: A selective modification model. *Cognitive Science, 12,* 485–527.

Smith, E. E., Shafir, E., & Osherson, D. (1993). Similarity, plausibility, and judgments of probability. *Cognition, 49,* 67–96.

Smith, E. E., Shoben, E. J., & Rips, L. J. (1974). Structure and process in semantic memory: A featural model for semantic decisions. *Psychological Review, 81,* 214–241.

Smith, E. M., Ford, J. K., Kozlowski, S. W. J. (1997). Building adaptive expertise: Implications for training design strategies. In M. A. Quinones, & A. Ehrenstein (Eds.), *Training for a rapidly changing workplace: Applications of psychological research* (pp. 89–118). Washington, DC: American Psychological Association.

Smith, E. R., Fazio, R. H., & Cejka, M. A. (1996). Accessible attitudes influence categorization of multiply categorizable objects. *Journal of Personality & Social Psychology, 71*(5), 888–898.

Smith, J. D., & Minda, J. P. (1998). Prototypes in the mist: The early epochs of category learning. *Journal of Experimental Psychology: Learning, Memory & Cognition, 24,* 1411–1436.

Smith, J. D., Murray, M. J. Jr., & Minda, J. P. (1997). Straight talk about linear separability. *Journal of Experimental Psychology: Learning, Memory, & Cognition, 23,* 659–680.

Smith, L. B. (1989). A model of perceptual classification in children and adults. *Psychological Review, 96,* 125–144.

Smith, S. M. (1979). Remembering in and out of context. *Journal of Experimental Psychology: Human Learning and Memory, 5,* 460–471.

Smith, S. M. (1986). Environmental context-dependent recognition memory using a short-term memory task for input. *Memory & Cognition, 14,* 347–354.

Smith, S. M. (1994) Theoretical principles of context-dependent memory. In P. E. Morris & M. Gruneberg (Eds.), *Theoretical aspects of memory (2nd ed.).* London: Routledge.

Smith, S. M., & Blankenship, S. E. (1991). Incubation and the persistence of fixation in problem solving. *American Journal of Psychology, 104,* 61–87.

Smith, S. M., Glenberg, A., & Bjork, R. A. (1978). Environmental context and human memory. *Memory & Cognition, 6,* 342–353.

Smith, S. M., & Rothkopf, E. Z. (1984). Contextual enrichment and distribution of practice in the classroom. *Cognition and Instruction, 1,* 341–358.

Smith, S. M., Ward, T. B., & Finke, R. A. (Eds) (1995). *The creative cognition approach.* Cambridge, MA: MIT Press.

Snyder, C. R. R. (1972). Selection inspection, and naming in visual search. *Journal of Experimental Psychology, 92,* 428–431.

Snyder, M., Tanke, E. D., & Berscheid, E. (1977). Social perception and interpersonal behavior: On the self-fulfilling nature of social stereotypes. *Journal of Personality and Social Psychology, 35,* 656–666.

Sokal, R. R. (1974). Classification: Purposes, principles, progress, prospects. *Science, 185,* 1115–1123.

Solomon, K. O., Medin, D. L., & Lynch, E. B. (1999). Concepts do more than categorize. *Trends in Cognitive Science, 3*(3), 99–105.

Solomon, R. L. (1977). An opponent-process theory of acquired motivation: The affective dynamics of addiction. In J. D. Maser & M. E. P. Seligman (Eds.), *Psychopathology: Experimental models.* San Francisco: W. H. Freeman.

Solomon, R. L., & Corbit, J. D. (1974). An opponent-process theory of motivation: I. The temporal dynamics of affect. *Psychological Review, 81,* 119–145.

Spelke, E. S. (1990). Principles of object perception. *Cognitive Science, 14,* 29–56.

Spelke, E. S., Phillips, A., & Woodward, A. L. (1995). Infants' knowledge of object motion and human action. In D. Sperber & D. Premack (Eds.), *Casual cognition: A multidisciplinary debate. Symposia of the Fyssen Foundation* (pp. 44–78). New York: Clarendon Press/Oxford University Press.

Spellman, B. A. (1996). Acting as intuitive scientists: Contingency judgments are made while controlling for alternative potential causes. *Psychological Science, 7*(6), 337–342.

Spellman, B. A., & Holyoak, K. J. (1996). Pragmatics in analogical mapping. *Cognitive Psychology, 31,* 307–346.

Sperber, D., Cara, F., & Girotto, V. (1995). Relevance theory explains the selection task. *Cognition, 57,* 31–95

Spilich, G. J., Vesonder, G. T., Chiesi, H. L., & Voss, J. F. (1979). Text processing of domain-related information for individuals with high and low domain knowledge. *Journal of Verbal Learning and Verbal Behavior, 18,* 275–290.

Squire, L. R., Knowlton, B., & Musen, G. (1993). The structure and organization of memory. *Annual Review of Psychology, 44,* 453–495.

Srull, T. K., & Wyer, R. S. (1979). The role of category accessibility in the interpretation of information about persons: Some determinants and applications. *Journal of Personality and Social Psychology, 37,* 1660–1672.

Standing, L. (1973). Learning 10,000 pictures. *Quarterly Journal of Experimental Psychology, 25,* 207–222.

Stanfill, C., & Waltz, D. (1986). Toward memory-based reasoning. *Communications of the ACM, 29,* 1213–1228.

Stein, B. S., & Bransford, J. D. (1979). Constraints on effective elaboration: Effects of precision and subject generation. *Journal of*

Verbal Learning and Verbal Behavior, 18, 769–777.

Sternberg, R. J. (1982). Natural, unnatural, and supernatural concepts. *Cognitive Psychology, 14,* 451–488.

Sternberg, R. J., & Lubart, T. I. (1999). The concept of creativity: Prospects and paradigms. In R. J. Sternberg (Ed.), *Handbook of creativity* (pp. 3–15). New York, NY: Cambridge University Press.

Sternberg, S. (1966). High-speed scanning in human memory. *Science, 153,* 652–654.

Stevens, A., & Coupe, P. (1978). Distortions in judged spatial relations. *Cognitive Psychology, 10,* 422–437.

Stickgold, R. (1998). Sleep: Off-line memory reprocessing. *Trends in Cognitive Sciences, 2,* 484–492.

Storms, G., De Boeck, P., Ruts, W. (in press). Prototype and exemplar based information in natural language categories. *Journal of Memory and Language.*

Storms, G., De Boeck, P., Van Mechelen, I., & Ruts, W. (1998). Not guppies, nor goldfish, but tumble dryers, Noriega, Jesse Jackson, panties, car crashes, bird books, and Stevie Wonder. *Memory and Cognition, 26,* 143–145.

Strange, W., & Dittmann, S. (1984). Effects of discrimination training on the perception of /4–l/ by Japanese adults learning English. *Perception and Psychophysics, 36,* 131–145.

Stroop, J. R. (1935). Studies of interference in serial verbal reactions. *Journal of Experimental Psychology, 18,* 643–662.

Studdert-Kennedy, M. (1976). Speech perception. In N. J. Lass (Ed.), *Contemporary issues in experimental phonetics.* Springfield, IL: Charles C. Thomas.

Sutherland, N. S. (1968). Outlines of a theory of visual pattern recognition in animals and man. *Proceedings of the Royal Society, 171,* 297–317.

Sutton, R. S., & Barto, A. G. (1981). Toward a modern theory of adaptive networks: Expectation and prediction. *Psychological Review, 88,* 135–170.

Swanson, J., Posner, M. I., Cantwell, D., Wigal, S., Crinella, F., Filipek, P., Emerson, J., Tucker, D., & Nalcioglu, O. (1997). Attention deficit/Hyperactivity disorder: Symptom domains, cognitive processes, and neural networks. In R. Parasurmann (Ed.), *The attentive brain* (pp. 445–460). Cambridge, MA: The MIT Press.

Sweller, J. (1988). Cognitive load during problem solving: Effects on learning. *Cognitive Science, 12,* 257–286.

Sweller, J., & Chandler, P. (1994). Why some material is difficult to learn. *Cognition and Instruction, 12,* 185–233.

Tajfel, H. (1981). *Human groups and social categories: Studies in social psychology.* Cambridge: Cambridge University Press.

Tajfel, H., & Wilkes, A. L. (1963). Classification and quantitative judgment. *British Journal of Psychology, 54,* 101–114.

Tan, H.-T., & Yates, J. F. (1995). Sunk cost effects: The influences of instruction and future return estimates. *Organizational Behavior & Human Decision Processes, 63*(3), 311–319.

Tanaka, J. W., & Sengco, J. A. (1997). Features and their configuration in face recognition. *Memory and Cognition, 25*(5), 583–592.

Tanaka, J. W., & Taylor, M. (1991). Object categories and expertise: Is the basic level in the eye of the beholder? *Cognitive Psychology, 23,* 457–482.

Tarr, M. J. (1995). Rotating objects to recognize them: A case study on the role of viewpoint dependency in the recognition of three-dimensional objects. *Psychonomic Bulletin and Review, 2,* 55–82.

Tarr, M. J., Bulthoff, H. H., Zabinski, M., & Blanz, V. (1997). To what extent do unique parts influence recognition across changes in viewpoint. *Psychological Science, 8*(4), 282–289.

Tarr, M. J., & Pinker, S. (1989). Mental rotation and orientation-dependence in shape recognition. *Cognitive Psychology, 21,* 233–282.

Taylor, H. A., Naylor, S. J., & Chechile, N. A. (1999). Goal-specific influences on the representation of spatial perspective. *Memory & Cognition, 27,* 309–319.

Taylor, H. A., & Tversky, B. (1992). Spatial mental models derived from survey and route descriptions. *Journal of Memory & Language, 31,* 261–292.

Taylor, S. E., Fiske, S. T., Etcoff, N. L., & Ruderman, A. J. (1978). Categorical and contextual bases of person memory and stereotyping. *Journal of Personality and Social Psychology, 36,* 778–793.

Tenbrunsel, A., & Messick, D. R. (in press). Sanctioning systems, decision frames, and cooperation. *Administrative Science Quarterly.*

Terr, L. (1994). *Unchained memories.* New York: Basic Books.

Testa, T. J. (1974). Causal relationships and the acquisition of avoidance responses. *Psychological Review, 81,* 491–505.

Tetewsky, S. J., & Sternberg, R. J. (1986). Conceptual and lexical determinants of nonentrenched thinking. *Journal of Memory and Language, 25,* 202–225.

Thaler, R. H. (1980). Toward a positive theory of consumer choice. *Journal of Economic Behavior and Organization, 1,* 39–60.

Thaler, R. H. (1985). Using mental accounting in a theory of purchasing behavior. *Marketing Science, 12–13.*

Thaler, R. H., & Johnson, E. J. (1990) Gambling with the house money and trying to break even: The effects of prior outcomes and trying to break even: The effects of prior outcomes on risky choice. *Management Science, 36,* 643–660.

Thorndyke, P., & Hayes-Roth, B. (1982). Differences in spatial knowledge acquired from maps and navigation. *Cognitive Psychology, 14,* 560–589.

Timberlake, W. (1994). Behavior systems, associationism, and Pavlovian conditioning. *Psychonomic Bulletin & Review, 1*(4), 405–420.

Tinklepaugh, O. L. (1928). An experimental study of representational factors in monkeys. *Journal of Comparative Psychology, 8,* 197–236.

Tinklepaugh, O. L. (1932). Multiple delayed reaction with chimpanzees and monkeys. *Journal of Comparative Psychology, 13,* 207–243.

Tooby, J., & Cosmides, L. (1990). The past explains the present: Emotional adaptations and the structure of ancestral environments. *Ethnology and Sociobiology, 11,* 375–424.

Townsend, J. T. (1971). A note on the identifiability of parallel and serial processes. *Perception & Psychophysics, 10,* 161–163.

Treiman, R., Mullenuix, J., Bijeljac-Babic, R., & Richmond-Wetty, E. D. (1995). The special role of rimes in the description, use, and acquisition of English orthography. *Journal of Experimental Psychology: General, 124,* 107–136.

Treisman, A. (1960). Contextual cues in selective listening. *Quarterly Journal of Experimental Psychology, 12,* 242–248.

Treisman, A. (1964). Effect of irrelevant material on the efficiency of selective listening. *American Journal of Psychology, 77,* 533–546.

Treisman, A. (1988). Features and objects: The fourteenth Bartlett memorial lecture. *Quarterly Journal of Experimental Psychology, 40A,* 201–237.

Treisman, A., & Gelade, G. (1980). A feature integration theory of attention. *Cognitive Psychology, 12,* 97–136.

Treisman, A., & Gormican, S. (1988). Feature analysis in early vision: Evidence from search asymmetries. *Psychological Review, 95,* 15–48.

Treisman, A., & Sato, S. (1990). Conjunction search revisited. *Journal of Experimental Psychology: Human Perception and Performance, 16,* 459–478.

Trueswell, J. C., & Kim, A. E. (1998). How to prune a garden path by nipping it in the bud: Fast priming of verb argument structure. *Journal of Memory and Language, 39,* 102–123.

Tulving, E. (1983). *Elements of episodic memory.* New York: Oxford University Press.

Tulving, E. (1985). How many memory systems are there? *American Psychologist, 40,* 385–398.

Tulving, E., & Thomson, D. M. (1973). Encoding specificity and retrieval processes in episodic memory. *Psychological Review, 80,* 352–373.

Tulving, E., Schacter, D. L., & Stark, H. A. (1982). Priming effects in word-fragment completion are independent of recognition memory. *Journal of Experimental Psychology: Learning, Memory, and Cognition, 8,* 336–342.

Turing, A. (1936). On computable numbers, with an application to the Entscheidungs problem. *Proceedings of the London Mathematical Society, 42,* 230–265.

Turing, A. (1958). Computing machinery and intelligence. *Mind, 59,* 433–460.

Tversky, A. (1972). Elimination by aspects: A theory of choice. *Psychological Review, 79,* 281–299.

Tversky, A. (1977). Features of similarity. *Psychological Review, 84,* 327–352.

Tversky, A., & Kahneman, D. (1974). Judgment under uncertainty: Heuristics and biases. *Science , 185,* 1124–1131.

Tversky, A., & Kahneman, D. (1981). The framing of decisions and the psychology of choice. *Science, 211,* 453–458.

Tversky, A., & Kahneman, D. (1983). Extensional versus intuitive reasoning: The conjunction fallacy in probability judgment. *Psychological Review, 90,* 293–315.

Tversky, A., Sattath, S., & Slovic, P. (1988). Contingent weighting in judgment and choice. *Psychological Review, 95,* 371–384.

Tversky, B. (1981). Distortions in memory for maps. *Cognitive Psychology, 13,* 407–433.

Tversky, B. (1991). Spatial mental models. In G. H. Bower (Ed.), *The psychology of learning and motivation, vol. 27.* New York: Academic Press.

Tversky, B. (1995). Cognitive origins of graphic conventions. In F. T. Marchese (Ed.) *Understanding images* (pp. 29–53). New York: Springer-Verlag.

Tversky, B., & Hemenway, K. (1984). Objects, parts, and categories. *Journal of Experimental Psychology: General, 113,* 169–193.

Tversky, B., & Tuchin, M. (1989). A reconciliation of the evidence on eyewitness testimony: Comments on McCloskey and Zaragoza. *Journal of Experimental Psychology: General, 118,* 86–91.

Tweney, R. D., Doherty, M. E., & Mynatt, C. R. (Eds.). (1981). *On scientific thinking.* New York: Columbia University Press.

Tyc, V. L., Mulhern, R. K., & Bieberich, A. A. (1997). Anticipatory nausea and vomiting in pediatric cancer patients: An analysis of conditioning and coping variables. *Journal of Developmental and Behavioral Pediatrics, 18,* 27–32.

Ullman, S. (1979). The interpretation of visual motion. Cambridge, MA: MIT Press.

Ullman, S. (1989). Aligning pictorial descriptions: An approach to object recognition. *Cognition, 32,* 193–254.

Ullman, S. (1996). *High-level Vision.* Cambridge, MA: The MIT Press.

Ungerleider, L. G., & Mishkin, M. (1982). Two cortical visual systems. In D. J. Ingle, M. A. Goodale, & R. J. W. Mansfield (Eds.), *Analysis of visual behavior.* Cambridge, MA: MIT Press.

Vaidya, C. J., Gabrieli, J. D. E., Keane, M. M., & Monti, L. A. (1995). Perceptual and conceptual memory in global amnesia. *Neuropsychology, 9,* 580–591.

Van Mechelen, I., Hampton, J., Michalski, R. S., & Theuns, P. (Eds.) (1993). *Categories and concepts: Theoretical views and inductive data analysis.* London: Academic.

Van Someren, M., Reimann, P., Boshuizen, H., de Jong, T. (Eds.) (1998). *Learning with multiple representations.* Oxford: Elsevier Science.

VanderStoep, S. W., & Seifert, C. M. (1993/1994). Learning "how" versus learning "when": Improving transfer of problem-solving principles. *Journal of Learning Sciences, 3,* 93–111.

VanLehn, K. (1989). Problem solving and cognitive skill acquisition. In M. Posner (Ed.), *Foundations of cognitive science.* Cambridge, MA: MIT Press.

VanLehn, K. (1998). Analogy events: How examples are used during problem solving. *Cognitive Science, 22,* 347–388.

Vicente, K. J., & Brewer, W. F., (1993). Reconstructive remembering of the scientific literature. *Cognition, 46,* 101–128.

Vollmeyer, R., Burns, B. D., Holyoak, K. J. (1996). The impact of goal specificity on strategy use and the acquisition of problem sructure. *Cognitive Science, 20,* 75–100.

Von Neumann, J., & Morgenstern, O. (1944). *Theory of games and economic behavior.* New York: Wiley.

Vosniadou, S., & Brewer, W. F. (1987). Theories of knowledge restructuring in development. *Review of Educational Research, 57,* 51–56.

Vosniadou, S., & Brewer W. F. (1994). Mental models of the day/night cycle. *Cognitive Science, 18,* 123–183.

Vosniadou, S., & Ortony, A. (Eds.). (1989). *Similarity and analogical reasoning.* Cambridge: Cambridge University Press.

Voss, J. F., & Post, T. A. (1988). On the solving of ill-structured problems. In M. T. H. Chi, R. Glaser, & M. J. Farr (Eds.), *The nature of expertise.* Hillsdale, NJ: Erlbaum.

Wagner, A. D., Schacter, D. L., Rotte, M., Koutstaal, W., Maril, A., Dale, A. M., Rosen, B. R., & Buckner, R. L. (1998). Building memories: Remembering and forgetting of verbal experiences as predicted by brain activity. *Science, 281,* 1188–1191.

Waldmann, M. R., Holyoak, K. J., & Fratianne, A. (1995). Causal models and the acquisition of category structure. *Journal of Experimental Psychology: General, 124,* 181–206.

Walker, S. J. (1992). Supernatural beliefs, natural kinds, and conceptual structure. *Memory and Cognition, 20,* 655–662.

Wallace, R. A. (1973). *The ecology and evolution of animal behavior.* Pacific Palisades, CA: Goodyear.

Wallas, G. (1926). *The art of thought.* New York: Harcourt Brace Jovanovich.

Waltz, D. (1975). Understanding line drawings of scenes with shadows. In P. H. Winston (Ed.), *The Psychology of Computer Vision.* New York: McGraw Hill

Wanner, E., & Maratsos, M. (1978). An ATN approach to comprehension. In M. Halle, J. Bresnan, & G. A. Miller (Eds.), *Linguistic theory and psychological reality.* Cambridge, MA: MIT Press.

Ward, T. B. (1994). Structured imagination: The role of category structure in exemplar generation. *Cognitive Psychology, 27,* 1–41.

Ward, T. B. (1995). What's old about new ideas? In S. M. Smith, T. B. Ward, & R. A. Finke (Eds.) *The creative cognition approach.* Cambridge, MA: The MIT Press.

Ward, T. B., Smith, S. M., Finke, R. A. (1999). Creative cognition. In R. J. Sternberg (Ed.), *Handbook of creativity* (pp. 189–212). New York, NY: Cambridge University Press.

Ward, W. C., & Jenkins, H. M. (1965). The display of information and the judgment of contingency. *Canadian Journal of Psychology, 19,* 231–241.

Warrington, E. K., & Shallice, T. (1984). Category-specific semantic impairment. *Brain,* 107, 829–854.

Wason, P. C. (1960). On the failure to eliminate hypotheses in a conceptual task. *Quarterly Journal of Experimental Psychology, 12,* 129–140.

Wason, P. C., & Evans, J. St. B. T. (1975). Dual processes in reasoning. *Cognition, 3,* 141–154.

Wason, P. C., & Green, D. W. (1984). Reasoning and mental representation. *Quarterly Journal of Experimental Psychology, 36A,* 597–610.

Wason, P. C., & Johnson-Laird, P. N. (1972). *Psychology of reasoning: Structure and content.* London: Batsford.

Wasow, T. (1989). Grammatical theory. In M. I. Posner (Ed.), *Foundations of cognitive science.* Cambridge, MA: MIT Press.

Wasserman, E. A. (1990a). Attributions of causality to common and distinctive elements of compound stimuli. *Psychological Science, 1,* 298–302.

Wasserman, E. A. (1990b). Detecting response-outcome relations: Toward an understanding of the causal texture of the environment. In G. H. Bower (Ed.), *The psychology of learning and motivation, vol. 26.* New York: Academic Press.

Wasserman, E. A., & Neunaber, D. J. (1986). College student's responding to and rating of contingency relations: The role of temporal contiguity. *Journal of the Experimental Analysis of Behavior, 46,* 15–35.

Watanabe, S. (1969). *Knowing and guessing: A formal and quantitative study.* New York: Wiley.

Watkins, M. J. (1975). Inhibition in recall with extralist "cues." *Journal of Verbal Learning and Verbal Behavior, 14,* 294–303.

Watson, S. E., & Kramer, A. F. (1999). Object-based visual selective attention and perceptual organization. *Perception and Psychophysics, 61*(1), 31–49.

Wattenmaker, W. D. (1995). Knowledge structures and linear separability: Integrating information in object and social categorization. *Cognitive Psychology, 28,* 274–328.

Wattenmaker, W. D., Nakamura, G. V., & Medin, D. L. (1988). Relationships between similarity-based and explanation-based categorization. In D. Hilton (Ed.), *Contemporary science and natural explanation: Commonsense conceptions of causality* (pp. 205–241). Sussex, England: Harvester Press.

Weber, E. U. & Hsee, C. K. (1999). Models and mosaics: Investigation of cultural differences in risk perception and risk preference. *Psychonomic Bulletin and Review.*

Weber, R. J., & Dixon, S. (1989). Invention and gain analysis. *Cognitive Psychology, 21,* 283–302.

Weisberg, R. W. (1986). *Creativity: Genius and other myths.* New York: W. H. Freeman.

Weisberg, R. W. (1993). *Creativity: Beyond the myth of genius.* New York: W. H. Freeman.

Weisberg, R. W., & Suls, J. (1973). An information processing model of Duncker's candle problem. *Cognitive Psychology, 4,* 255–276.

Weldon, M. S., & Coyote, K. C. (1996). Failure to find the picture superiority effect in implicit conceptual memory tests. *Journal of Experimental Psychology: Learning, Memory, and Cognition, 22,* 670–686.

Welford, A. T. (1952). The "psychological refractory period" and the timing of high speed performance. A review and a theory. *British Journal of Psychology, 43,* 2–19.

Wells, G. L., & Bradfield, A. L. (1999). Distortions in eyewitnesses' recollections: Can the postidentification-feedback effect be moderated? *Psychological Science, 10,* 138–144.

Wells, G. L., Luus, C. A. E., & Windschitl, P. D. (1994). Maximizing the utility of eyewitness identification evidence. *Current Direction in Psychological Science, 3,* 194–197.

Wertheimer, M. (1950). Laws of organization in perceptual forms. In W. D. Ellis (Ed.), *A Source Book of Gestalt Psychology* . New York: Humanities Press.

Wertheimer, M. (1945/1982). *Productive thinking.* Chicago: University of Chicago Press.

Wharton, C. M., Holyoak, K. J., Downing, P. E., Lange, T. E., Wickens, T. D., & Melz, E. R. (1994). Below the surface: Analogical similarity and retrieval competition in reminding. *Cognitive Psychology, 26,* 64–101.

White, T. L., Hornung, D. E., Kurtz, D. B., Treisman, M., & Sheehe, P. (1998). Phonological and perceptual components of short-term memory for odors. *American Journal of Psychology, 111,* 411–434.

Wickelgren, W. A. (1974). *How to solve problems: Elements of a theory of problems and problem solving.* San Francisco: W. H. Freeman.

Wickens, C. D. (1980). The structure of attentional resources. In R. S. Nickerson (Ed.), *Attention and performance VIII.* Hillsdale, NJ: Erlbaum.

Wickens, C. D. (1984). Processing resources in attention. In R. Parassurmant & D. R. Davies (Eds.), *Varieties of attention.* Orlando, FL: Academic Press.

Wickens, D. D. (1972). Characteristics of word encoding. In A. W. Melton & E. Martin (Eds.), *Coding processes in human memory.* Washington, DC: V. H. Winston & Sons.

Williams, D. R., & Williams, H. (1969). Automaintenance in the pigeon: Sustained pecking despite contingent non-reinforcement. *Journal of the Experimental Analysis of Behavior, 12,* 511–520.

Williams, M. D., & Hollan, J. D. (1981). The process of retrieval from very long-term memory. *Cognitive Science, 5,* 87–119.

Wilson, M., & Emmorey, K. (1998). A "word length effect" for sign language: Further evidence for the role of language in structuring working memory. *Memory & Cognition, 26,* 584–590.

Wilson, T. D., & Brekke, N. (1994). Mental contamination and mental correction: Unwanted influences on judgments and evaluations. *Psychological Bulletin, 116,* 117–142.

Wilson, T. D., Dunn, D., Kraft, D., & Lisle, D. J. (1989). Introspection, attitude change, and attitude behavior consistency: The disruptive effects of explaining why we feel the way we do. In L. Berkowitz (Ed.), *Advances in Experimental Social Psychology, 19,* 123–205.

Wilson, T. D., & Schooler, J. W. (1991). Thinking too much: Introspection can reduce the quality of preferences and decisions. *Journal of Personality & Social Psychology, 60*(2), 181–192.

Winograd, E., & Neisser, U. (Eds.). (1992). *Affect and accuracy in recall: Studies of "flashbulb memories."* Cambridge: Cambridge University Press.

Wisniewski, E. J. (1996). Construal and similarity in conceptual combination. *Journal of Memory and Language, 35,* 434–453

Wisniewski, E. J. (1997). When concepts combine. *Psychonomic Bulletin & Review, 4,* 167–183.

Wisniewski, E. J., & Gentner, D. (1991). On the combinatorial semantics of noun pairs: minor and major adjustments to meaning. In G. B. Simpson (Ed.), *Understanding Word and Sentence* (pp. 241–284). North Holland: Elsevier.

Wisniewski, E. J., Imai, M., & Casey, L. (1996). On the equivalence of superordinate concepts. *Cognition, 60,* 269–298.

Wisniewski, E. J., & Love, B. C. (1998). Properties versus relations in conceptual combination. *Journal of Memory and Language, 38,* 177–202.

Wisniewski, E. J., & Medin, D. L. (1994). On the interaction of theory and data in concept learning. *Cognitive Science, 18,* 221–281.

Wolfe, J. M. (1994). Guided search 2.0: A revised model of visual search. *Psychonomic Bulletin and Review, 1*(2), 202–238.

Yates, J. F., Lee, J.-W., & Shinotsuka, H. (1996). Beliefs about overconfidence, including its cross-national variation. *Organizational Behavior & Human Decision Processes, 65*(2), 138–147.

Yeni-Komshian, G. H., & Soli, S. D. (1981). Recognition of vowels from information in fricatives: Perceptual evidence of fricative-vowel coarticulation. *Journal of the Acoustical Society of America, 70,* 966–975.

Young, M. E. (1995). On the origin of personal causal theories. *Psychonomic Bulletin & Review, 2,* 83–104.

Zaragoza, M. S., & Lane, S. M. (1994) Source misattributions and the suggestibility of eyewitness testimony. Journal of Experimental Psychology: Learning, Memory, and Cognition, 20, 934–945.

Zaragoza, M. S., & McCloskey, M. (1989). Misleading postevent information and the memory impairment hypothesis: Comment on Belli and reply to Tversky and Tuchin. Journal of Experimental Psychology: General, 118, 92–99.

Zelizer, V. A. (1994). *The social meaning of money.* New York: Basic Books.

Zsambok, C. E., & Klein, G. (Eds.). (1997). *Naturalistic decision making.* Mahwah, NJ: Erlbaum.

Zurif, E. (1990). Language and the brain. In D. N. Osherson & H. Lasnik (Eds.), *Language: An invitation to cognitive science.* Cambridge, MA: MIT Press.

CREDITS

Table 1.1   From *Vision* by D. Marr, © 1982 by W. H. Freeman and Company. Used with permission.

Figure 1.1   D. A. Kleffner & V.S. Ramachandran, "On the perception of shape from shading." *Perception and Psychophysics* (1992) 52:18-36. Fig. 5A, p. 22. Reprinted by permission of the Psychonomics Society.

Figure 1.2   Figure by R.N. Shepard from *Perceptual organization*, ed. by M. Kubovy and J. R. Pomerantz, ©1981. Reprinted by permission of Lawrence Erlbaum Associates, Inc.

Figure 1.3   "PET Scans" from *American Psychologist*, Vol. 50, 1995, pp. 901-911. Courtesy of Marcus Raichle.

Figure 1.5   "On the control of automatic processes: A parallel distributed processing account of the Stroop Effect" by J. D. Cohen, et al. *Psychological Review* (1990)97:332-361. Copyright © 1990 by The American Psychological Association. Reprinted with permission.

Figure 2.1   From *The ecology and evolution of animal behavior*, by R. A. Wallace, © 1973, originally published by Goodyear Publications. Reprinted by permission of the author's estate.

Figure 2.2   "Scores on ASL" by E.L. Newport in *Cognitive Science 14,* 1990, pp. 11-28. Reprinted with permission from Ablex Publishing Corporation.

Figure 2.3   Reprinted with permission from "Behavioral regulation of the Milieu Interne in man and rat" by J. Garcia et al., from *Science*, Vol. 185, 9/6/74. Copyright © 1974 American Association for the Advancement of Science.

Figure 2.5   Unpublished study by W. K. Estes. Courtesy of W. K. Estes.

Figure 3.3   "Forest before trees: The precedence of global features in visual perception" by D. Navon, *Cognitive Psychology, 9,* 1977, pp. 353-383. Copyright © 1977 Academic Press, Inc. Reprinted by permission.

Photos 3.4   "Hybrid stimuli" by P. G. Schyns and A. Oliva in *Psychological Science* (1994)5:195-200. Reprinted by permission of Blackwell Publishers. (two photos)

Figure 3.10   Adapted from "Attached and cast shadows" in C. F. Nodine and D. F. Fisher (eds.), *Perception and pictorial representation*, © 1979 by Praeger Publishers. Reproduced with permission of Greenwood Publishing Group, Inc., Westport, CT.

Figure 3.11   Gibson, James J., *The perception of the visual world*. Copyright © 1977, 1950 by Houghton Mifflin Company. Used with permission.

Figure 3.12   "Retinal disparity" from *Perception*, 2/e by Hochberg, J., © 1964. Reprinted by permission of Prentice-Hall, Inc., Upper Saddle River, NJ.

Figure 3.13   "Feature analysis in early vision: Evidence from search asymmetrics" by A. Treisman and S. Gormican, *Psychological Review* (1988)85:15-48. Copyright © 1988 by The American Psychological Association. Reprinted with permission.

Figure 3.16   From "Recognition by components: A theory of human image understanding" by I. Biederman, *Computer, Vision, Graphics, and Image Processing*, Vol. 32, 1985, pp. 29-73. © Academic Press. Reprinted with permission.

Figure 3.17   From "Recognition by components: A theory of human image understanding" by I. Biederman, *Computer, Vision, Graphics, and Image Processing*, Vol. 32, 1985, pp. 29-73. © Academic Press. Reprinted with permission.

Figure 3.18   Reprinted by permission of the publisher from *Categories and concepts* by E. E. Smith and D. L. Medin, Cambridge, Mass.: Harvard University Press. Copyright © 1981 by the President and Fellows of Harvard College.

(1984)109:164-178. Copyright © 1984 by The American Psychological Association. Reprinted with permission.

Figure 7.2 From "Scripts in memory for text" by G. H. Bower et al., *Cognitive Psychology*, 11:177-200 (1979). Copyright © 1979 Academic Press. Reprinted by permission.

Figure 7.3 From "Semantic integration of verbal information into a visual memory" by E. F. Loftus et al., *Journal of Experimental Psychology: Human Learning and Memory*, Vol. 4, No. 1, 1978, p. 20. Courtesy of Elizabeth F. Loftus, University of Washington.

Table 7.4 Table from "Misleading postevent information and memory for events" by M. McCloskey and M. Zaragoza, *Journal of Experimental Psychology* (1985)114:1-16. Copyright © 1985 by The American Psychological Association. Reprinted with permission.

Table 7.5 Table from "Misleading suggestions can impair eyewitnesses" by D. S. Lindsay, *Journal of Experimental Psychology: Learning, Memory and Cognition* (1990)16:1077-1083. Copyright © 1990 by The American Psychological Association. Reprinted with permission.

Figure 8.2 From "Spatial mental models derived from survey and route descriptions" by A. A. Taylor and B. Tversky, *Journal of Memory and Language, 31,* 1992, pp. 261-292. Copyright © 1992 Academic Press. Reprinted by permission.

Figure 8.3 From "Spatial mental models derived from survey and route descriptions" by A. A. Taylor and B. Tversky, *Journal of Memory and Language, 31,* 1992, pp. 261-292. Copyright ©1992 Academic Press. Reprinted by permission.

Figure 8.4 From "Distortions in judged spatial relations" by A. Stevens and P. Coupe, *Cognitive Psychology, 10,* 1978, pp. 422-437. Copyright © 1978 Academic Press. Reprinted by permission.

Figure 8.5 From "Mental rotation of three-dimensional objects" by R. N. Shepard and J. Metzler, reprinted abstract with permission from *Science,* Vol. 171, 1971, pp. 701-703. Copyright © 1971 by the American Association for the Advancement of Science.

Figure 8.6 "Can mental images be ambiguous?" by D. Chambers and D. Reisberg, *Journal of Experimental Psychology: Human Perception and Performance, 11,* 1985, pp. 317-328. Copyright © 1985 by the American Psychological Association. Reprinted with permission.

Figure 8.7 From "Failure to detect changes to people during a real-world interaction" by D. J. Simons and D. T. Levin, *Psychonomic Bulletin & Review, 5,* 1998, pp. 644-649. Reprinted by permission of Psychonomics Society.

Figure 9.5 From "The interaction of syntax and semantics during sentence processing: Eye movements in the analyses of semantically based sentences" by K. Rayner, M. Carlson, and L. Frazier, *Journal of Verbal Learning and Verbal Behavior, 22,* 1983, pp. 358-378. Copyright © 1983 by Academic Press. Reprinted by permission.

Figure 9.6 From "Language disorders (APHASIA)" by H. Goodglass and N. Geschwind, *Handbook of Perception, 7,* 1976, pp. 389-428. Copyright © 1976 by Academic Press. Reprinted by permission.

Figure 9.7 From "Neuropsychological, neurological, and neuroanatomical profile of Williams Syndrome" by U. Bellugi et al., *American Journal of Medical Genetics Supplement, 6,* 1990, pp. 115-125. © 1990 John Wiley & Sons. Reprinted with permission.

Figure 10.2 From "Tall is typical" by E. B. Lynch et al., *Memory and Cognition*, Vol. 28, No. 1, January 2000, pp. 41-50. Copyright © 2000 Psychonomics Society, Inc. Reprinted by permission.

Figure 10.7 From "Respects for similarity" by D. L. Medin et al., *Psychological Review* (1993)100:254-278. Copyright © 1993 by The American Psychological Association. Reprinted with permission.

Figure 10.8 From "Categories and induction in young children" by S. A. Gelman and E. M. Markman. Reprinted from *Cognition* (1986)23: 183-209 with kind permission of Elsevier

Science—NL, Sara Bergerhartstraat 25. 1055 KV Amsterdam, The Netherlands.

Figure 11.2 "Children's conception of the earth as a cosmic body" by J. Nussbaum, *Science Education* (1979)63:838-93. © 1979 John Wiley & Sons. Reprinted with permission.

Figure 11.3 From "Development of intuitive theories of motion" by M. K. Kaiser, M. McCloskey and D. R. Proffitt, *Developmental Psychology* (1986)22:66-71. Copyright © 1986 by The American Psychological Association. Reprinted with permission.

Figure 11.4 From "Development of intuitive theories of motion" by M. K. Kaiser, M. McCloskey and D. R. Proffitt, *Developmental Psychology* (1986)22:66-71. Copyright © 1986 by The American Psychological Association. Reprinted with permission.

Table 12.1 "Why are some problems hard?" by K. Kotovsky et al., *Cognitive Psychology* (1985)17:248-294. Copyright © 1985 Academic Press, Inc. Reprinted by permission.

Figure 12.4 From *How to solve problems* by W. A. Wickelgren. Copyright © 1974 W. H. Freeman and Company. Used with permission.

Figure 12.8 "The effect of a diagram retrieval cue" by M. L. Gick, *Canadian Journal of Psychology* (1985)39:460-466. Copyright 1985. Canadian Psychological Association. Reprinted with permission.

Figure 13.1 "The mind's eye in chess" by W. G. Chase and H. A. Simon, *Visual information processing*. Copyright ©1973 Academic Press, Inc. Reprinted by permission.

Figure 13.2 "The mind's eye in chess" by W. G. Chase and H. A. Simon, *Visual information processing*. Copyright ©1973 Academic Press, Inc. Reprinted by permission.

Table 13.2 "New experimental attempts at preventing mechanization in problem solving" A. S. Luchins and E. H. Luchins, *The Journal of General Psychology*, Vol. 42, 1950, p. 280. Reprinted with permission of the Helen Dwight Reid Educational Foundation. Published by Heldref Publications, 1319 Eighteenth St., N.W., Washington, D.C. 20036-1802. Copyright © 1950.

Table 13.3 "Incubation and the persistence of fixation in problem solving" by S. M. Smith and S. E. Blankenship, *American Journal of Psychology* (1991)104:61-87. Copyright 1991 by Board of Trustees of the University of Illinois. Used with permission of the University of Illinois Press.

Figure 13.3 "Categorization and representation of physics problems by experts and novices" by M. T. H.Chi et al., *Cognitive Science* (1981)5:121-152. Copyright Cognitive Science Society, Incorporated. Used by permission.

Figure 13.5 "Invention and gain analyses" R. J. Weber and S. Dixon, *Cognitive Psychology* (1989)21:283-302. Copyright © 1989 Academic Press, Inc. Reprinted by permission.

Figure 13.6 "Structured imagination: The role of category structure in exemplar generation" by T. B. Ward, *Cognitive Psychology* (1994)27:1-41. Copyright © 1994 Academic Press, Inc. Reprinted by permission.

Table 14.1 "Two sets of options" by G. Loomes from *Economic Journal, 97,* 1987, pp. 188-124. © Basil Blackwell, Ltd.

Figure 14.2 "Prospect theory: An analysis of decision under risk" by D. Kahneman and A. Tversky, *Econometrica, 47,* 1979, pp. 263-291. © The Econometric Society, UK.

Figure 14.3 From "Physicians use of probabilistic information in a real clinical setting" by J. J. J. Christensen-Szalanski, *Journal of Experimental Psychology: Human Perception and Performance* (1981)7:928-935. Copyright © 1981 by The American Psychological Association. Reprinted with permission.

AUTHOR INDEX

Abelson, R., 257, 291
Abramson, A. S., 341
Adams, M. J., 315, 317
Ader, R., 63
Aguirre, G. K., 28
Aha, D. W., 380
Aikins, J. S., 503
Aitken, M. R. F., 77
Alcock, J., 79
Alfonso-Reese, L. A., 380
Alhakami, A., 539
Allais, M., 523-524
Allard, F., 485
Allen, S. W., 380
Allport, A., 141
Almaraz, J., 77
Altom, M. W., 376
Amabile, T. M., 509, 517
Ambadar, Z., 281, 283
Anderson, J. A., 44
Anderson, J. R., 31, 189, 207, 208,
    220, 223, 225, 226, 228, 242, 298,
    309, 324, 379, 401, 494, 495, 497-
    498, 517
Anderson, R. C., 252, 265
Anderson, S. J., 277
Andrasik, F., 177
Arbib, M. A., 39
Ardila, A., 360, 361, 364
Arkes, H. R., 73, 529, 542
Ashby, F. G., 380, 401
Atkinson, R. C., 69, 156, 189
Atran, S., 202, 374, 384, 392, 393,
    399, 400, 401
Au, T. K., 352, 391, 395
Avis, N. E., 424
Awh, E., 159, 220
Ayers, M. S., 273, 292
Ayton, P., 529

Baddeley, A. D., 159, 160, 161, 162,
    163, 167, 175, 195
Bahrick, A. S., 178
Bahrick, H. P., 178, 322
Bahrick, L. E., 178
Bahrick, P. E., 178
Bahrick, P. O., 322
Baker, D. P., 305

Balch, W. R., 175
Baldwin, D. A., 9
Ball, G. F., 53, 79
Ball, T. M., 309, 311
Balsam, P., 63
Banaji, M. R., 386
Bandura, A., 79
Barclay, J. R., 168, 223
Bargh, J. A., 386
Bar-Hillel, M., 424
Barkley, R. A., 145, 148
Barnes, L. L., 159, 220
Baron, J., 532, 549
Barsalou, L. W., 298, 299, 310, 324,
    371, 373, 379, 391, 396
Bartlett, F. C., 254
Barto, A. G., 64
Bassok, M., 466, 477, 493
Bates, E. A., 242
Batsell, W. R., Jr., 65
Bayes Braem, P., 383, 384
Baylis, G. C., 147
Bazerman, M. H., 526, 538, 549
Beattie, A. E., 371
Becker, H. C., 64
Bedard, J., 486
Begg, I. M., 475
Bell, D. E., 531
Bellezza, F. S., 177, 287, 292, 372
Belli, R. F., 272
Bellugi, U., 362
Bendiksen, M., 281, 283
Benjamin, A. S., 292
Benson, D. F., 360, 361, 364
Berkeley, G., 92
Berlin, B., 384
Bernstein, I. L., 56, 57, 79
Berscheid, E., 13
Berstein, I. D., 57
Berti, A., 305, 324
Bettman, J. R., 535, 536, 539, 549
Bever, T. G., 25, 348, 353, 364
Bieberich, A. A., 57, 79
Biederman, I., 99, 101, 103
Bihrle, A., 362
Bijeljac-Babic, R., 338
Bisiach, E., 305, 324
Bjork, R. A., 175, 181, 182, 292
Black, J. B., 259, 260

Black, T., 440
Blake, R., 114
Blank, H., 424
Blankenship, S. E., 509-511
Blanz, V., 106
Blaxton, T. A., 219
Bleske, A. L., 31
Blessing, S. B., 491
Blount, S., 526
Blumstein, S. E., 361
Bly, B., 332
Boden, M. A., 507
Bodenhausen, G. V., 386
Bolles, R. C., 57
Borgida, E., 371
Boring, E. G., 18
Borkan, B., 519
Borson, S., 57
Boshuizen, H., 469
Bouillard, J-B., 360
Bovbjerg, D. H., 65, 68
Bower, G. H., 64, 69, 158, 168, 175,
    189, 195, 220, 259, 260
Bowerman, M., 395
Bowers, K. S., 509
Bowlby, J., 52
Bradfield, A. L., 274
Braine, M. D. S., 419
Braitenberg, V., 48
Bransford, J. D., 168, 169, 223, 252,
    476, 219, 261
Breedin, S. D., 439
Breedlove, D., 384
Brekke, N., 22, 371
Brennan, S. E., 330
Bresnan, J., 349
Brewer, W. F., 256, 266, 275, 277,
    357, 434,
Broadbent, D. E., 22, 124, 128, 148
Broadbent, M. H. P., 128
Broca, P., 360
Brooks, K., 324, 451
Brooks, L. R., 307, 379, 380
Brown, A. L., 476
Brown, A. S., 65
Brown, J., 155, 208
Brown, P. L., 67
Brown, R., 273, 276, 292
Bruck, M., 292

Bryant, D. J., 303
Buchanan, B. G., 502
Buchanan, M., 161, 162
Buckner, R. L., 179
Budescu, D. V., 420
Bulthoff, H. H., 106
Burkhard, B., 64
Burns, B. D., 493
Burns, H. J., 268
Burtt, H. E., 183
Busemeyer, J. R., 539, 549
Bushyhead, J. B., 543
Buss, D. M., 31
Butters, N., 206
Byrne, R. M., 418
Byrne, R. W., 299, 324, 445
Byrnes, D., 65, 79

Cabeza, R., 180
Caharack, G., 139
Calvanio, R., 314
Camerer, C. F., 520
Cameron, J., 21, 43
Cantril, H., 4
Cantwell, D., 144
Caplan, D., 349
Cappa, S., 28
Cara, F., 416
Caramazza, A., 394
Cardoze, S., 424
Carey, S., 362, 390, 391, 395
Carlson, M., 354, 355
Carlson, R. A., 495
Carpenter, P. A., 309
Carr, T. H., 148
Carter-Sobell, L., 172
Casey, L., 384
Catrambone, R., 476, 477
Cattell, J. M., 117
Cavanagh, P., 89
Cave, K. R., 132
Ceci, S. J., 292
Cejka, M. A., 386
Cermak, L. S., 206
Chabris, C. F., 305
Chait, H., 376
Chalmers, D. J., 114
Chambers, D., 310
Chandler, P., 493
Chapman, G. B., 526
Chapman, J. P., 74
Chapman, L. J., 74
Charness, N., 490, 517

Charney, D. H., 169
Charniak, E., 251, 260
Chase, W. G., 266, 286, 483-484
Chater, N., 416
Chatterjee, S. H., 41
Chechile, N. A., 300, 324
Chedru, F., 305, 324
Cheney, D. L., 333, 334
Cheng, P. W., 75, 77, 140, 416, 419, 445
Cherniak, C., 43
Cherry, E. C., 123
Cherry, K. E., 169
Chi, M. T. H., 450, 477, 480, 486-487, 517
Chiesi, H. L., 285
Chiu, C. Y., 328
Chiu, M., 477
Choi, I., 401
Choi, S., 395
Chomsky, N., 21, 44, 346-347, 349, 364
Christensen-Szalanski, J. J. J., 543
Chun, M. M., 129
Church, B., 214
Clancey, W. J., 502
Clark, H. H., 328, 329, 330, 346,364
Clark, J. J., 94
Clark, M. C., 168
Clark, S. E., 194
Clawson, D. M., 504
Clement, C. A., 430
Cochran, B. P., 56
Cohen, J. D., 36-39, 40
Cohen, L. J., 520, 549
Cohen, M. M., 342
Cohen, N. J., 203, 205, 207, 209, 211, 212, 213, 237, 239, 242, 276
Cohen, N., 63
Coley, J. D., 202, 374, 379, 384, 391, 392, 399, 401
Collins, A. M., 198, 200, 201, 223, 226
Collins, A., 390
Collins, G. C., 390
Conrad, F. G., 497-498
Conrad, R., 24, 156
Converse, T. M., 476
Conway, M. A., 277, 279, 292
Cooke, N. J., 439
Cooper, L. A., 107, 307, 309
Copper, C., 312
Corbett, A. T., 497-498
Corbit, J. D., 64

Corkin, S., 203, 207
Corrigan, B., 549
Cosmides, L., 31, 416, 419, 445, 549
Coupe, P., 303, 304
Cover, T. M., 380
Cowan, N., 161
Cox, H. C., Jr., 528
Cox, J. R., 415
Coyote, K. C., 321
Craik, F. I. M., 166, 167, 174, 195, 215
Craik, K. H., 43
Crick, F., 30
Crinella, F., 144
Crowder, R. G., 118, 166
Crowe, E., 538
Crowell, C. R., 64
Csikszentmihalyi, M., 509, 512, 517
Curiel, J. M., 305
Cutmore, T. R. H., 65, 68

D'Esposito, M., 28
Dadds, M. R., 65, 68
Dafters, R., 68
Dagenback, D., 148
Dale, A. M., 179
Dallas, M., 215, 216, 217
Dallenbach, K. M., 184
Damasio, A. R., 539
Damasio, H., 394
Danks, J., 465
Dark, V. A., 132
Davidson, N., 517
Dawes, R. M., 520, 549
Day, R. H., 90
De Boeck, P., 379, 397, 401
De Groot, A. D., 266
de Jong, T., 469
de Leeuw, N., 477
Deci, E. L., 20
DeJong, G., 393
DeLange, N., 299, 300
Dell, G. S., 207
DeLoache, J. S., 431
Dempster, A., 477
Dennett, D. C., 93, 114
Denniston, J. C., 77
DePoot, C., 352
Dermatis, H., 68
Desimone, R., 148
D'Esposito, M., 163
Detweiler, M., 163

Deutsch, D., 126
Deutsch, J. A., 126
Devine, P. G., 371
Di Sessa, A. A., 440
Dickinson, A., 75, 77, 392
Diehl, R. L., 340
Die-Trill, M., 68
Dietterich, T. G., 393
Dittmann, S., 337
Diwadkar, V. A., 106
Dixon, S., 511-512
Doane, S. M., 504
Doherty, M. E., 442, 445
Doherty, S., 362
Domjan, M., 64
Donnelly, C. M., 277
Dovalina, I., 424
Downing, C., 132
Downing, P. E., 475
Drain, M., 105, 159, 220, 320
Driskell, J. E., 312
Driver, J., 133, 147
Duff, S., 430, 445
Dunbar, K., 36-39, 443, 513
Duncan, J., 132, 148
Duncker, K., 465, 470, 480
Dungca, R. G., 504
Dunlosky, J., 288
Dunn, D., 549

Ebbinghaus, H.,
Ebbinghaus, H., 154, 183, 211
Eddy, D. M., 425
Edelson, S. M., 376, 424
Edwards, W., 537
Egan, D., 484
Egeth, H. E., 132, 134
Egly, R., 133
Eich, E., 175, 195
Eichenbaum, H., 203, 209, 212, 242
Einhorn, H. J., 392, 543
Einstein, G. O., 287
Eisenberger, R., 21, 43
El-Ahmadi, A., 278
Ellis, A. W., 131, 207
Ellman, T., 393
Elman, J. L., 242
Emerson, J., 144
Emmorey, K., 163
Engstler-Schooler, T. Y., 321
Epstein, D., 437
Erdfelder, E., 261
Erickson, M. A., 380, 401

Ericsson, K. A., 22, 286, 292, 450, 485, 490, 491, 499, 517
Estes, W. K., 35, 70, 71, 79, 188, 376, 379, 400, 401
Estin, P., 384
Etcoff, N. L., 538
Ettinger, M., 477
Evans, J. St. B. T., 413, 415
Evenden, J., 392
Eyrolle, H., 489

Falkenhainer, B., 430
Farah, M. J., 105, 114, 162, 163, 310, 311, 312, 314, 320, 324
Farr, M. J., 517
Farvolden, P., 509
Fazio, F., 28
Fazio, R. H., 386
Fehling, M. R., 183
Feigenbaum, E. A., 500, 502, 503
Feltovich, P. J., 486-487, 488, 489
Ferguson, E. L., 300
Fernandez, P., 77
Fernandez-Duque, D., 130
Ferster, C. S., 19
Fiedler, K., 540
Fiez, J. A., 28
Filipek, P., 144
Finger, K., 280
Finke, R. A., 310, 312, 513
Finke, R. A., Ward, T. B., 517
Finkenauer, C., 278
Finucane, M. L., 539
Fischhoff, B., 424, 537, 542, 549
Fisher, R. P., 174
Fisher, S., 519
Fiske, A. P., 545, 546, 549
Fiske, S. T., 371, 538
Flaherty, C. F., 64
Flann, N. S., 393
Flannagan, M. J., 376
Flannagan, O., 30
Fleshner, M., 63, 79
Fodor, J. A., 25, 91, 114, 348, 364
Forbus, K. D., 430, 474
Forde, E. M. E., 394
Ford, J. K., 504
Foree, D. D., 62
Foss, M. A., 387
Fox, P. T., 28
Francis, M., 306, 467
Frank, R. H., 538
Franks, J. J., 168, 219, 223, 476

Fratianne, A., 390
Frazer, J. G., 391
Frazier, L., 354, 355
Fredrickson, B. L., 532-533
Freedman, J. L., 200
Freko, D., 376
French, R. M., 237, 239
Freud, S., 15, 18, 279
Freyd, J. J., 41
Friberg, L., 314
Fried, L. S., 376
Friedman, D., 113
Frieske, D. A., 169
Fujisaki, H., 342
Fusella, V., 307
Fussell, S. R., 364

Gabrieli, J. D. E., 207, 219, 242
Gadzar, G., 349
Gagne, C. L., 397
Gales, M. S., 272
Gall, F. J., 360
Gallistel, C. R., 63
Garcia, J., 58
Gardner, H., 361, 490
Garnsey, S. M., 355
Garrett, M. F., 25, 348, 364
Garry, M., 204
Gathercole, S., 162
Gati, I., 387
Gauthier, I., 321, 389
Gelade, G., 130, 131
Gelfund, H., 416
Gelman, S. A., 389, 391, 392, 393, 400, 401
Gennari, S., 401
Gentner, D., 257, 258, 387, 388, 394, 397, 428, 430, 432, 433, 434, 440, 445, 474
Gerrig, R. J., 397
Geschwind, N., 360-361
Gettys, C. F., 519
Getzels, J., 512
Giard, M. G., 313
Gibbon, J., 63
Gibbs, B. J., 134-135
Gibson, J. J., 31, 83, 90, 114
Gick, M. L., 470-471, 472, 475, 476, 517
Gigerenzer, G., 416, 424, 425, 520, 549
Gillie, S., 376
Gilovich, T., 532

Ginsberg, R., 519
Girotto, V., 416
Gisle, L., 278
Glaser, R., 63, 79, 477, 486-487,
488, 489, 517
Glass, J., 159, 220
Glenberg, A. M., 175, 176, 177,
357
Glisky, E. L., 207
Glisky, M. L., 310
Gluck, M. A., 212
Glucksberg, S., 372, 465
Glushko, R. J., 337
Gobet, F., 485
Godden, D. R., 175
Goetz, E. T., 252
Golding, E., 416
Goldmeier, E., 114
Goldowsky, B. N., 56
Goldstein, W. M., 549
Goldstone, R. L., 86, 97, 387, 388,
389, 432, 489
Gonon, M. A., 313
Goodglass, H., 360-361
Goodman, N., 388, 426, 445
Gopnik, A., 390, 395
Gordon, W. J. J., 512
Gormican, S., 97
Gosling, S. D., 43
Gotlib, I. H., 36
Gottfried, G. M., 392
Grabowecky, M., 145
Grabowski, T. J., 394
Graesser, A. C., 358, 359
Graf, A., 288
Graf, P., 212, 214, 217
Graham, N., 84
Grassi, F., 28
Gray, K. C., 475
Gray, W. D., 383, 384
Green, D. W., 416, 417
Greene, D., 20
Greene, R. L., 176, 177
Greenwald, A. G., 386
Greenwood, P. M., 147
Grether, D. M., 525
Grice, H. P., 331
Griggs, R. A., 415
Grimes, J., 95
Grove, E., 203
Guha, R. V., 260, 503
Guilford, J. P., 507
Gutheil, G., 401
Gutmann, M., 437

Ha, Y-W., 442, 445
Halle, M., 364
Halpern, A. R., 168
Halpin, J. A., 305
Hamel, R., 311, 324
Hamilton, D. L., 540
Hamilton, W. J., 52
Hammond, K. J., 476, 477
Hammond, K. M., 314
Hampton, J. A., 397, 400
Hardin, G., 547
Hardy, J. K., 305
Harkness, A. R., 73, 542
Harsch, N., 276, 277, 280
Hart, P. E., 380
Haselton, M. G., 31
Hashtroudi, S., 204, 241
Hastie, R., 549
Hastorf, A., 4
Hatano, G., 391
Hauser, M. D., 328, 333, 340
Haviland, S. E., 330
Hawkins, R. D., 64
Hawkins, W. G., 58
Hayes, J. R., 465-467, 480
Hayes-Roth, B., 299, 300
Hazelrigg, M. D., 299, 300
Heath, C., 529
Hegarty, M., 300
Heit, E. J., 373, 390, 400, 401
Hell, W., 424
Hellige, J. B., 305
Helmholtz, H., 18
Hemenway, K., 383
Henderson, P. W., 547
Henle, M., 418
Hepburn, C., 371
Herrmann, D. J., 499
Herz, R. S., 177
Hesse, M. B., 428
Hetherington, M., 68
Hichwa, R. D., 394
Hicks, J. L., 514
Higgins, E. T., 538
Hildreth, E. C., 96, 114
Hillyard, S. A., 27
Hilton, D. J., 10
Hinson, R. E., 64
Hinton, G. E., 234, 262
Hintzman, D. L., 176, 207, 220, 379,
401
Hirschfeld, L. A., 370, 393, 400
Hirsh, K. W., 207
Hirst, D. E., 546

Hirst, W., 139
Hirtle, S. C., 303
Hissis, W. K., 32
Hitch, G. J., 159, 160, 162, 163
Hochberg, J. E., 92
Hodge, D., 280
Hodgson, C., 207
Hoffman, H. W., 52
Hoffrage, U., 520, 549
Hogarth, R. M., 392, 537, 543, 544,
549
Holcomb, P. J., 27
Holding, D. H., 457
Hollan, J. D., 170
Holland, J. H., 60
Holland, P. C., 64
Hollis, K. L., 64, 79
Holyoak, K. J., 60,
Holyoak, K. J., 64, 75, 77, 79, 239,
262, 376, 390, 416, 419, 430, 445,
470-471, 472, 474, 475, 476, 477,
493, 503, 512
Homa, D., 376, 379
Hornung, D. E., 163
Howard, J., 370
Howe, M. L., 289
Hsee, C. K., 526, 549
Hubbard, M., 13
Hubel, D., 87
Huber, J., 526
Hug, K., 416
Hulse, S. H., 53, 79
Hummel, J. E., 101, 239, 262, 430
Humphreys, G. W., 132, 394
Hunter, I. M. L., 483
Hunter, L. E., 390
Hurley, S. M., 306, 467
Huttenlocher, J., 371
Hyde, T. S., 167

Imai, M., 384
Inagaki, K., 391
Intons-Peterson, M. J., 309
Irwin, D. E., 23, 94, 316
Isen, A. M., 539
Ivry, R. B., 84, 147, 305

Jackendoff, R., 364
Jacobs, W. J., 9, 58, 62, 282
Jacobson, P. B., 68
Jacoby, L. L., 208, 215, 216, 217, 272
James, W., 148

Jasechko, J., 208
Jefferson, G., 329
Jenkins, H. M., 67, 73
Jenkins, J. G., 184
Jenkins, J. J., 167
Jepson, D., 426
Jernigan, T., 362
Job, R., 394
Johnson, D. M., 383, 384
Johnson, E. J., 451, 526, 535, 536,
    545, 546, 549
Johnson, H. M., 182, 292, 475, 476
Johnson, J. S., 54
Johnson, K. E., 383
Johnson, M. H., 242
Johnson, M. K., 180, 204, 241, 252,
    270, 280,
Johnson, M. L., 130
Johnson, M., 323
Johnson-Laird, P. N., 96, 409, 414,
    415, 416, 418, 434, 445
Johnston, W. A., 132
Jones, D. M., 300
Jones, G. V., 315
Jones, L. E., 387
Jonides, J., 159, 162, 163, 220, 303,
    314
Joyce, E. J., 546
Ju, G., 101
Jusczyk, P. W., 53
Just, M. A., 309

Kahneman, D., 126,
Kahneman, D., 126, 127, 134-135,
    423, 424, 520, 524, 527, 529, 530,
    532-533, 537, 540, 541, 543, 544,
    549
Kaiser, M. K., 438
Kalat, J. W., 60
Kamin, L. J., 61
Kamp, H., 382
Kandel, E. R., 59
Kane, M. J., 476
Kanwisher, N. G., 128
Kaplan, C. A., 464
Karmiloff-Smith, A., 242, 514
Kass, A., 476
Katona, G., 493
Katz, N., 519
Kawashima, T., 342
Keane, M. M., 219, 396, 430, 445
Keil, F. C., 387, 390, 391, 392, 395,
    401

Kelley, C. M., 208, 272
Kelley, C., 208
Kelly, H. H., 43
Kemler-Nelson, D. G., 378
Kempton, W., 436
Kendall, R. E., 366
Kennedy, P. T., 475
Kennell, J. H., 52
Kerr, N. H., 311
Ketcham, K., 278, 280, 292
Keysar, B., 332
Kibler, D., 380
Kidd, J. B., 543
Kiecolt-Glaser, J. K., 63, 79
Kieras, D. E., 494
Kihlstrom, J. K., 310
Kilbane, M. C., 476
Kim, A. E., 355
Kim, J. J., 349
Kimberg, D. Y., 163
Kimchi, R., 33
Kinchla, R. A., 84
Kinsbourne, M., 93
Kintsch, W., 286, 291, 292, 485, 504
Klaczynski, P. A., 416
Klaus, M. H., 52
Klayman, J., 442, 445
Kleffner, D. A., 5
Klein, E., 349
Klein, G., 517
Klopfer, D., 488, 489
Kluender, K. R., 340
Knowlton, B. J., 212, 209, 241
Koch, C., 5, 30
Koedinger, K. R., 497-498
Koehler, J. J., 424, 442, 443, 445
Koenig, G., 324
Koh, K., 64, 474
Kolers, P. A., 211
Kolodner, J. L., 379, 476, 477, 480
Komatsu, L. K., 390
Kosslyn, S. M., 296, 298, 305, 307,
    309, 311, 324
Kotovsky, K., 465-467
Koutstaal, W., 179, 319
Kozlowski, S. W. J., 504
Kraft, D., 549
Kramer, A. F., 131, 134
Krampe, R. T., 490, 491
Krantz, D. H., 426
Krasner, L., 66
Krauss, R. M., 328
Kreuz, R. J., 364
Kristofferson, M., 137

Kruley, P., 357
Krumhansl, C. L., 82
Kruschke, J. K., 239, 380, 401
Kuhl, P. K., 342
Kuhn, D., 441, 443, 445
Kulik, J., 273, 276, 292
Kunreuther, H., 519
Kurbat, M. A., 101
Kurtz, D. B., 163
Kutas, M., 27

Lakoff, G., 323
Lamberts, K., 371, 379, 400
Lamon, M., 475
Landau, J. D., 514
Landauer, T. K., 181, 200
Landry, J. O., 63
Lane, S. M., 270
Lange, T. E., 475
Langston, C., 445
Langston, W. E., 357
Larkin, J. H., 486
Larkin, M. J. W., 77
Larrick, R. P., 528
Larsen, S. F., 277
Lasnik, H., 364
Lassaline, M. E., 140, 428, 432
Lau, I. Y. M., 328
Lauber, E. J., 159, 220
LaVancher, C., 477
Lebiere, C., 223, 242, 494, 495
Leclerc, Y. G., 89
Ledgeway, T., 430, 445
Lee, J.-W., 549
Legrenzi, M., 415
Legrenzi, P., 415
Lehmann, A. C., 490, 517
Lenat, D. B., 260, 503
Lepper, M. R., 13, 20
Lerner, M. J., 544
Lerner, M., 144
Lesgold, A. M., 168, 488, 489, 517
Leslie, A. M., 392
Letsinger, R., 502
Lettvin, J. Y., 97
Levelt, W. J. M., 364
Leventhal, H., 436, 437
Levin, D. T., 95, 316, 318
Levine, D. N., 314
Levine, M., 72, 78
Levinson, S. C., 395
Lewis, C. H., 226
Lewis, D. K., 417

Lewis, M. W., 477
Liberman, A. M., 340
Lichtenstein, S., 424, 524, 542
Light, L. L., 172
Lillard, A., 400
Lin, M., 371
Lindman, H., 537
Lindsay, D. S., 204, 241, 272
Lisker, L., 341
Lisle, D. J., 549
Lively, S. E., 336
Livingstone, M., 87
Lloyd, B. B., 400
Lock, T. G., 282
Lockhart, R. S., 166, 195, 475
Locksley, A., 371
Loewenstein, G. F., 526, 532, 533, 539
Loftus, E. F., 201, 204, 223, 268, 270, 272, 278, 279, 280, 281, 292, 330-331, 270, 272
Logan, G. D., 140
Logan, J. S., 336
Logie, R. H., 159, 277
LoLordo, V. M., 9, 58, 62
Loomes, G., 531
Lopez, A., 397-398, 401, 428
Lopez, F. J., 77
Lorayne, H., 287, 292
Lorch, E. P., 144
Lotocky, M. A., 355
Love, B. C., 43, 397
Lubart, T. I., 517
Lucas, J., 287, 292
Luce, M. F., 539
Luchins, A. S., 505-506
Luchins, E. H., 505-506
Luminet, O., 278
Lundsgaarde, H. P., 502
Luria, A. R., 288, 292
Luus, C. A. E., 268
Lynch, E. B., 202, 374, 375, 395, 399
Lynch, J. S., 415
Lynn, S. J., 282

MacCallum, R. C., 63, 79
MacDonald, J., 342
MacLeod, C. M., 36
Macnamara, J., 394
MacQueen, G. M., 63
Macrae, C. N., 386
Maddox, W. T., 401
Madigan, S. A., 177

Maier, S. F., 63, 79
Makin, V. S., 368, 375
Malt, B. C., 367, 376, 400, 401
Mandl, H., 517
Mandler, G., 212, 214, 257
Manis, M., 424
Manktelow, K. I., 415, 416
Mann, V. A., 341
Manning, C. G., 204
Manning, C., 519
Maratsos, M., 353
Marche, T. A., 289
Marcus, S. L., 412, 413
Maril, A., 179
Marine, C., 489
Markman, A. B., 98, 257, 258, 296, 324, 368, 375, 383, 430, 432, 433, 445
Markman, E. M., 9, 389, 393, 401
Marler, P., 53
Marr, D., 31-35, 43, 82, 92, 96, 101, 102
Marsh, R. L., 514
Martin, R. C., 162
Marucha, P. T., 63, 79
Massaro, D. W., 113, 342, 540
Mather, J., 539
Mattingly, I. G., 340
Maturana, H. R., 97
Matute, H., 76, 77, 79
McCann, C. D., 36
McCarthy, T. T., 272
McCartney, H., 68
McClelland, A. G. R., 277
McClelland, J. L., 36-39, 108, 111, 187, 220, 229, 234, 238, 239, 239, 242, 262
McCloskey, M., 44, 237, 239, 270, 271, 272, 275, 276, 297, 372, 438, 440
McCulloch, W. S., 97
McDaniel, M. A., 277, 287
McDermott, D., 260
McDermott, J., 486
McDermott, K. B., 205, 219, 220
McDonald, J. L., 56
McDougal, T. F., 476
McGarry, S. J., 475
McGurk, H., 342
McKenzie, B. E., 90
McKinley, S. C., 380, 401
McKoon, G., 23, 207, 218, 220, 224, 357, 358
McNamara, D. S., 504

McNamara, T. P., 106, 224, 303, 305, 392
McNaughton, B. L., 187, 220, 239
McNeil, B. J., 528
Meagher, R. B., Jr., 376
Mechelen, I., 400
Medin, D. L., 75, 77, 79, 86, 104, 202, 241, 373, 374, 375, 376, 378, 379, 380, 384, 387, 388, 390, 391, 392, 393, 395, 397, 399, 400, 401, 424, 432, 549
Medvec, V. H., 532
Meehl, P. E., 549
Mehle, T., 519
Melcher, J., 508
Melton, A. W., 176, 178
Meltzoff, A. N., 342, 390
Melz, E. R., 475
Mermigis, L., 509
Merton, R. K., 352
Mervis, C. B., 373, 374, 376, 383, 384, 387,
Messick, D. R., 545, 546
Metcalfe, J., 292, 509, 538
Metzler, J., 307, 308
Meyer, D. E., 23, 197, 224, 361, 517
Meyer, D., 436, 437
Michalski, R. S., 400
Michela, J., 43
Michimata, C., 305
Michotte, A., 392
Milberg, S. J., 371
Milich, R., 144
Miller, D. G., 268
Miller, D. T., 543, 544
Miller, G. A., 22, 25, 158, 161, 195
Miller, J. D., 342
Miller, J. L., 53, 340
Miller, K. F., 431
Miller, L., 519
Miller, N. E., 29
Miller, R. R., 76, 77, 79
Millis, K. K., 358
Millman, L., 391
Milne, A. B., 386
Milner, B., 152, 203, 210
Mims, M., 73
Minda, J. P., 378, 379
Mineka, S., 66
Minsky, M. L., 298, 378
Mischel, W., 538
Mishkin, M., 131
Mitchell, D. B., 309
Miyake, A., 195

Monti, L. A., 219
Moore-Glascock, J., 183
Moran, A., 312
Moray, N., 123, 124
Morey, L. C., 392
Morgan, J. N., 528
Morgan, K. I., 169
Morgenstern, O., 522
Morris, C. D., 219
Morton, J., 118
Mulhern, R. K., 57, 79
Mullenuix, J., 338
Muller, H. J., 132
Murnane, K., 175
Murphy, A. H., 543
Murphy, G. L., 383, 384, 388, 390,
    397, 401
Murray, M. J. Jr., 378
Musen, G., 209, 214, 241
Myers, B. P., 52
Myers, B., 282
Myers, D. M., 175
Myers, E., 355
Mynatt, C. R., 442, 445

Nadel, L., 282
Naigles, L., 395
Nakamura, G. V., 392
Nakayama, K., 95
Nalcioglu, O., 144
Narens, L., 288, 292
Navon, D., 83, 84, 127
Naylor, S. J., 300, 324
Needham, D. R., 475
Neely, J. H., 510
Neisser, U., 23, 139, 264, 276, 277,
    280
Nelson, J. M., 394
Nelson, T. O., 183, 288, 292
Nemeroff, C., 391
Nerenz, D., 436
Neuberg, S. L., 371
Neunaber, D. J., 63
Newell, A., 25, 453-456, 459, 462,
    463, 469, 476, 479, 480, 494, 500,
    512
Newport, E. L., 53, 54, 56
Nickerson, R. S., 315, 317
Nicolich, R., 496
Nisbett, R. E., 20, 43, 60, 64, 401,
    416, 426, 445, 528
Nolde, S. F., 180
Norman, D. A., 126

Norman, G. R., 380
Nosofsky, R. M., 379, 380, 401
Novick, L. R., 75, 306, 467, 474, 477
Nussbaum, J., 434
Nyberg, L., 180

O'Reilly, R. C., 187, 220, 239
Oaksford, M., 416
Obal, F., 64
Ohlsson, S., 324, 451
Oliva, A., 84, 86, 389, 390
Oliver, L. M., 416
Olseth, K. L., 466
O'Regan, J. K., 94
O'Reilly, R. C., 114
Orians, G. H., 52
Ortony, A., 254, 291, 387, 392, 480
Osherson, D. N., 28, 364, 382, 396,
    397-398, 399, 401, 426, 428
Osman, A. M., 23
Osterhout, L., 27, 355
Ostrum, E., 547
O'Sullivan, J. T., 289
Over, D. E., 416
Owen, E., 493

Page, G. G., 63, 79
Paivio, A., 320
Palmer, C., 82
Palmer, J. C., 331
Palmer, S. E., 33, 88, 99, 200, 296,
    298
Palmeri, T. J., 140, 379, 380, 401
Papagno, C., 162
Papert, S. A., 378
Papotto, C., 175
Parasuraman, R., 144, 147, 148
Parault, S. J., 56
Parisi, D., 242
Park, D. C., 169
Partee, B., 382
Pashler, H., 126, 129, 139, 141, 142,
    148
Patalano, A., 159, 220, 517
Pauker, S. G., 528
Pavlov, I., 60, 63, 65
Payne, D. G., 282
Payne, J. W., 526, 535, 536, 539, 549
Payne, S. J., 300
Pearlmutter, N. J., 355
Pelletier, R., 498
Penfield, W., 182

Pennebaker, J. W., 437
Pennington, N., 496, 549
Perani, D., 28, 305, 324
Perkins, D. N., 512
Peronnet, F., 312
Peters, E., 539
Peters, S., 53
Peterson, L. R., 155
Peterson, M. A., 310
Peterson, M. J., 155, 376
Peterson, R. A., 547
Peterson, S. E., 28
Pezdek, K., 280
Phelps, M. P., 175
Philippot, P., 278
Phillips, A., 395
Phillips, B., 542
Phillips, L. W., 165
Pichert, J. W., 265
Pickett, J. M., 334
Pinker, S., 106, 132, 310, 349, 361,
    395
Pirolli, P., 477
Pisoni, D. B., 336, 342
Pitts, W. H., 97
Plott, C. R., 525
Plunkett, K., 242
Poggio, T., 5, 92, 114
Pollack, I., 334
Polson, P. G., 494, 504
Polya, G., 496, 517
Pomerantz, J. R., 298
Posner, M. I., 131, 144, 148
Post, T. A., 448
Postman, L., 165
Prasada, S., 349
Prelec, D., 532, 533
Presson, C. C., 299, 300
Prince, A., 349
Proffitt, D. R., 438
Proffitt, J. B., 399
Provine, R. R., 50
Pullum, G., 349
Putnam, H., 25
Puto, C., 526
Pylyshyn, Z. W., 91, 114, 298, 324

Quillian, M. R., 198, 200, 201, 226

Raaijmakers, J. G., 189, 193, 194,
    195
Radvansky, G. A., 305

Rafal, R. D., 133
Rahm, J., 496
Raichle, M. E., 28, 148
Rajamoney, S., 393
Rajaram, S., 216
Ramachandran, V. S., 5
Ranney, M., 439
Ratcliff, R., 23, 194, 207, 218, 220, 224, 237, 357, 358
Ratner, A. M., 52
Rattermann, M. J., 430, 474
Raufaste, E., 489
Raven, P., 384
Rawles, R. E., 277
Raye, C. L., 180, 270
Rayner, K., 354, 355
Reaves, C. C., 139
Recker, M., 477
Redd, W. H., 65, 68
Redelmeier, D., 532-533
Reder, L. M., 169, 223, 227, 228, 242, 273, 292
Reed, S. K., 99, 107, 477
Reese, H. W., 416
Reeves, L. M., 474
Reicher, G. M., 108
Reimann, P., 469, 477, 517
Reisberg, D., 310, 311
Reiser, B. J., 309, 311, 419
Reitman, J. S., 484
Reitman, W., 448
Rensink, R. A., 94
Repp, B. H., 341
Rescorla, R. A., 62, 64, 76, 77, 79
Reuter-Lorenz, P. A., 159, 220
Reynolds, R. C., 252
Rhodes, G., 106
Richardson, J. T. E., 287, 307
Richman, C. L., 309
Richmond-Wetty, E. D., 338
Rickard, T. C., 140
Riesbeck, C. K., 476
Rips, L. J., 241, 373, 390, 396, 397, 401, 412, 413, 416, 418, 445
Roberts, W. A., 193
Robertson, L. C., 84, 145, 147, 305
Robins, A., 239
Robins, R. W., 43
Rodet, L., 389
Roediger, H. L., 205, 216, 219, 220, 510
Rogers, C., 19
Roland, P. E., 314
Romo, L. F., 391, 395

Rosch, E., 373, 374, 376, 383, 384, 387, 400
Rose, P., 310
Rosen, B. R., 179
Rosenbloom, P., 494
Rosengren, K. S., 431
Rosenthal, R., 43
Ross, B. H., 207, 208, 226, 227, 228, 368, 375, 380, 401, 449, 474, 475, 476, 491
Ross, L., 13, 43
Roth, A. E., 546
Roth, E. M., 377
Rothbart, M., 370
Rothkopf, E. Z., 176
Rotte, M., 179
Rouder, J. N., 43
Rouw, R., 311, 324
Rowley, R. L., 169
Rozin, P., 60, 65, 79, 391
Rubinson, H., 488, 489
Ruddle, R. A., 300
Ruderman, A. J., 538
Rumain, B., 419
Rumelhart, D. E., 108, 229, 234, 238, 239, 242, 254, 262, 291,
Rusiniak, K. W., 58
Russo, J. E., 451
Ruts, W., 379, 397, 401

Sacks, H., 329
Sag, I., 349
Sagi, P., 519
Samarapungavan, A., 434
Sanders, G. S., 12
Sanocki, T., 86
Sartori, G., 394
Sato, S., 132
Sattath, S., 524, 526
Savage, L. J., 537
Saville, P. D., 542
Schacter, D. L., 179, 183, 207, 209, 214, 216, 220, 239, 292, 319, 324
Schadewald, M. S., 546
Schaefer, E. F., 330
Schaffer, M. M., 376, 379
Schallert, D. L., 252
Schank, R. C., 257, 261, 291, 390, 476
Schegloff, E. A., 329
Schneider, W., 137, 138, 163, 496
Schnur, T., 28
Schober, M. F., 329, 330

Schoenfeld, A. H., 497, 499, 517
Schooler, J. W., 281, 283, 321, 324, 451, 508, 549
Schreiber, C. A., 532-533
Schumacher, E., 159, 220
Schvaneveldt, R. W., 197, 224, 361
Schwanenflugel, P. J., 378
Schwartz, B. L., 292
Schwartz, B., 484
Schwartz, D. L., 440
Schwartz, J. H., 59
Schyns, P. G., 84, 86, 97, 389, 390, 489
Segal, S. J., 307
Seidenberg, M. S., 44, 111
Seifert, C. M., 292, 475, 476, 517
Sekuler, R., 114
Seligman, M. E. P., 58
Semin, G. R., 352
Sengco, J. A., 106
Servan-Schreiber, D., 40
Seyfarth, R. M., 333, 334
Shackelford, T. K., 31
Shafir, E. B., 399, 426, 397-398, 401, 428, 525
Shah, P., 195
Shaklee, H., 73
Shallice, T., 394
Shanks, D. R., 73, 75, 76, 77, 79, 392, 400
Shannon, C. E., 22
Shapiro, K. L., 9, 58, 128
Shaw, J. C., 453, 512
Sheehe, P., 163
Shelton, J. R., 394
Shepard, R. N., 6, 41-42, 44, 95, 107, 295, 296, 298, 307, 308, 309, 317, 319, 324, 393
Sherman, S. J., 204
Sherman, V., 53
Sherry, D. F., 220
Sherwood, R. D., 476
Shi, M., 401
Shiamura, A. P., 292
Shiffrar, M., 41
Shiffrin, R. M., 137, 138, 156, 189, 193, 194, 195, 220
Shinotsuka, H., 549
Shoben, E. J., 241, 373, 377, 397
Shortliffe, E. H., 502
Shwartz, S. P., 324
Shweder, R. A., 391
Siegel, S., 63, 64, 79
Silverman, B., 32

Simmons, W. L., 12
Simon, D. P., 486
Simon, H. A., 11, 22, 25, 266, 448, 450, 453-456, 459, 462, 463, 464, 465-467, 469, 475, 476, 479, 480, 483-484, 485, 486, 492, 500, 512, 517, 520, 535, 549
Simons, D. J., 95, 316, 318, 391
Simonson, I., 525, 526
Simonton, D. K., 517
Simpson, R. L., 477
Singer, M., 359
Singley, M. K., 495
Skinner, B. F., 19-21, 44, 66
Slamecka, N. J., 217
Slobin, D., 351
Sloman, S. A., 239, 399, 401
Slovic, P., 424, 519, 524, 526, 527, 537, 539, 549,
Slugoski, B. R., 10
Smedslund, J., 72
Smith, E. E., 104, 159, 162, 163, 220, 241, 314, 373, 376, 382, 384, 396, 397-398, 399, 400, 401, 426, 428, 445
Smith, E. M., 504
Smith, E. R., 386
Smith, J. D., 378, 379
Smith, L. B., 388
Smith, S. M., 175, 176, 195, 509-511, 513, 517
Smolensky, P., 262
Snyder, A. Z., 28
Snyder, C. R. R., 131
Snyder, M., 13
Sokal, R. R., 372
Soli, S. D., 339
Solomon, K. O., 310, 375, 395
Solomon, R. L., 64
Spelke, E. S., 96, 139, 395
Spellman, B. A., 430, 441
Sperber, D., 416
Sperling, G., 117-119
Spilich, G. J., 285
Spranca, M., 549
Springston, F., 158
Squire, L. R., 205, 209, 211, 212, 213, 214, 241
Srinivas, K., 219
Srull, T. K., 386
Standing, L., 319
Stanfill, C., 380
Stark, H. A., 216
Starkes, J. L., 485

Stein, B. S., 169
Stephens, D. L., 451
Sternberg, R. J., 136, 426, 445, 517
Sternberg, S., 119
Stevens, A. L., 434, 440
Stevens, A., 303, 304
Steyvers, M., 194, 195
Stickgold, R., 210
Storms, G., 379, 397, 401
Strange, W., 337
Stroop, J. R., 36
Studdert-Kennedy, M., 342
Sugden, R., 531
Sullivan, E. V., 203
Sullivan, M. A., 496
Suls, J., 465
Suppalla, T., 53
Sutherland, N. S., 99
Sutton, R. S., 64
Swanson, J., 144
Sweller, J., 493
Swinney, D., 355

Tajfel, H., 369
Tajfel, H., 371
Tan, H.-T., 529
Tanaka, J. N., 105, 320
Tanaka, J. W., 106, 383, 384-385
Tanke, E. D., 13
Tarr, M. J., 104, 105, 106, 321, 389
Taylor, H. A., 300, 303, 324
Taylor, M., 383, 384-385
Taylor, S. E., 538
Tenbrunsel, A. E., 538, 545
Terr, L., 278, 279, 292
Tesch-Römer, C., 490, 491
Testa, T. J., 392
Tetewsky, S. J., 426, 445
Tetlock, P. E., 545, 546, 549
Thagard, P. R., 60, 430, 445, 512
Thaler, R. H., 528, 545, 546
Theuns, P., 400
Thibaut, J. P., 97, 389, 489
Thomson, D. M., 34, 172, 173
Thomson, N., 161, 162
Thorndyke, P., 299, 300
Timberlake, W., 64
Tinklepaugh, O. L., 19
Tohkura, Y., 336
Tooby, J., 31, 520, 549
Tootell, H. S., 90

Torrance, E.P., 507
Torre, V., 5
Townsend, J. T., 35, 120, 539
Trabasso, T., 359
Tranel, D., 394
Trauner, D., 362
Treadwell, J., 214
Treiman, R., 338
Treisman, A., 97, 120-121, 124, 126, 130, 131, 132, 134-134, 145,
Treisman, M., 163
Treyens, J. C., 256
Trueswell, J. C., 355
Tucker, D., 73, 144
Tulchin, M., 272
Tulving, E., 34, 166, 167, 172, 173, 180, 195, 202, 203, 207, 215, 216, 241, 379
Turing, A., 24-25
Turken, A. U., 380
Turner, T. F., 259, 260
Tverksy, A., 272
Tversky, A., 387, 423, 424, 520, 524, 525, 526, 527, 529, 530, 535, 537, 540, 541, 549
Tversky, B., 299, 300, 303, 305, 306, 324, 383
Tweney, R. D., 442, 445
Twitchell, T. E., 203
Tyc, V. L., 57, 79

Ullman, L. P., 66
Ullman, S., 96, 101, 105, 114
Ungerleider, L. G., 131

Vaidya, C. J., 219
Vallar, G., 305, 324
van der Linden, M., 278
van Dijk, T. A., 292
Van Mechelen, I., 397
Van Someren, M., 469
VanderStoep, S. W., 476
Vecera, S. P., 114
Vesonder, G. T., 285
Vicente, K. J., 266
Vollmeyer, R., 493
Von Neumann, J., 522
Vondruska, R. J., 387
Vosburgh, R., 376
Vosniadou, S., 434, 480
Voss, J. F., 285, 448
Vye, N. J., 476

Wade-Benzoni, K. A., 538
Wagner, A. D., 179
Wagner, A. R., 64, 77
Wakefield, J. C. 31
Waldmann, M. R., 390
Waldron, E. M., 380
Walker, S. J., 392
Wallace, R. A., 50
Wallas, G., 508, 512
Wallsten, T. S., 420
Waltz, D., 99, 102, 380
Wang, Y., 401, 488, 489
Wanner, E., 353
Ward, T. B., 511, 513, 514-515
Ward, W. C., 73
Warrington, E. K., 394
Wason, P. C., 414, 416, 417, 441
Wasow, T., 349
Wasserman, E. A., 62, 63, 75
Watanabe, S., 388
Watkins, L. R., 63, 79
Watkins, M. J., 184
Watson, J. B., 18
Watson, S. E., 131, 134
Wattenmaker, W. D., 378, 390, 392, 393
Weber, E. U., 549
Weber, R. J., 511-512
Weber, T. A., 131, 134
Webster, M. M., 57
Weisberg, R. W., 465, 474, 507, 508,
    511, 513, 517

Weldon, M. S., 219, 321
Welford, A. T., 142
Wellman, H. M., 393, 395
Wells, G. L., 268, 274
Wernicke, C., 360
Wertheimer, M., 114, 508, 517
Wharton, C. M., 475
White, A. R., 309
White, T. L., 163
Wible, C. G., 276
Wickelgren, W. A., 461-462, 480,
    517
Wickens, C. D., 127, 128, 156, 475
Wiebe, D., 509
Wigal, S., 144
Wilkes, A. L., 369
Wilkie, O., 397-398, 401, 428
Williams, D. R., 67
Williams, H., 67
Williams, L., 144
Williams, M. D., 170
Wilson, K. D., 105, 320
Wilson, M., 163
Wilson, T. D., 22, 549
Windschitl, P. D., 268
Winkler, H. B., 177
Winkler, R. C., 543
Winzenz, D., 168
Wisniewski, E. J., 43, 383, 384, 391,
    393, 397
Wittlinger, R. P., 322

Wolfe, J. M., 84, 132
Woloshyn, V., 208, 272
Woodward, A. L., 395
Wortmann, R. L., 542
Wrzesniewski, A., 65, 79
Wu, L. L., 310, 466
Wundt, W., 17, 18
Wyer, R. S., 386

Yamada, R. A., 336
Yamada, T., 336
Yamauchi, T., 375
Yaniv, I., 517
Yantis, S., 23, 132, 134
Yates, J. F., 529, 549
Yeni-Komshian, G. H., 339
Young, A. M., 131
Young, D. R., 177
Young, M. E., 76

Zabinski, M., 106
Zaragoza, M. S., 270, 271, 272,
    297
Zarahn, E., 28
Zelizer, V. A., 547
Zsambok, C. E., 517
Zucco, G. M., 159
Zurif, E., 361
Zwaan, R. A., 358

SUBJECT INDEX _____

Acoustic coding, 156
ACT-R, 224, 494, 497. *See also*
    Adaptive control of thought
    (ACT) theory
Ad hoc categories, 396
Adaptation, 63
Adaptive Control of Thought (ACT)
    theory, 220-229
  account of the typicality effect, 226
  fan effect, 225-226
  propositions in, 221-223, 225
  type-token distinction, 222-223
Affirming the antecedent. *See* Modus
    ponens, 411, 413
Affirming the consequent, 412
Algorithm, 456-457
Algorithmic level, 32
Allais paradox, 523-524, 530
Alzheimer's Disease, 147, 163
American Sign Language (ASL), 53-
    54
Amnesia, 202-208, 211-215.
Analog representation, 296-297, 305,
    308-309, 310-311, 427-433
Analogical reasoning, 427-433
Anchoring and adjustment strategy,
    541
Anterograde amnesia, 203. *See also*
    Amnesia
Apparent motion, 41, 95
Artificial intelligence, 7
Associated learning model, 77
Attention Deficit/Hyperactivity
    Disorder (ADHD), 144-145
Attention
  allocation to objects vs. locations
    debate, 132-135
  automaticity and, 136
  bottleneck model of, 124-126, 141-
    142, 143
  capacity theories of, 126-130
  dichotic listening task as measure
    of, 122-123
  disorders of, 144-147
  early vs. late selection theories of,
    126
  effects on response selection, 141-143
  feature integration theory of, 130-
    133

filter model of, 124-126
focused types of, 121-123
influence of learning and practice
    on, 136-141
multiple resources theories of, 127-
    128
spotlight as a metaphor for, 120,
    132-134
Attentional blink, 128
Attenuation theory, 124-125
Attraction effect, 526
Auditory theory of speech perception,
    340-342
Automaticity, 136, 138-140
  instance theory of, 140
Autoshaping, 67
Availability heuristic, 537

Backward chaining. *See* Text
    comprehension
Balint's syndrome, 146-147
Base rate, 421-425
  defined, 421
  neglect of, 423-425
Basic level category, 383
Behaviorism, 18-21
Blocking
  backward, 76
  defined, 62
  exceptions to, 62
  in humans and animals, 76-77
Bottleneck model of attention, 124-
    126, 141-142, 143
Bottom-up processing, 108
Bounded rationality, 520
Broca's aphasia, 361

Case-based reasoning, 476-478
Categorical perception of speech, 341-
    342
Categorization
  basic level, 383-385
  between-category structure in, 382-
    386
  in brain damaged patients, 394
  category defined, 367
  category-specific deficits, 394

central tendency, 373-374, 376
classical view of, 372
context-dependence in, 377, 379,
    387
cross-cultural studies of, 374-375,
    384-385, 391, 399
domain specificity in, 394-395
exemplar theory of, 378-381
functions of concepts and, 367-368
fuzzy characteristics of, 373, 375-
    378, 387-388
goal-derived types of, 373-374,
    394, 396
hierarchically-structured, 382-384
inductive reasoning in, 397-399
influence of naïve theories, 391-395
in-group favoritism in, 369-370
internal structure in, 372-381
linguistic influences on, 394-395
medical applications of, 366, 380-381
non-hierarchically-structured, 385-
    386
probabilistic view of, 373-381
prototype models of, 375-378, 379-
    380
in reasoning, 396-399
similarity in, 371-372, 375, 379,
    386-390, 391-393, 398
social types of, 370-371, 378, 384-
    385
theory-based approach to, 390-393
typicality effects in, 373-377
within-category structure in, 371-
    395
Category, 367
Category specific deficits, 394
Causal schema, 541-542
Central executive, 160
Certainty effect, 523
Change blindness, 94-95, 316-317
Chunking, 22-23, 286, 483-485
  defined, 157-158
Chunks, 22.
Classical conditioning, 392
  as adaptation to environment, 63-64
  affective types of, 65
  backwards, 57
  chemotherapy's relation to, 67-68
  compensatory response model, 64

Classical conditioning,—*cont'd*
conditioned response (CR), 60-61
conditioned stimulus (CS), 60-61
conditioned stimulus, predictive
  value of, 62
contingency vs. co-occurrence in,
  62
defined, 60
effects of time delay on, 62-63
extinction, 60
Garcia effect, 58
information value of, 61
medical uses of, 63
mental imagery used as a US in, 65
preparedness, 58
relation to instrumental learning, 67
substitution of CS for US in, 63-64
taste aversion, 56-57
unconditioned response (UR), 60-
  61
unconditioned stimulus (US), 60-61
Classical view, 372
Coarticulation, 339, 341
Cognitive heuristics, 536-537
Cognitive neuroscience, 26-30
defined, 26-27
measures used in, 27-30
Cognitive psychology
defined, 4
empirical knowledge, 12-15
experimentation, 15-16
history of, 18-21
information processing perspective
  of, 22-24
measures used in, 16
measures used in, 23-24
nonempirical knowledge, 11-12
Cognitive science, 24-26
Communication. *See* Language.
Compensatory response model, 64
Computational complexity, 8
Computational level, 32
Concept, 367. *See also* Categorization
Conceptual combination, 396-397
Consciousness, 30, 93
Conditioned response, 60.
  See also Classical conditioning
Conditioned stimulus, 60.
  See also Classical conditioning
Confirmation bias, 442-444
Confounding factor, 15
Conjunctive search, 130-132
Conjunction fallacy, 540
Connection weights, 233

Connectionist models, 36-39. *See also*
  Parallel Distributed Processing
  models (PDP)
Consistent mapping, 137-141
Constraints, 8
Contagion, 392
Context effects, 174-175, 192
Contingency learning
cell-a strategy, 73-74
effects of theories and expectations
  on, 74
Conversational maxims, 331
Correlation, 14
Creativity, 20-21, 505-51
cognitive analyses of, 509-511
creative cognition approach to,
  513-514
defined, 506-507
as incremental problem solving,
  511-512
as problem finding, 512-513
in problem solving, 505-506
stages of, 508-509
traditional views of, 507-508
Credit assignment, 48
Critical period
attachment, 52
development of birdsong, 52-53
imprinting, 52
language learning, 53-56
nature vs. nurture, 52

Decision-making
bounded rationality in,
Decision-making
categories of, 545-547
emotions in, 538-539
heuristics in, 536-541
hindsight bias, 542
minimalization of negative
  experience in, 532-533
mutability in, 543-544
overconfidence in, 542-543
rational model of, 519-520
results of biases in, 541-544
social rules in, 545
strategies for complex, 535
strategy adjustment in, 535-536
temporal component to, 532-534
Declarative memory, 187, 208, 228
Deductive argument, 407
Deductive reasoning, 409
Deep structure, 347

Deliberate practice, 491
Denying the antecedent, 411
Dependent variable, 15
Depth cues. *See* Distance cues
Depth of processing.
    See Levels of processing
Dichotic listening experiment
defined, 122-123
role of channels in, 122-123
shadowing in, 122
Distance cues, 88-92
monocular types of, 89
motion parallax, 91
stereoposis, 92
texture gradients, 90-91
Distributed representation, 235
Domain-specificity, 394-395
Dual-coding hypothesis, 320-321
Dual-task paradigm, 159

Early selection theory of attention,
    126. *See also* Bottleneck model
    of attention
Echoic memory, 118
Ecological validity, 40-41
Edge detection
defined, 83
low and high-spatial frequency
  information in, 84
mechanism of, 86
Einstellung, 506
Elaboration
memory and, 169
Elimination by aspects, 535
Empiricism, 12-13
Encoding, 166
Encoding specificity approach, 34-35
Encoding specificity effect, 171-174
Encoding specificity, 475
Episodic memory, 197, 202-208, 210
effects of amnesia on, 202-208
vs. semantic memory, 202-203
Essentialis
see Psychological essentialism
Event-related potentials (ERP), 27-28
Exemplar models, 378. *See also*
    Categorization
Expected utility theory, 522-523, 545,
    546
context effects in, 526-527
violations of, 523-529
Expected value theory, 521-522
Experimentation, 15-16

Expert system, 500-504
Expertise
  acquisition of skill in, 494-496
Expertise, 482-504
  adaptation to new situations, 503-504
  in chess, 8, 483-485, 488
  content effects in, 493
  decrease in skill with, 489
  development of, 492-499
  experts vs. Novices, 482-483, 486-
    487, 490-492
  heuristics in, 496-499
  in medicine, 488-489, 502
  in mental math, 483-485, 488
  talent in, 490-491
  use of computer systems to
    develop, 496-497
Explicit memory, 210, 215-220
Extinction, 60
Extrinsic motivation, 20-21
Eyewitness testimony, 268-273, 274-
  275, 330-331

Face recognition, 105-108
Family resemblance, 375
Feature detection theory, 96. *See also*
  Perception
Feature integration theory
  defined, 130-133
  "what" and "where" system
    components of, 131
Figure-ground relations, 87
Fixed action patterns, 50
Flashbulb memories, 273-278
Forgetting, 181-185
  causes of, 183
  in episodic and semantic memory,
    207
  inference in, 225
  intentional types of, 182
  interference as a cause of, 184, 192
  memory decay hypothesis, 184
  overwriting as a cause of, 185
  savings in relearning, 183
Forward chaining. *See* Text
  comprehension
Frame, 254. *See also* Schema
Framing effects, 527-529, 533-534
Free recall memory, 165, 171-174,
  182
Functional fixedness, 465
Functional Magnetic Resonance
  Imaging (fMRI), 28-30, 179

Gambler's fallacy, 541
Garcia effect, 58
Garden path sentences, 355
GENEPLORE model, 513-514
Generation effect, 217
Geons
  defined, 99
  nonaccidental properties, 99
  role in object recognition, 101-103
Gestalt, 87
Given-new strategy, 330
Global precedence, 84
Good continuation, 88
Government and binding theory, 349
Gricean maxims, 331-332, 415

Habituation, 59
Heuristics, 457-461
Hierarchical model of memory, 198-
  201, 223-224, 226
  activation tags, 200
  links, 199
  nodes, 198
  problems with, 200-201
  relatedness effect, 201
  typicality effect in, 200-201
High level vision, 82
Hill-climbing, 457-459, 510
Hindsight bias, 542
Homeopathy, 391
Hypothesis testing, 414-417, 441-444

Iconic memory, 118
Ill-defined problems, 448
Illusory correlation, 74
  effects on memory, 74-75
Illusory motion, 94
Imagery, 306-314
  involvement of visual system, 311-
    314
  mental rotation in, 307-309
  neuropsychological studies of, 312-
    314
  perception vs., 310-311
  of physical activity, 312-313
  selective inference in, 307, 313
  similarity to physical movement,
    309-310
  in the visually impaired, 311-312
Implementation level, 32
Implicit memory, 210-220
Imprinting, 52

Incidental learning, 167
Incubation, 508, 509-510
Independent variable, 15
Induction, 397-399
Inductive reasoning, 409-410, 419-426
Information processing, 22
Instrumental conditioning
  latent inhibition, 68
  use with chemotherapy, 68
Instrumental learning
  defined, 66
  operant behavior and, 66
  reinforcement, 66
  relation to classical conditioning, 67
  respondent behavior and, 66
  Skinner Box and, 66
Intelligent tutoring systems, 496-497
Intentional forgetting, 182
Interactive activation, 109
Intrinsic motivation, 20-21
Introspectionism, 18
Intuitive physics, 438-440
Invariants, 90

Joint action, 329

Korsakoff's Syndrome, 204-206, 213

Language comprehension device
  (LCD), 350-356
Language
  American Sign Language (ASL),
    53-54
  in animals, 333-334, 342
  and the brain, 360-362
  as communication, 328-332
  comprehension of text. *See* Text
    comprehension
  comprehension of, 350-356
  constraints in the acquisition of,
    338-339, 351-353
  conversational maxims in, 331
  conveying meaning, 329-330
  coordination in, 329
  deep structure, 347
  extraction of meaning, 344-345,
    347, 356-357
  formation of plurals in, 336-338
  given-new principle, 330
  government and binding theory,
    349

Language—*cont'd*
  Gricean maxims for
    communication, 415. *See also*
    Gricean maxims
  hierarchical structure of, 344-345
  indirect speech acts in, 331-332
  less-is-more hypothesis, 54-56
  loss and reacquisition of
    phonological distinctions, 336-
    337
  parsing, 353-356
  perception of speech. *See* Speech
    perception
  phonological aspects of, 335-342
  presuppositions in, 330-331
  processing in Broca's area, 360-361
  processing in Wernicke's area, 361
  productive nature of, 333-334
  pronunciation of, 336-339
  regularities in, 336-338
  resolution of ambiguity in, 334-335
  surface structure, 347
  syntax and structure, 343-350
  transformational grammar, 346-349
Late selection theory, 126
Law of contradiction, 520-521
Learner's model, 496-497
Learnin
  artificial intelligence and, 48
  associated learning model, 77
  basic types of, 59
  biases and constraints on, 9, 48, 49,
    57-58, 60, 68
  contingency learning in, 72-74
  credit assignment, 48
  critical periods and imprinting, 52
  defined, 49
  illusory correlation, 74-75
  innate behaviors in animals and
    humans, 50-53
  language, 53-56
  learning-performance distinction to
    assess, 71
  machine learning, 48
  meaningful types of, 75-76
  memory and, 49
  paired-associate procedure in study
    of, 68-71
  relationship between simple and
    complex learning, 76-77
  taste-aversion, 56-57
Learning performance distinction, 71
Less-is-more hypothesis,
  54-56

Levels of processing, 166-168
Lexical decision task, 197-198
Linear separability, 377-378
Links, 199
LISP programming language,
  497-498
Logic, 407. *See also* Reasoning
Long-term memory. *See* Memory,
  long-term
Low level vision, 82

Magnetic Resonance Imaging (MRI).
  See Functional Magnetic
  Resonance Imaging
Maintenance rehearsal, 156
Marr's three levels, 31-34
Mathematical models, 35
McGurk effect, 342
Means-end analysis, 459-460, 493
Memory decay hypothesis, 184
Memory
  ACT theory of. *See* Adaptive
    Control of Thought (ACT)
    theory
  chunking, 22-23, 157-158, 286,
    483-485
  comprehension of complex
    information, 250-253
  consolidation, 186
  decay, 184
  declarative, 187, 208, 228
  declarative, vs. procedural memory,
    228
  encoding-retrieval interaction, 263-
    265
  episodic, 197, 202-208, 210
    effects of amnesia on, 202-208
    vs. semantic memory, 202-204,
    220-240
  expertise and, 285
  explicit, 210, 215-220
  eyewitness testimony. *See*
    Eyewitness testimony
  for faces, 320-322
  false memories, 204-205
  flashbulb, 273-278
  free recall, 165, 171-174, 182
  functions of, 153-154
  hierarchical association model of.
    See Hierarchical model of
    memory
  hypnosis and, 282-283
  implicit, 210-220

  implicit, vs. explicit memory
    distinction, 210-220, 238-239
  improving, 284-286
  introduction to, 10-11
  lexical decision task, 197-198
  long-term, 164-185, 191, 485
    context effects, 174-175
  elaboration and, 169
  encoding, 166
  encoding interaction, 171
  encoding specificity effect, 171-
    174, 192
  forgetting, 181-185. *See also*
    Forgetting
  free recall measures of, 165
  hierarchical model.
    See Hierarchical model
    of memory
  olfaction and, 176-177
  organization and, 168-169
  retrieval, 170-171
  spacing effect, 175-179
  state-dependant effects, 175
  for meaning, 168
  metamemory, 287-290
  mnemonics, 287
  mnemonists, 286-287, 288-289
  multiple association model of, 188
  number of systems debate, 218-219
  PDP model of. *See* Parallel
    distributed processing (PDP)
  for pictures, 316-319
  procedural, 187, 209, 211, 228
  procedural, vs. declarative
    distinction, 238-239
  recognition, 167, 171-174, 182-183
  reconstructive, 263
  recovered, 278-282
  repetition priming in, 211-215
  repressed, 278-282
  retrieval processes, 170-171
  Search of Associative Memory
    (SAM) model of, 189-194. *See*
    also Forgetting
  semantic, 197
  short-term, 154-158, 166, 182, 190,
    483-485, 492. *See also* Memory,
    working
  chunking, 157-158.
    See also Chunking
  coding in, 156-157
  proactive interference in, 156
  rehearsal as a strategy of, 155-
    156

simple association model of, 187-188

span, 286

strategies in, 284-286

visual, 315-322

working, 158-163, 223

  central executive in, 160

  phonological loop, 160-162

  use of dual-task paradigm in, 158

  visuospatial sketchpad, 160-163

Mental accounting, 546-547

Mental models approach to reasoning

  defined, 434-440

  use in medicine, 436-437

Mental rotation, 307-309

Metamemory, 287-290

Method of loci, 287

Minimal attachment strategy, 354

Misinformation effect, 269-273

Mnemonics, 287

Mnemonists. *See* Memory, mnemonists

Modus ponens, 411, 413

Modus tollens, 411, 413

Morphemes, 336-337

Motion parallax, 91

Motor theory of speech perception, 340-342

Naïve physics, 438

Naïve realism, 4

Neglect, 145

  spatial types of, 305

Nodes, 198

Nonempirical knowledge, 11-12

Object centered representation, 106

Operant behavior, 66

Organization

  memory and, 168

Overconfidence, 542-543

Overwriting, 183, 185, 238, 270-273

Paired-associate learning

  gradual vs. All-or-none learning, 69

  keyword method, 69

  nonsense syllables as stimuli in, 70

Parallel distributed processing (PDP)

  model of memory, 229-240, 504

  connection weights, 233

introduction to, 36

layers, 229-231

valence, 229-230

Parse trees. *See* Language, parsing

Partial report technique, 117-119

Perception

  assumptions made by perceptual system, 5-7

  distance cues. *See* Distance cues

  echoic memory, 118

  edge detection, 83-86

  feature detection theories of, 96-98

  global precedence in, 84

  high level types of, 82

  iconic memory, 118

  imagery vs., 310-311

  low level types of, 83-92

  motion's role in, 94-96

  partial report technique as measure of, 117-118

  recognition-by-components theory, 99-104

  retina, 81

  search tasks. *See* visual search tasks

  segregation in, 87-88

  span of, 117

  structural description theories of, 99-104

  template matching theories of, 104-105

  visual, 82-96

Perceptual identification task, 215-216

Phonemes, 335

Phonetics, 335

Phonological loop, 160-163

  function of, 162

  subsystems of, 161

Phonology, 335

Phrase structure, 345-346

Picture-superiority effect, 319-321

Positive test strategy, 442

Positron emission tomography (PET), 27-29, 159, 162, 181, 314

Pragmatic reasoning schemas, 416-417

Pragmatics, 330

Preference reversals, 524-526

Primacy effect, 165-166, 191-192

Primary memory. *See* Memory, short-term

Primary rehearsal. *See* Maintenance rehearsal

Priming, 134, 198

Proactive interference, 156-157, 184-185

Probabilistic view, 373-381

Problem

  defined, 447. *See also* Problem solving

  ill-defined, 448

  well-defined, 448

Problem formation, 513

Problem operators, 455

Problem schemas, 486, 488, 492-494

Problem solving, 447-478

  computer simulation to study, 450-452

  content effects in, 465-467, 473-475

  difficulty accessing prior experience in, 472-475

  effects of varying problem representation in, 465-469

  experience in, 470-475

  functional fixedness in, 465

  heuristics in, 457-461

  improving ability to use prior experience in, 475-478

  information-processing system in, 453-455

  methods for evaluating, 448-452

  problem space in, 454-456

  problem, defined, 447

  representation of problem space, 461-465

  search of problem space in, 456-461

  task environment in, 455

  types of problems, 447

Problem space, 454-456

Problem state, 455

Problem

  defined, 447. *See also* Problem solving

  ill-defined, 448

  well-defined, 448

Procedural memory, 187, 209

Productions, 494-495, 498, 504

Propositional representation, 297-298, 305, 309

Propositions, 221-223

Prosopagnosia, 105

Prospect theory, 529-531

Prototype, 375. See also Categorization, prototype models of

Proximity principle, 88

Psychological essentialism, 392-393, 395

Psychological Refractory Period task, 142

Rapid Eye Movement (REM) sleep, 186-187
Rapid serial visual presentation, 128
Rational model, 519-520, 546-547
Real motion, 95
Reasoning schema, 406-408
Reasoning
    analogical, 427-433
    case-based, 476-478
    in children, 431
    conditional, 411-417
    conditional argument forms in, 411-414
    conditional probabilities in, 424-425
    content effects in, 408-409, 415-416, 426, 427
    deductive, 409-417
    hypothesis testing and, 414-417, 441-444
    inductive, 409-410, 419-426
    introduction to, 10
    intuitive theories used in, 438-440
    matching hypothesis, 415, 417
    mental models approach to, 418-419
    probabilistic, 420-425
    role of prior beliefs, 443-444
    scientific, 441-444
    similarity in, 431-433
    using social schemas, 416
    validity vs. truth of argument in, 408-409
Recency effect, 165-166
Recognition memory, 167, 171-174, 182-183
Reconstructive memory, 263
Recursive decomposition, 33
Reductionism, 33
Regret theory, 531
Rehearsal, 31-34
Reinforcement, 19, 20-21
    expectancy of reward in, 71-72
    role-learning tasks and, 72
Release from PI, 156-157
Releasers, 50
Remote Associates Test (RAT), 510-511
Repetition blindness, 129
Repetition priming, 211-215
Representation, 295
    analog vs. propositional types of, 296-298
Representativeness heuristic, 540-541
Retinal disparity, 92
Retrieval plan, 170

Retrieval, 191
Retroactive interference, 184
Retrograde amnesia, 203. See also Amnesia
Route knowledge, 299-303

Satisficing, 11, 535
Savings in relearning, 183
Schema, 254-257
    activation of, 261-262
    frame, 254
    problems of, 262
    relation to stereotypes, 265-267
    slots, 254
Schizophrenia, 40
Script, 261
Search of Associative Memory (SAM), 189-194
Search tasks. See Visual search tasks
Segregation
    figure-ground relations, 87
    good continuation, 88
    proximity principle, 88
Self-fulfilling prophecy, 13-14, 352-353
Semantic coding, 156
Semantic memory, 197
Semantics, 334-335
Sensory store of perception, 117-121
Serial position effect, 165-166
Shadowing, 122. See also Dichotic listening experiment
Shape constancy, 6
Short-term memory. See Memory, short-term
Similarity. See Categorization, similarity in
Size constancy, 90
Skinner box, 66
Slots, 254. See also schema
Source confusion, 270
Spacing effect, 175-179
Span of apprehension, 117
Spatial knowledge, 299-305
    acquisition from descriptions, 300-303
    hierarchical organization of, 303-305
    navigational experience in, 300
    route types of, 299-303
    survey types of, 299, 301-303
Spatial neglect, 305
Spectrograph, 339-340

Speech perception, 339-342
    auditory theory of, 340-342
    categorical nature of, 341-342
    coarticulation, 339, 341
    context-dependency of, 340
    integration of auditory and visual modalities, 342
    motor theory of, 340-342
Spreading activation model, 224-225, 228-229
Spotlight metaphor, 120, 132-134
State-dependant recall, 175
Stereoposis, 92
Stereotypes, 265-267, 370-371, 376
Stroop effect, 36-39
Structural description theories of perception
    defined, 99-104
    vs. template-matching, 106-107
Structure mapping theory, 428-430, 432-433
Subordinate, 383
Sunk costs, 528-529
Superordinate, 383
Surface structure, 347
Survey knowledge, 299, 301-303
Syntax, 343-350. See also Language
Systematicity, 430

Template matching theories of perception
    defined, 104-105
    vs. Structural description theories, 106-107
Text comprehension, 356-360
    use of inferences in, 357-359
Texture gradients, 90-91
Top-down processing, 108
Transfer appropriate processing, 219
Transformational grammar, 346
Transitivity, 521
Turing machine, 24-25
Turing test, 25-26
Type-token distinction, 222-223
Typicality, 373-377
Typicality effect, 200-201, 226

Unconditioned response, 60. See also Classical conditioning
Unconditioned stimulus, 60. See also Classical conditioning
unusualness heuristic, 60

Varied mapping, 137-141
Verbal protocol, 449-451
viewer centered representation, 106
Visual coding, 156
Visual perception. *See* Perception
Visual search tasks
  conjunctive search, 130-132
  consistent vs. Varied mapping task
    structure, 137-141
  defined, 119-121
  distractors, 137
  feature search, 130

  parallel vs. Serial search in, 120-
    121, 131-131
  role of task structure in reducing
    attentional demands, 136-137
Visuospatial sketchpad, 160-163
Voice onset time, 341
Von Restorff effect, 538-540

Wason selection task, 414-417
Well-defined problems, 448
Wernicke's aphasia, 361

What system, 131. *See also* Feature
  integration theory, 131
Where system. *See also* Feature
  integration theory, 131
Williams syndrome, 361-362
Word superiority effect
  defined, 109
  interactive activation model as
    explanation for, 109-111
Working backward heuristic,
  460-461
Working memory, 158-163, 223